Praise for **BEFORE THE STORM**

"Writing with the authority of an academic historian and the dash of a journalist, Mr. Perlstein manages to break free of the partisan *idées reçues* and doctrinal laziness that typify so much writing on recent history. There is something independent, un-bought-out and, in the best sense, radical about this book."

—Christopher Caldwell, *The New York Observer*

"Occasionally a book comes along which causes historians to rethink an entire era. Rick Perlstein's remarkable *Before the Storm* is such an achievement: elegantly written, copiously researched, brimming with fresh anecdotes. Perlstein illuminates how conservatism erupted into a mass political movement while the academic scholars and media pundits were embracing Great Society Liberalism and Counterculture Despair. A truly landmark study."

—Douglas Brinkley, author of *The Unfinished Presidency: Jimmy Carter's Journey Beyond the White House*

"Anyone who has read Perlstein's wonderfully colorful account of the Goldwater nomination and his subsequent defeat in November 1964 will be sorry that the book stops there . . . Let us hope that Perlstein is already at work on another book about it all."

—William A. Rusher, *National Review*

"Offer[s] much background on the remarkable fact of contemporary politics: most of our major political institutions . . . are today owned by the right, although, issue by issue, the causes of the right are unpopular . . . Perlstein has a nose for pungent detail. It is hard to imagine that he has missed any interesting or delicious fact about Goldwater or his circle of devotees."

—Todd Gitlin, *Boston Review*

"Perlstein is such a great storyteller—one of the most enjoyable historians I've ever read."

—Robert Sherrill, *The Nation*

"One of the finest studies of the American right to appear since the days of Hofstadter. Read it and understand where the mad public faiths of our own day came from."
—Thomas Frank, editor of *The Baffler* and author of *One Market Under God*

"Perlstein retells this story with energy and skill . . . His vibrant, detailed narrative moves swiftly and brings a large cast to life."
—Sam Tanenhaus, *The New Republic*

"Comprehensive and compelling . . . The heart of Perlstein's lengthy book is his colorful account of the intellectual giants, the canny political operatives, and the far-out fellow travelers in the conservative cause."
—Richard S. Dunham, *Business Week*

"*Before the Storm* is told dazzlingly. Perlstein re-creates the social and cultural milieu that gave rise to the conservative movement with earned authority and easy patience . . . Insightful, gracefully written, well-paced and sympathetic to its central characters' motivations."
—Michael Tomasky, *Newsday*

"Perlstein's narrative . . . is never less than compelling, brilliantly researched and reported."
—Sara Scribner and David Daley, *The Hartford Courant*

"Although conservative Republicans suffered a humilating defeat in 1964, the principles they had embraced and the organization they had built endured, soon to bring them local, state and then national victories. Perlstein tells this story with energy and insight, and in lively prose."
—Gary Gerstle, *Dissent*

"Finally, a gifted writer has told the full story of the difficult birth and exuberant adolescence of the conservative movement that went on to transform American politics. Rick Perlstein's indispensable history is stuffed with wit, learning, and drama. After reading it, you will never think of the 1960s in the same way again."
—Michael Kazin, co-author of
America Divided: The Civil War of the 1960s

Jerry Bauer

Rick Perlstein

BEFORE THE STORM: BARRY GOLDWATER
AND THE UNMAKING OF THE AMERICAN CONSENSUS

Rick Perlstein was born in 1969 and writes for *The Nation*, *The New York Observer*, *The New York Times*, and other publications. *Before the Storm*, his first book, was selected by *The New York Times*, the *Chicago Tribune*, and *The Washington Post* for their year-end "notable book" lists. Perlstein was named one of *The Village Voice*'s Writers on the Verge in 2000 and has received a National Endowment for the Humanities grant for independent scholars. He lives in Brooklyn, New York.

BEFORE THE STORM

BARRY GOLDWATER AND THE UNMAKING OF THE AMERICAN CONSENSUS

Rick Perlstein

🖐 Hill and Wang
A division of Farrar, Straus and Giroux
New York

For Kathy

Hill and Wang
A division of Farrar, Straus and Giroux
19 Union Square West, New York 10003

Copyright © 2001 by Rick Perlstein
All rights reserved
Distributed in Canada by Douglas & McIntyre Ltd.
Printed in the United States of America
Published in 2001 by Hill and Wang
First paperback edition, 2002

Owing to limitations of space, all acknowledgments for permission
to reprint previously published material can be found on page 672.

Library of Congress Cataloging-in-Publication Data
Perlstein, Rick, 1969–
    Before the storm : Barry Goldwater and the unmaking of the American consensus /
Rick Perlstein.— 1st ed.
        p. cm.
    Includes bibliographical references and index.
    ISBN 0-8090-2858-1 (pbk.)
        1. Goldwater, Barry M. (Barry Morris), 1909–1998.   2. United States—Politics and
government—1953–1961.   3. United States—Politics and government—1961–1963.
4. United States—Politics and government—1963–1969.   5. Conservatism—
United States—History—20th century.   6. Presidents—United States—Election—
1964.   I. Title.

E748.G64 P37 2001
973.92'092—dc21

                                                                00-033427

Frontispiece: Barry Goldwater and Lyndon Johnson supporters duel at the site of a Goldwater campaign appearance in central Pennsylvania, October 1964. Photograph courtesy the Arizona Historical Foundation.

www.fsgbooks.com

1   3   5   7   9   10   8   6   4   2

It is the folly of too many to mistake the echo of a London coffee-house for the voice of the kingdom.   —Jonathan Swift

Politics ain't bean bag.   —Mr. Dooley

CONTENTS

PREFACE

At their 1964 convention in San Francisco, the Republican Party emerged from a corrosive faction fight between its left and right wings to do something that was supposed to be impossible: they nominated a conservative. Barry Goldwater went down to devastating defeat in November at the hands of Lyndon Johnson, and there, for most observers, the matter stood: the American right had been rendered a political footnote—perhaps for good.

The wise men weighed in. Reston of the *Times*: "He has wrecked his party for a long time to come and is not even likely to control the wreckage." Rovere of *The New Yorker*: "The election has finished the Goldwater school of political reaction." "By every test we have," declared James MacGregor Burns, one of the nation's most esteemed scholars of the presidency, "this is as surely a liberal epoch as the late 19th Century was a conservative one."

Some, recalling the words of Thomas Dewey, worried for the future of the two-party system itself: if the parties realigned along ideological axes, he had said, "the Democrats would win every election and the Republicans would lose every election." Others imagined, in the words of a *Partisan Review* writer, "a recrudescence on American soil of precisely those super-nationalistic and right-wing trends that were finally defeated in Europe at the cost of a great war, untold misery, and many millions dead."

It was one of the most dramatic failures of collective discernment in the history of American journalism. After the off-year elections a mere two years later, conservatives so dominated Congress that Lyndon Johnson couldn't even get up a majority to appropriate money for rodent control in the slums. The House Republican Caucus elected as chair of its Policy Committee John Rhodes, one of Barry Goldwater's Arizona protégés. In 1964 there were sixteen Republican governors, all but two of them moderates; in 1966 ten new conservative Republican governors were voted in. In 1980 Americans elected one of them, Ronald Reagan, as their President. And in 1995 Bill Clinton paid Reagan tribute by adopting many of his political positions. Which had also been Barry Goldwater's positions. Here is one time, at least, in which history was written by the losers.

This is a book about how that story began.

It is hard, now, to grasp just how profoundly the tectonic plates of American politics have shifted between 1964 and today. Think of a senator winning the Democratic nomination in the year 2000 whose positions included halving the military budget, socializing the medical system, reregulating the communications and electrical industries, establishing a guaranteed minimum income for all Americans, and equalizing funding for all schools regardless of property valuations—and who promised to fire Alan Greenspan, counseled withdrawal from the World Trade Organization, and, for good measure, spoke warmly of adolescent sexual experimentation. He would lose in a landslide. He would be relegated to the ash heap of history. But if the precedent of 1964 were repeated, two years later the country would begin electing dozens of men and women just like him. And not many decades later, Republicans would have to proclaim softer versions of these positions just to get taken seriously for their party's nomination. The analogy wouldn't be exaggerating what has happened since 1964 too much. It might even be underplaying it. When commentators want to remark on today's sweeping embrace of market thinking, the retreat of the regulatory state, and America's military role as the "indispensable nation," a shorthand rolls off their tongue: "There Is No Alternative"—TINA. But such things have been said before.

Go back to 1952. When the first Republican President in twenty years was elected, liberals feared Dwight D. Eisenhower would try to roll back the Democratic achievements of the New Deal—minimum wage and agricultural price supports; the Tennessee Valley Authority, that massive complex of government-built dams that brought electricity to entire swatches of the Southeast that had never seen it before; Social Security; and many, many more. Instead, the Republican President further institutionalized and expanded such programs. He created the Department of Health, Education, and Welfare, championed low-income housing, chartered the federal interstate system, proclaimed Social Security as much an American institution as the free enterprise system—and extended its reach more than Roosevelt or Truman ever had. Black Americans' legal status as second-class citizens was beginning to be dismantled; it seemed only logical to assume that the racial attitudes that undergirded segregation would also wither once the general prosperity, and increased help from Washington, lifted white Southerners from their status as economic pariahs. Meanwhile, Senate Majority Leader Lyndon Johnson and the President were tripping over each other to declare their comity over matters of national defense. And under their shared watch another broad consensus formed: that the Soviet Union might be evil, but nothing "so dangerous to the United States that we can afford to burn up the world over it," as Walter Lippmann put it. America's history of ideological disputation seemed to be over. The nation had settled into a governing equilibrium. And commentators began speaking of the American "consensus." There was no alternative. New complexities brought new needs; government had to change—grow—to respond to them. "To meet the needs of the people," as *The Atlantic Monthly* neatly summarized the consensus's tenets, "the federal government must contribute to a solution of the manifold problems of modern urban life—housing, education, welfare, mass transportation, health, and civil rights—and it must promote policies that stimulate a healthy economy."

This was not ideology. This was *reality*. One did not argue with people who denied reality. Which was why the pundit Stewart Alsop wrote that conservatism was "not really a coherent, rational alternative at all—it is hardly more than an angry cry of protest against things as they are"; and why the Columbia University historian Richard Hofstadter joked that he welcomed the Goldwater-for-President movement when it sprang up because it was providing conservatives "a kind of vocational therapy, without which they might have to be committed."

Men like this did not detect the ground shifting beneath their feet. They didn't notice that year by year, crisis by crisis, America was slowly becoming more divided than it was united.

In 1961 John F. Kennedy scaled back an exile invasion of Cuba to overthrow Fidel Castro. Castro stood his ground. The next year the Soviets tried to make Cuba a base for nuclear missiles trained on North America. Millions of Americans were thus converted to the right-wing doctrine that any weakness in the face of the Soviets was an accommodation with evil, bringing the Communists one step closer to their goal of world domination. On the other hand, millions were converted to the left-wing position that the Soviets must be met halfway lest the world court Armageddon.

Blacks staged sit-ins at Southern lunch counters, rode through Dixie on buses alongside whites in defiance of local laws and in accordance with the rulings of the United States Supreme Court, marched through the streets of Southern cities in ever-escalating confrontation with the customs and codes of segregation. Millions thrilled to the moral transcendence of these heroic warriors for freedom. Millions of others decided that rabble-rousers—perhaps

Communist dupes—were spitting on law and order, overturning tradition, and might not stop until they had forced their way into their own Northern white neighborhoods.

Experts stepped forward to manage and coordinate people's problems; more and more people decided they wanted to be left alone. Union power was turning a proletariat into a middle class—and union members began wondering how much of their dues went to subsidize civil rights groups that were eager to break up their neighborhood school districts. Millions stirred to Lyndon Johnson's visions of governmental expertise distributing the bounty of an abundant society to those who had been left behind. But millions also looked at the bottom line on their tax returns and wondered why these people couldn't help themselves. They wondered why, when they tried to impress on government what they considered *their* interests, they were met with indifference, or incompetence, or were swallowed inside a bureaucratic maze—or were called extremists and reactionaries, even borderline mental cases. City councils proudly passed laws outlawing the refusal to sell property to people on the basis of their race. And in places as diverse as Seattle, Berkeley, Phoenix, Detroit, and Akron, citizens used any direct democratic means at their disposal to strike them from the books. They were slowly disproving the Establishment cliché that an increasingly complex, urban society would necessitate politicians committed to finding solutions for the manifold problems of modern urban life. The cliché was based on a demographic error anyway, which few noticed: perhaps half the people the U.S. Census Bureau classed as "urban" lived in the suburbs. And suburbanites would demand a different kind of politician.

If the Restons and the Lippmanns and the James MacGregor Burnses had tugged at such loose threads, they would have seen another entire, unwelcome story revealed beneath the upholstery. America was becoming a different place from the one they thought they knew. The best measure of a politician's electoral success was becoming not how successfully he could broker people's desires, but how well he could tap their fears.

This is a book, also, about how that story began.

Scratch a conservative today—a think-tank bookworm at Washington's Heritage Foundation or Milwaukee's Bradley Foundation (the people whose studies and position papers blazed the trails for ending welfare as we know it, for the school voucher movement, for the discussion over privatizing Social Security); a door-knocking church lady pressing pamphlets into her neighbors' palms about partial-birth abortion; the owner of a small or large business sitting across the table from a lobbyist plotting strategy on how to decimate corporate tax rates; an organizer of a training center for aspiring conservative activists or journalists; Republican precinct workers, fund-raisers, county chairs, state chairs, presidential candidates, congressmen, senators, even a Supreme Court justice—and the story comes out. How it all began for them: in the Goldwater campaign.

It was something more than just finding ideological soul mates. It was learning how to *act*: how letters got written, how doors got knocked on, how co-workers could be won over on the coffee break, how to print a bumper sticker and how to pry one off with a razor blade; how to put together a network whose force exceeded the sum of its parts by orders of magnitude; how to talk to a reporter, how to picket, and how, if need be, to infiltrate—how to make the anger boiling inside you ennobling, productive, *powerful*, instead of embittering. How to feel bigger than yourself. It was something beyond the week, the year, the campaign, even the decade; it was a cause. You lost in 1964. But something *remained* after 1964: a movement. An *army*. An army that could lose a battle, suck it up, regroup, then live to fight a thousand battles more. *Did You Ever See a Dream Walking?*—that was how William F. Buckley entitled an anthology of conservative writings in 1970. Later that year, his brother won a Senate seat from New York with the backing of the state's Conservative Party. The dream was walking. Maybe it wasn't even just an army. Maybe it was a moral majority.

America would remember the sixties as a decade of the left. It must be remembered instead as a decade when the polarization began. "We must assume that the conservative revival is *the* youth movement of the '60s," Murray Kempton wrote in 1961, in words that would sound laughable five years later. Forty years later, these are words that are, at the very least, arguable.

A new academic discipline formed in the early sixties that perfectly captured the liberal establishment's mood: "futurism." In the presidential year of 1964, the movement even spun off a parlor game, as the sociologist Daniel Bell lamented: "The year 2000 has all the ingredients for becoming, if it has not already become, a hoola-hoop craze." Lyndon Johnson was a prime offender. "Think of how wonderful the year 2000 will be," he would gush on the campaign trail. "I am just hoping that my heart and stroke and cancer committee can come up with some good results that will insure that all of us can live beyond a hundred so we can participate in that glorious day when all the fruits of our labors and our imaginations today are a reality! . . . I just hope the doctors hurry up and get busy and let me live that long."

Perhaps it is a blessing that he didn't live that long. History humiliated Lyndon Johnson. It was as a young boy, he told a crowd on the steps of the

Texas State Capitol in Austin in the closing days of the 1964 campaign, that "I first learned that the government is not an enemy of the people. It is the people." Three decades later, half of all Americans would be telling pollsters that "the federal government has become so large and powerful that it poses a threat to the rights and freedoms of ordinary citizens." In 1964 those who rejected the dominant vision of liberalism were classed as vestiges, soon to be overwhelmed by the inexorable spread of things as they are. In the year 2000, political pros would dismiss those who held on to that same creed as "paleoliberals." Which, along with its antonym, "neoconservative," would once have sounded as oxymoronic as "zebra elephant."

So it is appropriate that this story should begin with a little circle of political diehards whose every move was out of step with the times, who lived in a mental and social world presumed to have been in its death throes ever since Sinclair Lewis's *Babbitt* had driven a stake through its heart in 1922, but who managed to set the spark that lit the fire that consumed an entire ideological universe, and made the opening years of the twenty-first century as surely a conservative epoch as the era between the New Deal and the Great Society was a liberal one.

PART ONE

THE MANIONITES

I magine you live in a town of twenty, or fifty, or one hundred thousand souls—in Indiana, perhaps, or Illinois, or Missouri, or Tennessee—with a colonnaded red-brick city hall at its center, a Main Street running its breadth, avenues rimmed with modest bungalows and named for trees and exotic heroes and local luminaries, interrupted at intervals by high-steepled churches. On the outskirts of town are factories. It is June 1959, and, three shifts a day, they throw up great clouds of smoke, churning out vast pools of cement, cords of lumber, spools of rolled steel, machine parts of every size and description. Although no one who didn't have to would ever venture inside one of these factories, locals point to them with pride, because they are what make their little town prosper, and because all over the world foundries use machine parts inscribed with the town's name.

Imagine you are the proprietor of one of these concerns. Your father founded it; perhaps to start things up he cadged a loan from the father of the man you bank with now. Probably, by dint of their shared membership on any number of company boards and fraternal orders and community chests and church committees, the bank let it slide when your father—who had made sacrifices to expand his plant in the hopes that the town's grandchildren, too, might enjoy its fruits—was late a time or two paying off a note.

You grew up reading the adventure novels in the "Mark Tidd" series by Clarence Budington Kelland, an author prominent in the national Republican Party, and your favorite was the story in which a group of boys take over a run-down sawmill and get it to turn out a profit: "Up till then a river didn't mean anything to me but a thing to fish or swim in," the narrator said, "but before I was many months older I discovered that rivers weren't invented just for kids to monkey with, nor yet to make a home for fish. They have business, just like anybody else, and they're valuable just like any other business, getting more valuable the more business they do." Calvin Coolidge once said, "The man who builds a factory builds a temple; the man who works there worships there." You agreed. You liked Calvin Coolidge.

By the time you took over the plant, the additions you built were too expensive to finance through any of the banks in your town, which was now a small city. More and more you found yourself trudging to New York, hat in hand, for money. New York, after all, controlled over a quarter of the nation's banking reserves. Your letterhead soon bore an address in Manhattan as well as the one in your town, but it galled you what it took to get the Wall Street boys to take you seriously (you had worked much harder than any of them when you went to college with them back East).

When the union rep came by to try to sign up your men (there are hundreds, but you know most of them by name), you told the workers stories of the sacrifices your father made for their fathers; you reminded them of the times you kept everyone on the payroll when business was slack, of how you were always ready with an advance to help with the new baby or a sick mother. For fifty years they had seemed perfectly happy without a union, but when FDR signed the Wagner Act, the organizers came again, this time with a slogan: "The President wants you to join a union." A union came.

You hated Franklin Roosevelt. In 1932 he ran on a platform of balanced budgets, less bureaucracy, and removing the federal government from competition with private enterprise. Then the New Deal threw money at everyone and everything—everyone and everything, that is, but you and your plants. You thought it was a godsend to industrialists who managed thousands of workers, instead of hundreds, and their friends on Wall Street. Roosevelt's National Recovery Administration authorized executives in every industry to regulate their own. The men he picked were inevitably from the biggest companies, no one you knew. You had no say when they set floors so high that they destroyed the only edge you had over them in accessing the market—you could no longer undercut their prices. You had no say when your taxes ballooned to pay for Roosevelt's deficits, which you knew would only bring inflation.

Bigger companies licked at your heels all through the Depression. Government regulations—whose application was the same for large and small firms, but which invariably fell heavier on the small—began to feel more burdensome to you. The armies of unemployed were as uninterested in fine distinctions as the New Dealers were: when Roosevelt attacked the "economic royalists" at his acceptance speech in 1936, you found yourself as much the object of the poor's resentment as was the company that wanted to bury you. You felt like a victim.

Then came the Second World War. You hadn't asked for this fight; as a leader of the America First Committee you had agitated against U.S. involvement. You didn't pay your taxes so that Washington could fight England's quarrels. Lawyers from John Kenneth Galbraith's Office of Price Administration and the National War Labor Board, small, petty, jealous men who had never met a payroll in their life, now poked their heads into your plant, read your profit and loss statements, told you what to make and what to charge.

By the time it was over, Roosevelt, not happy just to sell out this country to the collectivists, was busy selling out the rest of the world as well: first by tying MacArthur's hands in the Philippines, and then by handing over vast tracts of China to Stalin to get him to join the war against Japan. His striped-pants diplomats had been busy signing secret agreements at Yalta that would leave the countries of Eastern Europe in the hands of the godless Communists—and one by one by one they entered the ranks of the "captive nations."

Japan's surrender did not end wartime price controls; it did, however, end wartime no-strike pledges. A rash of strikes swept your plants and plants across the country: 4,985 in the last six months of 1946 alone, during which 116 million working hours were lost to the labor bosses. The President wanted the workers to join a union. Now the factories were in the hands of the unions. So was the Democratic Party, now that the labor bosses could deliver them millions of votes.

Meanwhile Wendell Willkie's Wall Street internationalists had taken over the Republican Party, and they were selling out the country right alongside the Democrats. You had read Willkie's gauzy tract *One World* back in 1943: "What we need now is a council of the United Nations," he wrote. Well, now we had it—and we were forking over our riches to every last Hottentot in addition to the billions General Marshall had committed to Europe.

August 1949: China fell, Russia got the bomb. There would soon be an explanation. Russian spies had been at Los Alamos. Alger Hiss, architect of the United Nations; Harry Dexter White, wizard of Bretton Woods; Owen Lattimore, whispering in an enfeebled Roosevelt's ear as he handed over Poland to the Soviets—all were Communists. America was falling apart. You began spending more of your time serving on political committees, reading books, attending lectures, studying the newspapers, writing letters. You retired in 1952 to work for the Republican presidential nomination of Ohio's Senator Robert Taft, one of the few pro-Americans left in Washington—only to see him railroaded at the convention by the Wall Street kingmakers. Eisenhower talked a good game about returning government back to the states. Yet his first recommendation to Congress was to establish a new cabinet department of Health, Education, and Welfare! He left the heroic Senator McCarthy to twist in the gale-force winds issuing from the Eastern Establishment Press. He worked out a humiliating "truce" in Korea that tied us to the United Nations' war aims. You pledged to fight against our boys serving under any flag but the American flag, so long as you lived.

But the fight was getting harder and harder. In 1958, recession set in, and practically every *real* Republican was voted out of Congress. You watched as the presumptive nominee for 1960, Richard Nixon—the man who brought down Alger Hiss!—announced a trip to Moscow. Worse, you heard rumors that the archinternationalist of them all, Nelson Aldrich Rockefeller, would be the only one to challenge Nixon for the nomination.

You despaired of ever having a chance to vote against the socialistic Republocrats. You despaired of Washington ever balancing a budget. You despaired of ever again seeing a President who had read the Constitution. You despaired of real Republicans receiving anything but ridicule from Eastern "Republican" newspapers like the *Herald Tribune*, which wasn't too Republican not to run Eleanor Roosevelt's execrable column. You despaired for a country brainwashed into believing it was approaching paradise, and you despaired of anyone ever waking up. You sent more and more, bigger and bigger checks to any patriotic, pro-American, pro-Constitution organization, candidate, radio program, or publication that asked. Better they get your hard-earned money than the Internal Revenue Service.

On the first day of June 1959, you received a letter marked "CONFIDENTIAL" from Clarence Manion of South Bend, Indiana. Manion was a conservative lecturer and weekly radio commentator, one of the most stirring you had ever heard. You opened a letter from Manion eagerly. It invited you to join a "Goldwater Committee of 100" to draft Barry Goldwater, the junior senator from Arizona, for President. You put it down. Goldwater in the White House—Goldwater winning the Republican nomination—was an incredible, impossible notion. You sent Clarence Manion a letter, on the stationery with your factory's and Manhattan office's addresses on the top, telling him that you wished him well, but that this was a lost cause, hopeless, that a conservative would never win the Republican presidential nomination as long as you lived. You were an old man, tired, and you were through with fighting impossible battles.

Five years later, when you watched Barry Goldwater accept the 1964 Republican nomination for President with tears in your eyes, you wondered how it possibly could have come about.

The name of the man who started it all shows up in few history books. Clarence "Pat" Manion was a precocious kid from a small town in northern Kentucky, Democrat country, the son of a well-off sidewalk contractor with no particular interest in politics. Not long after Pat graduated from the local Catholic college after his twentieth birthday he traveled to Washington, D.C., to study philosophy at Catholic University. Woodrow Wilson had captured Washington from the stolid, stand-pat Republicans. The nation's capital was teeming with brash young intellectuals from all over the country who believed the progressive mood percolating through the states had finally found its fit exemplar in the former political science professor now in the White House. He had resisted the entreaties of Wall Street and had pledged that under his Administration no American would suffer entanglement in the blood feud then raging in Europe. Manion, too young to vote, was swept up in the excitement. The night before the 1916 election he stood in front of Democratic headquarters and led the chants for reelection: "We want peace, we don't want war. / We want Wilson four years more!"

Wilson won a second term, and then he went to Congress to ask for a declaration of war.

Pat Manion swallowed hard and elected to stick with the Democrats. Each party had its nationalists and its internationalists—and also its progressives and its stand-patters, its urban and rural elements, its reformers and its machine hacks. For an ambitious young man like him, demonstrations of party loyalty made more sense than demonstrations of principle. By the age of twenty-nine he was a law professor at Notre Dame, making his way up the ranks in the Indiana Democratic Party. In 1932 he lost his bid to be his district's nominee for U.S. Congress; in 1934 he failed in an attempt to win nomination for Senate—a New Dealer like him, at any rate, was unlikely to do very well in conservative, Republican Indiana. A textbook he wrote in 1939 for parochial school government courses, *Lessons in Liberty*, assured students that guaranteeing a decent standard of living to all Americans was government's sacred duty, and his few criticisms of Roosevelt fell foursquare within the emerging consensus of American liberalism: that the only things standing in the way of the federal bureaucracy efficiently spreading well-being to all citizens were problems of technique, their solution just a matter of time and governmental effort.

When Roosevelt began making noises for military mobilization in 1940, Manion once again joined the anti-interventionist cause, taking a leadership position in the left-right coalition America First. The next year he was named dean of the Notre Dame Law School. And by war's end, Dean Manion, as his admirers would come to call him, had joined a multitude for whom disillusionment with FDR over the war became a bridge to despising the President's every work. Manion had been swayed by two of the New Deal's most prominent critics: America First's national chairman, General Robert E. Wood, CEO of Sears, Roebuck; and the baronial publisher of the *Chicago Tribune*, Colonel Robert McCormick, America First's chief propagandist—who daily declared in his blustery editorial that Roosevelt aimed to create "a centralized, despotic government different in no essential detail from Hitler's despotism."

Exhibit A—one that Manion, a constitutional scholar, was particularly incensed by—was the Supreme Court's ruling in *Wickard* v. *Filburn* in 1942, one of the key cases institutionalizing the sweeping new powers Washington now claimed for itself. The defendant was a Montgomery County, Ohio, farmer who had made a custom of setting aside land on which he grew wheat to feed his poultry, livestock, and family, above and beyond the acreage allotted to him by the Department of Agriculture. He was assessed a $117.11 fine. When he refused to pay it, he was prohibited from selling his produce on the open market. "The power of Congress over interstate commerce is plenary and complete in itself, may be exercised to its utmost extent, and acknowledges no limitations other than are prescribed in the Constitution," the decision concluded. "It follows that no form of state activity can constitutionally thwart the regulatory power granted by the commerce clause to Congress." In *Lessons in Liberty*, Manion had assured high school students that the power given to Congress in Article I, Section 8, of the Constitution "to spend in the interest of the general welfare falls far short of the power to manage and control the general welfare directly." Now he had been shown the fool. His next book, *Key to Peace*, reversed his last with the zeal of the convert. "Government cannot make men good," he now explained; "neither can it make them prosperous and happy." When it tries, even—perhaps especially—"in the sweet name of 'human welfare,' " it "begins to do things that would be gravely offensive if done by individual citizens": robbing the industrious Peters to pay the indolent Pauls. He led a movement for the American Bar Association to purge its rolls of present or former members of Communist-front organizations.

He also became one of the nation's foremost advocates for the strange foreign policy mishmash cooked up by Ohio senator Robert Taft, leader of the conservative forces in Congress: anticommunism for isolationists. Like their internationalist cousins, Taftites held that the Communist conspiracy was America's eternal enemy. But they also believed that America's *antecedent* eternal enemy—what George Washington warned of in his farewell address as "entangling alliances"—was worse. The solution to this contradiction was the belief that policies such as signing mutual security pacts in the NATO mold and pledging foreign aid to vulnerable nations sapped America's ability to fight the menace *at home*, where the real threat was, from traitors like Alger Hiss and Owen Lattimore, and the agents in the federal government who would bring America to her knees through social spending that would cripple the economy through inflation—Russia's most devious offensive of all. (One theory had it that Harry Dexter White, the former Treasury Department official who went on to become director of the International Monetary Fund, stole U.S. Mint engraving plates so that Communism could flood the country with excess currency.) Though, incongruously, it also honored America's centuries-old sentimental attachment to China and distrust of Europe by demanding massive assistance for the nationalist forces fighting Red China under the command of Generalissimo Chiang Kai-shek.

In 1952 Manion retired from Notre Dame and worked tirelessly for Bob Taft's third bid in a row for the Republican presidential nomination. Manion was still a Democrat—the old kind of Democrat, before the party was captured by the Eastern internationalist big-government Wall Street boys and the radicals. At least in the Republican Party there still was hope: Taft went into the convention with a clear lead in delegates. So when he was defeated at the eleventh hour by a lowdown parliamentary trick pulled off by Eisenhower's Wall Street handlers—they availed themselves of a "Fair Play" resolution that allowed them to strip Southern Taft delegations of their credentials—it felt like a building had collapsed. Were it not for Taft's magnanimous pledge of support for the Eisenhower-Nixon ticket, many of his followers would have left politics altogether. Manion himself worked assiduously to build Democrats for Eisenhower. Taft, promised a voice in Administration appointments in return for his support, recommended Manion for attorney general. Instead Manion was given the chairmanship of a little blue-ribbon commission charged with reviewing the balance of power between the federal government and the states.

Given that he was now spending his time barnstorming the country for the Taftites' last, desperate stand, the Bricker Amendment, it was a miracle he was offered anything at all. The idea for a constitutional amendment to slash the President's power to negotiate and sign treaties—such as the United Nations' Genocide Convention, which conservatives feared would allow Communist countries to punish the United States for segregation, or the pending treaty to establish a UN World Court, which they feared the Communists would use to shut down every line of resistance against them—had been introduced in 1951 by Taft's junior colleague, Ohio senator John Bricker. Eisenhower would later call the fight against the proposed amendment the most important of his career. And Manion favored the most radical version of the amendment: it would require a referendum in all forty-eight states before *any* treaty could go into effect. Testifying for it before a judiciary subcommittee in April of 1953, he certainly hadn't looked like someone shopping for an Administration appointment. He insulted Secretary of State John Foster Dulles to his face—and inspired pro-Bricker senators to badger Dulles so mercilessly that the normally implacable diplomat exploded. Why, creating NATO alone had required no less than ten thousand executive agreements, he exclaimed. "Do you want all those brought down here? Every time we open a new privy, we have to have an executive agreement!" That, of course, was exactly what they wanted.

Manion worked quietly as chair of the Intergovernmental Relations Committee through 1953, dutifully ferreting out unconstitutional federal programs that should be killed, even as the Administration brought yet more to life. Eisenhower got around to firing him in February. Or, as the Taftite *Fort Wayne Sentinel* put it: "President Eisenhower finally yielded to the insistent clamor of a vicious internationalist cabal, spearheaded by the *New York Times* and the Henry Luce *Time-Life* smear brigade, *Washington Post* and New Deal columnists."

Manion was interviewed on TV the next night. "Some of the left-wing Communists, who have had an unfortunate effectiveness in this administration," he said, "served notice on me that I would be fired because of my advocacy of the Bricker Amendment." As usual, the strands of hair were arranged carefully over his bald dome. (His forehead seemed to get bigger each year, as if to make room for yet one more set of facts and figures on the Communist conspiracy, forcing the droopy ears, doughy cheeks, protruding lower lip, and picket-fence teeth to crowd ever more tightly at the bottom of his face.) His eyelids were raccooned, as ever, from too much work and too little sleep. But his eyes sparkled. He looked almost beatific. He was free. Now he could work to break the Wall Street boys' hammerlock on the Democrats and the Republicans once and for all.

The pledge was several notches shy of quixotic. Taft's Senate heir apparent, the unlovable California senator William Knowland, was fast being eclipsed in party councils by the Senate's "new nationalists"—conservatives like Richard Nixon and the former isolationist Arthur Vandenberg who rejected Taft's foreign-policy legacy outright and gladly joined the majority in appropriating $3.5 billion more for mutual security in Europe. Manion went down the same month the Bricker Amendment was defeated in the Senate by a single vote. On the domestic front, the right fared worse. On May 17, 1954—"Black Monday"—Manion was crushed by the Supreme Court's decision in *Brown* v. *Board of Education of Topeka*. A month later, the Army-McCarthy hearings (then the awful, humiliating censure vote against McCarthy in December) rung down the curtain on the political viability of the one other fit standard-bearer for Manion's crusade.

Manion's people did what conservatives always did when the going got tough: they started a new group. "For America" was co-chaired by Manion and General Wood. Its manifesto promised to fight for an "enlightened nationalism" to replace "our costly, imperialistic foreign policy of tragic super-interventionism and policing this world single-handed with American blood and treasure." When their first public appeal brought in five thousand telegrams and a like number of phone calls, they were convinced they had the internationalists on the run. They sent an emissary to Washington to meet with Senators Knowland, McCarran, Byrd, Bricker, Goldwater ("who is an outstanding, courageous young Senator"), even Vice President Nixon (perhaps he could yet be saved, they reasoned). Many of them sounded receptive. "Maybe it's time to call a conclave of 25 to 50 leading Republicans and Democrats to discuss the whole idea of realignment off the record," McCarran, a right-wing Democrat, remarked, although he also said that it would be nearly impossible to win over the public without an attractive leader like General Eisenhower.

From his office in the St. Joseph's Bank Building in downtown South Bend, Manion was laying the groundwork to open his own front in the war: a weekly radio broadcast. He decided he would reject commercial sponsorship so he could keep his independence. Instead, he bought a Robotype machine—a clattering behemoth that could spew forth hundreds of identical copies of a form letter, each with an individual address and salutation that the machine read off a punched tape, player piano–style. He dunned friends, friends of friends, and friends of friends of friends, and, mostly, family-owned manufacturers: "The Leftwing, please remember," ran his pitch, "is strong, well-organized and well-financed. Many gigantic fortunes, built by virtue of private enterprise under the Constitution, have fallen under the direction of Internationalists, One-Worlders, Socialists and Communists. Much of this vast horde of money is being used to 'socialize' the United States."

The Manion Forum of Opinion went on the air in October in a prime Sunday night slot just in time to announce the success liberal Democrats enjoyed in the off-year elections and the McCarthy censure vote in December. Listenership was sparse for these weekly preachments that the sky was falling; most Americans were looking out the window and seeing the glorious sunshine of postwar prosperity. Manion and Wood's little group For America looked to be little heard from, the Manion Forum to be little noted. And so, as the next few years wore on, it turned out to be.

In 1956 For America was almost single-handedly responsible for the presidential candidacy of T. Coleman Andrews, a former Eisenhower commissioner of public revenue who now called for abolishing the income tax. They were sure the time was ripe for a platform of bringing the Washington Leviathan to heel. The Supreme Court had delivered its "Brown II" decision, mandating that school integration go forward with "all deliberate speed," and a new political culture of "massive resistance" blossomed in Dixie almost

overnight. Nearly every Southern congressman signed a manifesto pledging to
defy the Court by "all lawful means." In Alabama a bus boycott organized by a
charismatic young minister named Martin Luther King was under way, even as
rioting broke out over the court-ordered integration of the state university in
Tuscaloosa. In Coleman Andrews's home state of Virginia, senator and former
Klansman Harry Flood Byrd's minions pushed through the state assembly an
order to close any school under federal court order to integrate, and the *Richmond News Leader*'s editorial page spun out arguments not unlike the ones
used one hundred years earlier to justify secession. In this context, Coleman's
stump speech wasn't just an argument about the IRS. "When the states ratified
the Sixteenth Amendment," he would cry, "the practical effect of their acquiescence was to have signed away the powers that were reserved to them by the
Constitution as a safeguard against degeneration of the union of states into an
all-powerful central government!"

Manion's Robotype clacked around the clock, printing missive after missive to raise funds and staff the petition drives that got Andrews on the ballot in
fifteen states. Manion visited all of them. He was confident that if only he
had succeeded in getting Andrews on the ballot in all fifty, a grassroots
groundswell would throw the election into the House of Representatives—an
exigency that had last occurred in 1824—where Southern and Northern conservative congressmen would provide a majority to a major-party candidate
only at the price of concession to their agendas. Some even thought Andrews
could win. "Don't waste precious time, energy, and money seeking to change
left-wingers," declared the conservative newsletter *Human Events*. "In the first
place, it's too late for that. In the second place, conservatives are already in the
majority—in your state, in almost every state." But even in his best state, Virginia, Andrews got only 6.1 percent of the vote.

Conservative fortunes hadn't bottomed out yet. In Manhattan a new
weekly, *National Review*, struggled just to keep its head above water, went
fortnightly, then begged readers outright for donations above and beyond the
subscription price. The 1958 off-year elections were a slaughter: in the House
of Representatives, 282 Democrats now lay poised to swamp 153 Republicans;
in the Senate there were now almost twice as many Democrats as Republicans,
the worst defeat ever for a party occupying the White House. The Democratic
Party, that tensile combine of urban machine hacks and their immigrant constituencies, Southern grandees and their anti-immigrant constituencies, and
egghead do-gooders—"gangs of natural enemies in a precarious state of sym-
biosis," H. L. Mencken once said—now pulled unmistakably in the direction
of the eggheads and the do-gooders: left. Twenty-five out of the thirty-two senatorial candidates supported by the AFL-CIO's Committee on Political Educa-

tion won. The Republicans who pulled off victories in 1958—among them Senator Kenneth B. Keating and Governor Nelson A. Rockefeller in New York—were mostly liberals. Everyone still liked Ike—even though in 1956 Eisenhower had been the first successful presidential candidate in 108 years not to carry either house of Congress, then had the temerity to declare this re-election a victory for liberal "Modern Republicanism" and posit that "gradually expanding federal government" was "the price of rapidly expanding national growth."

Ten days after this awful new Eighty-sixth Congress was seated, Manion's forces convened once more in Chicago to curse the darkness and plot their next move. With the Republicans and Democrats in hock to an Eastern Establishment that kept them from nominating a conservative, and with the majority of Americans being conservative—what was there to do but name a committee to explore organizing a third party?

They sent a young, energetic red-haired Yalie from Omaha named L. Brent Bozell around the country to raise funds for the effort. He had cowritten a book-length defense of Senator McCarthy in 1953 with his Yale classmate William F. Buckley Jr., then went on to write speeches for the Wisconsin senator and help edit Buckley's *National Review*. In 1958 Bozell ran for Maryland's House of Delegates and became one of the victims of the Democratic landslide. He saw the Republicans' defeat differently from the leaders of For America, who simply assumed a bedrock majority of Americans thought just like them. "A conservative electorate has to be created," Bozell countered in an article published after the election in *National Review*, "out of that vast uncommitted middle—the great majority of the American people who, though today they vote for Democratic or Modern Republican candidates, are not ideologically wedded to their programs or, for that matter, to any program. The problem is to reach them and to organize them."

It was a hard sell. His take was $1,667—all from a single donor. Others were more sophisticated—such as General Robert E. Wood, from whose purse had always flowed the right's most generous bequests and from whose bequests had always flowed those of myriad others. Wood had known at least since 1951—when Republican senators Karl Mundt, Albert Hawkes, and Owen Brewster joined to sponsor a "National Committee for Political Realignment"—that the recipe for a new conservative party was plain: one part Midwestern Taft Republican, one part Southern states' rights Democrat. Mundt, Hawkes, and Brewster's group had failed because it had not lured Southerners into its camp. Before General Wood opened his checkbook for Bozell, he needed to know: What inroads had For America's Northern leadership made in the Deep South?

They had made none. Southerners—for whom, falling heir to a deep and abiding tradition of military honor, isolationism was inscrutable—had never had much truck with Taftites like Manion. Their anti-Washington mood was a late development, in response to *Brown*. Whatever the ideological convergences of conservatives North and South now, there were too few abiding friendships, too few of those intimate bonds that make men willing to take risks together. And without risks from Southerners willing to bolt the Democrats, why should Wood risk bolting the Republicans? He closed his checkbook, and the committee made plans to dissolve. Manion was disconsolate.

He soon found hope in his mailbox in the form of a long missive on the letterhead of the Arkansas Supreme Court.

Jim Johnson was a young lawyer who made a name for himself after *Brown* as the head of the Arkansas branch of the Citizens Council movement—the respectable segregationist outfits popularly known as the "uptown Klan"—traveling up and down the state proclaiming, "Don't you know that the Communist plan for more than fifty years has been to destroy Southern civilization, one of the last patriotic and Christian strongholds, by mongrelization, and our Negroes are being exploited by them to effect their purposes?" He decided to challenge Orval Faubus because the incumbent governor—a native of the poor hill country in the northern part of the state where blacks were as rare as millionaires, and the son of a backcountry socialist who gave him the middle name Eugene, as in Debs—was a goddamned liberal who had proudly integrated the state Democratic Party. It seemed Johnson didn't stand a chance—before, that is, the Massive Resistance movement spread so thick and fast over the region in the summer of 1956 that politics even in a moderate state like Arkansas had turned from day to darkest night. Now, by calling Faubus "a traitor to the Southern way of life," Johnson had a chance to win. Manion, no fan of integration, had met Johnson while stumping in the state for Coleman Andrews and had gladly given some speeches to help him out. But Faubus's instincts for political preservation proved much deeper than his liberalism. He added a line to his standard speech: "No school district will be forced to mix the races as long as I am governor of Arkansas." By co-opting Johnson's bigotry and dressing it up in uptown language, Faubus won the primary hands down. He never looked back. A segregationist leader was born.

In the general election that year, Johnson both ran for a seat on the Arkansas Supreme Court and led a ballot initiative to give the state legislature the right to nullify any federal law it wished—"damned near a declaration of war against the United States," he later called it. The initiative passed with 56 percent of the vote, and Johnson won his Supreme Court seat. The next year,

Orval Faubus made the history books when he forced Eisenhower to send the Army to back up a federal court order to integrate Little Rock Central High. Faubus received 250,000 telegrams and letters of support for courageously standing up to Washington. A Gallup poll that spring listed the Arkansas governor as one of the ten most admired men in the world. Johnson slyly maneuvered himself into Faubus's inner circle to become his liaison with the conservative forces around the country who were clamoring for the governor to seek higher office. And Johnson hadn't forgotten his friend Clarence Manion.

"With the proper persuasion," Johnson wrote Manion, "I am convinced that Governor Orval Faubus can be prevailed upon to lead a States' Rights Party in the coming presidential election." Manion immediately called a Southern friend, U.S. Representative William Jennings Bryan Dorn of South Carolina. Dorn was a favorite politician of the textile manufacturers who had moved South from New England to escape the unions. South Carolina mill owners hated unions with a single-minded passion. In 1934, mill towns across Dixie had exploded in the largest coordinated walkout in American history—which ended quickly in the Palmetto State after armed guards in one town gunned down five strikers in cold blood. And after the Wagner Act federally guaranteed the right for employees to form a union, the mill owners hated Washington even more than they did the CIO. Dorn was their kind of fanatic. He loved to brag to reporters about sending money bound for his district *back* to the federal treasury.

Like Manion, Dorn mused constantly on the subject of political realignment. So when Manion got in touch to tell him the interesting news that Orval Faubus might be willing to run for President, Dorn was ready with an idea. Faubus should announce his candidacy for the Democratic presidential nomination on a conservative platform and enter primaries in the North, as Johnson suggested. At the same time, For America should line up some prominent conservative to run for the *Republican* nomination on the same platform. "*X* for President" clubs would be organized in the North, "Faubus for President" clubs in the South. And when both candidates were turned back at their respective party conventions, the two organizations would merge to form a new party to back *one* of the candidates—who, combining the votes of Dixiecrats and Taft Republicans, could finally block the major-party candidates from an electoral college majority.

Manion thought that was brilliant. Sixteen months remained before the 1960 party conventions. To Johnson, Manion wrote: "What you tell me about Governor Faubus is very interesting and very welcome news. . . . Be sure that you will find a great deal of sympathetic support in the North for the procedure you outlined." He scrawled a note to General Wood asking him for a meeting "on the prospects of a conservative candidate in the 1960 elections." He had an idea which Republican they could tap for their scheme, and he curled one more sentence into the margin: "Confidentially, what would you think about a committee to draft Goldwater for the Republican nomination for President? Such a movement may start a 'prairie fire.' "

The next day he left for an Easter vacation in Central America, leaving both letters on his desk to await his return. He was especially reluctant to send the one to General Wood. Barry Goldwater of Arizona seemed an unsteady rock on which to build their church. The man was an oddball, hard to place, not *quite* one of them. The people loved Barry in Arizona. But as one of Manion's friends reminded him, "It is all too obvious there is only one Arizona."

MERCHANT PRINCE

The story was told again and again, in a ribbon of biographical profiles as sunny and unchanging as a stretch of desert interstate: how Barry Goldwater's grandfather "Big Mike," one of twenty-two children, emigrated from Poland rather than face conscription in the czar's army, learned haute couture in Paris, steamed to Panama, crossed the isthmus by mule and by foot, got to gold-rush San Francisco and found it full up with dry-goods provisioners, whereupon, helped by a network of fellow Yiddish-speaking Jews, he opened a saloon—which doubled as a brothel. Then he made his way to a wide spot in the road—Phoenix. He went on to become Arizona Territory's retail potentate, bringing the shirtwaists, corsets, gloves, and parasols of the East to a grateful frontier and in the process bestowing on rough but grand Arizona its defining family.

Barry's father, Baron, was a dude with perfumed hair who was kicked out of the Prescott, Arizona, mayoralty for expanding the reach of the government too much. Barry's uncle Morris was the future senator's political role model— a states' rights advocate who founded the Arizona Democratic Party, got himself reelected mayor of Prescott nine times, paved her streets, founded her militia and fire brigade, and lobbied to bring a transcontinental railroad spur through town. His own man, he boldly kept his father's Jewish identity though his brother Baron converted to Episcopalianism.

Barry's mother, Josephine, descended from Puritan dissenter Roger Williams, was a tuberculosis patient ("lunger") sent to Arizona to be rehabilitated in the hot, dry air who recovered to become an outdoorswoman who slept with a loaded revolver under her pillow, and raised her children on camping trips deep into the desert wilderness, and trooped them off to the Phoenix Indian School every morning to salute the flag as it was raised. Barry's first memory, at three years old, was of his mother taking their own flag down to sew on a forty-seventh and forty-eighth star for the new states of Arizona and

New Mexico. (Other versions of the story have him serving as a ring bearer at a wedding when a man rushes into church to announce Arizona's statehood.)

Few politicians had a childhood more colorful than Barry Goldwater's, it was said. He rubbed shoulders with boys of all classes and races, was a basement tinkerer and a hellion who fired a miniature cannon at the steeple of the Methodist Church and flipped pats of butter onto the ceiling, read *Popular Mechanics* instead of his schoolbooks, and nearly flunked out of high school—then grew into a man at military school, graduating with the award for best all-around cadet. He left the University of Arizona after one year to take over the family business after his father's death (his great regret in life was not attending West Point). He was the company's master promoter, modest (he worked in a tiny basement office) and generous (always handing out advances, advice, and outright gifts to whatever supplicant should ask), who became famous by introducing the "antsy-pants" fad to the nation—boxer shorts printed with the critters scampering up the front and back.

Barry's exploits organizing relief flights for starving Navajo families as an Army Air Corps Reserves flier in the 1930s, shooting the Colorado River in a flimsy plywood boat in 1940, flying a ferry route during World War II so dangerous it was known as the "Aluminum Trail," were lovingly chronicled by the press through the 1950s and early 1960s—as was the story of how he became a politician: a fresh-scrubbed veteran who deplored the dissipation his city had fallen into in his absence, he was drafted onto a nonpartisan slate of reformist city councilmen. He preached self-help even if it hurt himself: opposing a bid by downtown merchants for the city to build them a parking structure, Goldwater—a downtown merchant—snapped, "Let them do it for themselves!" His colleagues appointed him vice chair for his plainspoken effectiveness; when speeches went on for too long he wound up his set of chattering toy teeth; he shut up one municipal grifter in mid-sentence with a booming "You're a liar!" He ended legal segregation in Phoenix schools and in his own beloved National Guard (his first Senate staff assistant was a black woman lawyer). He managed the successful campaign of Arizona's first Republican governor since the 1920s, shuttling him to every settlement in the state in his own plane. He became the state's first Republican senator by beating one of the country's most powerful Democrats in an outsider's campaign to beat them all.

To his chroniclers, Goldwater, and the Goldwaters, *were* Arizona; one of them even observed a resemblance between the senator's chiseled, angular face and the native geography. Goldwater encouraged the identification whenever he could. Stewart Alsop once wrote an article on Barry Goldwater in which he recorded the senator's utter delight, flying high above Phoenix, in telling the journalist, "If you'd dropped a five-dollar bill down there before the war, it would be worth a couple of hundred now." Alsop toured the house Goldwater had built in 1952—Bia-Nun-I-Kin, Navajo for "house on a hill"—on a deserted hillside. Goldwater called himself a conservative, but Alsop marveled that besides books, there wasn't a thing that was *old* in this house, all angles and odd shapes, a masterpiece of high desert modernism complete with a TV, burglar alarm, and outside lights that Goldwater could work from controls on the headboard of his bed. This was not a man who habitually looked backward. "Out here in the West," Goldwater told him, "we're not harassed by the fear of what might happen." Goldwaters, he said, "have always taken risks."

Some of it was even true. Reading profiles of Goldwater written in the eight or so years of his uninterrupted honeymoon with the press as a young senator is a bit like driving that stretch of desert interstate: the illusion of autonomy came courtesy of dollars and leadership from Washington; the sweeping view that seems to encompass the horizon hides everything beyond a narrow ribbon of reality. Barry Goldwater once wrote that flying an airplane is "the ultimate extension of individual freedom." He neglected to note that a pilot not hemmed in by the intricate regulatory apparatus of the skies may get only as far as the plane he collides with in midair.

Of his family he would say, "We didn't know the federal government. Everything that was done, we did it ourselves." But Big Mike's rise came from knowing the federal government intimately. The Arizona Territory he traveled to in 1860 to follow a gold strike developed as a virtual ward of the federal government, used as a base for fighting the Indian Wars. ("Hostilities in Arizona are kept up with a view of protecting inhabitants," a general sardonically observed, "most of whom are supported by the hostilities.") The money to build Big Mike's first Goldwater's store in 1872 came largely from contracts for provisioning Army camps and delivering mail. Pioneering days were long past, at any rate, by the time his grandchildren came along: Barry, born in 1909, and his sister and brother grew up with a nurse, chauffeur, and live-in maid. He hardly needed to take over at the store after his father's death because a hired manager, not Baron Goldwater, ran it; Barry later admitted he left college because he didn't like it. He never carried cash growing up; when he wanted to make a purchase in any store in Phoenix, he could charge it to his father.

His generation's coming marked the greatest confluence of all of federal largesse to Arizona and Goldwater fortune: the Roosevelt Dam, begun in 1905. The population of nearby Phoenix, fattened by construction money, doubled in five years. During World War I, thanks to the call for stepped-up production of the state economy's "Three C's"—cotton, copper, and cattle—it boomed some more. During the 1920s, three more reclamation projects gave federal handouts to farmers and ranchers, and federal outlays for health and highways and vocational education made up 15 percent of Arizona's economy, and the population of Phoenix nearly tripled.

Then came the New Deal. The economic development of the South and the West was one of Franklin Roosevelt's most cherished goals. Washington operated fifty different federal agencies in Arizona, in addition to the Hoover Dam project. Federal funds totaling $342 million went to the state, and less than $16 million in taxes were remitted in return.

By then Barry Goldwater and a brother were in charge of the family enterprise. They did not profess gratitude for the federal government's help. In 1934 they removed the blue eagle emblem of Roosevelt's National Recovery Administration from the windows of their stores to protest its price dictates. Their response to the Depression was that private citizens should take care of their own, the way they did: Goldwater's paid higher than the industry wage; provided health, accident, life, and pension benefits; provided profit sharing, a store psychiatrist, and a formal retirement plan. Later came a twenty-five-acre farm for employee recreation, and a day camp for children. The family allowed employees to examine the company's books whenever they wished.

In June of 1938, when the Works Progress Administration was putting money to spend in department stores in the hands of sixteen thousand WPA construction workers, Barry greeted the passage of the Fair Labor Standards Act, raising the minimum wage from 25 to 40 cents and limiting working hours to forty-four a week, with his first public political pronouncement, an open letter to the President in the *Phoenix Gazette*. "My friend," Goldwater began, mocking Roosevelt's fireside chat salutation, "you have, for over five years, been telling me about your plans; how much they were going to do and how much they were going to mean to me. Now I want to turn around and ask you just what have they done that would be of any value to me as a businessman and a citizen." He complained of astronomical taxes and alphabet-soup agencies; he argued that workmen had been able to win higher wages only because Roosevelt's economic policies forced factories to operate for fewer hours; he charged that the President had "turned over to the racketeering practices of ill-organized unions the future of the workingman. Witness the chaos they are creating in the Eastern cities. Witness the men thrown out of work, the riots, the bloodshed, and the ill feeling between labor and capital, and then decide for yourself if that plan worked."

"I would like to know just where you are leading us," he concluded. "I like the old-fashioned way of being an American a lot better than the way we are headed for now."

The ideal politician, it has been written, is an ordinary representative of his class with extraordinary abilities. Goldwater wrote as a member of an imaginary republic of beneficent businessmen-citizens just like himself. It was not for him to observe that the operating deficits brought on by the Goldwater's stores' generous benefits package were covered out of interest generated from his wife's trust fund. (Indiana-born Peggy was an heiress of the Borg-Warner fortune. Her family vacationed in Arizona, where they socialized with the most prominent local family—the Goldwaters—as a matter of course.) Goldwater's approach to any political problem invariably derived from the evidence of his own eyes—an attitude most visible in his views on discrimination. "There never was a lot of it," he recalled of the Phoenix of his youth. Yet when he was eleven the chamber of commerce took out an ad boasting of Phoenix's "very small percentage of Mexicans, Negroes, or foreigners." Barry Goldwater delighted in, and journalists delighted in repeating, his corny put-downs of anti-Semites. Why couldn't he play nine holes, he was supposed to have responded when kicked off a golf course, since he was only half Jewish? They reported how when he took over as president of Phoenix Country Club in 1949, he said if they didn't allow his friend Harry Rosenzweig to join he would blackball every name. Rosenzweig became the first Jew the club ever admitted. Left out of the tale was that another Jew wasn't allowed in for a decade.

Later he would be described as a political innocent. This was not exactly true. Never a ruthless politician, he was ever a politician, with a classic politician's upbringing: a doting mother who convinced him he could accomplish everything; a distant, moody father who convinced him that no accomplishment was enough. The letter to Roosevelt marked the moment a master salesman began selling himself to his state. He crisscrossed Arizona in his airplane delivering lectures on Native American handicrafts and Arizona's natural wonders. After his trip down the Colorado he presented his film of the adventure, sometimes five times a day, in rented theaters all over the state. (He descended from the sky, a witness who was ten years old at the time remembers, like a "bronze god who had just beaten the river.") The trip had been dangerous; making sure it was all captured on film even more so. Goldwater had a flair for self-dramatization. His gift for nature photography became renowned. But his most impressive photo is an extraordinarily complex and accomplished self-portrait: Barry in cowboy hat with smoldering cigarette, his face half obscured by shadow, the whole composition doubled in background silhouette.

When World War II came, Goldwater was too old to win a flying commission through normal channels. He got family friends—Senators McFarland and Hayden—to expedite the paperwork. When he returned, he signed on to head the retailers' wing of the Veterans Right to Work Committee. He did not see what a union shop could bring workers that enlightened employers like himself were not already giving them. "It's almost," a radio ad for the committee declared, "as if we were living in pre-war Germany. We just can't let that sort of thing happen here! These despotic little labor racketeers, the would-be Hitlers, must be crushed now—once and for all—before it's too late."

That same year Goldwater was appointed to the Colorado River Commission, an enormously important post in a state that relied on monumental irrigation projects for its very economic existence. In this, at least, he showed a keen appreciation of the federal government's role in supporting Arizona's bounty—and also showed a skilled political hand: to his California vendors he darkly warned of the "strangling of the life from California-Arizona trade relations" if Arizona were denied its fair share of Colorado River waters; he urged his Eastern suppliers to lobby their congressional representatives to save the "agricultural empire" that let him be such a good customer. A political career soon followed.

Arizona had entered statehood in 1912 with two political factions. One was a man: Governor George W. P. Hunt, a William Jennings Bryan–style populist crusader. The other consisted of the copper, cotton, and cattle interests who opposed him. All of them were Democrats—the magnates solely for the quadrennial privilege of attempting to deny Hunt the gubernatorial nomination. By the time Hunt finally rode off into the sunset in 1932, the Republican Party had practically ceased to exist in Arizona. Most of the state's Republicans were Midwestern transplants of maverick disposition—like the boys' novelist Clarence Budington Kelland, and Barry Goldwater's feisty mother Josephine, who came from an Illinois clan whose commitment to the party went back to Lincoln's day and who taught her children the GOP's virtues at her knee.

The war changed everything. The Pentagon, valuing Phoenix for its ideal flying weather—and its alacrity in donating land—built Luke Air Force Base, Williams Air Force Base, Falcon Field, and Thunderbird Field; plants for Goodyear Aircraft, Consolidated Aircraft, AiResearch, Alcoa, and Motorola followed—the companies also drawn by Arizona's right-to-work law. Young new families came to the Southwest after the war to vacation in the hot, dry air; many settled there. Arizona could then boast a fourth C: climate. The newcomers, a Democratic pol lamented, "altered the whole demography of the place": the newcomers were largely Republican.

The most important Republican came in 1946: Eugene Pulliam, owner of Indianapolis's *Star* and *News*. Pulliam spotted an opportunity in Phoenix. A moderate Republican internationalist, he loved a reform crusade. He had been vacationing in Phoenix for years and saw its potential during the squalid years when the place was celebrated as "sin city" by the servicemen who passed through. In 1946 he bought the morning and evening newspapers, the *Republic* and the *Gazette*, and set to work cleaning up the town. Part of the problem, he realized, was the Democrats' spoils-inducing political monopoly. Arizona needed a two-party system to keep officeholders honest; Phoenix needed a nonpartisan charter-style city government.

He knew who to turn to. There is no business relationship more symbiotic than that between newspapers and department stores, their most assiduous advertisers. Phoenix's grandest department stores happened to be operated by a Republican family. And when Pulliam put together his slate of twenty-seven reform candidates for city council in 1949, he talked that family's scion into leading it. Everyone knew Barry Goldwater, the former president of the chamber of commerce and chairman of the community chest; a board member of the YMCA, the art museum, two hospitals; a member of every club in town. The slate won in a sweep. Goldwater got three times as many votes as anyone else.

When his colleagues chose him as vice chair of the city council he suddenly found himself the highest Republican officeholder in the state. Mayor Nicholas Udall pegged this "young merchant prince who liked to get his picture taken and fly airplanes" as an aspirant for higher office. Udall had reason to fear. The reformers had reduced the number of city departments from twenty-seven to twelve and turned a projected $400,000 budget deficit into a $275,000 surplus. Corruption was decimated; business boomed. In 1950 *Look* magazine and the National Municipal League gave Phoenix their annual All-American City award "in recognition of progress achieved through intelligent citizen action."

Goldwater decided to run for governor. He struck a deal with another popular Republican aspirant, a sentimental radio personality named Howard Pyle: Pyle would plug Goldwater for the statehouse, and Goldwater would back Pyle for U.S. Senate. Then Pyle pulled a dirty trick, "letting" himself be drafted into the gubernatorial race at the state convention. Goldwater, committed to building the Republican Party in the state, didn't make a fuss; he swallowed his pride and signed on as Pyle's campaign manager—and committed himself to run hard for Senate. Though when the handsome young campaign manager emerged from the cockpit of his twin-engine Beachcraft Bonanza as the Pyle campaign arrived in a town, he usually upstaged the balding candidate. The incumbent, Susan Frohmiller, had a hard time taking all this seriously. She had won reelection time and again as state auditor for her brilliant management of Arizona's volcanic growth. Registered Democrats outnumbered registered Republicans five to one. She spent only $875 on her campaign—and Pyle won by 3,000 votes.

A year later, the honey-voiced, wild-maned, wrinkle-faced giant of the Senate from Illinois, Everett McKinley Dirksen, came to Phoenix to address the state Republican convention. He pulled Barry and Peggy Goldwater out of the cocktail-hour snarl and made the case that Barry should run for the U.S. Senate. Goldwater would later portray himself the startled naïf in the encounter, but he was already compiling a scrapbook on his opponent, junior senator Ernest McFarland, the popular author of the GI Bill and the Senate minority leader. Goldwater was the underdog: McFarland had been chosen leader by his party precisely because his seat seemed so safe, after the previous leader had been replaced by Dirksen for purported softness on Communism. When asked by a friend why he had the temerity to think he could beat McFarland, Goldwater replied: "I can call ten thousand people in this state by their first name."

One of them was the state's most effective political operative. Swarthy, intense, standoffish, Stephen Shadegg was a master of appearances, a man fascinated by the space between deception and detection; he was a trained actor and the author, under a pseudonym, of hundreds of True Crime stories. He made most of his money as proprietor of "S-K Research Laboratories"—which researched nothing, but manufactured an asthma remedy he had invented. Pulling on his pipe, he held journalists enthralled. "His interests range from 'lies' to 'God,' " the *New York Times* reported in a profile. It was a time when a man who was cynical enough to imply that truth was a relative thing was rare. And for a political campaign, valuable. "Approached in the right fashion at the right time," he once wrote, "a voter can be persuaded to give his ballot to a candidate whose philosophy is opposed to the cherished notions of the voter." He was neither a Republican nor a Democrat; his latest triumph was running the reelection bid of Arizona's senior senator, Carl Hayden.

Shadegg argued with himself: Could the merchant prince win? Years later Shadegg penned a primer called *How to Win an Election*. There were three types of voters, he theorized: Committeds, Undecideds, and Indifferents. The first step to victory was identifying the Indifferents—"those who don't vote at all, or vote only in response to an emotional appeal, or as a result of some carefully planned campaign technique which makes it easy for them to reach a decision." Indifferents were the kind of suckers another master of persuasion said were born every minute. And Shadegg decided that the evidence from 1950, when thousands of Arizona voters voted the straight Democrat line with one exception—crossing over to vote *against* the vastly more qualified woman—proved to him that Arizona was so lousy with Indifferents that just about anyone with a good campaign manager could win.

Shadegg agreed to manage Goldwater, if Goldwater would submit to his iron-clad rules: the candidate would do whatever he was told by the campaign manager, would follow his prepared speeches, and would take no stand without checking with Shadegg first. "Oh, so you think I'll pop off?" Goldwater replied—and accepted the conditions.

Shadegg reasoned that Goldwater needed the votes of 90 percent of the state's Republicans and 25 percent of the vastly greater number of Democrats. Arizona's new Republicans could be counted on to go to the polls in November to vote for President. For them to go for the Senate nominee, they would have to believe that their vote wouldn't be wasted. So Shadegg delegated Goldwater the task of finding a strong Republican candidate for every state office. For the first time, in a state whose ninety-member lower chamber held but two Republicans, it had to be possible for Republicans to vote a straight ticket. Goldwater was born for the job. He persuaded forty of the state's most dynamic young men, most of them postwar transplants, to run for office. Shadegg ran him ragged all autumn, sending him on as many coffee hours in the state's widely scattered Republicans' homes as he could fit in, to do the hard work of convincing them that 1952 was finally their year in Arizona. In the process, Goldwater built a remarkable network of activist Republicans who knew and trusted him. Even if he lost, he likely would emerge as party boss.

Shadegg worked on the Indifferents. Arizonans *trusted* McFarland, he decided. They must be made to distrust him. The opportunity came in September when McFarland made a gaffe. Shadegg decided to have Goldwater exploit it in his kickoff speech, delivered from the steps of the Yavapai County Courthouse in Prescott. He saved the sucker punch for the end: "The people of Arizona are entitled to know that in the past week the junior Senator described our Korean War as a 'cheap' war." *Gasps.* " 'Cheap,' he said, because we're killing nine Chinese for every American boy. And to justify his participation in this blunder of the Truman administration, he added to his statement these words: 'It is the Korean War which is making us prosperous.' "

Goldwater dug in the knife: "I challenge the junior senator from Arizona to find anywhere within the border of this state, or anywhere within the borders of the United States, a single mother or father who counts our casualties as cheap—who'd be willing to exchange the life of one American boy for the nine Communists or the nine hundred Red Communists or nine million Communists."

Eugene Pulliam helped with editorials and slanted news columns. Radio ads blanketed the state with the sounds of dive-bombers, machine guns, grunts in the trenches, and a disgusted voice-over: "This is what McFarland calls a cheap war." Shadegg devised a maddeningly catchy jingle for commercials that aired on the new medium of television:

> *Voter, voter, you'll be thinking*
> *What a fine land this will be*
> *When the taxes have been lowered*
> *Taxes less for you and me.*

McFarland, way ahead in the polls, hardly deigned to mount a campaign. Shadegg had workers scribble fifty thousand postcards timed to arrive at the homes of registered Democrats the day before the balloting. Each was signed "Barry."

Barry Goldwater was swept into the U.S. Senate on Ike's coattails by a slim seven thousand votes. That was shocking. Even more so was that the Republicans he had recruited won, too: John J. Rhodes, another handsome young jet-jockey, became a U.S. congressman. Thirty Republicans were sent to the state senate, thirty-five to the House. Arizona now had a Republican Party. It was made up of men like lawyer Richard Kleindienst: young (twenty-nine), smart (Harvard Phi Beta Kappa), deeply rooted in Arizona's cowboy mythos ("Any son of a bitch out there thinks he's big enough to run me and my family out of this town, come on up and try!" his granddad had announced, .45 in hand, when vigilantes set upon him for voting for Alf Landon)—and a close personal friend of Barry Goldwater. Goldwater would hug close to these men for the rest of his political career.

Barry Goldwater was not a well-known senator during Dwight D. Eisenhower's first term. He was not much missed on the floor when party leaders assigned him a job that took him very far from Washington, very often: chairman of the Senate Republican Campaign Committee, trouping countless miles to GOP gatherings of every imaginable kind to raise funds for Senate hopefuls. Neither did needy constituents much miss him; they knew that if you wanted something done in Washington, you got in touch with Carl Hayden, who was the powerful chair of the Senate Ways and Means Committee.

Goldwater loved the road, and he logged more miles than any other chairman in history. Whenever possible he booked talks on the side, at venues like the Marion County, Illinois, Soldiers and Sailors Reunion, the Southern Nevada Knife and Fork Club, the Michigan Christian Endeavor Convention— and, especially, with veterans' groups like the American Legion and business-

men's redoubts like the free-market-worshiping National Association of Manufacturers, where he nearly always brought down the house. He attacked the
liberals who were taking charge of the Democratic Party and the Republicans
who seemed to want the country to adopt a "dime store New Deal" (New Deal
programs, only cheaper)—a daring message in a season when nonpartisan bon-
homie was close to a Washington religion. Conservatives, accustomed to party
officials who blew into town to crow about the latest Republican successes
keeping up with the Lyndon Johnsons, began taking notice. So did the media;
Time ran a short, glowing profile of Goldwater in 1955 entitled "Jet-Age Senator with a Warning."

But by the time Eisenhower's second term approached, Goldwater's
prospects looked if anything to be diminishing. Some among the GOP leadership began wondering whether a man whose best speech was a defense of Joe
McCarthy was quite the man to represent a party wracked by internal dissen-
sion; others were hardly aware of what he stood for at all. Eisenhower confidant Paul Hoffman, in a polemic in *Collier's* the week before the 1956 election
entitled "How Eisenhower Saved the Republican Party" (answer: by making it
more like the Democrats), divided legislators to Eisenhower's right into two
categories: "unappeasables" and "faint hopes." Goldwater was a faint hope.

He would not be mislabeled for long. The national collegiate debating
topic for the 1957–58 school year was "Resolved—that the requirement of
membership in a labor union as a condition of employment should be illegal."
Nineteen fifty-eight was the year of the right-to-work debate. Right-to-work
was Barry Goldwater's issue. When he arrived in Washington, Goldwater, a
military buff and an outdoorsman, had asked Bob Taft for berths on the Armed
Services and Interior Committees. He was put on Banking and Labor instead.
Goldwater protested that he had run a department store, not a bank; that his
stores had never had unions because the workers had never wanted one. Taft
said he wanted a businessman on these committees. The decision shaped a
political destiny.

In 1957 the Democrats began control of the Senate. That made the former
minority counsel of the Government Operations Committee's Permanent
Subcommittee on Investigations, Robert F. Kennedy, the majority counsel.
Investigations was Joe McCarthy's old fiefdom. Determined to reclaim the
subcommittee's good name—and also determined to give his brother, who was
a member of the committee, a leg up on the field for the 1960 Democratic presidential nomination—Robert Kennedy began an inquiry into corruption among
contractors providing clothing for the military. The trail led him to the Mafia's
spectacular success making trade unions—especially the giant transport union,

the Teamsters—its playground. He convinced Senator John McClellan to chair
a select committee to investigate.

The series of hearings that followed were an extraordinary success. Americans sat glued to their TV screens for months on end as the panel questioned
thugs with names like Thomas "Three-Finger Brown" Lucchese, Frank "Lefty"
Rosenthal, and Anthony "Tony Ducks" Corallo. Two Chicago racketeers were
brought to testify straight from the Illinois State Prison in Joliet, handcuffed
together. Teamsters president Dave Beck Sr., asked if he knew one Dave Beck
Jr., replied, "I decline to answer this question on the grounds it might open up
avenues of questions that would tend to incriminate me." Jimmy Hoffa, elected
Beck's successor at a convention at which only 4.8 percent of the delegates
were legally entitled to vote, answered one question, "To the best of my recollection I must recall on my memory I cannot remember." RFK's staff was
pulling consecutive sixteen-hour stretches, processing six hundred letters a day
from frightened victims of harassment, crisscrossing the country to interview
anyone and everyone with information that might help nail a case, tracing
phone calls all the way down to third and fourth parties to a hustle. They turned
up millions of dollars of diverted—stolen—union dues. Genuine evil was
being exposed. And through it all, Democrats gave fulsome praise to the vast
majority of the nation's unions that were honest, decent, and patriotic. After
fearing a smear job at the outset, many unionists ended up praising the work
the three years of hearings did to clean up their movement.

All of the hearings, that is, except the one pursued in early 1958 by the
select committee's junior member, who had been put on the panel only at the last
minute when Joe McCarthy died: Barry Goldwater. Since he was on the Labor
Committee, the Republican leadership decided he must know something about
labor.

Goldwater had learned how to think about unions from the Phoenix lawyer
Denison Kitchel. The son of a partner at a prominent Wall Street law firm,
Kitchel was set to follow in his father's footsteps when, in 1934, he shocked his
blue-blooded family by announcing that he was moving to Arizona. ("What are
you going to practice on out there, cows?" his father asked.) He embraced his
adopted land with the zeal of the convert. Once he had been a liberal. Now
Kitchel seethed with resentment at the Eastern Establishment. He had joined
the *Arizona* Establishment—who looked east for their loans (New York controlled a quarter of the nation's banking reserves), leased their land from Washington (the federal government owned almost half of Arizona's land), and, if
they were baseball fans, listened to Harry Caray's broadcasts of the St. Louis
Cardinals, the closest major league team. Kitchel married Naomi Douglas,
niece of the baron who had created the copper empire in the southeast corner of

the state, now owned by the mining company Phelps Dodge. He became Phelps Dodge's labor counsel. He became Barry Goldwater's best friend.

For decades Phelps Dodge had operated as its own law in southeast Arizona. When Governor Hunt brokered a settlement to a 1915 strike that was favorable to the workers, and called in the National Guard to protect the deal, the company responded by bankrolling Hunt's defeat in 1916 by the suspicious total of 30 votes. The next year the mining company staged a dawn raid in which gun-toting agents herded union miners and "any suspicious-looking person" onto manure-laden cattle cars, hauled them across the state line, and dropped them off in the middle of the desert. Forced migrations were not unheard of in American industrial history. This one was the worst ever. It ended with two dead.

Not much had changed in Bisbee by the time Kitchel arrived in the 1930s. Another union-organizing drive began, and Phelps Dodge responded by firing the union members. But in Washington, everything had changed. The new Wagner Act had chartered the National Labor Relations Board, which ordered Phelps to hire the union workers back—and give them back pay. The company appealed all the way to the Supreme Court in 1941. Felix Frankfurter, Kitchel's professor at Harvard Law, handed down a decision that declared Kitchel's argument "textual mutilation"—and enshrined federal labor law's "Phelps Dodge rule" forcing companies to hire union members, which would haunt Kitchel for the rest of his days. Yet the humiliation had an upside. For Kitchel was among the first corporate lawyers to grasp the new reality of the Roosevelt era: the unions could no longer be beaten by intimidation, or even by being outlasted in strikes, let alone with industrial reenactments of the Trail of Tears. Now the name of the game was politics.

The key battleground was over right-to-work laws. The Wagner Act dictated that if a majority of workers at any company chose a union to represent them, that union became the sole bargaining agent for all the workers in the company. That stipulation posed a knotty problem: if a worker enjoyed the benefits of a contract whether he joined the union or not, why should he join? Labor's solution was to demand "union shop" provisions in contracts, requiring that all new hires must join up within a certain time. But from management's perspective, that provision didn't just give unions power on the shop floor; it gave them a steady, guaranteed stream of dues, ensuring the unions unprecedented *political* power to press their liberal agenda in Washington and every state capital in the country.

But management had its own special advantage. The same year that Kitchel argued in front of the Supreme Court, the right-wing *Dallas Morning News* ran an editorial headlined "MAGNA CARTA." It proposed an amendment to

the Constitution to make forcing a worker to join a union illegal—protecting
the "right to work." It was a masterstroke. Now, pressing for right-to-work
laws, companies could wield the most potent symbol in the American civil religion: liberty. Unions were left in the rhetorical dust. Labor lawyer Arthur J.
Goldberg was left to defend the union shop by claiming that unions weren't
exactly voluntary organizations in the first place, but more like armies: they
required conscription to exist. That didn't sound very American.

The right achieved a major victory when the Taft-Hartley Act in 1947 gave
states license to pass their own right-to-work laws. (Arizona was the first to do
so.) Every year afterward liberals fought to repeal the union shop exemption,
and conservatives fought to preserve it—and to pass more state right-to-work
laws. When the American Federation of Labor merged with the Congress of
Industrial Organizations in 1955, creating a confederation that represented a
quarter of the civilian workforce, and heavily funded its political arm, the
Committee on Political Education, the stakes were raised appreciably. In Arizona, Kitchel implored Gene Pulliam to give a group of businessmen a Sunday
column in the *Republic*, "Voice of Free Enterpise," to run alongside the one he
had given to the Arizona Labor Federation. Labor bosses, the typical businessmen's column would explain, were guilty of "the boldest bid for economic and
political power ever made by any group since the founding of our nation." For
if they could "arrange it that everyone who works has to be a union member in
good standing the money rolls in automatically." With that money they could
"overwhelm all who seek election to public office without their endorsement."
Companies who had fought all the way to the Supreme Court for the right to
fire workers whenever and however they liked, who had workers' blood on
their hands, could now effectively style themselves as the worker's best friend.

But labor was prevailing in the political war—thanks largely to Walter
Reuther, president of the United Automobile Workers. The son of a German
immigrant beer truck driver and militant socialist who raised his sons to save
the world, Reuther began his career as a labor organizer in the mid-1930s, just
as unions were developing a dazzlingly audacious new tactic: at the opening
whistle, activists simply sat down at their machines and refused to leave until
the owners agreed to bargain with them. Sit-down strikes were wars, naked
fights for power—struggles for control of the factory between the capitalists
who owned them and the workers who breathed them life, management
advancing with tear gas and blackjacks, the workers making their stand with
whatever heavy projectiles they could find. The grandest of all the actions
struck GM's giant works in Flint, Michigan. It was a watershed in labor history. At the height of the uprising, in early 1937, the new Michigan governor,
Frank Murphy, moved in the militia, and strikers prepared for the inevitable

blows to rain down upon their heads. They never came. Murphy was intervening on the *union*'s side—because he owed his office to the UAW's get-out-the-vote effort for him the previous November. This was an enormous lesson, the same lesson learned by Denison Kitchel, and Reuther was among the first labor leaders to grasp it: now the real battles were to be fought and won in the political arena. Previous labor leaders jealously guarded their independence from government. But Reuther rose by combining old-school shop-floor organizing, legislative-floor politicking to create a friendly legal climate, and precinct work to elect the politicians that believed in Walter Reuther's grand left-wing vision, inherited from his father, that business, labor, and government, working together, could more rationally run industries than could private enterprise alone. He never saw his dream fulfilled. But with more and more labor-friendly politicians in Washington and the state capitals willing to back him up, he did manage to negotiate the most splendid contracts—and some of the most liberal laws—American workers had ever won. And that, to his enemies, was bad enough.

Reuther became head of the UAW's General Motors division in the 1940s. He understood the massive, exquisitely calibrated production system of America's biggest corporation better than most of its executives. Knowing that just one small wildcat strike could render half a dozen plants useless, he began consolidating control of his members so that no wildcats would take place. Thus able to promise America's largest corporation what it wanted—labor peace—he was able to gain unheard-of concessions in return: a contractual "cost of living adjustment"; then, in 1955, a historic "guaranteed annual wage" whereby, for the first time, workers would be paid during layoffs—65 percent of full pay when state unemployment compensation levels (which UAW lobbying helped increase all around the country) were added in.

Walter Reuther soon became Public Enemy Number One in the offices of the kind of factory owner who supported Clarence Manion. Bargaining concessions won at the top of the industrial system had a tendency to trickle down as more and more workers demanded the same perks. But if the GMs of the world could afford these concessions—and, indeed, welcomed them because they greatly stabilized a company's labor relations—smaller manufacturers insisted they could not. Moreover, these company leaders believed with religious certainty that in this plague of Reuther-style contracts, which increased wages year by year regardless of productivity, were recipes for inflation. The contracts were also un-American: "Strict seniority without regard to individual merit, equal pay for unequal work," bathroom fixtures magnate Herbert Kohler said, "—these and similar bargaining demands of union leaders treat the workers en masse, not as individuals." If on top of supporting unions the government unbalanced its budget with reckless spending thanks to unions' undue influence in the political realm, inflation might race out of control. Union-shop provisions were the keystone of the entire edifice—so the right-to-work fight was the centerpiece of the effort to do "Reutherism" in. That 1955 GM contract, Clarence Manion railed in one of his first broadcasts, "moved Mr. Reuther close up to the supreme dictatorship of American organized labor as a prelude to a try for the presidency of the United States." It was "offered at the point of a strike threat to practically every big industry in the country by a labor monopoly that is exempt from the antitrust law and can, therefore, callously disregard the public interest that every other person, corporation, and organization is obliged to serve." (Reuther, of course, saw it just the opposite: the entire goal of the labor movement was to dignify the individual by removing him from the vagaries of market competition. *This* was the public interest.)

Manion and Kohler could rage at Reuther. But he was a useful adversary; years later conservatives should have lifted a glass in his honor. There would have likely not been much of a conservative movement without him as catalyst. The audience for sweaty appeals for isolationist anticommunism was shrinking with every passing month. The fight against Reuther, on the other hand, was one that everyone who owned a business—and everyone who aspired to owning a business—could understand. And the timing was propitious. In the South, the struggle against the civil rights carpetbaggers was also turning moderates into conservatives.

And in Washington, Barry Goldwater was inserting the fight against Reutherism into the McClellan Committee's proceedings on union corruption at every turn. He was looking for a wedge to get Walter Reuther into the witness chair.

The panel would ask a local Teamsters officer why the union had given $5,000 to the defense of a Portland district attorney indicted as a fixer for the city's gangsters. Goldwater would change the subject, asking about a $2,000 contribution to the campaign fund of a local politician. Colleagues zeroed in on an admission from a Pennsylvania union officer that he operated goon squads to keep union members from attending meetings when Goldwater interjected: "Suppose union membership was purely voluntary, with no union shop or anything like that. Don't you think attendance would be better?" The only effect these entreaties had on the hearings was to make them longer. The effect outside the hearing room, though, was to increase Goldwater's renown as a conservative spokesman. And the spokesman was growing into the role.

On the morning of April 8, Barry Goldwater's phone at the Old Senate Office Building rang with a pleasant invitation: lunch at the White House to help plan his Senate reelection bid in 1958. Goldwater paused; cast his eye over his comfortably cluttered office, at the desert landscapes pictured on his walls, the models of the dozens of airplanes he had flown, his prized Navajo kachina dolls; and drew in his breath. No, he said, he did not think it was the right time to come to lunch at the White House. That afternoon, he admitted, he was going to denounce his President on the floor of the Senate.

It was a crucial moment in the fiscal history of the United States. Conventional wisdom had always been that the symbol and substance of national economic health was a balanced budget. But with the Great Depression, Keynesian ideas began creeping into the thinking of the Democrats—that in times of stagnant private investment, government spending in excess of revenues could, by sloshing the citizenry in surplus cash, serve to "pump-prime" the economy back into life. For most Republicans such notions remained heresy. Now Eisenhower, buoyed by his landslide victory in November to break with the old Republican shibboleths and weighing the advice of his economic advisers that a recession was around the corner, had just submitted a record budget in March for FY 1958 of $71.8 billion.

And on April 8 Barry Goldwater stood up in a nearly empty Senate chamber and delivered himself of a tirade. "Until quite recently," he began, "I was personally satisfied that this administration was providing the responsible and realistic leadership so vital to the maintenance of a strong domestic economy which, in turn, is a vital factor in maintaining world peace.

"Now, however, I am not so sure. A $71.8 billion budget not only shocks me, but it weakens my faith."

He addressed "Mr. President" directly—to tell Eisenhower that he was a betrayer of the people's trust and a quisling in thrall to the Democrats' "economic inebriation." The President had embraced "the siren song of socialism," "government by bribe," "squanderbust government." And Goldwater was only warming up.

The junior senator now found himself cast in the press as the key player in the war rivening the GOP's left and right wings. *Time* ran another profile: below file photographs of dumpy Joe McCarthy, William Ezra Jenner, and George Malone, whom *Time* labeled "The Neanderthals," young Goldwater was pictured in the cockpit of a fighter plane. When the influential moderate Republican publisher John Shively Knight, proprietor of the *Chicago Daily News* and the *Detroit Free Press*, joined Goldwater's brief against the Administration budget ("WE'VE READ ALL 1,249 PAGES! AND BROTHER, IS IT LOADED WITH FRILLS AND BOONDOGGLES!" blared the *Daily News*), mentions of the dashing Arizona senator's name began cropping up in the press like dandelions.

Goldwater was eager to put the dispute with Eisenhower behind him. He had Walter Reuther in his sights. Throughout the spring, stories had appeared quoting "unnamed Republican Senators" as saying that McClellan Committee Democrats—the Kennedy brothers especially—were blocking hearings about the UAW's abuses in the calamitous strike at the Kohler Company outside Sheboygan, Wisconsin. In late May Goldwater stood before the 4,200 delegates to the forty-fifth annual Washington meeting of the United States Chamber of Commerce—and a goodly portion of the Washington press corps—to renew his call for $5 billion in cuts from the Eisenhower budget. Then he changed the subject: "Today, certain labor leaders bring to the bargaining table, not only the strength of their arguments, but the power of politics," he said. "What Mr. Reuther preaches is socialism."

Bobby Kennedy, feeling the heat, sent a staff investigator down to Sheboygan to investigate the Kohler strike. They found no evidence of UAW impropriety of which the company was not equally guilty. But Kennedy knew that politically he had no choice. In July he convinced McClellan to prepare for hearings on the Kohler strike, and he sent out another investigator—this one handpicked by the Republicans. Even as he did, *Newsweek* quoted an anonymous Republican senator accusing the Kennedys of running a "Reuther protection game." In fact, Jack Kennedy was not a fan of the labor left; journalists marveled at the senator's indifference to this powerful Democratic bloc. The calumny was useful to Barry Goldwater, though. Reuther, Goldwater told anyone who would listen, was the biggest threat the country faced. "Here is a man, a socialist," he spluttered to a group of unsuspecting Wellesley and Vassar girls who met with him on a field trip, "with all this power!" And he was zeroing in on a way to get that man into that witness chair.

If there had ever actually been a consensus in the party over "Modern Republicanism," the events at Herbert V. Kohler's great porcelain works outside Sheboygan, Wisconsin, would have broken its back. The plant was located in a town called Kohler—a company town that the family began building in 1912, a gorgeous place with vine-clad brick houses, lush parklands, peaceful streets, and, bounding the village on its east, the sprawling industrial complex that made the bathroom fixtures that made the name Kohler famous nationwide. The Kohler family was proud of how it took care of its people. The recreation facilities were top-notch, and free; a company band gave free Monday afternoon concerts at the factory; the family, which had placed two members in Wisconsin's governor's chair since the 1930s, built Sheboygan's harbor and its Home for the Friendless. Herb Kohler liked to brag that no worker was scared of him; he personally and proudly oversaw the naturalization process of his immigrant employees, many of whom lived in the lavish American Club boardinghouse in the center of Kohler Village. His factories anticipated Wisconsin's pioneering workmen's compensation law by two years.

But there were grievances at Kohler Village, and they mounted through the 1920s. The provision of company health insurance did not make up for the number of retired sandblasters suffering from tuberculosis in nearby Knoll Sanatorium (known locally as Kohler Pavilion). Kohler paid by the piece on the theory that workers should be treated as capitalists themselves—as individuals responsible for their own risks and rewards. But that policy hadn't kept him from hiring efficiency experts with stopwatches in their hands to weed out those workers who were unable to keep up the pace. If a crack was found on a piece taken out of storage for shipping, the man whose number it bore would find his paycheck docked years after the fact. Finally, in 1934, the workers struck. A dozen pickets were ambushed by eighty sheriff's deputies; several were shot in the back. Two workers died. Herb Kohler still refused to recognize the union.

By the 1950s Herb Kohler had added air-cooled industrial engines and precision controls for jet planes to his line. But he still ran his company town like a feudal manor. In 1952 the UAW won from Kohler workers the right to represent them. But it was only by the barest of majorities. This was worrisome: many of those who voted against the union were as zealous to turn back Reuther's men as Kohler was. In 1953 the company signed its first one-year contract with the UAW. The next year, UAW agents began renewal talks by asking for far more than they knew they would get, as would any good negotiator: a twenty-cent hourly raise, a seniority system, union-run pensions and health coverage, an arbitration clause, formalized layoff policies, a union shop. Then the union agents waited for the company to meet them halfway, like companies always had, at least since the battles of the 1930s had settled into the working comity between capital and labor that experts called the "Treaty of Detroit."

But Herbert Kohler refused to negotiate.

He had had enough of unions telling him how to run his company. His negotiator, Lyman Conger—an obligingly Dickensian villain, reedy-voiced, with a thin, cruel face, a hawkish nose, and a cleft chin—sent word through Kohler Village that there would be no slackening in operations in the event of a strike. Armed encampments were fashioned on plant rooftops; company officials held target practice on man-shaped targets. The union called a strike. Two thousand pickets surrounded the plant. Company loyalists who tried to make their way to work were harassed, sometimes beaten. A UAW official from

Detroit pummeled a scab at a saloon; another attacked someone at a filling station. When a court ordered the union to let those who wished cross the picket
lines, the action shifted to the community: those workers who dared to cross
were visited by "house parties"—jeering union mobs. Local chemical supply
houses did a brisk business in acid, used to deface property on both sides. The
company infiltrated the union with agents provocateurs, dispatched comely
lasses to entrap the leadership, and put a twenty-four-hour tail on National
Labor Relations Board investigators. Through it all the factories were kept running.

    This was just not done. The UAW, stunned, hardly knew what to do. To
save face, union agents abandoned their procedural demands; they would settle
for a seven-cent raise. They would have taken less. They wouldn't have got a
contract at any rate. Kohler had unilaterally severed its relationship with the
United Auto Workers—although, by the dictates of the Wagner Act, this action
was against the law. Herb Kohler hit the businessman's lecture circuit through
1955 and 1956 to advocate what amounted to Massive Resistance to the federal
government. The UAW, he thundered, was telling him he had no right to operate. "This union dictate has been and is being defied by Kohler Company and
by a host of men and women of courage who believe in their individual freedoms and rights, including the right to work!"

    The strike went on through 1957, an agonizing, slow war of attrition, the
violence piling up on both sides. On August 20 James Riddle Hoffa spent five
hours in the McClellan "Rackets" Committee's witness chair. Lights glaring,
cameras protruding, reporters climbing over each other to get a look, the Teamsters president was cornered into admitting to receiving $70,000 in outstanding
loans from parties with business before the union, without collateral or note; to
seventeen previous arrests; to returning $7,500 ("or maybe more") to grocers in
Detroit after he was brought up on charges of extortion. But when it came Senator Goldwater's turn to ask the questions, Hoffa enjoyed a respite. They
shared an enemy: Walter Reuther, whose idealistic, politicized unionism could
not have been more different from the Teamsters'. "I do not believe that it is
the original intention of labor organizations to try and control any . . . political
powers in this country for their own determination," Hoffa said. Goldwater
replied, "I think we both recognize that in the writing in the clouds today there
is an individual who would like to see that happen in this country. I do not like
to even suggest to let you and him fight, but for the good of the movement I am
very hopeful that your philosophy prevails."

    Two Sundays later on *Meet the Press*, Goldwater declared war. He said
that the Republicans were determined to get the McClellan Committee to hold

hearings on the UAW's abuses in Kohler. "And subsequent to that," he promised, "will be a full investigation into the affairs of Mr. Reuther's unions as they apply to his control, let us say, of the Democratic Party in Michigan, and pretty much his control of the Democratic Party across the country."

In actual fact, although the UAW controlled enough delegates at any Michigan Democratic conventions to give the union veto power over candidates, that was where Reuther's "control" ended. The Republicans' reach exceeded their grasp. Their hand-picked investigators returned from Sheboygan with a "report" consisting mostly of quotes from the National Labor Relations Board, minus the parts that criticized the company. The investigators promised imminent "sensational developments." Bobby Kennedy rushed down to Sheboygan to investigate. He discovered that one of the sensational developments—that $100,000 was missing from the union treasury—was an investigator's accounting error. The other stemmed from receipts from a Sheboygan butcher for yards and yards of sausage links, supposedly for the strike kitchen. The Republicans suspected a kickback: Who could possibly want to eat knockwurst every day? The answer was: The sausage-loving German-Americans of Sheboygan, who celebrate a Bratwurst Day each August. On the merits, the Republicans had little. Reuther gladly sent a decade's worth of UAW financial records to Washington. "Do you mean to tell me," asked an amazed committee accountant after wading through the ascetic leader's expense accounts, "that Walter Reuther pays for his own dry cleaning when he stays in a hotel?"

Goldwater was not deterred. "I would rather have Hoffa stealing my money," he declared, "than Reuther stealing my freedom." Extravagant rumors of a Kennedy-Reuther conspiracy developed; Senator Carl Curtis told Bobby he understood that all of the committee's incoming mail was being examined by AFL-CIO officers. Kennedy was enraged. He told Curtis that before the hearings he was indifferent to Walter Reuther, but that the Republicans were fast forcing him into Reuther's camp. Coming into a January 8 executive session, the McClellan Committee was on the verge of breaking up altogether over the issue of whether to schedule Kohler hearings. Then Jack Kennedy called the Republicans' bluff. He said he agreed with them. Kohler should have its day in court as soon as possible. Goldwater blanched; the Republican strategy was to drag out the affair, and drag the Kennedy brothers through the mud, for as long as possible. Wouldn't it be better to wait a few months? Bobby said no, it wouldn't be; Republican investigators had told him they would be ready to present their evidence in February. At which the Republicans were resigned: hearings would begin in February.

The Goldwater-Reuther feud escalated. Every year the Republicans celebrated Lincoln Day by putting on fund-raising dinners in a score of different cities linked by closed-circuit TV. Goldwater spoke at the one at Detroit's Masonic Temple. *Time*—which ran a picture of Goldwater in a Brando-esque T-shirt hefting a load of lumber, his squared-off, rugged face turned to the camera—reported that Goldwater elicited "whoops and hollers" with his speech:

> Underneath the Democrat label here in Michigan there is something new, and something dangerous—born of conspiracy and violence, sired by socialists and nurtured by the general treasury of the UAW-CIO. This is the pattern of men whose conscienceless use of violence and money to achieve political power belies the soothing, well-worded statements in favor of democratic processes, which they produce, at regular intervals, for public consumption.

He called Reuther "more dangerous than Soviet Russia and all the Sputniks."

The provocation couldn't have been more deliberate. The UAW was to take up residence at the same venue the following week for its convention to debate Reuther's bold "Share the Profits" plan—a demand that one-quarter of all corporate profits automatically go to workers. In Reuther's keynote address, though, the intricacies of bargaining gave way to red-faced diatribe. "Goldwater is a stooge for Republican politicians and big business," he cried, "undertaking a campaign of slander and smear to weaken democratic unions everywhere!" The Arizona senator was "mentally unbalanced and needs a psychiatrist." He was America's "number one political fanatic, peddler of class hatred, and union hater."

By March 27, the great Senate hearing room had rung for weeks with flat Germanic Midwestern accents declaiming with such acrimony on the events in Kohler that Counsel Kennedy could only compare the scene to what he had witnessed between Arabs and Jews in Israel. Now, finally, Reuther was going to testify. At last the two rivals would meet face to face. As the hour approached, the shadowboxing stepped up. Reuther told newsmen that Goldwater was "a political hypocrite and a moral coward"; Goldwater, schoolyard-style, rebounded that Reuther should "look into the mirror and see who is the coward." Their meeting promised to be the hottest ticket in town.

Once the hearings began, neither was long in drawing blood. Goldwater backed Reuther into an apology for the role union goons had played in Kohler. Reuther came back with an old quote from Goldwater that Kohler had a "right not to have a union if he can win a strike." But federal law—Reuther pointed out—said no company had the right to close down a union.

Reuther pressed: "I would like to know whether you think under the Taft-

Hartley law a company can decide not to have a union and destroy that union? I maintain they can't."

Goldwater was backed into a corner. "I will tell you what, someday you and I are going to get together and lock horns," he drawled.

Reuther: "We are together right now and I would like to ask you right now—"

Goldwater: "Wait a minute, Mr. Reuther. You are not asking the questions. I am asking the questions."

And so it went, until an exasperated entreaty issued from the chair: "Can you folks not get off somewhere and talk this out?"

As Reuther finished up his testimony, Goldwater leaned over to Bobby Kennedy to admit that Republican committee members had no case. "You were right," he said. "We never should have gotten into this matter." But Goldwater's feud with Walter Reuther was about more than the legal merits of the case. He had a reelection fight coming up. His crusade against Reuther would win it for him. It would also bring him more than what he had bargained for.

It was March 1958, and Goldwater feared for his reelection. Ernest McFarland was now the governor, and he was so eager to win his Senate seat back that he was descending upon every ribbon cutting and church picnic in the state. Goldwater wrote Shadegg worriedly about all the credit McFarland was getting for things he hadn't done. Shadegg gently chided his issues-minded boss: "People have short memories in politics." He might have added that many of the voters had no memory at all. Arizona's population had increased by a third since Goldwater had first won office. In Phoenix, streets like Rural Road became misnomers overnight. Roadrunners scurried for the hills just ahead of the bulldozers. But Shadegg wasn't taking any chances. In December, he had bought up every single billboard along the state's endless asphalt ribbons (YOUNG *COURAGEOUS*DEDICATED, they read, above a photo of Goldwater chosen by Shadegg that had been taken perhaps ten years earlier). Then he began setting up the cells.

The campaign manager, Shadegg explained in *How to Win an Election*, should follow Mao Tse-tung: "Give me just two or three men in a village," the dictator wrote, "and I will take the village." Shadegg's version of the technique was to pool the names of everyone in the state with whom he and his staff could claim personal association. Researchers uncovered each name's banking, church, business, lodge, media, and family connections to create a massive card file. People on the list got a "personal" letter from the senator about some piece of legislation that was threatening to them. When recipients replied, they were added to the names on the bulk mailing list that received various campaign letters "personally" addressed from their new friend. This produced over three thousand people loyally working in concert for the campaign, none aware of any other's efforts—spreading the right rumors, sending bits of intelligence to the office, setting up events and selling to their friends. Forty years later, labeled "one-to-one marketing" and aided by artificial intelligence technology, this approach would be advertising's cutting edge. Back in the late 1950s such practices were unheard of.

For fifteen months Shadegg had been sending out forms simply reading "Good Government Survey" that invited respondents to give a ten-word description of the senator, list their policy concerns, and the like. He discovered that water rights was an area of prime concern; he also discovered that no one perceived any difference on the issue between Goldwater and McFarland. So much for water rights. (McFarland wasted thousands of dollars on the issue.) He also learned that voters valued Goldwater as a kind of walking embodiment of Arizonans' independent streak. Then the United Auto Workers at their annual meeting in Miami announced that their number one political objective for the year was beating Barry Goldwater. And Shadegg had his campaign: Eastern labor bosses telling Arizonans who their representatives should be.

In May the AFL-CIO sent a staffer from its Committee on Political Education (COPE), Al Green, to move to a Tucson hotel and work on canvassing the labor vote. Painstakingly, all through the summer, Stadegg's private investigators sought to dig up dirt on Green. Mug shots were discovered and procured in California from two past arrests. Then Shadegg arranged with Eugene Pulliam for an exposé to be published in the *Republic* on Sunday, October 19—two and a half weeks before the election, a thin enough slice of time that there was little chance McFarland would be able to fight back.

The banner was an inch and a quarter high: "COPE AGENT 'MUSCLES IN': ARIZONA DEMOCRATS RESENT INVASION." Mug shots were splayed across the front page—with his eyes beady, hair slicked, face fleshy, and teeth bared, Green looked like he had come straight from the witness table of the McClellan Committee. The caption read: "This is the man sent to Arizona by Reuther and Hoffa to beat Goldwater . . . and get control of Arizona State Legislature." Articles claimed that Green was giving orders to state Democrats and that he had unlimited funds at his disposal, that the "Committee to Cancel Out People's Equality" was as powerful as "all other groups and individuals combined." The package took up two broadsheet pages. The heat kept up for weeks in both Pulliam papers. (It helped that readers had been softened up for the message by Kitchel's "Voice of Free Enterprise" column.) If "Big Labor can tear apart Goldwater," said the *Gazette*, "it can frighten all lesser figures into bondage."

A thirty-minute television commercial opened up with Goldwater's voice and a shot of a twelve-foot-high blowup of a labor newspaper bearing a derogatory headline about the candidate. "For six years newspapers such as this one have been telling you that Barry Goldwater hates the union men," the voice said, "and for six years I have been trying to get through this union curtain of thought control"—then the camera focused in as Goldwater burst through the scrim to explain his iron-clad support for the principle of collective bargaining.

It was all very impressive. It was also mostly nonsense. There was no Hoffa/Reuther cartel; Jimmy Hoffa, who liked Goldwater, had just been kicked out of the AFL-CIO by Walter Reuther. The *Republic* reported that COPE was spending $450,000 on state races in 1958. The actual amount was $14,000. Goldwater was, if anything, more guilty of dealings with non-Arizonans than McFarland was; most of his campaign contributions came from wealthy out-of-state conservatives, much of it from the mysterious Dallas oil tycoon H. L. Hunt and Massachusetts candy manufacturer Robert Welch. And in compiling his scoop, Pulliam was accessory to offenses arguably as damning as the fifteen-year-old ones that had earned Al Green his mug shots: the Dallas outfit of former FBI agents Shadegg hired as his dicks plied their law enforcement contacts to obtain the mug shots illegally. They also tracked Green's long-distance calls and photographed the license plates and faces of everyone who entered the state AFL-CIO's offices.

Election Day came. The Republicans, hoping to piggyback on anti-union sentiment from the McClellan hearings, had sponsored right-to-work initiatives in seven states. The strategy, and the election, was a disaster. Six of the initiatives were crushed, along with the candidates who supported them: gone were conservative stalwarts like Malone of California, Bricker of Ohio, and Jenner of Indiana, thirty-six years of seniority in the Senate among them. In California the party collapsed after Senator William Knowland decided to run for governor and the governor chose to run for Knowland's Senate seat, and both were defeated. COPE had a banner year: 25 of its chosen 32 Senate candidates won, 183 of 294 in the House. Democrats gained five new governorships and 700 new seats in state legislatures. Vice President Richard Nixon, the presumptive presidential nominee, tallied thousands of miles of travel for the party's candidates. Now he would go into 1960 with a bruised reputation.

Only in Arizona was 1958 a Republican year. Paul Fannin, a political neophyte whom Goldwater called the worst speaker he had ever heard, became one of two new Republican governors (Nelson Rockefeller of New York was the other). Johnny Rhodes once more won reelection to Congress. And Goldwater scored a come-from-behind upset, carrying eleven of fourteen counties and 56 percent of the vote.

He certainly dazzled the Eastern press. A September *Time* article on the race only mentioned the Democrat to note that he was the favorite—then gave over the rest to "the tall, bronzed, lean-jawed, silver-haired man of 49" whose grandfather "packed in behind a mule to found the mercantile business which now does $6,000,000 a year in five department stores, spawned a robustious breed whose reputation for high-jinks Barry did his best to uphold." The *Saturday Evening Post*, which was outgrowing its Norman Rockwell days to become perhaps the most sophisticated of the weekly slicks, gave over five pages to "The Glittering Mr. Goldwater."

3

WORKING TOGETHER
FOR THE WORLD

Clarence Manion returned from Guatemala with his family in April of 1959 and took the measure of his plan to build movements behind both a Republican and a Southern Democrat running on conservative platforms, watch as both were turned back at the respective party conventions, then merge the two organizations to form a new party to back one of the candidates, who, combining the votes of Dixiecrats and Taft Republicans, could finally block the major-party candidates from their electoral college majority. He was still unsure about Goldwater. And General Bonner Fellers, a full-time lobbyist against foreign aid and Manion's eyes and ears in Washington, noted that several claques of Southerners were scrambling to swing Faubus to their own various schemes to throw the election into the House of Representatives.

Manion decided definitely to go forward with the plan when a hero joined his movement. Four-star general Albert C. Wedemeyer had authored the Army War Plans Division's 1940 contingency document for America's joining the war. Its conclusions became a key piece of evidence for right-wingers who argued that Roosevelt had ignored evidence of Japan's plans to attack Pearl Harbor in order to draw America into the war. By 1944, Wedemeyer, a Chinese speaker, had risen to the command of the China-Burma-India theater. After V-J Day he was lent as chief of staff to Chiang Kai-shek. There, he filed another report, this one on the operational capabilities of the Chinese Communists and the ability of the Nationalists to beat them. He said that the Nationalists could handily overwhelm Mao if only America would make the commitment to help—10,000 military advisers would be needed to start, he suggested. When his advice was ignored, its author demoted, and China fell to the Communists, the Republican right anointed Wedemeyer as a prophet. And his renown did not stop there; his new book *Wedemeyer Reports!* was a best-seller, and he was featured on the television program *This Is Your Life*. Wedemeyer was a name to organize with.

When a columnist for the Hearst papers reported that Faubus was receiving "thousands and thousands" of letters urging him to run for President, Manion moved. He arranged to meet Dorn in Washington. He circulated to his inner circle a thirteen-page report written by his Arkansas friend Jim Johnson: "Orval Faubus can be elected president of these United States," it began—and then went on to spell out the strategy that would make George Wallace a presidential contender in years to come. "For every action there is a reaction," Johnson wrote. "Recent actions by the Federal judiciary which have tended to hasten at a frightening speed the Federal grab for power at the expense of the people and the States have placed the Federal judiciary squarely in the middle of the controversy. . . . States' Rights have become household words in Ohio as much as in Arkansas or Mississippi. . . . How well would Orval Faubus do in the North, the Midwest, and the West Coast states? There is only one way to answer that question: by encouraging him to enter presidential primaries in those states."

"This is the first step in our Committee strategy," Manion wrote his comrades.

There was still the matter of the second half of the plan.

Tentatively—three weeks after he penned it—Manion sent his feeler out to General Wood about backing Goldwater for President. "I think it would not be advisable," Wood wrote back on April 20, "because I think Nixon has the support of the whole organization." That was discouraging; so was the fact that Goldwater was by no means the obvious man for the job. He was a generation younger than them, and not exactly a perfect ideological fit. He had gone to the 1952 convention as an Eisenhower delegate, had voted for a higher minimum wage and to extend Social Security, and had voted for the 1957 and 1960 civil rights bills. And when one of Manion's friends dined with the Goldwaters in Washington in February of 1959 and said that Barry should run for President, the senator expressed horror at the very idea.

But when the Eighty-sixth Congress was seated in January, Goldwater was practically the Republicans' only star. As the McClellan hearings wound down into a debate on labor law reform, he was gaining national fame as the conservative tail wagging the centrist dog. Democrats Sam Ervin and John F. Kennedy put forward a bill narrowly tailored to stymie the schemes of a Hoffa or a Beck and gave management the sweetener of a ban on unions picketing where they had already lost elections; to labor it offered to allow replacement strikers to vote in union recognition elections. Goldwater thought it was anemic, and threatened to submit his own bill—a contingency that would likely result in no labor reform being passed at all—if the Democrats' bill were not challenged by a tougher Administration package. Kennedy's bill passed the Labor Committee and went to the Senate floor for debate in the middle of April. Goldwater proposed three poison-pill amendments and promised more. The vote on one was 46 to 46 (Vice President Nixon broke the tie for the Goldwater side); another passed without debate. Everyone assumed a compromise had been struck; Kennedy-Ervin was shaping up as that rare legislative sausage that actually pleased everyone. On April 25, 1959, just after Manion's return from Guatemala, the upper chamber assembled for the vote. Ninety senators voted *aye*. A single senator voted nay—Barry Goldwater. He called the bill "a flea bite to a bull elephant." The Manionites loved it. He was now their Republican.

Manion brought in Frank Cullen Brophy, an Arizona banker on For America's advisory board and a mover in the short-lived 1955 Campaign for the 48 States, a movement for constitutional amendments to cap the income tax and limit federal spending. Brophy, one of Phoenix's biggest landowners, had sold Goldwater the magnificent hilltop lot where his dream house now stood. They shared a curious passion of Arizona's elite: playing Indian. (On the heel of his left hand, Barry Goldwater wore a tattooed four-dot glyph signifying his initiation into the Smoki Clan, a Prescott "tribe" complete with its own creation myth—cobbled together from the publications of the Bureau of American Ethnology—and an annual dance pageant; Brophy led a similar outfit called the St. John's Mission Indian Dancers.) Manion was friends with Brophy. Brophy was friends with Goldwater. Maybe together they had a chance of convincing him.

One Monday in May, Brophy wrote Goldwater: When they got together later in the month, did he mind meeting with "several people whose opinion both you and I respect" to discuss a political project? Brophy hinted that General Wedemeyer might show up.

The audience was May 15, in Washington. First Manion met with Representative Dorn, who agreed that Goldwater was a good choice for the Republican half of their scheme. Then Manion joined his friends in imploring Barry to run—or at least let them form Goldwater Clubs to drum up support for him. They wanted to know if Goldwater would, even if he chose not to actively cooperate with them, at least stay out of their way—and whether he would yield gracefully to a draft if the boom they expected took shape. Goldwater gave a response he would echo many more times in the years to follow as supplicants paraded before him with arguments much the same: He was a loyal Republican, he said, and he would do nothing to harm the party. He supported Nixon. But it was his duty not to stand in the way of the wishes of the party's rank and file, were they made sufficiently clear. Though it seemed to him that someone with a Jewish name couldn't be an effective candidate.

Manion left for Indiana in a mood of cautious optimism. And Goldwater left for a speaking engagement in Greenville, South Carolina.

Goldwater traveled some ten thousand miles a month that year for the Senate Republican Campaign Committee, always giving the same speech to any local audience that would have him: "Balance our budgets . . . stop this utterly ridiculous agriculture program . . . get the federal government out of business—every business"; sell the Tennessee Valley Authority "if we can only get a dollar for it"; stop "the unbridled power of union bosses." He spoke in a dehydrated, movie-cowboy tenor, slipping his heavy black spectacles on and off to match his awkward rhythms, now and again raising his voice in anger, sometimes stammering awkwardly. And to the right audience he could barely get his words out for the applause.

The question was whether this was that audience. Goldwater didn't often visit the states of the Old Confederacy, since there were practically no Republican Senate candidates below the Mason-Dixon line. In the land where Faulkner said the past isn't even past, the word "Republican" still signified the political wing of the marauding Union Army. By the time Republican carpetbaggers were routed in the 1870s, the South was codifying a system of racial segregation to cow the potentially insurrectionary black population in its midst. And the ruling Bourbons had indoctrinated the people that if a second party were to grow up in the South, it would only have to court Negroes as its allies in order to take over—evoking visions of Negro domination and rape on the order of D. W. Griffith's *Birth of a Nation.*

State Republican organizations survived as shells, "post office parties" that existed only to deliver their "black-and-tan" delegations at Republican conventions in exchange for federal patronage if the GOP won the White House. They had a vested interest in remaining as meager and insular as possible—"rotten boroughs," in political parlance. Since convention delegations were apportioned by voting population, not by Republican population, the black-and-tans were unaccountable to any grass roots. The delegates were tractable black citizens proud to represent the Party of Lincoln even if only as puppets of Democratic bosses. In the South, went the joke, Republicans were all rank and damned little file. Mississippi's black Republican chair for thirty-six years didn't even live in Mississippi. In South Carolina it could be impossible to vote for a Republican even if you wanted to, lest the local sheriff come knocking on your door; the secret ballot had only been instituted there in 1950.

But the South, like Arizona, was changing. During and after World War II the South had also filled up with fortune-seeking outsiders unschooled in the curious political folkways of their new home. The newcomers formed a potential Republican base. And to the rest of the South's (white) citizenry, the Democratic Party was looking worse all the time. It started at the 1936 convention when the party first seated black delegates (a black minister gave the convocation; South Carolina senator "Cotton Ed" Smith walked out: "This mongrel meeting ain't no place for a white man!"). That convention also suspended a rule that candidates needed two-thirds of the delegates to win the nomination—and with it the South's veto power. In 1947 Truman tentatively welcomed the conclusions of his Committee on Civil Rights, whose report *To Secure These Rights* defined the legislative agenda for the modern civil rights movement. At the 1948 convention Minneapolis mayor Hubert H. Humphrey declared it was "time for the Democratic Party to get out of the shadow of states' rights and walk in the sunshine of human rights," and he maneuvered a robust civil rights plank into the platform. South Carolina governor Strom Thurmond led a walkout to form a third party.

Southern Democrats claimed the gestures toward civil rights were only demagogic and expedient attempts to hustle the votes of urban blacks in the North so the party could turn its back on the South. But where else could Southerners go? Until about 1958, Republicans were more liberal on race than the Democrats were (although it wasn't hard to take a liberal stand on race so long as it was seen as a Southern problem, and the Republicans didn't have any white Southerners to placate). Many chose to vote for General Eisenhower as their protest against the civil rightsters taking over the national Democratic Party, some for quite idealistic reasons: a second party would light a fire under lazy Democratic courthouse hacks. Ike won a majority of the region's electoral votes in 1956. Those gains were lost after he federalized the National Guard at Little Rock Central High in 1957—reluctantly, to be sure; a frequent visitor to the South, Eisenhower was rather fond of its folkways, truth be told. But the GOP was not ready to give up the fight: also in 1957, Republican National Committee chair Meade Alcorn put one of his best men, the affable Virginian I. Lee Potter, to building a rank and file in the South in a project called "Operation Dixie."

Its biggest success had been in South Carolina. The first state to bolt the Union had always been the surliest in the Democratic coalition. Its senior senator, Olin Johnston, already chaired the Post Office and Civil Service Committees, so South Carolinians didn't want for patronage. Strom Thurmond, now the junior senator, was hardly a Democratic loyalist after his 1948 Dixiecrat presidential run, and after threatening to bolt the party once again in 1956. Meanwhile, the state was eager to lure more right-to-work Republican industrialists. In 1956 Herb Kohler, in the heat of the strike, built a $12 million ceramics factory in South Carolina; in 1958 six new factories were built in the town of Spartanburg alone. In 1959, after Gerber chose to build a $3 million baby-food plant in a nearby town whose blue laws didn't prevent the company from running shifts on Sundays, Spartanburg voted to repeal its blue laws altogether.

Two men were instrumental in bringing the modern South Carolina Republican Party into the world. Gregory D. Shorey was a poster child for the latest New South. A Massachusetts native, he had settled in Greenville in 1950, founded a water-sports equipment company, and led the state's Eisenhower campaign in 1952. But it is unlikely that the Republican Party in South Carolina would have got so far so fast through the 1950s without the cover given potential recruits by Roger Milliken, one of the wealthiest and most powerful men in the state. Milliken came from a Northeastern textile family who had been Republican since the 1860s, and who began building mills in South Carolina in 1884. Shy and brilliant, a virtuoso in industrial modernization (his company would register almost fifteen hundred patents), Milliken took over the family's booming business in 1947 after graduating from Yale. He was a conservative's conservative: in 1956, when workers at his Darlington factory organized to form a union, Milliken shut it down permanently rather than negotiate.

Together, Shorey and Milliken had scared up enough genuine rank-and-file Republicans to hold a respectable convention in 1959, in Greenville. Goldwater's speech, on May 16, was broadcast live on statewide television. For saying that *Brown* v. *Board of Education* should "not be enforced by arms" because it was "not based on law," he became a sensation—the Republican Yankee who preached the states' rights gospel.

Shortly afterward, Manion received what should have been encouraging news from Arkansas—a letter, coded for security, from one of Faubus's administrative assistants announcing that the governor was considering the conservative group's offer. But by then the point was moot. When Dorn sent Manion the newspaper accounts of Goldwater's hero's welcome in Greenville, Manion realized that to go forward courting Faubus was entirely unnecessary. Goldwater would do for the South *and* the North. That was Wednesday. On Thursday Manion began sending out invitations and working the phones to assemble a Goldwater for President committee from among his most trusted friends and biggest donors. By the next week he had fired up the Robotype machine and had gone down his mailing list.

And so on the first day of June 1959, a phalanx of proprietors of small, family-owned manufacturing companies—men born in the waning years of the nineteenth century, who had fought the U.S. entry into World War II; who had their hearts broken once, then twice, then three times, when Robert Alonzo Taft was spurned by their party; who feared Communism only slightly more than they feared Walter Reuther and an unsound dollar if they didn't just believe they all amounted to the same thing—received a letter marked "CONFIDENTIAL" from Dean Clarence Manion of South Bend, Indiana.

> The subject of this personal and confidential message is conservative political action. In the past few months, a great volume of letters and continuing contacts with "live" audiences in all parts of the country have convinced me that there is tremendous popular sentiment for Senator Barry Goldwater. He has stood up manfully and *successfully* under every conservative test and I honestly believe that his nomination for President by the Republican Party is the *one* thing that will prevent the complete disintegration of that party once and for all in the 1960 election.
>
> By the same token, I believe that Goldwater, as the Republican candidate, can win the presidential election. It has been encouraging to find that politically experienced people agree with these conclusions and we are now in the process of assembling a National Committee of 100 prominent men and women to "draft" Goldwater for the Republican nomination. We hope that General Albert Wedemeyer will be Chairman of this Committee. . . . We hope that you will consent to serve. . . .
>
> It is felt that the Goldwater Movement will definitely establish a firm position far to the right of the "middle of the road" around which conservative popular sentiment throughout the country can rally with real enthusiasm.

And so he gathered the sons of Acme Steel of Chicago and of Wood River Oil & Refining Company of Wichita; of Uncle Johnny Mills of Houston and Lone Star Steel of Dallas; of Rockwell Manufacturing of Pittsburgh and Roberts Dairy of Omaha; of Kentucky Color and Chemical and Youngstown Sheet & Tube; of Lockport Felt and the Cincinnati Milling Machine Company; of United Specialties and Memphis Furniture Manufacturing and Avondale Mills and Henderson Mills and American Aggregates and Downing Coal and United Elastic, to go out to try to change the world.

To most of the country—to Brent Bozell's "vast uncommitted middle"—these maneuverings couldn't have been more obscure. A new decade dawned, and the Establishment had spoken: it was a time of enormous possibility—if only the greatest nation in the world weren't too much like a rich, portly old man to wake up and grab it. If it did, as Arthur Schlesinger wrote in a much discussed piece in the January 1960 issue of *Esquire* called "The New Mood in Politics," from the vantage point of the 1960s, the 1950s would appear as "a listless interlude, quickly forgotten, in which the American people collected itself for greater exertions and higher splendors in the future"—and "the central problem will be increasingly that of fighting for individual dignity, identity and fulfillment in an affluent society."

Like sentiments crowded the magazines on the nation's coffee tables. There had never been a decade rung in with such heady self-consciousness of high purpose. John F. Kennedy was the new mood's self-proclaimed political prophet, kicking off his campaign for the Democratic presidential nomination warning of a "trend in the direction of a slide downhill into dust, dullness, languor, and decay." Such phrases—taunts, almost—would ring through his campaign speeches over the coming summer and fall: "If we stand still here at home, we stand still around the world. . . . If you are tired and don't want to move, then stay with the Republicans. . . . I promise you no sure solutions, no easy life." Under his administration there would be "new frontiers for America to conquer in education, in science, in national purpose—not frontiers on a map, but frontiers of the mind, the will, the spirit of man."

Kennedy was styled the very incarnation of action, of youth, of vigor, of everything conservatism was presumed not to be. "Do you remember that in classical times when Cicero had finished speaking," Adlai Stevenson said, introducing the candidate in California, "the people said, 'How well he spoke!,' but when Demosthenes had finished speaking, they said, 'Let us march'?" When Harris showed the "America is going soft" refrain as Kennedy's highest-scoring campaign theme by far, Richard Nixon added to his own speeches an amen chorus: "So I say, yes, there are new frontiers, new frontiers here in America, new frontiers all over the universe in which we live. . . . The United States needs more roads, more schools, more hospitals. This is what our opponent says. But we can do it better—because they want to send the job to Washington and do it by massive spending."

The youth were stirring. The Student YMCA-YWCA drew thousands to a conference called "The Search for Authentic Experience"; the same year an editor of the student newspaper at Cornell led students in a rock-throwing riot against the doctrine of in loco parentis; at the University of California's massive Berkeley campus a coalition of self-professed radicals overturned the Greek machine for leadership of student government. Everywhere on campuses paperbacks of a certain description were avidly passed from hand to hand: William H. Whyte's *The Organization Man*, David Riesman's *The Lonely Crowd*, Paul Goodman's *Growing Up Absurd*, John Kenneth Galbraith's *The Affluent Society*; Sartre, Camus, Ayn Rand, Vance Packard,

C. Wright Mills; George Orwell's *1984* and Aldous Huxley's *Brave New World*—glorifications of stalwart, lone individuals who chose authenticity and autonomy and risk over conformity and prosperity and ease, a philosophy embodied by the four black college students who had almost on a whim done no more than order coffee at a Greensboro, North Carolina, lunch counter in February and sparked a movement in seventy cities that winter in which well-scrubbed young black men and women put their bodies on the line to challenge the social order of an entire region.

The "new mood in politics" did not seem to bode well for Clarence Manion's cadres—rich, portly old men, in the main. They would have been as shocked as anyone else to find out that the man who ended up spearheading their crusade would express the zeitgeist as well as the handsome young senator from Massachusetts.

Recruitment had been slower than the dean had hoped through the summer of 1959. Some prospects were already committed to Nixon; others said Goldwater didn't have "a Chinaman's chance" (Gene Pulliam's words); some insisted any candidate be vetted for his position on a pet nostrum like repeal of the income tax or withdrawal from the United Nations. Some Southerners Manion called still held onto the fantastic notion that one of their own might sweep the Democratic nomination. Many told him they were just too old.

But by July, Manion had a hook. "We hope to publish a 100 page booklet on Americanism by Senator Goldwater," he now wrote in his entreaties, "which can be purchased by corporations and distributed by the hundreds of thousands."

The idea for the booklet had come in the middle of June. Through the ministrations of Frank Brophy, Manion had negotiated the grudging noninterference of Goldwater in their efforts to publish something under his name. In exchange for Manion keeping the Goldwater for President committee secret until the pamphlet was released, and going no further without the prospective candidate's permission, Goldwater promised to endorse no one for the 1960 nomination, thus keeping his own name open. He probably agreed to that much in the certain belief that nothing would come of it. "I doubt there's much money to be made by mass sale of a Goldwater manifesto," *National Review* editor Bill Buckley told Manion, citing "the difficulties Taft had in 1952 peddling his foreign policy book."

Recruitment picked up. Manion already had his friend J. Bracken Lee, recently voted out as governor of Utah after he refused to pay federal income tax, and whose Committee of 50 States was working on a constitutional amendment to dissolve the federal government when U.S. debt reached a specified amount. Now Herb Kohler signed on to the Manion committee, and his fame drew dozens more prominent conservative names: movie stars and HUAC-friendly witnesses Joel McCrea and Adolphe Menjou; erstwhile FDR Naval Secretary and New Jersey governor Charles Edison, son of the inventor; Spruille Braden, former U.S. ambassador to Colombia and Chile; Robert Welch, a former candy executive, now convening mysterious two-day symposia across the country laying out a sweeping and gothic new vision for fighting the Communist conspiracy; the fire-breathing anticommunist lecturer from Alton, Illinois, Phyllis Schlafly. Now Manion had a movement. "Dear Clarence: Please pardon the informality of this salutation," one committeeman began a letter. "If we are working together for the world, first names are now respectably in order."

There was considerable doubt whether Manion was worthy of this man's confidence. He didn't have a publisher. He had hired Brent Bozell as ghostwriter, but then the ghostwriter promptly went missing for the next three weeks. (He was sojourning in Spain, where he had begun a romance with Catholic monarchism.) When Bozell resurfaced, Manion celebrated by announcing in mid-July that the booklet would "appear about the time our Committee is announced—not sooner than 60 days hence."

That wasn't even in the ballpark. For, sixty-two days hence, Khrushchev would visit the United States, in a trip just announced, and presently all other political activity on the right ground to a halt. Bozell convened a Committee for the Freedom of All Peoples, Manion a National Committee of Mourning (to greet Khrushchev, he announced, with public prayers, the tolling of bells, and black arm bands). Robert Welch's Committee Against Summit Entanglements circulated petitions accusing Eisenhower of treason; Buckley's *National Review* held a melodramatic rally at Carnegie Hall, with Buckley promising in a press conference to dye the Hudson River red to greet the Butcher of Moscow. Milwaukee's Allen-Bradley Company bought a full page in the *Wall Street Journal*: "To Khrushchev, 'Peace and Friendship' means the total enslavement of all nations, of all peoples, of all things, under the God-denying Communist conspiracy of which he is the current Czar. . . . Don't let it happen here!"

Khrushchev left; the republic stood; new headaches arose. Manion had secured a publisher—Publishers Printing Co., in tiny Shepherdsville, Kentucky, whose specialty was trade magazines (it was the only printer that didn't say it was impossible to publish and distribute a book in time for the Republican Convention in July). But now a rival group, We, The People!, hosted Goldwater at the group's fifth annual "Constitution Day Convention" in Chicago, where there was much backroom talk of drafting him for President. Manion let the leaders in on his plans, and they agreed to back off. No sooner had Manion tamped down those flames than the wild-eyed New Orleansian Kent Courtney, the most scabrous pamphleteer on the right, and his wife, Phoebe, held an "Independent American Forum and New Party Rally" in Chicago. "I have been busy on the phone continuously trying to keep this group from going off half-cocked," Manion wrote despairingly to Dorn. It took a trip to New Orleans, and negotiations until 2 a.m., to ward off the Courtneys. Manion, losing heart, had even considered joining Jim Johnson in an attempt to draft Governor Ernest "Fritz" Hollings of South Carolina for an independent elector scheme, or perhaps dropping Goldwater in favor of General Wedemeyer. There was still no text for what was tentatively being called "What Americanism Means to Me." On November 16, Manion penned a stiff note to Hub Russell: *"Keep after Bozell!"*

By then Brent Bozell was at home in Chevy Chase writing like a house afire, starting and finishing the Goldwater manuscript within six weeks. All he had needed was an incentive. Nelson Aldrich Rockefeller provided it. Rocky had begun approaching party activists around the country to back him in a run for President. And if Nixon and Rockefeller deadlocked at the convention—perhaps Goldwater's moment would come.

The second son of John Davison Rockefeller Jr. had been the first of his clan to broach the unseemly world of politics. It was a matter of family temperament. If the reserve, discipline, and Baptist discretion of the patriarch John D. Rockefeller Sr. was legendary, these traits were only bested by John D. Jr. His "never-ending preoccupation," wrote one of the family's many chroniclers, was "with what being a Rockefeller *meant*." It did not mean slapping boozy ward bosses on their overly broad backs.

There was also the matter of a certain realism. A spawn of the houses of Aldrich and Rockefeller could not exactly have been expected to inspire devotion among the unwashed masses: there had never been a more forthright defender of the prerogatives of Big Business than Nelson Aldrich, the industrial magnate that muckraker Lincoln Steffens labeled "the boss of the United States." John D. Rockefeller Sr. did not exactly win his oil monopoly in a manner calculated to win his progeny the loyalty of 50 percent plus one of the voters. When the idea of running Nelson Rockefeller for New York governor was proposed in high Republican councils in 1954, the room erupted in laughter: "For the Republican Party to nominate a Rockefeller," chortled one, "would be *suicidal!*"

For Rockefellers there were better—quieter—ways to place one's stamp on the world. If some exquisitely principled soul sought to avoid the taint of the Rockefeller billions he would have a job on his hands. If he were the descendant of slaves he might want to forgo a university education (Rockefeller funds kept the nation's Negro colleges in the black); if he were a New Yorker he should boycott milk (the Rockefeller Institute for Medical Research had sanitized the city's supply); if he were Chinese he'd better stay healthy (the family's China Medical Board trained a generation of physicians); if he was of a wandering bent he would forgo the pleasures of Versailles (renovated with Rockefeller cash), Grand Teton National Park (Rockefeller land), the Agora in Greece (excavated thanks to the family's largesse), and Tokyo's Imperial University (rebuilt by the Rockefeller Foundation after the disastrous earthquake of 1923). And on and on—all welcome expense for the privilege of serving God and country without ever having to venture into the distasteful task of grubbing for votes.

Nelson was a different story.

He grew up in the typical family fashion: born at the vacation cottage at Seal Harbor, Maine, shuttled in childhood between the 3,500-acre family estate on the banks of the Hudson, Pocantico Hills (the rambling, two-story Tudor "Playhouse" had a bowling alley, billiard room, squash court, indoor tennis court, and swimming pool), and the nine-story townhouse at 10 West 54th Street in Manhattan—but compelled all the same to mend his clothes, weed the garden, keep strict accounts of his thirty-cent-a-week allowance, and conduct himself with the modesty and dignity befitting a Rockefeller. But he was a scampish, impatient boy—qualities much in the way of his beloved and vivacious mother, but unbecoming to his towering father. So early on Nelson developed an unmistakable gift to, as a biographer put it, "diligently attend to the Rockefeller rituals, while stealthily subverting them at the same time." For all his advantages in life, he honed a skill for working the system more proper to a man without means. He grew up seeking something that would resist him. Late in his life an interviewer asked him how long he had wanted to become President of the United States. "Ever since I was a kid," he answered. "After all, when you think of what I had, what else was there to aspire to?"

In 1937, around the time Goldwater was penning nasty open letters to Franklin D. Roosevelt, Rockefeller, not yet thirty, began consummating that aspiration in earnest. He had invested much of his massive trust in the Venezuelan arm of Standard Oil of New Jersey. Long fascinated by Latin America (some said it was the hot-blooded, effusive, and physical Latin temperament—his temperament—that attracted him), he spent two months traveling its length and breadth on the pretense of inspecting his holdings. The unspeakable poverty in the squatter towns that had grown up around the oil fields, and the imperial condescension with which workers were treated, overwhelmed him. Upon returning, he addressed Standard's board of directors in perhaps the most succinct statement he would ever make of his evolving patrician liberalism: "The only justification for ownership is that it serves the broad interests of the people. We must recognize the social responsibilities of corporations and the corporation must use its ownership of assets to reflect the best interests of the people."

By 1940, with the Nazis making diplomatic and commercial inroads into South America, Rockefeller bluffed and hustled his way to an appointment by President Roosevelt to a position he invented: "Coordinator of Inter-American Affairs." By the height of the war Nelson had seven personal secretaries and 1,413 employees and projects ranging from producing propaganda cartoons by Walt Disney to a failed scheme to manufacture wooden, sail-powered warships in Latin American shipyards (which Navy man FDR latched onto with delight); he had even, incredibly, persuaded FDR to insert an unnoticed clause into the Appropriations Act of July 1942 giving his office power to act "without regard to the provisions of law regulating the expenditure, accounting for and audit of government funds." By 1943 he was laying fantastic plans for a massive (American-funded) social welfare program for the entire South American continent—budgeted all the way through 1953. Later it would serve as blueprint for a key aspect of U.S. foreign policy: using foreign aid to win the loyalty of the world's multitudes in the struggle against Communism.

When the Republicans—the Rockefeller family's ancestral party—took over the White House in 1953, Nelson made an even greater imprint in Washington, first as undersecretary of the new Department of Health, Education, and Welfare—where, practically serving as acting secretary, he was the guiding hand in the agency's every attempt to preserve or extend the welfare state, from Social Security to his own failed plan for instituting guaranteed national health care—then in the State Department's top propaganda post. He was in line for the number two job at State when he was blackballed by Ike's thrifty treasury secretary, George Humphrey, who blanched at Rockefeller's reputation for fiscal profligacy. The experience galvanized Rockefeller: checked by bureaucracy, he decided his ticket upward was the electorate. He saw no reason in his first campaign, in 1958, not to run for what was widely regarded as the second most powerful office in the nation: governor of New York. Three men had made the governorship of New York a stepping-stone to the presidency; Nelson Rockefeller wanted to be the fourth. He made his political ambitions impossible for the state Republican Party to ignore. They tried to shunt him into the New York City postmastership or a congressional seat from Westchester County. These he rejected. They suggested a run for U.S. Senate. "All they do there is talk," he grumbled.

He planned his gubernatorial campaign by refining a political vision. After he quit his State Department post he joined his brothers in assembling the best minds of the American establishment in a half-million-dollar project to produce a series of definitive reports on . . . everything. The goal of the Rockefeller Brothers Foundation's Special Study Fund was to define an American mission for the 1960s. Its eight subpanels ("The Moral Framework of National Purpose," and so forth) included magnates like Justin Dart of Rexall Drug, Thomas McCabe of Scott Paper, and Charles Percy of Bell & Howell; generals like Lucius Clay, former U.S. commander in Europe; media impresarios Henry Luce and David Sarnoff; university presidents, union leaders, and foundation bosses. Their reports were digested by the project administrator, a young Harvard professor named Henry Kissinger, into some twenty volumes over three years and finally distilled into a summary paperback, *Prospects for America: The Rockefeller Panel Reports*. It became a literary touchstone of the ideology—Rockefeller's ideology—future generations of scholars would label consensus, managerial, or pragmatic liberalism: the belief that any problem, once identified, could be solved through the disinterested application of managerial expertise.

Rockefeller surprised the world with his effortless populism on the campaign trail (though to be sure he was a populist who instinctively threw his arms back whenever he stepped outdoors to accommodate whomever—there was always someone—was putting his coat on for him). Some days he reached out with his muscular right arm to shake two thousand hands, giving most people his trademark salutation, "Hiyah, fella!" At a county fair he rode a harness racer's sulky at full gallop. At Coney Island he stripped to swim trunks and plunged into the Atlantic Ocean. In Rockland County he spoke in the rain atop a wooden plank suspended between two oil drums. ("I hope my platform is stronger than this plank," he said in that ever so slightly patrician voice with the rumble at the bottom.) And in an encounter that came to symbolize the Rockefeller campaign style, he trooped into Ratner's delicatessen on New York's Lower East Side and stuffed cheese blintzes, one after the other, into his chiseled, handsome face. "I recommend the blintzes," he told anyone who would listen, shaking a hand, autographing a napkin, flashing a billion-dollar grin with a double wink of his left eye. He won handily. The planning for a presidential campaign began soon after.

A year later, he launched his opening salvo, in Los Angeles. The Republican Party was holding its Western states meeting the weekend of November 14, 1959, at the Biltmore in Pasadena. Rockefeller rented a hall at the Sheraton nearby for a luncheon. He delivered a technical address carefully calibrated to establish his foreign policy bona fides—the classic move for a governor seeking presidential credibility. Reporters exhibited little interest in his views on strengthening the Western alliance. They wanted to know whether all these efforts meant he was challenging Richard Nixon for the nomination. He would reply with a grin that he was only an innocent "toiler in the Republican vine-yards" working for victory in 1960. Then he sped off for a series of back-room meetings with Republican chieftains. For Nelson Rockefeller was an innocent toiler in the Republican vineyards that fall like the family's 107-room redoubt at Seal Harbor was a cottage. The machine he built merely to explore the possi-bility of a presidential run was larger than the machine Kennedy's "Irish Mafia" built to *execute* a presidential run. Within the two three-story buildings at Nos. 20 and 22 West 55th Street in Manhattan that served as the governor's executive offices whenever the legislature wasn't in session, some seventy deputies probed the Republican waters that autumn and devised methods to bring them to a Rockefeller boil. The names, faces, and dispositions of every local GOP grandee worthy of note from Maine to Malibu were filed by the Research Division for quick consultation by the Logistics Division, which planned one-on-one backslapping sessions, luncheon meetings, and conference-room dinners after addresses written by the Speechwriting Division, while the Citizens Division worked with the local "grassroots" Rockefeller Clubs which, one veteran correspondent marveled, "seemed ready to sprout fully armed like a dragon seed, all across the country." There was also an Image Division and an office where an author scribbled away at a book-length Rockefeller biography.

In Los Angeles it did him little good. Rockefeller was received by his 2,600 lunch guests with the polite applause befitting a dry speech written by committee. Behind the closed doors the panjandrums told the governor they would back Nixon against all comers. And the next day, Rockefeller was resoundingly upstaged.

Goldwater had just wrapped up a marathon forty-three-state tour for the Senate Republican Campaign Committee with a morning hearing in southeast Arizona on water rights. He hopped into his Beechcraft, speechwriter Shadegg in tow, for a two-and-a-half-hour routine flight to a routine speech at a routine party conclave at the Pasadena Biltmore. The expanse of his beloved state passed beneath his eyes for the hundredth time, then California's eastern desert; he then approached the stunning pass that threads through the San Bernardino and San Jacinto Mountains. Low, menacing clouds rolled in. He prepared an approach on instruments. Forty miles out he opened his flight case with a start: the tables he needed to execute a blind landing at Burbank Airport were miss-ing. Only at the last minute did the clouds break and he was cleared for a visual landing. His luck ran out at the airport. It was the taxi driver's first day on the job. "Have either of you gentlemen ever been to the Biltmore before?" he asked. When they finally arrived at the hotel, the desk clerk wouldn't cash a check Goldwater wrote for pocket money (he kept to habits from childhood: he never carried cash). By the time he got to the meeting it was already in progress. A sergeant at arms, who didn't recognize him, refused him entrance to the overflowing hall. Goldwater said to hell with it and went to grab a bite to eat. He was persuaded to return to the hall by the pleas of the chairman of the Western Conference. They were counting on him, he said. An appeal to duty was always the best way to Barry Goldwater's heart.

Maybe it was the adrenaline from the day's wild rides. Maybe there was something in the rubber chicken. Whatever it was, when Barry Goldwater spoke, the room sparked to life in a way that startled even those who had seen Goldwater do this many times before.

First came the body blow to the Democrats: *"Not long ago, Senator John Kennedy stated bluntly that the American people had gone soft. I am glad to discover he has finally recognized that government policies which create dependent citizens inevitably rob a nation and its people of both moral and physical strength."*

Then there were the home truths of his pioneer forebears: *"Life was not meant to be easy. The American people are adult—eager to hear the bold, blunt truth, weary of being kept in a state of perpetual adolescence."*

Then he made an appeal to the timelessness of his cause: *"Abraham Lincoln chose to be called conservative—one who would conserve and protect the best of the past and apply the wisdom of the ages to the problems of the future"*—and of its inherent popularity—*"We have, at times, offered candidates and policies which were little more than hollow echoes of the siren songs of the welfare-staters; and when we have fallen from grace, the American public has made it abundantly clear that we were in error."*

He landed a right-hook to the bloated midsection of the federal government: *"Government is the biggest restaurant operator and clothier, it spends almost $1.3 billion in these operations"*—followed by another aimed at Walter Reuther: *"At the opening of this Congress, we were told the majority of the Senate and the majority of the House were owned by the labor unions."*

Then, in defiance of the defensive trend of a party convinced it had suffered its blows at the ballot box in 1958 by moving away from the center, he delivered the knockout punch: *"Republicans across this great nation of ours have been telling me we can win the elections of 1960—they tell me we will win if we thrust aside timidity, plant our flag squarely on those conservative principles which made this nation great and speak forthrightly to the American public."*

Somewhere amidst the convention-sized ovation that followed, Earl Mazo of the *New York Herald Tribune* was heard to utter in amazement that Barry

Goldwater had just challenged Nixon and Rockefeller for the Republican presidential nomination—and that he would place his bets on Goldwater. The next
morning Goldwater dutifully stepped up to a press conference microphone and
assured the buzzing reporters (backsliding on his promise to the Manionites not
to declare for a candidate) that Vice President Richard Nixon was his and the
party's choice for the nomination. But something was happening. People were
crazy for Barry Goldwater. The same day in South Carolina, a newspaper interview was printed in which Republican chair Shorey bragged he would corral at
least two-thirds of the 310 Southern Republican delegates for Goldwater.
(Manion sent the clip to his committee members: "Please get it reprinted and
distributed as widely as possible among the Republicans who expect to attend
the national convention.") The *Los Angeles Times*'s Kyle Palmer, who had virtually minted Richard Nixon as a political star in the 1940s, printed four paragraphs of Goldwater's remarks for his readers to savor over their coffee the
next morning (the *Times* printed but two sentences of Rockefeller's address).
The publisher, Norman Chandler, invited Goldwater to lunch with the newspaper's editorial board.

A historian once wrote of the Chandler family and their *Times*, "it would
take in the East a combination of the Rockefellers *and* the Sulzbergers to match
their power and influence." Much of it stemmed from that moment in 1890
when a printer's strike shut down the plants of Los Angeles's four newspapers
and only the *Times*'s patriarch, General Harrison Gray Otis, Norman Chandler's grandfather, kept his machines running. For this—and his attendant crusade to make southern California the most union-free region in America—
thugs in 1910 blew up the printing plant (and Otis began tooling around town
in an armored car with machine guns mounted on the hood). The *Times*, its
news columns as much as its editorial pages—its news columns sometimes
more than its editorial pages—had been a blaring, smearing voice for conservatism ever since. But in 1958 Chandler named a new managing editor with the
mandate to make the paper professional and fair. From that point forward, the
editorializing would go on the editorial page. Which meant that the newspaper
needed more people to do the editorializing. The editorial board offered Goldwater a thrice-weekly column. After securing Steve Shadegg as his ghostwriter, Barry agreed to a January 1960 debut.

Meanwhile Rockefeller traveled to California, Oregon, Missouri, Indiana,
Minnesota, Wisconsin, Oklahoma, Texas, Florida. Occasionally he would be
received warmly; more often his appearances were debacles. Nixon loyalists
would arrange for only one hundred tickets to be sold at a two-hundred-seat
hall so the press would report that Nelson had spoken to a half-filled house. In
New Hampshire Nixon's people infiltrated a press conference to needle Rocke-

feller with embarrassing questions. At Chicago no one met him at the airport. "The more I campaign," he lamented, "the more I drive the party to the right." He didn't understand why. Nelson Rockefeller could never understand why.

You could almost imagine him, traveling across the nation in his private jet, entourage in tow, bestirring in Republicans long-buried folk memories: the ghost of John D. Rockefeller Sr., the brilliant and ruthless young oil man, rumbling across Ohio wantonly buying up every refinery in his path through means fair and foul but mostly foul, neatly folding enterprises built up through the sweat of generations into the Standard Oil juggernaut and rendering once-proud independent men mere nodes within a great and impersonal bureaucracy. His grandson grew up to make it his career to spend money he hadn't earned— his grandfather's first, then, as governor, that of millions of ordinary, hard-working New Yorkers. *"Many gigantic fortunes, built by virtue of private enterprise under the Constitution, have fallen under the direction of Internationalists, One-Worlders, Socialists and Communists,"* the old Manion fundraising appeal ran. *"Much of this vast horde of money is being used to 'socialize' the United States."* Rockefeller spoke once at the Advertising Club in Chicago. He was introduced as Nelson Roosevelt—"another Republican who wants to betray his class and go to Washington and wreck the economy."

He returned home from the disastrous tour and, the day after Christmas, released a statement announcing that his presidential explorations had come to a "definite and final" close.

4

CONSCIENCE

Over the holidays Goldwater skimmed Bozell's manuscript and pronounced it fine. On January 23, 1960, his column, "How Do You Stand, Sir?," debuted in the *Los Angeles Times*. And twenty-nine members of Manion's Goldwater for President committee finally met in person. It was the same locale as his For America third-party meeting almost a year earlier, the posh Union League Club in downtown Chicago. They were getting more politically savvy. W. W. Wannamaker Jr., the new Republican chair from South Carolina, said that his organization was ready to commit its thirteen convention delegates to Goldwater—though, should it be judged bad publicity to launch the cause in Dixie, his people would publicly back Nixon for the time being.

Manion explained the plans for the book. "Victor Publishing," the dummy imprint he had set up and licensed as a Kentucky-based not-for-profit, would publish 50,000 copies in March. Friendly businesses would be approached to make bulk purchases, which would be tax deductible as a business expense. (Since his radio show had gone on the air in 1954 as a "Non-Profit Educational Trusteeship, Politically Non-Partisan," Manion had been packaging transcripts of his programs just this way: 175,000 copies of a fusillade against the Tennessee Valley Authority—characterized as "wholesale fraud"—for power companies to distribute to customers with their bills; a like number of blasts at Social Security—"wholesale humbug"—for life insurance company stockholders.) The members of Americans for Goldwater—as the committee, which had never quite got up to one hundred, was now called—would buy the copies at $1 each and resell them for $3, keeping a dollar vig for themselves and remitting the rest to the organization.

Now Clarence Manion was in the book business. Throughout February, pages were sent in batches to the printer in Kentucky and Shadegg in Arizona (who was vetting them for the senator) almost as they rolled off Bozell's type-writer. Manion had sent an announcement to all the names on his Robotype punched tapes. Now he was taking orders. Brent Bozell dropped in on a board meeting of Robert Welch's new John Birch Society to announce that the book was almost ready for shipping; the Birchers watched, amazed, as Fred Koch, a Wichita oil refiner, ordered 2,500 copies, then turned to his friend Bob Love, a county Republican chair who owned a box factory, and ordered him: "You send it out." The 2,500 were dutifully earmarked for Mr. Love's warehouse, to be circulated to every library, newspaper, and VIP in Kansas. The publication date was set for April 15. Manion promised Roger Milliken that he would move heaven and earth to deliver 500 hand-sewn copies for Goldwater's tri-umphant return to the South Carolina Republican convention on March 26. Soon 10,000 copies were committed.

But Publishers Printing Company would not recoup its investment unless 50,000 copies were sold. To do that Manion would need to get the thing into bookstores. So they sent out review copies and took out newspaper ads. Before long booksellers were dutifully contacting one Victor Publishing Company in Shepherdsville, Kentucky, with orders. That was a problem. The Shep-herdsville operator had not yet been apprised of the existence of a Victor Pub-lishing Company. That crisis resolved, the first boxes were shipped to stores on April 7. April 8, the president of Publishers Printing, Frank Simon, began answering his private line "Victor Publishing."

Manion and Simon were offering bookstores what seemed to them a fair deal: books were shipped upon receipt of a dollar per unit, and the booksellers could keep $2 profit on each book sold. They were unaware that in retail book-selling inventory is shipped to stores on credit, and unsold copies are returned to the publisher, so the risk of trading in an unsaleable book belongs to the pub-lisher, not the bookseller (Simon soon found this out from booksellers who called to fulminate over his private line). Meanwhile Manion fielded angry telegrams from his people that the book was unavailable in their hometown bookstores. But the angriest telegram came from Senator Goldwater. He had not yet received his two hundred author's copies. The next day Manion and Simon tracked Barry's cartons to a warehouse in D.C., where they had sat for three days with the labels stripped off. They suspected union sabotage; Gold-water agreed and contacted the FBI. It was the most interest he had taken in the project to date.

A slim hardback called *Conscience of a Conservative*, 127 pages, red, white, and blue on the front, a picture of Goldwater on the back, eventually did find its way into the stores that spring. A month later *Barron's* published an article on its front page about a phenomenon. The book debuted at number ten on *Time* magazine's best-seller list on June 6, and number fourteen on the *New York Times*'s list on June 26—alongside books by authors like James Michener, Leon Uris, and Allen Drury. By the time voters went to the polls in November to choose between Richard Nixon and John Kennedy, there were half a million copies in print. Shepherdsville, Kentucky, was, for a brief, shining moment, a mover and shaker in the publishing world. The book was selling fastest in college bookstores—typically scooped up, the *Wall Street Journal* reported, alongside the perennial adolescent best-seller *The Catcher in the Rye*.

Why, a year and a half after the electorate had turned nearly every last conservative out of Congress, was America buying *Conscience of a Conservative*?

Think of a college bookstore, perhaps at one of the new universities in California, its sprawling, bland, concrete campus as big as a medium-sized town. Imagine a pimply college freshman wandering in. He is wearied from his first soul-crushing run-in with Big Bureaucracy, after complying with the procedures for securing his place in next semester's classes. After purchasing the closely printed required texts for the major he had just been compelled to declare, his eyes alight upon the red, white, and blue cover of *Conscience of a Conservative*. He picks it up, weighs it in his hand—127 pages, large type, space between each little paragraph. He turns it over and sees a handsome, serious, welcoming face; the shoulders of a sharp, well-cut suit are visible, the tie reed-slender in the current style. He opens the book and, standing, reads fourteen short pages inviting him to join an idealistic struggle to defend the individual against the encroachments of the mass.

"We have heard much in our time about 'the common man,' " he reads.

It is a concept that pays little attention to the history of a nation that grew great through the initiative and ambition of uncommon men. The conservative knows that to regard man as part of an undifferentiated mass is to consign him to ultimate slavery. . . . Every man, for his individual good and for the good of his society, is responsible for his own development. The choices that govern his life are choices that he must make; they cannot be made by any other human being. . . . The conscience of the Conservative is pricked by anyone who would debase the dignity of the individual human being.

Liberal demagogues had produced "a Leviathan, a vast national authority out of touch with the people, and out of control." Conservatives believed in a politics that ministered to the "whole man." And nothing could change, he read—in italics—until *"we entrust the conduct of our affairs to men who understand that their first duty as public officials is to divest themselves of the power they have been given."*

The student buys the book. Freedom, autonomy, authenticity: he has rarely read a writer who speaks so clearly about the things he worries about, who was so cavalier about authority, so *idealistic.*

It was a brilliant rhetorical performance. Only after this introduction did Bozell—or, as far as the public knew, Goldwater—mention specific policy prescriptions that might turn off the prejudiced reader. Or, more accurately, the book discussed policy *pro*scriptions:

> I have little interest in streamlining government or making it more effi-cient for I mean to reduce its size. I do not undertake to promote wel-fare for I propose to extend freedom. My aim is not to pass laws, but to repeal them. It is not to inaugurate new programs, but to cancel old ones that do violence to the Constitution, or that have failed in their purpose, or that impose on the people an unwarranted financial burden.

The ideas that followed—in chapters like "Freedom for the Farmer," "Freedom for Labor," "Taxes and Spending," "The Welfare State," "Some Notes on Education," and "The Soviet Menace"—were radical. *Conscience of a Conservative* domesticated them—as surely as nineteenth-century European socialist movements domesticated such radical ideas as the progressive income tax and universal education. Federal grants-in-aid to states providing matching funds for specified ends, it argued, were "a mixture of blackmail and bribery." Segregation was abhorrent. But if Congress and the Supreme Court did not leave to the states what was not specifically reserved for the federal govern-ment, what was to stop them from dictating *anything* to the states? He called, in italics, for *"prompt and final termination of the farm subsidy program."* The graduated income tax defied the principle of equality under the law: *"govern-ment has a right to claim an equal percentage of each man's wealth, and no more."* As for the federal budget itself, he recommended "a staged with-drawal . . . 10% spending reduction each year in all of the fields in which federal participation is undesirable," because economic growth could only be achieved "not by government harnessing the nation's economic forces, but by"—a pow-erful word—"emancipating them."

Few, perhaps, among the millions of people who read *Conscience of a Conservative* came to adopt its positions as their own who didn't already have conservative instincts, who didn't already agree with lines like "The ancient and tested truths that guided our Republic through its early days will do equally well for us" and "The laws of God, and of nature, have no dateline." Many likely didn't get past the assertion "I am . . . not impressed by the claim that the Supreme Court's decision on school integration is the law of the land." Others fell in love with the political ideals of autonomy and liberty through *Conscience of a Conservative*, only to later come to believe that the welfare state (or even later in the decade, Marxist revolution) was their most worthy guarantor.

That wasn't the point. *Conscience* had stolen conservatism from the sole possession of the old men. *Time* noted how the book "thoroughly belies the U.S. Liberals' caricature-belief that an Old Guardist is a deep dyed isolationist endowed with nothing but penny-pinching inhumanity and slavish devotion to Big Business." "Its success," agreed *Barron's*, "springs in part from the author's ability to give humanitarian reasons for following policies which usually have been associated with a lust for gain."

The Manionites' conservatism was a conservatism of fear. They harped endlessly on the "communistic income tax," how the economy would be decimated by inflation every time workers got a raise. (Taft Republicans, joked *The Nation*, feared "only God and inflation.") Their scapegoats were unnamed subversives who were invisibly destroying the system from within: "I am at a loss to understand the current public attitude deflating the inflation psychology," Fred Koch wrote in a self-published pamphlet. "Perhaps it is propaganda, of which we have been fed much of late—pink propaganda, in as much as, in my opinion, Russia's first objective is to destroy our economy through inflation." Politically the philosophy lost when it won: if you removed the fear of subversion by catching subversives, you ended the fear that brought you to power in the first place—although, of course, you could never catch all the subversives, for the conspiracy was a bottomless murk, a hall of mirrors, a menace that grew greater the more it was flushed out. "The Communists have infiltrated both the Democrat and Republican Parties for many years," Koch wrote. "If we could only see behind the political scenes, I am sure we would be shocked."

Conscience of a Conservative didn't blame invisible Communists for America's problems. It blamed all-too-visible liberals. Its anticommunism was not about raising nameless dreads but about *fighting*—hard and in the open. America, said *Conscience*, was not losing the Cold War because of Alger Hiss, Julius Rosenberg, or the striped-pants diplomats of the State Department. The enemy was in the mirror. "A craven fear of death is entering the American consciousness." It "repudiates everything that is courageous and honorable and dignified in the human being. We must—as the first step toward saving American freedom—affirm the contrary view and make it the cornerstone of our foreign policy: that we would rather die than lose our freedom."

The Cold War had whipsawed since 1955 when President Eisenhower and Premier Khrushchev met in Geneva for the first East-West summit conference. The 1956 GOP platform boasted: "The threat of global war has receded. The advance of Communism has been checked and, at key points, thrown back." Then came Hungary; then, on the eve of the elections, French and English bombs pounded Egypt for nationalizing the Suez Canal, and Russia threatened to intervene on Egypt's behalf. There was a glimmer of hope when Russia ceased nuclear testing in October of 1958. Then, in November, Khrushchev first threatened to take over Berlin. Now he had just been mollified by his 1959 American visit. Was peace *finally* at hand?

Conscience of a Conservative answered that Soviet expansionism was *enabled* by the fantasy of coexistence. Russia was "determined to win the conflict, and we are not." So the Kremlin used arms control agreements and testing suspensions and the rest to seduce the American populace with romantic fantasies of peace. "The Kremlin can create crisis after crisis, and force the U.S., because of our greater fear of war, to back down every time." Then the Soviets looked forward happily to the next phase of coexistence—legitimating their crimes by relabeling them "disagreements" amenable to "negotiation."

"If an enemy power is bent on conquering you, he is at war with you: and you—unless you contemplate surrender—are at war with him. Moreover—unless you contemplate treason—your objective, like his, will be victory." The logical conclusion: "A tolerable peace . . . must *follow* victory over Communism."

Conscience of a Conservative drew to a close by ticking off the tenets of American foreign policy, asking of each: "Does it help us defeat the enemy?" Alliances were important—but since our alliances did not yet girdle the globe and were defensive in outlook, we must be willing to act alone. Foreign aid (unconstitutional unless it could be shown to promote the national interest) should be limited to military and technical support. Diplomatic ties to the Soviet Union should be reexamined: "I am quite certain that our entire approach to the Cold War would change for the better the moment we announced that the United States does not regard Mr. Khrushchev's murderous claque as the legitimate rulers of the Russian people or any other people." The United Nations, which reduced the struggle for world freedom to the lowest common denominator agreement of eighty-odd nations, should be looked upon circumspectly. As for arms talks: "No nation in its right mind will give up the means of defending itself without first making sure that hostile powers are no longer in a position to threaten it." Since the Soviets understood the nature of the conflict, they wouldn't dismantle their nuclear weapons despite assurances to the contrary; then, once we dismantled ours, "aggressive Communist forces will be free to maneuver under the umbrella of nuclear terror."

To prevent that, *Conscience of a Conservative* offered a quietly extraordinary argument, in a few short paragraphs passing blithely over the simple, awful paradox of the Cold War: in a world where weapons possessed the power to destroy civilization, to attack an enemy with the most effective weapon at your disposal would be to ensure your own destruction through retaliation. This was the "balance of terror" experts believed kept the Cold War peace, but *Conscience* insisted it did no such thing: the Communists tested us in Hungary, in the Suez, in West Berlin because they knew we wouldn't stop them. We feared any military altercation might escalate to the unthinkable. The audacious solution: make nuclear war *more thinkable*—"perfect a variety of small, clean nuclear weapons," designed to be used locally, on the battlefield. "Overt hostilities should always be avoided," *Conscience* averred, "especially is this so when a shooting war may cause the death of many millions of people, including our own. But we cannot, for that reason, make the avoidance of a shooting war our chief objective. If we do that"—if war is rendered *unthinkable*—"we are committed to a course that has only one terminal point: surrender."

To many young readers the argument had almost a Gandhian appeal—the same appeal, on the left, held by valiant Southern blacks laying their bodies on the line for the freedom to eat where they wished. Freedom was indivisible. It was worth dying for. Thus *Conscience of a Conservative* reached its stirring dénouement, read, one imagines, by our pimply freshman with steadily mounting glandular thrust:

> The future, as I see it, will unfold along one of two paths. Either the Communists will retain the offensive; will lay down one challenge after another; will invite us in local crisis after local crisis to choose between all-out war and limited retreat; and will force us, ultimately, to surrender or accept war under the most disadvantageous circumstances. Or we will summon the will and the means for taking the initiative, and wage a war of attrition against them—and hope, thereby, to bring about the international disintegration of the Communist empire. One course runs the risk of war, and leads, in any case, to

probable defeat. The other runs the risk of war, and holds forth the promise of victory. For Americans who cherish their lives, but their freedom more, the choice cannot be difficult.

Our student then sets the book down, blinking twice, stretching his limbs, silently intoning: Let us march.

5

The Meeting of the Blue
and White Nile

In 1957 Khrushchev announced that the Soviet Union would imminently catch up to the United States in the production of meat, milk, and butter. The Soviets began testing an intercontinental ballistic missile. Then, in October, Russia sent its bleeping medicine ball around the planet. America's space-race debut was rushed to the launching pad, where it rose five feet before disintegrating into a fireball (headline: "FLOPNIK"). And a panicked nation busied itself with rituals of compensation. One of them was the National Defense Education Act, designed to enrich science, math, and engineering education. The NDEA included among its provisions the by then routine requirement that beneficiaries forswear allegiance to "any organization that believes in or teaches the overthrow of the United States government by force or violence by any illegal or unconstitutional methods." But loyalty oaths were in bad odor after the ugly implosion of Senator McCarthy. A coalition of Ivy League administrators campaigned to strike the NDEA loyalty oath from the law as a threat to academic freedom. Senator Kennedy, courting left-wing support for 1960, drafted a bill to drop it. Two eager young conservatives decided the loyalty oath was worth fighting for—and that Kennedy and horsey-set liberals like Yale president A. Whitney Griswold were worth fighting against. It was the beginnings of a youth conservative movement.

David Franke and Douglas Caddy had met in 1957 at a summer journalism school in Washington sponsored by *Human Events*, a political magazine founded during World War II by right-wing veterans of America First, that by the late 1950s had settled into a comfortable niche as a scrappy Washington newsletter consisting of two sections: four pages of news, and a long article or speech by a McCarthy, Knowland, or Goldwater. Its calling card was its gung ho proselytizing. ("MULTIPLY YOURSELF by mailing to someone each section of 'Human Events' after you have read it," read the banner at the top of each page. "As a bonus for ordering $65.00 or more in gift subscriptions, you

can get the annual bound volume of 'Human Events' free," ran a typical promotion.) The summer journalism school was an outgrowth of the evangelism.
After the course was over, Franke returned to Del Mar Community College in
Corpus Christi, Texas, from where he edited the magazines of the Intercollegiate Society of Individualists and the College Young Republicans; Caddy
went back to the Georgetown University School of Foreign Service, where he
was chair of the D.C. College Republicans. The two kept in touch. After
Kennedy introduced his bill, they decided to form a Student Committee for the
Loyalty Oath.

They launched an armada of press releases; they exploited *Human Events*
connections to persuade conservatives to enter their documents into the *Congressional Record*. Few in Washington paid attention. The nation's capital
even then was replete with faux organizations consisting of no more than a letterhead and a mail drop. But when Caddy and Franke announced that they had
thirty college chapters petitioning to save the oath around the country—even at
Harvard, where the first signature they got was "Attila the Hun" and the second
was "Adolf Hitler"—the liberals at *The New Republic* took notice, and none
too defensively: Caddy and Franke's group was evidence, they editorialized,
that liberal arts colleges, properly devoted to the cultivation of liberty, were
"carrying a 35 percent overload of the ineducable."

But when Caddy challenged a representative of the student wing of the liberal Americans for Democratic Action to debate on the radio, ADA director
Sheldon Pollack warned a colleague that the ineducable were precisely *not*
what they were dealing with: "I can't think of any of our students who would
be able to hold his own against Caddy," he said. "He is a junior edition of
Buckley and a rather vicious debater."

Buckley. The young conservatives tried to talk like him, dress like him, write
like him—and, of course, think like him. There was his sophistication, which
came from his father, William Buckley Sr., a Texas oil millionaire of learning
and style who sought to defy every stereotype of Wild West new money. There
was Buckley Jr.'s bottomless well of self-confidence, the outlaw demeanor, the
devil-may-care grace—and underlying it all, somehow, an orthodox Catholi-
cism so heartfelt it was bracing. That came from his father, too; for William
Sr., as it would be for his son, rebellion against the status quo was one of the
definitions of conservatism. William Buckley Sr. made his name lawyering to
the wildcatters of the Tampico, Mexico, oil boom of the teens. Then the revolutionary forces of Obregón, Villa, and Zapata began demanding taxes from
the oil men on pain of expropriation, which was bad enough. When Obregón
called the Catholic church a "cancerous tumor," Buckley père joined the counter-

revolutionary underground and helped coordinate a failed coup in Mexico City. When he was kicked out of the country he bought a mansion, Great Elm, built in 1763 in the town of Sharon, Connecticut, that had once sheltered the governor. It boasted the state's largest elm tree, the Great Elm itself—symbol of all that was good and enduring in Yankee patrimony. After striking a gusher in Venezuela in the late 1930s, Will Buckley showed how much he cared about the Yankee patrimony. He built an addition nearly larger than the original house, complete with three-story Mexican-style patio, with tiles smuggled on his way out of the country. His obsession became educating his six children against the depredations of a fallen world. The youngest children were taught Spanish by their Mexican *nanas*. At five they began tutorials in French. Professional instructors dropped in to teach the children subjects ranging from art to tennis, from typing to woodcarving. Family dinners were salons, with rewards bestowed on the child who could deliver the most brilliant, witty, and stylish ripostes. The kids published a family newspaper to spread the patriarch's isolationist, laissez-faire, orthodox Catholic gospel.

Buckleys went to Yale the way Kennedy boys went to Harvard: ready to challenge the WASP stronghold as much as master it. Bill Buckley soon made his voice heard. Three freshmen were selected for the debating squad; he was one. Another was a tall New Dealer from Nebraska, the president of the campus World Federalists, L. Brent Bozell. Bozell was the only Yalie Buckley judged to be as morally and intellectually intense as he was. The two became inseparable. Bill won Brent to his conservatism; Brent won Bill away from isolationism. Brent married Bill's sister Patricia.

It would be 1968 before Yale saw hell-raisers as audacious. Yale was known as the most conservative of the Ivies. It wasn't conservative enough for Buckley. In his first semester Bill led a fight against the establishment of a student council (he feared it would be captured by liberals). When the rest of campus was welcoming the third-party bid of the left-wing, Communist-backed Henry Wallace as the royal road to Dewey victory, Buckley, a friend, and two of his sisters invaded a Wallace rally at the New Haven arena in mock "radical" attire (no makeup for the girls; hair laid flat with grease for the boys) and circulated signs reading "LET'S PROVE WE WANT PEACE—GIVE RUSSIA THE ATOM BOMB." Authorities foiled the planned coup de grace: the release of a flock of doves.

Buckley was chosen unanimously to be chairman of the *Yale Daily News* his senior year, the most powerful student position on campus, where his editorials inspired wonder and fear. One attacked a popular anthropology professor for "undermining religion through bawdy and slap-stick humor." Since Yale students did not lecture Yale professors, an issue had to be published without advertisements to make way for the letters of protest. For his valedictory in

1950 he convened a dinner to honor the retiring Yale president. The guests of honor included such fellow college presidents as Harold Stassen of Penn and General Dwight D. Eisenhower of Columbia, both 1952 White House contenders. Chairman Buckley stepped to the podium and browbeat them for letting enemies of religion and free enterprise reign in their classrooms under cover of academic freedom. His conclusion brought stunned silence: trustees of elite universities must compel their employees—professors as much as administrators—to show a proper measure of piety and patriotism. "And if they cannot, Godspeed on their way to an institution that is more liberal."

That was, more or less, the argument of his first book, *God and Man at Yale: The Superstitions of "Academic Freedom,"* published after Buckley completed a short stint with the CIA in Mexico. Yale's attempt to suppress publication only whetted the public's curiosity; Yale's attempts to discredit it (alum McGeorge Bundy's *Atlantic Monthly* review called Buckley a "twisted and ignorant young man"; Yale distributed two thousand reprints) made it a bestseller. His next book, coauthored with Bozell, was an unabashed attempt to defend a family friend: Joe McCarthy. By evaluating the senator's early cases in narrowly legalistic terms, they managed to acquit McCarthy to their own satisfaction as someone around which "men of good will and stern morality may close ranks." But what was most remarkable about *McCarthy and Its Enemies*, what makes it in retrospect a signal document of a new conservatism struggling to be born, was the number of *critical* references to McCarthy it included. Just as for Goldwater, the hunt for subversives appeared inadequate to the greater task at hand. "We are interested in talking, not about 'who is loyal?,' " Buckley and Bozell emphasized, "but about *'who favors those politicians that are not in the national interest as we see it.' "*

Buckley's next project would make criticizing those politicians into a merry art—a mighty engine for massing right-wing fellow travelers into a community, a *force*, a band of brothers and sisters ready to take on the (liberal) world. Buckley founded *National Review* after a spell of barnstorming colleges on behalf of a new conservative organization, the Intercollegiate Society of Individualists. ISI was modeled on the Intercollegiate Socialist Society, founded by Jack London in 1905. The conservative group's founders were convinced that the nation's enthusiasm for the socialistic schemes of the New Deal and after was traceable to the propaganda efforts of ISS alumni who had graduated to positions of power and influence—youthful socialists like Walter Lippmann, whose recollection of his ISS days at Harvard they never tired of quoting: "Our object was to make reactionaries stand-patters; stand-patters, conservative liberals; conservatives, liberals, and liberals, radicals; and radicals, Socialists." ISI sought to work the operation in reverse. College students were sent books like Henry Hazlitt's *Economics in One Lesson*, Friedrich A. Hayek's *Road to Serfdom*, and Frank Chodorov's *The Income Tax: Root of All Evil*, along with postcards asking if they wished to continue receiving literature. The group sent out one million pamphlets and books in 1953 alone.

Buckley loved sparring with the liberals on his campus recruiting trips for ISI (if the liberals hadn't already convinced administrators to bar the incendiary speaker from the campus outright). But he had greater ambitions. He had already been rebuffed by the owners of *Human Events* in a proposal to buy the newsletter and turn in into a full-fledged magazine. Meanwhile Willi Schlamm, a brilliant ex-Communist expatriate of the Luce empire, was witnessing at close range the crackup of an earlier attempt at a mass-circulation conservative magazine, *The Freeman*, for which he served as literary editor. One faction of editors sought to remain aloof from unseemly day-to-day political battles in Washington, while another—Schlamm's—yearned to engage them. The magazine folded from the strain. Schlamm was all ready to settle into his next job, editing a new journal of high-minded reflection on current events for Henry Luce, when Luce got cold feet during the 1954 recession. Schlamm, left at the altar, and Buckley, all dressed up with no place to go, discovered one another, and *National Review* was born. Or at least a business plan was born. It offered two classes of stock. Class A held no financial value but included voting rights. Class B was $1 a share and had no voting rights. All Class A shares—all decision-making authority—were possessed by a single man: William F. Buckley Jr. This new magazine, the two founders were determined, wouldn't be brought down by power struggles like *The Freeman*.

Buckley spent over a year on the road peddling *NR* debentures to businessmen who could afford to lose money. His prospectus began: "The New Deal revolution could hardly have happened save for the cumulative impact of *The Nation* and *The New Republic*, and a few other publications, on several American college generations during the twenties and thirties." That was ISI talking. The rest was pure Buckley: "New Deal journalism has degenerated into a jaded defense of the status quo. . . . Middle-of-the-Road, *qua* Middle-of-the-Road, is politically, intellectually, and morally repugnant." The Millikens proved generous; L.A. oil magnate Henry Salvatori gave $50,000. Most people gave nothing. It did not surprise Buckley's father to see his experience reconfirmed: the task of preserving capitalism was too important to leave to the capitalists. The Buckley family stepped in to finance the rest of the endeavor.

The first issue rolled off the presses in November of 1955. The baffled criticisms came soon after. That of John Fischer, editor of *Harper's*, was typical. He said he had high hopes for *National Review* as "a remarkably useful addition to the American scene." Those hopes "did not survive the first half-dozen issues. By that time it was plain that the new magazine was an organ, not of conservatism, but of radicalism." His conclusion: "it will have a certain interest for students of political splinter movements." He wondered why these "conservatives" could not abide a fellow like Dwight Eisenhower, who was so judiciously *conserving* the progress of the FDR years, without recklessly expanding them. In the immediate postwar years, in fact, the meaning of "conservatism" had been up in the air. When Senators Nixon and Kennedy first ran for Congress in 1946, the former ran as a "practical liberal," the latter as a "fighting conservative." The poet and political philosopher Peter Viereck, the first to argue that conservatism was a rebellion against a liberal status quo, argued that a true conservative should welcome the welfare state as a stabilizing force. As did Tory journalist Peregrine Worsthorne: "For only if the many are spared economic hardship can the few expect to enjoy economic and social privilege." But *National Review*'s conservatives seemed scarcely concerned with anything so pedestrian, so *materialist*, as economic and social privilege.

"Are you for majority rule in the U.S.A.?" Mike Wallace asked Buckley on his television interview program.

"Yes," came the exhalation from the graceful man leaning back in his chair across from him. "Unless the majority decides we should go Communist. I would try to subvert any Communist society."

Wallace: "You mean you would turn revolutionary?"

Buckley: "Yes. I am already a revolutionary against the present liberal order. An intellectual revolutionary."

There hadn't been anything like *National Review* since the Marxist weeklies of the 1930s—not surprising, since many of its editors were veterans. "The Tranquil World of Dwight Eisenhower" (an article that ran in the January 18, 1958, issue) was boring. *National Review* never was. "We are an opposition," wrote *NR* chief theoretician Frank Meyer, "and we have to fight conformity." Arch wit and stylistic daring were revered in the cramped offices on East 37th Street. Garry Wills, a young Midwestern seminarian brought on board as drama critic on the strength of one unsolicited manuscript, and two of the most influential critical stylists of the 1960s, John Leonard and Joan Didion, got their start in the the magazine's culture pages. But culture was the undercard. The main event was exposing the Liberals (the word was always capitalized, sticking out like an unlovely anomaly in the march of Western Civilization) as an unaccountable establishment—a mission formalized, in early issues, by eleven separate columns, each devoted to monitoring a single redoubt: the intelligentsia (Willmoore Kendall on "The Liberal Line"), foreign policy (James Burnham on "The Third Cold War"), newspapers (Karl Hess on "The Press of Freedom"), and on and on.

National Review rode an impressive postwar tide of conservative intellectual work that, wrote an observer, "would tax the dialectical agility of a thirty-third degree Trotskyite." They believed that the bulwark of any civilization was not industry or riches or men under arms, but *ideas*. The West was imperiled because it was infected by error: by materialism, in the philosophical sense of the word, believing the world to be wholly composed of ordinary physical matter and of valuing physical well-being as an ultimate end. And materialism's handmaids: humanism and egalitarianism, which assumed man had unlimited power to order his own world; pragmatism, which said whatever worked was right; and utopianism, the doomed attempt to establish the kingdom of heaven on earth (Buckley liked to call that "immanentizing the eschaton"). The offenders were both Democrats (Kennedy: "Our problems are man-made; they can be solved by man. And man can be as big as he wants") and Republicans (Rockefeller: The ideal politician "goes in and says, 'I want to find out what the facts are.' Then he adapts his program and his approach to the realities"). It was the political water America was swimming in—a swamp, Buckley's acolytes thought.

If this was abstruse stuff, that only added to the thrill of belonging to the club. Young *National Review* readers were discovering one another. The spring that *Conscience of a Conservative* was published, the Midwest Federation of College Republicans meeting in Des Moines, overwhelmed with a record 435 delegates, resolved by voice vote to endorse Barry Goldwater for vice president. A group of them who had met through the loyalty oath fight formed Youth for Goldwater for Vice President, headed by Caddy and a University of Indiana student who was active in ISI, Robert Croll. Within a few weeks Youth for Goldwater had sixty-four campus chapters in thirty-two states, a headquarters in Washington, and a mentor: an edgy right-wing publicist named Marvin Liebman, for whom Caddy was working that summer, and who was going to the Republican National Convention to plump for an old China Lobby stalwart, Republican Walter Judd of Minnesota, for vice president.

Restless, lonely teenagers discovering their first intellectual and political high; craggy old Midwestern foundry men counting their inflation-addled dollars and chasing the unions from their gates; the newly wealthy in a changing South—and the gruff and glamorous cowboy aristocrat whom they all pictured when they closed their eyes and imagined their political beau ideal: quietly, just below the notice of a media and political establishment for whom such a confluence was unimaginable, something was happening—"like the meeting of the Blue and White Nile," as William Rusher, publisher of *National Review*, would describe it much later, although at the time he chose a different metaphor: "I think we had better pull in our belts and buckle down to a long period of real impotence. Hell, the catacombs were good enough for the Christians!"

The tributaries would converge in Chicago that summer at Richard Nixon's Republican National Convention. Croll began organizing National Youth for Goldwater for Vice President full-time out of a Chicago attic with funds raised via a *National Review* ad and a dollar-a-head membership fee. Manion's allies in the South Carolina Republican Party at their state convention on March 26, clutching advance copies of *Conscience of a Conservative*, listened to Goldwater criticize Nixon's "complacent attitude" toward the South and, in a move coordinated by Manion that caught Goldwater quite by surprise, pledged their thirteen convention delegates to him. Manion immediately began mobilizing for a repeat performance in Mississippi in April. He opened an Americans for Goldwater headquarters in Chicago on July 7; a full-page ad ran in the *Tribune* on July 13. People were coming to the dean and asking how to organize their own clubs; soon there were hundreds of Americans for Goldwater chapters.

And, almost incidentally, there was a flesh-and-blood man named Barry Goldwater, the one who gave twenty-three speeches in thirteen states in the first two months of 1960 on behalf of the Republican Party. Three months after its debut, the *Los Angeles Times* column with his name at its head had drawn a thousand fan letters, three of four expressing a desire to vote for Goldwater for President; in April the column went into syndication. The book with his name on the cover would soon be selling in a torrent. A bit shaken by it all, the man behind the byline, a loyal party soldier, met with the vice president to assure him how startled and dismayed he had been when the crowd in South Carolina got so out of hand. But he added that if Nixon ignored the amazing swell in conservative sentiment in the country, he might be sorry. Privately he resolved to force Nixon's hand. "In the last six weeks Dick has shown a decided tendency to drift far to the left," he wrote a friend, Phoenix lawyer William Rehnquist, in a letter instructing the Arizona delegation to vote for Nixon at the convention, "and this has caused such consternation among the party workers across the country that we must employ means to get him back on track."

He concluded: "I would rather see the Republicans lose in 1960 fighting on principle, than I would care to see us win standing on grounds we know are wrong and on which we will ultimately destroy ourselves."

There was ample provocation that spring and summer for Goldwater's Cold War hard line to resonate: It seemed as if Communism was on the march. In April, student riots in South Korea brought down the government of ally Syngman Rhee; in Turkey another friendly government held on by a thread after riots in May. Soviet foreign minister Anastas Mikoyan visited Cuba, to an unusually warm reception, as part of Khrushchev's campaign for Third World countries to rise up against "capitalist imperialism"; then Castro nationalized the oil refineries. Eisenhower, in the Far East on a final goodwill tour, was kept from Japan for fear for his safety after students took to the streets in outrage at a mutual security pact Japan's government had signed with the United States; in Africa, independence celebrations in the new nation of the Democratic Republic of the Congo were followed by the secession of the mineral-rich province of Katanga, then an invitation by prime minister Patrice Lumumba to the Soviet Union to intervene, then by Westerners fleeing by the thousands one step ahead of—a new household phrase—"anti-American mobs." Were the swarms in Turkey and Korea and Japan and the Congo, rising so close in succession, directed by the Communists? What, for that matter, about the student mobs from Berkeley who rioted that May in protest against hearings held in San Francisco by the House Committee on Un-American Activities?

But it wasn't Goldwater who seized the moment. It was Nelson Rockefeller.

Rockefeller was a Cold War hawk almost to the degree (if not exactly the kind) of Goldwater. An early proposal he put forward as governor was to assess each New York family the over $300 it would require to build a bomb shelter for every household in the state. The argument was the same as in *Conscience*: whichever side was able to render nuclear war less unthinkable had the advantage. "Are we going to arrive at a point some day," he asked at a civil defense seminar in March, "when the president will say: 'Well, how can we afford to stand for freedom? With the people exposed, can we run that risk?' " He introduced a new phrase to the American lexicon that summer: "missile gap"—the assertion that the Soviets had hundreds more nuclear projectiles than did the United States. He based the charge on one of his Rockefeller Brothers Special Studies Fund reports. Then he amplified it to revive his presidential bid.

In fact, data from U2 spy planes had demonstrated that the USSR's arsenal of bombers and missiles that could reach the United States was nearly nonexistent. But that intelligence was top secret, unknown even to a New York governor—a rule of espionage being that you can't let your enemy know what you know about them. ("I can't understand the United States being quite as panicky as they are," Eisenhower once said, forgetting that he was one of only a handful of people who knew that the empire that threatened to bury us could in fact do no such thing.) Republican leaders scurried to shut Rockefeller up. Nixon leaked that the governor was first choice for vice president; Kentucky senator Thruston Morton, chair of the Republican National Convention, offered him the keynote speech in Chicago. Rocky rebuffed them. "I hate the thought of Dick Nixon being president of the United States," he told confidants.

Events turned up the temperature. Another East-West summit was coming up, and it was so eagerly anticipated that it became a pop culture phenomenon: when Frank Sinatra, Dean Martin, Peter Lawford, Joey Bishop, and Sammy Davis Jr. began performing together at the Sands in Las Vegas, the act was billed as "The Summit." But then a U2 plane was felled by a Soviet S-75 missile 1,300 miles deep in Russian territory, and the Soviets canceled the honeymoon—vindicating Goldwater's *Conscience of a Conservative* argument that Cold War thaws were reliable predictors of imminent Communist outrages. In Vegas, "The Summit" was rechristened the Rat Pack. And in Albany, Rockefeller launched himself back into the nomination race with a grandiloquent statement on June 8. "The failure of the Paris Conference," Rockefeller declared, "places in serious question some of the illusions, as well as the procedures, that led to the summit itself." He was, he said, "deeply concerned that those now assuming control of the Republican Party have failed to make clear where this party is heading and where it proposes to lead the nation," a dilemma that was the "gravest in its history." The party's "destiny," he concluded, "is to save the nation by saving itself." For his program, Rockefeller Brothers Special Studies Fund reports were knocked into a series of campaign position papers—a nine-movement symphony of Immanentized Eschatons, internationalist idealism, and managerial expertise, delivered in installments across the country in any forum where his handlers could book him and in any publication that would grant him space.

Rockefeller hoped to use the convention platform as a wedge to pry open a nominating process every other Republican presumed was sealed. A platform draft is composed by a functionary; a resolutions committee (colloquially called a platform committee) of a hundred or so delegates, usually pledged to one candidate or another, hears dreary testimony on proposed amendments; committee members "debate," then vote the amendments up or down mostly by instruction of the campaign to which they owe their loyalty—making the contest interesting only to the tea-leaf readers seeking to gauge the relative strengths of the contenders. (The Democrats in 1944 manfully pledged "such additional humanitarian, labor, social and farm legislation as time and experience may require"; Woodrow Wilson's platform in 1912 opposed second terms.) But Rockefeller rather fantastically assumed that if he could just demonstrate intellectually how inadequate the platform draft was to modern needs, concerned Republicans couldn't but flock to his banner.

When Rockefeller read the draft that July, he summoned Charles Percy, chair of the platform committee, an overpoweringly vital man who was the Fortune 500's youngest CEO, to West 55th Street for a bit of unsubtle persuasion. The nation, Rockefeller reminded Percy, was in a state of Cold War emergency. The platform didn't convey that at all. What's more, there were *problems* out there, problems amenable to can-do government solutions, that the platform glossed over: civil rights, declining health among the aged, declining rates of capital investment in sectors ripe for federal stimulation. If these problems were not addressed in the document, Rockefeller said, he could not promise his support—hinting darkly at a divisive floor fight. It was with considerable agitation that Percy traveled on to Washington to meet with Nixon, with twelve days to go before his committee was to convene for its opening session in Chicago and seven days before the state delegations were to arrive, and heard Nixon reassure him that the authority over the platform was the platform committee's to wield. If Rockefeller wanted to influence the proceedings, Nixon promised, he would have to line up to testify just like anyone else.

And so from every state and territory they came, the 103 members of the Republican platform committee, two by two and one from each territory, straggling into the Crystal Ballroom at the Blackstone Hotel on South Michigan Avenue in Chicago on July 18, 1960, to begin the painstaking and unedifying work of bending the planks toward that elusive most banal common denominator. The only relief from the tedium came when Barry Goldwater presented his "Suggested Declaration of Republican Principles" before the committee members on the twentieth. "To our undying shame, there are those among us who would prefer to crawl on their bellies rather than to face the possibility of an atomic war," he said. He earned a standing ovation. It sure beat listening to the Ford Foundation rep report that 7 percent of gifted children grow up maladjusted, versus 14 percent of the general student population.

As the platform committee's work wound down, the rest of the Republican delegates came straggling into Chicago—as they had before in 1952, 1944, 1920, 1916, and 1912 (when the convention ran two days over because of a knock-down-drag-out floor fight between William Howard Taft's conservatives and Teddy Roosevelt's "Bull Moose" progressives); and in 1908, 1904, 1888, 1884, 1868, and, in the first successful nominating convention of the new party formed to fight the expansion of slavery into the Western territories, 1860. Taxi drivers, by order of Chicago's Public Vehicle License Commission wearing fresh, clean shirts, massed on the South Michigan Avenue blocks across the street from Grant Park's strip of greensward hard to Lake Michigan that contained the city's finest hotel rooms. Republicans set down their valises amidst an imbroglio of sound trucks and pickets, pamphleteers and sandwich-board men, "Nixon Girls" parading up and down the street in pink-and-white gingham—and, led by activist Bayard Rustin, a civil rights march twice as large as the one held a few weeks before at the Democratic National Convention in Los Angeles.

At the entrance to the convention hall, each delegate received an instruction card: "You're on television," it warned, admonishing them in verse:

> *Don't read papers in the hall,*
> *Even the latest issue.*
> *If you hold them up before your face,*
> *The folks at home will miss you.*

These were golden years for political conventions: television audiences tuned in hoping for a showdown like the one between Taft and Eisenhower in 1952, the parties not yet having learned how to script the events so as to make a showdown impossible. Factions, meanwhile, began playing for TV, hoping for some dramatic breakthrough that would inspire the folks back home to stampede their delegates with telegrams and phone calls—as had almost seemed possible at the Democratic Convention a few weeks back after the surprising roof-raising demonstration that greeted dark-horse candidate Adlai Stevenson when he took his seat with the Illinois delegation. Many conservatives hoped to do the same thing for Goldwater.

But the real action still took place behind the scenes. Unbeknownst to the platform committee, at the Sheraton headquarters of the New York delegation (a rumor had it that Rockefeller had rented the entire hotel; it was only an entire wing), Rocky's political chieftains were monitoring the committee's every move. On Friday, his Albany press secretary delivered a surprise statement: "The Governor has been keeping in touch with all developments on shaping the platform. . . . He is deeply concerned that the reports reaching him clearly indicate that the draft on a number of matters—including national defense, foreign policy, and some critical domestic issues—are still seriously lacking in strength and specifics."

Richard Nixon's coronation threatened to break into war, and the vice president was nervous. *Lacking strength and specifics*—the idea was absurd. All platforms lack in strength and specifics! Was this pretext for the New York delegation—nearly 10 percent of the votes needed for nomination—to lead a stampede for Rockefeller?

Nixon had been working for this moment, sweating for it, slaving for it, cringing for it, *bowing and scraping* for it, since—since when? Since he was denied the chance to go to Harvard because he could only afford to live at home; since he was blacklisted from Whittier College's one social club because he was too poor; since he was reduced to sharing that one-room shack without heat or indoor plumbing with four fellow students while working his way through Duke Law and finished third in his class; since he begged Los Angeles's plutocrats, Navy cap in hand, for their sufferance of his first congressional bid; since he trundled across California in his wood-paneled station wagon to bring his Senate campaign "into every county, city, town, precinct, and home in the state of California"; since he was forced to plead cloth-coated poverty on television to keep his spot as vice-presidential candidate in 1952; since his vice-presidential career was interrupted every off year when he hit the road to campaign for other Republicans, pounding whiskey in the back rooms when his companions pounded whiskey, drinking juice in church basements when his companions drank juice. Richard Nixon: collector of chits. And now, when it was finally time to call them in, would the whole thing disintegrate before his eyes?

And so over the heads of the lowly platform committee, behind the back of Charlie Percy—behind the backs of his own inner circle—Richard Nixon reached a decision. He would bow and scrape once more, before Nelson Rockefeller. Through Attorney General Herbert Brownell, Nixon relayed the message that he would come to New York whenever Rockefeller wished. Rockefeller's lieutenants dictated the terms: a meeting at Rockefeller's apartment that very night, in secret, followed by the announcement that the meeting had taken place at the vice president's request, accompanied by a "joint" agreement over platform changes. Nixon flew to New York with a single mid-level aide in tow, arriving at 7:30 in the evening, Friday, July 23.

They drove directly to Rockefeller's apartment in the fading summer light. Nixon was led up the stairs of 810 Fifth Avenue, whose two upper apartments Nelson had purchased as his private home in 1934 upon receiving his $12 million trust—around the time Nixon was cranking a mimeograph machine in a sweltering basement to earn his keep at Duke Law. The bottom third of the building Rockefeller bought in 1938, around the same time Nixon married Patricia Ryan—for her money, he would joke: she had saved up for the honeymoon out of her teacher's salary.

Rockefeller might have been wearing the open-necked shirts and soft-soled shoes he favored; Nixon's dress shoes would have *click-clacked* his presence as he traversed the eighteenth-century parquet floors Nelson had imported from France to match the rococo moldings his decorator had chosen to evoke Louis XIV's Versailles. Rockefeller honored his guest with dinner, during which he refused Nixon's entreaties to become his running mate. Rockefeller led Nixon up to the penthouse, his study. They would have swept first through the apartment's showpiece, the living room. Rockefeller's passion was modern art. The centerpiece of the living room was twin fireplaces, the andirons custom-designed by the sculptor Alberto Giacometti, their mantels stretching nearly to the ceiling and painted with specially commissioned murals by Fernand Léger and Henri Matisse depicting languid female figures and sinuous plantlike morphs. ("I always liked forms of art where I could feel the artist, feel the material," Nelson said.) Ascending the circular marble staircase, the eye of the nation's premiere tribune of middle-class morality might have been drawn by paintings by Picasso and Braque, glass cases filled with primitive carvings collected on their owner's journeys to the four corners of the globe, sculptures by Alexander Calder, one of Gaston Lachaise's over-endowed bronze Amazons.

Then to the penthouse. Nixon was given a seat at Rockefeller's desk; Rockefeller lounged on a nearby bed. Nixon spied the glorious floodlit expanse of Central Park; when Rockefeller had bought the place, a stone balustrade blocked the view, so he had the floor raised several inches. Nixon was handed a draft of fourteen points that Rockefeller wanted to see in the platform. As the governor's people established a four-way phone line to Percy at the Blackstone and Rockefeller's command center at the Sheraton, as well as extensions for both Rockefeller and Nixon, the two spent three hours haggling, tweaking, talking, listening—mostly Rockefeller talking and Nixon listening; most of the changes Nixon made to Rockefeller's working paper were cosmetic. At 3:20 a.m. Nixon left for La Guardia. From there, Rockefeller phoned Chicago to give his people the first hint of the extraordinary event that had just transpired. Nixon's press secretary Herb Klein was awakened by reporters who asked for confirmation that a meeting between Nixon and Rockefeller had taken place. Klein denied it. He was called a liar. He had no idea what they were talking about.

Members of the Rockefeller apparat at the penthouse busied themselves editing and mimeographing the fourteen-point text for a 5 a.m. release: "The Vice-President and I met today at my home in New York City. The meeting took place at the Vice-President's request."

Richard Nixon ignored hints that summer that he should be taking Goldwater and his conservatives seriously. In spring the Arizonan made his grandest tour yet, fourteen speeches in eleven states in May alone. In June he gave the keynote speech at the Mississippi Republican convention and appeared on *Meet the Press*, where he challenged Nixon to clarify his wishy-washy positions. The Arizona Republican convention pledged its delegate votes to Goldwater on the first ballot. So did Louisiana's Republican convention. The July 4 *Newsweek* published remarkable news: "It was conceded in top party echelons that in a truly open convention, Republicans would probably nominate Goldwater for Vice President." (National Youth for Goldwater for Vice President sent out two thousand copies of the clip with an arrow pointing to that line and the ominous question *"Is it going to be an 'open' convention?"*) Delegates were besieged with postcards and telegrams plumping Goldwater for the top spot. The ones orchestrated by Robert Welch read: "Nominate anybody you please. I'm voting for Goldwater." Indiana College Republicans chair James Abstine sent Nixon a letter so threatening it could only have come from someone too young to know better: "We have worked, are now working, and will continue to work actively for your election as President, but if to so work for you requires the accommodation of our thinking so that we agree with you on all issues at all times just for the sake of agreeing with you, then, I suppose, that many of us would prefer the freedom to think our own thoughts than to be active politically in such a way that we could not do so." Ignore Goldwater at your peril, warned a top Republican from Nixon's home territory, Orange County, American Bar Association president Loyd Wright: "Thousands and thousands of people every day are singing his praises for furnishing Republican leadership . . . people upon whom we must rely to punch doorbells and put up money."

Nixon took it all in, dutifully put Goldwater on a list of potential vice presidents, and presumed that was the end of it. Never one to get hung up on ideology, Nixon was dismissive. "They are against any change whatsoever, including good change," he complained. "Whenever we talk about good ends, they charge us with being 'me too.' " Even in the feverish summer of *Conscience of a Conservative*, only 1 percent of Republican voters thought Barry Goldwater should be nominated for the top spot over Nixon. But they were overrepresented at the convention in Chicago. And they were so sure in their convictions that they took on the aura of multitudes.

The hottest ticket that weekend was a Hawaiian "Hukilau" to honor the newest state in the union, thrown by Illinois Federation of Republican Women president Phyllis Schlafly, with Goldwater as the featured speaker. Everywhere in Chicago one tripped over the new paperback edition of *Conscience*—distributed, along with fifteen thousand Goldwater buttons, by Croll and Caddy's Youth for Goldwater for Vice President. Doug Caddy talked like a power broker: "Nixon has a right to the nomination," he said, and young conservatives would support him—because he "has been kept fairly well in line by Goldwater." On newsstands, the August 1 *Newsweek* featured an article by Goldwater: "I am convinced we will lose the 1960 elections if we embrace the false notion that a majority of American citizens are eager to trade their birthright of responsible freedom for the mess-of-pottage promise of subsidy and support." Delegations arriving early pestered Goldwater's little gray-haired secretary Edna Coerver unsuccessfully for an audience. Nonplused, they stalked his suite at the Blackstone, a red-white-and-blue sea for him to part everywhere he went.

"The country needs you, Barry!"

"Autograph my Bible!" (A copy of *Conscience* would be pushed into his face.)

"I want to shake your hand! You're the only real Republican in the running!"

Goldwater did his best to muster a thin smile and not break his stride while hiding his irritation, and to avoid the urge to snap—he was prone to snapping—*"I am not in the running!"*

"Those damned Goldwater people are everywhere," Nixon aides muttered, relaxing, dining, their work, they thought, complete.

Dawn, Saturday, July 23. In the press room at the Hilton, reporters scrambled to digest the detailed statement coming over the teletype and complete the brain-twisting task of cross-checking it against the finished platform draft. The AP was first into print with news of the "Compact of Fifth Avenue." Nixon's campaign manager Leonard Hall learned about it from them. Blinded by rage, streaming profanity, he sought out Barry Goldwater.

Goldwater was about to address a breakfast meeting to the Republican finance committee. A messenger told him to see Len Hall immediately. Goldwater said he would just have to wait. The emissary whispered something in his ear. Goldwater excused himself from the room. He couldn't believe what he was hearing. He had to get it from Hall himself.

Goldwater's incredulity pointed to a facet of his character: slow to trust, once he accepted someone as a confidant he presumed in them the same deep-seated sense of honor that motivated him. It was why long after many Republicans abandoned McCarthy to his fate, Goldwater defended him: McCarthy had extended him important help in his 1952 Senate run. Almost alone among successful politicians, he took slights personally. What he thought was not that Nixon must have had his reasons, or that Nixon was selling out the party, or that Nixon was just being Nixon. What he thought was that Nixon had assured him *personally* that he wouldn't meet with Rockefeller until after the convention, and that when he had talked to him only the morning before, Nixon told him nothing about any meeting with Rockefeller, and that Richard Nixon would not lie to him.

He soon learned from Hall, who was as angry as any man Goldwater had ever seen, screaming "This might cost Nixon the election!," that Nixon had done just that. Goldwater was scheduled for a 10 a.m. press conference to magnanimously release his Arizona and South Carolina delegates to Nixon. He tore up his statement and spoke from hasty notes instead.

"I think the Republican Party would both be breaking faith with itself and shirking its duty to the nation should we fail to identify ourselves with the conservative point of view in both domestic and foreign affairs," he said. He continued: "Early today came the disturbing news that Mr. Nixon himself has felt it necessary to make overtures and concessions to the liberals." It was "a sellout on nearly every point that once separated the Vice President and the Governor." Goldwater removed his black-rimmed glasses. "I believe this to be immoral politics. I also believe it to be self-defeating. . . . Alienate the conservatives—as the party is now in the process of doing—and the handful of liberal militants that are seeking to take over the Republican Party will inherit a mess of pottage." If Nixon folded before "a spokesman for the ultra-liberals," he, Goldwater, would be forced to fight Rockefeller's platform changes on the floor. "If the Fourteen Point agreement—both the substance of it and the process by which it was reached—is allowed to go unchallenged, it will live in history as the Munich of the Republican Party. It will be a Munich in two senses, that it subordinated principle to expediency; and that it guaranteed precisely the evil it was designed to prevent—in this case a Republican defeat in November."

Edna Coerver prepared Goldwater's remarks for release to the press, toning them down slightly for diplomacy, typing so fast that the liberals were scored for their "shoeking unrealism." In his diary Goldwater wrote of Nixon, "This man is a two-fisted, four-square liar." Technically, the senator was still a candidate for the nomination. His wheels were turning.

Rockefeller flew to Chicago and declared that since the platform was more important than the nominee, and that there was a "very good chance" his fourteen points would be written into it without protest, he could now support the ticket. "Hell, he's playing elder statesman without waiting to be a statesman," one reporter muttered. So much the statesman, in fact, he didn't even bother to pay court to the small but fervid band of young Rockefeller for President enthusiasts who seemed to be everywhere, placing Rockefeller banners within the field of every television camera and Rockefeller cheers in range of every radio mike.

Goldwater couldn't have ignored his supporters if he tried. Kicked up like a sandstorm by the "Munich of the Republican Party," shrieking conservatives made Michigan Avenue and its hostelries a cloud of scrawled picket signs: "LOUISIANA IS TIRED OF DICTATORS!"; "DON'T GO DOWN THE ROCKY ROAD TO *RUIN*!"; "PLATFORM COMMITTEE—DON'T BE RAILROADED!" A significant plurality were Southerners. The convention had become a proxy fight in America's second civil war. The day's newspapers reported that Greensboro, birthplace twenty-two weeks earlier of the still-spreading sit-in movement, was on the verge of yielding to pressure to desegregate its restaurants. Congress debated whether the Temporary Commission on Civil Rights authorized by the 1957 Civil Rights Act would become a permanent Fair Employment Practices Commission. Liberal Republicans pointed out that their party owed Negro voters for one hundred years of loyalty. But the party was increasingly becoming a redoubt for those who either wished blacks ill or viewed them with indifference.

It was point nine of the fourteen points that the Southerners were protesting:

> Our program for civil rights must assure aggressive action to remove the remaining vestiges of segregation or discrimination in all areas of national life—voting and housing, schools and jobs. It will express support for the objectives of the sit-in demonstrators and will commend the action of those businessmen who have abandoned the practice of refusing to serve food at their lunch counters to their Negro customers and will urge all others to follow their example.

To Nixon deputies, states like Louisiana relayed threats: expect no campaign labor or money from them. Texas, legally pledged to Nixon, called a hasty caucus. Its leader, a quiet but dominating political science professor named John Tower who had resigned his teaching position to run for the Senate, said he could not in good conscience prevent them from voting for whichever candidate they wished—which was tantamount to delivering the delegation to Goldwater.

Tower was a member of the platform's civil rights subcommittee. Since platform delegates were apportioned to subcommittees based on their area of interest, the civil rights subcommittee was a self-selected gathering of pit bulls. Its hearings were chaired by New York assembly speaker Joseph Carlino—as a Rockefeller deputy, the de facto leader of the Northern, pro–civil rights faction. They were mêlées. Tower's group had the majority. Their will was fought at every turn by Carlino, wielding the gavel like a jackhammer. The Tower faction's desired draft platform plank was a pitch-perfect expression of what passed for the "moderate" position in the South on civil rights: although the sit-ins had been peaceful—so far—the protests were vulnerable to Communist infiltration, had they not fallen already; the likely result of continued protests would be violence of the sort that had rocked Ankara, Tokyo, Kinshasa, and Berkeley; and although orderly progress toward Negro rights should be sup-ported, if a Federal Employment Practices Commission could tell private business who to hire the government would be trespassing America's most sacred liberties.

Point nine would also, added Louisiana's flamboyant Tom Stagg, "kill the Republican Party in the South. Lyndon Johnson is going to come across the border and talk 'magnolia' to them and they'll vote Democratic."

Eisenhower, drafting his valedictory address for the Tuesday of the convention at his "summer White House" in Newport, was enraged by the Compact's defense points. They had sold out his legacy—the most valuable thing a former President had. The document spouted off on nuclear strategy, calling for "a nuclear retaliatory power capable of surviving surprise attack to inflict devas-tating punishment on any aggressor . . . a modern, flexible and balanced mili-tary establishment with forces capable of deterring or meeting any local aggression"—as if Rockefeller knew what he was talking about. Eisenhower, knowing what only a President and a few others *could* know, wondered whether an arms race wouldn't bankrupt us before it could save us; whether, in fact, the whole dismal business didn't deliver more *in*security than security. He called Nixon in Washington and shamed him. How could he assent to calling for weapons there was no money to pay for? Kennedy had already picked up Rockefeller's "missile gap" charge and gladly made it his own. How could Nixon run on a platform echoing the charges of the Democratic nominee? Ike called Thruston Morton, a loyal political friend, and told him to tell Rockefeller to get in line to testify before the platform committee like everyone else. Rocke-feller had never given a single thought to any platform committee. He blithely assumed that Nixon could simply impose his will from on high.

Now, to save his coronation, Nixon had to compromise. He knew that if he didn't placate Rockefeller, the New York governor would do all he could to crush him. Nixon would also lose face, having already informed the world that the fourteen points were *his* idea. He had to compromise. The only possible compromise was to defend either the civil rights part (offending Goldwater's conservatives) or the foreign policy part (betraying Eisenhower), then try to sell the result as best he could to the full platform committee.

So would he sell out Ike, or would he sell out the conservatives?

.   .   .

You can imagine Nixon's brooding, in his mind, taking form in the typical style of his speeches: Richard Nixon debating Richard Nixon. *Now we come to the key question: what should the answer be? Some might say, why, give in to Rockefeller on foreign policy. Some would say that Rockefeller should have his way on domestic issues, of which the most pressing, of course, is the question of civil rights. But the former, of course, means relinquishing control of our party's position in the worldwide struggle for Freedom. . . .*

As in all his little rhetorical dialogues, victory for one side was fore-ordained. Nixon wanted to become President to command America in the Cold War. He was obsessed with the details of foreign affairs; domestic policy, he said famously a decade later, just takes care of itself. One of the aides Nixon brought with him to Chicago, a thoughtful young political science instructor named Chuck Lichenstein, had produced a campaign book, *The Challenges We Face*, from Nixon's speeches. When Nixon had thumbed through it and got to the section on agricultural price subsidies, he asked, "Have I really said all of these things?"

"Yes, every word," replied Lichenstein.

"Well, that's interesting, because I can't tell."

"But do you accept this as your views?" the nervous deputy asked.

"Oh, yes, oh, yes," Nixon reassured him.

The internal dialogue continued: *I am not going to waste your time on a dispute over the details of domestic policy, for these things take care of themselves.*

Sunday the twenty-fourth, Rockefeller was on Michigan Avenue—not at its luxurious hotels, but miles to the south on the stretch that would later be renamed after Martin Luther King Jr., the man who sat on the pulpit next to Rockefeller. It was King's more established colleague, however, Roy Wilkins of the NAACP, who was the featured speaker, calling Nelson Rockefeller the man who "made a backbone plank out of a spaghetti plank." The six thousand Negroes packing the pews of Liberty Baptist Church interrupted Rockefeller thirty-three times with applause. Though, of course, he had only proposed a strengthened platform plank on civil rights, not made one. That was the job of the platform committee, whose meeting, miles to the north, was now spiraling out of control.

At Eisenhower's behest, Thruston Morton had published each subcommittee's draft planks and distributed them to reporters along with Rockefeller's proposals, trying to keep Nixon from choking off deliberations and simply imposing the Compact's terms. Subcommittee chairmen, meanwhile, sought to fool reporters into believing that the planks were already finished—thus making Rockefeller look even more like a spoiler. When the full platform committee finally settled down at the Blackstone after midnight to hash out a solution, members competed to demand most strenuously that not a single word of their subcommittee's draft planks be changed—even as Rockefeller's loyal New York delegates made what parliamentary maneuvers they could to bring up the planks for debate.

Blood was in the air. Mrs. A. Dabney Barnes of South Carolina won the floor to defend Tower's civil rights majority report. She pulled out a book and read a stirring defense of the go-slow approach to Negro rights. "Nixon could never agree with that," liberals cried—then Mrs. Barnes revealed she was reading from Nixon's *The Challenges We Face*. Outside, conservatives, supplemented by ringers Caddy had bused in from the Chicago suburbs, chanted from behind hand-lettered placards ("NO ROCKS IN OUR HEADS, HOW ABOUT YOURS?") in the still night air. Working like a convention floor manager, John Tower wrung enough votes hour by hour to get his subcommittee report through the platform committee. The meeting adjourned toward dawn. Still, this was just a preliminary step; the plank could be changed. Every precedent gave the putative nominee the prerogative to dictate the platform. The Southerners were determined to tell the putative nominee to go straight to hell.

The convention was a mess, and the opening gavel had not even been struck. Goldwater leaders observed the chaos and were delighted. Greg Shorey ran a Goldwater clearinghouse out of the South Carolina delegation's headquarters at the La Salle. He told the press that 120 nomination votes were in hand. Whenever his booster could get the great man's ear, they plied him with extravagant promises of 300 if he would only announce his candidacy. It just made Goldwater aggravated. "I've heard enough rumors to be elected king," he complained. "I can still count only 61 votes." That was generous; at that point, there were only South Carolina's and Arizona's delegations—40—who were willing to stand up on the convention floor for Goldwater and risk political and patronage exile if Nixon won the election. Goldwater told *Life* what to him seemed obvious: "We can't expect to come here and change 900 delegates in three days. But if we work hard for the next four years, maybe we can do it."

He might be an ideologue. But he revered the "pros," those value-neutral party mechanics whose behind-the-scenes work left him free to range over the fruited plain to deliver his grand ideological pronouncements. He didn't see any of *them* showing up at his doorstep. Sick and tired of the entreaties of amateurs, Goldwater finally snapped: "Get me three hundred names of delegates on paper. Show me." Then, and only then, he'd begin to campaign. "It's my political neck they are putting on this chopping block, and I don't know that I like it."

Nixon arrived at O'Hare the morning of Monday the twenty-fifth for the convention's opening day, met by a friendly crowd of three thousand and a knot of photographers begging him for a display of affection for his little girls, Julie in ivory and Tricia in blue-and-white checks. (He obliged under duress: "I don't go for all this kissing in public.") A brass band favored him on the tarmac with a rousing "California Here I Come"—a dispiriting selection for one to whom returning to California would be the worst possible outcome. At his Blackstone headquarters he was favored with a sidewalk demonstration organized by Robert Croll: Barry Goldwater's face on hundreds of identical placards, "GOLDWATER FOR PRESIDENT," "GOLDWATER FOR PRESIDENT," "GOLDWATER FOR PRESIDENT," as if he were in a hall of mirrors.

Nixon crossed the street to the Hilton for a televised news conference. He answered the first question, on civil rights, as Rockefeller's ventriloquist: "I believe it is essential that the Republican convention adopt a strong civil rights platform, an honest one, which does deal specifically and not in generalities with the problems and with the goals we desire to reach in these fields. . . . The statement which Governor Rockefeller and I agreed upon provides that we support the objectives for which the sit-in demonstrators were working." He denied that Nelson Rockefeller was his vice-presidential choice. Already the rumor mill had as his choice the Eastern Establishmentarian Henry Cabot Lodge—a key plotter, conservatives recalled, in the 1952 Eisenhower convention cabal against Taft. Nixon was selling them out.

Nixon got down to work on his compromise. He quickly sent word to the platform committee at the Blackstone to go ahead and approve the original—non-Rockefeller—foreign policy plank. Then, one at a time, he summoned into his Blackstone suite platform committee members who had voted with the South on civil rights, and began calling in chits.

As twilight approached, an exodus made its way southwest from Michigan Avenue to the cavernous International Amphitheater at 42nd and Halsted—nicknamed "The Stockyards" after its occasional and original purpose as showroom for the adjacent endless-maze of cattle pens (a coincidence unimaginative wags never tired of remarking upon when political candidates began dishing out bovine fundament from the podium). Amidst the neat rows of folding chairs on the delegate floor, Nixon deputies—the ones who had thought their work complete—worked on platform committee members, over the steady drone of ceremonial greetings and parliamentary business going on at the podium. They pressed the tactical argument that by matching the Democrats' pro–civil rights platform, the GOP could win as many votes from blacks as they would lose from Southern whites. And they called in chits.

Halfway through the opening session their job got harder. Herbert Hoover, eighty-five years old, gave an address to polite applause. Then Barry Goldwater, tapped to give the routine formal introduction of Republican Senate candidates, was presented. The din that followed his approach to the podium lasted a full eight minutes. Thruston Morton madly clopped his gavel for order. Goldwater gave his speech, on conservatism, the "heart and soul of our great historic Party." And the frenzy was repeated.

Downtown other Nixon deputies were coordinating telephone negotiations with Newport, begging Ike to throw Rockefeller just a bone on the foreign policy plank to keep Rockefeller from starting a floor fight—adding the word "intensified" here, a mention of Polaris missiles there, and—a painful concession for a man planning a farewell address in which he would decry the new "military-industrial complex"—allowing Rockefeller's favorite phrase from the Compact to be slipped in: "There is no price ceiling on American security."

The opening session closed with the keynote address, a McCarthyite stemwinder delivered by vice-presidential long shot Walter Judd: *"Was it the Republicans who, at Teheran, against the urgent advice of Mr. Churchill, agreed to give the Russians a free hand in the Balkans?"* [*"NO!!!"*] *"Was it the Republicans who secretly divided Poland and gave half of it to the Soviet Union?"* [*"NO!!!"*] It was television mummery, hiding smoke-filled bargains struck in plain sight.

"NIXON SAYS RIGHTS PLANK MUST BE MADE STRONGER," the *New York Times* headline announced Tuesday morning. The platform committee met in its last official session; Percy's gavel now passed to a more accomplished parliamentarian, Wisconsin congressman Melvin Laird. Nixon/Rockefeller's civil rights plank beat Tower's 56 delegates to 28. For those reluctant to allow chits to be cashed against their conservatism, Nixon's people allowed face-saving abstentions. Fence-sitters may have been won by the sounds of the angry chants wafting up from the streets below—the largest civil rights picket yet of the convention, during which Martin Luther King Jr. galvanized the crowd in a way no NAACP Old Guarder ever could. Rockefeller finally announced he was definitely, officially, not a candidate for President. Nixon breathed a final sigh of relief.

The garrotes had been tightened. The platform passed by voice vote, viewers on television unaware that there had been a scrap of discord. The coronation was on. The outgoing monarchs Mamie and the General (in retirement Ike demanded the honorific "General") arrived to a ticker-tape parade.

Eisenhower's speech contained an unsubtle dig at Rockefeller, in the guise of a dig at Kennedy: "Just as the Biblical Job had his boils, we have a cult of professional pessimists, who . . . continually mouth the allegations that America has become a second-rate military power." He was proceeded at the podium by his black special assistant E. Frederic Morrow, who had flown in with the President on Air Force One. "One hundred years ago my grandfather was a slave," radio and TV audiences heard. "Tonight I stand before you as a trusted assistant to the President of the United"—and then the networks cut away for fear of offending their Southern affiliates.

When Goldwater arrived back at the Blackstone that night he was besieged once again by his would-be drafters as they straggled back from the Stockyards. He delivered an ultimatum: "All right. You go out and get those delegates you say are willing to vote for me. I'll sit in this room all night. You bring them in. I want them to sign a paper saying they'll vote for me."

He sat up all night, perhaps sipping his favorite drink, Old Crow whiskey on the rocks, to calm his nerves. Not a single delegate came. It was Nixon's show now. Wednesday morning Goldwater sent word to the Arizona delegation that he did not want his name to be placed in nomination. Then he went to the South Carolina delegation to tell them the same thing. Roger Milliken stood up. "We were instructed by our state convention to vote this delegation for Senator Goldwater," he said, "and that's what we intend to do." He said that his delegates would claim the floor to put his name in nomination whether he liked it or not.

Goldwater retreated to confer with friends. "You aren't going to let these country bumpkins push you into this, are you?" Steve Shadegg asked him. That's just what Goldwater wanted to do—for he had an idea. Arizona would nominate Goldwater, and the requisite seconding speeches would be given. Then Goldwater would give a speech withdrawing his name from contention. He would give everyone a piece of his mind—on national TV.

As an aide got to work drafting the speech, Goldwater repaired to the Youth for Goldwater for Vice President office at the Pick-Congress Hotel to pay his respects. They seemed to him one of the only bright spots in an exceptionally annoying convention—a hell of a lot more practical in their sensible vice-presidential talk than the South Carolinians. "Turn your group into a permanent organization of young conservatives," he advised. "The man is not important. The principles you espouse are. Do this, and I shall support you in any way I can."

Nixon's acceptance speech Thursday night made Manion cringe: promising "plenty and hope to the unfortunates of the earth," explaining, "it may be just as essential to the national interest to build a dam in India as in California." The dean didn't want the federal government building dams in India *or* in California. For conservatives, the convention had ended the night before, when pointy-eared Paul Fannin had stepped up to the podium to place Goldwater's name in nomination for President of the United States.

There had followed a demonstration—the traditional ostentatious ritual display of emotion that followed the nomination of every candidate at a political convention. The Goldwater ranks had swelled far beyond what troops Croll, Caddy, Shorey, and Manion had come to Chicago with: now his supporters included disgruntled platform drafters, most of the Southern delegations, old Taftites who thought they had come to Chicago to rubber-stamp decisions made from on high—perhaps even stragglers who joined the cause after devouring *Conscience of a Conservative* up in their hotel rooms. It was their last chance to assure they would not be ignored, to show them all—Goldwater's enemies as much as Goldwater—that they were ready for war.

The intensity even amazed themselves.

Nixon's demonstration later in the evening would include exploding rockets, a sing-along, costumed brigades. Goldwater's, planned on a few hours' notice (and, in some parts of the convention hall—like the Illinois delegation, where Phyllis Schlafly simply barked to the burly guy next to her to hoist their state's standard and fall in—not planned at all) just had guts. For three minutes they marched around the hall, accompanied by the strains of "Dixie" played by the convention orchestra. The college kids—who had battled security to convince the guards that their fake credentials were real—were the loudest. In the family box, Goldwater's wife and daughters wept. It began to look like an insurgency. At the podium, movie star George Murphy, Nixon's stage manager, leaned into Goldwater's ear: "We're running overtime. This must be stopped." Ushers herded the marchers out the door—into the parking lot. Still the noise did not stop. It swelled. It continued for eleven minutes. Goldwater raised his hands for silence. Nothing happened. He couldn't control them.

Finally the cheers died down. Conservatives were shaking with anticipation: perhaps Goldwater would stampede the convention. From the spectator gallery a lone voice yelled, "God bless you, Barry." The cheering reignited.

"Thank you," he began. The cheering spluttered.

"Mr. Chairman, delegates to the convention, and fellow Republicans: I respectfully ask the chairman to withdraw my name from nomination."

The cry of *"No!!!"* that roared back was oceanic. Nixon deputies secretly rooting for Goldwater in their command trailer zoomed their closed-circuit TV camera in on his face: he was clearly moved.

"Please," he implored.

"I release my delegation from their pledge to me, and while I am not a delegate, I would suggest that they give these votes to Richard Nixon."

Nixon partisans cheered. Goldwater partisans groaned.

He addressed his fans. "We are conservatives," he began.

This great Republican Party is our historic house. This is our home.

Some of us do not agree with every statement in the official platform of our party, but I might remind you that this is always true in every platform of an American political party. . . . We can be absolutely certain of one thing—in spite of the individual points of difference, the Republican platform deserves the support of every American over the blueprint for socialism presented by the Democrats. . . .

Yet, if each segment, each section of our great party were to insist on the complete and unqualified acceptance of its views, if each viewpoint were to be enforced by a Russian-type veto [he referred to the Soviets' power to stymie any action of the UN Security Council], the Republican Party would not long survive. . . .

Now, radical Democrats, who rightfully fear that the American people will reject their extreme program in November, are watching this convention with eager hope that some split may occur in our party. I am telling them now that no such split will take place. Let them know that the conservatives of the Republican Party do not intend by any act of theirs to turn this country over, by default, to a party which has lost its belief in the dignity of man, a party which has no faith in our economic system, a party which has come to the belief that the United States is a second-rate power. . . .

While Dick and I may disagree on some points, there are not many. I would not want any negative action of mine to enhance the possibility of victory going to those who by their very words have lost faith in America. . . . Republicans have not been losing elections because of more Democrat votes—now get this—we have been losing elections because conservatives often fail to vote.

Why is this? And you conservatives think this over. We don't gain anything when you get mad at a candidate because you don't agree with his every philosophy. We don't gain anything when you disagree with the platform and then do not go out and work and vote for your party. I know what you say, "I will get even with that fellow. I will show this party something." But what are you doing when you stay at home? You are helping the opposition party elect candidates dedicated to the destruction of this country. . . . Now, I implore you, forget it.

We have had our chance and I think the conservatives have made a splendid showing at this Convention. We have had our chance. We have fought our battle. Now, let's put our shoulders to the wheel for Dick Nixon and push him across the line.

Now his voice was raised, the right corner of his mouth curled slightly above the left, his eyes narrowed; he was a stern father working over a recalcitrant child.

This country is too important for anyone's feelings. This country, in its majesty, is too great for any man, be he conservative or liberal, to stay home and not work just because he doesn't agree. Let's grow up, conservatives. If we want to take this Party back, and I think we can someday, let's get to work.

Goldwater was falling in behind the party establishment. It was all Brent Bozell could do to turn to the person next to him and mouth, "That son of a bitch."

PART TWO

6

QUICKENING

To much of the nation, January 20, 1961, felt like a rebirth. It certainly did to most of the nation's press corps. They would record how Washington, captured once again from the stolid stand-pat Republicans, crackled back to life at the arrival of John F. Kennedy's brash young band of brothers, the day breaking cold and clear, the man, coatless and hatless in the stinging wind, still aglow from the birth of his second child.

> Let the word go forth from this time and place, to friend and foe alike, that the torch has been passed to a new generation of Americans—born in this century, tempered by war, disciplined by a hard and bitter peace, proud of our ancient heritage—and unwilling to witness or permit the slow undoing of those human rights to which this nation has always been committed, and to which we are committed today at home and around the world. . . . And so, my fellow Americans, ask not what your country can do for you—ask what you can do for your country.

The joy of new life, of idealism, the promise of youth: this is how the day would be remembered. But another set of symbols could have been mined from these same events—omens of just how frightening the year 1961 would turn out to be.

The night before the inaugural a black-tied multitude fought its way through one of the biggest snowfalls in Washington history to an extravagant gala at the D.C. Armory, headlined by Frank Sinatra's Rat Pack. The Rat Pack, that is, minus Sammy Davis Jr. Since he was about to marry a statuesque blonde, he was politely but firmly disinvited at the last minute so as not to risk Kennedy's Southern support. Inaugural morning, after uniformed soldiers had swept the vicinity with flamethrowers to clear the snow, Richard Cardinal

Cushing of Boston began offering the invocation, then halted with a start: blue smoke, then flames, were issuing from his lectern from a short-circuit in the wiring. The nation's beloved old poet, Robert Frost, reading the first stanza of the inaugural poem he had just composed ("Summoning artists to participate / In the august occasions of the state / Seems something artists ought to celebrate"), stopped and looked away helplessly—blinded by the sun.

Three days earlier Americans had tuned in to their TVs for a bit of comforting sentimentality from their warm and wise national grandfather. They witnessed instead a jeremiad. President Eisenhower's boyish Midwestern-by-way-of-Southern voice darkened with gravity as he began his farewell address. He reminded his listeners of the century's great wars ("holocausts," he called them), of the "indefinite duration" of the Cold War.

Then, with the obliqueness of a difficult truth struggling for expression, he spoke of the psychic consequence of this indefiniteness—"a recurring temptation to feel that some spectacular and costly action could become the miraculous solution to all current difficulties." He warned, "Good judgment seeks balance and progress; lack of it eventually finds imbalance and frustration."

Then he broached another subject: "a permanent armaments industry of vast proportions." The admission was startling: "we annually spend on military security more than the net income of all United States corporations." He called it a "military-industrial complex," and said it had "grave implications" for "the very structure of our society. . . . We must never let the weight of this combination endanger our liberties or democratic processes." The consequences of permanent war was a wartime mentality. America "must avoid becoming a community of dreadful fear and hate."

Must never, must avoid, must guard: the minatory commands came eleven times. In contrast, Kennedy's rhetoric on January 20 was a cascade of permissions: the word "let" rang out fourteen times. It was as if, liberated from the daily tasks of administration, stepping back to survey the new America the Cold War had made, Eisenhower recognized an Icarus, a Tower of Babel, a fallible nation, angrier than it knew.

His speech was shrugged off as a puzzlement. Evidence supporting its wisdom piled up that week. But because America *was* seized by a wartime mentality, much of that evidence was secret. The Central Intelligence Agency was training Cuban exiles deep in the Guatemalan bush for an invasion to overthrow the Castro government; on January 17 the files were closed on a completed CIA mission in which rebels led by a military officer named Joseph Mobutu hunted down and killed the Republic of the Congo's Soviet-leaning prime minister, Patrice Lumumba, on the country's 203rd day of independence. The next day Adlai Stevenson denounced the coup at the UN. And the Kremlin officially declared "the only way to bring imperialism to heel" was through the "sacred struggle of colonial peoples, wars of colonial liberation." On January 19, the American nuclear program suffered its thirteenth "broken arrow" when a B-52 exploded in midair in Utah, luckily without any of the missiles armed; the fourteenth was ten days later when a B-52 flying a routine Strategic Air Command training mission out of Seymour-Johnson Air Force Base crashed near a North Carolina farm. The aircraft's two nuclear bombs jettisoned, and five of their six safety mechanisms were unlatched by the fall.

One day at an auditorium at Rutgers University in New Jersey a standing-room-only crowd of six hundred students back from Christmas break engaged in the kind of debate that had never taken place in the course of the presidential race that had just passed—sanguinary ideological combat, students facing off on radically opposed visions of what was moral and what was not, arguing politics as if their lives depended on it.

They had waded through a forest of pickets in order to watch what papers were calling the nation's most talked-about film. *Communist-Led Riots Against the House Committee on Un-American Activities in San Francisco, May 12–14, 1960* was better known by its informal title, *Operation Abolition*. HUAC claimed to have derived the nickname from the label "the Communist Party itself has given to its current, greatly intensified drive to have the committee abolished." The events the film depicted were rooted back in 1959, when HUAC subpoenaed 110 Bay Area teachers for one of its road-show hearings. HUAC was a lunatic outfit; its latest project involved hunting down the officer responsible for withdrawing an Air Force Reserve training manual because it contained the claim that "Communists had infiltrated our churches" to "teach Soviet Gospel from the Pulpit." HUAC was not popular in liberal San Francisco. When the targeted teachers' names were published in the local press, the outcry that ensued was such that the committee had to postpone its planned West Coast tour. By May of 1960, when HUAC finally rolled into town, a politically charged academic year was just winding to a close at UC Berkeley. A student began a hunger strike to protest compulsory ROTC participation. (President Clark Kerr responded by strengthening rules against students speaking on campus about "off-campus" issues.) The Congress of Racial Equality chapter picketed the local Woolworth's; students massed in a vigil outside San Quentin protesting the execution of Caryl Chessman; and when the Board of Regents prostrated themselves before J. Edgar Hoover after a university document criticized the FBI, the *Daily Californian* editorialized that

Hoover's FBI was America's own homegrown Gestapo. An anti-HUAC movement began.

On May 12 dozens of students went to San Francisco's City Hall expecting
to be able to observe HUAC's public hearings. Barred entry, they lined up on
an outdoor second-floor rotunda outside the hearing room and attempted a literal exercise of their First Amendment rights, delivering a document reading,
"We petition this arm of the United States Congress either to move to a larger
hearing room or to open its doors on a first come, first served basis." Security
officers were unmoved. The next day even more spectators were denied
entrance to the proceedings. They beat on the doors and began singing "The
Battle Hymn of the Republic." After San Francisco's most open and unapolo-
getic Communist, the wizened longshoreman Archie Brown, raised a cry from
the witness table—"Open the doors! Open the doors! What are you afraid
of?"—white-helmeted police closed in on him as he bleated, "Here come their
goon squads!" The hearing room went up in pandemonium. A group in the
back of the hall took up a rousing chorus of "The Star-Spangled Banner." Outside, police pointed a firehose at the crowd of students, now sitting down civil
rights–style. And, in a scene that looked like a visitation from some far-off
world, white kids, most well-scrubbed and neatly dressed, were brutally
washed down the stairs by firehoses. Slicing through fifties decorum as if
through butter, they got back up and were washed right down again, the stairs
now slicked by their blood.

HUAC subpoenaed news footage of the event. Representative James Roosevelt of California, FDR's son, had recently introduced a daring bill to end
HUAC's congressional authorization once and for all. HUAC wanted to make
a documentary demonstrating just how vital the committee's work remained—
by demonstrating how the Communist Party had duped innocent students into
working on its behalf. *Operation Abolition* began with a still of a document
labeled "Communist-front Literature"—a speech delivered by Jimmie Roosevelt. It went on to explain that Students for Civil Liberties had issued a
"directive" on the front page of the *Daily Californian* to sabotage HUAC hearings. A scene was shown of a kid defending himself against a cop's blows; but
since HUAC assembled the shots out of order, it looked like he was assaulting
the cop. The narration explained that the guerrilla attack on the police had been
signaled by the singing of "We Shall Not Be Moved," a song "lifted from the
old Communist *People's Song Book*."

Operation Abolition was little noticed until J. Edgar Hoover published his
own report on "the successful Communist exploitation and manipulation of
youth and student groups throughout the world today," *Communist Target—
Youth* (later made into a film narrated by Attorney General Robert Kennedy). In

a summer of left-wing student unrest on three continents, the idea that the Berkeley students had been duped by the Communists caught on. Private groups, first a trickle, then a flood, began screening *Operation Abolition* (the commercial film company that HUAC hired to produce it sold five hundred prints at $100 apiece). Soon it was being shown to entire staffs of cabinet departments. By the winter of 1960–61, its narrator, Fulton "Buddy" Lewis III, a young staffer on HUAC and the son of McCarthyite radio host Fulton Lewis Jr., and Herb Romerstein, an ex-Communist HUAC investigator, began touring it around colleges.

Thus the scene that January evening at Rutgers University.

It began when the MC, head of the county conservative club, rushed in late and announced, "I heard there were pickets from SANE here"—the National Committee for a Sane Nuclear Policy, a disarmament group—"and I wanted to see how you picketed while crawling on your belly." (It was the same language Barry Goldwater had used before the platform committee in July.) He was answered by the first of the evening's many choruses of boos. The film was rolled, interrupted throughout by laughter, applause, jeers. Romerstein took the floor. "I hope that those students who have been brave enough to jeer in the dark would be brave enough to stand up in the light, give their names, and make their comments." They were, and they did. Angry, passionate debate ensued: on Communism, on anticommunism, on civil liberties, civil rights, questioning authority, respecting authority—an evening of sweaty brows, flailing arms, and outbursts, ending four hours after it began when a dean ordered dormitory dwellers back in time for curfew.

Then Lewis and Romerstein packed up for the next school. The same thing happened everywhere they went—which wasn't supposed to be *possible* in consensus America. A history professor named John Higham had recently published an article in the liberal magazine *Commentary* called "The Cult of American Consensus: Homogenizing Our History." In it, he complained that his colleagues were unaccountably bleaching out all the conflict in the American past—as if such conflicts weren't important to the story at all. He watched, surprised, as those colleagues proudly claimed the epithet "consensus historians" for themselves. Conflict in America, in those rare moments it occurred, *was* an epiphenomenon, they argued—a footnote, in the past as much as the present. The political scientist Seymour Martin Lipset published a book called *Political Man* whose final chapter, "The End of Ideology," reported that domestic politics were now "boring" because "the fundamental political problems of the industrial revolution have been solved."

It was a nice idea—and, since no one paid much attention to what politically active kids under the age of thirty were doing, it was catching.

. . .

The fifteen activists from Youth for Goldwater for Vice President at the Chicago convention whom Goldwater urged to make their group permanent did exactly that. They made their public debut as Young Americans for Freedom on January 2, 1961, picketing against HUAC abolitionists in front of the White House.

Their mentor had been instrumental in putting it all together. Marvin Liebman had begun a long romance with the Communist Party in high school; he joined the Army during the war, drew a dishonorable discharge for homosexuality, then settled down to what he thought would be a life of confirmed bohemianism in Greenwich Village. Desperate for cash, he took a job with a Zionist organization and found his calling. He designed a brochure, black with a jagged cutout that opened to reveal in stark white letters the words "HEBREW BLOOD." The yield from the fund-raising campaign it announced broke the bank. Marvin Liebman began a new career. Soon he would also have a new ideology.

Liebman was taken on as an apprentice by top-drawer New York publicist Harold L. Oran. Oran asked him to help with a fund-raising campaign for a humanitarian committee led by Elinor Lipper, who had spent eleven years in a slave labor camp in Siberia. Liebman refused. "There are no slave labor camps in the USSR," he told Oran. "The woman is obviously a fraud." His boss asked him to meet her just once, as a favor. The two met for drinks at the Algonquin. Lipper calmly looked Liebman in the eye and related her experience in Stalin's camps. A wave of revulsion washed over him. He felt personally responsible.

The experience was a common one among former-Communist leaders of the right—Whittaker Chambers, Frank Meyer, John Dos Passos, and Herb Romerstein, among others. A chiliastic struggle between light and darkness was unfolding, they had believed as Communists. *Everyone* was responsible to one side or the other. And when they realized the side they had thought was the bearer of light was really the embodiment of evil, no less convinced of the stakes, no less fervent, no less driven—Communists became anticommunist warriors.

What made this anticommumist warrior unique was that he had received the best public relations education money couldn't buy. He went into business for himself and became the right's P. T. Barnum, the publicity arm of *National Review*'s literary revolution—maestro of the bipartisan committees, the testimonial dinners, the rallies, the full-page ads, the crowded letterheads with the preprinted signatures for committees with long names. His masterpiece was the Committee of One Million, which had supposedly collected a million signatures to keep Red China out of the United Nations.

Doug Caddy was one of Liebman's apprentices. Liebman persuaded Bill

Buckley to loan Great Elm, the family estate, as the site for an organizational meeting for their new conservative youth group on September 10. A call was posted from Liebman's Madison Avenue office to 120 conservative student activists and journalists. "Now is the time for Conservative youth to take action to make their full force and influence felt," it declared. "By action we mean *political action!*" He sent another letter to his prime contributors' lists.

Almost one hundred students came to Sharon, Connecticut, that September weekend. For young conservatives who had discovered their idiosyncratic political faith from *National Review*, from ISI and Foundation for Economic Education pamphlets, from *Human Events*, who were ridiculed whenever they spoke up in class about the spiritual crisis of the West and against "peaceful coexistence" with a slave empire—for many of them, for the very first time they felt like they were not alone.

A disproportionate number of those who came were serious Catholics. Pope Pius XII had made fighting Communism a church priority in 1947 as Italy's first postwar general election approached—excommunicating party members, ordering propaganda films shown in village squares of Communists hurling church bells from their towers. In the United States the mandate was taken up in a thousand parish pulpits, and in church publications such as *Our Sunday Visitor, The Brooklyn Tablet*, and *The Tidings*, filled with dramatic tales of martyrs like Hungary's Cardinal Mindzenty and the heroes of the 1956 uprising there. Kids had the lesson reinforced on their round-screened Philcos and RCAs when they watched the heroic young rebels of Budapest burning portraits of Stalin in public squares and facing down Moscow's tanks with paving-stone barricades—and the Eisenhower Administration doing nothing, even though it was Dulles's "rollback" doctrine that had spurred them into the streets in the first place. The event was an epiphany shared by thousands of future anticommunist militants.

They read schoolboy equivalents of the Pope's encyclical *Divini Redemptoris* ("Atheistic Communism")—James Michener's slim, stirring narrative of the struggle in Hungary, *The Bridge at Andau* (a Catholic Digest Book Club selection); Thomas Dooley's memoir of rescuing Catholics from North Vietnam, *Deliver Us from Evil*; Whittaker Chambers's *Witness*. They discovered *National Review*. They saw how John F. Kennedy was unthinkingly lionized by their parochial school peers (and New Dealer parents). They viewed the Democratic Party as a moribund establishment—especially if they lived in cities like Baltimore or Jersey City, where mobbed-up political machines choked liberty as surely as any Dixie courthouse gang. Fidel Castro, a former student at a Jesuit high school, noted that moralistic young Catholics made the best revolutionaries. Goldwater would soon discover the same thing.

The Saturday of the Sharon Conference broke warm and sunny. A knot of students gathered in parliamentary session under the spreading bows of the Great Elm itself. Someone moved that the maximum age of group members be set at twenty-seven; in a close vote, the age was set at thirty-five—that way they could recruit some congressmen. At dinner in the Mexican patio, Buckley, Liebman, Edison, John Dos Passos, and *NR* editor Frank Meyer struggled mightily not to dominate the conversation as the group debated the manifesto that M. Stanton Evans, the twenty-six-year-old boy-wonder editor of Gene Pulliam's *Indianapolis News*, had drafted on the plane on the way in. (The document had been edited the night before the conference with the help of Caddy and Carol Dawson, a star student journalist and Youth for Nixon leader from Washington, D.C., then mimeographed for distribution on a machine they found in a local theater shortly before midnight.)

The short text was a distillation of Buckley-and-Bozell-style conservatism: insisting that government be limited to the administration of justice and the preservation of order to maximize "the individual's use of his God-given free will"; urging "victory over, rather than co-existence with" Communism; and pledging—closely paraphrasing *Conscience of a Conservative*—to evaluate foreign policy by a single criterion: "Does it serve the just interests of the United States?" The only dispute was over the mention of God. A cadre of agnostics and atheists opened debate to strike it. They were defeated 44 to 40. The next item on the agenda was choosing the name of the organization. Suggestions containing the word "conservative" were avoided; it was public relations poison. The members settled on Young Americans for Freedom—following the precedent of American Youth for Democracy, which had once been the Young Communist League.

On Sunday morning the insurgents trundled off to church. In the afternoon they elected officers. Caddy had appointed himself president. He urged a young Yale law student, Bob Schuchman, as chairman. Schuchman had been a member of a tiny weekend conservative study group at the prestigious Bronx High School of Science (their clubhouse was the NYU economics department, where the Austrian free-market absolutist Ludwig von Mises let them sit in on his weekly seminar). Schuchman was Jewish—an advantage, making it harder for opponents to smear the group as fascist. A board was chosen and vested with broad powers; regional chairs were named. The Sharon Conference adjourned, and Buckley could not believe what he had just seen. "What was so striking in the students who met at Sharon is their appetite for power," he wrote in *NR*. "Ten years ago the struggle seemed so long, so endless, even, that we did not dream of victory. . . . The difference in psychological attitude is tremendous. They talk about *affecting* history; we have talked about *educating* people to want to affect history."

Young Americans for Freedom set up to affect history in an unused corner of Liebman's offices, piled high with books and periodicals, presided over by a gargantuan poster of Barry Goldwater that "smiled down at visitors," observed a rare liberal guest, "as Nikita Khrushchev does in the foyer of the Soviet Union's United Nations delegation headquarters." They started counting members at 10,000, the combined rolls of existing groups voting to affiliate with YAF; Manion financed the distribution of a copy of *Conscience of a Conservative* to each new member. They began planning a public rally for March, when they would also debut their magazine, *New Guard* (the opposite of "Old Guard," the nickname for conservative congressmen in the 1940s and 1950s). The publication was edited by Lee Edwards, the son of a *Chicago Tribune* Washington correspondent who had also been a McCarthy speechwriter. On November 19 there was the first YAF wedding, between Carol Dawson and Republican House cloakroom staffer Bob Bauman. When Bauman had gone shopping for a tux, the clerk explained that the choice of tie was very important. The ascot was more proper "since President-elect Kennedy and his bride chose them when they were married."

Bauman instantly cut off the clerk and chose the four-in-hand.

In front of the White House gates on January 2, 1961, YAFers outnumbered anti-HUAC pickets two to one. But the *New York Times* dispatch didn't even mention their presence.

The young conservatives would not be ignored for long. The February 10 *Time* reported that the Republicans had won mock presidential elections at Michigan, Indiana, Northwestern, and Ohio; that students were picketing movies written by the blacklisted Dalton Trumbo and reading the hyperindividualist novelist Ayn Rand; that a conservative had been elected student council president at Harvard. *Time* didn't notice that Howard Phillips won the post for his success chairing the Harvard Combined Charities Drive, despite his conservatism, not because of it. Or perhaps *Time* knew and didn't mention it; the man-bites-dog angle of what Scotty Reston of the *New York Times* called the "young fogies" made fantastic copy. Yale conservatives got five hundred signatures in two hours on a petition urging the President "to expel Communist imperialism from its beach-head in the Americas represented by the Communist regime of Fidel Castro." Their manifesto declared: "The American student lives in a dream world. His life is comfortable, and it would seem that his future is secure. But the realities of today dash these pleasing assumptions upon the rocks of war, massacre, and revolution." A dozen Yalies hiked 55 miles from New Haven to the Groton shipyards to defend the honor of the Polaris missile.

YAF soon reported 24,000 members at 115 schools. "You walk around with your Goldwater button and you feel the thrill of treason," a University of Wisconsin student told *Time*. Madison was one of the few places in America besides Berkeley where one could actually find living, breathing Marxists. Every year left-wing radicals put on an "Anti-military Ball" to spoof the annual ROTC dance. The gung ho Conservative Club countered with an annual McCarthy-Evjue lecture series—William Evjue being the editor of the *Capital Times*, the left-leaning sheet Bill Buckley labeled *Prairie Pravda*. In case anyone missed the joke, the publicity for the lectures went out on pink paper.

The pages of the Conservative Club's handsomely produced magazine *Insight and Outlook* (*Hindsight and Outhouse*, according to the campus humor magazine) revealed a secret of their success. College students in the market for 12,000-horsepower engines, iron castings, weldments, or "the new line of motor starters everyone's talking about" could shop among the advertisements taken out by Manionite manufacturing companies in Wisconsin like Nordberg, Grede Foundries, Falk, and Allen-Bradley. There was no generation gap here: the Manionites didn't go away. Now they were just one more force in the conservative wave.

In February YAF published a directory of ninety-seven campus conservative clubs in twenty-five states. "A flock of little Buckleys now torment social scientists in colleges large and small," wrote an observer. They read twice as much as anyone else, the enemy's ideas and their own, delighting in dangling bait before unsuspecting peers who didn't know their assumptions *required* arguments, then slaughtering them in debate. (A favorite debating trick against the progressive income tax was to point out that the *Communist Manifesto* called it one of the "inroads on the rights of property that will inevitably bring on the centralization of all instruments of production in the hands of the State.") The *Michigan Daily* compared the school's new conservative club to the Hitler Youth. This did not keep the *Daily*'s editor, Tom Hayden, from giving conservatives the most space in an article he wrote for the annual college issue of *Mademoiselle*, "Who Are the Student Boat Rockers?" When it came to student activism, conservatism was practically the only thing around. Hayden had recently been recruited to join a new group called Students for a Democratic Society. It had about 250 members.

YAF's Greater New York Council, which had nearly ten times that number, made the best copy of all. The Hunter College chapter was started by a black woman; the Greenwich Village one debuted with a showing of *Operation*

Abolition at a hip downtown theater. Its members—civil libertarians, anarchists, Ayn Randites, longshoremen, a Teamster—drank at the legendary White Horse Tavern, joining members of the Young People's Socialist League in rousing choruses of radical songs. "We had more common ground of conversation and interest with one another than with all those people who didn't give a hoot about politics, the great yawning masses of the middle," said a socialist. One spring day New York YAFers picketed blacklisted singer Pete Seeger on the West Side, then dashed across Central Park to join a demonstration of anti-Castro Cuban exiles at the Soviet UN mission headquarters. ("We still feel sheepish on the line," the picket captain told liberal journalist Marvin Kitman. "I mean, it isn't natural for a conservative.")

On March 3, over three thousand young conservatives packed the Manhattan Center for YAF's first rally. The three thousand turned away at the door glared across Ninth Avenue at the 150 pickets from the New York Youth Council to Abolish HUAC. Now the *Times* noticed—reporting the rally on page 1. When Goldwater took the stage there was an eruption: placards emblazoned with his visage waved above thousands of heads, roving spots picked up the yellows, pinks, and blues from the flock of balloons released from the rafters, and white noise bathed the arena. It was all so thrilling that few in the crowd noticed that Goldwater's speech was calibrated to dampen their enthusiasm. "Sometimes," he said, "the objectives we work toward can't be realized overnight and we must train ourselves to understand that there is such a thing as timing and patience in the conduct of political affairs."

They didn't need the lecture. They knew how to do politics. At his first State of the Union address President Kennedy had announced plans for something called a Peace Corps. Later that spring, the National Student Association convened three hundred delegates in Washington for a "Youth Service Abroad" conference inspired by the idea. The NSA was constitutionally nonpartisan, de facto liberal. Student governments, four hundred of them by the early 1960s, generally decided to affiliate their student bodies with the NSA as a matter of course. The NSA thus ostensibly placed the voice of 1.3 million American college students behind its annual resolutions against nuclear testing, in favor of the Southern sit-ins and the immediate decolonization in the Third World, and for the abolition of HUAC. And this was unacceptable.

Eight operatives led by Schuchman set up camp near the NSA conference with a mimeograph machine and created a simulacrum of a popular groundswell for proposals that the Peace Corps's name be changed to the Anti-Communist Freedom Corps and that all volunteers be screened to make sure they were strong enough anticommunists. At parliamentary sessions YAFers monopolized the microphones, then group members would move out across the room in diamond formation, an old Communist trick to give the appearance of greater number to manufacture acclaim for their speakers. The next day, the surprising degree of conservatism among college students was widely noted in newspapers around the country. Murray Kempton would write in *The Progressive*, "We must assume that the conservative revival is *the* youth movement of the '60s." And another wave of disaffected young collegians read the reports and signed on with the battalions Barry Goldwater was not sure he wanted to lead.

The day Young Americans for Freedom rallied in New York, an issue of *Time* reporting on a group that made YAF look tame found its way to mailboxes.

The John Birch Society, apparently, believed General Dwight David Eisenhower to be a secret agent of the International Communist Conspiracy. The group's absolute leader was a man named Robert Welch; there was a governing council (including Manion and several of his Americans for Goldwater stalwarts, and three past presidents of the National Association of Manufacturers), but it was said that its main purpose was to choose a successor should Welch be assassinated by Communists. Every year the Society published a "scoreboard" of how far down the road to complete Communist subversion each country was; the United States was 50 to 60 percent, Iceland 80 to 100 percent. According to *Time*, the John Birch Society was "a goose step away from the formation of goon squads."

To congressmen, the eerily uniform flood of letters they had been receiving calling for the impeachment of Supreme Court Chief Justice Earl Warren finally made sense: that was one of the Society's four goals—along with saving HUAC, abolishing the income tax, and banning the sale of goods manufactured in Communist countries. The media coverage opened the eyes of community groups whose meetings were being disrupted by unfamiliar faces shouting "republic!" every time someone called America a "democracy" (it was Society doctrine that "democracy" meant rule by mob, and Society tactics to press the case through heckling) and the eyes of PTA leaders who had learned to rue sudden spikes in membership: Welch urged members to join the local PTA and "go to work to take it over."

By April of 1961 you had to have been living in a cave not to know about Robert Welch and his John Birch Society. The daily barrage of reports left Americans baffled and scared at this freakish power suddenly revealed in their midst. It also left some eager to learn where they could sign up.

Robert Harold Winborne Welch was born in 1899 on a farm in Chowan County, North Carolina. His people were simple farmers and Southern Baptist ministers. Young Robert was a genius. He left home to enroll at the state university at twelve, then earned a commission to the Naval Academy when he was seventeen. He decided he wanted to be a writer. The Navy being overstocked with officers at the close of the Great War, he was let go. But his nerve failed him. He enrolled at the Harvard Law School instead—then quit to quickly raise the means to win the hand of the daughter of a wealthy Akron, Ohio, businessman. His brother had a candy business outside Boston. So candy it would be.

Welch specialized in sales. The frustrated writer's first book, in 1941, *The Road to Salesmanship*, proclaimed selling a profession more important than law or medicine. "Instead of the bread and circuses handed out to idle mobs by politicians," salesmen drove progress itself by inducing Americans to want more things and then to strive to better themselves in order to earn enough to buy them. Wartime experience as an Office of Price Administration consultant for the candy industry hardened Welch's conservatism; lobbying as chair of the Washington Committee of the National Confectioners Association (he was named Candy Industry Man of the Year in 1947) petrified it. He mastered the signal vocation of America's domestic Cold Warriors: compiling, organizing, and cross-referencing files—who had belonged to what? who had been where? who knew whom? He devoured history, newspapers, socialist organs; and became convinced (incredulous that anyone would *want* to deliver more power into the hands of an all-powerful central government) that Western Europe's welfare states were products of a Communist conspiracy—and that the conspiracy was gaining ground here, too. He began taking longer and longer trips abroad, winning audiences with men like Chiang Kai-shek and Konrad Adenauer. In 1950 Welch ran for the Republican nomination for lieutenant governor of Massachusetts. He declared his platform the United States Constitution. He came in fourth. Elective office would not be his métier.

The next April, President Truman relieved General MacArthur of his command in Korea. There followed an unprecedented outpouring of popular emotion for the general—he was, said one Republican congressman, "a great hunk of God in the flesh"—and a triumphant national tour. Alongside McCarthy's ongoing inquisition, it marked a new tendency on the American right: it was that much easier to believe you were doing patriotic work even—perhaps especially—if you defied the government. In 1951 Welch traveled New England decrying the aid and comfort Dean Acheson's State Department was providing to the Communists. In one town a listener wrote a critical open letter to a local newspaper: Wasn't McCarthyism fast becoming a political liability for the Republican Party? Welch, compelled to answer, spent the next two weeks in a graphomaniacal stupor.

His eighty-page response defined a method that would hardly waver over the next thirty years and untold thousands of pages. It was a letter, beginning with an apology for length ("For I have to go far afield, and build up these facts step by step, in order to show the ultimate impact and significance of the partly completed pattern as it now appears to me"). Welch expressed befuddlement that august congressional investigators who had looked at the same facts neither "knew, nor took the trouble to find out, the right questions to ask." Then came the eye-popping, awful revelations, thick with documentation, deduced with unshakable confidence—in this case concerning how "at every step Mao could have been stopped by our government. . . . Instead we deliberately turned over rule of China's four hundred million people to Stalin's stooge." He was sorry he was the one who had to discover the ugly news.

He sent the letter to three friends. Friends asked for copies for their friends. Soon, as if by mitosis, Welch was mailing out hundreds, then thousands of copies—although it was not, as Welch might have put it, an accident. The master salesman had incorporated a "Welch Mailing Committee"—five energetic young Bay Staters "frightened to death of what is happening to our country"— to drum up readers. He called his tract *May God Forgive Us.*

In November, he submitted the piece to Henry Regnery, the shy, cerebral son of a Midwestern Quaker pacifist family whose Regnery Company was the most respected of the nation's handful of conservative publishers. They had been nearly bankrupt—as they would be many times in the future—when Regnery published Buckley's *God and Man at Yale.* Welch bet Henry Regnery a good dinner "that within the next twelve months you sell more than twice as many copies of *May God Forgive Us.*" It was a token of the man's very curious arrogance and innocence. Welch believed that if you only told the American people the truth—the truth he had had the bad luck to discover in his investigations—they would respond and set things right. Years later, at the opening meeting of Manion's Americans for Goldwater committee, Welch said that Goldwater had only to take the lead in opposing Eisenhower's planned May summit with Khrushchev for a grateful Republican rank and file to ring him into nomination by acclamation.

When *May God*'s first sales figures were tallied, Regnery told Welch the book was flying off the shelves by the tens of thousands. Welch was incredulous. Why wasn't it selling in the hundreds of thousands? Regnery protested that there simply wasn't that kind of demand for this kind of book. This Welch simply could not accept. So he revived the Welch Mailing Committee, bought out Regnery's inventory, and sold the books while campaigning for Robert Taft. After the 1952 Republican Convention, Welch was one more who reluctantly went to work for Ike; in December he wrote Regnery that the Republican presidential victory "highlighted a definite turn back from the left, which will make it easier for the soundly factual books which you publish to obtain a wider readership." Welch offered to buy enough stock to join his board of directors. Regnery refused—then he refused to publish Welch's hulking allegorical novel on the civilization of ants who were seduced into accepting a paternalistic government that soon came to enslave them.

Regnery accepted one more book from Welch. *The Life of John Birch: In the Story of One American Boy, the Ordeal of His Age* told the tale of a young American Baptist missionary-cum-spy who learned at the close of World War II of the Communists' secret plan to take over China. He was assassinated, and his murder was supposedly covered up by State Department quislings who knew if the story got out their own complicity in Mao's victory would be revealed. John Birch was "the first casualty of the Cold War." If he had lived, how different the world would have been! If every American knew this story, how ready everyone would be to do what was right! Regnery's stubborn refusal to realize his obligation to Western civilization—not to stop until he had put the book into the hands of every American—convinced Welch that he once more would have to do this job himself. The hour was dark. For now he had discovered how Dwight Eisenhower's career-long liaison and cooperation with the Communist Party had led to the fall of Eastern Europe. He circulated his three-hundred-page letter on the subject, *The Politician*, to a few close friends who could handle this level of truth.

Robert Welch built the John Birch Society on the foundation of two important earlier groups that kept alive the conservative message during the right's years in the wilderness. One was the National Association of Manufacturers. Welch was chair of its Education Committee, an important job: NAM was a group with a keen, even prescient appreciation of how to use public relations to shape political opinion. "We have allowed our detractors to put over on us their symbols," its president declared. Businesses had to counter with symbols of their own. The organization spent millions to drive home the message that it was employers, not unions, who were the natural allies of workers. In 1947 NAM took out ads in 265 daily papers ("We are all workers, we are all capitalists") and issued two million pieces of literature; in 1950 it launched a $1.5 million radio program, *Industry on Parade*—more popular in its time slot than *Meet the Press*, which did not boast its own singing group. A full-time staff of debaters fanned out to appear on local radio shows; other staff gave two-day seminars to businessmen on how "to become better champions of the American way."

Then there was the Foundation for Economic Education, on whose board Welch served. Founded in 1946, FEE spread a libertarian gospel so uncompromising it bordered on anarchism. And they spread it *everywhere*. The organization had pamphlets designed for placement on bookracks in factory break rooms (*31 Cents*, on the amount of taxes extracted from each dollar earned; *The First Leftists*, on the French Revolution's Great Terror). At FEE seminars, businessmen learned the words, phrases, and ideas to freeze liberals in debate. The Foundation searched out cash-strapped high schools to whom it distributed free conservative textbooks. And after *The Freeman* folded, FEE revived it as a controlled circulation magazine that businessmen could pay to have sent free to employees, vendors, and clients.

FEE and NAM were conservative media empires. Welch took inspiration from them to build a media empire of his own. First he put out his own magazine, *One Man's Opinion*; when it had passed a few thousand in circulation, he changed the name to *American Opinion*. He did all this after work and on weekends. In 1957 he retired from business, contemplated a run against Massachusetts's blue-blooded Senator Leverett Saltonstall, then changed his mind. The Communists, after all, did not work their domination through electoral politics. They did it by seizing institutions from within. If he recruited enough people to *explain* the conspiracy (for instance, how the Communists bamboozled Americans into believing they lived in a democracy, not a republic), the conspiracy could not work. He figured he'd need about a million people to rout the Communists altogether.

He founded the John Birch Society on December 8, 1958, at an Indianapolis lecture delivered to eleven wealthy men, three of them past presidents of NAM, that lasted two straight days—breaking only for lunch, coffee, and dinner. Identical meetings were held in a dozen more cities in the year to come. The transcript of the lecture would later become the Society's catechism, *The Blue Book*. The invitees were men like Harry Lynd Bradley, CEO of Allen-Bradley, whose electronics factory lorded over Milwaukee's South Side with the biggest four-sided clock tower in the world; and Robert W. Stoddard, who owned the world's largest manufacturer of metal forgings, the morning and evening newspapers in Worcester, Massachusetts, and the city's leading radio station. Men like Bradley and Stoddard listened to Welch with awe. "These were two of the most worthwhile days I have ever spent," one textile-mill owner wrote Manion. "Here for the first time is hope—hope of success instead of more frustrated shadow boxing."

"We are living in America today," Welch's lesson began, "in such a fool's paradise as the people of China lived in twenty years ago, as the people of Czechoslovakia lived in a dozen years ago, as the people of North Vietnam lived in five years ago, and as the people of Iraq lived in only yesterday." Lenin had declared a three-stage strategy for world conquest: "First, we will take

Eastern Europe. Next, the masses of Asia. Then we shall encircle that last bastion of capitalism, the United States of America. We shall not have to attack; it will fall like overripe fruit into our hands." Welch said the fruit was already one-quarter loosened.

Only rarely, Welch explained, did Communists take over countries through force. More often they disguised theirs as just another political party, then struck peacefully from within the system; or they slipped the noose over a people through steady and subtle propaganda, colonizing their very minds. That, he concluded, was what was happening in America. "The trouble in our southern states has been fomented almost entirely by the Communists for this purpose," he explained by way of example, "to stir up such bitterness between whites and blacks in the South that small flames of civil disorder would inevitably result. They could then fan and coalesce these little flames into one great conflagration of civil war. . . . The whole slogan of 'civil rights,' as used to make trouble in the South today, is an exact parallel to the slogan of 'agrarian reform' which they used in China." It was all part of the plan: elites surrendering American sovereignty to the UN; foreign aid rotting our balance of payments; skyrocketing taxes, unbalanced budgets, inflation. There was only one way to explain it: our labor unions, churches, schools, *the government*—all had been infiltrated. Voices of opposition were censored: not by outright ban, but the way Stalin censored Trotsky—by holding down his press runs because there wasn't enough "demand."

Two days, dozens of conspiracy theories, and God knows how many cups of coffee later, Welch explained what the members of his group were going to do about it.

The message of the organic unity of the American welfare state and Russian imperial expansion was not new to them; it was a commonplace of organizations like Kent and Phoebe Courtney's Conservative Society of America, Chicago's We, The People!, and H. L. Hunt's Life Line, and of radio ministries like Carl McIntire's and Billy James Hargis's. What differed was the clarity of Welch's solution. All it would require was a coordinated body of patriots, disciplined under a single command: not running for office, not taking up guns—but *educating*. For if America had only learned the truth about John Birch in time, then Communism's spread might have ended then and there. Welch doubted he was up to the task of directing the effort, but as a dedicated patriot he was willing to answer the call. The only condition for membership in the Society was that members follow his dictates absolutely. They could quit if they didn't like it. Otherwise internal power struggles would kill them. The Communists hadn't won their gains through parliamentary procedure.

He started by hiring a staff of bright young salesmen who believed in the product, would not question the boss, and would work long hours on commission (they focused their pitches on houses flying the American flag out front). By the time of the John Birch Society's sudden national coming-out in the spring of 1961, they had 20,000 members (or 60,000, or 100,000; estimates varied—but even 20,000 was greater than the membership of the Communist Party of the United States in its 1930s heyday). An office down the road from Welch's fieldstone-and-frame home in the Boston suburb of Belmont employed some twenty-eight full-time staffers and an equal number of volunteers, who dumped $4,000 worth of mail each week at the Belmont post office next door. An Iowa pen company gave an expensive fountain model as a premium to each new member. Centralia, Missouri, was a virtual Birch fiefdom; the owner of the factory that employed half the town's workforce made membership practically a condition for advancement. By 1962 Welch was raising over a million dollars a year.

Since McCarthy's day, liberals had been wondering why apparently intelligent people could believe that the wrong kind of politics in the United States would inexorably hasten its takeover by the USSR. It was concluded that these were people who feared for their status in a rapidly changing, complex urban society, who pined for a simpler past (they were for the "repeal of industrialism," said *Commentary*, which was odd, since most Birch leaders were industrialists). The cognoscenti neglected the simplest answer: people were afraid of internal Communist takeover because the government had been telling them to be afraid—at least since 1947, when George F. Kennan argued in "The Sources of Soviet Conduct," the founding document of U.S. Cold War doctrine, excerpted in *Reader's Digest,* that "exhibitions of indecision, disunity, and internal disintegration within this country have an exhilarating effect on the whole Communist movement." Through the 1960s, AFL-CIO president George Meany loved to flatter rank-and-file members that they were the first line of resistance against the Communists: in Czechoslovakia, he said, "they controlled the trade union movement, and within seven days they controlled the country." Attorney General Robert Kennedy told a 1961 press conference, "Communist espionage here in this country is more active than it has ever been." (There had been none to speak of since World War II.) Army recruits saw films like *Red Nightmare*, narrated by Jack Webb, which depicted an ersatz American town deep within the Soviet interior where spies were supposedly training in indigenous American arts like sipping sodas at drugstore fountains in order to infiltrate the United States. You could no less avoid breathing in a bit of paranoia in Cold War America, in fact, than you could soot in Charles Dickens's Manchester. Did Birchers and their ideological cognates claim that dangerous "fallout" from nuclear testing was a hoax? So did the

Atomic Energy Commission, all through the 1950s. And it was the "discoveries" of the CIA chief of counterintelligence, James Jesus Angleton, not Robert Welch, that a KGB "Master Plan" allowed no Soviet to defect to the United States except as a KGB double agent (thus bona fide Soviet defectors were often kept naked in isolation in a brightly lit room and had to submit to cruel three-year interrogations to force them to give up their KGB secrets); and that there was a second, secret Kremlin *inside* the official Kremlin whose existence could only be inferred because no one who had ever been inside it was ever allowed beyond its walls.

It shouldn't have been surprising that the John Birch Society was able to win a membership in the tens of thousands in an officially encouraged atmosphere of fear and suspicion. The John Birch Society was also a voice for conservatism—its motto was "Less government and more responsibility"—at a time when the Republican Party was turning more liberal. At a time when a housewife from suburban New York, Betty Friedan, was writing a book arguing that the alienation and boredom of housewives was America's "problem that has no name," the Society gave housewives world-historic purpose to their lives. ("I just don't have time for anything," one told a *Time* magazine interviewer. "I'm fighting Communism three nights a week.") And last but not least, being a Bircher was *fun*. The fellowship was vouchsafed by the rule that when a chapter grew bigger than two dozen, it was split in half—the rationale being that unwieldy chapters were easier for the Communists to infiltrate. The groups' main activity was monthly meetings in members' living rooms (at which the main activity might be watching a film of a lecture given by Welch, who looked a bit like TV's Mr. McGoo and, eerily, recited his interminable talks from memory); and group members would carry out whatever suggestions they cared to that were handed down in Welch's monthly *Bulletin*. They might write the director of the Boy Scouts to ask why the president of the Communist-infiltrated National Council of Churches addressed the National Jamboree; or they might send postcards to congressmen showing the map the "Negro Soviet Republic" Communists proposed be carved out of the American South in 1928. They might be asked to attend meetings of "Communist fronts" like the ACLU to shout down "disloyal" speakers, or to urge their dentist and the airlines to display *National Review* and *Human Events* on their magazine racks, or to form a local chapter of a Birch front organization like Support Your Local Police. And, most of all, members were instructed to keep informed by reading books like *Tito: Moscow's Trojan Horse* and *I Saw Poland Betrayed*.

Welch could have remained obscure forever if not for his success. Disillusionment with the GOP after Nixon's 1960 defeat swelled the membership rolls; by February of 1961 the John Birch Society was large enough that when members read in the *Bulletin* that Welch wanted them to write their congressmen demanding the impeachment of Earl Warren for his decisions favoring civil libertarians over red-hunters, letters flooded in to Capitol Hill. Enterprising reporters took notice. And the story spread like wildfire.

By April 1 the Birchers made page 1 of the *New York Times*; by the twelfth Ohio's aging, acid-tongued Senator Stephen Young, labeling Welch a "Hitler," commandeered a copy of Welch's notorious *The Politician* and entered into the *Congressional Record* its claim that Eisenhower "has been sympathetic to ultimate Communist aims, realistically willing to use Communist means to help them achieve their goals, knowingly accepting and abiding by Communist orders, and consciously serving the Communist conspiracy for all of his adult life." Cries went up for congressional investigations; Welch proposed that the proceedings be carried out by Senate Internal Security Committee chair James Eastland of Mississippi, who praised the society as "patriotic." Cardinal Cushing, three months after giving the benediction at the Kennedy inauguration, announced that he was a Welch admirer; two southern California congressmen, Edgar Hiestand and John Rousselot—Rousselot was chair of the congressional Republican freshmen caucus and a Nixon protégé—announced that they were proud members (as did all Society members, they creepily referred to Welch as "The Founder"). Ezra Taft Benson, Eisenhower's agriculture secretary and a Mormon elder, was also a member. Barry Goldwater, reached in Los Angeles, volunteered that "a lot of people in my home town have been attracted to the society, and I am impressed by the type of people in it. They are the kind we need in politics."

Welch devoted his April *Bulletin* to the uproar. "On February 25, 1961," he explained,

> *The People's World*, official communist newspaper published in San Francisco, attacked the John Birch Society. *Time* magazine attacked on March 10, 1961, using the word "cells" in reference to Birch Society chapters, just as the communist newspaper had done; and singling out the same Birch Society Council members that the communists had singled out. Within two weeks, more than a hundred newspapers throughout the nation ran articles, practically all of them inaccurately condemning the Society for things it has never done or does not believe in. A good many of these so slavishly followed the line set down in San Francisco that the communist attack can reasonably be called the "mother article" for scores of tirades against the Society in big metropolitan dailies all over the nation.

Things intensified. On April 14 the *New York Times* splashed a sensational
story on page 1: an officer stationed in Germany, General Edwin Walker, was
indoctrinating his troops with Birch literature. Then the *Times* thundered
against him on the editorial page. On April 17 Walker was removed from his
post.

Then, on the eighteenth, the John Birch Society was knocked off the
nation's front pages. A force of 1,400 CIA-trained Cuban exiles landed at
Cuba's Bay of Pigs for an assault on Fidel Castro's government. Cuba's meager air force, which was supposed to have been wiped out in air strikes that
President Kennedy scaled back at the last minute so he could plausibly deny
American involvement, strafed the force's landing boats, and 1,000 survivors
made a quick surrender. Kennedy's advisers saw him weep. The news came
just six days after another crushing Cold War humiliation: the world's first
space flight, by a Russian, Yuri Gagarin. And for a time, the right-wing scare
seemed hardly worth the candle.

7

STORIES OF ORANGE COUNTY

T here was one place in the United States where there was no sudden alarm at a failed invasion of Cuba; there, alarm was a constant. Long before the Bay of Pigs, the signs graced Orange County, California, windows: "THEY'RE NOT JUST 90 MILES AWAY. THEY'RE HERE." On April 18, 1961, at any rate, Orange County was paying more attention to the struggle against "their" attempts to subvert a local school board.

Joel Dvorman, a New York native and liberal Democrat, had been elected as a trustee of the Magnolia School District board the previous summer. That he was also the membership secretary of the Orange County chapter of the American Civil Liberties Union, and had once belonged to American Youth for Democracy, was unknown or ignored at the time. In June of 1960 Dvorman invited an organizer of the protests at the San Francisco HUAC hearings to his home to speak at a meeting.

James Wallace, a production supervisor at a local aerospace firm who lived near Dvorman, got word of the meeting an hour before it started. A new report from the California state legislature's own local version of HUAC had just noted that the ACLU's southern California division "devoted an unusually large part of its time and energies to the protection and defense of Communist Party members." Wallace decided to drop in to check out what his neighbor was up to. He reported what he saw in a letter to the *Santa Ana Register*: Joel Dvorman was entertaining traitors. "I wonder what we would have done in 1942 if Mr. Dvorman had a German-American Bund meeting at his home," he wrote. At a subsequent school board meeting, Dvorman was asked if he had ever been a member of the Communist Party. A committee was hastily gotten up to fight a "threat to our heritage, to expose it and to combat it with every weapon at our command." The weapon of choice, a recall petition, warned that Dvorman might "subtly impose his beliefs upon students through selection of textbooks, establishment of curriculum, selection of teachers."

James Wallace soon formed Anaheim's first chapter of the John Birch Society. (Robert Welch, he said, "awakened us out of our selfish apathy and indifference to what is happening in America.") Soon there were five chapters in Anaheim, and thirty-eight in Orange County. In January of 1961 Orange County State College and Fullerton Evening Junior College announced a series of lectures, "Understanding the Goals and Techniques of World Communism." The course was promptly oversubscribed, as was Santa Ana College political science instructor John G. Schmitz's course "Communist Aggression." In March a coalition of civic leaders hosted a rally by the barnstorming Australian minister Fred C. Schwarz's Christian Anti-Communism Crusade (whose unique contribution to right-wing discourse was to draw on his background in disease pathology and to contend that the Communist Party held sway over the people of Russia via "the techniques of animal husbandry"). The publicity for Schwarz's event warned of "communist plans for a flag of the USSR flying over every American city by 1973." Principals were urged to suspend school; seven thousand children were obligingly trooped off to attend the all-day affair. Soon the ninety thousand parents of the Garden Grove School District were sent flyers assuring them that their children recited the Pledge of Allegiance every morning, in schools where "any type of propaganda in conflict with county, state, and national laws is prohibited."

And on April 18, 1961, residents of Orange County's six-thousand-pupil Magnolia School District recalled Joel Dvorman and two other liberals at the polls by a ratio of 3 to 1. Even during the McCarthy years a public official had never been recalled from office for membership in the American Civil Liberties Union. But even during the McCarthy era there had never been a place quite like Orange County was in the 1960s.

Orange County had caught anticommunism fever. On any given weekend, interested citizens of Anaheim, Santa Ana, Fullerton, Costa Mesa, and half a dozen other Los Angeles–area suburbs could drop in on one, two, or five different showings of films like *Operation Abolition* or *Communism on the Map*, a geopolitical melodrama in which blood- or pink-colored ink leached over country after country, sparing only Spain, Switzerland, and the United States (which was covered by a big question mark). On any given night they could find a study group assiduously poring over the organizational structure of what J. Edgar Hoover called the "state within a state"—the American Communist Party.

Orange County's VFW halls and school auditoriums were Meccas for traveling lecturers like former double agent Herb Philbrick (whose claim to fame was announced in the title of his book, *I Led Three Lives*); Korean War

POW John Noble (*I Was a Slave in Russia*); and World War I fighting ace Eddie Rickenbacker (*The Socialistic Sixteenth—A National Cancer*). Another perennial was W. Cleon Skousen, who was so right-wing he had been fired as Salt Lake City police chief by Mayor J. Bracken Lee, the tax resister working to dissolve the federal government, for running his department "like a Gestapo." Another favorite was Ronald Reagan. It was glamorous having a movie star talk to your Republican precinct club. And he preached anticommunist hellfire as well as anyone else on the circuit.

Reagan's showbiz fortunes had declined considerably since his peak after the war when he commanded a salary just below that of Errol Flynn. In 1954 he took a job as an MC in Vegas, an experience he likened to "going over Niagara Falls in a tub." Partly it was the rise of television; partly it was fashion (he was no T-shirt-wearing method actor); partly it was that he spent so much time with politics. As a liberal who worshiped FDR, Reagan became president of the Screen Actors Guild in 1947 just as a jurisdictional struggle with deceitful, violent craft unionists whom Reagan suspected of being Communists gave him very good reason to fear for the safety of himself and his family. It was a formative experience. In his mind, Communism became an everyday threat, looming just around the corner.

He was still a liberal. But his remarriage in 1952 to the daughter of a conservative, politically connected Chicago surgeon (whose Phoenix vacation home the couple visited each Easter) and his work negotiating with studio chiefs were beginning to change that. That year he worked for Democrats for Eisenhower. The entrepreneur, not the union, the government, or the crusader for social justice, moved ever closer to the center of his moral imagination. In 1955 he became a charter subscriber to *National Review*.

TV and politics had doomed him; now they saved him. In 1954 General Electric was looking for an attractive, smart, straight-arrow actor who could think like a salesman to take a demanding double job as actor-host of TV's weekly *General Electric Theater* and as a motivational speaker for G.E.'s hundreds of thousands of employees in 125 separate facilities across the country, making everything from light bulbs to locomotives. The fact that *General Electric Theater* was produced by Reagan's talent agency, MCA—an agency that SAG president Reagan had helped to receive a blanket waiver of a union rule that talent agencies could not produce television programs—helped his chances. But it had to be said that Reagan was a natural for the job.

G.E. was an unusual company. It had always considered communicating a precisely calibrated corporate image as much a part of the company's business as making the products it sold—as much inside their 125 plants as outside them. The image G.E. hoped to convey was of a company that was an indispensable cog in America's well-being. In the 1930s and 1940s, when G.E.'s top brass was liberal (one executive chartered Roosevelt's National Recovery Administration), that meant that the company backed the New Deal vision of a strong welfare state and a vigorously enforced Wagner Act (G.E. was among the few big manufacturing companies to avoid labor strife in the 1930s by simply offering the CIO a national contract). But when a 1946 strike shuttered every electrical plant in the country, that vision began changing. New management came in and hired a man named Lemuel Boulware to a new post: vice president for employee and community relations. Boulware was a marketing expert. The key to successful labor relations, he believed, was to "achieve ultimately the same success in *job marketing* that we had accomplished in *product marketing*." A crucial part of the task was explaining how free enterprise created a virtuous circle harmoniously joining labor, management, customer, and community. In this scheme, Bouwarism (as labor leaders, with a shudder, pronounced it), unions were but irritants, as was the welfare state. The United States, he would lament in the many addresses in which he spread his gospel to business leaders, "is well down the road to a collectivist revolution."

Reagan was an integral component in the Boulwarite system. The actor, crackling charm, would walk the floor of the yawning thirty-acre plants—squinting a little because he couldn't wear his contact lenses for the smoke and dust—shaking hands and chatting up the workers. Then he would speak to an assembly. "Today," he would say, "there is an increasing number who can't see a fat man standing beside a thin one without automatically coming to the conclusion that the fat man got that way by taking advantage of the thin one. So they would seek the answer to all the problems of human need through government." Lem Boulware couldn't have said it better.

On Reagan's first tour, his handler was approached because a convention speaker had canceled at the last minute, leaving several thousand teachers waiting in the town armory. "Let's give it a try," Ronnie said gamely. He performed famously. After that, nearly every factory stop was followed up by a freelance appearance before some civic or business group or another.

Reagan stepped up his outside political work after resigning from his SAG responsibilities in 1960. He still hadn't bothered to change his party registration. But he was aghast enough at John F. Kennedy's convention acceptance speech to be moved to write Richard Nixon a letter. "Shouldn't someone tag Mr. Kennedy's *bold new imaginative program* with its proper age? Under the tousled boyish hair cut it is still old Karl Marx." Nixon, delighted, appended a note to his staff: "Use him as speaker wherever possible. He *used* to be liberal." In 1960 Reagan ended up running Democrats for Nixon in California. And after Nixon's loss, Reagan's disillusionment took him in the same direction as it did so many of his southern Californian neighbors—to the right. When he wasn't on the road for G.E. or on the set, he spread the gospel in front of any audience that invited him. His family hardly saw him. "The inescapable truth is that we are at war," he would say, "and we are losing that war simply because we don't or won't realize we are in it. We have ten years. Not ten years to make up our mind, but ten years to win or lose—by 1970 the world will be all slave or all free."

In Orange County that kind of talk was making Reagan a hero. He was like them—a Midwestern transplant, from small-town Illinois. He almost belonged more to them than he did to Hollywood.

It was first said in the nineteenth century that California was "America, only more so." Orange County was California, only more so. It had been the commandment to Americans after World War II to go forth and multiply. Orange County listened, and exploded. The government said to fight Communism. Orange County listened, and went berserk.

California had always been a territory of booms and busts. Orange County's boom came during World War II. Opening up to the Pacific, possessed of a mild climate, southern California was the perfect place for defense installations. As in Phoenix, the aircraft manufacturers followed. Unions were weak. Venture capital was abundant. And when the jet and missile age arrived in the 1950s, it turned out that southern California had a competitive advantage: unlike more established companies back East, which preferred safe construction contracts, the tinkerers in California welcomed long-term research and development deals. New York State lost 34 percent of its share of the Defense Department's procurement between 1950 and 1956; by 1965 California would have almost a quarter of the Defense Department's prime contracts and 41 percent of NASA's. Aerospace accounted for a staggering 10 percent of all personal income in the state of California and perhaps a quarter of its economic growth. And Orange County, the formerly rural area south of Los Angeles—whose municipalities were so eager to play host to the War Department that the town of Santa Ana leased the U.S. government a 412-acre former berry ranch for a dollar a year—did best of all. Orange County's population, 100,000 in 1940, approached a million by 1960. Washington had called forth a new suburban civilization in southern California. Orange County was its hub.

Real estate speculators turned ranches into subdivisions virtually overnight—an entire municipality, Irvine, from a single orange grove. Men who got a taste of the Sunshine State as Pacific Theater veterans flocked back after the war to settle there with their families; all you had to do was visit a real estate office at the edge of some former citrus grove, point to a site on a tract map, and lay down a $200 down payment (less if you were a veteran), and you'd bought yourself a house. But with mortgage debt a constant, silent presence, the new homesteaders were not keen on squandering their precious salaries, their only assets, on high taxes to help out the other guy. In 1959 Orange County congressman James Utt reintroduced an effort to add a "Liberty Amendment" to the Constitution—which would repeal all federal income, estate, and gift taxes and ban all government enterprises that competed with the private sector. Utt likened the federal government to a "child molester who offers candy before his evil act."

Orange County had always been a Republican stronghold. As in the rest of southern California suburbia, much of the county's population hailed from Taft's Midwest (every year a massive "Iowa Day" celebration was held in L.A.'s Griffith Park). The first time a Democratic President carried the county was 1932, the last 1936. That was two times too many for Raymond Cyrus Hoiles, publisher of the *Santa Ana Register*, who said the world would have been better off if Franklin D. Roosevelt had never learned to read or write. Hoiles's editorials railed against the government stake in what he called "tax-supported schools, roads, and parks"—and called for an end to child labor and pure food and drug laws. As for the area's racial attitudes, in 1954 a Korean-American Olympic Gold Medal winner was able to purchase a home in Garden Grove only after an outcry in the international media, and the Magnolia District's first black teacher was forced to quit after a year when she couldn't find housing. Orange County tended to draw people who found such politics amiable. Once there, they often moved further to the right.

New postwar migrants, unmoored from the familiar Main Streets of their youth, burst the churches of conservative preachers like "Fighting Bob" Wells at the seams. Many were fundamentalists and Evangelicals of a new kind: they mixed politics with religion, a diversion much more associated with liberal clergymen. ("Preachers are not called to be politicians, but to be soul winners," as the young pastor of the Lynchburg, Tennessee, Thomas Road Baptist Church, Jerry Falwell, put it.) When fundamentalists and Evangelicals were political they weren't necessarily conservative: the Southern Baptist Convention endorsed *Brown* v. *Board of Education*, and the Reverend Billy Graham called Martin Luther King's Montgomery bus boycott "an example of Christian love." But Joe McCarthy's 1953 charge that prominent Methodist bishop G. Bromley Oxnam was a Communist—and the ensuing claim of McCarthyites that perhaps 5 percent of Protestant clergymen followed the Soviet line—boosted the right-wing radio "parachurches" of Billy James Hargis, Carl McIntire, and Edgar C. Bundy; a 1960 Federal Communication Commission ruling that encouraged networks to sell air time to religious broadcasters as a public service—and Evangelical terror of the possibility of a Catholic U.S. President—helped even more. Orange County church vestibule tables were thick with publications the radio hosts produced, like *The United Nations, A Smoke-Screen for Communist Aggression* and *Disarmament, An Invitation to Communist Takeover*.

Disarmament may or may not have been an invitation to Communist takeover. It certainly was a threat to the southern California economy. A 1961 issue of *Orange County Industrial News* admitted that its growth projections presumed "that there will be no agreements on disarmament or on limitation of nuclear weapons"—although their dependency on government contracts didn't increase their love for Washington any more than it did the nineteenth-century Arizona merchants who had been put in business by the Indian Wars. "Show me one, just one, from Southern California who helps make policy at Washington!" the mayor of Los Angeles seethed in a speech to Orange County service clubs as the crowd whistled him on. It was a curious relationship. The trade journal *Missiles and Rockets* expected Kennedy to penalize California contractors because the state went for Nixon. In fact, it was to Kennedy that they owed their continued good fortune. Eisenhower worried that high military budgets would superheat the economy toward recession; Kennedy's Keynesian economic advisers proposed a virtuous circle: grand designs abroad put money into workers' pockets, vouchsafing economic growth at home. Southern Californians might not be working in Washington, but their money certainly was. North American Aviation, where James Wallace started his career, paid its D.C. lobbyist $14,000 a month, an executive's salary, just for part-time work.

As for the internal security paranoia, in Orange County, hundreds of engineers went home from working on top secret defense projects to children who could not know what their fathers had done at the office that day. The example was Los Alamos: it took only one disloyal American to hasten catastrophe. Local business leaders developed complete dossiers on the two thousand southern Californians identified as having once been Communist Party members. They had two million index cards for suspected—as Robert Welch coined it— comsymps. James Wallace was an ordinary representative of his community.

Another was Walter Knott. Orange County residents loved to tell his story: An itinerant day laborer from one of the poorest families in Pomona, at age thirty-one Knott managed to rent a forlorn berry plot in Buena Park. His wife, Cordelia, sold delectable berry pies from a roadside stand; then, noting the increasing traffic from yachters on their way to the harbors at Newport Beach and Balboa, she convinced her wary husband to let her have a try at selling chicken dinners. Cordelia's savory cooking and homey kindness brought customers back again and again; a banker offered Knott a loan to open a restaurant. Knott refused the debt but built the restaurant anyway.

He did well as a restaurateur. But in true Orange County fashion, it was technology that made him rich. Painstakingly, over the course of three years, Knott had been nursing a new hybrid: a cross between the loganberry, blackberry, and raspberry, marvelously fat and juicy, that a certain Mr. Boysen had invented, then abandoned when he found the prickly bramble too difficult to cultivate. Knott had the entrepreneurial spirit to persevere. "Boysenberries" yielded Knott a Depression-era fortune. In 1940 he expanded the restaurant and opened a restored Western ghost town, a tourist monument to the pioneer spirit that had built the West—and to the entrepreneurial pioneers like himself who kept it great. Through the years an abandoned schoolhouse was shipped from Kansas, a hotel from Arizona, and rolling stock from around the country to build a working railroad line. In 1951 Knott moved in an entire abandoned Mojave Desert silver mining town in which he had once toiled as a day laborer. By the 1960s Knott's Berry Farm was drawing seven thousand visitors on a busy weekend and was the region's second biggest tourist attraction, behind Disneyland. Knott shared the welfare-capitalist business philosophy of Barry Goldwater and Herb Kohler: his employees had profit-sharing, health insurance, and a generous retirement plan; he also headed the fight for a California right-to-work law in 1958.

Knott also added a "Freedom Center" to the grounds—a two-story restored farmhouse where a former college president and a former minister toiled full-time spreading the free-market gospel. Knott wrote the Freedom Center off on his taxes as a business expense; no use giving Washington any more of his money to waste than he had to. "We've seen government grow until it is all out of proportion," he told *Reader's Digest* in a profile called "One Man's Crusade for Everybody's Freedom." "Every time it grows, it takes bits of freedom out of our lives, and we become more dependent on it and less on ourselves."

But Orange County residents and *Reader's Digest* left out the most telling part of Walter Knott's story: the boysenberry was a welfare case. It all started when the Department of Agriculture's Bureau of Plant Industry's experimental station at Beltsville, Maryland, received a letter reporting a rumor of a marvelous new berry developed by a Mr. Boysen of Orange County, California. An agent at the Bureau did what he was paid taxpayer money to do: he made the trip out to California to investigate. He began asking local berrymen what they knew. None had heard of the boysenberry. Walter Knott was intrigued, though, and asked if he could tag along on the agent's investigation. They located Rudolph Boysen, who was working as a "tax-supported" (as Ray

Hoiles would have put it) park superintendent in Anaheim. The three of them found the abandoned vines amidst the weeds at Boysen's old farm. Boysen gave Knott the right to try to cultivate the berry for profit.

The men who led their families on weekends to Knott's Berry Farm as if to secular worship were like Walter Knott's boysenberries: in a way not quite apparent to the naked eye, they were welfare cases. Veterans who returned home from World War II to a country terrified of sinking back into depression benefited mightily from federal schemes to boost consumer spending by subsidizing homeownership; before the war, a typical mortgage required a down payment of 50 percent and came due in ten years; now a mortgage involved a down payment of 10 percent, was financed at 4 percent, lasted three decades, and was tax deductible—one of the most generous redistributions of wealth in American history. The irrigation projects that were the lifeline of the arid region were funded by taxes from the forty-nine other states. People like James Wallace cursed Washington at John Birch Society meetings after spending their days inside firms built lock, stock, and barrel with government contracts and after earning their engineering degrees in California's tuition-free, state-run university system, or buying them with GI Bill money. They delighted in Ronald Reagan's sparkling professions of free-market faith. But even his faith had its limits. When Reagan began saying that the Tennessee Valley Authority drained the U.S. Treasury better than its own basin, he was reminded that G.E. had a $50 million bid in for TVA generators. Reagan gladly dropped the reference.

All the way across the country, on the banks of the Hudson River in New York State, there was another Orange County. Like the one in California, it was rock-ribbed Republican, also shot through with orchards and berry fields and thriving manufacturing companies, and also a favorite terminal for postwar migrants seeking their fortune. In 1952 a handsome little town there called Newburgh, population 32,000, won *Look* magazine's All-American City award.

But this Orange County turned out to be less blessed than the other one by the tides of economic history. Work in its needlework plants, sporadic in the best of times, stagnated; Eisenhower's interstate neutralized its best economic advantage, the Hudson River frontage that had made it a bustling transportation hub; factories pulled up stakes to head south and west; rivalries among municipalities kept them from working together to lure new ones. In 1957 the Labor Department declared the region an "area of substantial unemployment." And in Newburgh every other downtown storefront fell vacant.

Hurt most of all were the African-Americans who had migrated there from the South upon hearing rumors that jobs were to be had in the Hudson River Valley—and who then found themselves last hired and first fired for what dwindling work there was. The residential district along the waterfront, which custom reserved for blacks, deteriorated, a process exacerbated by Newburgh's city government's being too apathetic to revise and enforce its health and sanitation codes, and the unscrupulous landlords' neglecting to keep up the properties they rented there at gouging rates. Crime doubled. One city council member, a plumbing contractor named George McKneally who displayed a "KHRUSHCHEV NOT WELCOME HERE" sign in his shop, barely failed in 1959 to get the other city council members to authorize the purchase of police dogs to patrol the waterfront. "The colored people of this city are our biggest police problem, our biggest sanitation problem, and our biggest health problem," he said at a meeting. "We cannot put up with their behavior any longer. We have been too lenient with them. They must be made to adhere to the standards of the rest of the community. If necessary we will enforce our ideas on them." The black community was enraged. The city manager, convinced they had averted another Little Rock only by a whisker, quit when his contract came up in the fall of 1960. George McKneally led the search for a replacement.

The city council received sixty applications. A balding career bureaucrat named Joseph Mitchell, who had just finished up a disastrous tenure in a township in Pennsylvania, impressed McKneally the most. Mitchell agreed with McKneally's theory that the reason for the town's troubles was the share of the budget taken up by relief payments to Southern blacks who came to Newburgh because of its reputation as an "easy relief town." Joe Mitchell got the job. He proceeded to turn "Newburgh" into a household word.

As city manager Mitchell made his first policy decision in February. Newburgh had been hit hard by the same squall that blanketed Washington on the eve of the inauguration. To make up a deficit brought on by snow removal costs, he decided to close out thirty "borderline" relief cases and reduce the food relief allotment. Welfare, he said, was bringing "the dregs of humanity into this city" in a "never-ending pilgrimage from North Carolina to New York."

That move provoked an injunction from the state welfare department; Mitchell was not deterred. In April, the city sent out letters to all relief recipients: "Your welfare check is being held for you at the police department. Please report to the police department and pick up your check there. This procedure is effective for this check only. Future checks will be mailed to you as in the past." And so they came: women, mostly, many with infants in their arms, and elderly home-relief recipients leaning on canes. Some came on foot, others in buses, still others, police reported, in Cadillacs. (The police report was the first of many politically charged misapprehensions to come, since the Cadillacs belonged to members of the town's Junior League who were shepherding the oldest and frailest citizens to city hall to save them the shame of hobbling through the center of town.) The welfare recipients all milled about the police station confusedly as officers tried hopelessly to organize an orderly queue. The mayor, William D. Ryan, who had not been apprised of the muster, stormed in from his office to find out what was going on. "This is nothing more than a routine audit," Mitchell told him. "We're just trying to weed out the chisellers." The mayor, the only Democratic voice on the five-member city council, ordered Mitchell to stop. "I'll stop," Mitchell retorted, "when I'm finished."

No cases of fraud were found. Mitchell did not back down. He claimed Newburgh's reliefers, 5 percent of the city's population, cost the city $1 million annually, one-third of the town budget. He commissioned a report, by a panel of his allies in the town, that found that save for "the care of worthy folk in the city home and infirmary," relief payments were "a total loss," much of the money going to indulgences like liquor and fancy cars. "The gradual changes and widening in the philosophy of public welfare has merely changed the behavior of certain elements of the community to take advantage of it," the report concluded. "The broadening of the base of public welfare has not curtailed social problems—it has increased them." And so on June 19 Mitchell pushed through the city council thirteen provisos for the administration of the city's welfare system.

The first demand was that all cash aid be converted into vouchers for food, clothing, and rent. Then: "All able-bodied adult males on relief of any kind who are capable of working are to be assigned to the chief of building maintenance for work assignment on a 40-hour week." If recipients were offered a private-sector job but refused it, "regardless of the type of employment involved," they would lose their relief. "All mothers of illegitimate children are to be advised that should they have any more children out of wedlock, they shall be denied relief." No relief package for any one family could exceed the take-home pay of the lowest-paid city employee. Newcomers to the city would have to demonstrate a concrete offer of employment, "similar to that required for foreign immigrants." Any payment of aid would be limited to three months in a year. The relief budget would be slashed; the city's corporation counsel would review all cases monthly. Finally, "prior to certifying or continuing any more Aid to Dependent Children cases, a determination shall be made as to the home environment. If the home environment is not satisfactory, the children in that home shall be placed in foster care in lieu of Welfare aid to the family adults."

The state department of welfare responded to the draconian strictures with alarm. Local welfare spending was subsidized by Washington and Albany; both reserved the right to regulate how that money was spent. In a special meeting in New York City on June 22, the state declared that Mitchell's new code fell well afoul of the rules. Mitchell responded that his Thirteen Points would be implemented in full by July 15. The *New York Times*, which had been covering the battle of wills since May as a story of local interest, now put the long-faced, balding forty-one-year-old career civil servant on the front page and ran an editorial on the fracas, "The Dark Ages in Newburgh": "Cruelty anywhere is the concern of mankind everywhere." A dispatch over the AP wire saw the Thirteen Points reprinted in newspapers around the country. Hubert H. Humphrey denounced them as "a substitute of police methods for welfare methods."

The critics were in the minority. "I willingly join those you defame as 'know nothings,' " read a typical letter to the *Times*. Newburgh's "people have a good deal to protect from this creeping modern malady which well may be softening us up for the cold war." Another letter writer wondered why "those receiving unearned benefits from the public purse" should not "suffer the social stigma that is rightfully theirs." "Responsible municipal officials everywhere watch with anxiety the constantly increasing welfare fund burden," said the *Cleveland Plain Dealer*; "Detroit and other large cities with oppressive welfare loads and a comparable problem of rising costs into other municipal projects would well take a lesson from Newburgh," echoed the *Detroit Free Press*. Even critics could not resist praise. The clause denying further relief to mothers of illegitimate children, said a *Life* editorial, "is not only dubious but quite unrealistic since it is simply not in the American character to let anyone starve." Be that as it may. "Newburgh provides a healthy example of local government assuming due initiative and responsibility."

Liberals, advocates for the poor, policy experts, welfare officials: All leapt confidently into the fray with a bunch of data suggesting that Mitchell's system would be *more* bureaucratic and expensive than the present methods. They pointed out that Newburgh had spent $338,000, not $1 million, on relief the previous year. Mitchell said that real estate valuations had gone down by $1 million owing to migrants' slovenly housekeeping; values had actually gone up slightly. Newburgh, in fact, carried less of a welfare burden than comparable cities around the state, and among a sample of the thirty "borderline cases" Mitchell tried to close after the winter snowstorm, twenty of twenty-three had resided in Newburgh for over three years, and eleven were lifelong natives. They added that work requirements for able-bodied men were already written into state law—and pointed out Mitchell's shocking display of ignorance in demanding that women have their children in wedlock in order to get their relief: federal law prevented families from receiving Aid to Dependent Children if there was a man in the house.

The Board of Social Welfare expected that public hearings slated to be held in Albany on July 7 would scotch the whole sorry affair once and for all. Instead Joseph Mitchell emerged as a hero. The *Wall Street Journal* editorialized, "It's a fine commentary on public morality in this country when a local community's effort to correct flagrant welfare abuse is declared illegal under both state and federal law." Mitchell bragged of receiving hundreds of letters from the public, 60 to 1 in his favor. It was Albany's "social work mentality," he told reporters, that was the problem; it would result in a "form of government that truly does smack of an ideology we are all fighting today." Since the Leopold and Loeb case, he said, "criminal lawyers and all the mushy rabble of do-gooders and bleeding hearts in society have marched under the Freudian flag toward the omnipotent state of Karl Marx."

The day of reckoning came, July 15. All able-bodied men on relief were to show up for a work detail. Television cameras and reporters massed to meet them. An hour passed, then another. A single able-bodied male reliefer arrived—the only one in town, it turned out. He was a thirty-three-year-old former ironworker with one eye who lived with his wife and six small children in a house without a stove, heat, or hot water, and who had been searching for a job in vain for months. Once again liberals claimed vindication. Once again victory was only apparent. Mitchell went to Washington that very night to speak at the biannual *Human Events* political action conference. The huzzahs were predictable. But it was not just the *Human Events* crowd that was lionizing him. "I find myself in the unenviable position of not having public support," lamented his most vocal critic, Mayor Ryan. Social welfare professionals felt blindsided. Kennedy's new Health, Education, and Welfare secretary, Abraham Ribicoff, had made reforming welfare his priority. His goals paralleled Mitchell's: fighting illegitimacy, reducing dependency, moving recipients to work—even, as many experts were insisting, women with children. Now suddenly came this demagogue from a tiny town brandishing the experts' own ideas and casting them as the enemy.

They warded off the menace with more statistics: Spiraling welfare costs were a myth; in fact costs were declining. The very dynamism of the American economy left whole sectors behind when markets shifted, and automation wiped out thousands of unskilled jobs a month. How could you blame a helpless individual for that? The city manager Mitchell had replaced, now secretary to the New York state senate, called the whole scandal "a microscopic example of the deterioration of the German middle class under Hitler." On July 28 a sixty-year-old reliefer in Oneida County assigned to shovel debris on a 90-degree day died of heat prostration; the same day, in Newburgh, Mitchell hired a local gym teacher as commissioner of welfare. Social work professionals said that was like replacing atomic engineers with tenth graders to build missiles.

It was no use; Mitchell's critics were impotent. Americans in the millions who were not Birchers, who had not read *Conscience of a Conservative*, who had not heard of *National Review*; whose families did not own factories, who did not live in military-industrial-libertarian enclaves like Orange County—all read the Thirteen Points, liked what they saw, then tuned out the voices of the experts who pointed to their unimpeachable evidence, moralists who demanded that they care more, and highbrows who compared them to Nazis. Nothing quite like it had ever happened before.

Mitchell was now a right-wing hero. Two hundred YAFers took a festive boat ride up the Hudson from Manhattan to march down Newburgh's Main Street to present him with a two-foot-long plaque, which Mitchell accepted, banana republic–style, speaking from a second-floor balcony: "What more could a Communist want? Here is the realization of a dream of conquest: How to wreck cities, then counties, then states, and then the national government; how to ruin the moral fiber and social and economic structures without the expenditure of anything but an idea." (Later, when the affair concluded, Marvin Liebman arranged to take possession of the cartons full of citizens' letters, adding seven thousand new names to his mailing lists.)

Goldwater adored Mitchell. He wrote him an exuberant telegram: "Reading the account of your stand on welfarism in this week's *Life* magazine was as refreshing as breathing the clean air of my native Arizona. . . . The abuses in the welfare field are mounting and the only way to curtail them are the steps which you have already taken." When Mitchell traveled to Washington, he met privately for twenty minutes with Goldwater, who was immediately mobbed by reporters: surely his meeting with Mitchell was a warning to Nelson Rockefeller, the Republican front-runner for President, to beware of a Goldwater challenge.

The reasoning was sound: Rocky was the officer ultimately responsible for the disposition of the Newburgh case. "There's nothing political in this," Goldwater responded. His protestations were genuine. But few believed him. Goldwater was now the hottest politician in Washington. Everyone assumed that his lust for higher office would erupt at any moment; that was how Washington worked. Rockefeller knew how it worked; he knew the law was on the side of the liberals, but he commissioned a poll: one-third of New Yorkers believed half of welfare recipients were chiselers, so Rockefeller responded to his political dilemma by retreating to his Venezuelan *finca* until things blew over.

Barry Goldwater's fame had been steadily increasing ever since the Republican Convention the previous summer. He made 177 speeches across twenty-six states for the GOP ticket, a good portion in Dixie. Nixon staffers seeded the crowds with buttons reading "GOLDWATER SAYS DON'T DODGE: VOTE NIXON AND LODGE." Many already wore ones reading "GOLDWATER FOR PRESIDENT."

By the month before the election, with the presidential candidate professing timid echoes of the Democrat line, a *Times* reporter remarked to Goldwater that he was hearing the word "Nixon" less and less often in the Arizonan's speeches. Goldwater denied it—then undercut himself by saying that if Nixon lost the race, he might run for the nomination in 1964. On October 15, two nights after Premier Khrushchev was seen on TV banging his shoe on the table at the United Nations in rage at the American imperialists, Goldwater treated Nixon to a bruising private workout session at the Westward Ho Hotel in Phoenix in an effort to get him to put more partisan blood into his campaign. They stepped out together into the Thunderbird Room to greet an assembly of Republican campaign workers, a fifteen-foot cactus scrim as backdrop. Nixon was intimidated. "I traveled the country in '58. It was not a pleasant job, I can assure you," he said self-pityingly in his speech. "Frankly, if the time ever comes when I'm not proud of my party and proud of the candidates I'm running with, then, of course, the thing for me to do is get out of the party. So I can only say, since I don't intend that, I'm going to continue to support every Republican candidate in this state, and also in the nation."

In the last televised debate, Nixon performed atrociously. It wasn't even his fault: Kennedy, in a legendary dirty trick, cheated by asking why the Eisenhower Administration hadn't attempted to take back Cuba militarily—exploiting the fact that he had been given a top secret briefing that that very thing was being planned. It forced Nixon to sound like a dove so he wouldn't blow the invasion's cover. But Goldwater didn't know that any more than any other viewer. He promptly wrote Nixon: "What this nation wants is firmness in its president. . . . They want to hear a tough attitude toward Russia—an attitude that might run the risk of war but which would guarantee us a fight for our freedom instead of the slow dribbling away such as the Democrats have been doing at Versailles, Potsdam, Yalta, Tehran, and Korea." He warned Len Hall, "Conservatives of both parties are now speaking of staying home. They are being prodded in this by Dan Smoot and Bob Welch, each of whom has a large following."

In the desperate final days before the 1960 election, Nixon, Rockefeller, Lodge, and Eisenhower met in New York to regroup and plot strategy. Goldwater was not invited—an absence so conspicuous that Senator Kennedy joked, while campaigning in Phoenix, that those Republican potentates would have invited Barry to the New York meeting, "if they can just get Barry out of that Confederate uniform that he has been using in the South." The laughter was nervous. Opinion polls were showing that Kennedy might become the first Democrat in over a hundred years to lose Dixie. If he did, Barry Goldwater would be a prophet.

It had been an autumn of reckoning for the parties. When the Senate passed a mild civil rights bill in 1957, Republicans unanimously hewed to the tradition of the Party of Lincoln and voted for it. Sixty-two percent of Democrats supported it. When the Senate passed the Civil Rights Act of 1960 in April, once again the Republican senators were unanimously in favor—or at least the ones who voted; thirty-one GOP senators stuck their finger in shifting winds and avoided the session entirely. Thanks to Rockefeller, Nixon hit the campaign trail with a platform supporting voting rights, desegregation, and a commission on equal job opportunity. But in Los Angeles the Democrats— whose 1956 platform complimented the South for resisting *Brown*—did the GOP one better: their unprecedentedly liberal platform (the platform hearings had been chaired by *National Review* whipping boy Chester Bowles) demanded timetables for federal integration efforts. It almost dared Dixiecrats to do anything about it—a passel of them immediately obliging by coming out for Nixon.

Richard Nixon's first campaign tour was through the South. What greeted him there was a revelation: the biggest party in Atlanta, wrote liberal *Atlanta Constitution* editor Ralph McGill, "since the premiere of *Gone With the Wind*." A crowd of 150,000 spectators blanketed the route; on the platform with Nixon at Hurt Park before acres of delirious fans, the most enthusiastic demonstration Nixon had seen in fourteen years in politics, the Democratic mayor William Hartsfield warmly welcomed the coming of the two-party system to the South. In the capital of South Carolina, Columbia, Nixon drew 35,000 rooters. Kennedy drew 10,000.

The turnout for Nixon in the South presented a dilemma. Conventional campaign wisdom held that all America was divided in three: some states tended to go or always went Republican (Midwestern strongholds like Indiana and Ohio, New England ones like Vermont and Maine); others never did (the Southern states). The swing states that decided elections were the "Big Six," the industrial states Illinois, Pennsylvania, New York, Ohio, Michigan, and California. And the swing voters in these states—it was believed—were blacks. Nixon's original strategy was to concentrate on the Big Six, which meant saying things that would scare off the Southern Democrats who suddenly seemed so tantalizingly within his grasp. After Kennedy's nomination, the Reverend Billy Graham, an old Nixon friend, shaken at the thought of a Catholic president, dangled before the Republicans hints concerning his two-million-name, overwhelmingly Southern Democrat mailing list. Race was not on Graham's mind; his other advice to Nixon was to draw closer to Martin Luther King. But Richard Nixon, not so high-minded, understood how you won elections in the South.

The Democrats whistle-stopped Lyndon Johnson through the South in a train reporters tagged "the Cornpone Special." In town after town the Texan, in exaggerated drawl, would speak of the rewards loyalty to the Democratic Party had brought and would bring. In a tiny hamlet in Virginia he delivered the most memorable line of the campaign: "What has Dick Nixon ever done for Culpeper?" (What, indeed, compared to Virginia senators Harry Flood Byrd and A. Willis Robertson, and their congressman Howard Worth Smith, each of whom had served since 1933?) Goldwater toured the South, too; he called Johnson a "counterfeit Confederate." In the North, Nixon sat on the fence concerning civil rights. But when Henry Cabot Lodge impulsively promised (others heard him predicting) in Harlem that a Nixon-Lodge Administration would include a Negro cabinet member, Nixon raged at him.

Then, an astonishing development: Martin Luther King was arrested and sentenced to four months at hard labor for taking part in his first sit-in, in Atlanta. Kennedy's civil rights point men Harris Wofford and Sargent Shriver fervently lobbied his campaign managers to have the candidate issue a call for King's release. The managers—Bobby Kennedy foremost among them—were horrified at the thought of scaring off Southern whites. Shriver rushed to the candidate's Chicago hotel room, waited until backs were turned, and buttonholed Kennedy with the suggestion that he phone King's wife, Coretta, with a few words of comfort. Offhandedly, oblivious to his high command's urgent efforts to head off just such a prospect, Kennedy agreed.

That Sunday, Nelson Rockefeller spoke against the King arrest from pulpits at four black churches in Brooklyn. At his side was Jackie Robinson, a longtime friend of Nixon who had nearly broken down in tears trying to convince him to throw in for King. Robinson's argument wasn't only moral; he had been warning Nixon over the course of the entire campaign that his neglect of blacks might lose him the election. Goldwater had been warning Nixon during the entire campaign that his neglect of the South might lose him the election. It is unlikely that this purebred political animal misunderstood the portent of the decision he would have to make: Speak for King and lose the Southern vote; ignore him and lose the black vote. Nixon's final campaign stop broadcast which bloc he had chosen to court: he spoke at the South Carolina statehouse.

Meanwhile Mrs. King told the *New York Times* about John F. Kennedy's call. Since King, coincidentally, was released at almost exactly the same time, Shriver and Wofford spotted an opportunity. Behind the Kennedy brothers' backs they hastily cobbled together a pamphlet, *"No Comment" Nixon versus a Candidate with a Heart, Senator Kennedy*. Two million copies—nicknamed the "Blue Bomb" after its flimsy paper stock—were distributed the Sunday before Election Day at black churches around the country. They were clutched with reverence by people startled that Kennedy would take this risk in support of their freedom. Georgia Republicans responded with a pleading last-minute flyer: with a President Nixon, "there will be no compromises between the national administration and southern segregationists to pay off for votes. . . . PLAY SAFE! VOTE FOR NIXON AND LODGE!" When the ballots were counted, Kennedy overwhelmingly won the black vote. So has every Democratic presidential candidate since.

Kennedy also won the election—by an average of one-tenth of a vote per precinct. Republicans affixed blame to a hundred factors: Nixon would have won if Eisenhower had stumped more; if Eisenhower had pump-primed the economy; if not for Henry Cabot Lodge's afternoon naps; if not for the Chicago Democratic machine; if Henry Luce hadn't at the last minute timorously pulled a *Life* article by Billy Graham preaching that it was wrong to vote for a candidate simply because he was "more handsome or charming." (Ironically, this last one was among Nixon's favorite explanations.) Liberals said that Nixon lost because he didn't speak against segregationism; conservatives said he lost because he didn't speak for states' rights. They also pointed out that in Illinois sixty thousand voters who marked their ballots for House and Senate, the majority for Republicans, didn't indicate a preference for President. The fact shored up a conservative nostrum: millions of people would rather stay home than endorse the Republicans' leftward drift.

This last message was heard most loudly from the party's conservative star. "It's just what I've been saying," Goldwater told *Time*. "We cannot win as a dime-store copy of the opposition's platform." He began acting like he was positioning himself for something. For the first time he hired a press secretary, a former newsman and chamber of commerce staffer named Tony Smith. He turned to Brent Bozell, the hardest of *National Review*'s hard-liners, to write

him a head-turning speech on declining American prestige for an appearance at
the Air War College November 14, the first foreign affairs address for a politician who "[had] no foreign policy to speak of," Bill Buckley had complained
only a year and a half earlier. The next month, speaking to the Congress of
American Industry in New York, Goldwater lambasted the Eisenhower
Administration's parting stroke of authorizing $500 million in foreign aid for
Latin America. The following morning the *New York Herald Tribune*'s cartoonist had Barry ministering to an elephant stretched on a psychoanalyst's
couch: "You've been in the hands of quacks."

After the New Year, the GOP's most liberal senator, blunt, intense Jacob
Javits of New York, organized an effort to try to dump Goldwater as chair of
the Republican Senatorial Campaign Committee. It gained momentum within
the caucus, then sputtered when senators were swamped with protests from
conservatives. On January 11 Goldwater took to the floor to deliver "A Statement of Proposed Republican Principles, Programs, and Objectives"—a stem-
to-stern Republican legislative agenda for the 1960s, perhaps what the
Republican presidential campaign would have looked like with Barry Goldwater at the helm. In the address, later dubbed the "Forgotten American"
speech, Goldwater argued that in a political scene jammed with minority and
pressure groups, the only population left unorganized were those Americans
"who quietly go about the business of paying and praying, working and saving." The GOP, he said, must become the party of these "silent Americans."
This language would become influential in Republican presidential campaigning—seven years hence. In 1961 Goldwater made no attempt to build a coalition around these ideas or shepherd the statement's clauses into bills; soon he
dropped them.

He spent more energy that winter organizing a congressional wing of the
Air National Guard, the 9999th Air Reserve Squadron. He was never one for
legislating. His business was casting "no" votes: against an emergency increase
in price supports for grain; against restricting federal aid to states making
progress on segregation; against the foreign aid package; against aid to
depressed areas to relieve chronic unemployment in places like New York's
Orange County; against a wilderness preservation bill years in the making (it
passed 78 to 8); against the Educational and Cultural Exchange Act (93 percent
of Republicans voted in favor); against an authorization of money to irrigate
Navajo lands in New Mexico (although he introduced a bill to authorize funds
for the dam-building Central Arizona Project). In a monumental statement, he
said Kennedy's school assistance bill was a farce, designed to address a teacher
shortage that did not in fact exist. Then, naturally, he voted against it.

The word "no," apparently, was all it took to get him on the cover of *Time*.

"Salesman for a Cause," the cover line read. It went on to call Goldwater the "hottest political figure this side of Jack Kennedy." A fawning feature in the March 25 *Business Week* reported that "the most sought-after man on Capitol Hill for speaking engagements around the country used to be a glamorous, liberal senator named John F. Kennedy. Today he is a glamorous, conservative senator named Barry Goldwater." *Conscience of a Conservative* had sold three-quarters of a million copies. *Newsweek* put Goldwater on the cover on April 10—"a handsome jet aircraft pilot with curly gray hair, dazzling white teeth, and a tan on his desert-cured face," who began his day by swinging "out of his bed as though he hadn't partied until the small hours the night before." Even the country's most liberal major daily, the *New York Post*, fawned: "Like Kennedy, he has a devastating impact on the ladies; he also projects an aura of rugged masculine competence with which men like to identify." The number of newspapers featuring Goldwater's opinion column climbed from 26 in April to 104 by summer. His suite in the Old Senate Office Building, besieged by eight hundred pieces of mail each day, was mobbed every morning by well-wishing families on summer vacations craving a scrawled autograph, eye contact, a handclasp—anything. ("If you'd like to see the Vice President, he's right over there," a reporter overheard a guide say. She was answered by a chorus: "Where's Senator Goldwater?") "GOLDWATER IN 1964" bumper stickers began appearing ("GOLDWATER IN 1864" stickers soon followed). A negative profile in *Life* by the novelist Gore Vidal, who called Goldwater a fascist, came off making Vidal look like the crank, the intended victim an altogether affable fellow.

Kennedy, meanwhile, was floundering politically in his first year in office. His only real legislative victory had come in the second week of his term, when the House voted to enlarge the size of the Rules Committee to dilute the power its reactionary majority of Northern Republicans and Southern Democrats had used to bog down enough social legislation to render the liberal Democratic triumph in 1958 moot. But he won the victory by only a single vote, through the severest arm-twisting by House Speaker Sam Rayburn. Kennedy's only big foreign policy move was the shameful loss at the Bay of Pigs. His Rules Committee coup availed him nothing: the school bill died a slow death; his depressed areas bill was only able to pass at half strength after Southern obstructionists were bought off with far more patronage than they deserved; the minimum wage was increased slightly, but thanks to business lobbying, the number of workers it covered decreased. A sweeping federal housing bill and one providing medical care to the aged through Social Security appeared ready to meet the same fate.

There was no mistaking it, though: the large majority of Americans adored their dashing young President. He enjoyed a 79 percent approval rating at the beginning of April, 83 percent after the Bay of Pigs. All the same, it was strange: even as the slice of America that disdained Kennedy grew slimmer, it was growing more distinct, better organized, more articulate. This constituency was on the move. It had a hero. Barry Goldwater gave 225 speeches on the road in 1961. He was becoming, in the words of an astute young *Fortune* reporter, "the favorite son of a state of mind." And by the end of the summer, events would see to it that this state of mind would spread impressively.

8

APOCALYPTICS

I n the midst of one of those myriad foreign policy crises of his Administration when a wrong decision might doom the entire earth, the bedraggled President looked up at aide Walt Whitman Rostow and muttered, "Sometimes, I'm afraid that the good Lord put me on earth to start a nuclear war."

Leading the free world in 1961 was enough to haunt any man. In the Southeast Asian nation of Laos, a pro-American regime was defending itself against a guerrilla band backed by Communist North Vietnam. In Berlin the problem was more immediate. The two Germanys were in a kind of bureaucratic limbo, still officially "occupation zones." That made Berlin, divided by postwar agreement but deep within the Soviet zone, the one place in the world where the forces of the West (12,000 troops) and the East (500,000 troops) mingled at the distance of a shouted insult or a tossed grenade. For the Soviets, Berlin was an open wound through which East Germany's most gifted citizens bled. For the NATO countries, the tumbledown misery of the Soviet district was a splendid everyday rebuke to propaganda that Communism could build a paradise on earth. Militarily, the city carried incredible strategic value. It was, said Khrushchev in November of 1958 before demanding that the U.S. accede to placing Berlin under Soviet control, "the testicles of the West," which he need only squeeze to make Presidents scream.

The 1958 crisis dissolved with Eisenhower's invitation to Khrushchev to visit the United States. In 1961 Berlin heated up again because of a chain of events taking place half a world away. On April 1 Khrushchev agreed to meet with Kennedy in Vienna in June over Laos. Two weeks later, the Bay of Pigs shattered the young, untested President's bargaining position. Kennedy well remembered the only other time he had met the Soviet premier: when he paid court to the Senate Foreign Relations Committee during his September 1959 visit, Khrushchev said that Kennedy looked awfully young to be a senator. In anticipation of the April meeting with the premier, Kennedy frantically back-filled to broadcast his toughness and resolve by calling up twelve thousand new Marines.

It was harder to control events at home. An inconvenience of making foreign policy during the high tide of the American Century was that since the nation was possessed of a simple faith in its omnipotence, any presidential compromise looked like failure, even unto treason—thereby minting new right-wing critics continually. Kennedy was trying to bargain with Castro to free the prisoners from the Bay of Pigs in exchange for a shipment of American tractors. In Rockford, Illinois, Barry Goldwater held an audience spellbound bemoaning "the disgusting, sickening spectacle of four Americans groveling before a cheap, dirty dictator" (the audience, and Goldwater, didn't know about the $50 million budget for CIA efforts to overthrow Castro). The appearance of national disunity would hurt Kennedy in Vienna. So would the latest outbreak of civil rights disturbances in the South: young activists from the Congress of Racial Equality testing the Supreme Court ban on segregation in interstate bus facilities on a dramatic "Freedom Ride" through the region. In Birmingham they were beaten, in Anniston their bus was torched, in Montgomery they hid from a mob in a church like cornered rats.

In Vienna, just as Kennedy feared, Khrushchev came after him like a playground bully, brazenly repeating his 1958 ultimatum: NATO must remove its troops from Berlin or the Soviet Union would sign a separate peace treaty with East Germany making it an "independent" nation with sole rights to the city. "And if that means war," the premier fulminated, "the Soviet Union will accept the challenge." The next day he went on Moscow TV to say that the treaty would be signed within the year. If America tried to stop them, he boomed, "it would mean war, and a thermonuclear war at that."

It might come to World War III over Berlin: Kennedy spent the summer thinking of little else. Again and again he worked through the military scenarios with his advisers. They all boiled down to one of two options: surrender or nuclear war. They differed only in the number of steps it took to get there. A nuclear first strike was considered, then the pulverization of a Hiroshima-sized Russian city at the first sign of a Soviet move. Dean Acheson told Kennedy that America should be put on immediate footing for total war, including wage and price controls. Finally, at the Kennedy family compound in Hyannisport, an initial course of action was decided upon. The gambit would be a speech, delivered on television on July 25. It was the most terrifying of the Cold War. Later Barry Goldwater would say the same kinds of things during the 1964 presidential campaign, and people would call him a madman.

Kennedy spoke in front of a flag emblazoned with the presidential seal, draped in such a way that, intentionally or not, the only part visible was the clutch of arrows in the eagle's right talon, not the olive branch in its left. "An attack on that city will be regarded as an attack upon us all . . . we cannot separate its safety from our own." Berlin was "the great testing place of Western courage and will, a focal point where our solemn commitments stretching back over the years since 1945, and Soviet ambitions, now meet in basic confrontation." Our only course there was to find a path between "humiliation" and "all-out nuclear action." The Soviets had made the "mistake of assuming that the West was too selfish and too soft and too divided to resist invasions of freedom in other lands." They were wrong. He explained that he would ask Congress for $3.2 billion in new military appropriations, triple draft calls, order reserve and National Guard units to active duty, and put long-range bombers on fifteen minutes' alert. In previous wars, he said, "serious misjudgments were made on both sides of the intentions of others, which brought about great devastation. Now, in the thermonuclear age, misjudgment on either side about the intentions of the other could rain more devastation in several hours than has been wrought in all the wars of human history." Americans must begin preparing for that eventuality immediately: "In the event of an attack, the lives of those families which are not hit in a nuclear blast can still be saved—*if* they can be warned to take shelter and *if* that shelter is available."

In the space of an evening the end of the world became routine business. The bomb shelter—only recently the province of neighborhood eccentrics—was now presidential mandate. Thomas J. Watson of IBM gave his employees $1,000 loans to build them; the Rabbinical Council of America recommended construction of bomb shelters beneath all new synagogues. New companies sprang up: Acme Bomb and Fallout Shelter Company, Peace-O-Mind Shelter Company, Nuclear Survival Company. Specialized products appeared on shelves: "Foam-Ettes—the Toothpaste Tablet You Can Use ANYTIME, ANY-WHERE—WHEREVER YOU ARE, even in a family fallout shelter."

The grim trade illuminated dark corners of the American psyche. An article called "Gun Thy Neighbor" in *Time* reported on a suburban Chicagoan who planned to mount a machine gun on the hatch of his shelter, and described a civil defense coordinator for Riverside County in southern California who recommended that families stock survival kits with pistols to ward off Angelenos who might head for the sticks. The article appeared in *Time*'s religion section. Its main point was that religious leaders were sanctioning this kind of thing. "If you allow a tramp to take the place of your children in your shelter, you are in error," said the dean of a Baptist seminary. "A Christian has the obligation to ensure the safety of those who depend on him." Jesuit father L. C. McHugh branded as "misguided charity" the refusal to repel invaders by "whatever means to effectively deter their assault." Rod Serling rushed into production an episode of *The Twilight Zone* to run September 29—if the world made it that far. It depicted a neighborhood birthday party for the beloved town doctor, interrupted by a radio announcement of imminent alien attack. The doctor takes his wife and son to the family shelter and battens down the hatches. Just as the shelterless mob pounds their way in, the radio informs them it was a false alarm. The people face each other in shame, their trust in one another forever shattered.

The situation in Europe escalated. On August 12, East German soldiers began sealing off the Soviet sector with barbed wire; within days there was a concrete wall, interrupted only by watchtowers. West Berlin mayor Willy Brandt sent Kennedy an open letter demanding "not merely words but political action" to preserve his city. Berlin students sent the President a Neville Chamberlain–style umbrella—a sucker punch to the man whose father was famous, while serving as ambassador to Great Britain, for having a soft spot for Hitler. Kennedy sent Lyndon Johnson to Berlin to pledge "our lives, our fortunes, our sacred honor" to Berlin's defense. Then he sent a fifteen-hundred-man battle group along the 110-mile single roadway that linked the West to Berlin—a game of chicken that so whitened his knuckles that talking to him, according to an aide, was like talking to a statue. The Soviets announced that they would resume atmospheric nuclear tests. Then they exploded a bomb bigger than all the tonnage in World War II put together. The White House scuttled ongoing disarmament talks.

It wasn't just international strategy; it was domestic politics. The growing popularity of Goldwaterite conservatism and popular resentment over the failure at the Bay of Pigs were very much in the President's thoughts. "They'd kick me in the nuts," Kennedy told an adviser who warned against a game of tit-for-tat on nuclear testing. "I couldn't get away with it." On September 5 he announced that the United States, too, would resume tests.

The Cold War social contract was stretched near the breaking point. *Life* manfully tried to make it all sound like an episode out of the era of Teddy Roosevelt: "the American people are willing to face nuclear war for Berlin," an editorial boasted, citing "our spontaneous boom in shelter building as proof." The issue that followed, introduced by a letter from President Kennedy, demonstrated how, "prepared, you and your family could have 97 chances out of 100 to survive." (Time Inc. even helped the Administration draft a civil defense pamphlet to send to every family in the country, part of which would explain that community fallout shelters could double as "after school hang-outs" where "gregarious teenagers" could "relax with sodas and play the jukebox.") General Eisenhower was so disgusted by the charade that he came out and said that America could "survive" a nuclear attack only as a garrison state. "I would not want to face that kind of world," he proclaimed.

But in fact the crisis was over. Kennedy's July 25 speech had telegraphed a sort of coded message to the Soviets proposing a middle course between surrender and war: that America would not fight over what Khrushchev did on *his* side of Berlin. While Kennedy publicly professed outrage at the concrete monstrosity dividing Berlin, privately, he was relieved: "A wall is a hell of a lot better than a war."

The near miss was a hinge in the history of the Cold War. "Now we have a problem in making our power credible," Kennedy told James "Scotty" Reston of the *New York Times*, "and Vietnam is the place." Kennedy meant that it was the safest place: one could signal resolve to draw the line against Communist aggression in a land so godforsaken that neither the Soviets nor China would ever risk escalation over it—escalation that could only lead, inexorably, to nuclear war. It was one of those secrets that only the President and a few of his closest advisers were allowed to know: amidst all the bluster, the only Cold War option conscience truly allowed was local, limited war. The ultramilitant publisher of the *Dallas Morning News*, E. M. Dealey, as guest at the White House, once insulted President Kennedy to his face: "We need a man on horseback to lead this nation, and many people in Texas and the Southwest think that you are riding Caroline's bicycle." The President replied sternly: "I have the responsibility for the lives of 180 million Americans, which you have not." Only those who didn't have all the facts could counsel unchecked belligerence.

On October 26, Kennedy sent President Ngo Dinh Diem, whose brutal South Vietnamese government existed at the sufferance of the U.S., a note promising continued American assistance. In November, Walt Rostow and General Maxwell Taylor recommended adding 8,000 "advisers" to the 800 already stationed in Vietnam. Secretary of State Dean Rusk agreed, with one eye on the Goldwater boom: losing Vietnam "would stimulate bitter domestic controversies in the United States and would be seized upon by extreme elements to divide the country and harass the administration." At mid-month Kennedy sat down with his Joint Chiefs of Staff to discuss the idea. They thought it splendid. Kennedy was ambivalent, worried about justifying sending thousands of troops to Southeast Asia given that he had sent none to Cuba, 90 miles from our shores. The abrasive chairman of the Joint Chiefs, Lyman Lemnitzer, spat out that the Chiefs thought the United States should pour troops into Cuba, too.

This intemperate, nearly insubordinate, right-wing drift of certain top military brass and an accompanying militant cast infecting much of the body politic were worries very much on Kennedy's mind then. He was giving a speech on the subject in Seattle in two days, in fact.

It was as if the fear he was addressing had flowed uninterrupted from Berlin.

In California, Democratic governor Pat Brown had ordered his attorney general, Stanley Mosk, to submit a report on the John Birch Society. It came out in July and was excerpted in the *New York Times Magazine* in August. Mosk reported that Birchers defined Communism as "any idea differing from their own," that to fight it they were "willing to give up a large measure of the freedoms guaranteed them by the United States Constitution in favor of accepting the dictates of their founder," and that they sought "by fair means or foul, to force the rest of us to follow their example." Birchers "do the work of the Communists," Mosk concluded, by undermining the integrity of the United States.

It had been only three weeks since a shocking memo from Democratic senator J. William Fulbright of Arkansas, chairman of the Foreign Relations Committee, addressed to Kennedy's defense secretary, Robert McNamara, had been made public. In 1956 Army psychiatrist William E. Mayer released a report, which became a media sensation, that Korean War POWs had been brainwashed with alarming ease because they had been sent out into the field with a profound lack of understanding of the meaning of America. It led in 1958 to a National Security Council directive that military authorities begin educating the troops in their charge, and the public in their community, in basic facts about the Cold War. Commanding officers were supplied literature and suggestions but were allowed wide latitude in carrying out the directive. And in some cases that latitude, Fulbright reported, had created a monster. A private outfit, the Foreign Policy Research Institute, bankrolled by the conservative Richardson Foundation, was being retained by military bases nationwide—and by the Army War College, under the auspices of no less than the Joint Chiefs of Staff—to convene "strategy seminars" to carry out the NSC Cold War directive. Among their teachings was that Defense Secretary McNamara's project to replace bombers with missiles as the centerpiece of American nuclear strategy was in fact a deliberate, covert plan for unilateral disarmament. The civilian arm of the Foreign Policy Research Institute instructed civic leaders on how entire American states might be turned into "civilian war colleges" to train the populace in "Catonic" strategy—the right-wing doctrine, named for the Roman general who ended his every Senate speech with the declaration "Carthage must be destroyed," that preparations for protracted total war to annihilate the Soviet Union should begin immediately.

In Pensacola (a town so dominated by the right that a local theater company presenting Arthur Miller's *The Crucible* interpreted the play as a critique of the persecution of anticommunists), the chief of naval air training set up a series of mandatory, weeklong seminars for officers that taught that the progressive income tax, the Federal Reserve, and increased business regulations were, just as Robert Welch believed, part of the Soviet takeover of the United States. Then the show was taken on the road in mass rallies for civilians. At one of them, in Los Angeles, Loyd Wright educated the audience on the imperative of "preventive war"—a doctrine proposed in 1953 by Air Force general Jimmy Doolittle, rejected with horror by President Eisenhower, to issue an ultimatum that the Soviet Union leave Eastern Europe by a certain date on pain of nuclear retaliation. "If we have to blow up Moscow," said Wright, "that's too bad."

Fulbright's startling revelation that military personnel were being indoctrinated with the idea that the policies of the Commander in Chief were treasonous dovetailed with the return to the news of the strange case of General Edwin Walker. Walker had always been an odd one; he volunteered to lead a paratroopers unit in World War II without ever having jumped out of a plane ("How do you put this thing on?" he reportedly asked a subordinate as the plane took off for his first jump). His long, spectacular disillusionment with his civilian masters began in the Korean War. "I saw stalemate become the substitute for victory," he later recalled. The disillusionment continued when he served as a military adviser for Chiang Kai-shek: Why wasn't America preparing Taiwan for the final assault on the mainland? (The Cold War was a war, and Walker, like all West Point graduates, had been taught that in a war, "the only real victory was total victory, the complete annihilation of the enemy and its power to wage war.") Fulbright gained public prominence in 1957 by commanding the regiment guarding Little Rock's Central High. And this bastardization of the military was the last straw. "In my opinion the 5th column conspiracy and influence in the United States minimize or nullify the effectiveness of my ideals and principles," he soon wrote in a letter resigning from the Army. His resignation was refused. If every old salt who felt the same way were to leave, it would decimate the officer corps. Instead Walker was promoted, sent to command the Twenty-fourth Infantry Division in Augsberg, Germany. And immediately upon arrival, he set to work implementing the National Security Council Cold War directive.

In June 1961, the Army released a report as thick as a telephone directory documenting how Walker had been lecturing his troops about the suspicious loyalties of Harry Truman, Eleanor Roosevelt, Dean Acheson, Walter Lippmann, and Edward R. Murrow. Before the 1960 elections Walker had distributed the Americans for Constitutional Action voting index. ACA had been founded by former admiral Ben Morreel in 1958 upon his retirement as chairman of the board of Jones & Laughlin, a steel manufacturer so brutish that its workers once dubbed its works "Little Siberia." ACA's goal of "repeal of the socialistic laws now on our books" was abetted by its famous index, which rated congressmen from 1 to 100 in categories such as "FOR Sound Money and AGAINST Inflation" and "FOR Individual Liberty and AGAINST Coercion." Senator Kennedy scored zero on "FOR Private Ownership and AGAINST Government Ownership and Control of the Means of Production"; even Barry Goldwater was two points short of a perfect score. Walker also prescribed what he called a "Pro-Blue" reading program—consisting largely of the publications of the John Birch Society and like groups.

The Army feared if it punished Walker he would become a right-wing martyr. So he was given the lightest sanction possible. It didn't work. Instead Strom Thurmond held hearings on this "dastardly attempt to intimidate the commanders of the U.S. Armed Forces." Robert McNamara was jeered from the gallery when he testified. From California, eleven-year-old James Quinlan wrote the President: "I heard that you pulled out a general for teaching Americanism. Would you rather for him to teach communism to all those men?" Editorialized the *New York Mirror*, "No matter how it is sliced, General Walker seems to have committed the crime of being excessively patriotic, of preferring his own country to Soviet Russia." The Texas state senate pledged its "unqualified support"; the newspaper columnist Paul Harvey lamented, "Today, the loyal American is being defamed, demoted, discharged, destroyed if he militantly defends the American 'ism' against all its enemies, foreign and domestic." Barry Goldwater declared: "When we reach the point where we have a bunch of namby-pambies as our generals, men who cannot use a little strong language once in a while, particularly as it concerns enemies who say, 'We will bury you' and 'Your children will live under socialism' . . . I think we are farther down the road than we realize."

The centrist press panicked too; it tended to imply that the nation was on the verge of having a military putsch. *Look* magazine reporter Fletcher Knebel began drafting a novel called *Seven Days in May* in which military leaders plot to overthrow a President after he signs a nuclear disarmament treaty—of the sort Kennedy had dreamed of, eloquently, in a September 25 speech at the United Nations before signing a bill establishing the United States Arms Control Agency.

On October 16 the spectacle in Washington was joined by Dr. Fred Schwarz's Christian Anti-Communism Crusade at the Hollywood Bowl, which was broadcast across the state—then, a few weeks later, shown again in New York City. This required monumental sums of money. It came from two of southern California's most prominent businesses: Richfield Oil, whose filling stations dotted the West Coast; and Coast Federal Savings & Loan, the third largest S&L in the country. Coast dedicated 4 percent of its net revenue to far-right propaganda, distributing two million pieces of literature in 1961 alone. In a typical blitz, account holders received a red postcard bearing a spurious quote from Khrushchev: "We cannot expect the Americans to jump from capitalism to communism, but we can assist their elected leaders in giving Americans small doses of socialism, until they suddenly awake to find they have communism."

The Schwarz crusade made President Kennedy jump out of his skin. The podium at the Hollywood Bowl was graced with stars like John Wayne, Jimmy Stewart, and Roy Rogers. But the most remarkable presence was that of C. D. Jackson, the publisher of *Life*. He was there to proffer a groveling apology for running an article critical of Dr. Schwarz. "It is a great privilege to be with you tonight," he said, "because it affords me an opportunity to align *Life* in a very personal way with a number of stalwart fighters." Then it was back to the program, Walter Judd proclaiming that Khrushchev possessed a "well-disciplined" apparatus to "start a riot or a strike in any major city any time he wants to." The extremist fringe had humbled the mighty Luce empire. Kennedy had a legislative agenda to pass, a foreign policy to manage—tasks complicated when the most powerful media institution in the country was joining forces with those who would declare both treasonous. The day after the news, Bobby Kennedy breakfasted with Walter Reuther and his brother Victor, and lawyer Joseph Rauh, to begin plotting a counterstrategy.

The temperature rose. Four days later the AP printed a dispatch from a tiny Illinois hamlet where police had seized an arsenal of machine guns and 81-mm mortars belonging to a shadowy group dedicated to training civilians in anti-communist guerrilla warfare. They called themselves the "Minutemen," and soon they had worked their way to the front page of the *New York Times*. No one knew how many of them there were (they had no organizational structure so as to minimize the chance of Communist infiltration). Their ideology was Birchite. Their founder, Robert DePugh, a manufacturer of veterinary pharmaceuticals in Missouri, told the press that while waiting for the final showdown on American soil, his men would monitor and check subversive activities in their hometowns. "On a local basis we feel we're in a better position to know our friends and neighbors" than the FBI, he explained. He claimed that his inspiration had been a speech Kennedy had delivered in January: "We need a nation of Minutemen, citizens who are not only prepared to take up arms, but citizens who regard the preservation of freedom as a basic purpose of their daily life."

Kennedy spoke often in these absolutist, apocalyptic terms; he had done so in his inaugural when he asked Americans to "pay any price, bear any burden, meet any hardship," and all the rest. Vigilantism of some sort was perhaps an understandable result. Kennedy's rhetoric now haunted him. Eisenhower's farewell address had been prophetic: a permanent sense of Cold War emergency was indeed giving birth to "a recurring temptation to feel that some spectacular and costly action could become the miraculous solution to all current difficulties" to a citizenry wracked with "imbalance and frustration." There had been scores of threats on Kennedy's life already. Thirty-four had come from Texas. And when the next disturbing right-wing rally was held in Dallas, Kennedy chose to act.

Dallas was second only to Orange County as a right-wing redoubt. Like Orange County, it owed its good fortune to government; it had been desolate until local boosters persuaded the state legislature to route the Texas & Pacific Railroad through it. Its population had doubled since 1940—rising out of the thankless desert, according to the latest generation of boosters, by the sheer force of will of men on horseback, proud of their ability to thrive without outsiders' help. Once again the chief propagandist was a newspaper publisher— E. M. Dealey, he of the "Caroline's bicycle" crack, whose *Dallas Morning News* saw Reds beneath, beside, and on top of every bed.

Dallas was also less than ashamed of its reputation for outlaw violence. Shortly before Election Day in 1960, Lyndon Johnson and his wife were on their way to a campaign luncheon when they were set upon by a hissing mob. A gob of spit found Lady Bird. One of the men holding a placard was Republican U.S. Congressman Bruce Alger, who told the press he wanted "to show Johnson that he was not wanted in Dallas" and who defended the disturbance as merely the "hubbub of a large gathering fighting for a society free from federal control." Four days later, Dallas resoundingly sent Alger back to Congress. It was a place that made its resident psychologists, social workers, and sociology professors nervous.

In early November a local insurance man published a letter in the *Dallas Morning News* reporting that Yugoslav pilots—Communists!—were training at a nearby Air Force base. When further investigation revealed that America was also selling mothballed fighters to Yugoslavia, it took a young Bircher named Frank McGhee only thirty-six hours to mobilize an auto caravan to parade around the base in protest. To the foreign policy establishment, Yugoslavia was a complicated piece in the Cold War puzzle: Tito, although a socialist, had broken with Moscow, and winning a friend on the Eastern frontier was an unmatched strategic opportunity. To Dallas, Yugoslavia was the enemy, and dealing with her was treason. McGhee called a rally, and two hundred people showed up. He held one the next night, and a thousand people came. Fifteen hundred appeared on the third night, and McGhee decided to make the protest a movement.

Seven weeks later two thousand delegates from ninety cities across the country packed Dallas's cavernous new Memorial Auditorium for McGhee's "National Indignation Convention." The featured speaker was rancher J. Evetts Haley, head of For America's Texas branch. Haley, a local celebrity as the writer of books on Lone Star history, had appealed a suit in the 1950s to nullify all federal agricultural programs all the way up to the Supreme Court. He then led a successful campaign in 1960 to have several textbooks that spoke favorably of the UN, integration, Social Security, and the income tax scotched from the state curriculum. That fall Texans for America won a hand in approving every history and geography textbook up for adoption. Haley won even more local fame when he pummeled a history professor who said that *Operation Abolition* was slanted. At the Memorial Auditorium, decked out in black boots, cowboy plaid, and a white ten-gallon Stetson, Haley looked for all the world like Gary Cooper. The MC, an itinerant lecturer for the John Birch Society, introduced him, and Haley turned to him to remark, "Tom Anderson here has turned moderate! All he wants to do is impeach Warren. I'm for hanging him!" The audience roared. Kennedy ordered an aide to begin preparing monthly reports on the right, he asked the director of audits at the IRS to gather intelligence on organizations receiving tax exemptions, and he told his speechwriters to whip up addresses to educate the people on the menace of right-wing extremism for his upcoming Western tour.

Kennedy's first speech was in Seattle. He echoed Eisenhower's farewell address. The radical rightists, he explained, "lack confidence in our long-run capacity to survive and succeed; hating Communists, yet they see Communism in the long run, perhaps, as the wave of the future. And they want some quick and easy and final and cheap solution—now." Two nights later he was in Los Angeles for a $100-a-plate fund-raiser for Governor Brown at the Los Angeles Palladium. Nat King Cole sang; at the head table, Mayor Sam Yorty was joined by Frank Sinatra and Vic Damone. The L.A. metropolitan area was now home to a quarter of the John Birch Society's membership, and a good portion of them were outside the Palladium that night—having marched four abreast to the site, roughly shunting aside the disarmament activists led by Rita Moreno (star of the year's hit film *West Side Story*), chanting "No Aid to Tito!" and carrying signs reading "MUZZLES FOR DOGS NOT FOR THE MILITARY," "DISARMAMENT IS SUICIDE," "GENERAL WALKER FOR PRESIDENT," and "COMMUNISM IS OUR ENEMY."

Inside, Kennedy reminded the glittering audience that strident peddlers of

panaceas have always arisen in America in times of trial. "Now we are face to
face once again with a period of peril," he said. "The discordant voices of
extremism are heard once again in the land. Men who are unwilling to face up
to the danger from without are convinced that the real danger comes from
within. They look suspiciously at their neighbors and their leaders. They call
for 'a man on horseback' "—a jab at the *Dallas Morning News*'s Dealey—
"because they do not trust the people." He told the audience that America's
military might was enough to assure she would prevail against Communism,
that there was no need for the corrosive suspicion of enemies within. He didn't
realize he was playing into the protesters' hands. If America possessed all this
power, how did one explain any defeat *but* by pointing to the presence of subversives in high places?

   Time put the issue on its next cover. The *New York Times* gave the speeches
its front page. The brown scare was on. The annual meetings of the National
Catholic Welfare Conference and the Union of American Hebrew Congregations resolved that right-wing extremists were "unwittingly aiding the Communist cause by dividing and confusing Americans" and were "stirring division
and hysteria." Dwight D. Eisenhower clucked to Walter Cronkite, "Those who
take the extreme positions in American political and economic life are always
wrong." On Sunday, the *New York Times Magazine* ran an article entitled
"Report on the Rampageous Right," which explained, "Frustration, which produces tantrums in babies, can lead to equally irrational fits of rage in adults."
Henry Luce's next *Life* editorial parroted the President's Seattle speech.

   At the end of 1961, report after report probed the storms suddenly revealed
beneath the placid surface of consensus America. *Communism on the Map*'s
producer, tiny Harding College in Searcy, Arkansas, had an eleven-building
factory of right-wing propaganda that lent out a hundred prints of its films each
day to schools around the country. Children were being subjected to jarring
mock Communist "takeovers" of their schools. Municipal officials who dutifully followed the advice of public health experts to fluoridate their water
supplies found themselves the target of late-night threatening phone calls
denouncing fluoridation as a Communist plot. The lunatic Dallas oil billionaire
H. L. Hunt, reputedly the richest man in the world (and the author of a utopian
novel called *Alpaca* in which the richer you were, the more votes you could
cast, but you couldn't cast any if you took government aid), was beaming his
radio show over three hundred stations in forty-two states. Its host, an ex–FBI
man named Dan Smoot, reported discovering plans, under cover of a congressional act supposedly designed to provide community mental health services in
Alaska, which he claimed actually constituted "the beginning of the American
Siberia," where those who exposed subversion in American government would

be herded. More recently he had published a book arguing that the Council on Foreign Relations, a benign educational enterprise whose small, exclusive membership unfortunately consisted of hundreds of the most powerful people in the country, was the center of an "Invisible Government" determined "to convert America into a socialist state and then make it a unit in a one-world socialist system."

"Communist subversion" was becoming the channel through which a hundred ordinary political grievances were now sluiced. When the Housing Act of 1961 passed Congress on June 28, increasing the funding authorized for urban renewal from $2 million to $4.5 million, and then Kennedy announced he would propose a new cabinet-level urban affairs department, the panic came in a torrent. Urban renewal meant seizure of property—from Administration critics? for secret government projects? Kent Courtney published a pamphlet, *Kennedy's Power Grab: The Department of Urban Affairs*, calling Kennedy's plan "a blueprint for the destruction of private property in the United States." A Memphis bank sent out a copy with every customer's monthly statement. A Los Angeles landowner threatened with seizure of his home to make way for the new Dodger Stadium at Chavez Ravine set up a "Committee for Public Morality": "Could a foreign enemy propose more brutal treatment? How much more brazen a declaration of war do *you* need?" In Phoenix a group called "Stay American" put up a slate of municipal candidates to oppose the city manager system as a Moscow-inspired monstrosity: after Communists gained their municipal toehold, one of their candidates declared, they would "blow up state capitols at a certain signal."

Discerning observers were beginning to notice that the American right was coming to comprise two circles. Each was of roughly the same size, expanding at about the same rate; each intersected the other. And each, somehow, defined Barry Goldwater as its center. It was becoming increasingly clear to *National Review* that such a situation was no more viable in politics than it was in geometry. Buckley and Company set out to claim the Goldwater movement for themselves—and wrench it away from those who believed that the Communists were ready to blow up state capitols.

This storm had been gathering for years. Bill Buckley and Robert Welch were friends, introduced in 1954 by their common publisher, Henry Regnery. In 1955 and again in 1957 Welch wrote $1,000 checks to buoy Buckley's struggling magazine (although the second was accompanied with a note chiding Buckley for his naïveté in not realizing that Eisenhower was "on the other side"). The next year, Welch circulated a few score of *The Politician*, his letter about Dwight D. Eisenhower's Communist proclivities, bound in individually numbered black binders, to select friends. Buckley got copy number 58. The letter he sent back to Welch was gently chiding. Goldwater, blunter, said what Buckley was really thinking: "If you were smart," he wrote Welch, "you'd burn every copy you have. It will do great damage to the conservative cause."

National Review's first steps toward a break with Welch were gingerly. Some of the publication's most important benefactors—Spruille Braden, Adolphe Menjou, Manion, and, most of all, Roger Milliken—were Birchers. After Welch made the incredible declaration in his magazine *American Opinion* that Boris Pasternak, author of *Doctor Zhivago*, was a Communist agent, Eugene Lyons, editor of *Reader's Digest*, submitted an article to Buckley criticizing *American Opinion*. Buckley wrote Welch a letter of warning before he published Lyons's article: "Probably a little friendly controversy among ourselves every now and then is not too bad an idea!" Welch wrote back, to Buckley's relief, that he agreed. Other readers proved less generous. "I was about to repeat my last year's $100 contribution when I picked up your April 11th issue," read one angry letter. "I will send my money to Robert Welch."

The argument raged in the editorial offices through 1961: Was the groundswell to their right an opportunity or a nightmare? "There now exists in this country a conservative anti-Communist apparat that we all have hoped for," Marvin Liebman wrote to the *NR* circle despairingly. "It is controlled by Robert Welch." Bill Rusher, esteemed among the staff for his political savvy, gravely worried that "as the scope and pace of the free world's collapse becomes apparent to the American people and desire for a scapegoat takes hold" Welch might find himself at the head of a literal fascist movement—a prospect that horrified these conservative pragmatists as much as it did their liberal enemies. Scotty Reston wrote in the *New York Times* that at the rate the far right was siphoning off its contributions, there wouldn't *be* a Republican Party to nominate Goldwater in 1964.

The question was whether the broad conservative movement itself was strong enough to survive a faction fight. Publicly, conservatives hid their dirty laundry and closed ranks: *pas d'ennemi du droite*. "Next to the Twist and barely knee-length skirts," the YAF newsletter declared after Tom Hayden's *Michigan Daily* compared YAF to the Hitler Youth, "the most fashionable thing of the season is a rousing, vitriolic attack on the so-called 'Extreme Right.' " Privately, Buckley brooded. He pored over a report on the John Birch Society in *Commentary* speculating that if Goldwater lost the 1964 nomination to Rockefeller, he might take up the assembled forces of the extreme right as *his* fascist army. "Result: An American Raskol'niki," Buckley scribbled in the margin. He glimpsed the abyss. Buckley liked to say that *National Review*'s purpose was "to articulate a position on world affairs which a conservative candidate can adhere to without fear of intellectual embarrassment or political surrealism." If political surrealists like Welch ended up in control of the movement, all might be lost. But if *National Review* lost the Roger Millikens and Adolphe Menjous and couldn't continue to raise enough money to stay in business . . .

He chose a stopgap: a signed editorial, worded with the delicacy of a hostage negotiation, that ran in the April 22 issue, in which Buckley availed himself of his Jesuitical temper to reduce Robert Welch's sin to a logical fallacy: "I hope the Society thrives," the editorial concluded, "provided, of course, it resists such false assumptions as that a man's subjective motives can automatically be deduced from the objective consequences of his acts."

National Review already possessed an informal controlling interest in a membership organization—Young Americans for Freedom. But a feud was developing within its leadership that threatened to tear it apart. A mere six months after its founding, YAF president Caddy instituted a policy change to (he claimed) smooth the liaison procedures with local chapters. David Franke, his old partner, knew it was a power play, and lined up forces with the intention of purging Caddy. Caddy countered by organizing a faction within the twenty-five-member board—in which much of the group's executive authority was vested—to wrest YAF from the *National Review* orbit altogether.

The plotters were strange bedfellows. One, Harvard's Howard Phillips, was frustrated by the older conservatives' dominion over what was supposed to be a student organization. Another was said to harbor secret loyalties to Nelson Rockefeller. Others simply saw in the coup a way to advance their own ambitions. But one of the coup members, Scott Stanley of Kansas, was a Bircher—determined, the *National Review* editors decided, to place YAF under Robert Welch's discipline.

Meanwhile, two hundred YAFers descended on Madison for the fifteenth National Student Association Congress. Students for a Democratic Society hoped to use the meeting to establish a beachhead; YAF aimed to do the same. The conservative group's efforts dwarfed the exercises in Washington the previous spring. An advance guard arrived early to set up shop like a general staff in a military campaign. When the sessions began, walkie-talkies were used to coordinate attacks on every live microphone and roll-call vote; to recognize friend from foe at long distances, YAFers wore suspenders. Meanwhile, at headquarters at the expensive Madison Inn, a staff of secretaries knocked out press releases, speech typescripts, flyers, and meeting proceedings (transcribed from clandestine tape recordings) full-time. They lined up a dummy "middle-of-the-road caucus" of enough unsuspecting dupes to keep the usual string of pro–civil rights and anti-anticommunist resolutions from even getting past committee. Spokesmen plied reporters with continual press conferences.

It was incredible. And it nearly didn't come off at all. Howard Phillips had raised thousands of dollars to finance the effort. Bill Rusher somehow got control of the escrow account that held the money. Phillips's general staff encamped in Madison and started running up bills. Rusher called and told Phillips that unless he promised to vote against severing ties with *National Review* at the upcoming YAF board meeting, Phillips would have to pay all the bills himself. Phillips was not so easily intimidated—he was a veteran of hardball Boston politics, having run the campaign of Tip O'Neill's Republican opponent at the ripe age of seventeen. He won back control of his money by threatening to expose the "middle-of-the-road caucus" as a sham.

In January, Jay Hall—a GM publicist and close Goldwater adviser—Russell Kirk, Steve Shadegg, Bill Buckley, and William J. Baroody Jr., head of American Enterprise Institute, joined Goldwater at the palatial Breakers Hotel in Palm Beach for a council of war. It was time to settle the Birch issue once and for all.

The attendees fell into two camps. Buckley and Kirk said they were ready to write the Birchers out of the conservative movement altogether. Goldwater and others counseled accommodation. He thought there were a lot of "nice guys" in the Society, not just kooks, and that it wasn't the time to precipitate breaks in the conservatives' fragile movement. They settled on a compromise: *National Review* would attack Robert Welch, not the John Birch Society. Goldwater would take the line that Robert Welch was a crazy extremist but that the Society itself was full of fine, upstanding citizens working hard and well for the cause of Americanism.

The White House was undertaking parallel machinations. A few weeks earlier the Reuther brothers had delivered their study on the radical right. Its forces, "bounded on the left by Senator Goldwater and on the right by Robert Welch," were strong and well organized, they warned. "It is late in the day to start dealing with these problems." Another White House report urged that organizations allied with *National Review*—YAF, the Committee of One Million, the New York Conservative Party—not the Birchers, were the true danger, because they were focused on "the winning of national elections" and "the re-education of the governing classes," not on numskull crusades. "The real goal may be to replace the erratic Welch with a man whose thinking parallels that of *National Review*"—to "channel the frenzied emotional energy presently expended on futile projects to impeach Warren and repeal the Income Tax into effective political action." Meanwhile a group called Group Research Incorporated, bankrolled by the UAW, was about to open up shop in Washington. It was the mirror image of the political intelligence businesses that monitored left-wingers in the 1950s, identifying fellow-traveling organizations by counting the number of members and officers shared with purported Communist Party fronts. Group Research did the same thing, substituting the John Birch Society for the reds.

It was a moment dense with opportunity, fraught with peril. Bill Buckley was about to begin writing a syndicated column; Goldwater's column—the fastest-growing feature in Times-Mirror Syndicate history—appeared in over 150 papers. The Republican Party was weak—ripe for takeover. Maneuvers for the 1964 presidential nomination were beginning; the President was contemplating ways to turn his fire on the conservative movement. The stakes seemed inordinately high.

9

OFF YEAR

The Republican Party was going broke. The debt from the Nixon campaign approached a million dollars, which in itself was no great problem; the parties always borrowed in presidential election season and paid off the deficit in between. This time, though, money wasn't coming in. Every Friday night the Republicans' creaky old Senate and House leaders Everett Dirksen and Charlie Halleck went on TV to retail the tired argument that too much spending promised recession just around the corner ("Not *this* corner, *that* one. No, not *that* one, *that* one over *there*," Bill Buckley japed); with economists predicting 10 percent economic growth in 1962 against 3.2 percent yearly during Eisenhower's terms, the counsel of doom just wouldn't take. The "Ev and Charlie Show" played so poorly against John F. Kennedy's sparkling weekly press conferences that in a poll of thirty GOP congressmen, only two admitted liking it: Ev and Charlie. A program to sell "sustaining memberships" in the Republican Party for $10 showed promise. If only the leadership could agree on what they were selling.

It was an embodiment of the parable of the blind men poking the elephant, each one describing a different beast: here was Jacob Javits claiming that "when a composite of our Party is taken, the thinking is Eisenhower (modern) thinking"; there Chicago Republicans were convening a banquet called "Real Republicanism versus Modern Republicanism." Each was correct. Abraham Lincoln's party was formed in the 1850s to fight the spread of slavery, and also to fight *for* something: the ideal that would later be called liberal capitalism—every man making the best for himself through his own hard work, every farmhand aspiring to be a farmer, every factory hand aspiring to own a factory. On this much the Republican homesteaders of the West and the industrialists and artisans in the East could agree. America prospered under Republican rule through the Gilded Age. But the Republicans themselves split. The Easterners desired, and got, high tariff walls that protected their manufactures from foreign competition. The Midwesterners—beholden to the Easterners for credit to buy machinery and finance mortgages, to their railroads to bring their goods to market—wanted free trade.

In later years the issues would change. The split endured. As Eastern entrepreneurs became an Eastern Establishment, they came to prefer a settled economic order to a wide-open one; as America became an equal partner with Europe, the Eastern business titans became free-trade internationalists. Their noblesse oblige gave way to a taste for liberal reform. Republicans in the heartland, meanwhile, were protectionist, isolationist, and laissez-faire. Each faction decried the other's monopoly in party councils. Here, too, both sides were right: Midwesterners sent a powerful obstructionist bloc of conservative congressmen to the Capitol; Wall Streeters got the presidential nominees by intimidating the Midwesterners at national conventions by threatening to call in loans or shut off credit. As long as a charismatic difference-splitter like Teddy Roosevelt held sway, the cracks could be papered over well enough. But that only delayed fixing the disrepair in the foundation.

After FDR won his second term with a record 61 percent of the vote with the slogan "If you want to live like a Republican, vote Democratic"—then a third and a fourth—party elites in the East began to take stock of realities: in some years registered Democrats outnumbered registered Republicans by as much as three to two. The Eastern elites decided that the only way to win was to find candidates who appealed to Democrats and Independents. The prototype was Alf Landon. The apotheosis was Wendell Willkie—"the Republican quisling," according to Colonel McCormick's *Tribune*. The gifted Wall Street lawyer from Indiana began his public career speechifying for American entrance into the European war—the very antithesis of Midwestern Republicanism. Willkie's presidential draft in 1940 was the earnest doing of low-level Manhattan professionals acting spontaneously. But since his star was picked up by the likes of Ogden Reid, publisher of the *New York Herald Tribune*, and Raymond Moley and Alfred P. Sloan—and Democrats like Al Smith—the Willkie boom smelled of conspiracy. His improbable nomination on the sixth ballot a week after France fell to Hitler heightened the suspicion; so many phony telegrams were sent to delegates that Alf Landon, returning home to Topeka, sent out eighteen sacks of notes acknowledging pro-Willkie missives—and received eighteen sacks in return marked "ADDRESS UNKNOWN."

Meanwhile the Republicans kept losing. Liberals said it was because the congressional Old Guard scared the majority of voters, who liked the New Deal, and they quoted Al Smith: "No one shoots Santa Claus." Conservatives, meanwhile, said that Republican presidential candidates lost because millions of disgusted heartlanders stayed home rather than vote for so unnatural a beast as the "me-too Republican." The distrust reached a peak at the 1952 Republican National Convention. On its eve, Taft controlled enough delegates to win. Tom Dewey, Henry Cabot Lodge, and Herbert Brownell—the "Wrecking Crew of '52" to conservatives—who had manufactured the candidacy of General Eisenhower (who entered the race out of fear that isolationism would gain sway in the country) rammed through a phony "fair play" resolution that let them uncredential a number of key Southern Taft delegations. Taft's loyal army entered the hall singing "Onward Christian Soldiers," and left decrying the steal of the century.

With Ike's retirement and Nixon's razor-thin loss in 1960 just behind them, the old feuds festered worse than ever. "The Republican Party is just a little bit pregnant with New Dealism," Senator Jenner told Indiana convention delegates in 1960, "and you ladies know you can't be just a little bit pregnant."

It fell to the RNC chair, Kentucky senator Thruston Morton, to heal the wounds. *Winning* would be a start. There was a congressional election coming up. Census statistics showed that an unprecedented 70 percent of Americans were living in urban areas. Precinct data from 1960 suggested that Kennedy's margin of victory came from voters in the big cities. So Morton assigned Raymond Bliss, a high-strung, chain-smoking Ohio Republican leader who had dropped his Taft conservatism for a career as a nonideological political professional, the task of shaping up the party's urban precinct organizations. One dreary afternoon in the middle of the Republican National Committee's annual conclave, in Oklahoma City, fourteen months after the Nixon defeat, a committee Bliss chaired delivered their entirely technical solution on how to take the White House back.

It was very much in the spirit of an age that was turning anti-ideological pragmatism into a fetish. Critics who scored the "far right" always accompanied their criticism with a token jab at the "far left." At this prosperous moment in American history, President Kennedy insisted, we just didn't need "the sort of great passionate movements which have stirred this country so often in the past." Just what counted as pragmatism, however, and what as ideology, was not always immediately apparent. L. Judson Morhouse, the New York GOP chairman and Nelson Rockefeller's political right-hand man, explained to the press that the most pragmatic strategy for the Republicans to win the cities was to do what the Democrats did, only better: identify the people's problems, then find government programs—urban renewal, health insurance, relief, and so forth—to solve them. It was the kind of plan only a Nelson Rockefeller could love.

But Nelson Rockefeller hated it. His *other* top political deputy, suave, charming George Hinman, had been spending 1961 unobtrusively sucking up to conservatives around the country. His boss was willing to do whatever it took to win the Republican nomination in 1964. That meant placating the conservatives who had stonewalled him in 1960.

Rockefeller quickly, angrily, disassociated himself from Morhouse's ideas. Lincoln Day was coming up, the evening when Republicans across the country united in stolid bacchanals to pay tribute, literally and figuratively, to their party. There would be the usual fund-raisers linked by closed-circuit TV; Rocky would be speaking live from Des Moines. The crowd that watched him on TV at the Mayflower in D.C. was loaded with conservatives. When he began to speak, instinct kicked in: they booed. Then they stopped. They couldn't believe their ears. The face on the screen talking about Kennedy's Department of Urban Affairs proposal looked like Nelson Rockefeller. But he sounded a hell of a lot like Kent Courtney. The new department, Rocky said, "might well be used, in the form proposed, as a subterfuge to bypass the Constitutional sovereignty of the states and to gain direct political control over the nation's cities. . . . What is this but political fakery?"

It might have had something to do with the secret breakfasts. It was Thruston Morton who had proposed informal peace conferences between Rocky and Barry Goldwater on how to join the party's warring wings. Rocky hadn't cared anything about party unity back at the Chicago convention. Times change; now "unifier" was a title he coveted. Goldwater, who always worried about Republican unity, agreed to go along. It turned out they enjoyed each other's company—they absorbed each other's brashness—and found plenty they shared in common: a mutual antipathy for Richard Nixon, a disaffection with Eisenhower, an annoyance with overenthusiastic, out-of-control party volunteers. Goldwater also welcomed the chance to advocate conservatism with the person all the pros were saying would be the 1964 nominee. He was sick of people asking when he would begin running for President. Once he had toyed with the idea; no more. "I have no plans for it," he told *Time*. "I have no staff for it, no program for it, and no ambition for it."

Steve Shadegg, who was serving as Arizona Republican chair, had corralled Goldwater to a meeting the previous November, ostensibly to talk about party unity—and soon Roger Milliken and Senator Norris Cotton and others were all but begging him to run. Goldwater told reporters that all the draft organizations popping up without his permission caused him "deep embarrassment." By the time the Senate adjourned in September of 1961, Goldwater was so fed up he booked a cruise to Europe—on a cargo ship. He drafted his next book, on foreign policy, which would be entitled *Why Not Victory?* Just because he didn't want to be President didn't mean he didn't want to advocate hard for a conservative political agenda.

The breakfasts began upon his return. It wasn't a moment too soon for Nelson Rockefeller. He was about to get a divorce. The people who nominated Republican presidential candidates, even if they had no problem with the minimum wage or negotiations with the Soviets, could be a puritanical bunch. There had been a divorced presidential candidate before. That candidate had been Adlai Stevenson. But no one knew how, exactly, Republicans would react to the same news about one of *their* presidential contenders.

Goldwater, a live-and-let-live kind of guy, certainly did not look down his nose at his new breakfast partner for the fact that his marriage was breaking up. Soon he was doing favors for Rocky: making personal phone calls to Republican leaders urging a warm reception for a friend about to speak in their city. "He's not really such a bad fellow," Goldwater would say. "He's more conservative than you would imagine. You ought to talk to him someday." Goldwater, in turn, received the satisfaction of hearing Rocky mouthing conservative positions—although in private Rockefeller compared Goldwater's supporters to "cattle that aren't going anywhere. They're scared and they'll fly off in any direction." Rockefeller shot past Goldwater in the polls at the beginning of 1962. Everyone who was anyone put short odds on him for the nomination.

Everyone-who-was-anyone did not include febrile college kids, southern California right-wingers, or Southern segregationists. And these groups had different ideas.

Young Americans for Freedom had weathered its rocky patch. Rusher and Liebman had consolidated their purge of Caddy's faction by taking out an ad in the back of *National Review* for an executive director. It was read by a young lawyer from Houston, Richard Viguerie—one of those devout Catholics with Democratic parents. He had spent all his time in the office of the Harris County Republican Party, fell in love with the nuts-and-bolts side of political organizing, was desperate to go out East to work in the conservative movement, and got an interview on the strength of testimonials from his Texas friend David Franke. When Viguerie came to New York, Liebman showed him his mail room: thousands and thousands of three-by-five cards, a Robotype machine, the accoutrements of a veritable propaganda factory. Seeing Viguerie's eyes widen, Liebman knew he had their man. When Viguerie reported to begin the job, the first thing Liebman told him was that YAF was $20,000 in debt, with only 2,000 paid members, although the organization claimed a membership of 25,000: "It's important that membership be perceived at 25,000," Liebman explained. He gave him a list of 1,200 conservative donors and showed him the phone. Viguerie's first three calls brought in $4,500.

Young Americans for Freedom reserved Madison Square Garden on March 7 for the group's second rally, and it spooked them to the bone. JFK's popularity rating was approaching 80 percent. Where would YAF find 18,000 conservatives in New York City? Senator Thomas J. Dodd of Connecticut, a former FBI agent and the Democrats' most assiduous red-hunter, was lined up to speak at the rally—but when he returned from a trip to Africa and learned that the honorees included General Walker, he withdrew his name. Walker's participation was also too much for publicity-savvy Liebman—who made his living crafting massive bipartisan anticommunist coalitions for his groaning letterheads backing some beleaguered pro-West government or other. He promptly resigned from his consulting position with YAF. A month before the rally, Dodd released a statement attacking the "extremist coloration of the gathering"—at which *Goldwater* briefly refused to appear. YAF finally cut Walker loose. The contretemps was reported widely in the press.

The Tshombe affair brought more bad publicity. When the southern African state of Katanga seceded from the Republic of the Congo, it took half of the country's mineral wealth with it. The new state's leader was a pro-West, virulently anticommunist Methodist named Moise Tshombe ("Uncle Tshombe," to the American black press). Lumumba had accepted Soviet aid to put down the rebellion. The White House chose to publicly back UN forces supporting Lumumba, which put the United States on the record in an apparently Soviet-sponsored enterprise (at the same time, the CIA soon saw to Lumumba's assassination). Mineral companies began a massive PR campaign for their friend Tshombe's claim on Katanga. The publicists found an active partner in conservatives eager to preserve a "Christian West" bulwark in Central Africa. Tshombe was scheduled for a U.S. tour that would include an appearance at the YAF rally—which had the potential to pose enormous complications for Kennedy's Africa policy. So, as the date for Tshombe's junket approached, the State Department denied Tshombe a visa.

But this time the silver lining trumped the cloud: by March, everyone in New York knew about Young Americans for Freedom and their rally. Even though a vicious storm whipped the entire Atlantic Coast for the occasion, thousands had to be turned away at the doors. They were forced to yell at the counterdemonstration instead.

At first it seemed that the left-out conservatives might have gotten the better part of the bargain: outside, lefties, having earlier almost broken up on the shoals of a disagreement between the Americans for Democratic Action kids and Students for a Democratic Society over what to print on the leaflets, were now advancing to fisticuffs. Inside, the program was a bore. Platform guests invited to say a few words droned on and on. Bob Schuchman couldn't begin the awards presentation because of the noisy claque chanting "We Want Walker! We Want Walker!" Brent Bozell, flown in from Spain, was supposed to be warming up the crowd for Goldwater. But he began sententiously lecturing the crowd on something called the "Gnostic Heresy." The rafters were buzzing with paper airplanes fashioned from the glossy special edition of *New Guard* when Bozell finally changed his rhetorical tack. And suddenly the grand old auditorium came to life as he ripped into the peroration:

"To the Joint Chiefs of Staff: *Prepare an immediate landing in Havana!*

"To the Commander in Berlin: *Tear down the wall!*

"To our chief of mission in the Congo: *Change sides!*"

The crowd leapt to their feet.

It was almost 11 p.m. when John Tower, who had won Vice President Johnson's Senate seat (thanks, in part, to the help of Stephen Shadegg), and who was the first Republican senator from the Old Confederacy since Reconstruction, took the stage to give the penultimate speech. Now the place was pulsing with energy. It was something special; something to remember your whole life.

Barry Goldwater was unimpressed. The thought of addressing a rally that was designed to look like a nominating convention—*his* nominating convention—made him nauseous. The hours of speeches had tested his patience. And backstage he let loose a stream of profanity—against Bozell, against YAF, against all these damned amateurs who were so eager to decide his political future—that would have done a sailor proud.

Goldwater's impatience made his introduction, by a kid named William Schulz, the shortest speech of the evening: "Ladies and gentlemen, I give you the conservatives' choice for president, Barry Goldwater!" It was also the best received: five minutes of applause broke over Goldwater in waves, as he stood at the podium in plain annoyance. Streamers and balloons fell from the ceiling. Banners waved. The crowd began chanting "We Want Barry! We Want Barry!" When he finally got an opening, he snarled, "Well, if you'll shut up, you'll get him."

The next morning the *New York Times* gave over three columns on its front page to a dramatic photograph taken from the stage, a sea of faces, balloons, placards, and American flags. YAF took home $80,000. Leaders laid plans to fill Yankee Stadium the next year. They were so carried away that few noticed that Goldwater's speech, streamers still dribbling down from the rafters, was more appropriate to the rubber-chicken circuit than to a rally. Supposedly entitled "To Win the Cold War," it turned out to be a dry examination of the Republicans' electoral chances in New York City in 1962. The *New York Times* gave half its space to sympathetic coverage of the counterdemonstration.

Three thousand miles to the west, Richard Nixon was suffering.

The pressure for him to run for governor had begun shortly after he had moved into his little apartment on Wilshire Boulevard in Los Angeles in February of 1961. The California GOP, decimated from 1958, needed a strong figure to bring it back to health. The incumbent Pat Brown's popularity was at an all-time low. The idea of running was tempting. Boredom was driving Nixon out of his mind. Perhaps he really believed that summer that he was still undecided. But anybody who advised him *not* to run, state Republican chair Caspar Weinberger recalled, "he barely spoke to again." Nixon felt no great desire to be governor of California. The plan was to cruise to an easy victory; then he would have an excuse not to run for President in 1964. He had had enough of running against the Kennedys. They fought dirty. He would wait and reach for the brass ring in 1968 with a unified California Republican Party as his base.

Little did he know that the political rules had been rewritten in California: the Orange County style was taking over the Republican Party. Nixon had never considered that another announced Republican candidate, a far-out conservative state assembly minority leader from Orange County and erstwhile University of Southern California football star, Joe Shell, would stay in the race. Shell had 2 percent in the polls. He would be running against a former U.S. vice president and Republican presidential nominee. But Shell had no interest in withdrawing. Doing so would mean making an accommodation with the liberal Republicans, which in Orange County Republican circles was but a few steps removed from accommodation with Communists.

California's unusually weak party system, created by early-century progressives who viewed the two parties as mere instrumentalities by which the railroads expedited graft, profoundly amplified the power of extra-party volunteer organizations such as the Young Republicans and the California Republican Assembly. Nixon assumed he would own such groups, given the tacit accord that had long obtained in California Republican circles: conservatives supported moderate candidates in exchange for back-room influence in party and policy decisions. That, he learned, was then.

Young Republicans nationwide had a reputation for being innocent spoils-seeking toadies—energetic but harmless, like their mascot, the cute little boxing elephant "Punchy." Nixon, the returned veteran made good, had once been their hero. But the Los Angeles County Young Republicans brought Nixon his first shock of the gubernatorial primary season. The "difference between a 'lib-

eral' Republican and a 'liberal' Democrat," wrote the organization's new president, a pale, silver-haired, mercurial fellow named Bob Gaston, "is the difference between creeping socialism and galloping socialism." The movement that
swept Gaston into office was experienced by the old regulars as if it were an
alien invasion. Two thousand attended meetings where once there had been
two hundred; the two hundred were branded "country club Republicans" and
red-baited. In return, they Birch-baited the newcomers. Nixon's first move in
the campaign seemed obvious: denounce the group that was causing all the
trouble, the John Birch Society. The LACYR responded by censuring Nixon
for attacking "patriotic organizations"; then they endorsed Shell.

Going into the annual California Republican Assembly convention, Nixon
could write off all this business as the impetuousness of youth. Nixon's strong
right hand, Murray Chotiner, was a former CRA president. The CRA was Earl
Warren's creation—like Warren himself, leaning toward the progressive wing
of the party. Nixon and California's popular senator Thomas Kuchel, the
minority whip, who was up for reelection, brought a resolution to the convention condemning the "dictatorial and totalitarian" John Birch Society. But
the CRA, too, now included a swarm of right-wingers. A Newport Beach
optometrist named Nolan Frizzelle had spearheaded an effort to charter dozens
of new CRA chapters, and for conservatives to flood existing ones. They had
turned the CRA inside out. "I don't consider the John Birch Society extremists," Frizzelle said. "Except maybe extremely American."

Nixon left the CRA convention with an embarrassingly close endorsement
vote and a humiliating compromise on his resolution, condemning Robert
Welch but professing neutrality on the group that was constitutionally an
extension of Robert Welch's will. Shell called the result "a major move in
breaking the old Establishment machine in California." Kuchel was enraged.
Two right-wing nuts were scratching each other's eyes out to replace the senator in the primary. Loyd Wright, a divorce lawyer whose campaign was chaired
by Ronald Reagan (after Reagan turned down entreaties to run himself), advocated an offensive nuclear strike against the Soviet Union. Howard Jarvis was
a loud, angry man who proclaimed himself "to the right of Barry Goldwater."
(His campaign was led, Nixon was aghast to learn, by Murray Chotiner.)

This was Shell's army. It was lubricated by some of Nixon's wealthiest
supporters from 1960: Walter Knott; Union Oil's Cy Rubel; Western Geophys-
ical's Henry Salvatori; dog-food king D. B. Lewis; Joe Crail of Coast Federal
S&L; Patrick Frawley, maestro of Paper Mate, Schick Safety Razor, and Technicolor. Shell campaigned with veiled threats. At a May 23 rally, aided by the
benisons of a sixty-two-voice choir and pom-pom-waving "Shell's Belles," he
hinted to the fifteen thousand assembled at the L.A. Sports Arena that "a large

number of Republicans would not vote for Richard Nixon" in a general election. "A sizable part would not get out and work for him." And thanks to powerhouse organizing by Shell's campaign manager, Rus Walton, a brilliant, driven former corporate publicist and National Association of Manufacturers administrator who had somehow managed to pull together the chaos of southern California's multitude of conservative groups into an integrated strike force, Shell had the power to make good on the threat.

Nixon hadn't even expected to have to campaign. Now he found himself once more bumping along forlorn highways in the most remote corners of this enormous state, just as he'd done back in 1950 when he ran for the Senate. The highways were less bumpy now, but they were also dotted with billboards with Earl Warren's face: "WANTED FOR IMPEACHMENT FOR GIVING AID AND COMFORT TO THE COMMUNIST CONSPIRACY," "THE MORTAL ENEMY OF THE UNITED STATES AND THE AMERICAN PEOPLE." While Shell addressed rallies, Nixon was spending an interminable 100-degree afternoon shaking hands in the desert in the southeast of the state. Pat Brown had pulled ahead of Nixon in the polls for the first time. Day after day, fanatics pressed into his hand yet another copy of that damned little blue pamphlet with the United Nations insignia on the cover, Department of State Publication 7277, which they claimed was proof that the government was about to sign over America's armed forces to a Soviet colonel. (Actually it was a woolly UN report setting a course for atomic disarmament over something like a century "through the progressive strengthening of international institutions under the United Nations and by creating a United Nations Peace Force to enforce the peace as the disarmament process proceeds." One of the assistant secretary-generals of the UN was a Russian colonel. Q.E.D.) It could have been just then that Richard Nixon cemented his title as the Job of American politics.

Shell won 35 percent of the ballots in the June 5 primary. In return for delivering his supporters in the fall, he demanded control of one-third of the state's delegation to the 1964 GOP Convention, and that Nixon pledge to slash the state budget. Nixon refused the deal. Shell said Nixon would be sorry.

The RNC chair who replaced Thruston Morton in 1962, Bill Miller, a brash conservative from upstate New York, poured resources into Operation Dixie, the party's Southern organizing drive. It had paid off handsomely. *Time* enshrined the young Republican operatives as "The New Breed": "furrow-browed, button-down, college-trained amateurs who, one by one, took control of the state parties from apathetic and aging professionals." Alabama's John Grenier had registered as a Republican after reading the Democrats' liberal 1960 convention platform. At twenty-nine he became the chairman of Birmingham's twelve-member Young Republicans chapter. Now, as part of Operation Dixie, he traveled the state five nights a week on the RNC's dime—conducting forty-four meetings in one forty-day stretch, sometimes in a town's general store. In South Carolina, colleague J. Drake Edens Jr. used the AFL-CIO manual *How to Win* to organize precincts. His rule was that a precinct had to have six members. He wouldn't give up until a county had three precincts. For some counties it took a dozen trips. "We've got a product and a sales force, just like a business," Grenier told *Time*. "The product is conservatism."

Regulars in other regions were cooking up schemes just to keep the party from shrinking. Conservative Wisconsin congressman Melvin Laird led an ecumenical committee of conservatives and moderates that produced a boiler-plate "Declaration of Republican Principle and Policy." General Eisenhower convened an "All-Republican Conference" at the Gettysburg farm to which he had retired to charter a "National Citizens Committee"—to attract the great quantities of Americans he assumed were sympathetic to Republican values but blanched at the Republican Party. Goldwater smelled a liberal power grab, but kept his criticisms from the General out of respect. Not so his new Dixie acolytes. "The fact that you were politically naive has been obvious for quite some time," thirty-two-year-old Mississippi chair and insurance executive Wirt Yerger wrote the man who had faced down Adolf Hitler. "I don't blame all the troubles of the Republican Party on you, but I do think that you will have to take responsibility for a great many." He then laid plans to convene a meeting of Republican state chairmen in Dallas after the November 1962 elections to force a reckoning with a new balance of power in the party.

In South Carolina, Drake Edens managed the campaign of William D. Workman Jr. for Senate. The campaign perfectly crystallized what the Republican Party was up to in the South—and the incredible progress it would make in 1962.

Workman was a popular columnist and TV commentator, and his 1960 book *The Case for the South* was a masterpiece of courtly segregationism: the Southerner, he wrote, merely demanded "the right to administer his own domestic affairs, and he demands for himself the right to rear his children in the school atmosphere most conducive to their learning." His campaign was based on the argument that although his opponent, the legendary sixty-six-year-old three-termer Olin D. Johnston, was a fine segregationist himself, any Democrat was necessarily in hock to the national party leadership. And since the "Kennedy Klan" had staked the party's future on cynical civil rights dema-goguery, Johnston would be helpless to preserve the Southern way of life.

It was tough sledding. Workman tried to tie Johnston to the dreaded Kennedy Klan's tail by reminding voters that he had been a leader in the fight for Kennedy's Medicare plan and a point man for the Administration's farm support legislation. But most South Carolinians *liked* farm supports and the idea of medical insurance for the aged. And they still instinctually recoiled at the idea of joining the party of the carpetbaggers. Whenever Edens received a letter of support, he answered it by asking the correspondent to join or start a GOP precinct organization. Few had the courage to do so. They feared they would become local pariahs.

Then the campaign received a boost: South Carolina, like the rest of Dixie, would soon come to hate Washington more than ever. In late September federal marshals began massing to protect the matriculation of the first Negro student at the University of Mississippi in Oxford. Thousands of Oxfordians massed behind Confederate battle flags and prepared for a vigilante war. (Such flags were everywhere in 1962, a year of centennial observances of the War Between the States. The South Carolina legislature even decided to fly a Confederate flag temporarily above the statehouse.) General Walker came to lend moral support, announcing that he had been on the "wrong side" in Little Rock. On September 30, President Kennedy announced that the White House was committed to seeing James Meredith enter Ole Miss. There immediately followed an attempt to breach the building holding the federal marshals, the oldest and most venerated on campus—first with bullets, then with a bulldozer, then with an armada of cars. The violence escalated to furious rioting. By the end of the week two were dead, and 23,000 federal troops were stationed in Oxford, Mississippi. The South called it another invasion, same as the one a hundred years earlier.

Goldwater immediately criticized the Kennedy Administration's actions. "We haven't turned over to the federal government the power to run the schools. . . . I don't like segregation. But I don't like the Constitution kicked around, either." He also said that the Administration was now the "best tool the Republican Party has." And South Carolina's Workman, at least, was proving Goldwater right. Now the candidate for the Senate spoke with Confederate flags behind him and cried that the Oxford invasion "takes on the earmarks of a cold-blooded, premeditated effort to crush the sovereign state of Mississippi into submission." He readily compared Kennedy to Hitler. "When South Carolina's turn comes, she'll defend her rights," he promised. A high school band struck up "Dixie"; he shouted, "I just hope that song could be heard all the way from Oxford, Mississippi, to Washington, D.C." There was little for Senator Johnston to do. He agreed with Workman. It was all he could say to implore voters not to abandon "the sacred party of their fathers." And on Election Day, the Republican Workman won 44 percent of the vote. Anywhere else that would have been considered a landslide victory for his opponent. But in South

Carolina—where a more typical general election vote was "W. J. Bryan Dorn, Democrat, 65,920; write-ins, 47"—44 percent of the vote for a Republican was a revolution.

In Alabama, thirty-seven-year congressional veteran Lister Hill was challenged for the first time in a general election. His Republican opponent, Gadsen oil distributor James Martin, lost by nine-tenths of a percent. In the race for the congressional seat representing Tennessee's Ninth District, Memphis— which hadn't seen a GOP *candidate* since 1936—the Republican came even closer. GOP congressional candidates across the South polled over two million votes in 1962. They had received 606,000 in the last off-year election. The Republicans, for an ever increasing number of Southerners, were carpetbaggers no more.

The pundits declared the off-year elections nationwide a draw. In Republican races moderates prevailed statistically over conservatives; among the gubernatorial winners were such pitch-perfect Republican moderates as Chafee in Rhode Island, Romney in Michigan, Love in Colorado, and Rhodes in Ohio. Forty-two percent of Americans thought Kennedy was pushing integration too fast. That kept Democratic totals down, although the Democrats still kept both houses of Congress. Though the Republicans likely would have done better if the world hadn't nearly ended.

On October 22, President Kennedy went on television to announce a quarantine of Soviet ships that had been fortifying a nuclear battery in Cuba capable of striking two-thirds of the territory of the United States. Then he went eyeball-to-eyeball with the Russians to demand the missiles' removal. A dull shock fell over the nation: the Armageddon that had been merely possible during the Berlin crisis was suddenly probable. The other guy blinked. The nation closed ranks around its President.

10

SUITE 3505

The pundits who declared the off-year elections yet one more endorsement of the responsible center had not read between the lines. To conservatives, the 1962 elections were a historic triumph.

Politics is not, except on the most elementary level, a game of raw numbers. It is one of margins. In a Senate party-line vote, 51 votes is as good as 91; in presidential nominations, the received wisdom on which states are "Republican" and which "Democratic," once upset, forever shifts calculations about which kind of candidate is a sure thing and which a hopeless case. Any game of margins is one of portents—where a trend, once rumored, can become the gust that blows the straw that settles on the proverbial camel's back. That is why the "Big Six" states and their black swing vote were so doted upon in conventional political speculations. More imaginative prognosticators, however, were beginning to argue that the next tipping point might be found somewhere else.

Or so *National Review* publisher Bill Rusher argued in an article published the winter after the 1962 elections called "Crossroads for the GOP." Rusher was sure that the message of the 1962 elections was that the Republican Party had to nominate Barry Goldwater over Nelson Rockefeller or face certain doom. The reason was the South. "Goldwater, *and Goldwater alone*, can carry enough Southern and border states to offset the inevitable Kennedy conquests in the big industrial states of the North and still stand a serious chance of winning the election," he wrote. He asked readers not just to take his word for it; he cited a Southern senator who claimed Bobby Kennedy had told him that the people in the White House considered Rockefeller a pushover, but were terrified of facing Goldwater.

Perhaps Goldwater could even win the second biggest state in the country. In California, Richard Nixon, without real issues to campaign on against an effective incumbent, was reduced to telling California voters that he would make an excellent governor because he knew how to handle Khrushchev. His attempt to win back Joe Shell's conservatives was doomed by an initiative on the ballot, the proposed Francis Amendment, to give grand juries power to identify "subversive organizations" and bar their members from public employment. Nixon's conscience wouldn't let him support it. So the Orange County types who voted for Shell in the primary refused to vote for Nixon in the general election—just as Shell had darkly warned months earlier. Nixon lost, 47 to 53. Nixon's ticket mate, Tom Kuchel, won by 700,000 votes. "You won't have Richard Nixon to kick around any more," Nixon growled in his acid concession speech, in which he also announced his retirement from politics. ABC broadcast a special called "The Political Obituary of Richard Nixon."

And the media's ongoing exposés of conservative excesses did nothing to stop California's far right from doing well. Every candidate who was a member of the John Birch Society got over 45 percent of the vote. John Rousselot lost only because his district was ruthlessly gerrymandered against him. And a stunning upset in the state school superintendent race, usually fought quietly on issues of competence, was won by Max Rafferty, a man who claimed progressive education could render students the tools of "red psychological warfare."

The *New York Times*'s top pundit, James "Scotty" Reston, wrote that Rockefeller had about as much chance of losing the Republican nomination as "going broke." It was a dubious claim. Rockefeller had been judged such a shoo-in for reelection in 1962 that New York Democrats had to go to extraordinary lengths just to find someone willing to run against him. The lucky fellow, State Attorney General Robert Morgenthau, was believed to be such a weak candidate that the party refused to waste more than $420,000 on his campaign. Rockefeller spent $2,184,000. On election eve it was widely reported that Rockefeller's margin of victory would be a million votes. He won by only 500,000. It was his ticket mate Jacob Javits, his ideological twin, who won by a million. And, most tellingly, a poll concluded that 80 percent of New York Democrats who voted for Rockefeller said they would vote for John F. Kennedy against Rockefeller in the 1964 presidential election. This was hardly the recipe for an ideal presidential nominee. But Reston knew who always controlled Republican presidential nominations; and this year, Rockefeller was the Establishment's man. There seemed nothing else to say. He was unaware of the extraordinary underground insurgency that was determined to write another ending to the story. He wouldn't have made anything of it if he was.

The revolutionary was never seen without a bow tie. Tall, gangly, gracious, Frederick Clifton White was a country boy from upstate New York who only partially overcame his shyness in public by becoming the star of his high school debating team. He also made it onto the basketball team, although it took him four years of untiring practice. His grades were below par. But there was also that aw-shucks charm. He entered Colgate University after talking his way into a personal meeting with the dean. He studied to be a schoolteacher and earned pin money giving patriotic speeches to local Kiwanis and Daughters of the American Revolution chapters. He entered the Army Air Corps as a private and emerged with a Distinguished Flying Cross. He reminded friends of Jimmy Stewart; you almost expected him to say "gee whiz." When he entered politics as a profession, he found his calling working behind the scenes. There, he was tougher than steel—Mr. Smith gone to Washington, exchanging intimacies with Plunkett of Tammany Hall.

White found his calling after the war, entering graduate school to study political science at Cornell and forming a chapter of the American Veterans Committee, a left-wing advocacy group. No leftist himself, he simply wanted to organize to fight the gouging Ithaca landlords who were taking advantage of a housing shortage and students rich with GI Bill cash. He found he liked doing politics much more than he liked studying it. It thrilled him. He became a statewide organizer for the AVC. That was how he learned that the AVC, like many liberal groups at the time, was the object of a takeover attempt by the American Communist Party. At the next state convention, he decided to run for chairman. He was on his way to easy victory when, during the balloting, a rumor suddenly swept the floor that the married White had shacked up with his secretary, using AVC funds to maintain their love nest. White was stunned.

But his floor manager, Gus Tyler, a veteran of the 1930s wars between socialists and Communists for control of the garment unions in New York, recognized exactly what was happening. The Communists had lain in wait to discredit White. That meant they were about to present their own candidate as an eleventh-hour white knight while their minions scurried about the floor convincing delegates that the Communists' secret man was the very embodiment of sweetness and light. Tyler hurriedly withdrew White's candidacy and substituted another from their faction, a respected law professor, but it was too late: the Communists had already lined up their votes—including two from White's own Cornell chapter. Now White was disconsolate. He felt violated. Tyler reassured him that the Communists had won because they were peerless organizers. "Learn from them," he said. "I've been fighting these bastards for a long time. The first thing you need to know is whom you can trust, who will stand up with you, whom you can work with."

And so, with customary earnestness, White learned. The Communists organized as cells, small face-to-face groups under the discipline of a single benign dictator, chosen for his willingness to act as an extension of the Party's will. White organized his AVC chapter into cells. "Each leader," he told his people, "will be personally responsible for his ten men, and he's going to tell them that we have an AVC meeting they all have to attend. I don't care what else is going on, short of death. When there's a vote coming up, everyone has to attend and cast his vote against the Communists"—even if the Communists put up a resolution in favor of motherhood and apple pie. That often was the opening wedge to ram through a resolution endorsing accommodation with Stalin.

The Communists deployed honeyed words to seize the chairmanship of a meeting, then manipulated parliamentary procedure to control it: by relocating a meeting to a room so small that they could crowd into it before others arrived and turn their minority into a majority; by making endless stalling motions to hold off critical votes until the wee hours of the morning, when only their troops remained; by slowly calling the roll votes that were going against them, using the window of time to lobby the swing votes, in then jacking the roll call to lightning speed once they had them; by maneuvering for their forces to vote at the point in a roll call where a candidate had 49 percent so they could negotiate concessions in exchange for putting him over the top; by imposing the unit rule—whereby a delegation votes as a bloc so that a proposal with majority support can be made to appear unanimous—whenever the vote was auspicious to them; by calling a lightning vote when enough of their opposition's forces were out of the room, and then calling for adjournment.

There was no reason, White decided, that anticommunists couldn't use the same techniques to defeat them. Later he would use them to take over the Republican Party.

The next year, when White came up for reelection as chair of his AVC chapter, he gaveled the meeting to order and his Communist opponent immediately rose to observe that, as a candidate and an honorable man, surely he was going to relinquish the chair. No way, White said. The opponent put forward a heartfelt motion for "fair play." White ruled it out of order. At the national convention in Milwaukee, White booked his delegation's block of rooms far enough in advance to assure they would stay in the hotel where the meetings took place—so that, when the Communists began their predawn maneuvers, he could ring his soundly sleeping deputies in their rooms and call them down to vote. *Robert's Rules of Order* was a Promethean tool.

While teaching political science at Cornell and Ithaca College from 1949 to 1951, he attracted the notice of a Republican reform group seeking a congressional candidate to run against the local machine. He ran and was defeated.

Then he joined the machine. He would do any menial job they asked; every-thing was an education. Driving little old ladies to the polls election after elec-tion, he found they began asking for his advice on whom to vote for: loyalty was powerful; so was getting your people to the polls on Election Day. Before long he was Tompkins County GOP chair—an exceptionally inventive one, with a thousand little political tricks up his sleeve. Mayoral candidates in small towns were advised to introduce themselves personally to every registered voter, then "pray for a low turnout." Party poll-watchers were instructed, "Never leave anything to people's imaginations. When you go through a [sam-ple] ballot form with voters, mark it up the way you want them to vote."

All the while he got swept up in Young Republican politics. It had nothing to do with ideology; members of the Young Republican National Federation were constitutionally bound to help elect whatever candidates the party hap-pened to nominate. It was a hobby. In 1948 White had struck up a friendship with Bill Rusher, then a young Wall Street lawyer who was eager to have upstate allies in the Hatfield-and-McCoy-like feud his New York YR faction was fighting with another faction led by the charismatic young John Lindsay. No one really remembered its origins; all were moderate Republican loyalists of Governor Thomas Dewey. It seemed more a cultural thing than anything else. Rusher and his friends bristled at the blue-bloodism of Lindsay's group; a third group set itself apart because its members worked in midtown Manhattan, as opposed to Lindsay's and Rusher's Wall Street, and were mostly Jewish. Rusher and White's team prevailed. They dubbed themselves the Action Fac-tion. And they decided their next project would be to build a national Young Republican political machine.

The key was manipulating regional balances of power. Midwesterners controlled the national organization. So at the 1949 convention in Salt Lake City the Action Faction ran a Michigander, John Tope. That gave them two of the biggest delegations, theirs and Michigan's, right out of the gate, meaning that they needed only a few more states to win—which they did. In 1951 they perfected the technique of finding a nonentity willing to submit to their disci-pline. The man was Herbert Warburton, from Delaware. White, Rusher, and deputies sprinted across the convention hall with voting instructions to their people on how to handle the tortuous procedural votes, meanwhile lining up delegates for a Willkie-style upset that took five ballots. It took a week of advance work at the site, during which time they had gotten the equivalent of a single night's sleep between them. Rusher was so spent at the climax that he sat down on the convention floor and cried tears of exhaustion and euphoria.

White sat alone in his hotel room, beset by an enveloping gloom, watching bland Herb Warburton harvesting accolades on television. "How would you like to be chairman of the Young Republican National Federation?" he had asked Warburton long ago. For the first time in days the phone wasn't ringing.

Clif White began his ten-year rule as puppeteer of the Young Republican National Federation from behind the desk of a patronage job at the Department of Motor Vehicles in Albany, quid pro quo for running National Youth for Eisenhower in 1952. The YR's geographical margins were shifting: at the 1953 convention White won by getting loyalists from the South and West. These delegates were considerably more conservative. But the Action Faction was tacking to the right, too. Rusher heard Barry Goldwater speak for the first time in 1955 and found a hero. The next year he left Wall Street to become a counsel to the Senate Internal Security Committee, the upper chamber's HUAC. By 1957, shortly after Goldwater won his first spurt of renown with his speech savaging Ike's budget, Rusher and White's faction won handily by running a fierce conservative, Ohio's John Ashbrook. The resolutions committee, traditionally a fount of milquetoast pronouncements on patriotism and the grandness of the Grand Old Party, now won a front-page headline in the *New York Times*: "YOUNG GOP HITS IKE ON 4 OUT OF 5 ISSUES."

By then Governor Dewey was out of office. Clif White had gone into business. His company, Public Affairs Counselors, ran seminars for corporate executives interested in getting involved in politics, which once would have seemed a thankless task: for Fortune 500 executives, politics had long meant little more than sending along a few well-placed checks and making a few phone calls every fourth summer to vouchsafe an acceptable nominee at the Republican Convention. Politics, as opposed to lobbying, meant taking a side; lobbying a congressman was difficult if you'd just filled his opponent's coffers to the gills. Customers, suppliers, employees, local governments—all stood to be offended when a corporation took a stand. And if there was one thing that marked the corporate world in the 1950s, it was a disinclination to offend. The success of the AFL-CIO's Committee on Political Education in getting out the labor vote in 1958 to decimate pro-business congressmen began changing all that. Suddenly White had the corner on a new industry. GM hired him to create a system of seminars for its entire executive staff. Allen-Bradley did the same. And such was Harry Bradley's stature in Wisconsin—and so powerful was the example of the Kohler strike—that just about every sizable company in the Dairy State followed suit. Newspapers began to speak of the businessmen-in-politics movement as a new force to be reckoned with.

For White, it was another chance for him to expand his political education. Public Affairs Counselors' approach was relentlessly local. In every city where he spoke, White compiled a booklet explaining the local election codes—how Democratic and Republican convention delegates were selected, how precinct meetings were organized, how the city and state governments were arranged, and on and on. Sometimes there had never been such a publication before; most times the information was out of date—and in Missouri (the Show-Me State, supposedly) electoral rules had never been fully *codified* before (White presented his work to the state as a gift). White's political erudition was becoming epic. So was his political network. It was said that Franklin Roosevelt used to impress visitors to the Oval Office by telling them to draw a line across a map of the United States; then he would proceed to name every county through which it passed and the political peculiarities of each. Clif White might have been the only other human being by the end of the 1950s who could have worked the same trick. And he was about to get a chance to put it to work.

In 1959 White lost control of the New York Young Republicans to an influx of loyalists of the new governor, Nelson Rockefeller. Without White's New York keystone, many assumed his control of the national body was over. The judgment was premature. His coalition earned a new nickname after that 1959 convention: the Syndicate. They won by stretching their South-West-Midwest conservative coalition—New York notwithstanding—to the breaking point. It got White thinking. Young Republican delegations mirrored Republican National Convention delegations. Could a *presidential* candidate now do what Bob Taft could not—eschew New York and still win the nomination?

One day in the summer of 1961 Bill Rusher, by this time *National Review* publisher, lunched in Washington at the House restaurant at the Capitol with his friend John Ashbrook, then a freshman congressman. They fell to nostalgic reverie; then talk turned, as it always did when Republicans gathered in 1961, to their party's pathetic condition. "If we held a meeting of our old Young Republican group," Rusher said, "it would probably comprise about the third or fourth largest faction in the Republican Party."

It was an offhand remark. But Ashbrook perked up. There hadn't been a contested Republican nomination since the Taft-Eisenhower fight in 1952. Most of the old Establishment pros were too old and tired to win one if they tried. Ashbrook dragged Rusher back to his office and pulled open a file drawer: there was his correspondence from 1957 to 1959, when he was Young Republican chair, all of it arranged alphabetically by state, then alphabetically within state, folder after folder. Many of their old allies were now powerful men. Rusher and Ashbrook looked at each other, exchanged a few words, and began copying down names.

Rusher called Clif White. White had sold his stake in PAC when he became organizing chairman for Volunteers for Nixon-Lodge in 1960. The

Nixon presidential loss had disillusioned White badly. It was his staff that had discovered the notorious irregularities that had so famously and closely swung Illinois for Kennedy. When Nixon declined to demand a recount, White wondered what damage all those ideological twists and turns had done to Nixon's soul. White was forty-one, a full-time political operative—one of the best. And he was at a crossroads. He began to wonder just what all this expertise was *for*.

His midlife crisis had come at the right time.

Rusher and White met for lunch in the city. Rusher related his conversation with Ashbrook three days earlier about all those tired old pros. "Sitting ducks," White agreed. By a coincidence worthy of a novel, at a nearby table sat two of those ducks: Tom Stephens, Ike's old appointment secretary, and Bill Pfeiffer, the former New York GOP chair. "They are plotting nothing less than the election of Nelson Rockefeller as the next president of the United States," White joked. It was a bit of psychological projection. Rusher and White were the ones doing the plotting. Rusher introduced the idea of reorganizing their old Young Republican machine to nominate the next President. But White was already one step ahead of him. He unspooled his own plan to do the very same thing.

White called Charlie Barr in Chicago, an old business contact and lobbyist for Standard Oil of Indiana, for advice. It was said of Barr that whatever he didn't know about politics in the Midwest wasn't worth knowing. Barr was not a wide-eyed ideologue; neither did he suffer fools gladly. He was the acid test. And he liked their idea. It couldn't be that crazy.

That week Rusher, White, and Ashbrook chose twenty-six people to invite to a secret meeting in Chicago on October 8, 1961. Barry Goldwater had just appeared on ABC's *Issues and Answers* and said, "I am not interested at all in 1964 in any way."

The twenty-six men were told only that Rusher, White, and Ashbrook were getting together some old friends to talk politics in Chicago, and that it was important that they come. The bonds were tight: on the strength of that call alone, twenty-two made the trip. Two were congressmen, another a state treasurer, two were lobbyists. There was a small-town newspaper publisher, a national party committeeman, and the chairman of Maine's Republican Party. Another was chief counsel of the Senate Internal Security Committee. A few were political affairs officers at large corporations. Gerrish Milliken, Roger's brother, represented one of the biggest fortunes in the conservative movement. These men were not dilettante factory owners; they were political professionals.

They met incognito, at a Chicago motel best known as a place for romantic assignations. They felt delight at just being together once again. White did the talking; it took him three hours to explain his strategy to upend the Republican Party and nominate a conservative for President. He didn't dare mention the name Goldwater—as if that would be tempting fate. They all knew who he meant. They adjourned, forgetting that the fourth game of the World Series had just taken place. No one asked the score. They were so engrossed that they hadn't given the Series a thought.

Rusher contacted Goldwater to ask for a Washington meeting on behalf of the group, including Roger Milliken and John Ashbrook. Smelling one more outfit wanting to run him for President, but casting his eye over the list and seeing that the people were not influential enough in the Republican Party to do too much damage, yet were of sufficient stature not to warrant offense, he told his secretary to fit them in. When the day came, the man before them wearing the vest with the Navajo glyphs under his suit jacket was not pleased. He had been promised Rusher, a magazine publisher, Ashbrook, a congressman, and Milliken, one of the richest men in the South; he saw before him only Rusher and a failed candidate for Nebraska lieutenant governor, Charlie Thone. Goldwater was mollified, at least, to hear that the men were only interested in doing a little organizing for the conservative electoral cause for the 1962 elections, a year away, and perhaps to get a hard start thinking about nominating a conservative for the presidential race. (Their secret hope was that by the time their effort was well under way, their momentum would be so undeniable that Goldwater would have no choice but to commit to a run.) They left the meeting with a copy of his speaking schedule. He promised to make time for their people whenever they crossed his path. White breathed a sigh of relief.

They filled out their roster with a few more trusted friends and scheduled a meeting for December. White unfurled a map of the United States and explained the grand strategy. States were colored in blue, green, or red, for those that possibly, probably, or almost certainly would go for Goldwater at the 1964 Republican Convention. Bob Taft's ugly convention defeat at the hands of the Northeastern swing vote in 1952 had been a formative political memory for these men. When White explained that a convention could be won *without* the Northeast, they understood that what he was describing was a revolution. No one had ever convincingly claimed that a Republican presidential candidate could be nominated without winning New York. He said 637 of the 655 delegates needed to win the nomination were likely already in the bag. Many Republican organizations across the country, he explained, withered from eight slack years under Eisenhower, enervated by the agonizing 1960 Nixon loss, weren't really organizations at all. If five people showed up for precinct meetings, it took only six conservatives to take the precinct over. Enough precincts and you had a county. Then a congressional district. If you got enough congressional districts, then you had a state. With just the people in this room and a network of loyal friends, they could have the Republican Party, as easy as pushing on an open door.

The room was buzzing.

He explained their base: the Midwest, the Southwest—and the South. In 1964 their delegates wouldn't be available to the highest bidder as in the old "post office" days. Now there were real Republican organizations in Dixie. And their members worshiped Goldwater. White gestured at his map, and proceeded to explain in dizzying detail what hardly anybody else in the nation understood: the occult process by which a presidential candidate won delegates to the Republican National Convention.

At the convention, he explained, each state got four at-large delegates plus a delegate for each congressional district that cast two thousand votes for either Nixon in 1960 or the Republican House candidate in 1962; plus an extra at-large delegate for each Republican congressman; and six additional delegates-at-large if the state had gone for Nixon or elected a Republican senator or governor in 1960. The formula overrepresented the smaller states, where Republican activists were most conservative. And the balance of power, he explained, had been turning in their favor. In 1940 34.9 percent of the convention's votes came from the South and West. In 1964 it would be 43.4 percent.

He talked about the Rube Goldberg–like system for selecting delegates. Different in each state, the rules were generally set by statute, usually in concert with a body of obscure tradition. Sixteen states had binding primaries, and together these states selected about a third of the delegates to the convention. They would enter few of these. Winning pluralities in the beauty pageants was an expensive, wild-card proposition; dark horses like Nixon could be expected to pour massive resources into the "Big Six" states with early primaries, like Illinois, to signal their electability. No candidate was ever guaranteed a nomination because of a dramatic primary win; but plenty—Stassen in Oregon in 1948, Humphrey in West Virginia in 1960—had slunk away after an embarrassing loss.

The fact was, most delegates were chosen not in voting booths but in hotel ballrooms at state party conventions. The old saw was that state delegates were highly susceptible to manipulation by congressmen, senators, governors, and mayors—now dangling, now withholding patronage to delegates to get them to agree to run for a berth at the national convention "uncommitted," whence power brokers could cash them in for a candidate desperate to go over the top in exchange for a handsome consideration. But bosses only controlled delegates if their bait was taken, and White's plotters would search for conservatives who were more interested in saving Western civilization than in gaining a spot on the streets and sanitation commission. The rules were often so obscure and complex that just *knowing* them would give the insurgents an enormous advantage.

Their work would begin at the dewiest grassroots level, recruiting and training candidates to stand for election to the precinct conventions; those people, in turn, would select delegates to the county conventions; these, finally, would choose the national convention delegates. Some states nominated favorite sons for President, a gambit that allowed them to hold their delegates in reserve on the first ballot and to sell them to the highest bidder on the second. Where appropriate White and his people would encourage this—a favorite-son delegation could become a powerful Trojan horse if all the members were really gung ho for Goldwater. Sometimes it paid to look weak. That made you more intimidating once you proved yourself strong.

It was just as Clif White learned from the Communists—and also from John F. Kennedy's Irish Mafia, who had started working the precincts shortly after the 1956 convention. A single small organization, from a distance and with minimal resources, working in stealth, could take on an entire party. They didn't need the big fish, the governors, senators, mayors. They didn't need the little fish, the individual voters. They just needed enough middling fish. The plotters left the meeting with their heads spinning. Roger Milliken pledged $30,000 on the spot. They were on their way.

White rented an office high atop the Chanin Building, across from Grand Central Terminal. It was an art deco masterpiece, surely a monument to the glories of the civilization he had consecrated himself to save. But White just liked his suite because it was tucked into the back corner of the floor, invisible from the elevator. The door read, simply, "3505." That became the group's code name: Suite 3505. He squeezed desks for himself and a secretary between forests of file cabinets, filled with intelligence on every Republican worth knowing in the country. White then set out to assemble his nationwide team. His wife, Bunny, steeled herself for political widowhood.

He prepared for his first organizing trip by having his comrades identify the solid, trustworthy conservatives in their region, whom White would gather for slide talks. In Texas, that effort was superfluous; he learned that their Goldwater organization was nearly in place already. In Jackson, Mississippi, he ran down his national delegate projections with Wirt Yerger and came up with an estimate that they had two hundred more than were needed to nominate a candidate. In Shreveport, Louisiana, he talked the night away with an oil man,

Charlton H. Lyons, who said he'd never gotten involved in politics before, but would be glad to join the Goldwater effort now. (In a few months, Lyons would be running for governor of Louisiana.) White hit the Midwest, then the West, posting confidential memoranda with no return address to his co-conspirators on his progress. In March he hit California. That was a sticky situation. The Birch wars in the gubernatorial primary were going full tilt, *National Review* had gone to press with its attack on Robert Welch, and the YAF-Walker controversy had boiled over. Two ministers' homes in the San Fernando Valley had been bombed after they decried right-wing extremism. Congressman John Rousselot had been one of the twenty-six at White and Rusher's original meeting. Now they had to decide whether it was safe to invite him to the second. If the press found out that their group existed, that would be bad enough. If they found out that the group harbored a Bircher, that could be their end. Rusher wanted to find out if Rousselot still took this Robert Welch nonsense seriously. He gave Rousselot a call—and the congressman asked Rusher how he could be absolutely *certain* that Eisenhower was not a Communist. Upon hearing this, White decided that it would be better to keep Rousselot off their rolls. He was asked to work on their behalf in secret. Rousselot—a good soldier and a good spy—agreed.

The third meeting, on April 13, was at a fishing camp in the still-frozen Minnesota lake country owned by 3M, one of White's old corporate clients. The big news that week was that U.S. Steel had defied the Kennedy Administration's voluntary "wage-price guideposts." That morning's *Herald Tribune* quoted Kennedy as saying that "businessmen were a bunch of s.o.b.'s." Those who thrilled at one of their number defying the creeping advance of the central planners responded with buttons reading "S.O.B.: SONS OF BUSINESS." For these particular s.o.b.'s, reading the news was like a pep rally. Fired up, they got an enormous amount of work done—when they weren't sitting in front of roaring fires clinking whiskey glasses or horsing around like frat boys. They had appointed regional directors; now these were presented with state-by-state rundowns of delegate procedures to memorize. White said it would take five grand a month to keep him on the road. They went around the room, and each pledged to raise generous amounts. White set a deadline of December to have in place a chairman, a women's chair, and a finance chair for each state. Things were going better than expected. Going to the Republican Convention with a majority of delegates now seemed within their reach. And, as White reminded them in his closing pep talk, even if they didn't go in with a majority—they knew every trick it would take in order to leave with one. They left Minnesota in a glow.

Then they hit a brick wall.

Suite 3505's plan was secret. If they named their goal—a Goldwater nomination—Goldwater would get wind of it and shut them down. If they didn't name their goal, why would people give money to them at all? All that White's new full-time fund-raiser could reveal when he made a pitch was that a group of important people (he couldn't say who) were working to advance the conservative cause (he couldn't say how) and ask them to make out the check to something called the "Tope-Fernald Agency Account"—not quite the accounting practice your typical sober-sided Republican businessman (like Pennsylvania's Richard Mellon Scaife, who turned them down indignantly) preferred. Meanwhile, back in November, White had squirmed through a meeting in which representatives of every major conservative organization in the country lines up behind Americans for Constitutional Action's push to put eighteen field men on the road for conservative candidates in the 1962 congressional elections. Who would want to give money to some vague idea about electing a conservative President in 1964 when an army for 1962 was being mustered? Clif White watched that spring as ACA sucked in thousands that might have gone to *them*—$6,000 alone from G.E.'s Lem Boulware, *Reader's Digest*'s DeWitt Wallace, and Johnson & Johnson's Robert W. Johnson. That was the exact amount White had already siphoned off from his children's college fund.

Again and again he returned to Washington to get his hands on the card files of Nixon delegates to the 1960 convention. He failed, with ever greater frustration, every time. In June he attended an RNC meeting in Seattle. So did a gang of Harvard kids, led by Bruce Chapman, a member of the team that had drafted the Compact of Fifth Avenue in 1960, and George Gilder, David Rockefeller's godson, who put out a new magazine called *Advance*—"flaming moderates," they called themselves. Chapman and Gilder had recently drummed up a movement that once again almost got Goldwater dumped as chairman of the Republican Senatorial Campaign Committee. *Advance* was all anyone talked about all weekend. While in Seattle, White was offered a corporate job. He almost took it. Suite 3505 took in a grand total of $300 in June. The organization let the rent slide.

It was excruciating: the broker they got, the more celebrated Barry Goldwater seemed to become. Washington State Republicans passed a resolution to declare Goldwater the party's only genuine spokesman. The 1960 delegates—the ones whose names and addresses White was still so desperate to obtain—were polled by the AP: 264 for Goldwater, 203 for Rockefeller, 137 for Nixon, 32 for Romney. In Texas, a straw poll gave Goldwater 1,115 votes to Rockefeller's 90. At Yale University, of all places, the senator was awarded the prestigious Chubb Fellowship, whose holder visited the campus for a week of lectures and casual interactions with the student body. The honor had previously seemed to be reserved for liberals—people like Abe Ribicoff and Adlai Stevenson. Campus conservatives joked that the idea must have been to exhibit Goldwater as a two-headed calf. Instead he held crowds spellbound: speaking on the necessity of using force in Southeast Asia, on the disastrous effects of unbalanced budgets—and on how his grandfather once had an Indian bullet extracted from his hide without benefit of anesthesia. Political science professors argued with him that a true conservative should embrace the stabilizing forces of the New Deal. Students were unmoved—or at least the twenty-five who marched into President A. Whitney Griswold's office with a thick petition demanding that more conservative faculty members be hired.

But Goldwater proved overwhelmed by all the attention. He removed himself from the lecture circuit for the first time in half a decade. The *Wall Street Journal*'s Robert Novak described it as "all but a Sherman-style disclaimer"— referring to Civil War hero General William Tecumseh Sherman's famous wire to the 1884 Republican National Convention: "I will not accept if nominated and will not serve if elected." And White had to decide what to do. Goldwater's amiable partnership with Rockefeller was by then well known. White, on the verge of eviction from the Chanin Building, told Rusher that Goldwater's retreat was the last straw: he was throwing in the towel. Rusher convinced him to press on. He pointed out that their most valuable assets lay elsewhere—in the network of county party chairs, precinct captains, and conservative activists White had won through hard organizing efforts over the past six months. And Rusher reminded White of his success in winning three crucial organizational beachheads. These were bases of power no amount of money could replace.

The first was the National Federation of Republican Women. The tradition in that group since time immemorial was for the annual September convention to rubber-stamp those officer candidates picked by a nominating committee. This year, Suite 3505 had run a slate of candidates to oppose them. Their candidates swept the election. This was invaluable. Women made up perhaps a fifth of the delegates to the Republican National Convention. Now Suite 3505 had taken over the organization best able to deliver these delegates to Goldwater.

Then there was the American Medical Association. The AMA had been organizing physicians against the specter of socialized medicine ever since Earl Warren began pushing for guaranteed health care in California in the early 1940s. When Harry Truman proposed a national health insurance system, the AMA retained the California PR firm Whittaker & Baxter to convince the country that Truman's goal was "to gain control over all fields of human endeavor." Soon the AMA was lobbying tirelessly against *any* expansion of federal power—fighting for the Bricker Amendment; against a federal Department of Health, Education, and Welfare; against JFK's campaign to expand the House Rules Committee. In the wake of the Rules Committee fight, the AMA formed the American Medical Political Action Committee. One of the committee's first actions was distributing LPs featuring Ronald Reagan warning that Kennedy's "Medicare" idea was "a foot in the door of a government takeover of *all* medicine." White had no trouble convincing the group's president-elect and the head of AMA-PAC to join Suite 3505 in a tactical alliance for 1964.

Finally, there was the Young Republican National Federation. In 1961 White had let the YR chairmanship slip away. He had handed down Syndicate leadership to a new generation of activists, and they had made an awful botch of the job. Now, in time-honored fashion, the YR machine faced a reform faction. Its candidate was a genial Minnesota corporate publicist named Leonard Nadasdy who pledged to bring the organization back to its constitutional mission as a neutral clearinghouse for all Republicans—not a playground for ideologues. Nadasdy trounced the Syndicate candidate. And as chair he performed flawlessly. Literature flurried off the presses—manuals for organizing college chapters and teenage clubs, guides to programming speakers and fund-raising and registering voters, a thick primer on running a campaign. Elaborate civil rights conferences were organized to convince Negroes to stay in the Republican column. Membership had stagnated under the Syndicate (they had more interest in putting together tractable paper chapters than in expanding membership). Under Nadasdy the organization's numbers were swelling. Now all fifty states had strong organizations, and thousands of members were ready to volunteer in the 1962 congressional elections. Nadasdy himself traveled the country campaigning for any Republican, conservative or liberal, who asked.

The Syndicate, however, kept the college chairmanship and Young Republican co-chair, a position reserved for a woman, for which they had an ace in the hole: their candidate, Chicago society girl Pat Hutar, was beauty-pageant stunning. She also hid an iron fist in her velvet glove. As for college chair, that was a job no reform faction could touch. College Republican conventions were like the old Southern Republican Party: all it took to control them was to set up rotten boroughs at dozens of colleges and load the convention with loyal Syndicate delegates. The Syndicate's college chair, Jim Harff of Northwestern, was as tough as Hutar. And for them, all of Nadasdy's evenhanded efforts were not good government; they were the malicious spoiling efforts of an ideological villain. Hutar and Harff sabotaged Nadasdy's efforts when they could—especially the civil rights conferences. And it wasn't two weeks before Hutar, Harff, and White met in Chicago to begin plotting to dominate the 1963 Young Republican national convention. White raised a travel budget for Hutar to begin lining up state delegations. And they got to work discrediting Nadasdy: learning he was about to leave for a European honeymoon, they circulated a rumor that he was abandoning the country for a month at the height of the congressional campaign.

Still, for Suite 3505, all seemed for naught. "I have never sought the nomination," Goldwater wrote pesky Wirt Yerger in September, "as I have told you many times. I have many reasons, but I wouldn't put money and organization last and neither of these has reared its ugly head." Of White's magnificent organization, he was oblivious.

The 1962 congressional elections—the "Crossroads for the GOP" that Rusher later celebrated in his *National Review* article—came and went. Conservatives' promising showing opened Suite 3505's fund-raising spigots. They had one party auxiliary and were on their way to taking back the other—both guaranteeing control of a nationwide organization, publicity apparatus, and a fat budget from the Republican National Committee's coffers. Their alliance with the American Medical Association was an insurance policy against financial ruin. State conventions to pick national presidential delegates were less than a year away. Their cover hadn't been blown. White met with Goldwater the week after the election and showed off his thick book of organizational charts, budgets, timetables, and delegate estimates. Once again the senator was neither encouraging nor discouraging—good enough for them. Suite 3505 had survived its Valley Forge. White called the company that had offered him that lucrative job and turned it down once and for all.

The key meeting was around the corner, December 1 and 2, 1962, in Chicago, the week before the annual RNC meeting. This time, White was confident enough to expand his circle of plotters to fifty-five. "This meeting will determine where we go," he wrote his original group, "—whether we are serious or dilettantes." Rocky, he assured them, was serious—attaching a memo from Jud Morhouse to New York county chairmen listing twenty-eight supposedly "conservative" positions the New York governor had recently taken, "for your use in talking to people who feel the Governor is strictly a Liberal." Morhouse concluded, "It must be used cautiously and should not be published because we do not want to emphasize the conservative side so much that we lose other votes." Meanwhile, Rockefeller, Romney, Scranton, Javits, Senator John Sherman Cooper of Kentucky, and Senator Hugh Scott of Pennsylvania, reported the *Herald Tribune*, had been convened in some sort of meeting by Senator Clifford Case of New Jersey. They were likely hashing out an idea for a moderate unified front behind Rocky for the 1964 nomination. The stakes were being raised.

When White's fifty-five settled around the big table at the jet-set-modern Essex Motel, he did something bold: he introduced the organization as one specifically committed to a Goldwater nomination. The session was opened with a prayer for God's blessing on their enterprise. Then he got down to politics. He displayed his map, delineating the twenty-eight states he had visited in the past year. They needed 655 convention votes to nominate. He said their goal was controlling 700 before the opening gavel. Of this number, 451 would come from nineteen states mostly in the West and South, and these states were already solid for Goldwater. Georgia, Kentucky, South Dakota, Tennessee, Illinois, Iowa, and Ohio could be counted on for 81 more—142 "with extra hard work." They would enter Goldwater in the California primary on June 2; the winner of that contest was guaranteed the state's entire 86-vote bloc. That was for insurance. White's budget for the previous year had been $65,000. For the nineteen months remaining he presented a budget of $3.2 million. Then a roly-poly millionaire with a big cowboy hat—"Stets" Coleman, from Virginia—hoisted himself out of his chair and announced: "Look, everybody's been talking about how we need all this money, but who's going to put some up? I pledge $25,000." Within an hour $200,000 was on the table; by the end of the meeting, $285,000. Alabama put up $25,000. The fifty-five divided themselves up into working committees. White proposed unveiling their secret fourteen weeks hence—by which time their momentum would be impossible to deny. Someone piped up that at last they would redeem Dwight D. Eisenhower's theft of the nomination in 1952 and nominate an honest-to-God conservative Republican candidate for President. All they had to do was work hard, keep the faith—and keep things quiet until they were ready to trap the liberals in the magnificent conservative web they had spun.

The next morning, back in Alabama, John Grenier answered his phone to find Arthur Edson of the Associated Press on the other end. Edson asked Grenier why he had just been to Chicago (for a Bears game, he said). Edson asked if Grenier had been at the Clif White meeting (silence). And where was he going to raise $25,000?

There had been a liberal Republican spy at the meeting, and no one ever discovered who it was.

The story went out over the AP wires that afternoon:

A secret, highly confidential meeting of leading Republicans who want Senator Barry Goldwater of Arizona for president was held in Chicago on Sunday.

The objective is to get, as one put it, "an honest-to-God conservative Republican candidate for president"—and incidentally, to try to block the road for Governor Nelson A. Rockefeller of New York.

Walter Cronkite rushed down to Chicago to do a stand-up in front of the meeting room at the Essex. His report was accompanied by a near-perfect reproduction of White's electoral map. Front-page headlines blared: "SECRET MEET TO PUSH GOLDWATER IN 1964"; "GOLDWATER '64 BOOM: MOVE TO BLOCK ROCKY." The *Herald Tribune* editorial bemoaned the group's strategy as "bad timing, narrow motives, and poor politics." Columnist Joe Alsop, describing the effort as an attempt to turn the Republican Party over to the segregationists, just called it immoral.

White was able to get through to Goldwater before the reporters did, but the spy got there first—and did his best to convince Goldwater that White was a opportunist paying himself a lavish salary out of funds raised using Goldwater's name. In his marathon of telephone calls to important Republicans begging forgiveness for disrupting the party, White kept hearing pledges of support from ones he hadn't considered conservative.

And the annual Republican National Committee meeting threatened to become an ugly forty-eight-hour disputation into what was now being called Clif White's "Southern strategy."

In a session closed to the press, in front of a transparency of a montage of sensational newspaper headlines reporting on White's Southern strategy, RNC chair Bill Miller declared, "Our successes in the South need no apology." The fur was not long in flying. Northeasterners like Jake Javits called the White strategy a threat to "the very existence of the Republican party" and a conspiracy against liberal Republicans who needed black voters to stay in office. Conservatives shot back that they were making an effort to become the only truly *national* party—one that left special appeals to minorities to the Democrats.

Another session was even uglier. That was when the finance committee gave its report that the RNC was limping along on a $100,000 emergency loan from the New York GOP, and that the budget for 1963 had been slashed. The party's ideological wounds had been reexposed; now committeemen learned that it was also broke.

Goldwater appeared cool to the Southern strategy. "I think you have summed up the problem of any conservative for the Republican nomination in 1964," he wrote a South Dakota friend, Kenneth Kellard, the day of the RNC meeting. "No one from the larger states who might be delegates or who would head delegations have shown any interest in that type of philosophy." Though perhaps he was bluffing. His problem with the strategy might really have been that it would push him into presidential contention.

At the Phoenix Country Club, amidst the Christmas decorations, he and his cronies evaluated the "Chicago secret meeting" and the many other draft efforts that were competing for Goldwater's attention. They agreed that it was within the realm of possibility that he could win the nomination, but that Kennedy was unbeatable in the general election. Since Goldwater had chased around the country in 1960 accusing Lyndon Johnson of the blackest perfidy for running for vice president and the U.S. Senate at the same time, he could not very well credibly run for both the presidency and the U.S. Senate in 1964. And if he ran for President and lost, he wouldn't have *any* influence in moving his party to the right.

On January 14 White traveled to Capitol Hill to try to set things right. The suggestion that White was profiting off Goldwater lingered. Besides, Goldwater's notions about how nominations came about were entirely conventional: senators, key congressmen, newspaper publishers—these were the people who controlled convention delegations. White had no such names on his rolls. There was also the matter of temperament. White had a tendency to display forced familiarity among people he was intimidated by; Goldwater was slow to trust, especially with Easterners like White: in the same room, they jostled.

Goldwater was late for the meeting, and when he arrived he was furious. In Birmingham, Alabama, that day, a new governor, George Wallace, had delivered his inaugural address. It was a pure distillation of Deep South id: "We will tolerate their boot in our face no longer. . . . Segregation now! Segregation tomorrow! Segregation forever!" In Harrisburg, Pennsylvania, a young, handsome, moderate blue-blood named William Warren Scranton was inaugurated governor and was immediately dubbed by *The New Republic* (which preferred to identify the senator from Arizona as "Barry Sundust") as "the first of the Kennedy Republicans" and pegged as a presidential dark horse. Perhaps the contrast between Republicans who would compete with Wallace and those who could be compared to Kennedy contributed to the mood in the room of Republican senators who had voted Barry Goldwater off the caucus's policy committee that morning.

Goldwater ushered White into his inner office, and White briefed him on why his group was so eager for Goldwater to become a presidential candidate. He was stopped cold after five minutes.

"Clif, I'm not a candidate. And I'm not going to be. I have no intention of running for the presidency."

White plowed on. "Well, we thought we would have to draft you."

"Draft, nothin'! I told you I'm not going to run. And I'm telling you now, don't paint me into a corner. It's my political neck and I intend to have something to say about what happens to it."

White mustered his best Mr.-Smith-Goes-to-Washington voice. "Senator," he said, "I'm not painting you into a corner. You painted yourself there by opening your mouth for the last eight years. You're the leader of the conservative cause in the United States of America, and thousands—millions—of people want you to be their nominee for President. I can't do anything about that and neither can you."

"Well, I'm just not going to run," Goldwater said finally. "My wife loves me, but she'd leave me if I ran for this thing."

White trudged down Capitol Hill considering another line of work. Rusher wrote Goldwater imploring him not to pull the rug out from under an unprecedented nationwide organization of dedicated rank-and-file conservatives, built up painstakingly over fifteen months. Goldwater wrote back that he felt double-crossed, *used*: no one had ever told him these "old friends" were a Goldwater for President group, or that White was on salary full-time, or that the group was raising money in the hundreds of thousands of dollars on his behalf. He said that since he was running for Senate, charges of presidential campaigning could irreparably hurt his reputation. That didn't stop Rusher from writing an even more pleading letter the next day. Frank Meyer, one of *National Review*'s stable of apocalyptic ex-Communists, chimed in with a letter to Goldwater that "providence" had picked him to save the United States from "the verge of disaster."

Rusher's "Crossroads for the GOP" article came out. Offered as a pamphlet, it became the most popular reprint the magazine had ever sold. Conservatives were sending Goldwater copies in the dozens. Rumors had it that he had read it—and was impressed with its reasoning. Perhaps that was true; not long ago, after all, Goldwater had given a speech to Georgia Republican activists proclaiming he "would bend every muscle to see that the South has a voice in everything that affects the life of the South," and that since the GOP was never going to win back the Negro vote, the party "ought to go hunting where the ducks are"—that is, among white "states' rights" audiences like the one he was presently addressing.

But when White made his way again to the Old Senate Office Building on February 5, Charlie Barr in tow for backup, Goldwater cut him short once again.

This time it was level-headed old Charlie Barr who piped up: "It's a free country," he said, leveling a glance at Goldwater. "We're free to draft a candidate if we choose and there isn't much you or anyone else can do about it."

The senator smiled archly and said that they might discover what he could do if they kept pushing.

Half a dozen Suite 3505 leaders gathered in Chicago once more, wearied at their increasingly hopeless efforts to keep their recruits in the fold as word got out that Goldwater was absolutely refusing to run. It was as glum a conclave as any of them had ever attended. It certainly *felt* like a last meeting. They turned their dilemma over and over—Goldwater was the only possible candidate; Goldwater was determined to shun them—until, finally, a single brash voice rang out among the disconsolate. It was the normally colorless Indiana state treasurer, Bob Hughes. "There's only one thing we *can* do. Let's draft the son of a bitch."

He was answered by a voice of reason: "What if he won't let us draft him?"

Hughes: "Then let's draft him *anyway*."

The room sparked to life. That was exactly what they would do. They decided they needed a front man of sufficient stature to impress Goldwater that they were serious. They settled as first choice on the new senator from Colorado, Peter Dominick, and as alternate, one of the men in the room: Peter O'Donnell, the brash new Texas GOP chair who was a legend in the party for winning Dallas for Nixon with a massive house-to-house canvass and for managing John Tower's Senate campaign. O'Donnell was a Harvard Phi Beta Kappa, a young millionaire: how could Goldwater refuse him? A waiter arrived at their suite with the plate of sandwiches they had ordered, just in time to celebrate what they decided was a breakthrough.

In fact Goldwater had exaggerated his reluctance. He always returned White's calls within a few hours; he was willing to keep his options open. He just wanted to retain stewardship of his own political neck. In March he brought Denison Kitchel out to Washington and installed him in an office across the street from his, claiming that Kitchel was there to manage his 1964 Senate race. His friend and secret adviser, Jay Hall, the GM executive, prepared a confidential survey of Goldwater's presidential prospects in all fifty states.

Publicly—and even privately, because even Kitchel did not know about the secret survey—nothing had changed. On March 22 Goldwater appeared on *The Jack Paar Show*. Paar asked if Goldwater was running for President. "Well, I have said hundreds of times that I am not," he responded. "I'm running for the United States Senate. I would hate to think the Republican Party has gotten so hard up for candidates they would only talk about two." He certainly didn't act like a presidential candidate. He told self-effacing little stories about getting arrested in Mexico in a barroom brawl; then he put the audience to sleep with an endless disquisition on a pet subject: military hardware ("The RS-70 has been abandoned. Skybolt has been dropped, manned bombers are being phased out, Nike-Zeus is being delayed, the Dyna-Soar is being re-examined for possible junking . . .").

Goldwater was still breakfasting with Governor Rockefeller, who was still harvesting newspaper clippings anointing him heir apparent to the Republican presidential nomination—and also harvesting grassroots Republican disgust. If it hadn't been for Goldwater's interposition, the biggest political testimonial dinner in Nebraska political history, for Senator Roman Hruska, would have been the biggest humiliation in Nebraska political history; when Nelson Rockefeller was put on the program, conservatives began planning a boycott that would have left the room half empty—until one phone call from Goldwater shut the protest down.

Kitchel shuttled between Phoenix and Washington, but spent precious little time on Arizona affairs. Robert Snowden, a Manion confederate from Arkansas who had fielded an independent elector scheme in 1960, paid court with a promise to raise $3 million for a Goldwater presidential campaign. ("A great guy and a fine gentleman [who] talks a little more than he produces," Goldwater remarked about Snowden to Kitchel, laughing off the news.) Piles of mail were forwarded from Goldwater's office to Kitchel's from groups like the National Association of Americans for Goldwater (Tennessee), Americans for Goldwater (Phoenix), Grassroots for Goldwater, Inc. (Missouri), Citizens for Goldwater (Pennsylvania), the National Committee to Draft Goldwater (New York), the Goldwater Association (New Jersey)—and, from California alone, the Advisory Committee for Goldwater, the Goldwater Leadership Conference, and Californians for Goldwater, whose newsletter, *The Goldrush*, proclaimed, "Since Mississippi is visibly considered a far worse enemy of the federal government than Tito's Yugoslavia, couldn't we follow the usual pattern, and send Governor Barnett a few million in foreign aid?" White could have at least taken heart that Barry opened his stuff before sending it on to Kitchel.

The cherry blossoms popped in Washington, and no one took much notice of one more press conference in the city's endless cavalcade. Since Senator Dominick had excused himself from chairing the group ("I don't think freshmen senators ought to be making Presidents"), it was Peter O'Donnell standing up in front of one of the Mayflower's smaller meeting rooms, fiddling with the podium, alongside co-chair Mrs. Ione Harrington of Indiana, a sweet-natured matron except when the subject was conservative politics. White flitted about anxiously making sure everything was in order, briefed the speakers one more time, then retreated behind the scenes as usual. It was April 8, 1963. Suite 3505, in existence for a year and a half to the day, was about to go public as the National Draft Goldwater Committee, P.O. Box 1964, Washington, D.C.—frippery, because the group had no Washington office.

O'Donnell delivered a version of Rusher's "Crossroads for the GOP" argument to a couple dozen reporters. He was patronized. No, O'Donnell answered, the National Draft Goldwater Committee wasn't endorsed by Goldwater; no, they didn't expect to get his permission to run him in any primaries; no, they didn't know whether he was going to run for President. O'Donnell announced a rally for Goldwater on Independence Day in Washington, D.C.; no, they couldn't promise Goldwater would be there, but they had invited him.

The reporters retreated to file their stories (the *New York Times*'s stringer botched the job: "Another 'draft Goldwater' movement was mounted from Chicago late last winter, but apparently never got far"); on their way out they picked up full-color National Draft Goldwater Committee paraphernalia stamped all over with the slogan "THE REPUBLICAN OPPORTUNITY TO *WIN* IN 1964" (a long-memoried rebuke of the Easterners' slogan in 1952, "Taft Can't Win"). Behind his hand, O'Donnell told a clump of reporters that winning it for Goldwater would be "a cup of tea"; the question was not whether their candidate would win, but by how much. "We have got the only show in town," he said, smiling. He had a long face, a slightly bulbous nose, and droopy ears, and bore a passing resemblance in speech and visage to a young LBJ. The reporters tried to make it seem like they were laughing with him, not at him. The week before, Walter Lippmann had written in his *Newsweek* column that the Republicans would nominate Rockefeller, "barring miracles and accidents." This crowd hardly seemed the stuff of miracles.

The man who counted wasn't laughing. Goldwater had just entertained Bill Middendorf, Draft Goldwater's powerhouse treasurer and a top Republican donor, in Phoenix. The senator was plied with a $1,000 check for a May 9 testimonial dinner in his honor. He also might have been slipped a copy of the group's extensive top secret strategy memo: "If the Republicans can shake off their fixation with the idea that they are engaged in a national plebiscite"—as opposed to an effort to win the majority of the electoral college by capturing the right strategic margins—"then it is quite possible Kennedy can be beaten. . . . In its hypnotic concentration on carrying New York, and in tailoring its candidates and program to appeal to the minority-bloc vote there, the GOP has put an intolerable strain on the Midwestern segment of the party." And, it hardly needed saying, its new base in the South.

However Middendorf did it, he seemed to have gotten to Goldwater. Shortly before O'Donnell's press conference, Goldwater authorized Kitchel to release to a few key allies copies of a letter he had recently written to a Phoenix friend. In it, he explained that he had no more idea of running for President than he had of running for the Senate in 1952, but he was certain of carrying the South if he did. That was an encouraging hint. For Goldwater *had*, of course, run for the Senate in 1952.

His office refused public comment on the White-O'Donnell committee. But reporters knew Goldwater usually forgot such strictures if you found him in a convivial enough social setting. A band of reporters cornered him at an afternoon reception of the District of Columbia Republican Committee, and recorded him growling, "I am not taking any position on this draft movement. It's their time and their money. But they are going to have to get along without me." The National Draft Goldwater Committee chose to identify that utterance as not-too-distant a cousin to an endorsement. They hired the YAFer who had handled the staging of the Madison Square Garden rally to do their planned Independence Day show, for which the committee had rented the 1,350-seat Federal Hall at 13th and M Streets. That was modest next to Madison Square Garden. But the capital emptied in the sweltering summer. They would be lucky to attract that many people. Goldwater would not be there. He rode his palomino, Sunny, every July 4 in the Rodeo Days parade in Prescott, Arizona.

Nelson Rockefeller was behaving strangely.

As soon as the pundits began declaring his nomination a lock, opportunistic politicians naturally began lining up to endorse him. As soon as they offered, he turned them down. An explanation would arrive soon enough. Among the first to receive it was Rockefeller's friend Barry Goldwater. The Arizona senator was up on his roof high above Paradise Valley puttering with the TV antenna when Rockefeller called. Peggy answered the phone.

"This is Nelson Rockefeller."

"Well, hello yourself," she replied. "This is Mamie Eisenhower." (Barry's friends liked practical jokes.)

Peggy was finally convinced. Goldwater climbed down from the roof to answer the phone. What Rockefeller told him so shocked him that it was a good thing he had climbed down from the roof. The most shocking part of all was that Rockefeller seemed not to realize just how shocking it was. Probably Rockefeller had been misled by his divorce a year earlier, which produced a sharp dip in the polls that was made up within a few weeks. Divorce was a tragedy; people accepted that sometimes it had to happen. Rockefeller's shocked no one who had eyes to see; the flaws in his pairing with Mary Todhunter ("Tod") Clark, a flinty Philadelphia society girl whom he had married just six days out of college in 1930, were evident before the union took place.

The affairs began within the decade, abetted by Rocky's tendency to administrative overreach: even in his wartime office he carried seven secretaries, each more lovely, clever, and voluble than the last; serially, he would set up a secretary almost as a second wife in the townhouse he kept eight blocks down from his 810 Fifth Avenue home. "I want you to know that Tod and I have an agreement that we will never get divorced but will live our own separate lives," he would say. When divorce did come, most presumed that Rockefeller would remain a playboy bachelor (there were rumors that he was dating Joan Crawford). That would have served him in better stead. But that was never his intention. For he was in love. And now he was getting remarried. Which was a political disaster.

Margaretta Fitler ("Happy") Murphy had volunteered in his 1958 campaign. She lived with her husband, a microbiologist for the Rockefeller Institute, and four children aged three to twelve, within the vast Rockefeller compound at Pocantico Hills. She was thirty-six; Nelson and Tod were both fifty-five. Happy got a divorce on April 1, immediately signing away custody of her children to her husband. The presiding judge announced that the case would be sealed "in order to protect the children"—a privilege rarely extended to those not about to marry billionaires. Four Sunday afternoons later, the couple wed at the cottage of Nelson's brother Laurance at Pocantico with a handful of guests, the Reverend Marshall L. Smith from the family's church nearby (a simple New England–style clapboard with stained-glass windows designed by Marc Chagall and Henri Matisse) presiding. A bulletin was dispatched to the press. The couple jetted off to the Venezuelan *finca*, thither to a Rockefeller-owned hotel in the Virgin Islands. Photographs reached the wires: girlish Happy and beaming Rocky striding through the Caribbean surf in matching shorts and low-buttoned shirts as if ready to reprise *From Here to Eternity*.

Rockefeller's enemies couldn't have planned it better if they tried. Now he looked like a corrupter of the nation's husbands and an accomplice to child abandonment. What if all men got the idea to dump their middle-aged wives? What if all women abandoned their children?

It is hard to understand the response now, given the revolution separating their time and our own. Since women were expected to give up virtually everything else when they gave themselves to a man to form a family, losing a husband seemed to most women equal to losing everything. It was a time, according to Betty Friedan, when it was easier to find an abortionist than a minister willing to marry a divorcé. "It is the plain fact," the esteemed Columbia University literary critic Lionel Trilling wrote in 1950, "that nowadays there are no conservative or reactionary ideas in general circulation." Politically, he may have had something. But the popular graduate text *The Psychology of*

Women clearly had not entered into his researches; it pronounced, "Woman's intellectuality is to a large extent paid for by the loss of valuable feminine qualities." Nor had *Modern Woman: The Lost Sex*, which suggested banning women from college teaching outright and identified feminism as "at its core a deep illness." Adlai Stevenson, the divorcé, speaking at a Smith College commencement in 1955, said: "I think there is much you can do about our crisis in the humble role of housewife." (He spoke of the spiritual crisis of the West.) "You may be hitched to one of these creatures we call 'Western man,' " Stevenson continued, "and I think part of your job is to keep him Western, to keep him purposeful, to keep him whole. . . . You can do it in the living-room with a baby in your lap or in the kitchen with a can-opener in your hand." The week after Rocky's nuptials, the Pulitzer board rejected the drama jury's recommendation of Edward Albee's *Who's Afraid of Virginia Woolf?* because the play depicted adultery. And that was among the intellectuals. The same message was repeated a thousandfold every day in every medium. A culture's unspoken assumptions were laid bare by the reaction to the Rockefeller remarriage.

"Have we come to the point in our life as a nation where the governor of a great state can desert a good wife, mother of his grown children, divorce her," railed Connecticut senator Prescott Bush at a prep school graduation, in a tongue-lashing *Time* called the most wrathful any politician had suffered in recent memory, "then persuade a young mother of youngsters to abandon her husband and their four children and marry the governor?" (No one bothered to call Happy's ex, who remarried as quickly as she did, to ask if he felt "abandoned.") The Hudson River presbytery brought up for censure the minister who had performed the ceremony, branding him "a disturber of the peace and unity of the church"; he expressed "deep regret" at violating the Church's requirement of a one-year waiting period before divorced people could remarry. Rockefeller attended the convention of the National Federation of Republican Women with Happy on his arm. They made their entrance into the ballroom to stony silence. An entire table of bejeweled, begloved matrons rose and marched out. The same matrons raised the roof when Barry and Peggy arrived.

Cadres of forward-thinking psychologists and sociologists leapt at the chance to wax knowingly that the nation was ready to take it all in stride. Rockefeller's backers did likewise. "I don't think this marriage changes his political picture at all," said the Michigan state chair; "Just because no divorced man has ever been elected president doesn't mean we won't have one sometime," said a New Jersey committeeman. Rocky was still "the logical nominee," proclaimed Thomas Dewey—the logical nominee from 1948. Politically it didn't matter; for now public servants started hearing from their constituents. A Maryland woman's club previously scheduled to meet its liberal Republican congressmen on an urgent matter of policy never got to it: the women begged him to cut loose from Rockefeller instead. A Denver representative heard from a woman who would "rather have Liz Taylor in the White House than that Happy." In Randall County, Texas, the GOP chair declared he would have to quit his job if Rockefeller was nominated.

The following Sunday, clergymen right and left sermonized in massed chorus. Theologian Reinhold Niebuhr, one of the towering figures of American liberalism, reported that his pious Baptist cleaning woman was disgusted, paused a beat, then added, "I share that view." Khrushchev denounced "parasitic capitalists who live a life of luxury, drinking, carousing, and changing wives." Hearst columnist Frank Conniff borrowed the argot of another celebrity brought low by remarriage: "As a presidential possibility, Nelson Rockefeller is in deadsville." On May 26, three days after Rockefeller returned from his honeymoon, Gallup pronounced the last word. Previously 43 percent of Republicans had been for Rocky, 26 percent for Barry. Now it was Goldwater 35 to 30 percent. The *New York Times* reported on mail received by New York congressmen—1 percent pro-Rockefeller, 99 percent against. And Rockefeller, the object of so much conspiracy theorizing, began spinning theories of his own: he suspected Goldwater was somehow behind it all. Goldwater, for his part, thought the reaction might have something to do with Richard Nixon.

Rockefeller's support had always been thin on the ground. A *Congressional Quarterly* poll had reported a month earlier that most 1960 delegates assumed Rockefeller would be the nominee. But they vastly *preferred* Goldwater. The conservatives Rockefeller had won through his recent insinuation that Kennedy was "appeasing" the Soviets in Cuba welcomed the remarriage as an excuse to cut loose from someone they were never excited about in the first place. His efforts to woo conservatives had already driven away much of his liberal Republican support (the *Herald Tribune* called his Cuba speech "unworthy of a presidential aspirant and quite revealing of the Governor's qualifications, or, rather, the lack thereof"). And Rockefeller was in the doghouse in his home state. New Yorkers were incredulous at his attempt to disguise a $105 million tax increase as a mere increase in "fees." His deputy Jud Morhouse resigned under a cloud during an investigation of corruption in the State Liquor Authority. The governor kept on trying to assess several hundreds of dollars per family for bomb shelters, embarrassingly oblivious of how few could afford the financial sacrifice. If it weren't for a newspaper strike in New York City, Rockefeller would have been doing even worse.

·   ·   ·

Deadsville for Rockefeller was ring-a-ding-ding for Goldwater. On April 20, Oklahoma Republicans resolved at their annual convention "that the HONOR-ABLE BARRY GOLDWATER, Senator from the state of Arizona, champions the political beliefs of the Oklahoma Republican Party"—the closest thing to a del-egate pledge state law would allow. From Suite 3505, one million copies of a brilliant petition form had gone out the door—signers pledged to donate one dollar when Senator Goldwater announced he was running for President, an efficient way to convince Goldwater that people were serious about supporting him, in addition to raising money—and were being returned to Box 1964 with exuberant abandon. White was so successful on a California trip that a report by the *Los Angeles Times*'s top political correspondent estimated that the National Draft Goldwater Committee had half a million dollars in its coffers—a vast exaggeration, but a handy lubricant for the bandwagon. Thruston Morton told *Fortune* that the power center in the party had lurched: "It's out there beyond the Appalachians," he said, "and its heart belongs to Barry." Two Washington reporters, Rowland Evans and Robert Novak, joined forces in a new column for the *Herald Tribune*, "Inside Report," specializing in what Washington called the "inside dope" piece. In one of their first filings they reported that with his legislative agenda stalled worse than ever, and his dream of a European Common Market on hold, Kennedy could not coast on image forever—and that a presidential race with Goldwater could prove very compet-itive.

Perhaps the most impressive indicator of Goldwater's strength was the quality of the gossip: one rumor carpeting the South claimed that he had sent an emissary to ask H. L. Hunt for a million dollars to fund his campaign for the California primary. That couldn't have been more wrong; when a friend told him he looked like the front-runner, Goldwater's face turned ashen. "Don't say that," he implored. "Please don't say that."

Other, more eager, entrants were jockeying in his stead. On May 2, Richard Nixon announced that he was moving to New York to take up a posi-tion with a Wall Street law firm. Nixon's witty appearances on Jack Paar's show were already the talk of Manhattan that spring. ("Which one?" he had quipped when asked if he would face Kennedy in 1964; thirty-year-old Teddy had just entered the Senate). As was his speech at the American Society of Newspaper Editors conference, where he made a graceful, self-deprecating aside on his famous "Last Press Conference." The media critic Marshall McLuhan opined that had Nixon displayed that same unhurried ease—"cool-ness"—on TV in 1960, he would now be President. With the assistance of a friendly Santa Monica newspaper that was sending out the ASNE speech in bulk as a "Freedom Doctrine for the Americas," Nixon was settling into a reputation as the Republicans' foreign policy guru. His people even tried to hire Clif White to run his presidential explorations. (White of course refused out of hand.)

That same May 2 a *New York Times* front-page article brought a new name to the fore. Eisenhower and Nixon, it reported, favored George Wilcken Romney, the first Republican Michigan governor in fourteen years. Romney was one of the unique ones in American politics, and for a while he looked like the answer to the Republican Party's prayers. He had the square jaw and booming mien (and dramatic middle name) of a President; he gave off an air of victory. He had taken over the American Motors Corporation back in 1956 when it was losing some $20 million a year; by 1959 the company was showing $60 million in profits. A Mormon bishop who brought a missionary's zeal, integrity, asceticism—and self-righteousness—to his every activity (he reminded many of his friends of Walter Reuther, whose COPE machine he had beaten to become governor), Romney gained national notoriety testifying at a 1958 hearing on administered prices. First he suggested that any company with a market share bigger than 35 percent should be broken up (that is, GM and Ford). Then he said that the UAW should be broken up. For good measure, he hit on "excessive concentration of government power." Groups constantly misread his idiosyncratic agenda as their own. Off he went to $100-a-plate Republican dinners where he reviled the idea of $100-a-plate dinners, to radical right conclaves where he called for bountiful foreign aid. Even before his run for governor he was talked about as a presidential possibility. Then came a newspaper editorial from the governor's biggest backer that yanked Romney out of contention as soon as the *Times* had ushered him in: "Come home, George," wrote the *Detroit News*'s John S. Knight, "and let's get on with the chores."

Meanwhile Pennsylvania national committeeman Craig Truax and gubernatorial aide Bill Keisling inaugurated a "Draft Scranton" movement. They had to do it behind Scranton's back. When Thomas McCabe, chairman of Scott Paper, wrote Scranton, "My young son, Jim, who like many of his contemporaries can be quite critical of public figures, told me he liked you immensely and thought you were real presidential timber," Scranton wrote back tartly, asking McCabe to "tell him for me that I hope he makes it as president, not me." Scranton had turned down four thousand speaking invitations since November.

The nomination seemed Barry Goldwater's to lose. Washington correspondents hung on his every word at an airport press conference in Massachusetts, before one of Goldwater's many speeches to young audiences, this one to a prep school. (He made backhanded swipes at attempts to draft him, then made himself sound like a candidate by complaining that Eisenhower and Nixon were behaving like "kingmakers" by trying to boost Romney on the sly.)

Every Republican who mattered was in Washington the next night for the fête of the season: the $1,000-a-plater honoring Barry Goldwater. Four hundred people paid the sum. Only Rockefeller was missing—he cabled "regrets from Mrs. Rockefeller and me" from Venezuela. It was read at the dinner to a chorus of adolescent giggles—more inauspicious, really, than mere booing.

It was enough to inspire Goldwater to call another meeting with his brain trust in Florida. All agreed he could win the nomination. Only two doubted he could win the presidency. He now searched his soul. "I ask myself, what's my responsibility to conservatism?" he told *Newsweek* in a May 20 cover article. "Is the country ready to buy conservatism? If I am beaten at the convention, how much will conservatism be set back? If I'm nominated, and then roundly beaten by Kennedy, it could be the end of the conservative movement in this country. And I'd be through in politics." The nation enjoyed a zesty romance with its young president—59 percent of those surveyed claimed to have voted for him, though, of course, only 49.7 percent had. But the conservative message was resonating more and more—even with sophisticated Eastern journalists like Irving Kristol, who sounded for all the world like the free-market economist F. A. Hayek when he asserted of big government in *Harper's* that "only in rare instances . . . can a large-scale plan encompass all the factors on which its success or failure depends."

Goldwater was now searching his soul. He was on the record saying he would consider running if he thought he could get within 5 percent of victory— because that would advance the conservative cause. He announced he would decide what to do by the middle of November. But very soon afterward, events began unfolding that forced the issue.

MOBS

To its white citizens, Birmingham, Alabama, was a proud and grimy symbol of the South's industrial future, presided over by United States Steel Company's dwarfing works on its outskirts and a fifty-six-foot statue of Vulcan, Roman god of fire, in its bustling downtown—"Magic City," they called it, in wonderment at its population's doubling since the war. To its black residents, who could hardly be called citizens, Birmingham was an everyday hell of quiet humiliation and frequent terror. No segregation code was stricter ("It shall be unlawful for a Negro and a white person to play together . . . in any game of cards or dice, dominoes or checkers"); nowhere were the consequences of transgression more terrifying. In 1957 a local black minister named Fred Shuttlesworth announced his intention to send his children to white schools. In retaliation, the Klan abducted a black man at random, castrated him, and poured turpentine on the wound. Blacks lived on the east side of Center Street in Birmingham, whites on the west, and not for nothing were the borderlands in between nicknamed "Dynamite Hill."

Violence was burned into the city's soul. U.S. Steel had been the last and the most vicious of the blue chips to accept industrial unionism in the 1930s. The savagery of the battle shaped Birmingham's political culture. In the early 1950s, U.S. Steel slowed down its hiring, then took advantage of the ensuing anxieties to demagogically install a low-tax, low-service city government. As public safety commissioner, they chose a notorious savage who had got his start in police work as a union-busting goon: Eugene "Bull" Connor.

In 1962 Martin Luther King's Southern Christian Leadership Conference had chosen the Georgia township of Albany as a wedge in their movement against segregation. Months of desultory marching and jailing had yielded but small concessions from officials, quickly broken; then a series of church burnings, quickly ignored. King's method of nonviolence worked by putting evil on display, by absorbing oppression's blows in a spirit of loving-kindness. But

Albany's police, smartly, handled their arrests peacefully—undramatically—or simply neglected to make any arrests at all. In 1963 King decided the movement would do better in Birmingham. He counted on Bull Connor as a more reliable outrage to the nation's conscience.

On April 3, protesters moved out in waves from their staging ground, Birmingham's majestic big red-brick Sixteenth Street Baptist Church, to sit in at five different downtown lunch counters. Waitresses, having been carefully trained, turned off the lights and went home, and Bull Connor never got his chance to bash heads. A new plan was formulated: taking to Connor's streets. This time there were a satisfactory number of arrests. Then there came new problems: recruitment for willing martyrs was slowed when the local Negro paper, outraged at the SCLC's uncivil tactics, staged a news blackout. The SCLC's activities were relegated to the back pages of the national papers if they were covered at all—even as Alabama governor George Wallace rushed through a bill raising maximum appeal bonds from $300 to $2,500, effective in exactly one city: Birmingham.

Easter weekend was a proper time for a resurrection, and on Good Friday, King himself decided he would march. He was duly arrested and put in solitary confinement. Still nothing. A new, "moderate" city council and mayor, Albert Boutwell, was to be sworn in soon; there might follow an era of "mutual respect and equality of opportunity," the *New York Times* editorialized—if King would only give things a chance. King, who knew better, could handle the wound to his strategy. An article that appeared in an issue of the *Birmingham News* smuggled into his jail cell, however, wounded his pride. Several of the city's most liberal divines—some of whom had risked terror by admitting black worshipers to their congregations—now told the *News*, "Just as we formerly pointed out that 'hatred and violence have no sanction in our religious and political traditions,' we also point out that such actions as incite hatred and violence, however technically peaceful those actions may be, have not contributed to the resolution of our local problems. We do not believe that these days of new hope are days when extreme measures are justified in Birmingham."

It was the word "extreme" that leapt out at him—implying that, just by the act of straying from the mainstream, however evil the mainstream, *his* movement was responsible for creating hatred. He had a pencil; he had newspaper margins to write on; and, in that dank and fetid cell, surreptitiously, patiently, over the next few days he betook himself to write. "Though I was initially disappointed at being categorized as an extremist, as I continued to think about the matter I gradually gained a measure of satisfaction from the label," he scrawled at a rhetorical high point. Was not Jesus an extremist? The prophet Amos? The disciple Paul? Abraham Lincoln, Thomas Jefferson? "The question is not whether we will be extremists, but what kind of extremists we will be. . . . Justice too long delayed is justice denied."

The press was still ignoring King's protesters. Four days later, an eccentric white postman from Baltimore embarked on a quixotic walk from Chattanooga, across Alabama, to Mississippi, wearing a signboard and pushing a shopping cart full of civil rights literature. He got as far a roadside near Attalla, Alabama, before he was shot twice through the head. The President's press conference the next day was unburdened by questions about the killing or about the twenty-one unbroken days of demonstrations in Birmingham. No one seemed to care.

King's forces decided to raise the stakes. After grave debate, they invited the young people who had been packing their mass meetings to take to the streets with them. May 2 began with yet another line of protesters stepping off from the Sixteenth Street Baptist Church, Connor's police preparing to haul one more thin rank of singing Negroes off to jail. Only this time the ranks kept coming. The cavernous church disgorged hundreds of people: college students, high school students, even elementary school students, herded seventy-five at a time into cells built for eight—685 prisoners in all. "The whole world is watching Birmingham tonight," a leader cried. And for the first time, it was true. The next day, another thousand radiant souls prepared to repeat the ritual. Connor prepared for them with new fire hoses capable of punching a brick out of a wall at thirty yards. That evening the nation saw shrieking children on TV, some as young as six, pinned down to the pavement from one end of the street to the other, refusing to retreat even as Bull Connor brought out his "K-9 Corps"—dogs set loose to tear chunks of flesh from their hides. The *New York Times* displayed three dramatic photos on its front page. The paper editorialized that the President must act. The President, for his part, said he had no authority to act.

By this time 178 reporters were encamped in Birmingham, hailing from as far as away as the Soviet Union (*Pravda* reported "MONSTROUS CRIMES AMONG RACISTS IN THE UNITED STATES"). Politicians began weighing in; in Massachusetts, Goldwater said, "If I were a Negro I don't think I would be very patient either," adding that under "no circumstances" should the federal government intervene unless local officials could not keep order. But they couldn't keep order. Since the demonstrators who had been trained in the exacting tactics of nonviolence were all in jail, the field was left to ruffians who attacked the police with rocks and bottles—and law enforcement responded with truncheons, dogs, and water canons. Kennedy announced he was monitoring the crisis for violations of federal law. By May 10 the Justice Department brokered

a truce: the demonstrations would stop; so would segregation in public accommodations, slowly, in carefully calibrated steps ("Colored" signs were to be
removed from the water fountains within the month). From Venezuela, the
honeymooning Rockefeller secretly authorized a massive transfusion of cash
from his brother's Chase Manhattan Bank to bail the black kids out of jail. The
crisis seemed over.

At the White House, Kennedy dined with his friend Ben Bradlee,
Newsweek Washington bureau chief. As was their custom, Bradlee told the
President about next week's cover story: Barry Goldwater's bully prospects for
the nomination. "I can't believe we'll be that lucky," Kennedy exclaimed. "If
he's the nominee, people will start asking him questions, and he's so damned
quick on the trigger that he will answer them. And when he does, it will be
over."

The next day the Klan massed on the outskirts of Birmingham. Outgoing
mayor Art Hanes refused to vacate his office, denouncing the businessmen
who had negotiated with Washington as "gutless traitors." Shortly before midnight explosions broke the heavy night air. The first bomb hit the home of
Martin Luther King's brother, and the second hit King's hotel room (he was
out of town). Dawn broke—Mother's Day—with Birmingham in full riot. And,
for the first time since Reconstruction, America recognized a national racial
crisis.

More stories on the subject of race showed up in the *New York Times* in two
weeks than had in the previous year. "Wherever the problem of race festered,"
declared a newsmagazine, "the name of Birmingham was invoked as a warning,
a symbol, and an epithet." In Chicago, blacks stoned policemen; in Nashville,
white and black mobs did battle on the streets with knives; in Harlem, six thousand greeted black separatist Malcolm X with full-throated cheers and heckled a
minister who praised integrationism. Civil rights protests broke out at Air Force
bases in South Dakota and Nova Scotia; Cambridge, Maryland; Raleigh and
Greensboro, North Carolina; Knoxville, Tennessee; Selma, Alabama; and
Albany, Georgia; and by the next week it was news when a Southern city
acceded to a court order *without* violence. Disturbances were reported only if
they provided novelty—as in Jackson, Mississippi, where police ran out of
paddy wagons and hauled hundreds of children to jail in fetid garbage trucks.

From Washington, Kennedy went on TV to declare that he would not permit the settlement "to be sabotaged by a few extremists"—that word again—
"on either side." He called up three thousand troops. The next day the
Newsweek with Goldwater on the cover that had been so eagerly anticipated by
the President was spoiled by the article that appeared on page 25: "Explosion in
Alabama." Kennedy's inner circle hunkered down to devise some way to cut

off the prospect of sending three thousand soldiers to every Cambridge, Raleigh, Greensboro, Harlem, and Knoxville in the country. The President first suggested legislating "a reasonable limitation of the right to demonstrate." Only then did the discussion shift to the idea of a civil rights bill with teeth.

This was a novel proposition. At the beginning of the year King had implored President Kennedy to win his place in history by honoring the one-hundredth anniversary of Lincoln's Emancipation Proclamation by calling for an end to segregation in his State of the Union address; the event came and went with barely a word on civil rights. The Senate debated Rule 22—the filibuster, which, ever since the Supreme Court had nullified the Fourteenth Amendment's application to the states in the 1880s, had been used to stonewall hundreds of civil rights bills; Kennedy remained aloof. He defended a policy of pursuing racial justice through a few federal appointments; when it was observed that four of his judicial nominees were virulent segregationists, one of whom referred to blacks from the bench as "monkeys," the President blandly replied that he thought they were doing a "remarkable job." When he did propose some civil rights legislation, in late February, it was so meager it marked the nadir of the civil rights movement's expectations of him. Privately, Kennedy spoke of blacks mostly as a political constituency to be bought, appeased, or written off, as the occasion demanded.

The President's civil rights aides protected him from the facts; race was a Pandora's box they preferred not to open. One told him that blacks were "pretty much at peace." Kennedy's own civil rights commission reported that in Mississippi, black businesses, then the Jackson office of the Student Nonviolent Coordinating Committee, were being burned to the ground, shots were fired at voting rights activists, and one hundred would-be voters had stood in line outside polling places for hours before being scattered by police dogs. When the President demanded an explanation, Burke Marshall of the Justice Department told him that the department had just entered suit on behalf of the one unfairly menaced registration worker of whom he was aware. (Marshall didn't add that the suit was to get a charge of disturbing the peace dropped against a man charged with disturbing the peace by getting whipped with the butt end of a pistol.)

But the President was beginning to get the picture. For his brother was involved in ongoing negotiations with George Wallace. Wallace's inaugural address was penned by the KKK man responsible for the 1957 Birmingham castration, Asa Carter. The new governor had changed the name of the Alabama Highway Patrol to the Alabama State Troopers, bolted Confederate battle flags onto their vehicles, appointed a ferociously cruel friend, Albert J. Lingo, to head the force, and mobilized it as a personal terror squad—a state militia that could not be federalized. In late April, Bobby Kennedy traveled down to the state capital to impress upon Wallace the Justice Department's determination to integrate his university. He was greeted by protest signs reading NO KENNEDY CONGO HERE and the laying of a wreath, "to keep the enemy off sacred ground," on the spot upon which Jefferson Davis (and George Wallace) had been inaugurated. On May 13 Wallace dispatched Al Lingo's troops to smoldering Birmingham. "Those guns are not needed," pleaded Birmingham's police chief. "Somebody's going to get killed." "You're damned right it'll get somebody killed!" Lingo responded, and then he led 250 men in a charge down the street clubbing any black man, woman, or child they could find.

By May 21—a day on which the White House dispatched greetings to a summit of African neutralists and got back an official protest against the "snarling dogs" of Birmingham—Kennedy was committed to a civil rights bill of unprecedented breadth, one that would ban discrimination in any place of public accommodations, a notion that struck political terror in the hearts of even many a liberal legislator. Senator Tower promised a lengthy filibuster unless the public accommodations clause, which "would take a virtual police state to enforce," was struck—an ominous political portent, for Tower, a Republican, was out of reach of the political threats Kennedy could issue as a Democrat. White House strategists felt they had no choice. "Biting the bullet," they called it, might be dangerous politically, but the alternative was worse: more protest, more chaos, more troops. After the introduction of the bill, Bobby Kennedy met with a group of key senators privately and desperately described the train of horrors that would follow if they failed to pass it.

In their conclusions the White House betrayed a constellation of unspoken assumptions about race relations—about social relations—in the United States: introduce bold legislation and the troublemakers would quit, like kidnappers who had been paid their ransom. Theirs was an almost desperate belief that America was by definition a placid place, if only "extremists" could be kept in check. That didn't just mean the racists who perpetrated the violence—but also those who "disturbed the peace" on the other side by *protesting* racism. The assumption was shared alike by Birmingham's liberal ministers and the *New York Times*, which implored Martin Luther King to give the city a chance to change slowly; by Birmingham's "moderate" mayor-elect, who proclaimed the citizens of Birmingham "innocent victims"; and by the Jackson, Mississippi, cops who charged pistol-whipped folks with disturbing the peace. All of them implied that everything had been just fine before irresponsible people began stirring the pot. It was the zeitgeist. "Responsibility" was a mantle even militants craved. Barry Goldwater was one of the very rare politicians who actually *welcomed* identification as a partisan. But his supporters on the Los

Angeles Republican Central Committee called themselves the "Responsible Republicans"—to distinguish themselves from Howard Jarvis's breakaway Conservative Party. "Americans for Democratic Action are more extreme than we are," YAF's Richard Viguerie assured a reporter. Colonel Laurence E. Bunker, General MacArthur's old aide-de-camp, now a Birch leader, was quoted in the *New York Post* in a series called "Far Right and Far Left": "We're right down the middle. Some groups advocate violence, others shrug their shoulders and read a book. We don't believe in either." The editor of *The Worker*, the paper of the American Communist Party, was quoted as saying: "This is the headquarters for the responsible left. Over there"—pointing downtown in the direction of the office of the Trotskyist Progressive Workers Party— "is the irresponsible left."

The zeitgeist, though, seemed to be beginning a retreat. On May 24 Bobby Kennedy was berated in a meeting with young Negro leaders who said they would sooner take up a gun to fight their racist countrymen than to fight on their nation's behalf overseas; tear gas marred the civil rights demonstrations on Memorial Day weekend in half a dozen cities; in Ohio two men chained themselves to furniture at the Capitol, vowing to stay until segregation was ended. And suddenly the White House seemed a little more worried about the political threat represented by Barry Goldwater. On the twenty-ninth—with a distressed-areas bill doomed to defeat at the hands of Southerners vowing not to deal with the Administration as long as it persisted in pushing civil rights— staffers staged an impromptu presidential birthday party. Press Secretary Pierre Salinger emceed ("Two score and six years ago there was brought forth at Brookline, Mass. . . .") and presented the gifts: a pair of boxing gloves for the showdown with Wallace and a model space capsule to be passed to Goldwater with a card reading "Hope you have a good trip, Barry."

They were back to work within the half hour. The next day—Saturday— they worked through the night, scratching for a public accommodations clause that could quiet the snarling dogs. They comforted themselves with the assumption that their responsibility would make the extremism stop.

Sunday morning the snarlingest dog of them all showed up on *Meet the Press* and proved he could look as winsome as a puppy when occasion demanded. "I will stand in the schoolhouse door," George Wallace responded confidently when asked what he would do on June 11, registration day for new students at the University of Alabama. He proceeded to make it sound like the most reasonable thing in the world. He pulled out a card from his pocket and began reading: The Supreme Court had "improperly set itself up as a third house of Congress, a superlegislature." FDR said that in 1937, Wallace explained with a grin. "I concur in it." Editorial pages around the country on Monday morning rang with praise for the governor's position. Declared the *Winona* (Kansas) *Leader*, "The very people who have the greatest stake in preserving the constitution"—Negroes—"are doing the most to destroy it" with their intemperate protests. Such editorials only made the Kennedys more determined in their belief that if they could only give the protesters what they were demanding, they could stop the George Wallaces of the world in their tracks.

The night before the showdown at the university in Tuscaloosa, Kennedy, speaking at a commencement at American University in Washington, D.C., gave one of the most magnanimous speeches of the Cold War. Intoning that "enmities between nations—and conflicts of ideology—do not last forever," he announced the unilateral suspension of atmospheric testing of nuclear weapons. The decision brought a refreshing outpouring of good feelings from abroad. Perhaps that was on Kennedy's mind when he read over breakfast that Martin Luther King was promising a massive march on Washington unless the White House put its full weight behind the passage of civil rights legislation—then, hours later, when news filtered in that George Wallace had fulfilled the letter of his pledge to stand in the schoolhouse door in Tuscaloosa—then the news, hard upon lunchtime, that cops in Danville, Virginia, had wielded their nightsticks and fire hoses to send forty-eight members of a city hall prayer vigil to the hospital. He proceeded to make what might have been the most portentously rash decision in the history of the American presidency: he decided to go on television that very night to introduce his civil rights bill to the nation. His aides remonstrated that there was no time to write a speech. He brushed them off. There was little calculation in his decision, little more in the outpouring of untutored emotion from the President that the American people saw on television that night. "We are confronted primarily with a moral issue," he said that June 11. "It is as old as the scriptures and is as clear as the American Constitution. The heart of the question is whether all Americans are to be afforded equal rights and equal opportunities, whether we are going to treat our fellow Americans as we want to be treated." Can we say to the world, he asked, "that this is a land of the free except for the Negroes?" No President had said anything like it since Abraham Lincoln.

In Jackson, Mississippi, an NAACP official coordinating a voter registration campaign—nonconfrontationally, self-consciously counterpoised to the supposed violence-provoking style of Martin Luther King—returned home from his evening's work well past midnight, as his family eagerly waited to tell him about the astonishing speech they had just witnessed on TV. Before he could make it to the door, Medgar Evers lay facedown in a pool of his own blood. His assassination rang in another week of violent civil rights demonstra-

Clarence Manion (right), an unreconstructed follower of the late Joseph McCarthy, led the group which sparked the first Goldwater for President drive in 1960 by commissioning and publishing Goldwater's ghostwritten book, *Conscience of a Conservative*. But the first politician Manion approached was not Goldwater but segregationist Arkansas governor Orval Faubus (below).

During Dwight D. Eisenhower's second term, Goldwater distinguished himself from an older generation of congressional conservatives, whom *Time* labeled "the Neanderthals," by his youth, charm, and vigor.

KNOW YOUR OPPONENTS
Here's the Labor Slate. Study it carefully.

For Governor, Walter Reuther

For Lieut.-Governor, Walter Reuther

For State Senator, Walter Reuther

For Atty.-General, Walter Reuther

For Treasurer, Walter Reuther

For Secretary of State, Walter Reuther

Goldwater gathered his first national following as the archenemy of United Automobile Workers president Walter Reuther, notorious among businessmen for his aggressive attempts to increase labor's political muscle. A dramatic televised showdown between Goldwater and Reuther at a Senate hearing over the violent strike at the Kohler Company, near Sheboygan, Wisconsin, minted Goldwater as a national political star.

Liberal Republican billionaire Nelson A. Rockefeller (right) won an upset victory to become governor of New York, then immediately trained his sights on winning an upset victory over Richard Nixon for the 1960 Republican nomination. During the campaign, the right and left wings of the party warred for Richard Nixon's soul over the issue of civil rights. Goldwater and Nixon (below) appeared in Phoenix after Goldwater had warned the presidential candidate to pay more attention to a conservative upsurge.

Young Americans for Freedom, inspired by the antiestablishment brio of William F. Buckley (above) and his magazine *National Review*, demolished stereotypes about the forbidding stodginess of conservatives, filling Madison Square Garden within a year and a half of the organization's founding . . .

. . . even as another conservative group, the John Birch Society, formed by Robert Welch, prompted press accounts depicting it as the front for a possible American fascist groundswell.

Throughout 1961, amid anxieties over the Bay of Pigs and Berlin crises, a string of scares from the right haunted the Kennedy Administration. Dr. Fred Schwarz, a barnstorming anticommunist lecturer from Australia, grew increasingly adept at winning the support of celebrities like Pat Boone, Ronald Reagan, and *Life* publisher C. D. Jackson for rallies, such as this one in Los Angeles, warning of a Communist takeover of the United States (right and below).

The center of far-right activity was southern California, especially suburban Orange County. Here, during a John F. Kennedy speech, marchers protest on behalf of Edwin Walker, an Army general censured for telling his troops that the loyalty of figures such as Harry Truman and Dean Acheson was suspect.

F. Clifton White (left) stealthily organized the disciplined network that gave Barry Goldwater the Republican nomination in 1964. Still, he was kept busy policing right-wing fringe groups given to activities such as burning baskets alleged to have been manufactured behind the Iron Curtain, as in the case of this Indiana YAF chapter (above).

The divorced Nelson Rockefeller was the hands-down favorite for the Republican nomination—until he married a woman twenty years his junior and was labeled an accessory to child abandonment. The incident laid bare many of the day's unspoken assumptions about gender and morality.

George Wallace became the face of violence in September 1963, after the Klan bombing of a Birmingham, Alabama, church that killed four little girls. When John F. Kennedy was assassinated two months later, many Americans blamed Goldwater for helping to foment a violent mood in the nation.

With Goldwater apparently out of contention for the nomination, moderate Republicans—including, clockwise from top left, George Romney, Henry Cabot Lodge, Harold E. Stassen, and William Warren Scranton—put themselves forward, or were put forward, as alternatives.

FINAL ★★

DAILY ☀ NEWS
NEW YORK'S PICTURE NEWSPAPER ®

5¢

Vol. 45. No. 186 Copr. 1964 News Syndicate Co. Inc.   New York, N.Y. 10017, Tuesday, January 28, 1964★   WEATHER: Mostly sunny, windy, cool.

MAGGIE SMITH FOR PRESIDENT

Maine Senator Says She Means It

None of the moderates entered the race with more enthusiasm than Maine senator Margaret Chase Smith. The first female major-party presidential candidate in history was soon drowned in ridicule and condescension.

tions, even riots. It wasn't supposed to happen. Kennedy thought he had given the civil rights protesters what they had demanded. What a nation thought it knew about itself disintegrated alongside John F. Kennedy's tidy notions about what it took to pacify a people four hundred years oppressed.

"A rising tide lifts all boats," the nation's sailor-president liked to say, the implication being that there *could be* no intractable problems in booming America. Most of the problems the country faced, he had recently told the policy intellectuals of the Brookings Institution—who, as staffers at the epicenter of the doctrine of managerial expertise, could only agree—"are technical problems, are administrative problems." Those few writers who demurred were spending most of their energy begging people to just open their eyes. Three masterpieces of left-wing social criticism appeared around the same time in bookstores in 1963: in *The Other America* Michael Harrington argued forcefully that there appeared to be little poverty in the United States because in the United States poverty was *hidden*; Betty Friedan's *The Feminine Mystique* said women were miserable because they could not call out their problem's name; and a book by Rachel Carson on the subtle, progressive degradation of the environment was called *Silent Spring*. *National Review* mobilized the same tropes every time it argued that the big-government liberalism Americans took most for granted was exactly the thing that should be at issue. Or when another Catholic-bred existentialist, Tom Hayden, wrote in 1962, in the (ignored) manifesto of Students for a Democratic Society, that America's purported consensus might "better be called a glaze above deeply felt anxieties." *The Fire Next Time*, the black author James Baldwin entitled an eye-opening collection of essays on race in America; few were aware there was even any kindling on the ground.

In his annual one-hour interview with *CBS Reports*, Walter Lippmann, the seventy-two-year-old dean of American pundits, ran down the tenets of the consensus as if reciting a catechism: the Soviet bloc was to be lamented, but it was nothing "so dangerous to the United States that we can afford to burn up the world over it," and could be contained "magnanimously, patiently and with restraint"; Castroism could be kept from South America by curing its nations' backwardness and illiteracy through foreign aid; budget deficits would vouchsafe economic growth; the Republicans' "only hope is to be able to convince the country that they can do substantially what Kennedy is trying to do, only do it better." For in America "the pull to the center is very strong."

The night after that May 3 broadcast Lippmann was mocked by Bull Connor's fire hoses.

Within the space of a week, the *New York Times* published a harrowing profile of the black separatists led in Harlem by the fearsome and brilliant Malcolm X, and *Life* published photos of Nation of Islam members learning how to strangle police dogs. In Missouri, when thousands of Catholic parochial school students were denied the same bus service as public school students by the state legislature on First Amendment grounds, their parents transferred them into the public schools to so clog them that the schools would have to shut down. In the St. Louis suburb of Florissant, five hundred children and parents were pressing their grievances the same way they saw Negroes doing in Birmingham: they marched on the schools singing civil rights anthems. "I am here as a taxpayer," declared one mother. "An irate, angry and broke taxpayer." (In his broadcast, Lippmann had dismissed the festering problem of parochial school parents' anger at being denied federal funding as "not beyond the wit of man.")

From far afield May 8 came news of the slaughter at the order of Vietnam's Catholic President Diem of seven men protesting for religious liberty on Buddha's birthday. On May 10, the same day as the Birmingham settlement-cum-riot, the far right returned to the news when Tom Kuchel stood up in the Senate to declare that 10 percent of the letters coming into his office—six thousand a month—were "fright mail," mostly centering on two astonishing, and astonishingly widespread, rumors: that Chinese commandos were training in Mexico for an invasion of the United States through San Diego; and that 100,000 UN troops—16,000 of them "African Negro troops, who are cannibals" [sic]—were secretly rehearsing in the Georgia swamps under the command of a Russian colonel for a UN martial-law takeover of the United States.

The latter rumor, which spread like wildfire after it showed up in the newsletter of Representative James Utt of California's Orange County, spoke volumes about the psychological paradoxes of running a democracy in a Cold War. In America citizens are charged with making their own sense of the world around them. But they were refused the information to do so by Cold War secrecy. So they did what they could with the facts available. Secret armies trained in out-of-the-way forests *did* try to take over countries; we had tried it at the Bay of Pigs. The United Nations, founded in 1945 with nine Asian and three African members, *did* now house a majority Afro-Asian bloc that was voting more often with the Soviets than with the United States. And seventeen Free World nations had indeed sent six hundred officers (four from Liberia, many more from South Vietnam) to participate in field exercises at the Army's Special Warfare Center at Fort Stewart, Georgia, to study "counterinsurgency"—the romantic Kennedy-era military doctrine that held that grassroots Communist advances must be met not through the deployment of superior force but with cleverness and surprise, by soldiers living off the land in tactical alliance with the native populace. To folks in nearby Claxton, Georgia, though, in the nerve-wracking wake of the civil rights uprising in nearby Albany, it just looked like a lot of darkies were running around in the woods. Imaginations took flight. Scary things were happening every day. Who could say things wouldn't get scarier? How could people explain a world that seemed to be falling apart?

In Boston, school board members were wondering the same thing. On May 22, at the height of Birmingham's fires, a community group aligned with the NAACP, Citizens for Boston Public Schools, released a report claiming that the city's schools were segregated. The group thought its case clear enough: of the thirteen city schools with student bodies over 90 percent black, eleven were housed in buildings over fifty years old (the other two were over twenty-five years old). In the white-majority schools, the average per pupil funding was $350; in black schools it was as low as $228.98.

But school administrators absorbed the allegation of racial bias with bafflement. Boston was still a city lived largely at the level of the parish and the precinct. Its school committee, elected at large in citywide elections, was a patronage organization more than an educational one; its members, and the ethnic communities they represented, got what they got by following the age-old rules of big-city politics. No one needed to be a racist—though many were—to install a racist school system. Boston's black population, which increased 342 percent between 1940 and 1970 while the city's white population drained off by a third to the suburbs, was represented by a Republican shadow organization living off table scraps and relying for its survival on low voter turnout. The power brokers in the black community were traditionally scions of middle-class families resentful of the new poor Southern migrants giving them a bad name and dragging down their schools. They were in no position to muscle requisitions for better schools even if they had the inclination to cause trouble in the first place. But with the postwar migration, a new black political class was coming up—educated, aggressive, and idealistic children of Martin Luther King, in a city run by Boss Curley's rules. What to them was a crusade for justice looked to others like merely jumping the queue.

The chair of the school committee, Louise Day Hicks, a prim and proper lace-curtain Irish Catholic, a juvenile court lawyer who had run on a platform to take politics out of the school committee, responded respectfully to the complaints, immediately meeting with the petitioners and promising to do what she could to right the wrong. For three weeks the two sides talked. The stumbling block was language. The NAACP wanted a simple admission that de facto segregation existed in Boston's schools. The school committee reacted as if to the Versailles Treaty's requirement that the Germans acknowledge sole responsibility for World War I. Talks broke down. Both sides agreed to try one more meeting before giving up. The date was set for June 11.

Three hundred NAACP members and sympathizers were turned away from the packed hearing room. Rather than return home to tune into the President's historic civil rights speech, they stood out in the rain and sang "We Shall Overcome." Inside, the parties spoke past one another. "I know the word 'demand' is a word that is disliked by many public officials," the NAACP education committee chair told school committee members, "but I am afraid that it is too late for pleading, begging, requesting, or even reasoning." Superintendent Gillis, aghast at the charge that Boston, which had been legally integrated in 1855, had anything to do with Birmingham, was indignant: "The Boston public school districts are determined by school population in relation to building capacities, distances between homes and schools, and unusual traffic patterns. They aren't bound by ethnic or religious factors." (He did not consider how those "traffic patterns"—blacks shunted by racist real estate practices into bursting ghettos—had come about.

Over seven hours of hard negotiation on the fifteenth, the school committee either accepted or agreed to study almost every one of the NAACP's fourteen demands, including new training for teachers, guidance programs, class-size reductions, new textbooks, and less racially biased intelligence tests. But the school committee rejected the one demand the activists considered nonnegotiable: "an immediate public acknowledgment of the existence of de facto segregation in the Boston Public School System." It was a stalemate that even mediation by Governor Endicott Peabody couldn't break. On June 18, the day before Kennedy introduced the text of his civil rights bill to Congress, an estimated 8,260 students boycotted Boston public schools. The revolution had gone north. So had the counterrevolution. "Our schools and our public officials preach obedience to the law," cried Louise Day Hicks, "yet here we have our Negro children being encouraged to flaunt the law!"

Flaunting the law was not, it arrived, the sole province of civil rights militants. Earlier the Supreme Court had handed down its ruling on *Abington Township* v. *Schempp*, outlawing Bible reading in schools. Carl Sanders, running for the Georgia governorship, had promised he would "not only go to jail, but give up my life" fighting for school prayer. More and more Americans, in fact, were beginning to look at politics as Martin Luther King did—and as Barry Goldwater, Michael Harrington, Rachel Carson, James Baldwin, and Betty Friedan did—as a theater of morality, of absolutes. "You're either for us or you're against us," a right-wing Orange County electronics executive told *Time*. "There's no middle ground anymore." Even moderates were becoming militant; they militated against extremism. "The mediator needs to become a gladiator," University of California president Clark Kerr said in a Harvard lecture published as an influential book, *The Uses of the University*, for "when

the extremists get in control . . . the 'delicate balance of interests' becomes an
actual war."

Reporters on the civil rights beat hardly noticed Boston. It was drowned out by
two straight days of history conspiring to change places with Shakespeare. The
President spoke of peace with our mortal enemy; George Wallace offered his
body against the forces of the federal government; Jackson, Mississippi, and
half a dozen other cities rioted; around the world, newspapers ran a photograph
of an elderly Vietnamese monk setting himself aflame to protest the policies of
his U.S.-sponsored government—and far from public view, in a seedy jail in
Sunflower County, Mississippi, the local sheriff was asserting his power over
the body of a sharecropper named Fannie Lou Hamer, who was in jail for trying to register to vote. "You bitch, we gon' make you wish you was dead," the
officer grunted, before ordering two other black inmates to take turns beating
her senseless with a blackjack. *This* was the archetype of the struggle for civil
rights. Boston didn't fit the script. When civil rights protests broke out in the
North, they were treated as sympathy strikes for Birmingham—the implication
being that blacks could not have grievances to press anywhere else. That the
same day of the President's speech, June 11, 650 picketers shut down construction on an annex to Harlem Hospital to protest segregated unions, immediately after which nervous Philadelphia officials negotiated for a handful of
Negro plumbers to work a school construction site that was being picketed by
civil rights protesters, then looked on in horror as white workers attacked the
protesters—this the media tended to disregard.

Politicians noticed. Some remembered the news from April of the supposedly liberal California municipality—Berkeley—that had voted down a law
banning discrimination in home rentals and sales, and the whispers from
Michigan that the reason George Romney had won the governorship was that
union members were angry at Democrat-backed antidiscrimination laws. An
economist named Ted Humes began polling three cities with large Polish-
American populations to test the hypothesis that urban white ethnics were leaning toward Goldwater in increasing numbers; in Pittsburgh, he learned, one
beauty shop owner in a blue-collar, iron-clad Democratic neighborhood had
secured one thousand signatures on her Goldwater for President petition. *U.S.
News* editor David Lawrence reported on whites terrified of "reverse discrimination": acting under "the President's order to advance Negro employees without regard to Civil Service procedures," Lawrence said, a post office was
goosing blacks 400 places up the promotion register. Stewart Alsop traveled
with pollster Oliver Quayle and interviewed some five hundred Northern
whites on race issues. They concluded that there was "a political goldmine" for

"a politician willing to exploit" the fears that Lawrence observed. Soon Clif White recruited Ted Humes for the National Draft Goldwater Committee. His campaign plan, after all, ranked "Conservatism revival" and "dedicated supporters" far below "civil rights" as Goldwater's political assets.

On June 25 a remarkable memo had begun circulating in Republican circles. Its writer, Peter H. Clayton, had been executive director of Citizens for Eisenhower-Nixon, a moderate redoubt. "As late as mid-March, I firmly held the view that Governor Nelson Rockefeller would be the Republican nominee," he wrote. "I was equally certain that a Kennedy-Johnson ticket would be overwhelmingly re-elected in 1964." But travels in twenty-four different states had convinced him that only Goldwater would win. The "dramatic change in the past 90 days has not involved anything good that Senator Goldwater has said or done," he explained. It was, simply, that the electorate now identified John F. Kennedy with *extremism*. "The abandonment of peaceful, hopeful striving for social justice," he said, "the hostility of the new Negro militancy," which "has seemingly spread like wildfire from the South to the entire country . . . seemingly undeterred by the antagonisms which these actions create"— these were associated in voters' minds with the White House. Citizens "seem to be looking for an alternative to Kennedy, a clear-cut alternative. As of this writing, that alternative is Senator Goldwater . . . he has apparently chosen a course of speaking understandingly for the aspirations of the minorities while reiterating the convictions that local problems must be solved locally. This course might elect him." Goldwater was, in other words, a candidate for voters in Boston as much as those in Birmingham—catering to white voters who were against the idea of federal civil rights legislation but at the same time desperate to receive assurances that this didn't make them bad people.

Clayton's hunch was being confirmed. Goldwater was receiving so much mail against Kennedy's civil rights bill that Kitchel complained of being "snowed under." In Pete O'Donnell's Texas, disenchanted Democrats by the hundreds were renouncing their party affiliation in mass rallies and joining the Republicans as if receiving Christ. Word was that some Southern congressmen were considering joining them. On May 20, in Montgomery County, Maryland—a wealthy D.C. suburb—a Goldwater rally brought out fifteen hundred. On May 24 O'Donnell urged it was time to move the National Draft Goldwater Committee to Washington. On May 25 South Carolina GOP county chairmen unanimously reconstituted themselves as the state's Draft Goldwater Committee. Clif White laid plans to move the Draft Goldwater Committee's Independence Day rally to Uline Arena, which held thousands more than Federal Hall. The *Washington Star*'s political correspondent David Broder reported of the attendees at a Republican workshop in Pennsylvania the weekend after

Kennedy announced his civil rights legislation, "A surprising number—considering the scarcity of strong conservatives in the group—indicated a willingness, if not an eagerness, to see the nomination go to Senator Goldwater." *Time* put Goldwater on its cover. Columnists Evans and Novak called the Goldwater boom "the closest thing to a spontaneous mass movement in modern American politics." White canceled Uline Arena and booked the much larger D.C. Armory.

It was also time to scout out first-in-the-nation New Hampshire. White met with New Hampshire YAF leaders, who bragged that they were ready to begin organizing for the primary. "Fine," White responded. "Show me a card file of every voter in a township indicating whether each one is pro-Goldwater, anti-Goldwater, or for some other candidate." Seeing them stunned to silence (of course they had no such thing), White continued: "When you have something close to that for every town and city in New Hampshire, let me know, and *then* we could announce a state Draft Goldwater committee."

The same week he hit the RNC meeting in Denver—a conclave ringing, Joe Alsop wrote, "with sanguine discussion of the Republican party's chance of victory as a 'white man's party' " (which strategy, the *Herald Tribune* said, amounted to a plot "to scrap the Republican Party"). Goldwater kitsch was everywhere. Nelson Rockefeller's empty hospitality suite in Denver looked so forlorn that just seeing it sent White into a sympathetic funk. At the podium, Wirt Yerger accused the Kennedy Administration of fomenting the spring's racial uprisings to help his ticket in 1964. Senator Gordon Allot of Colorado, previously a robust civil rights backer, did a credible imitation of John C. Calhoun. And Evans and Novak told their readers that what was unfolding at the meeting added up to a "quiet revolt": "The aggressive post-war club of conservative young Republicans from the small states of the West and South are seizing power, displacing the Eastern party chiefs who have dictated Republican policy and candidates for a generation." These same chiefs raised the old cry about the disaster of writing off black voters and losing the Big Six. "This isn't South Africa," responded a conservative. "The white man outnumbers the Negro 9 to 1 in this country."

The next week, as the rest of the nation contemplated reports of a madhouse, White checked off another success for the old hardball style.

Len Nadasdy had spent 1962 soldiering on in his smiling quest for a better, stronger, fairer Young Republican National Federation—convening civil rights conferences that showcased the party's black leadership, expanding participation in the YR's leadership schools, producing films like *The Case for a Republican Congress*, printing wallet-sized cards of the Young Republican National

Federation credo. Hutar and Harff, meanwhile, seeking to further their back-room plans to take back the Federation, spent the year circulating furtive communiqués with instructions for recipients to destroy the message after reading. They made Nadasdy a creature of their imagination, automatically assuming that he was seeding Rockefeller cash all around the country. Actually, when Bruce Chapman of *Advance* had sat down with Rockefeller's deputy George Hinman, showed him proof that Goldwaterite Young Republicans had locked up twelve states, and asked him outright for $50,000 to forestall a conservative takeover, Hinman couldn't give him the cold shoulder fast enough. Rocky was busy *courting* conservatives. Nadasdy began sending confidential organizational memos to his backers, too. First they came weekly. Then monthly. Then less often than that. Mostly, they wondered about things like where Pat Hutar was getting all that money she was spending.

The Young Republican national convention began on Tuesday evening, June 25, at San Francisco's grand old Sheraton-Palace Hotel. Bill Middendorf remitted thousands from the Draft Goldwater treasury for the fight. But by no means did Clif White's team have a lock. No sooner had they chosen their candidate, D.C. Young Republican chair, Air Force reservist, and congressional staffer Donald "Buz" Lukens, by the usual method—he appeared attractive and tractable—than they began regretting their decision. He was a bull in the china shop. His first move as the designated candidate was to insinuate himself into the nasty fight for California YR chair. One contender was Bob Gaston, backed by John Rousselot—now the John Birch Society's West Coast director. Gaston's opponent, Ron Garver, was an actual Society member. Lukens plumped for Garver. Gaston won. Somehow the White faction had to find a way to placate Gaston to win the gargantuan delegation he controlled. They failed. The media had covered the California YR race closely and labeled both candidates Birchers. To foreclose a public relations nightmare, White's people did what they could to shut out the Californians from leadership positions at the convention. Gaston retaliated by putting himself up as a candidate for national chair.

Now there were three candidates. All, including Nadasdy's candidate, Chuck McDevitt, who was a member of the Idaho state legislature, were conservatives who supported the "Liberty Amendment" to outlaw the income tax. McDevitt's conservatism didn't help him. White's goal was not to elect a conservative; it was to produce a YR chair who would answer directly to him. McDevitt pledged to honor Federation rules not to endorse any presidential candidate. So he had to go.

The plan White developed was this: Delegates to the convention preferred Goldwater to Rockefeller by a ratio of 8 to 1. McDevitt held a 100-vote advantage on the eve of the convention. White's faction would destroy that lead by painting McDevitt as a Rockefeller stalking horse. They would work on Gaston to get him to throw his 40 California votes to Lukens. Meanwhile, Draft Goldwater would exploit his Californians' wild-eyed zealotry to foment a useful chaos. As outgoing chair, Nadasdy would be wielding the sessions' gavel, a potentially enormous parliamentary boon. But if it looked like he couldn't control the convention, he would be badly discredited. It would give Draft Goldwater time and breathing room to line up a majority. The wizard behind the curtain, White, told reporters he didn't even know Buz Lukens.

One need only have surveyed the scene in the Sheraton-Palace lobby on Tuesday, the opening day of the convention, to see the wisdom of the plan of exploiting loyalty to Barry Goldwater. Bellhops trundled in fifteen hundred pounds of Goldwater paraphernalia (a pound's worth for each delegate) from the Texas delegation alone. During the keynote address Wednesday night by Mark Hatfield the hall was half-empty because Draft Goldwater had organized a boycott to humiliate Nadasdy. But when Bill Knowland, speaking next, ticked off the possible presidential candidates in alphabetical order, he was held up by a fifty-second demonstration when he got to the one starting with *G*. Back at the formerly elegant corridors of the Sheraton-Palace, the Texas kids, who were mostly college students, were using pictures of Bobby and Jack, California governor Pat Brown, Supreme Court Justice Arthur Goldberg, and Walter Lippmann for dart practice.

The first order of business Thursday was the selection of the Young Republican college chairman. Twenty of the eighty delegates were contested for eligibility to vote. California arrived with two separate, warring delegations. The key to power in this contest was to control the credentialing process. Nadasdy insisted he had the power to name the credentials committee. Harff said he did. Harff called a voice vote on which credentials committee to credential; Nadasdy questioned Harff's credentials to do so. Harff pressed on; the *ayes* equaled the *nays*; and Harff ruled for the *ayes*. The conclave descended into bedlam. Nadasdy dissolved the proceedings, opened up a sliding partition in the middle of the room, and reconvened the meeting on the other side. Forty-one delegates followed him; under his chairmanship, they elected the anti-Syndicate candidate. Pat Hutar, diaphanous in a stunning white dress, arrived to preside over a rump convention of thirty-nine; they elected the Syndicate's man. It did not bode well for peace in the days to come.

The senior convention opened the morning after the college convention with formalities that were usually crushingly boring. Usually. Now Clif White's Syndicate forces ceaselessly appealed rulings from the chair and made endless demands for roll-call votes. Nadasdy supporters screamed bloody murder. Delegates who had never attended a big convention before (that is, most delegates) thought they were witnessing spontaneous chaos. It was, of course, chaos choreographed with the precision of a Busby Berkeley picture. The Syndicate could start a pro-Lukens demonstration within the space of thirty seconds—and the man in front with the gavel, Nadasdy, who had not been able to organize his way out of a paper bag, could not do a thing about it. If he tried to reveal the Syndicate's game he would just look paranoid to most of the assembly. By the end of the afternoon he was panicking.

The night's featured attraction was a speech by Goldwater. He arrived at the airport to such an ecstatic reception that Nadasdy became convinced that Goldwater was the only hope to calm the mob. He buttonholed the senator for a meeting. Goldwater smiled warmly—he liked Nadasdy—and asked how the convention was going. Nadasdy related the madness that was unfolding on the senator's behalf. Lukens's people, he explained, were claiming that Lukens was the *official* Goldwater candidate, and Goldwater need only issue a statement that *either* McDevitt or Lukens was acceptable to him to let the air out of that balloon.

Goldwater found Nadasdy's counsel hard to credit, because the Syndicate had already told him that *McDevitt* had claimed Goldwater's endorsement. He thought Lukens and McDevitt were both fine candidates, and he didn't want to play favorites. But he couldn't say so without also saying that Gaston, whom he thought a disaster, was acceptable—or else he *would* be playing favorites. "A spirited convention is a good thing," he finally said. "Get the biggest gavel you can get hold of and the rule book and beat down the people trying to operate outside the rules." He promised to do what he could to stress party unity in his speech. That wasn't hard; he always stressed party unity in his speeches. But then, he always stressed conservatism in his speeches, too.

The convention had rented out the three-thousand-seat Longshoreman's Hall, the stomping ground of America's most militant trade unionist, Harry Bridges, then as always under suspicion for membership in the Communist Party. It was Bridges who had brought solidarity to the waterfront by ending the cruel "shape up" system in which longshoremen scratched each others' eyes out every morning for the attention of the dock bosses in order to get work. Solidarity was supposed to be a left-wing ideal—feeling the power of thousands of voices joining as one to blot out an encroaching, malign power that seemed to stretch from horizon to horizon. Now the solidarity belonged to Harry Bridges's enemies: thousands of young businessmen and professionals and segregationists and union-busters were crying themselves hoarse to the tune of Barry Goldwater:

The young people of this country are realizing that there is something profoundly wrong with the way things are going. . . . Can you imagine what level—what economic peak—we should have reached by now if we had not been carrying the tremendous and steadily increasing burdens of the last thirty years? Can you imagine the rocketing effect on the economy, the vast increase in employment, if some of the tax brakes had been taken off and the basic productive forces really let lose? . . . Modern liberalism is only a form of rigor mortis. The old, respectable—sometimes noble—liberalism of fifty years ago is gone for good!

Then came the seven-minute ovation. Nadasdy sighed. Barry had only inflamed the conventiongoers' passions further.

The next morning the delegates arrived at the hotel ballroom to find pamphlets attacking Nelson Rockefeller on their seats (most, of course, relished them). The parliamentary session that followed lasted for twenty-two hours. Clif White's old Communist Party enemies from the 1940s could have learned a thing or two.

Nadasdy gaveled open the proceedings; Lukens's campaign manager, Iowa's Ed Failor, immediately leapt up with a motion challenging the New Jersey delegation. Nadasdy ruled the motion out of order. Failor appealed. Syndicate operatives spread out in the old diamond formation to argue "spontaneously" that Nadasdy was being unfair; argument became shouting; and Nadasdy, in control of the mixing board for the microphones scattered throughout the hall, strategically switched off the ones the Syndicate domineered. The debate was soon a shouting match.

It was sometime during the keening that ensued that the organ was fired up.

I. Lee Potter, an RNC official who had been dispatched to observe the proceedings, was an amateur musician. An electric organ had been set up in the ballroom for festivities scheduled for later in the evening. He sat down, turned up the volume full blast, and launched into a spirited rendition of "The Star-Spangled Banner." It was like a scene out of the Marx Brothers: patriotic Americans, veterans, couldn't but stand up at the sound of their national anthem, put their hands over their hearts, and sing. The chaos was stilled.

The New Jersey fight ground on. The Syndicate lost the first roll call by 30 votes. They challenged more credentials; the rumble started up all over again. As Potter took to the keyboard (an unmercifully shrill Syndicate soprano was piping, "Mr. Chairman! Mr. Chairman!"), White's floor workers went to work targeting wavering delegates. Each worked his or her own special arts of persuasion: Bill Middendorf, the stentorian Wall Street tycoon; Stan Evans, the master debater; sexy Pat Hutar; even two United States congressmen, expertly exploiting the majesty of their office. Texas, heavy for Nadasdy's side, was assigned a college student, a Louisianan named Mort Blackwell. "Isn't this outrageous? Are you proud of this?" he said as Nadasdy clomped his gavel one more time to try to shut off the drone. One Texan, convinced, switched to the Syndicate's side.

"Oh, say can you see . . ."

"What they're doing is clearly unfair," whispered Blackwell. Another switched vote.

With each roll call Nadasdy's side slipped a little more. Hours passed, other credentials fights were waged, waves of shouting and organ-playing arose at intervals. Shoving broke out in front of the microphones. Fistfights broke out—the worst in the solidly liberal New York delegation, which was now divided into Nadasdy and anti-Nadasdy factions. The New Yorkers began throwing chairs at each other. Dave Broder turned to a colleague from South Dakota and told him he'd never seen anything like it—and he'd seen a lot.

The only thing that kept an exhausted Len Nadasdy going was the knowledge that the gavel would pass to Hutar if he faded. Fatigued, he would issue a mistaken ruling, recognize the error, then lavish attention on the next—making it look like he was playing favorites. The loudest protests came from Gaston's Californians—steeled against the wiles of left-wing subversion by their Orange County study sessions, ready to see it anywhere, making common cause against the infidels. A squad from Milwaukee located the cable that connected the organ to the loudspeakers and sliced through it—sliced through Nadasdy's strongest line of resistance.

At long last, with dark descending, the roll was called to elect the Federation chairman.

Nadasdy ordered the sergeant at arms to clear the floor of all but the delegates. A YR vice chair, a Nadasdy floor manager, immediately sicced a cluster of rent-a-cops on a Lukens floor manager—who was only kept out of handcuffs when someone managed to produce a printed list to prove that he was a delegate. The first roll call ended with a McDevitt plurality, but not the majority needed to elect. Someone cut the cable to the electronic scoreboard. Nadasdy, confused, declared McDevitt the winner. A bedlam of complaint broke out. Nadasdy numbly declined to start a second ballot. The Syndicate grabbed big black felt-tipped markers and scrawled Lukens's vote totals on the back of Goldwater signs and paraded them around the hall. Nadasdy cried "Illegal demonstration!" A group attempted to rush the platform and seize the gavel. Police arrived. "This is incredible," Nadasdy mumbled. He agreed to a second ballot; at wit's end, he also agreed to a Syndicate motion that a running count be called by the secretary, who was a Syndicate loyalist. During a rare lazy interval, someone began passing out free samples of instant mashed potatoes. During another, Syndicate negotiators prevailed upon Bob Gaston, to release his votes for Lukens, in exchange for a patronage job for Gaston's wife.

By the time Wyoming voted, Lukens seemed to have the chairmanship clinched. It was close to dawn. The secretary began a sentence: "And the final totals are . . ." What followed was the sort of event the truth of which eyewitnesses continue to debate for decades afterward. Some saw Nadasdy, believing that the secretary had outstripped her authority by announcing the total rather than merely keeping track of it, shoving her off the platform; others saw Nadasdy merely taking the microphone and accidentally knocking the secretary over. Still others thought she took an intentional pratfall.

Either way, the secretary fell off the dais with a thud.

Nadasdy himself wasn't sure what happened after that. Police rimmed the room. Chairs were scrambled everywhere. Coats and ties lay distended upon the carpeting, the sour reek of cigarette smoke and sweat hanging thick in the air. History would record that Nadasdy had declared Lukens the winner by two votes. The convention adjourned at 5:15 a.m. Two-thirds of the agenda was still left to go.

The fiasco made the news around the country. The delegates were described as "well-dressed beatniks" and "well-scrubbed monsters"—and, usually, as Birchers, even though Syndicate delegations forced their members to swear affidavits that they didn't belong to the Society. "We thought we knew exactly what it meant to be conservative until we saw these people," a leader of the South Dakota delegation told a reporter. "We found ourselves—mostly pro-Goldwater—becoming 'middle-of-the-roaders' in comparison to the extremists." Minnesota's Democratic lieutenant governor called the convention "a basic threat to the free workings of our governmental institutions as set forth by the Constitution." The *Herald Tribune* said that if the Republicans embraced Lukens's advocacy of the Southern strategy, it would be "as immoral a political act as any by a major party in American history."

Clif White had a lot of Republican conventions to win in 1964 if he wanted his man to win the nomination. And to Len Nadasdy, San Francisco looked like exactly what Clif White intended it to be: a dress rehearsal. "We'll see this radical right running a slate of delegate candidates for Senator Barry Goldwater for President," Nadasdy promised the *St. Paul Pioneer Press*. He wrote Goldwater, advising him to disown these radicals before it was too late: "Why not do it now—openly and clearly—rather than waiting until Rockefeller or, even worse, Kennedy forces you to do it in the heat of the campaign?"

•   •   •

The National Draft Goldwater Committee workers hardly worried about the atrocious publicity. They had an armory to fill, and they didn't have Goldwater as a draw. O'Donnell was so awed by the size of the D.C. Armory (it had been filled only for the Eisenhower and Kennedy inaugural balls and a Billy Graham crusade) and its stifling temperature (even Graham wasn't confident enough to schedule the space for the middle of summer) that he begged White to cancel. Shortly before curtain time the committee peered onto the floor from a dining room in the building's upper reaches. A band was playing patriotic songs; the spots danced on platform guests—Governor Paul Fannin, grade-B stars Efrem Zimbalist Jr. and Chill Wills; there were enough buntings and banners for two national conventions. But only one-third of the seats were filled. Prayers were mumbled.

They needn't have fretted. When Clif White stepped outside later, he had to blink: chartered buses from as far away as Texas stretched practically to the horizon. By the time the spectacular reached its peak—some thought it was White's slide presentation of "The Republican Opportunity to Win"; others Zimbalist's speech, in which he told the story of Goldwater's life, pausing expertly before declaring, "He didn't go to Harvard," bringing down the house—they had a fire hazard on their hands. The Washington press corps left awed by the crowd's zeal—and, incidentally, by the fact that there were as many Confederate flags in the hall as American flags. The *Washington Star* ran two front-page stories, one by Mary McGrory and another by David Broder, who wrote: "The entire evening—from the first bit of oratory to the last button on the costumes of the Goldwater Girls—showed a professionalism surprising in a group that opened its headquarters less than a month ago." It was reported that moderate Charlie Percy, in his bid for the Illinois gubernatorial nomination in 1964, was frantically tacking to the right as a result of the rally. *New York Times* columnist Arthur Krock found anti-Goldwater forces in the party suddenly "less visible" now.

The National Draft Goldwater Committee could not lose. Goldwater's support among independents had tripled since November of 1962. Goldwater was running twenty points ahead in early primary polling in California. Half the Republican county chairs in patronage-heavy Pennsylvania favored him over their own governor Bill Scranton.

Nobody seemed to worry over the fact that Goldwater's momentum rose the more the peace was disturbed. On Independence Day in Chicago, Mayor Richard Daley, who had proudly hosted Martin Luther King on his triumphant post-Birmingham tour, was booed off the stage at the Grant Park Bandshell because he had recently stated that there were no ghettos in Chicago. (Later in the year, two black college students tested the mayor's contention by renting a bungalow a block and a half from the Daley family home. The Eleventh Ward Regular Democratic Organization broke in, spirited the kids' possessions to a nearby police station, and invited locals to have their way with the place. After the real estate agent was forced to sign over the lease to two young local white men—real estate licenses were controlled by the Daley machine—neighbors pitched in to clean up the excrement they themselves had smeared on the walls.) "The Polish-American community," a director of the city's Polish National Alliance told Ted Humes, "quite generally imputes racial stirring to the Kennedys and are moving out of Chicago as fast as they can." Kennedy's ambassador to the Dominican Republic, John Bartlow Martin, on a trip home to the Chicago suburbs, was amazed at the rancor his well-off neighbors were expressing at the Administration.

In Oxford, Mississippi, three hundred troops remained to safeguard James Meredith's life. At the Commerce Committee hearings on the Kennedy civil rights bill, Mississippi governor Ross Barnett (whose state maintained a surveillance apparatus within its "Sovereignty Commission" with no analog closer than that of the East German Stasi) reminded senators that Communists were "championing the cause of the Negroes in America as an important part of their drive to mobilize both colored and white for the overthrow of our government." George Wallace showed a photograph of Martin Luther King at the Highlander Folk School, a camp that instructed activists in nonviolent methods. He declared Highlander a "communist training school" (King had the bad fortune to be sitting next to a member of the Communist Party in the photograph). President Kennedy was worried enough that Wallace was right, and terrified enough of the political consequences, that he spent the rest of the morning investigating. If he had known that Wallace borrowed the gambit from billboards put up by the John Birch Society, he mightn't have taken it so seriously.

Nelson Rockefeller preferred to launch his bombshells on weekends. This one came on Sunday, July 14, Bastille Day. It was said that his staff at the townhouse on 55th Street could knock out a statement or a speech on any subject in thirty minutes. The Bastille Day declaration they belabored over. They were searching for a way to use the events at the Young Republican convention in San Francisco to fan the dying embers of Rockefeller's presidential hopes.

An investigation had appeared in *Look,* a magazine with a circulation of seven million. "The Rampant Right Invades the GOP" depicted a California Republican Assembly chapter meeting in which a hostess expecting fifteen members was set upon by a roving band of eighty-seven Birchers, who voted out the previous officers, installed their own, absconded with the club records and checkbook, and left behind cigarette burns in the carpeting and an unplugged refrigerator, dashing off to do it all over again somewhere else. A tuxedoed William F. Buckley was shown addressing a staid Manhattan banquet; below that, an Indiana YAF chapter ("led by an adult counselor") was shown feeding a raging bonfire with wicker baskets because they had been manufactured in Yugoslavia. The placement of the two photographs conveyed an argument: behind the conservative movement's respectable façade lay jeering fascist mobs.

Rockefeller's July 14 statement placed the responsibility at Barry Goldwater's feet. The Republican Party, it began, "is in real danger of subversion by a radical, well-financed, and highly disciplined minority." They were "wholly alien to the broad middle course that accommodates the mainstream of Republican principle." They "have no program for the Republican party or the American people except distrust, disunity, and the ultimate destruction of the confidence of the people in themselves. They are purveyors of hate and distrust in a time when, as never before, the need of the world is for love and understanding." The conservatives "have no concern with and offer no solution to the problems of chronic unemployment, of education and training, of housing, of racial injustice and strife." Instead they would destroy the Republican Party with a chimerical strategy to write off the Northeast and black Americans everywhere.

> The transparent purpose behind this plan is to erect political power on the outlawed and immoral base of segregation and to transform the Republican party from a national party of all the people to a sectional party for some of the people. . . . It cannot stand the light of day. It will be rejected out of hand by the party. It will be rejected by the nation. It will be rejected by the South. . . . A program based on racism or sectionalism would in and of itself not only defeat the Republican party in 1964, but would destroy it altogether.

The Bastille Day declaration backfired. It was incoherent. On the one hand, it said that the conservatives' sin was sponsoring a grand conspiracy under cover of night (evidence never ranged beyond what the statement termed the "totalitarianism" in the Sheraton-Palace ballroom) because conservatives couldn't win any other way. On the other, Rockefeller said that the conservatives' sin was to win masses through a demagogic appeal to racism. This was a contradiction—one sharpened by the fact that the statement also called Republicans who had not spoken out against the conservatives' demagoguery "opportunists." By arguing that "the path to victory is in seeking out the people in the areas where they live" and in "accepting the responsibilities of leadership in the solution of their problems," the statement embraced the very approach Nelson Rockefeller had *rejected* in 1962 while *courting* conservatives. And the larger message was politically foolish: the millions of ordinary, honest Americans who agreed with conservative positions were now being equated with "vociferous and well-drilled extremist elements."

Rockefeller was the real opportunist. The immediate goal appeared to be winning Senator Tom Kuchel to head his delegate slate in the California primary by joining Kuchel's battle against the far right. It didn't help. The accuser—who only months before had been proud of his role as healer between the right and left wings of the GOP—was judged more extreme than the accused. "Our party is in no position to incite political mayhem by ruthless intramural attacks," said Mark Hatfield. Even New York senator Ken Keating moved away from an alliance with his governor, saying he didn't consider Goldwater in league with the far right at all. The main effect of the speech was to unify conservatives even more virulently against Rockefeller. The Bastille Day declaration, said *Newsweek*, was "an act of desperation that failed."

The leaders of the proverbial Eastern Establishment had already cut themselves loose from the Rockefeller presidential bid in the wake of his remarriage. Nonetheless his Bastille Day declaration bespoke their deepest fears. Stewart Alsop quoted one of them on the prospect of a Goldwater candidacy. The source nearly choked on his tongue: "My God, we'd be the *apartheid* party!" Jackie Robinson, a loyal Republican, published an article in the *Saturday Evening Post* pointing out a "striking parallel" between the Black Muslims and the Goldwaterites: Both "want to detour from the highway to racial integration. Both groups feel they can reach their goals by traveling the road of racial separation." One party blue-blood told the *San Francisco Chronicle*: "Barry doesn't know any more about the world than my 8-year-old grandson."

It was time, someone in some leather-lined boardroom deep within some marble-columned Wall Street edifice seemed to have intoned, to put the nonsense to a stop. And all at once, a cabal seemed to have spoken. The Harris poll had reported that only 19 percent of Americans recognized Pennsylvania governor William Warren Scranton's name. Yet there it was: suddenly, every newspaper editorial page in the country seemed to be haughtily presuming that he would be the Republican nominee in 1964.

An insider explained the mystery to *Life* magazine: "People fail to realize there's a difference in kinds of money. There's old money and there's new money. Old money has political power but new money has only purchasing power. Sure, everyone knows that when you get to a convention, you don't buy delegates. But you do put the pressure on people who control the delegates—the people who owe the old money for their stake." The first sign that Old Money had spoken came from *Time* magazine in its June 14 cover story on Goldwater. It had included a sidebar article: "Bill?" Those in the know understood: Pennsylvania governor William Warren Scranton's brother-in-law James Linen was president of Time Incorporated. *Time* was the Establishment's newsmagazine. The word had passed: Scranton was Old Money's man. *Newsweek* soon ran a lead story "The Block-Goldwater Movement in the GOP." The last word was given to White House sources predicting that Scranton would be the one to do the blocking.

New Money's man seemed to be doing everything he could to block himself. "You know, I think we ought to sell the TVA," Barry Goldwater told Stewart Alsop in a major interview for the *Saturday Evening Post*. Alsop was so incredulous he asked the question a second time—and Goldwater repeated the conviction. Republican Richard Fulton of Tennessee wrote Goldwater: You don't really mean to *sell* the dams that had brought great swaths of the American Southeast electricity for the first time? Goldwater—speaking in a time before the more sonorous designation "privatization" had been coined—released the letter and his response to the press: He meant it. Pete O'Donnell shot off a memo warning about "shooting from the hip": "your entire position should be spelled out at one time, rather than spread out over a period of days and weeks as the original statement is clarified, amended, or supplemented. . . . TVA puts your supporters in an important area on the defensive." (And so it did. Telegrams flooded his office: "I HAVE CONTRIBUTED TO YOUR CAMPAIGN AND HELPED ORGANIZE THE GOLDWATER CLUB HERE . . . I AM TAKING OFF MY GOLDWATER STICKERS." A Dixie GOP committeeman announced that Goldwater would have to choose between his TVA position and his support.) "Keep your ammunition fresh," O'Donnell advised. "If you spell out your position on all issues at this time, you will have fewer new things to say come next October. Also you will be presenting a nice, fat target to some group or other every time you take a stand." Goldwater ignored the advice. *Who the hell was Pete O'Donnell to tell him what to do?*

This was not how successful presidential candidates were supposed to behave. Pundits took note of the TVA affair and began numbering Barry Goldwater's days. Few noticed what Clif White was doing in the hinterlands. He had 200,000 one-dollar petition signatures. He was sucking in cash through a state-of-the-art program of direct mailings to subscribers of conservative magazines and the like. Many who might have deplored the YR tactics in San Francisco nodded appreciatively at Goldwater when he called the Kennedy civil rights bill a threat to their property rights. A Capitol Hill insider told Stew Alsop, "A few race riots in the North and Barry might make it."

Riot fears, just then, centered on the civil rights movement's massive "March for Jobs and Freedom" scheduled for August 28 in Washington, D.C. Later generations would remember it as an apogee of democratic idealism. As it loomed, however, public opinion was divided, broadly, in three parts. A small minority (around 20 percent, according to Gallup) considered the demonstration a welcome expression of black aspirations for overdue justice. Most, though, thought that the protest was insolent and ungrateful considering Kennedy's recent gestures, and that there was a dangerous potential for violence. Another minority wondered whether the event wouldn't spark a race war. "I'd kill," a white South Dakota housewife told *Newsweek* in an interview for a special issue, "What the White Man Thinks of the Negro Revolt," when asked what she would do if she suffered the same indignities as a Negro. "And I'm not a violent person."

It was hard for white America to see anything benign in a mass gathering of Negroes. The fears were primal, subliminal. "I don't like to touch them. It just makes me squeamish," one Northerner told *Newsweek*. Another said, "It's the idea of rubbing up against them. It won't rub off, but it don't feel right either." The magazine's polling showed that 55 percent of whites would object to living next door to a black person—and 90 percent would object if their teenage daughter dated one. Over half thought that "Negroes laugh a lot," "tend to have less ambition," and "smell different." "It is an oft-repeated statement among humans that the color of the hair and the pigment of the skin produce certain recognizable characteristics," observed the latest edition of *Training You to Train Your Dog* by Blanche Saunders (preface by Walter Lippmann)—the "excitable nature" of those with dark skin, for example. "If this be true, there is no reason why color of coat and pigmentation should not affect dogs as well." In an article that year, *Harper's* editor John Fischer congratulated himself for his courage in pointing out that much antiblack prejudice "is not altogether baseless": "Take the case of five Negro drivers who worked for a taxi company in Williamsburg, Virginia. On the first day of the fishing season, not one of them showed up for work." Even among the right-thinking and the respectable, seeing Negroes as civic equals was sometimes a stretch.

Washington emptied as the day of the march approached. On *Meet the Press*, Martin Luther King and NAACP head Roger Wilkins were asked whether "it would be impossible to bring more than 100,000 militant Negroes into Washington without incidents and possible rioting." President Kennedy worried discreetly about the specter of marchers rushing the aisles of Congress.

The Pentagon readied 4,000 troops in the suburbs; hospitals set aside beds. A contest between the Minnesota Twins and the Washington Senators at Griffith Stadium four miles away was canceled on account of what *National Review* called the "mob deployment."

The event itself proved transcendent. Martin Luther King's remarkable speech was shown live on all three networks: "I have a dream that one day, down in Alabama, with its vicious racists, with its governor having his lips dripping with the words of interposition and nullification, one day right there in Alabama, little black boys and black girls will be able to join hands with little white boys and white girls and walk together as sisters and brothers."

But the situation it left behind could only be called peaceful in the sense that Soviet-U.S. relations were peaceful: even if tensions were relaxing, that didn't mean that the world might not blow up. The sum total of the dread among the 50 percent of Americans who thought Kennedy was pushing civil rights "too fast" was hardly diminished. Civil rights supporter the Reverend Billy Graham, for one, was pessimistic: "Only when Christ comes again will the little white children of Alabama walk hand in hand with little black children."

The dialectic sharpened as summer became autumn: America became more frightening, Goldwater's stature grew; that made the world appear to the Establishment all the scarier—and Goldwater's stature among those who distrusted the Establishment grew all the more in the shadow of the Establishment's denunciations.

On August 29, the President had secretly passed the point of no return in Vietnam, maneuvered by zealous aides into approving a plan to overthrow the inconveniently corrupt Saigon government. On September 2 Walter Cronkite debuted his groundbreaking half-hour evening news format (all the other networks ran 15 minutes of news), instituted to establish CBS's news dominance in time to reap an advertising bounty during full coverage of the 1964 conventions. On that evening the entire show consisted of an interview with President Kennedy. "In the final analysis, it's their war," he told Walter Cronkite of the exotic land where forty-seven Americans had already met their end.

It must have felt good for Kennedy to feel he could covertly shape events in a jungle thousands of miles away, given the mess he faced back home. Gallup had the President getting trounced in Dixie. Even in Lyndon Johnson's Texas, Kennedy's approval rating was only 38 percent. The press did not report the savagery that lay behind the numbers. A theater in Georgia showed the JFK-glorifying film *PT 109*, the marquee reading "SEE THE JAPS ALMOST GET KENNEDY!" (as Pete O'Donnell reported with delight in a September report to Draft Goldwater activists). It was a challenge for enterprising reporters to get a quote on the record from one of the 40 percent of Southerners that polls said supported their President; the least angry statement a *Newsweek* reporter could find was "He's stirred up all the colored people to get their vote." Billboards across Alabama reading "KAYO THE KENNEDYS!" competed for attention with ones labeling Martin Luther King a Communist and bumper stickers reading "KENNEDY FOR KING—GOLDWATER FOR PRESIDENT."

Polls suggested that as much as 5 percent of the American public could be said to hew to Birch-like views. The President had just been given a report by his White House counsel on twenty-six conservative organizations that together raised between $15 and $25 million annually—"successful, politically . . . all the way down to the various state capitals, to county seats, and to local communities at the grass-roots." Since many of these groups were tax-exempt, the attorney general ordered IRS commissioner Mortimer Caplin to start in on aggressive audits.

In Northern cities, activists met the new school year with a bold new remedy for de facto segregation. The President was asked about it at his September 12, 1963, press conference: "As a parent, do you think it is right to wrench children away from their neighborhood-family area and cart them off to strange, far-away schools to force racial balance?" He began his answer optimistically— "Passage of the civil rights bill in the Senate . . . would surely improve the atmosphere"—then fell back into realism: "The country will by lucky to get by without a summer of violence that could have incalculable effect on the election next fall."

The country would have been lucky to get through the week. Governor Wallace was now standing in the doors of his state's elementary and high schools. If integration went ahead, he said, he didn't want any bloodshed— although if it happened, he said, civil rights agitators would be held responsible. Klansmen in Birmingham took the hint. The explosion inside the Sixteenth Street Baptist Church on September 15 was heard for two miles. Four little girls died in their Sunday school dresses. King wired Kennedy during the tensions that ensued: only the President's intercession could prevent the "worst racial holocaust this nation has ever seen." Ten days later another incendiary device exploded on Dynamite Hill, then a second, a shrapnel bomb intended to wound police if they investigated the first. The Klansmen who were responsible copped pleas for misdemeanor possession of dynamite.

Cronkite's next half-hour interview was given to Goldwater. The *New York Times* reported that he had already reserved the entire fifteenth floor of San Francisco's Mark Hopkins Hotel for the convention (the hotel, coincidentally, that Khrushchev had decided during his 1959 visit to someday make the headquarters for the International Communist Conspiracy, according to Dr. Fred

Schwarz of the Christian Anti-Communism Crusade). Kitchel's new field deputy, Phoenix attorney and recent past Arizona party chair Richard Kleindienst, reported that party rank-and-filers were telling him that if Goldwater wasn't nominated, there wouldn't *be* a rank and file. In Massachusetts, Establishmentarians like Senator Leverett Saltonstall were cowering under Clif White's back-room threats that his people would organize their way past the Massachusetts party leaders' traditional prerogative to name the state's delegates-at-large. No one had thought to challenge that prerogative before.

Goldwater was traveling: a ten-state tour, including New Hampshire, throngs of cheering young conservatives following him like iron filings to a magnet. It felt like a campaign, but for the fact that he refused the basic technique of having a few aides tag along to build a card file of the names behind the hands he shook. "You leave me alone," he told the aide who suggested it. "I'm doing all right just pooping around."

Rockefeller, who traveled with an entire research staff, corralled a major chunk of the Washington press onto his Convair jet for a visit to the humble Ogle Country Fair in central Illinois. All the candidates in the three-way Republican gubernatorial primary had already declined the chance to appear with him. The reporters watched as the crowd at the fair ignored Rockefeller and his wife as if they had the mange. (Yet the *New York Times* reported, incredibly, that "Rockefeller's surprisingly successful visit to this Goldwater bastion yesterday was evidence that the Governor could command conservative support in a race for the presidency.") The week after, the three Illinois gubernatorial candidates virtually pawed the clothes off Goldwater when he visited Chicago for the National Federation of Republican Women convention. He had to give his speech twice to accommodate all his fans. Behind the scenes at the meeting—Draft Goldwater operatives worked behind the scenes at every Republican meeting—Pat Hutar set in motion a purge of delegates who had voted against Goldwater in a straw poll.

White was traveling too, more than ever, working eighteen-hour days with a new partner, former RNC finance committee staffer Frank Kovac. "I have never been with Frank Kovac when he showed any compunction whatever about asking for a contribution," he noted in amazement. At the new Washington Draft Goldwater office—which was accumulating enough half-filled coffee cups, full ashtrays, and envelope-licking housewives to resemble a party headquarters a month before Election Day—petitions were pouring in with checks attached, $1,000 a day. *Roll Call* reported that the Goldwater campaign organization had $7.5 million in the bank. It was really $125,000, although White hardly minded the publicity; it would only bring in more. He brought a full-time finance director aboard (Dan Gainey of Minnesota, retired CEO of class-ring manufacturer Josten's, a former RNC treasurer who wintered in Arizona); on September 16, Carol Bauman (née Dawson) began work full-time putting together a nationwide Goldwater youth organization.

The date was auspicious. That night, in California, where there were already some one hundred Goldwater youth groups in operation, Robert Gaston's organization, despite a concerted sabotage attempt by party regulars, filled Dodger Stadium for a Goldwater rally—on an odd-numbered year, on a Monday night when the pennant-chasing Dodgers were playing a crucial game on TV, for a man who wasn't even officially a presidential candidate. The crowd groaned when Goldwater said he had to fly back to Washington afterward to debate the test-ban treaty; they gave him a bone-crunching roar when he said that he was voting against it.

"Almost everybody in Washington has violent views about it pro or con," wrote Scotty Reston of Goldwater's front-runner status for the nomination, "except Barry himself." Mary McGrory followed Goldwater back to Washington as he ducked in at the Chevy Chase Women's Republican Club for an off-the-cuff Q&A; one of the ladies asked about that awful Bobby Kennedy, and Goldwater responded by speaking about the attorney general with touching affection. McGrory recalled how Jack Kennedy behaved at a similar stage in *his* campaign: spouting statistics, attacking carefully chosen enemies and puffing all the right friends, quoting dead Greeks, never cracking a joke lest he remind the voters how young he was. "Senator Goldwater doesn't strain at all," she marveled. "He is entirely himself."

Kennedy certainly wouldn't have voted with only eighteen other senators against the Partial Test Ban Treaty, as Goldwater was about to do. The treaty marked a transforming moment in America's relationship with the atom. It began as a friendship. Within hours of the bombing of Hiroshima, the Washington Press Club had an "Atomic Cocktail" on offer; no one blanched at naming a sexy new bathing suit after an atoll that had been nearly wiped from the Earth in a hydrogen bomb test in 1952. That same year, in fact, an airborne nuclear test was broadcast on TV to Chet Huntley's thrilled commentary. Casinos scheduled outings to watch tests at the Atomic Energy Commission Proving Grounds northwest of Las Vegas. The AEC's propagandistic "Project Plowshare" produced glowing stories of the possibilities of using nuclear devices to carve a new canal in Central America and a new harbor in Alaska. The bomb was something to be proud of. It protected us. Its more imminent dangers were only discussed behind scientists' closed doors.

Atomic testing began showing a darker face in the mid-1950s, when physicist Ralph Lapp and chemist Linus Pauling began publishing widely on the dangers of "nuclear fallout," a mysterious toxin that "cannot be felt and possesses the terror of the unknown"—although it was known that it was released in the air in tests, was linked to cancer and genetic damage, and had a half-life of twenty-eight years. A full-blown fallout scare ensued in 1959 when high levels of strontium 90 were discovered in the bones of children under four. Anti-testing forces launched a brilliant scientific and public relations project, the "Baby Tooth Survey," which collected teeth from 80,000 children and released findings in 1962 of a fourteenfold increase in strontium 90 levels in children born in 1957 compared to those born in 1949. It might have been an ad that ran in newspapers in April 1963 that clinched public opinion: "Dr. Spock Is Worried," it read. "*Your* children's teeth contain strontium 90."

Test-ban talks began in Moscow in June 1963, around the time of Kennedy's American University address arguing that peace that "does not require that each man love his neighbors—it requires only that they live together in mutual tolerance." It was a message that, for the most part, only the kind of conservatives who went to Dodger Stadium rallies weren't thrilled to hear. Negotiations were completed in record time; the treaty was signed on July 25. (An informal part of the agreement was being carried out even as Martin Luther King delivered his stirring peroration on the steps of the Lincoln Memorial: a "hotline" was installed connecting the White House and the Kremlin.) And the ratification vote was quickly set for early September—just in time for Goldwater to vote against it at the height of his boom. He saw the treaty as an inexcusable strategic compromise. "If it means political suicide to vote for my country and against this treaty," he said on the Senate floor, "then I commit it gladly."

It wasn't that Goldwater wasn't interested in running for President. In fact, he had been flabbergasted by his reception of Dodger Stadium and promptly appointed a twenty-three-member committee, chaired by former senator Bill Knowland, to advise him on entering the California primary. One early October morning, the customary bustle at Draft Goldwater headquarters was parted by the screech of the switchboard operator. "It's Barry Goldwater!" she cried. "He's on the line now!" White hadn't spoken to him for months. Goldwater had never set foot in their office. Now the man in the bow tie was summoned down to Capitol Hill and given the order to travel to San Francisco to begin preparations for the national convention. Goldwater had checked with the Arizona attorney general: it was legal to run for both President and senator.

As early as his 1922 book *Public Opinion*, Walter Lippmann had come to believe that the world was so complex that political decisions would best be left to a specialized class of experts. Three years later the Scopes "monkey trial" confirmed his conviction that a public uninstructed by expert opinion would succumb to the tyranny of the majority—the very worst tyranny of all. Ideologically, the columnist vacillated from decade to decade, sometimes coming out liberal in foreign affairs and conservative in domestic, sometimes vice versa. But always, always, his thinking betrayed a constant: that he and his fellow pundits—Hindi for "wise men," a title first given to him by an admiring Henry Luce—were the nation's best defense against the terror of the mob.

With World War II within the living memory of almost every adult in the early 1960s, that did not seem an idle fear. In 1961 Adolf Eichmann's trial in Jerusalem for genocide was a television staple. Highbrow readers absorbed Hannah Arendt's courtroom reports for *The New Yorker* with a terrible awe: she argued that what made Eichmann so frightening was not that he was a monster but that he was an ordinary man. Her articles were published as a book in 1963, and the ensuing ferment among intellectuals was so enveloping that *Look* assigned a reporter to do an article on the debate—the same month that the magazine ran a photo of Indiana YAFers hurling Communist-made wicker baskets into a raging fire. "The most essential criterion for judging the events of our time," Arendt had written elsewhere, was "Will it lead to totalitarian rule or not?" What led to totalitarian rule, it seemed to most educated Americans, was when an extraordinary man, bound by the same limited moral horizon as everyone else, became swept up in the act of anointing himself a nation's redeemer.

That was the subject of Robert Penn Warren's Pulitzer Prize–winning novel *All the King's Men* (1946): the story of a rootless man (named Burden) who heals his alienation by filling himself with devotion for a charismatic strongman modeled after Louisiana governor Huey Long, then frees himself over the course of the story from what he increasingly realizes is an existential horror. Warren had Burden exclaim, "There is nothing like the roar of a crowd when it swells up, all of a sudden at the same time, out of the thing which is in every man in the crowd but is not himself." Teddy White, in *The Making of the President 1960*, used similar language in pondering a delirious moment at the 1960 Democratic Convention: "If demonstrations and noise alone can sway a national decision at a nerve center of national politics," he wrote, "then American politics could be reduced to that naked violence that has so frequently and tragically swayed the history of France and Germany." That the object of the crowd's roar was hardly führer material—quiet, cerebral Adlai Stevenson—hardly mattered. After Hitler, the crowd's roar was frightening enough in itself.

The American two-party system, it was thought, was a sublime bulwark against just such dangers. "Each party is like some huge bazaar," wrote the sociologist Daniel Bell, "with hundreds of hucksters clamoring for attention." To win party leadership, the successful huckster must be bargainer, splitting most issues down the middle—and as long as that was the case, extremists like Huey Long could never be more than a single yelping voice among the teeming throng. So it was that Walter Lippmann wrote in August that Goldwater's candidacy "strikes at the heart of the American party system." So it was that, faced with the spectacle of a stadium of youth chanting Barry Goldwater's name, Lippmann had but two choices: predict Goldwater's imminent movement to the ideological center, or brand him a fascist in the making.

He chose to retreat into the cocoon of theory rather than record the evidence of his senses: Goldwater, he reported, was becoming a moderate. "It is interesting to watch him, and comforting to think that the system is working so well." Lemminglike, others rushed to confirm the master. Pay attention to "a fascinating political biological process," *The New Republic*'s columnist TRB instructed readers, "like watching a polliwog turn into a frog."

These journalists didn't consider Goldwater's test-ban vote, or his recent correction of the *Congressional Record* to revise a passage giving the mistaken impression that he had denounced the radical right, or, indeed, the day after Lippmann's pronunciamento, a major speech Goldwater made on the Senate floor reaffirming his conviction that "profits are the surest sign of responsible behavior"—or that he was only becoming more popular in the event. "Barry Goldwater could give Kennedy a breathlessly close race," the *Time* then on the newsstands reported. *Look* ran the banner "JFK COULD LOSE." On the best-seller list sat *JFK: The Man and the Myth*, in which conservative journalist Victor Lasky, who had made his career attacking Alger Hiss, portrayed Kennedy as a pretty-boy empty suit. (It reduced dignified Republican outlets to spluttering. "Mr. Lasky," lamented the *Herald Tribune*, "knows how to use the knee." The *Wall Street Journal* deemed it "a hatchet job.") Like Lippmann, many liberals simply denied facts that seemed too unlikely to countenance. At a party celebrating the opening of a press liaison office in D.C., the AP's top political analyst, James Marley, sniffed disdainfully over his cocktail that the polls showing Goldwater's overwhelming popularity over Rockefeller simply couldn't be true.

John F. Kennedy was not a theoretical man. He read the polls—and had a brother-in-law open discussions with an ad agency for 1964. The "conservation trip" he embarked on at the end of September was suspiciously sudden. He started in Scranton's Pennsylvania and moved to Barry Goldwater's West, where he spoke on campuses, joining Goldwater in the battle for young hearts. He preached about the accelerated public works program he had passed the previous year, which had produced a million man-months of new employment. At the University of North Dakota he spoke of the 97 percent of farms that had gone without electricity in the state before the Democrats instituted the Rural Electrification Administration; at the University of Wyoming he bragged about the government's massive subsidies for petroleum research. (No one shoots Santa Claus.) He also made a rare assertion that nuclear war could mean the deaths of 100 million people in a day. It was a week of parrying and feinting with Barry Goldwater.

Then, at the Mormon Tabernacle in Salt Lake City, the sturdiest redoubt of the Republican right in America, Kennedy went on the attack—going for the flank that had been softened by Nelson Rockefeller in July. It was testament to the novelty of paying serious attention to conservatism that Kennedy's speechwriters' blows shot past Barry Goldwater and landed on Robert Alonzo Taft. "It is little wonder that there is a desire in the country to go back to the time when our nation lived alone," Kennedy said, patronizing the members of a church renowned for the sweep of its foreign missions.

> It is little wonder that we increasingly want an end to entangling alliances, an end to all help to foreign countries, a cessation of diplomatic relations with countries or states whose principles we dislike, that we get the United Nations out of the United States, and the United States out of the United Nations, and that we retreat to our own hemisphere, or even within our own boundaries, to take refuge behind a wall of force.

Not one of these positions could Goldwater fairly be said to hold. The President was not yet in any kind of shape to face the conservative senator from Arizona on ideological turf.

Kennedy would get plenty of training; trips were scheduled to Florida, Texas, and California before the year was out. The Democratic National Committee had filled two filing cabinets with Goldwater intelligence. At the Western States Democratic Meeting, Frank Church devoted his keynote to a new wedge issue. Goldwater had stated that America should consider nuclear retaliation against any Soviet territorial encroachment, Church noted. "Any American president," he answered, who "tampers cavalierly with the delicate balance of terror upon which the peace presently depends, might well be the last American president." At the Midwestern States Democratic Meeting, DNC chair John Bailey said that the GOP was "infiltrated by right-wing fanatics and fear mongers who think former President Eisenhower is a Communist dupe." Only Nebraska's loudmouth governor Frank Morrison spoke a certain fear aloud— predicting that Goldwater would carry every state west of the Mississippi but one. Sargent Shriver began mixing political errands with his Peace Corps travels. Martin Luther King began worrying that Goldwater had won an important victory already—Kennedy, King said, was moving appreciably to the right.

If Kennedy was moving to the right, he was only following the electorate. His approval rating was down from its usual perch in the mid-seventies to 57; even among Catholic Democrats he was down 11 points and falling. The political star of the moment was Louise Day Hicks, who was gaveling Boston School Committee meetings to adjournment at the very mention of the forbidden word "segregation"; with every *bang!* her favor soared. As she campaigned for reelection she rebuffed overtures from George Wallace. ("He's a segregationist," she said. "I don't want to be connected with him.") The White House offered her a judgeship—which seemed, at the time, like playing it safe, for cognoscenti were calling her appeal to racism political suicide. Two days before the school committee election, the NAACP held a march to one of the most tumbledown schoolhouses in the ghetto. The next day the building mysteriously burned to the ground. Now the cognoscenti prepared Hicks's political last rites; who would vote for a figure who inspired this kind of incivility? She ended up winning an unbelievable landslide. Many voted for her without even bothering to mark their ballots in the mayoral race. "Every time the Negroes demonstrated," she trilled, "they campaigned for me."

Evans and Novak called her victory a "glimpse of the iceberg." The DNC began preparing for a massive voter registration drive among urban black voters to replace suddenly unreliable urban white ones. In New York City, demonstrations for immediate school integration, under the leadership of a militant preacher named Milton Galamison, were daily newscast fare. Soon Galamison's Parents Workshop for Equality had competition: Parents and Taxpayers, a white group formed to protest the board of education's plan to blend the student bodies of two neighboring Queens elementary schools, one white, one black.

In Albany, New York's state capital, protesters held sit-ins demanding equal employment in state-financed construction. "There is only one standard for entrance into the United Association and that is the man's qualifications," the leader of the plumbers' union retorted. "We do not believe in rejecting an applicant because of his race, color, or creed, and we likewise cannot be expected to admit an applicant *because* of his race, color, or creed." Governor Rockefeller concurred: "Their program would destroy the whole concept of free unions." That sounded nice, but then, many building-trades locals automatically gave an applicant an extra ten points on the apprenticeship exam if a blood relative belonged to the union. Brooklyn's plumbers' local had only three black journeymen out of several thousand members. The carpenters' union confined black members to a Harlem branch. The electricians refused them altogether.

In the Mississippi governor's race the Democrat Paul Johnson won only because he convinced the electorate he hated John F. Kennedy more than the Republican candidate did. George Wallace appeared at Kennedy's alma mater, Harvard, and as the flower of American youth approached the microphone to show up a yokel, one by one they were folded up into a master debater's pocket. (Outside, the flower of American youth slashed the tires of his limo.) In Berkeley, the Jaycees canceled the annual Festival of Football Queens because one of the chosen queens was black. Coming hard upon inflammatory addresses by James Farmer and Malcolm X, Berkeley activists, many of them veterans of the 1960 anti-HUAC campaign, got up an Ad Hoc Committee Against Discrimination and marched off to San Francisco to picket racist hiring practices at a drive-in owned by the Republican mayoral candidate; 111 were arrested. In Chicago, Mayor Daley was flatly refusing to push an equal housing law through the city council on what, for the leader of a machine, was the soundest of reasons: he wouldn't reward a voting bloc for threatening a school boycott. The blacks protested for *their* soundest of reasons: pleas for relief from calamitous school crowding had been answered with the deployment of a few mobile homes plunked in the middle of parking lots—called "Willis Wagons" after the dyspeptic school superintendent, Benjamin Willis. It was just as with Hicks in Boston: the more the blacks protested Willis, the more popular he became. Chicago voters scared Daley by giving him the closest Republican challenge he would face in his life; Democratic mayors also received reelection scares in Indianapolis and Philadelphia.

Jack Kennedy had to wonder what would happen in 1964 to the Chicago machine that had delivered him the presidency in 1960 if Dick Daley dared get behind his civil rights program. His nervousness showed when he was asked at his October 31 press conference about a Goldwater charge made earlier in the day that the President was attempting to control the news to perpetuate himself in office. His eyes narrowed and he shook his head in annoyance before finding his feet with a trademark dry—if, this time, defensive—witticism: Goldwater had had "a busy week selling TVA and to, ah, giving permission, suggesting that military commanders overseas be permitted to use nuclear weapons. . . . So I thought it really would not be fair for me this week to reply to him." A pleased grin; gales of laughter.

History has not preserved a detailed account of what the Kennedy brothers and seven others discussed on November 12, 1963, at the first White House strategy session for the upcoming presidential election. They may well have started with small talk: a consideration of the significance of Norris Cotton, the moderate New Hampshire senator who was burning up the airwaves on behalf of Goldwater; or Goldwater's delirious reception at a massive Republican rally in Pennsylvania where Scranton barely mentioned Goldwater's name while Senator Hugh Scott used it for embarrassing puns; or the latest on George Romney, whose moral purity the President found surreal. Perhaps they discussed the Henry Luce editorial that accompanied a recent triumphant appearance of Goldwater's on the cover of *Life*: "Barry Goldwater represents a valuable impulse in the American politics of '64," Henry Luce wrote. " 'Guts without depth' and 'a man of one-sentence solutions' are the epithets of his critics. The time has come for him to rebut them if they can." And what if Goldwater was able to march before Henry Luce and do just that?

It likely wasn't long before the Kennedy strategy session moved on to a discussion of race. *Newsweek*'s "What the White Man Thinks About the Negro" issue, out recently, concluded, "Except for civil-rights troubles, Mr. Kennedy could expect re-election by a landslide." Now, the newsmagazine concluded, "he could lose." A *Look* feature was headlined, " 'Never Wrong' Iowa Township Forecasts the 1961 race: JFK Could Lose." The citizens were split down the middle on who they preferred for President—but they agreed that they held the White House responsible for racial violence. "I think Kennedy is too damned lenient with them damned niggers," one local farmer was quoted as saying. George Wallace, back from his successful Ivy League tour, proudly read his mail for a *Time* reporter: " 'God willin' I won't vote for Martin Luther Kennedy. . . . You have my vote in the Presidential election.' That's from Detroit. Dayton, Ohio . . . 'Strongly recommend you to run for President Against Nigger Kennedy . . .' " Wallace said he was thinking about entering some Democratic primaries.

Perhaps Kennedy and his men discussed the idea of Walter Heller, chairman of the Council of Economic Advisers, to divert more of the economy's swelling resources to wiping out "pockets of poverty." Kennedy had weighed, then tabled, the idea, for strategic reasons: the poor were loyal to him already, but the plan might lose him some votes in the new suburbs, where he and his advisers agreed the election would be decided.

Vietnam may have been on these Democrats' minds. Through September and early October, a flurry of cables between Washington and Saigon wrestled with a contradiction at the heart of the Pax Americana. American power wanted to be innocent. But once it became clear that South Vietnamese president Ngo Dinh Diem would not be cowed into moving toward American-style democracy by threats of losing $1 million a day in U.S subsidies, arrangements were made with a cabal of Vietnamese generals for a "totally secure and fully deniable" coup—to advance the cause of democracy, of course. Usually the CIA

carried out such orders at a remove from the presidential gaze; this coup, however, was directed from the White House. On November 1, a group of South
Vietnamese generals secured Diem's surrender by promising him safe passage
out of the country. Then they shot him in the back. Kennedy, incredulous,
almost convinced himself to believe the generals' story that Diem had killed
himself. National Security Adviser McGeorge Bundy brought him back to
earth by reminding him of the photographs of the corpse with his hands tied
behind his back—"not," he quipped, "the preferred way to commit suicide." It
haunted the President's conscience, what had happened there, what he had not
been able to control. Soon a *New York Times* investigation revealed American
involvement in the plot. Now it was a political problem.

Surely during the November 12 White House strategy session they discussed the President's upcoming trip to Texas. If any looked to be a swing state
in 1964, it was Texas. Goldwater—away on a ten-day hunting and fishing trip,
mulling over his final decision whether to run or not—was still ahead there.
Dick Maguire had been urging a visit to Texas for years to goose its share of
the DNC's coffers: there was all that oil money to tap, if the faction behind liberal senator Ralph Yarborough didn't drive the folks behind conservative governor John Connally into the Republican Party at one of Pete O'Donnell's
resignation rallies. The Kennedys planned a powerhouse fund-raising junket;
even Jackie had set a goal of raising $1 million.

Kennedy was with friends; perhaps he also noted that Texas would be his
first trip with Jackie since the haunting premature birth and sudden death of
their third child. Perhaps consideration was given to the wisdom of bothering
to visit Dallas at all, a Republican town so inhospitable to Washington that the
suburb of Richardson—an electronics industry stronghold—had raised a four-
thousand-signature petition to refuse to receive its share of federal money for
school lunches and milk. On October 20, UN Day (which the far right
answered by declaring "U.S. Day"), Adlai Stevenson, leaving Memorial Auditorium after giving a speech, had been clomped on the head by a yelping picket
wielding a sign reading "DOWN WITH THE UN." Stevenson insisted on con-
fronting the woman before policemen whisked her away. "What is wrong?" he
asked. "What do you want?" Mrs. Cora Frederickson, forty-seven, her face
contorted, responded with gnomic fury: "Why are you like you are? Why
don't you understand? If you don't know what's wrong, I don't know why.
Everybody else does." "A City Disgraced" was *Time*'s verdict; "nut country"
was Kennedy's. Perhaps he even laughed over the escalating shrillness of the
attacks broadcast over billionaire H. L. Hunt's radio show after the Administration began toying with cutting the depletion allowance, oilmen's favorite tax
break.

The evening of November 12, America was once again reminded of the well-organized underbrush of Washington-hating kooks in their midst when CBS aired a special called "Case History of a Rumor" on the UN-takeover-in-Georgia canard. The next day Dan Foley, the new National Commander of the American Legion, sat down to write his first editorial for the American Legion's magazine. He blasted the alarming rise in political extremism:

> I mean those individuals who would save America by forsaking its free institutions. I mean not just Communists and neo-Fascists who openly assail our system but, more especially, those who, in the conviction that theirs is the only right view, have lost sight of—and faith in—the fundamental processes of self-government. They claim to have the one true answer to every problem. They talk of setting aside the law when the law offends them. They are quick to cry "treason," slow to admit error, and indifferent to arguments and facts that do not support their beliefs. They are not really leftists or rightists—but simply anarchists.

Just that week his critique could have referred to the Congress of Racial Equality, which was directing increasingly uncompromising anger at de facto employment segregation outside the South; in San Diego, the group's pickets against the San Diego Gas & Electric Company brought a temporary restraining order. (The demonstrators continued to picket until they were hauled off by the cops.) Or he could be alluding to far-right reaction to Kennedy's recent decision to sell surplus wheat to the Soviet Union; or the latest development in the case of Otto Otepka, the cashiered State Department security officer who embarrassed the Administration by claiming that Foggy Bottom was back to putting subversives on the payroll. Or perhaps to events at the University of Alabama, where one of two black students dropped out after suffering a nervous breakdown; shortly thereafter a bomb carved a crater out of the street in front of the dorm of the remaining black student. (How long, George Wallace lamented, would it take "to get the nigger bitch out of the dormitory?") Foley's critique could even be taken to encompass the John Birch Society's tactic, on October 31, of dropping anti-UN leaflets into trick-or-treaters' little UNICEF boxes instead of coins.

Kennedy was grumpy, tired, feeling a bit alarmed as the trip approached. On November 20 the CIA had shown him a Cuban rifle that had been salvaged from the Venezuelan countryside—proof positive that Castro was violating the letter of the Missile Crisis settlement by disobeying his promise not to aid uprisings in South America (though the Kennedy brothers surely violated the spirit of the agreement by engaging in an ongoing CIA attempt to assassinate him). Kennedy had been rather snappish on his unimpressive trip to Florida ("While the federal net debt was growing less than 20 percent in these years, total corporate debt—*your* debt," he remarked superciliously to the chamber of commerce, "was growing nearly 200 percent!"). Perhaps intelligence reached him that the only thing keeping Goldwater from announcing his candidacy was a trip to Muncie, Indiana, to mourn the death of his mother-in-law. Perhaps he noted that *J. F. K.: The Man and the Myth* now topped the *New York Times* best-seller list, that *Publishers Weekly* reported that Putnam had paid an advance "on the high side of the five-figure bracket" to another ideologue from the conservatives' perfervid hack army, Ralph de Toledano, for his *The Winning Side: The Case for Goldwater Republicanism*, a mass-market restatement of the Draft Goldwater strategy, and was ordering up a second large printing before publication.

Kennedy's press secretary, Pierre Salinger, was spooked. He had received a letter on November 19 from a Dallas woman: "Don't let the President come down here. I'm worried about him. I think something terrible will happen to him." Salinger answered the letter personally: "I appreciate your concern for the president, but it would be a sad day for this country if there were any city in the United States he could not visit without fear of violence. I am confident the people of Dallas will greet him warmly." Richard Nixon, on a short visit to Dallas on November 21 for a board meeting at Pepsi-Cola, one of the legal clients that was making him, for the first time in his life, comfortably rich, urged "a courteous reception" for Kennedy.

It was too late for that. Extremists were distributing in the street a "WANTED FOR TREASON" handbill produced by General Walker's Dallas business partner, with face-forward and profile "mug shots" of the President. The *Dallas Morning News* editorialized: "If the speech is about boating you will be among the warmest of admirers. If it is about Cuber [sic], civil rights, taxes, or Vietnam, there will sure as shootin' be some who heave to and let go with a broadside of grapeshot in the presidential rigging." A full-page ad was set in type for the next morning's *News*, but only after consultation with libel lawyers:

WHY have you approved the sale of wheat and corn to our enemies when you know the Communist soldiers "travel on their stomachs" just as ours do? . . .

WHY did you host, salute and entertain Tito—Moscow's Trojan Horse—just a short time after our sworn enemy, Khrushchev, embraced the Yugoslav dictator as a great hero and leader of Communism? . . .

WHY have you banned the showing at U.S. military bases of the film "Operation Abolition"—the movie by the House Committee on Un-American Activities exposing Communism in America? . . .

WHY has the Foreign Policy of the United States degenerated to the point that the C.I.A. is arranging coups and having staunch Anti-Communist Allies of the U.S. bloodily exterminated?

The newspaper hit the streets as H. L. Hunt, whose son had helped bankroll the ad, took to the radio in full-throated bray to predict that Kennedy's next move after passing the civil rights bill would be revoking the right to bear arms. "In dictatorships," he said, "no firearms are permitted, because they would then have the weapons with which to rise up against their oppressors." The *Morning News* was joined on the newsstand by the second installment in a series by Teddy White in *Life* that intimated that the civil rights movement was heading toward racial Armageddon: Adam Clayton Powell was calling for "a Birmingham explosion in New York City" this fall; a "Communist effort" was said to be attempting to penetrate Martin Luther King's circles; civil rights leaders feared they would be labeled as "a front for the white man" unless peaceful marches were converted "into a violent *putsch* on government offices." Some black protesters were calling for cash reparations for slavery, he wrote. "There is the warning that, if such sin-gold is not paid by white Americans to black Americans, the 'power structure' is inviting 'social chaos.' "

The President planned to address the mounting sense of national unease that afternoon in his speech at the Dallas Trade Mart. "In a world of complex and continuing problems, in a world full of frustrations and irritations," the text ran,

> other voices are heard in the land—voices preaching doctrines wholly unrelated to reality, wholly unsuited to the sixties, doctrines which apparently assume that . . . vituperation is as good as victory and that peace is a sign of weakness. . . . At a time when we are steadily reducing the number of Federal employees serving every thousand citizens, they fear those supposed hordes of civil servants far more than the actual hordes of opposing armies.

But the first morning stop was Fort Worth, a pleasing sojourn in Democratic territory. The President warned that "without the United States, South Vietnam would collapse overnight." He repaired to his eighth-floor suite and relaxed with hapless vice president Johnson—who was spending manic hours working to vouchsafe a pleasant reception for his boss in Johnson's home state. Kennedy was comfortable; the reception so far was fine. "We're going to carry two states next year if we don't carry any others: Massachusetts and Texas," Kennedy, cheered, told Johnson in a rare moment of intimacy with the man who most often had been shunted ruthlessly into the background in the previous three years. Then they left for Dallas. And before the afternoon was through, the bottom had dropped out of the United States of America.

PART THREE

NEW MOOD IN POLITICS

A t the offices of the National Draft Goldwater Committee off Farragut Square in Washington, the new publicist was taking his lunch. Lee Edwards had been working his way up conservative movement ranks since signing on as press assistant for Maryland senator John Marshall Butler in 1959: the first editor of YAF's *New Guard*; speechwriter for the July 4 rally. Now he had landed the job of a lifetime. November 22 was his first day.

The secretaries started answering the phones to death threats. *"You sons of bitches, you killed him!"*—SLAM! *"You'll get yours."*—SLAM!

They looked up: a mob was banging on the door. *"Murderers! Murderers!"* They shut the office down—locked the doors, turned off all the lights—and huddled in a back room to take in the broadcasts, nervously. Lee Harvey Oswald: they wracked their brains to remember if they had seen his name before, at some meeting, on one of their mailing lists.

Denison Kitchel and Tony Smith wound up a lunch at the D.C. Sheraton-Carlton with two columnists. The four hopped into a taxi. They heard about the shooting over the radio. It was a few stunned blocks before Tony Smith broke the silence. "My God, one of those Birchers did it."

There was no radio in the cab Richard Nixon found after his flight back east from Dallas. A man leaned into the car window at a stoplight on the Queens side of the 59th Street Bridge and said that Kennedy had been shot. Nixon chose to write it off as a prank. When he got home his doorman rushed out to greet him with tears streaming down his cheeks. Nixon called J. Edgar Hoover. No small talk: "What happened, was it one of the right-wing nuts?"

Much of the country had already decided it was. The Voice of America's bulletin announcing the shooting had described Dallas as "the center of the extreme right wing." Clips of Adlai Stevenson being jabbed with anti–United Nations picket signs a month earlier were shown again and again on TV. Under the headline "DALLAS, LONG A RADICAL'S HAVEN," the *Herald Tribune* pointed out, "Texas is one of the few states that has a Senator ranking with Arizona's Barry Goldwater in conservatism"—that was John Tower, who, in the wake of the assassination, had to put up his family in a hotel because of the threats against them. Senator Maurine Neuberger of Oregon fixed her gaze at the television cameras and pinned the responsibility on H. L. Hunt. Walter Cronkite, on the air nonstop, was handed a slip of paper amid the chaos of CBS's studios and read aloud that Goldwater's reaction to the news while hustling to a political function had been a curt "No comment." (Cronkite skirted libel: Goldwater, in Muncie for the funeral of his mother-in-law, had given no such interview.) A deranged gunman pumped two shots through the window of a John Birch Society office in Phoenix, crying "You killed my man!" In man-in-the-street interviews, a lawyer told the *New York Times*, "We have allowed certain factions to work up such a furor in the South with fanatic criticism of the office of President that a demented person can feel confident that such atrocious action is justifiable," and a Russian immigrant said, "I'm angry at these groups who call themselves Americans and don't know the meaning—the Birchers, General Walker. Is this what they wanted?"

Before long the news of the arrest of Lee Harvey Oswald, a defector to the Soviet Union, was on the street. But the suspicion that the right was somehow to blame did not go away. In Kentucky the YAF chair resigned. "I am now satisfied that the climate of political degeneracy and moral hysteria masquerading as 'true Americanism,' " he said, "bears substantial culpability for the murder of the President of the United States." Police had arrested a Communist; the public blamed conservatives. "When right wing racist fanatics are told over and over again that the President is a traitor, a Red, a 'nigger-lover,' " columnist Max Lerner wrote, "that he has traduced the Constitution and is handing America over to a mongrelized world-state, there are bound to be some fanatics dull-witted enough to follow the logic of the indictment all the way and rid America of the man who is betraying it." As Bishop James A. Pike ruefully said, right-wingers, after all, "have consistently supplied the fuel which would fire up such an assassin."

Partly the irrationality was rooted in fear; the thought that the killer was an agent of the Communist conspiracy was almost too awful to contemplate. (Desperate to close off such suspicions, which he thought might pin him to a commitment to retaliate against the Soviet Union, Lyndon Johnson spent much of his first weeks in office maneuvering hurriedly to close the books on the case by putting together a commission of inquiry led by Chief Justice Warren.) When the news of Oswald's arrest and Communist ties arrived, the public seemed almost willfully to forget the lessons of eighteen years—that Communism was a devious, unitary global conspiracy that would stop at nothing to accomplish its aims—and gladly chose another, less threatening scapegoat. Against the shocks of the recent past—the civil rights uprising, the nuclear close calls—Americans had inoculated themselves by repeating ever more fervidly that we were a good nation, a unified nation, peaceful, safe. The assassination was experienced as a sign that somehow America had let herself become the opposite. A word was repeated again and again, on the streets, before the television cameras, in the newspapers: *hate*. Americans read an indictment on themselves: *hate* killed Kennedy, our own hate—hate that might consume us in violence, hate rife on both sides of the ideological spectrum, hate bred precisely by the act of veering too close to the extremes of the ideological spectrum. Extremism had killed Kennedy.

A typical expression of the sentiment can be seen in a letter the Episcopal bishop of Fond du Lac, Wisconsin, wrote to his flock: "I know that very often each of us did not just disagree, we poured forth our vituperation. The accumulation of this hatred expressed itself in the bullet that killed John Kennedy. I think we know this, and I think it makes us realize just how dreadful we people can be." A young journalist, Hunter S. Thompson, wrote a friend, "The savage nuts have destroyed the great myth of American decency." Senator Frank Church's Intelligence Committee hearings blamed a "conspiratorial atmosphere of violence" for the assassination. Chief Justice Warren—a prominent target of right-wing agitation—said in a service in the Capitol Rotunda that we might never know exactly why Lee Harvey Oswald had shot John F. Kennedy, "but we do know that such acts are commonly stimulated by forces of hatred and malevolence, such as today are eating their way into the bloodstream of American life. What a price we pay for such fanaticism!"

With the far left but a feeble remnant in 1963, the right received the brunt of the outrage; they were the fanatics closest to hand. The fallout would do much to shape the politics of 1964.

The new president was a perfect match for a traumatized nation. Consensus was Lyndon Johnson's religion.

He was a liberal—a liberal in an older, Southern sense of the word: liberalism as *liberality*, as the large-souled dispensing of generosities. Only twenty-seven when he became Texas administrator for the National Youth Administration, a subsidiary of Franklin Roosevelt's Works Progress Administration, he had been shaped by watching dirt-poor districts bloom under the touch of the New Deal. His forte became cultivating relationships with businessmen who could help broker the WPA's largesse. He saw nothing in liberalism that need conflict with businessmen of goodwill, which was why, when he became a congressman in 1937, one liberal tenet he could never embrace was ending the oil depletion allowance. It enriched his district and gave him a hand with the power brokers; what was the harm in that? With business help, his district got the largest rural electrical cooperative in the country (Washington remitted $14 million in four years for the dams), four new hospitals, an air base, a highway. Lyndon Johnson, unlike the young department store owner in Arizona, saw no reason to resent the Southwest's special relationship with the federal government.

Johnson had lost a bid for the Senate in 1941 because of his loyalty to the New Deal. It did nothing to dull his ardor. In his mind, liberals were beaten not by an opposing ideology but by recalcitrant fat cats conspiring against the public interest—which interest *was* liberalism, liberality, the haves sharing with the have-nots and emerging better-off for doing so. By the time Johnson acceded to the Senate in 1948, the Employment Act of 1946 had formalized the federal government's responsibility to do what Johnson had tried to do in his congressional district: guarantee prosperity for all by rising the tide to lift all boats. His own ideology—in its substance as much as in its refusal to recognize itself *as* an ideology—was now the nation's. The *Dallas Morning News* marveled at this new species, the consensus politician: "Business tycoons, left-wing laborites, corporation lawyers, New Dealers, anti–New Dealers, etc."—all, somehow, supported Lyndon Johnson. As Johnson somehow supported all of them.

As Senate majority leader in the 1950s, he concentrated his prodigious energy into dissolving any visible signs of discord—and, some said, of deliberation—in the world's greatest deliberative body. Exploiting party leaders' sovereign power to "motion up" bills for consideration, Johnson kept the number of contested roll calls in the Eighty-fourth Congress under a dozen. Real conflict was taken care of behind the scenes: substituting this favor for that, disbursing from the majority leader's overflowing store of liberalities, *compromising*. A secret to Johnson's success was known around the Capitol as "The Treatment": he planted his gunboat-feet straight in front of your toes, grabbed at your lapel, breathed down on you with hot Texas breath the message that your one vote was what stood between hell everlasting and paradise on earth (or at least between your biggest donor and a federal paving contract). Wheeling and dealing, for him, was nearly the sum of politics. Ideologues baffled him. Under Johnson, the Senate was a machine for getting things done and bringing people together, not for making lots of partisan noise. So, Lyndon Johnson was determined, would be his presidency.

John F. Kennedy's complicated legacy—soaring liberal rhetoric competing with stalled legislative initiatives, stirring preachments of peace with apocalyptic Cold War bellicosity—was dissolving in a warm bath of nostalgia. Jacqueline Kennedy gave her first post-assassination interview to Teddy White, whose *The Making of the President 1960* had clearly preferred JFK to Nixon. She regaled him with tales of how she and Jack used to play their favorite song on an old record player:

> *Don't let it be forgot*
> *That once there was a spot*
> *For one brief shining moment*
> *That was known as Camelot.*

And so the next article Teddy White filed for *Life*, after his dark speculation that racial holocaust was around the corner, retroactively crowned a king who was supposed to have presided over a golden age. Within the month, the JFK fifty-cent coin was approved, New York's Idlewild Field was renamed for him, and three or four Kennedy books were on the best-seller list. Lyndon Johnson was too practical a politician not to spot an opportunity.

"All that I have I would have gladly given not to be standing here today," he began his televised speech to a joint session of Congress two days after the funeral. "On the 20th day of January, in 1961, John F. Kennedy told his countrymen that our national work would not be finished 'in the first thousand days, nor in the life of this administration, nor even perhaps in our lifetime on this planet. *But*,' he said, '*let us begin.*' " The President leaned forward, sticking out his neck for emphasis, as was his wont, as if pecking the audience like a chicken, his Southern drawl smoothed for the occasion. "Today, in this moment of new resolve, I would say to all my fellow Americans, *let us continue!*"

Decisive legislative action would redeem the martyr. Johnson called for expeditious passage of the historic civil rights bill, the education bill, bills for employing youth, developing impoverished areas—passage "with the utmost thrift and frugality."

"This does not mean that we will not meet our unfilled needs or that we will not honor our commitments," he said. *"We will do both."*

Both: it was shaping up as the one-word motto of the new Administration. The hottest political book of 1963—President Kennedy studied it—had been James MacGregor Burns's *The Deadlock of Democracy*. It decried the impossibility of passing substantive new laws because of built-in structural impasses between the legislative and executive branches. Under Johnson the supposed deadlock promptly yielded. He played Congress like a 535-stop church organ.

He was the first President to come from the inner circle of the Senate, the first Southerner since Zachary Taylor, a drinking buddy of the Dixiecrats who controlled Congress through their committee chairmanships. Shortly before his death, Kennedy had sought to cement goodwill from the test-ban treaty by letting the Soviet Union buy U.S. wheat on credit. There was no issue more controversial than foreign aid to Communists. Calling the House into emergency session on Christmas Eve—breaking his own call for a one-month political moratorium—Johnson made controversy melt: House members, dozens returning from home districts to make the vote, answered their President's call to honor the memory of John F. Kennedy by approving the sale. In turn Johnson gave conservatives a relatively frugal $97 billion budget (until they got it below a hundred, he had warned his economic advisers, they "wouldn't pee a drop")—and began with a symbolic effort to cut costs in the White House, most conspicuously by turning off lights in empty rooms. LBJ, Barry Goldwater joked cuttingly, now stood for "Light Bulb Johnson."

Another thing was evident those first few weeks of the Johnson presidency. Two great humiliations had scarred this vain man, this nurser of grievances. The first had come in 1948, when he "won" his Senate seat by 87 votes—the difference coming in a Spanish-speaking rotten borough controlled by a friendly boss. It earned him the nickname "Landslide Lyndon." The second came in 1961. It was, simply, his demotion from his job as the second most powerful man in the United States to the vice presidency, a job he found so depressing—almost clinically so—that he sometimes had to be prodded out of bed in the morning. Now Johnson was President—with Kennedy's advisers, Kennedy's program, and Kennedy's cabinet (including, as attorney general, Kennedy's brother, whom Johnson detested). Johnson had not honestly won a contested election since 1937. He was haunted by feelings of illegitimacy. Before that black November evening in 1963 was over, he realized when he might redeem them both: a November day in 1964. His first calls for guidance were to General Eisenhower and Supreme Court Justice Arthur Goldberg. The next was to a man of considerably less stature: the DNC's chief fund-raiser, Richard Maguire. "You be giving some thought to what needs to be done," the President told him, "and we'll get together in the next day or two."

In Republican circles that fancied themselves polite, the conclusion was drawn quietly. The press, less courtly, didn't let a decent interval pass: Lee Harvey Oswald had cut down Barry Goldwater's chances as surely as he had John Kennedy's life. Dixie would never reject one of their own for President in the voting booth. And without a member of the Eastern Establishment as his opponent, it was thought, Goldwater lost much of his appeal. No, said the *Herald Tribune*'s Robert Novak, the new front-runner would have to be "a proper Republican candidate"—a moderate who could win the Big Six. Gallup confirmed the trend: Goldwater's approval rating since the assassination was down sixteen points. And so, one by one, proper—moderate—Republicans began floating to the fore.

On December 8, President Johnson's first morning waking up in the White House, the *New York Times*'s lead story claimed—no sources, no quotes—that Dwight Eisenhower, after satisfying himself that he bore no responsibility in the Diem assassination, endorsed Henry Cabot Lodge, America's ambassador to Vietnam, for President. No matter that Lodge was reported farther down the column to have rejected the idea outright—or that farther down still, an AP dispatch had Eisenhower denying from his favorite golf course in Georgia that he had spoken to Lodge about the presidency in the first place. The idea had been planted.

It wasn't a few days before the papers had Richard Nixon hustling down to Gettysburg to call on the General. Insiders saw it coming. Shortly before the assassination, Nixon, deciding he was out of the running, was on the verge of signing a contract to publish a chronicle of the 1964 election. After the assassination, he broke the deal and began campaigning for party elder statesman: setting up magazine articles, speaking tours, and trips abroad on "official" duties for his law firm. Rumors were he wanted to swoop down to dutifully accept the prize after maneuvering for a convention deadlock. In Gallup's first December sounding of which candidate Republicans preferred for the nomination, Nixon scored highest, with 29 percent. (Before, it had been Goldwater, with well over half.) The *Washington Post*'s Herblock, long a Nixon bête noire, drew Goldwater and Rockefeller unsuspectingly striding forth as Nixon waited for them to stumble into twin graves he had dug in their path.

Goldwater was digging his own grave. "I'm still wishing something would happen to get me out of all this," he told *Time* in an interview that ran in the issue dated November 22, 1963. The assassination, and a bone injury in his right heel that left him in searing pain, had sent him into a tailspin of depression, to which he was prone; within days he told Denny Kitchel to spread the word that he would not run. He wrote people like the editor of *Human Events* to implore them to stop watering the grass roots. Goldwater had relished the idea of running against JFK, whom he found an honorable man. He hated the idea of running against LBJ—whom he considered a ruthless opportunist. When their names had begun to show up together as convenient, charismatic bookends for lazy reporters seeking to frame the political scene, Goldwater and

Kennedy had started taking pleasure in displaying their mutual affection in public, and had talked idly about sharing a campaign plane and debating at every campaign stop, Lincoln-and-Douglas-style. (Goldwater seemed not to notice that Kennedy was ruthless, too; Goldwater always had trouble thinking anything but the best of his friends.)

He liked his freedom: flying himself to speeches, maybe dropping in at an Air Force base somewhere and begging a turn at the controls of the latest model, overflying Navajo country, poking around on his ham rig, listening to Dixieland jazz records full blast and then fussing with his trombone, or cranking up the air-conditioning full blast, building a roaring fire in his library, and settling in with a good Western or *Indian Art of the Americas*. He liked rocketing around Washington in his two-seat Thunderbird, the dashboard built to look like a jet cockpit, or ducking down to the Capitol's basement machine shop to pull some gadget apart and put it back together. Twice a year he liked flying to Michigan to buy the new Heathkit electric hobby kits the day they came off the line.

And he was scared. He had a favorite Western maxim: A good man knows the length of his rope. "Doggone it," he told the *Chicago Tribune*, "I'm not even sure that I've got the brains to be President of the United States." He worried whether he had the courage to do what he said he wanted to do in the White House. And what if lightning struck and he won? What would he be then but master of the world's most Byzantine bureaucracy?

Any day now, Clif White feared, Goldwater might file that dreaded Sherman statement: he would not run if nominated, would not serve if elected. And White had to decide whether to continue.

The answer came with the mail. In the seven days following the assassination, Draft Goldwater pulled in the same $25,000 in donations they did just about every week. They decided to do what they always did: act like it didn't matter what Barry Goldwater did or didn't say. Telegrams urging Goldwater to run were pouring in from young conservatives who were unaware that the office had no official connection to the senator; now Carol Bauman and Lee Edwards began to tap YAF's mailing lists to coordinate a deluge. The next week White was off to New Mexico, to continue his lonely tour of party district conventions: wandering the ballroom, working the phones, making sure his deputy's hand-picked candidates had the votes they needed and knew their orders to the letter. He would do just what his President counseled: he would continue.

He had to pretend it didn't matter that the previous fall, Denison Kitchel had moved to Washington—into Goldwater's building—to take over contingency plans for the possible presidential bid. White was singularly unimpressed by this short, introverted man whose manner was as bristly as his flat-top haircut. It was said that no one was better at beating a union organizing drive. Could anyone be worse at organizing a political campaign? When Kitchel asked him how national conventions worked, White had to pitch the explanation at a kindergarten level.

At first there was just Kitchel and a secretary. Then Dick Kleindienst began working in the field. Then came an administrative assistant, Dean Burch, a Tucson lawyer and former Goldwater Senate staffer. None had a day's experience in national elections. The rumor around Washington was that Burch had never crossed the Mississippi before he went to work for Goldwater at the age of twenty-eight. "A bunch of cowboys," they called themselves; proud, almost, of what they didn't know. They were dubbed the "Arizona Mafia." They socialized mostly with the senator—cursing like sailors in Navajo, sharing inscrutable Southwestern maxims about breaking one's pick and the length of one's rope—and they seemed uncomfortable around anyone else. Burch wore dark suits and black ties and was perennially asked if he was heading to a funeral. "I always wear black ties," he would reply serenely. "I like them."

White had even more reason to fear because the previous fall dark, stout, suave William J. Baroody, head of the conservative American Enterprise Institute "think tank," had begun offloading the cream of his associates to Kitchel's staff: Edward McCabe, Eisenhower's old congressional liaison, became director of research; Karl Hess, AEI's director of special projects, a Buddha-like man whom an admiring Goldwater called "Shakespeare," wrote speeches; Austrian émigré Robert Strausz-Hupé, a hard-line Cold War theorist, became foreign policy consultant; Chuck Lichenstein, a Yale teacher and ex–Nixon staffer, became a factotum. Baroody was exploiting the vacuum of political experience in Goldwater's new inner circle to become its brain.

First, after buttering up Kitchel with intellectual flattery (the Arizonan studied constitutional law in his spare time), Baroody humbly offered himself up to Kitchel as a guide to Washington's curious ways. Then he moved to eliminate a possible rival. Goldwater's association with *National Review*, Baroody told Kitchel, would play into the hands of enemies who wished to isolate Goldwater on the right-wing fringe. Bill Buckley had approached Jay Hall with some ideas for the campaign. Hall lured him to a dinner with Kitchel and Baroody to discuss them. Then Baroody leaked news of the meeting to one of his contacts at the *New York Times*—who dutifully ventriloquized Baroody's story that "the Goldwater for President ship just repelled a boarding party" that had "cornered some Goldwater aides" for a "share of the Goldwater command." No more William F. Buckley.

That was in character. Baroody was cagey, Machiavellian, hungry—a conservative empire builder. A devout Maronite Christian, like his father, who was an immigrant Lebanese stonecutter from Manchester, New Hampshire, he also did not know how to compromise when it came to principle.

His American Enterprise Institute began in 1943 as the American Enterprise Association, a little business lobby against wartime price controls. By 1953 it was little more than a luncheon club for visiting executives. The outfit was on the verge of shutting down when Baroody, then a chamber of commerce staffer, was brought in to see if he could resuscitate it. His partner, W. Glenn Campbell, a Harvard-trained economist, assembled a top-notch stable of scholars; Baroody worked tirelessly to make them indispensable to the city's workings. Washington was complex, and AEA made its name by making it simpler—providing legislators with a steady stream of issue guides that meticulously and fairly spelled out both sides of a pending bill, amendment, or policy question. Every word was vetted by an advisory council of professors.

In 1962 Baroody changed AEA's name to the American Enterprise Institute—trade groups in Washington were called "Associations," and he was selling a research center. He took in enormous sums of money; Howard J. Pew gave $100,000 that year alone. AEI began producing scholarship—monograph after monograph, with dozens of tables and graphs, promising things like "essential cost data, much of it never before assembled, on which any rational policy of public education must be based" (any rational policy of public education, it turned out, reserved no role for the federal government). Ideas once enforced at union-busting manufacturies by goon squad and court injunction now received scientific demonstration by economists with Austrian names. At his home, Bill Baroody convened grand salons where he sketched dreams of a conservative counterestablishment. To reporters he blandly proclaimed, "I really can't say whether I am a liberal or a conservative." He called himself a social, not political, friend of Goldwater's. He kept pictures of himself with people like Hubert Humphrey on his office walls. That was for the feds: AEI had a tax exemption to preserve. Admirers called this style intellectual entrepreneurship.

White was unmoved. The first project of Kitchel's eggheads was contracting for a "Recordak"—a computer programmed to file everything Goldwater ever said on any subject on punched cards for handy cross-referencing. White found the $10,000 expense about as relevant to the task at hand—lining up delegates—as, well, hiring a foreign policy consultant. White collected stories of Denison Kitchel's incompetence. "Who's Arthur Summerfield?" Kitchel asked when advised to consult the former RNC chair; "What line of work are you in?" he queried an uncommitted Republican senator. (It was then that White prepared a detailed notebook outlining the peculiarities, loyalties, and pecca-dilloes of every important name in the Republican Party for Kitchel to consult whenever one should happen to call.) When White learned Kitchel was hard of hearing—in a field where the most important work was done in whispers!—that clinched it: it was only a matter of time before Goldwater recognized the web spun out from Suite 3505 for the rare and marvelous thing that it was and relegated Kitchel to the background.

If he ever decided to seek the nomination.

The day the *New York Times* revealed Eisenhower's fondness for Henry Cabot Lodge, both White's and Kitchel's top men—along with Republican Johnny Rhodes, former senator Bill Knowland, and current senators Carl Curtis and Norris Cotton—teamed up to confront Barry Goldwater in his Washington apartment. They spoke in terms he understood best: duty. "Barry," began Carl Curtis, who had been the first politician to openly identify himself as a Gold-water delegate way back in May of 1963, "the time has come to either fish or cut bait."

The moral authority in the room belonged to Norris Cotton. He was a mod-erate—perhaps, by the flinty standards of New Hampshire, a liberal. He had gone far out on a limb for Goldwater the previous fall by becoming the first GOP leader in New Hampshire to back him, and Goldwater's refusal to back him up in return with an announcement of his candidacy had created a political hardship. So Cotton spoke last. He compared Goldwater to de Gaulle holding out against the Nazis; he brought much of the room to tears. It wasn't enough. Goldwater interrupted the waterworks to politely inform them that he wasn't yet ready to make a decision. It was excruciatingly awkward. Goldwater felt trapped. He had felt trapped ever since Clarence Manion had shoved him for-ward as a potential nominee in 1960. And he also felt obligated. Conservatism was his life's cause.

The crowd dispersed, leaving behind only two old friends, two glasses of Old Crow, and a plenitude of silence. "Barry," Denison Kitchel finally said, "I don't think you can back down." He reminded Goldwater of the thousands upon thousands of lesser Norris Cottons who had staked so much on him. There was no opinion Barry Goldwater respected more than Denison Kitchel's. Goldwater told him to inform his two Senate colleagues, in confidence, that he would run. Publicly, he kept his counsel for another agonizing three weeks.

Draft Goldwater met on December 11. A new strategy of entering as many pri-maries as possible to prove Goldwater's popularity was discussed. The committee turned over the idea of recruiting Len Hall, the party's top operative, as campaign manager. The finance committee reported that fund-raising was ahead of schedule.

They were going through the motions. The meeting had been called by White to inform them that their organization was being absorbed into the new Goldwater for President Committee, overseen by Denison Kitchel. When White had learned that Goldwater would announce his candidacy after the New Year at his home in Phoenix, he prepared for Kitchel a list of National Draft Goldwater Committee volunteers who deserved recognition in Goldwater's speech. White booked hotel rooms and a banquet hall in Phoenix to celebrate with his comrades. Then he was told that Barry wanted only his Arizonan political team present. And White canceled his reservations.

Soon afterward Len Hall rebuffed a plea to run Rockefeller's campaign. It was rumored he wanted to go to work for Goldwater. Kitchel met him for lunch. Washington protocol demanded that newcomer Kitchel address old hand Hall as supplicant. Instead Kitchel blustered: "I want you to understand, Mr. Hall, that we're not *asking* you to work for us." The Republicans' most competent operative, trusted by all factions, glad to oblige, never set foot inside the Goldwater nominating campaign. Clif White, an old friend, probably could have won Hall in a heartbeat.

New Year's Eve: Governor Rockefeller announced the expected arrival of a child in early June (the *Washington Post* also reported that Rockefeller would make a nationwide TV and radio broadcast to plea for "tolerance and understanding" on the issue of remarriage, but apparently someone talked him out of it). Lyndon Johnson had just signed a $4.4 billion public works bill; six liberal Republican senators announced a measure to guarantee medical care for the elderly, financed, as JFK wished, out of Social Security. In Pasadena, General Eisenhower grand-marshaled the Rose Bowl Parade (he told the Kiwanis Club Kickoff Luncheon that football helped mold the American character and that "every game means something to the United States"). Among those crowded streetside was Richard G. Kleindienst. He was heading back home on January 3 when he was greeted by a highway patrolman at the Arizona Border Inspection Station: "Dick Kleindienst? You are to proceed directly to Senator Goldwater's home in Phoenix."

"Why, is there anything wrong?" (He hadn't been told that his friend had decided to run.)

"Don't ask me—that's all that I know."

He drove faster than he should have. He snaked up the steep, winding road just outside the city limits to the base of Goldwater's still-steeper, windier driveway and was waved through by the Young Republican girls tending the electric gate with its Navajo-style crest. Local press had begun arriving at 7 a.m. Goldwater, who had recently announced that his daughter was to wed in June, ambled out in jeans and bedroom slippers and joked to the familiar faces that he had called them out to his home to announce that his daughter had been knocked up and they were having the wedding next week.

Kleindienst marveled at the scene. He glimpsed Peg, looking entirely too listless, herding Maricopa County sheriffs in tight brown slacks and ten-gallon hats to their appointed positions. Her mother had just died; her brother was ailing. The cops were there because of a bomb threat. She couldn't be pleased at turning over her garage to Western Union and the telephone company, or at the TV crews trampling her yellow roses, marigolds, bougainvillea, and desert blooms (may they back into an organ-pipe cactus!), or at catering tuna-fish sandwiches for the strangers who had banged and clanked their way through the night in her backyard. Peggy was part deaf, and abhorred publicity. She had given up dreams of becoming an artist to be a politician's wife. She and Barry had a good marriage, taking Caribbean cruises one year for her and outdoor adventures the next for him. Barry never asked her to appear on television with him except late on the last day of a campaign. But he had first informed Kitchel of his intentions—and only then his wife. She was a creature of her generation. She said, "If that's what you want to do, go ahead and do it. I don't particularly want you to run, but I'm not going to stand in your way."

Kleindienst handed over his keys to the Young Republican men parking cars, feeling a bit conspicuous in his casual dress, and was led across Bia-Nun-I-Kin's shining green floor (slate mined from Navajo country), past tables inlaid with silver-and-turquoise Indian designs, to the master bedroom in the back, where Kitchel, Burch, and Goldwater—the crutches from his recent bone surgery by his side—awaited him. He wondered where Steve Shadegg was.

The answer was: in the doghouse. In 1962, to ensure passage of crucial water legislation, Arizona Republican leaders had planned to let eighty-five-year-old Carl Hayden run unopposed. Then a hotheaded Pontiac dealer, Evan Mecham, a Bircher who considered Goldwater's bunch an unaccountable establishment, decided to run for the Republican nomination. Shadegg entered the primary to block him—against Goldwater's wishes. Goldwater was a stickler for loyalty. Shadegg was never close to him after that—although one wonders whether the resentment hadn't been building up for some time before. Shadegg had run Goldwater's Senate campaigns all the way down to what he wore and what he said. Now Goldwater was caught up in this whole business again, this time with Clif White's grasping hotheads trying to call the shots. That, in fact, was why these men were here. Goldwater had decided this campaign would be different. He would run it his way. Kitchel learned he was going to be campaign manager. Burch would be his assistant. And Kleindienst would be director of field operations.

"And what am I supposed to do as—what did you call it?—director of field operations?" Kleindienst asked, more irritated than amused.

What he was supposed to do was ensure Goldwater the 655 delegates he needed to be nominated—although Kleindienst had never worked on a primary before, and had barely attended a political convention outside of Arizona. Kleindienst told his dear friend he was crazy.

"Listen, and get this straight," Goldwater growled in response. "I'm not going to turn my life over to people I don't know and trust if I'm going to go through with this. Either the three of you agree to go through this with me or I'm not going to do it!"

It was a Friday—as President Johnson observed that night after cutting short a tour for reporters of the Texas hill country to watch a tape of the announcement on the *Huntley-Brinkley Report*. Johnson wondered why Goldwater didn't announce on a Sunday: "He'd get more space in the Monday morning papers." Goldwater's advisers had said the same thing. They also insisted he would get more coverage announcing from Washington. But Barry was determined to do this his way or not at all.

Goldwater stepped out from the bedroom to the living room, where thirty Arizona Republican leaders were gathered around the coffee table supported by a fifteen-hundred-pound ironwood log. Outside, a radio broadcaster said, "Any comment on his intentions would be premature at this time." (Somewhere in New York, Rockefeller's men transcribed the broadcast.) Inside, a cheer went up. The drapes opened. Camera shutters exploded. Goldwater prepared to hobble out onto his patio and into a typically beautiful Arizona day. He had a great photo of himself on that patio, on one knee, a shotgun resting on the other, in jeans, rawhide jacket, and a cowboy hat, a saguaro by his side and Camelback Mountain (and, dimly visible, slightly spoiling the effect, a set of pool furniture) in the background. Now, dressed in a dark blue suit, microphone draped around his neck, he looked uncomfortable. He paused. "Come on in, Barry, the water's fine," an Arizona reporter quipped to scattered laughs.

The candidate placed two sheets of paper on the lectern. The words were stirring: "I will not change my beliefs to win votes. I will offer a choice, not an echo." Their delivery was not. It came in a slow, drab monotone. He barely looked up.

Reporters asked him what role students had played in the rise of his political fortunes. He said they did "more than any other one factor." He was asked

to repeat the name of his field manager—"That's K-L-E-I-N-D-I-E-N-S-T."
(They whispered baffled inquiries.) Then they asked for another name he had
mentioned. "Dean Burch. That's not related to John Birch. B-U-R-C-H." The
reporters laughed, then remembered to ask Goldwater one more question:
Would he accept the support of the John Birch Society? (Back at his office in
Washington, White winced to hear his candidate expose his Achilles' heel.)
Goldwater gave the same answer as always: "I see no reason to take a stand
against any organization just because they're using their constitutional prerogatives even though I disagree with most of them." White's office girls broke
out bottles of champagne. White was in no mood to celebrate. He had already
been told Kleindienst was taking his job. He had, reluctantly, close to tears,
taken a position as Kleindienst's subordinate.

Lyndon Johnson broke into a broad smile when Chet Huntley pronounced,
"At the LBJ Ranch, meanwhile, the nation's business went forward." Between
bites of gulf shrimp and smoked venison, LBJ's guests asked him if he thought
Richard Nixon would run. "I don't know," the President replied. "I don't even
know whether I will." His close aide Walter Jenkins had just reported to him on
a poll that 93 percent of Californians were "favorably impressed" with how he
had taken over the presidency. The morning's Gallup poll had him scoring
around 70 percent against every Republican. Walter Heller, chair of the Council of Economic Advisors, flew out to the ranch to tell the President that the
gross national product had risen $30 billion in 1963 and that 6.5 percent growth
was predicted in 1964. But Lyndon Johnson was a man prone to melancholy.

Nelson Rockefeller was in the midst of his second campaign swing in New
Hampshire, dispelling rumors he was running as a placeholder until the Eastern
Establishment united behind someone more electable. "I am neither a summer
soldier nor a sunshine patriot of the political wars," he told a crowd at
Portsmouth High School. Then he told them he would save their navy yard.

It looked like a Rockefeller-Goldwater showdown in New Hampshire—which
led the more hard-nosed among Republican operatives to heave hearty sighs of
relief. Now one or the other of these bothersome characters would receive the
knockout blow each so richly deserved.

The afternoon after Labor Day, 1963, Rockefeller had invited his neighbor, Richard Nixon, over for a cocktail. (As if in some fit of masochism, Nixon
had bought an apartment next door to the very lair where he had capitulated to
Rockefeller in 1960.) "I'm going for the nomination," Rockefeller said. "I'm
not going to back out this time. I have nothing to lose." He leaned in: "What
you and I both have to recognize is that you and I are the only ones qualified."
Nixon screwed on a poker face. It became difficult to maintain. "What I want

you to suggest," Rockefeller continued, "is that if you will support me now, if there is a deadlock at the convention, I will support you." Nixon, having made enough deals within these particular precincts to last a lifetime, hastily turned Rockefeller down.

Rockefeller had announced his candidacy on November 7, 1963, early in the morning for broadcast live on the *Today* show on NBC, then winged away for his first New Hampshire trip, ignoring every hint that he didn't have a chance. One day that week he chartered a plane to bring forty-two Maryland Republicans to lunch in Manhattan. Then he traveled to Miami for a speech; then he was back to New York to speak to the AFL-CIO convention; then he ended the day in Missouri, with a speech to the St. Louis Press Club. Virtually all he had to show for such exertions was perhaps the most hedged endorsement in electoral history, from Baltimore mayor Theodore Roosevelt McKeldin— "Until I find a better qualified man, I'm for Governor Rockefeller"—and the unqualified endorsement of Jimmy Hoffa.

He tried everything. He borrowed Richard Nixon's strategy of statesmanship through high-minded speechifying: to the American Political Science Association (for a national transportation policy); in hardscrabble Appalachian coal country (promising programs for the 20 million predicted to be unemployed by 1970); to the Indiana Bar Association (on civil liberties). He pressed the flesh, old school–style, in Illinois, in Oregon (where he hired a lighting consultant), in California (where his personal film crew tramped along to provide footage to local network affiliates). He arranged ostentatious meetings with clergymen to neutralize the only issue really on anyone's mind—even, adding poignancy to the old saw that every presidential candidate visits Ireland, Israel, and Italy, arranging a private audience with the Pope. For an appearance at a closed-circuit Republican fund-raiser, his PR director prepared a long memo on the lighting, the makeup, what color to wear, and the distance the TelePrompTer would be from his face. There were paid Rockefeller staffers at work by the beginning of the year in states from Florida to Alaska.

But his only promising gambit was negative. "Can you imagine the prospect of these policies being presented to the American people next year?" he said in Miami. "Advocacy of such proposals as having the U.S. withdraw from the United Nations . . . of selling TVA, of ending immediately support prices for farmers, of leaving the protection of human rights up to the states— including Mississippi and Alabama. These ideas are not in the mainstream of American thinking."

And deep within the recesses of 22 West 55th a department was hard at work to provide him with stronger stuff. The effort was headed by a former undercover operative from the chief of staff's office whose specialty had been destroying the public reputations of politicians in dozens of countries around the world. "I can take anybody—I don't care who it is—and develop material that would annihilate them," Graham Thomas Tate Molitor liked to brag, embracing the label of Barry Goldwater's "political assassin."

Molitor made arrangements with friendly reporters to record for transcription virtually every word Goldwater said in public. Agents would shout embarrassing questions at Goldwater, then shove a microphone into his face. Meanwhile, his staff clipped and filed every Goldwater utterance they could find going back to the 1930s, trolling them for gaffes which, if publicized correctly, could knock Goldwater flat on his back. By May, major speeches were being recorded by multiple operatives running tapes in relays to a nearby real-time transcription center at ten-minute intervals; sometimes they set up a telephone system so Goldwater speeches could be transcribed live at Rockefeller headquarters. Reporters—and operatives in the guise of reporters—strode into Goldwater headquarters to beg advance copies of speeches or, if need be, steal one off a desk.

Rockefeller needed Molitor. He hadn't a teaspoon of bargaining power within his own party leadership. His only hope was with the voters—the vast, fickle public. If he could win New Hampshire on March 10, he could capture momentum. If he could win in California on June 2—adding the second biggest delegate block to the biggest one, New York, which he already owned—he might have the base for a convention stampede.

He was on the verge, his people were convinced, of owning California. Money had the advantage there; money could retain the best publicity agencies. The state's open initiative system had concentrated the energies of wealthy groups to seek out ever-more-elaborate ways to bend the system to their ends. Aggressive and creative PR firms sprang up to help them. (One initiative passed with the slogan "Keep California Green"; it was a tax break to private country clubs.) Soon these publicists invented a new job description: full-service campaign consultant, covering everything from walking the (inordinately sprawling) precincts, to fund-raising, to building the candidate's image—and, especially, advertising.

By the time Rockefeller came looking for a firm in the summer of 1963, one was playing the game better than anyone else: Spencer-Roberts & Associates. They were wizards. A candidate with no experience they would package as a citizen politician, a lifetime hack as an elder statesman. But they worked only for candidates they thought could win. Rockefeller was twenty percentage points behind in the early polling. His political chief, George Hinman, begged; they turned him down flat. Then Rockefeller himself did the begging, on an October trip, armed with a persuasive tool no politician in history could match.

Spencer-Roberts, after all, was a business. The $2 million operating budget Rockefeller offered the firm was unprecedented. They took the job. First they snapped up all of California's prime outdoor advertising spots. No campaign had ever been able to do anything like that; advertising agencies demanded cash up front, and no other campaign could ever have dreamed of having enough.

For his next task Hinman took up full-time residence in a bungalow at L.A.'s Ambassador Hotel. In the California primary, voters picked not the candidate, but a delegate slate pledged to him. Hinman's aim was to assemble a stellar cast of familiar names. He won over San Francisco mayor George Christopher; movie mogul Jack Warner; Eisenhower labor secretary Jim Mitchell; a member of the family who owned the *Los Angeles Times*; a scion of the Firestone tire family. Thomas Kuchel, preeminent heir of his state's Progressive Era anti-partisanism, was reluctant to get involved in a primary. Hinman persuaded him to sign on as campaign chair. Kuchel came out fighting, with a statement calling for a party "that speaks the same political gospel on both sides of the Mason-Dixon line," that would "not abandon the courageous doctrine it espoused in Lincoln's day and through the years to Eisenhower's time" to fight "for equality for all Americans before the law." The enemy, on the other hand (he didn't name names), "would endanger, if not destroy, the American two-party system."

Hinman convinced Kuchel the same way he had convinced most of his delegates. These were the men watching in horror as *their* party slipped away to the right-wing lunatics—people like the new state school superintendent, Max Rafferty. The board of education was about to vote on his recommendation challenging the teaching of evolution. "There is a new wind blowing in politics," Rafferty told *Fortune*, "but it isn't really political. I liken it to religion." Hinman told his Rockefeller delegates that they weren't *really* Rockefeller delegates, hinting that Rockefeller would step aside for another, more electable, moderate at the convention: they were fighting a crusade to save their party from the infidels.

GRANITE STATE

In the first new year after the President was slain, the nation mustered a determined optimism. The *New York Times* ran a multi-article package on January 6, headlined "COMPANY PROFITS ASTOUND EXPERTS; EXCEED ALL EXPECTATIONS—RECORD FIGURES CERTAIN." The *Los Angeles Times* was thrilled to be reporting "UCLA PUPILS NOT RADICAL, POLL SHOWS; MIDDLE-OF-THE-ROAD VIEWS PREVAIL."

Not all tidings were glad, to be sure; traffic deaths rose, farm incomes stagnated; in Washington, Labor Secretary Willard Wirtz, concluding a study of the draft pool, found one in three young men part of a "human slag heap of unemployables." The *Los Angeles Times* was obliged to report of the UCLA students, in a subhead, "Sex Ideas May Shock." The Surgeon General delivered a report that smoking was hazardous to your health. In Philadelphia, civil rights activists had attempted to get an injunction to ban the city's celebrated, nationally televised Mummers' Parade—a holiday-time tradition since 1834, in which hundreds of white revelers marched downtown in blackface as thousands lined the streets. The magistrate, declaring no harm intended, ruled that the spectacle, for which upwards of a million spectators were expected, could go forward so long as marchers "don't poke fun at anybody." The police chief canceled all vacation leaves for officers in order to get up a big enough force to ensure peace. But only 35,000 spectators showed up.

There was the usual background noise of the Cold War: Chou En-lai attacking Tito as a "U.S. tool"; Ceylon nationalizing the oil fields; Britain and France selling buses and trucks to Cuba; France recognizing Red China. But in the wake of the test-ban treaty, said *U.S. News*, "It's been a generation or more since the world was as quiet as now." Vietnam, the magazine reported, was "a local war. . . . *Big war* is not threatened." A *New York Times* subhead noted, of rocketing levels of consumer debt, "Experts Unworried." In January of 1964, experts weren't worried about much. Worrying was out of style.

Perhaps that was why Barry Goldwater's nine-year string of good press was about to vanish in a puff of smoke.

His first public appearance as a presidential candidate came on a cool, clear Sunday, on NBC's *Meet the Press*. Chafing at the idleness enforced by the injury to his foot, he refused a ride to the studio. (The thing on his foot was called a walking cast, after all.) It was the first mistake of his campaign. He tried not to betray the agonizing throb when the *Washington Star*'s David Broder asked him if he'd been briefed. No, he explained; the last time he had been on the show he hadn't even been asked the questions he was briefed on.

That was the second mistake.

The half hour was excruciating. Barry hurt so badly he couldn't think straight. Asked about his avowals that he would like to see the United States withdraw diplomatic recognition from the Soviet Union, he said that ultimately the decision was up to the Senate—although the Constitution vested that power in the President. He said he would break the test-ban treaty if he thought it would be to our military advantage, citing Dr. Hans Morgenthau, "one of the greatest physicists in the world," as his authority—although Morgenthau was a political scientist and supported the treaty (months later, Morgenthau would write that Goldwater embodied "the threat of fascism in America"). Broder asked him if he would have used federal troops at Ole Miss. Goldwater said, wrongly, "If you will recall, he didn't use federal troops. . . . He sent federal marshals in." He said, bafflingly, that he didn't worry about most of the countries lost to Communism because they were "going to go through the same period of growth that the United States did, when we spent 110 or 112 years experimenting with socialism and communism and egalitarianism and monarchy and everything else, arriving at our constitutional republic."

Gaffes aside, the substance of his remarks wouldn't surprise any reader of *Conscience of a Conservative*, *Why Not Victory?*, or the thrice-weekly column he had only recently stopped producing. Those numbers included practically all of the top Republicans—who were just then arriving in Washington for the annual Republican National Committee meeting. Which was just it; fence-sitters in the RNC, the ones still thinking about which candidate to back—like Len Hall, described as "a jockey looking for a mount"—were seeing Barry Goldwater perform under real pressure for the first time. They knew he had a reputation for loose talk. But if this was Goldwater under the studio lights with sweet-tempered Dave Broder, what would he be like across the table from Khrushchev? Then there were the millions who had never read, heard, or seen Barry Goldwater for any extended period. Many just found him unpleasant. Some thought he was terrifying.

"If you were elected President of the United States, would you under no circumstances negotiate with the Communists on disarmament?" asked host Lawrence Spivak. "I don't think negotiations are possible," Goldwater answered. If invited to parley, he would respond, "If you mean what you say, Mr. Khrushchev, put up or shut up—as we Western poker players say."

Goldwater didn't have time to rest before he was whisked off to Grand Rapids to give his first speech of the campaign, at a Michigan Republican Party dinner. He was met upon landing by over one thousand screaming fans, on a night almost too snowy to land the plane.

The demonstration was coordinated by Young Americans for Freedom, which was thriving. The group had moved from New York to Washington and hired a new executive director—which freed Richard Viguerie to pursue his true love, direct mail. One letter to donors brought in $10,000 in three weeks. Missives to prospective members were attracting four to five hundred new YAFers a month—true believers as ready to muster on a tarmac at a moment's notice as the Eighty-second Airborne.

The Kent County Republican Finance Committee was thrilled to find its routine fund-raising dinner suddenly a national event. Every Republican from miles around now wanted to hear what Barry Goldwater sounded like when he spoke not just to them, but to the nation. The answer was: the same. He gave his standard fusillade against the Democratic Party—it was "no longer the party of Jefferson and of Wilson, of principle and principled liberalism" and "seeks political conformity, social sameness, and regimented rules," measuring "welfare by the number of votes it produces"; its youth and vigor had "vanished into the creaking gears of machine politics all over America." He merely replaced the name Kennedy with Johnson. His opponent for the nomination was Nelson Rockefeller. The dinner attendees had just paid $100 to learn they shouldn't vote for Lyndon Johnson.

Two-thirds of the way through his speech, he did mention the campaign— to disclaim interest: "I want to assure you quickly that I haven't sought this role. My conscience and the principles I hold have led me to it, and it's because I believe in those principles and because I see no clear way to give this nation a choice that I have decided to seek the nomination of my party." The next day he was asked if he expected pressure in New Hampshire to change his views. There hadn't been any pressure in the past, he said, so he didn't expect any now.

The cognac was being poured in Michigan as Goldwater settled into his seat on the rented DC-3 for his first three-day trip for the March 10 New Hampshire primary. When he heard the itinerary Norris Cotton's people had prepared for him, he cursed the New Hampshire senator's very name. Wednesday began with an hour's drive to a 9:30 a.m. coffee hour—a half hour, actually—at a home in Nashua; 11:30 at a parish house in someplace called Milford; 1:15 in Amherst. The next day—just about every day—began with an early-morning press conference.

At Concord Airport, the snow was worse than it had been in Michigan. They landed in the middle of the night. The candidate lifted his cast for the first painful first step down the staircase to the tarmac—where hundreds of chanting fans awaited.

He growled to Cotton, who was waiting at the bottom to meet him: "Don't you New Hampshire people believe in going to bed?"

They did, of course, and early—or so the stereotypes said. It was part of the Granite State's political catechism. New Hampshire as we know it was invented in 1952, when Estes Kefauver, strapped for cash against commanding favorite Adlai Stevenson, took up the fool's errand of visiting every hamlet big enough to have a room to host him. The sight of this lanky, drawling Tennesseean—taciturn and hardy like them—slogging through the snow up around the 45th parallel so impressed the natives that they gave him a surprise success that launched him into contention for the Democratic nomination. And the word was handed down for all time: A New Hampshire voter must see the candidate in the flesh, not just driving by in a car. He must not knock on a door, for Granite Staters loathed to be disturbed in the sanctity of their home. You must never pass up a town your opponent deems worthy of a visit. Then there was the handshake: it must not be too soft; nor should it be too firm.

And if you were a Republican, you'd best get on the good side of William Loeb.

Loeb published the biggest newspaper in the state, the *Manchester Union Leader*, with 40 percent of the state's readers, three times more than his nearest competitor—its influence all the greater in a state with only one TV station, receiving the rest of its television news from Boston. Bill Loeb was a surpassingly strange man to control a state. He carried a pearl-handled revolver everywhere he went, claimed to have personally infiltrated the New Hampshire arm of the Communist conspiracy, reported the death of Joseph McCarthy in 1957 with the headline "MURDERED!" (His suspect was "that stinking hypocrite in the White House.") He saw to it that any local office seeker who proposed raising taxes could expect not to live to see another political day. A presidential primary candidate whom he disfavored could expect daily front-page editorials of the sort Nelson Rockefeller was suffering now—"spoiled, rich glamour boy" and "wife-swapper" Nelson Rockefeller (Loeb was twice divorced himself). For Baroody (who was a native) and Kitchel (who had gone to prep school in the state), Loeb's support clinched the case: New Hampshire was Goldwater country.

No matter that almost everyone with any experience in the matter disagreed. In December Peter O'Donnell made a post-assassination inspection tour and told Kitchel they might get clobbered. Raymond Moley, the former Roosevelt brain truster (he coined the phrase "New Deal") who wrote a conservative column in *Newsweek*, told Burch that if Goldwater won, the media would call it predictable, and if he lost, it might sink him altogether. Even Loeb (who sported a perpetual ruddy tan from his frequent visits to Arizona, where a favorite social companion was Barry Goldwater) thought that Goldwater should pass on New Hampshire. The Arizona Mafia listened—and lined up twenty-one days in New Hampshire, beginning January 7. White dutifully worked up a numbingly thorough advance report on every town Goldwater would visit and every luminary he would meet for his first trip. And suddenly the day was upon them.

Goldwater got his three or four hours of sleep, then hobbled into his state headquarters on Main Street in Concord to entertain reporters' questions. They covered the waterfront, and his answers economically laid out the positions he had been advocating for years: for considering withdrawal of diplomatic recognition of the USSR; against a progressive income tax, which "penalizes success"; for solving the poverty problem by getting government off the backs of business. He was in favor of the United Nations, so long as the charter was honored—which meant that Red China could never be allowed in—or perhaps revised to exclude countries from voting who haven't paid their dues. Cuban exiles should be armed for a second go at Castro. Republicans shouldn't divide the party by debating Republicans. There were no extremists in the Republican Party because extremists were those who called for violent overthrow of the government. America should reassure its allies by affirming the existing doctrine that the NATO commander had discretion to use tactical nuclear weapons in case of a surprise Russian attack. Then Social Security: "I would like to suggest one change," he said, "that Social Security be made voluntary, that if a person can provide better for himself, let him do it"—a position he had been spelling out in lesser or greater detail (mostly lesser) since *Conscience of a Conservative*.

It would have been a good performance—if the audience had been a group of *National Review* readers. To much of the press it seemed a blizzard of solecisms. What did he *mean* when he said there were no liberals in America? (He meant it in the classic European sense of a supporter of laissez-faire economics.) Why would loosening control of nuclear weapons *reassure* our allies? Did he really *believe* laissez-faire economics could end poverty? At the *Concord*

Monitor, an editor slapped this headline on his paper's report: "GOLDWATER SETS GOALS: END SOCIAL SECURITY, HIT CASTRO" (substituting his own actuarial projections for Goldwater's words, he was implying that to make Social Security voluntary was perforce to bankrupt it). In the *New York Times* a caption read: "Barry Goldwater, aspirant for the Republican Presidential nomination, with the widow of Senator Styles Bridges in East Concord. She holds dog"— just in case New Yorkers were unable to tell dowagers in pillbox hats from senators in black-rimmed glasses.

The slights were redeemed by a splendid day on the campaign trail. Four hundred Nashuans were shoehorned into one of Goldwater's house visits where fifty had been expected; his evening speech at Baroody's alma mater, St. Anselm's College, had to be moved from the campus theater to the field house. In tiny Amherst the candidate charmed the voters at George and Phyllis Brown's stately colonial by solemnly discussing the meaning of democracy with local grammar school pupils gathered on the lawn. Then he ducked in on a Rotary Club meeting. ("Greetings, fellow Rotarians, this gives me a chance to make up a missed meeting back home.") If this was New Hampshire campaigning, he was doing fine.

It didn't last a day. He kicked off the next morning's press conference by holding forth on the President's State of the Union address, given the previous afternoon, in which LBJ had concluded by intoning, "In these last seven sorrowful weeks, we have learned anew that nothing is so enduring as faith, and nothing is so degrading as hate. John Kennedy was a victim of hate." Goldwater heard it as a gratuitous swipe at the right.

"This hate theme, which is the most overdone, most untruthful attack ever made in my—in this country!" Goldwater spluttered. "To simply say it was an act of hate is an attempt to obscure the real issue. The assassin was a product of the sort of hate taught by Communists, not by Americans." To imply otherwise, he said, was to join "an attack that was started immediately after the trigger was pulled against the conservative members of the population. . . . The only time my life was threatened, bodily harm ever threatened me, came as a result of these writings and these announcements over the radio."

He moved to a favorite theme. Johnson had avowed that "even in the absence of agreement, we must not stockpile arms beyond our needs or seek an excess of military power that could be provocative as well as wasteful." Goldwater said he heard in that a call for unilateral disarmament. "Our strength doesn't provoke communist aggression," he countered; "it only deters it."

Later a reporter asked what he meant. Goldwater began riffing out a response—any verbal discipline he might have mustered for the day vanishing with every word. "Now, when Russia says, 'We want to disarm,' and they start

showing us they want to, then I'd say is the time to go ahead with it. But we, I
don't think, should now be downgrading our Strategic Air Command air fleet,
for example, just because we feel we're safe with our missiles in our silos over
here. I don't feel safe at all about those missiles, if you want to know the truth.
I wish the administration . . . would tell the American people how undependable they actually are."

The reporters began scribbling madly; this was something. "Senator," one
asked, "how undependable are they actually?"

Goldwater: "I can't tell you, you have to get that—that's classified information, but they're not dependable, I can tell you that, and I'll probably catch
hell for saying it, but they're not dependable."

Reporters snuck off to the phones to be the first to file on this remarkable
news. Before the day was through, Defense Secretary Robert McNamara made
a rare political appearance before the television cameras: Goldwater's charges,
he said, were "completely misleading, politically irresponsible, and damaging
to the national security. . . . There is no information, classified or otherwise, to
support the false implication that our long-range missiles can't be depended
upon to accomplish their mission."

The facts were not entirely in McNamara's favor. "I think both'em went to
extremes on it," Georgia senator Richard Russell, Goldwater's colleague on
the Armed Services Committee, told LBJ. "We have never fired a Minuteman
missile with a warhead in it, and that's where we put most of our billions, and I
raised the devil about it and tried my best to get them to fire at least one before
we ever got into that test-ban business, but they never did, so no man can take
an absolutely categorical oath that he knows that it will deliver." Soon Mississippi's John Stennis, chair of the preparedness subcommittee, would order his
staff to look into hearings on the issue.

But politically, the technical merits of the case were moot. Taking on the
Defense Department was another impolitic dinner-party habit Goldwater failed
to break. In airing the missile charge, Goldwater publicly took a side in the
complex behind-the-scenes Kulturkampf roiling the Pentagon. McNamara had
been plucked to serve in the Kennedy Administration after rising to the presidency of Ford as one of the Harvard-bred "whiz kids" who won back market
supremacy from GM through the method of "statistical control"—counting
everything that could be counted, comparing everything that could be compared, and devising coldly rational solutions to the problems thus revealed.
Senior officers who had been loyal to the military through the lean years of the
1920s and the 1930s, when it was small, insular, and unpopular, now found
their beloved institution overrun with "computer types," as Strategic Air Command chief Thomas Power put it, who "didn't know their ass from a hole in the

ground"—who demanded that Defense Department staff race hither and yon to collect statistics to justify policies and programs that had existed since Adam.

When Kennedy had cruelly scapegoated his Joint Chiefs of Staff for the Bay of Pigs fiasco, the distrust had become almost total. The following fall, when Kennedy called in the Joint Chiefs to tell them of the deal that settled the Cuban Missile Crisis and to congratulate them for their assistance, Navy chief George W. Anderson shouted, "We have been had!" and Air Force chief Curtis LeMay—who was inordinately proud of commanding an operation that rained down more destruction on Tokyo in one day than Hiroshima and Nagasaki combined—thought the American naval blockade was "almost as bad as the appeasement at Munich." He pounded the table, bemoaning "the greatest defeat in our history." Anderson was kicked upstairs to the Portugese embassy. LeMay was given a sort of one-year probation.

The missile/bomber debate was but an emblem of the trouble. McNamara had committed the country to a "triad" standard of deterrence: enough each of bombers, land-based missiles, and submarine missiles to survive attack and still be able to independently obliterate the Soviet Union. Since the United States already had more than enough bombers to do that, the result of Mc-Namara's policies was massive new commitments to computer-guided missiles—the apotheosis of the technowar mentality these seat-of-the-pants old-timers distrusted. Since its founding in 1947, the Air Force had suffered from a looming low-level paranoia that the rest of the military considered its untested core doctrine of strategic bombing illegitimate and useless. Now McNamara's new "whiz kids" wanted to base American strategy on the even more untested "deterrence" theory—which held that old-fashioned saber-rattling via fleets of B-52s had been rendered obsolete by the weapons they now carried on their wings. At the 1963 military appropriations hearings Tommy Power said, "This is the first time in our history that much or even most of the nation's striking power is to be entrusted to weapons that have never been fully tested operationally." He didn't mention that with missiles went the romance of the air, the manly daring sacralized in a dozen World War II pictures, renewed for the nuclear era in Jimmy Stewart's *Strategic Air Command* (1955).

When McNamara sought to kill development of two new high-speed, high-altitude bombers, code names B-70 and RS-70, Congress ordered an extension instead; there were, after all, 24,000 jobs depending on the project. It wasn't the jobs that moved Barry Goldwater. He cited the strategic vision of the brass—whom he identified with entirely. He had won his dream berth on the Senate Armed Services Committee, and its top secret intelligence and pre-paredness subcommittees, in 1962. His closest Washington friends were the military men who testified before him; their words were his own. "I say fear the civilians," Goldwater told a convention of the Military Order of the World Wars in October of 1963. "They're taking over." During the test-ban hearings he boasted that America's missiles were accurate enough "to lob one into the men's room at the Kremlin" (if they could be counted on to get into the air first).

Now he was plunged neck-deep into a debate with McNamara on the "dependability gap." But his opponent held all the cards. Once upon a time—in August of 1961, perhaps, when Gallup found that 71 percent of Americans supported going to war over Berlin shortly after Kennedy warned that such an engagement could mean "more devastation in several hours than has been wrought in all the wars of human history"; when hardly an eyebrow was raised when President Kennedy told Stewart Alsop, "In some circumstances we must be prepared to use the nuclear weapon at the start, come what may"—Goldwater might have gotten away with it. Not after the Cuban Missile Crisis. Not after the test-ban treaty. Now, raising terrifying doubts about the entire nuclear program, alone, on the fly, with no more cover than vague promises of "classified information," was enough to make it sound like Goldwater was courting either political or planetary suicide. Goldwater's friends could only defend him by revealing classified information or by defying their civilian leader, McNamara. So McNamara simply denied the charges, isolating Goldwater as an extremist.

ABC Reports ran the obligatory shot of old coots talking politics around a rural New Hampshire cracker barrel. Began one:

"He's a real Republican, regardless of what—"

"Yeah, he's a real Republican. He's going to get us in a batch of trouble, that's all."

"Oh no he won't, either."

"How's that?"

"Well, he's going around making statements which are going to absolutely eliminate him as a possibility for the election."

To add to Goldwater's troubles, complaints were filtering into his office about his language. "What the hell's that?" he asked of a boom lurking overhead, while he was on the air, and he said during another broadcast that he would be fine as soon as he was "rid of this damned cane." It was a time when political candidates skipped campaigning on Sundays for fear of seeming impious. New Hampshire was shocked.

At headquarters, meanwhile, his people were poring over the results of a canvass they had made in the little town of Pittsfield during Goldwater's first

day in the state—twelve hours before he had a chance to embarrass himself at
his first press conference: 130 Pittsfieldians were for him, 50 against; 300 were
undecided. The rosy predictions that New Hampshire was Barry Goldwater's
state were coming a cropper.

The tour ended with a whimper. The temperature began dropping as Goldwater spoke at an American Legion Hall that was so crowded he could touch
the audience surrounding him on all sides. When it was time to leave for a kaf-
feeklatsch at the home of a pair of widows in Exeter, icy conditions were setting in at the airport. He stood the old ladies up.

Rockefeller workers braved the chill. They were papering Exeter and
every other town with flyers: "GOLDWATER SETS GOALS: END SOCIAL SECURITY,
HIT CASTRO."

Goldwater might have dropped the missile charge and cut his losses. Instead,
at the annual Republican National Committee conclave in Washington that
weekend, he asked for a congressional probe. When the assembled Republicans saw him surrounded everywhere by his obscure Arizona cronies and
learned that this was his campaign team (and that Clif White had been relegated to a subsidiary role, and that Pete O'Donnell had been purged entirely),
the response was incredulity. Except among liberals, who responded with
glee. They had come to Washington to find someone to knock Goldwater out.
And to knock out Rockefeller, too—who arrived with his pregnant wife on his
arm chirping, "I want to be with my husband as much as possible in the campaign." Others came in the hope of being anointed. George Romney spoke at
the National Press Club. Afterward he was asked the question he was waiting
for: was he running? A grin spread across his jutting jaw: "I was afraid that
question would not be asked," he said, in Roosevelt-like deadpan. "I am not an
active candidate seeking the nomination, but if it should come to me, I'd have
a duty to accept it."

It wouldn't come. George Romney was finished. The new man of the hour
was "the first of the Kennedy Republicans": William Warren Scranton of
Pennsylvania. A week before the assassination, a meeting of Establishment
giants straight out of a conspiracy theorist's dream took place in the offices of
Thomas McCabe, the septuagenarian chairman of Scott Paper and the former
head of the board of governors of the Federal Reserve. Among those present
were publishers Walter Annenberg and Walter Thayer, CBS's William S.
Paley, Robert Woodruff of Coca-Cola, Pierre Du Pont, former Eisenhower
defense secretary and financier Thomas Gates, and Eisenhower attorney general Herb Brownell. Scranton was the guest of honor. The official agenda was
to congratulate him on his "effective and far-reaching program of industrial

development" in Pennsylvania. It was more like he was a Yalie being tapped for Skull and Bones. They wanted him to run for President. He seemed perfect; he answered every need. He didn't have enemies. He was a man of the center (the AFL-CIO gave him a 50 rating, Americans for Constitutional Action 58, Americans for Democratic Action 40). He had *breeding*.

Scrantons were to the Keystone State as Goldwaters were to Arizona. Puritans who first came to these shores in the 1630s, they migrated to the central Pennsylvania county of Lackawanna in the 1830s, and by 1866 their town honored the family that had bestowed on them an industrial empire—and had helped found the Republican Party—by taking its name. Commissions from Abraham Lincoln hung over the mantle of the family manse where Bill Scranton grew up—tokens of a family history that perfectly described the arc of the Republican Party's Northeastern wing. The forefather was a robber baron who organized an armed posse to shoot down workers in cold blood during the great rail strike of 1877. The son made amends through great philanthropies. And by the middle of the twentieth century, the grandchildren embraced business-tinged liberalism as the governing philosophy for a nation.

Bill Scranton was born in 1917—like Nelson Rockefeller, in the family vacation cottage. He grew up under the shaping influence of his mother, Marion Margery Warren Scranton (of the Mayflower Warrens), whose favorite things were orchids, diamonds, flamboyant hats, and politics. She began picketing for women's suffrage at the age of sixteen. Her son was gathering precinct returns by telephone on election night at age nine. The next year he joined his mother at the 1928 Republican Convention. At Yale he wrote a column in the *Daily News* that ran alongside McGeorge Bundy's. Only wartime service delayed Scranton's matriculation at Yale Law School. His fraternity pledge class there was nicknamed "Destiny's Men"; it included future Supreme Court Justices Byron "Whizzer" White and Potter Stewart, Cyrus Vance, Sargent Shriver, and Gerald Ford (and, owing to some occult Ivy League formula that would have a conservative minted for each dozen moderates or liberals, future Colorado senator and Goldwater booster Peter Dominick).

There was an organic reason that Bill Scranton became a liberal. It was the exact opposite of why Barry Goldwater became a conservative. A Pennsylvania squire who said that the free market brought only blessings would be run out of town on a rail. Scranton, the city, had been the anthracite coal capital of the world before the market for the fuel collapsed in mid-century, the nation's industrial center began sliding southwest, and radical new automation techniques began sluicing off some 40,000 industrial jobs a month nationwide. In Pennsylvania, unemployment was 50 percent above the national average and fifty-six of fifty-seven counties were federally designated as depressed areas; in the same years that Phoenix grew from 50,000 residents to 500,000, Scranton shrunk. It was a quiet, underlying dread in the 1960s that these economic forces, as Rhode Island's liberal Republican governor John Chafee put it, would "dump the unskilled and the semi-skilled worker into the human slag heap"—perhaps to evolve into some social Armageddon led by residents of industrial ghost towns like Scranton who couldn't move because all of their assets were tied up in now worthless houses.

Only activist government, it was thought, could stave off that awful day. Bill Scranton's father was the architect of a new kind of centrist liberalism: combining private and public resources to spur industrial redevelopment. He helped lure fifty industries and twenty thousand jobs back to Lackawanna County. Upon his father's death in 1955, Bill took over the "Scranton Plan," which was already internationally celebrated, and led his city to win a *Look* All-American City award. By the time he was plucked to become a State Department briefing officer in 1959 (he was so trusted by the secretary of state that the press called him John Foster Dulles's "private leak"), the chamber of commerce's executive secretary described him as "the best-informed man in the United States on how to bring jobs back to depressed areas." He burned with one of the core convictions of managerial liberalism: In a complex modern economy, only "labor market coordination" by centralized government could save the free market from bringing about waste, inefficiency, and ruin as a side effect of prosperity.

It was no coincidence that the best-informed expert on industrial job creation in the country was a stalwart civil rights man. As Martin Luther King had taken to pointing out, automation's social costs were borne by the last hired and first fired: the Negroes who had streamed north by the millions after World War II just as factory gates were slamming shut. Detroit, for example, lost half its manufacturing base in the 1950s—during which time 75 percent of job listings were reserved specifically for whites. In Philadelphia 70 percent of young black men were unemployed. Federal social legislation required racial covenants to win Southern support (Kennedy got his 1961 minimum wage hike by barring laundry, hotel, and food service workers—mostly black—from coverage). It was a far cry from the agriculture depression of the 1920s and 1930s, to which Washington responded by subsidizing farm incomes and pegging commodity prices to pre-Depression levels. No such response was forthcoming when industry in the urban North began to decay. In places like Newburgh, the problem was addressed by other means.

When Scranton took a seat in the House of Representatives in 1961, he was one of only twenty-one Republicans to vote with Kennedy on the Rules

Committee fight. He went on to vote with the Administration over half the time, and he introduced a depressed areas bill that was *stronger* than Kennedy's. In 1962 General Eisenhower prevailed upon Scranton to take back the Pennsylvania State House for the Republicans: "What it boils down to, Bill," Eisenhower said, "is a four-letter word—duty." Scranton won the governorship in a contest so brawling that it ensured him a reputation as a political comer. Then unemployment in Pennsylvania began dropping by percentage points. Liberal Republican leaders began paying court at the governor's mansion at Indiantown Gap. Scranton was, simply, the anti-Goldwater: he answered every fear that Goldwater only seemed to stoke. One by one they came, waited patiently in a vestibule graced by framed copies of ads he had commissioned to promote his state ("Governor Bill Scranton Says, 'You'll Like the New Pennsylvania' "; "The New Pennsylvania Means *Business*"), and begged him to run for President—and heard him, after his customary scintillating banter, once more repeat that his duty was to serve out his four-year term.

The week after Scranton had been summoned to the star chamber at the offices of Thomas McCabe, General Eisenhower docked his private Pullman car in Harrisburg and told Scranton it was now his duty to save the party of his grandfathers from capture by the radical right. Scranton emerged from that meeting seven hours later. He told the newsmen who had patiently staked out the rail yard, "I probably will give even deeper thought to this matter than I had expected"—nothing more. It was enough to yield reports that "Scranton appears to have opened a door for a build-up similar to that which won the GOP nomination in 1940" for Wendell Willkie. Walter Thayer's *Herald Tribune* ran an editorial titled "Calling Governor Scranton." On the *Today* show's year-end political wrap-up Sander Vanocur predicted that Scranton would get the nomination. Scotty Reston predicted he would have it "forced on him." *Life* assigned Teddy White, fresh off his historic "Camelot" scoop, to do a cover profile. "His unblemished record," *Life*'s seven million readers were told by the nation's most respected chronicler of presidential elections, was "an insurance policy against GOP disaster."

At the January RNC conclave, party leaders were determined to cash in the insurance policy. Len Hall, Meade Alcorn, and party general counsel Fred Scribner, Three Musketeers of the GOP's Eastern wing (or, depending on your loyalties, Three Horsemen of the Apocalypse), were reportedly now Scrantonites; so were RNC head Bill Miller and his predecessor, Senator Thruston Morton. In Washington, as the convention was getting started, Scranton's energetic young aides Bill Keisling and Craig Truax begged Eisenhower to pledge as a Scranton delegate and claimed that Walter Thayer had already done so. The boys from *Advance*, the liberal Republican journal from Harvard, distributed a 3,600-word manifesto announcing a new organization, the Ripon Society, calling for a presidential candidate with "those qualities of vision, intellectual force, humanness and courage that America saw and admired in John F. Kennedy, not in a specious effort to fall heir to his mantle, but because our times demand no lesser greatness."

Meanwhile their candidate of choice was back in Harrisburg, forbidding his 1962 campaign manager from starting a write-in effort in New Hampshire and presiding over a year-end joint session of the state legislature where he urged all Pennsylvanians to spend the year seeking "greater charity, greater equality, in relationships between the races."

Scranton eventually did make it to that Washington meeting. Coagulations of young admirers followed his every step. Bill Keisling, the twenty-seven-year-old political deputy who looked up to his boss as a puppy to a master, steered him into the paths of VIPs at dinners and receptions like a chess grand master moving a pawn. A reporter asked Tom McCabe why, if Scranton wasn't running for President, he was wearing a Scranton button on his lapel. "The governor doesn't know I'm wearing it," he said. Meanwhile Rockefeller was in a corner, neglected, busying himself signing autographs for the porters and kitchen workers.

That evening, Keisling and another aide threw a press party for Scranton, although the governor himself was not invited. It was the hottest ticket in town—besides Scranton's press conference the next evening, which everyone agreed was the perfect opportunity for him to announce a presidential campaign. "Are we looking at our next President?" one state chairman asked another as Scranton parted the crowd to take to the podium—where, with great ease, assurance, and grace (the audience whispering comparisons to Kennedy), he announced that he was in D.C. to meet with his state's congressional delegation, nothing more. Reporters pounced. If he wasn't running, why the party on his behalf? "Why, I don't know anything about that," he answered. He turned to his hotheaded young aide. "Is that right, Bill?" Keisling, sheepish, answered: "Yes, sir, governor."

The boom was on, his wishes notwithstanding. The *New York Times Magazine* ran an article entitled "Portrait of a Not-So-Dark Horse"; the *Saturday Evening Post* did a profile packed with homey pictures of the Scranton brood, accompanied by a Stewart Alsop column headed "The Logical Candidate" explaining confidently that in Republican nominations "the candidate with the best chance to win has usually been chosen before the convention was called to order by a process of consensus among the party's Grand Panjandrums." And, opined his columnist brother Joseph, Goldwater, "the great favorite of the early winter books," had "few remaining betters." *Newsweek* put Scranton on the cover.

On January 17 there was another all-star luncheon in Tom McCabe's boardroom. The participants entered through an Eisenhower Administration revolving door: Jim Hagerty, press secretary, now an ABC executive; Secretary of Defense Neil McElroy, head of Procter & Gamble; White House special counsel David Kendall, now at Chrysler. They were joined by Bill Miller, Len Hall, and Meade Alcorn. Scranton emerged with the same message: "Only if faced with a series of highly unlikely circumstances would I feel it my duty to become a candidate for the presidency." Then again, when a supporter filed his name for candidacy in New Hampshire without his permission—a quirk New Hampshire election law allowed—Scranton didn't file to withdraw it. At the White House, President Johnson inquired anxiously of Walter Jenkins about a new poll; "What does it show Johnson-Scranton?" (He needn't have worried. The President still scored nearly 80 percent against all comers.) But then again Scranton refused to attend the Young Republicans' annual training seminar on the twenty-fourth despite Eisenhower's urging.

His fervent admirers still held out hope. There was, after all, GO-Day coming up.

"GO-Day" was the GOP's annual closed-circuit TV fund-raising extravaganza. It ended up doing little more than neatly showcasing all the weaknesses of a party split clean down the middle: Goldwater's Pittsburgh appearance was nearly sabotaged by liberals who put on sale only 500 tickets for a 2,000-seat room (Clif White's western Pennsylvania chairman Ben Chapple saved the day, deploying his Draft Goldwater organization to sell the room to capacity); in Los Angeles, brigades of Young Republicans picketed Rockefeller with Goldwater signs. The speeches were flat, duds—except in Indiana, where the room thrummed with anticipation that the speaker, Bill Scranton, would throw his hat in the ring.

He wouldn't. His wife had hated the trip to Indianapolis—the campaign-style flesh-pressing, the constant comparisons to Jackie Kennedy, the awful accommodations. First she forbade Keisling's attempt to put an opening witticism in the speech about "feeling a presidential draft." Then she exercised the matrimonial veto: no more out-of-state political excursions. On February 3 Scranton removed his name from the New Hampshire primary rolls. It had been a whirlwind journey. But now it seemed over.

Heading out each morning in his respectable Republican cloth coat—a belted-back model out of style for years—chatting up the barbershops, banks, and general stores, buying ice-cream cones for the kids as his grandfather used to hand out dimes, Rocky knocked them dead in New Hampshire. NBC's cameras caught him in conversation with a little boy. Why are you running for President? "So that a nice boy like you will have a real chance to grow up in a country where there's freedom and where there's opportunity. And you are a wonderful boy." They caught Goldwater in an off-color quip: "I don't kiss babies because I lose track of their age too soon." Rocky even babbled away in French to woo New Hampshire's 18 percent French-Canadian population.

But even in New Hampshire you can't shake everybody's hand. And if you are Nelson Rockefeller, when you shake a hand with a glowing and conspicuously swollen Happy by your side, you are as likely to lose a vote as to gain one. As one stern matron told a reporter, eyes flashing with Old Testament wrath: "What can we tell our young people about this man's immoral living? How many wives did God make Adam?" Goldwater was so solid with the state's rock-ribbed Republican activists that Rockefeller hadn't been able to hire a decent campaign team or delegate slate for love or money. Voters would choose twenty-eight names from scores of candidates for delegates and alternates, with only their candidate preferences to identify them. On the "bedsheet ballot," familiarity bred success. And the Arizona Mafia had locked in the state's most familiar Republican names: Delores Bridges, widow of the late senator Styles Bridges; former governor Lane Dwinell; ex-Communist FBI double agent Herb Philbrick, whose autobiography was the inspiration for the TV show *I Led Three Lives.*

Rockefeller might have compensated with his customary blitzkrieg approach to staffing. But his New Hampshire managers insisted that local tastes demanded a puritanical front, limiting him to only three traveling companions (and a state police captain who insisted since the Kennedy assassination on accompanying him everywhere he went). He rode in the press bus and hired freelance stenographers by the day. (The effort at folksiness was blunted when NBC happened to run a special showcasing the country's greatest private collections of art, his own most prominently.) One of his greatest political gifts had always been his ability to absorb facts and figures in complex briefing sessions. But now the men who fed him the facts and figures were languishing back at 22 West 55th, so he responded to reporters with mumbled generalities. He retailed his plan to save small business, played to Granite Staters' fabled fiscal reserve, and worried over the projected 20 million people who would be unemployed by 1970; mostly, though, he bashed Goldwater. "How can there be solvency when Senator Goldwater is against the graduated income tax? How can there be security when he wants to take the United States out of the United Nations? . . . Americans will not and should not respond to a political creed that cherishes the past solely because it offers an excuse for shutting out the hard facts and difficult tasks of the present." A student at Keene Teacher's College said he agreed with Goldwater that relief rolls were packed with freeloaders and called Rockefeller "a Robin Hood in a gray flannel suit." Rockefeller replied that it was no wonder Goldwater thought that way, being a "Southern leader."

Other fronts were opened: a "Rockefeller Campaign Express" ersatz newspaper; a Manhattan campaign office; a D.C. headquarters—a ten-room suite on Connecticut Avenue across the street from the Goldwater for President Committee office, both campaign offices emblazoned with enormous likenesses of their candidates that looked out onto the White House a few blocks away. White learned from a banker close to David Rockefeller that Rocky was allegedly willing to spend $50 million to win the nomination. "All a public relations man has to do to get on the payroll is ask," he said. The exertion seemed futile. Rockefeller's popularity was plummeting, his chances of reversal remote.

Goldwater had problems of his own throughout the winter. It was possible to find two Republicans in New Hampshire who got along with each other after the corrosive three-way gubernatorial primary back in 1962, but his local campaign managers, Senator Cotton and House Speaker Stuart Lamphrey, weren't them. Lamphrey insisted on a state-of-the-art campaign with computer voter identification, door-to-door canvassing, and blanket TV ads. Cotton said over his dead body, and set up the traditional killing New Hampshire schedule for Goldwater—a dozen or more coffees a day, some in rooms smaller than the candidate's Senate inner office—ignoring the fact that Goldwater's ankle injury still shot pain with every step. Goldwater's old right hand, Tony Smith, was down with an ulcer, replaced by the far-too-inexperienced YAFer Lee Edwards (Kitchel had been floundering unsuccessfully since the previous fall trying to line up an experienced campaign publicist). At each stop came the same annoying questions—Social Security (the candidate now stuck to the argument that the true enemy of Social Security was the inflation that was eating away at benefits), the UN, nuclear weapons—as if audience members were reading from a script. (And, thanks to Graham Molitor, some of them—Harvard law students hired as audience moles—were.) Then it was on to the next picturesque village hall, which often, thanks to poor planning, was halfway across the state, to talk at the people again. Then back on the road—in the pitch dark, if it was past 4:00 p.m.—perhaps to hear on the car radio news of a widely publicized speech by Dean Thaddeus Seymour of Dartmouth: "The voters of the Granite State will largely determine whether unsophistication bordering on the supernatural becomes the foreign policy platform of one of our two major parties," he had said. "Goldwater may be a joke to most of us, but he has a well-financed, well-organized, and fanatical following which will stop at nothing to make their hero president."

It didn't help that the Birch Society had come roaring back into the news. In a small town in Washington State, a former state representative, John Gold-mark, a Harvard Law School graduate and ACLU board member, was suing a weekly Birchite newspaper for libel. Goldmark's wife had been a member of the Communist Party in the 1930s. When Goldmark had come up for reelection, the paper revived old saws from the McCarthy days: that the Communist Party never let anyone leave; that there was no such thing as a Communist wife and a noncommunist husband. "You know the Communists have forced marriage," said the newspaper's defense counsel. "Why would he marry a gal as homely as Sally if he wasn't forced into it?" A cavalcade of witnesses, including Herbert Philbrick, the New Hampshire Goldwater delegate, unfurled baroque conspiracy theories to demonstrate the peril Mrs. Goldmark represented to free people everywhere; another cavalcade pronounced them ridiculous. The circus made the papers all the way to frosty New Hampshire—where Barry Goldwater presently made his way through a torchlight parade in a tiny cart pulled by a Shetland pony, following a drum and bugle corps in Indian bonnets playing "Blue Moon" led by a pudgy high school girl, knees blue from the cold, carrying, of all things, a United Nations flag. It was hard to tell if Goldwater was grinning or if he had something painful stuck in his teeth.

"Why the hell am I doing this?" he would ask Norris Cotton after such adventures.

"That's the way we campaign in New Hampshire," Cotton would answer.

It wasn't helping. Kennedy had been right: Goldwater's loose lips were sinking the ship. *Newsweek* quoted a supporter: "I'm glad he has one foot in a cast or he'd have that in his mouth, too." The AP's Walter Mears—who had to file stories every few hours—remarked that all they had to do was pepper Goldwater with a few questions and wait for him to slip, and they had their headlines. Then it was back to the nonstop frat party at the Manchester Sheraton.

New Hampshire's movie theaters campaigned diligently against Barry Goldwater. Some were featuring a documentary called *Point of Order*, consisting of footage from the epic showdown in the Senate Hearing Room between Senator Joseph McCarthy (whom Goldwater had supported to the end) and the United States Army in 1954, a film that was gripping enough to make it one of the few documentaries in the history of American cinema to receive nationwide theatrical distribution. Others were showing *Seven Days in May*, the film version of the novel Fletcher Knebel began banging out when the strange case of General Walker was gripping the nation back in the autumn of 1961. Burt Lancaster played General William Maltoon Scott, a would-be führer who came within a hairsbreadth of leading a military takeover of the United States after the President signed a disarmament treaty with the Soviet Union. Like Barry Goldwater, Scott gave speeches in stadiums in which the crowd chanted rhythmically, "We want Scott!" He was abetted by a militarist senator from the Southwest, like Barry Goldwater. His key accomplice was the sort of right-wing radio commentator who constantly sang the praises of Barry Goldwater. "For some men it's a Senator McCarthy," the idealistic President stirringly intoned at the end. "For some it's a General Walker. Now it's a General Scott." He might as well have been saying "It's a Barry Goldwater."

Seven Days in May was a soppy morality play whose power to move minds paled in comparison to a third film gracing the screens of the nation as the New Hampshire primary hit its stride. *Dr. Strangelove, Or: How I Learned to Stop Worrying and Love the Bomb* was a war picture. But the country that heard Jimmy Stewart, in *Strategic Air Command,* exclaim of his B-47, "She's the most beautiful thing I've ever seen in my life!" had never seen a war picture like this. It was a slapstick comedy, whose subject was the damaged psyche of an age. *The New Yorker*'s movie critic Dwight Macdonald, reviewing the film before the theatrical release, was amazed that Columbia Pictures ever let the thing be made. He predicted picket lines. Instead there were lines of people around the block waiting to get in. It was a hit. It touched a nerve.

Since the dawn of the nuclear age, new Presidents—and, in the Soviet Union, new premiers—had received a briefing on the nuclear realities that no politician besides a President was allowed to know. There usually followed the spectacle of strong men reduced to jelly. When Johnson reported on his meeting with the chairman of the Atomic Energy Commission, he told the Speaker of the House that the AEC chair had told him something only Kennedy had known. "And when he walked out, I wished I hadn't known it." He spent the next day dazedly sprinkling the phrase "39 million" into nearly every conversation.

Presidents sometimes expressed this terrible awe in public. Mostly they did not. McNamara told Kennedy, then Johnson, to publicly affirm NATO policy that the United States would answer a Soviet attack of Europe with nuclear weapons—and to ignore it in practice as unthinkable. McNamara didn't think the attack would ever happen. The existence of our nuclear arsenal made it crazy for the Russians to try. That was the doctrine of "deterrence"—borne of a paradox unknown in the entire history of warfare: the superpowers were now so powerful that they were helpless to use their power. They were, said J. Robert Oppenheimer, as "two scorpions in a bottle, each capable of killing the other, but only at the risk of his own life."

It was a concept even congressmen had a hard time grasping. "After years on this committee it strikes me that we have no plan to win," spluttered Mississippi's Jamie L. Whitten to McNamara at the 1963 military appropriation hearings. The secretary of defense tied himself in knots to explain that stalemate—a "balance of terror"—and not superiority was a better goal, because an increase in our nuclear capability might be interpreted by Russia as enough to destroy their second-strike capability, perhaps to provoke a surprise preemptive strike out of fear America might do it first and leave the Soviets without the means to defend themselves. Though, spoken out loud, the idea sounded rather insane.

Dr. Strangelove's director, Stanley Kubrick, paid very close attention to these sorts of things. For years his bedside reading had been treatises thick with the mathematical formulae of "game theory," purporting to rationally explain the best strategies to deter a nuclear war—or, should it come to that, to win one. When he started working on a way to put these absurdities up on the screen, he was overwhelmed by the feeling that people would laugh at them. He decided that people should laugh. He would make a comedy.

The story begins in the office of the commander of Burpleson Air Force Base, one General Jack D. Ripper. (Grunting and growling, incessantly chomping his cigar, he looked suspiciously like the mad-bombing former Air Force chief of staff Curtis LeMay.) He cuts off communications to the outside world, then orders transmission of an attack code to the bomber wing he commands. The narrator explains (correctly) how America kept a fleet of bombers in the air twenty-four hours a day, each two hours from their targets within the USSR, each prepared to deliver a payload sixteen times greater than all the tonnage exploded by all sides in World War II.

Cut to the interior of one of these bombers (known in real life, unofficially, as "doomsday planes"), where the captain exchanges his flight helmet for a cowboy hat: "Well, boys, I reckon this is it—nuclear combat, toe to toe with the Russkies!" He predicts medals and promotions all around.

General Ripper, it arrives, is a madman, possessed of the Birchite conviction that the Communists have fluoridated the water supply to sap Americans' "precious bodily fluids," and that preventive war is America's only hope. By exploiting a top secret contingency plan for the possibility that a Russian sneak attack might take out the President—which the President doesn't remember approving—General Ripper exercises his authority to launch his own attack. He paraphrases Clemenceau: "Today, war is too important to be left to politicians," who have "neither the time, the training, nor the inclination for strategic thought." Kubrick could not have known that McGeorge Bundy had warned Kennedy in January of 1961 that "a subordinate commander, faced with a substantial Russian military action, could start the thermonuclear holocaust on his own initiative if he could not reach you (by failure of communication at either end of the line)." Kubrick understood nuclear war's built-in absurdities well enough to be able to imagine it.

Cut to the cavernous War Room, where the President's top military and civilian advisers are gathered around a giant table (just like the conclave President Kennedy convened to defuse the 1962 Cuban Missile Crisis, where Strategic Air Command chief Tommy Power's advice was to preempt the problem by—in the words of his alter ego in *Strangelove*, General Buck Turgidson— "hitting them with everything we've got"). As the simpering President (he looks like Adlai Stevenson) fervidly negotiates with the Soviet premier over the phone to convince him not to unleash his arsenal in retaliation, the Soviet ambassador steps into the room to explain the futility of the entire discussion: *Any* nuclear explosion over the Motherland, he dryly explains, will automatically set off a new, top secret "doomsday machine" with the power to destroy all life on earth.

Out of the shadows glides a queer man in a wheelchair—Dr. Strangelove, America's director of weapons research—who muses, impressed, in a thick German accent (suggesting at once the three towering émigré giants of American strategic thinking: Edward Teller, Harvard professor Henry Kissinger, and Herman Kahn, whose boast that America could limit its casualties in a nuclear exchange to a mere twenty million people inspired the movie's best joke) about how perfectly logical all of it is.

"*Deterrence,*" he hisses, "ees the art of producing in zee mind of zee enemy zee *fear* to attack." In the paradoxical world of nuclear combat, a doomsday machine is a splendid idea: "Because of zee irrevocable and unalterable decision-making process zat rules out human meddling, zee doomsday machine ees terrifying, and seemple to understand, and *complete*-ly credible and conveencing." ("Gee, I wish we had one of those doomsday machines!" General Turgidson whispers lustily.) Then Dr. Strangelove screams: "Zee only problem is that the whole point of a doomsday machine ees lost if you keep it a secret! *Vye didn't you tell the world, ehhh?*"

It was to be unveiled, the Soviet ambassador explains, at the next Party Congress on Monday. "As you know, the premier loves surprises." Another sardonic joke: the doomsday machine, the purest possible manifestation of automation, is precisely that which is supposed to *eliminate* the possibility of surprise.

The balance of terror, delicate or not, is too clever by far more than half.

As they speak, a single B-52 gets through the Soviets' defenses. Dr. Strangelove, the only one who grasps the whole mad system, is revealed to be a madman himself—the maddest of all, in fact. The gung ho pilot rides his payload to earth like a bronco. A wild proliferation of mushroom clouds fills the screen. Thus the final satire. The whiz kids of the McNamara stripe, the LeMays of the old school: one sets up the system the other trips, each assuming the other thought just like them. The madness only begins with the madmen. In a world that coexists with the power to destroy itself, Stanley Kubrick had seen the enemy. It was us.

Attentive viewers couldn't fail to understand that Kubrick was satirizing an entire system, not any of the system's cogs. But most viewers were not attentive. Americans prefer to isolate villains who despoil a preexisting innocence, rather than admit that there might not have been any innocence there in the first place. In this case, the villain became the man chasing around New Hampshire talking incessantly of "another Pearl Harbor" unless we commissioned new nuclear bombers, distributed tactical nuclear weapons to our allies, and returned to John Foster Dulles's "brinkmanship" policy. The man, in other words, who did what ordinary politicians avoided wherever possible: reminded America that it coexisted with the power to destroy itself. For the sin, more and more people began viewing Barry Goldwater as an outright menace.

By January 20, four out of ten New Hampshire Republicans told pollsters they preferred anyone but Rockefeller and Goldwater. And the New Hampshire primary abhors a vacuum. A political cartoonist caricatured the two generals ousted in the recent coup in Vietnam—the second coup, as it happened, in ten weeks—sitting on a jailhouse bench. "If we get out of here," one says, "we can always run in that New Hampshire primary."

All it took to run as a pledged delegate was $10 and one hundred signatures. It did not require the candidate's prior permission. By January 28 voters could choose from among delegates for Rockefeller, Goldwater, Nixon, Lodge, Stassen—only Romney and Scranton had taken the necessary steps to strike their names from the ballot—and a few more for whom running was a quadrennial hobby, such as Lar Daly, the eccentric Illinois furniture upholsterer who had run for President in an Uncle Sam suit as nominee of his own "America First" party since the 1950s.

And there was one more candidate, whose presence made history.

Maine senator Margaret Chase Smith's admirers had been approaching her to run for President ever since she issued her courageous 1950 "Declaration of Conscience" condemning Joseph McCarthy. With the Kennedy assassination the cries increased. At the podium of a January meeting of the Women's

National Press Club, Smith listed all the reasons that a woman could never realistically run for President. She concluded, "So, because of all these impelling reasons against my running, I have decided"—long pause—"I shall." The first female major-party presidential candidate brought down the house.

She had begun her career by taking up the House seat of her husband when he died, in the days when congressional wives were expected to spend half the week calling on embassies, the homes of Supreme Court justices, and the White House—a thrilling exercise consisting of leaving callings cards on a silver tray at the East Gate. After she served out her husband's term she was reelected by greater margins than her husband ever was. In 1948 she became the first woman to win a Senate seat in her own right; in 1960 Democrats decided to no avail that their only chance to beat her was to nominate a woman. (It was the first time two women faced off for a Senate seat, and the last until 1986.) The "Conscience of the Senate" was a bracingly unpredictable voter, a foe of both COPE and HUAC; whenever a colleague asked for her vote on an issue, she automatically voted the other way. She answered all her mail by hand, never took a dime of campaign contributions, and once held up Jimmy Stewart's promotion to brigadier general in the Air Force Reserve because "there are others more deserving."

Her style bore all the contradictions of a society coming upon a switching point. The Johnson White House would soon announce the appointments of ten women to high executive positions; the best-selling nonfiction book of 1964 would be *The Feminine Mystique*; the previous year Congress had passed an Equal Pay Act. But there Margaret Chase Smith was, before the *Women's* National Press Club—women being barred from the original National Press Club until 1971. Membership in the WNPC was largely confined to society reporters and "Inquiring Camera Girls"—attractive young women who trolled city streets for cute human interest stories (Jacqueline Bouvier was one when she met Jack Kennedy). When debate began on the Kennedy-Johnson civil rights bill at the end of January, Representative Howard Smith had thought it a clever tactic to derail it by adding "sex" as a protected category. There followed a bout of locker-room talk among the 424 representatives who were not women about henpecking wives and a "surplus of spinsters"; then Congresswoman Martha Griffiths of Michigan stood up and gravely spoke out for Judge Smith's motion as an idea whose time had come. The great chamber reverberated with shock.

Margaret Chase Smith's motto was "Women are people. A woman's place is everywhere." All the same, she unironically embraced the most rigid feminine stereotypes. Interviewed in a new magazine for federal employees, *Government Girl* (filled, mostly, with ads for party dresses, dance lessons, and dictation machines), she gave this advice: "We all want to be mothers and wives. Many of us can't be. Many who don't have a home go out into the world and follow some business or profession. . . . And one thing a girl should do is pay a great deal of attention to her clothes." She said that was how she chose her secretaries. She herself wouldn't dream of appearing outdoors without the frilly, flowery bonnets and architectural studio hats every woman over the age of fifty was still sporting in 1964, and her trademark rose corsage.

Her foray into New Hampshire was serious—serious enough for her to prove herself by ostentatiously starting out the campaign up at the 45th parallel, halfway to the North Pole, where it was 28 degrees below zero, posing for a photograph with her press corps as the only one not wearing a hat. Then she drove her own sedan 1,000 miles, crisscrossing the state in six days—the same way she covered 8,000 miles in Maine for two months every summer. "You got a lot of zip to be up here this morning," an amazed logger said. Out of earshot other men called her "a disgrace to the Republican Party." It remained to be seen whether she would be taken seriously.

Everyone took Richard Nixon seriously. A Harris poll had already come out listing him as the most popular Republican in New Hampshire. He had a reputation as a sterling New Hampshire vote-getter ever since he had won 22,000 "spontaneous" write-in votes for vice president after Harold Stassen tried to dump him from the ticket in 1956. It had actually been a concerted campaign to make the votes *look* spontaneous. But this time the spontaneity was (almost) real. New Hampshire voters were craving familiarity. Nixon responded by stepping up his speaking schedule—appearing but rarely in primary states, and never in New Hampshire, which would destroy his above-the-fray image. His speeches were loaded with so many stories of all the foreign dignitaries he'd called upon in his career that he sounded like a guy who had pinioned his neighbors into watching his vacation slides. The day after the Harris poll he appeared on Arthur Godfrey's radio show with Jackie Gleason. Gleason and Godfrey started to gab, awkwardly, about how none of the three of them seemed ever to wear hats; Nixon chimed in, "I never wear a hat. So it must always be in the ring." The joke certainly sounded like a setup.

Foreign policy brush fires abounded in those *Strangelove*-obsessed weeks. In Panama, anti-American students rioted and burned the flag; in Cuba, Castro shut off water to the Marine base at Guantánamo Bay; General de Gaulle was shopping neutralization deals for Southeast Asia and, with the United Kingdom, was selling durable goods to Cuba. Goldwater called for sending in the Marines to Cuba and Panama and said that de Gaulle wouldn't defy American policy if we would only give him more nuclear weapons. Johnson resolved the first two crises through negotiation, without, apparently, getting anything in return, and seemed to be doing nothing about the third. This laid down a perfect middle road upon which Nixon, in his speeches, gladly cruised to an admiring response. At the White House, President Johnson began to prepare for the eventuality of running against Nixon by taking steps to meet with Khrushchev and ordering the Democratic National Committee to prepare a memo on every flip-flop Nixon had made in his eighteen-year career.

Nixon was about to make one on race. On February 12, two days after the House began debate on the civil rights bill, 450,000 of New York's one million public school students had boycotted class to protest de facto segregation—a disruption designed to artificially lower school populations during the week when the state gauged attendance to decide how much education money to dole out to municipalities. Evidence of discontent among blacks in the North still had the power and terror of revelation. It was partly because newspapers honored gentleman's agreements with local authorities not to report racial disturbances; in Chicago, few outside Mayor Daley's high command knew, for example, that his Human Relations Commission had documented 260 such occurrences in July of 1961 alone. But you couldn't hide a school boycott. Bayard Rustin told reporters: "By running to the suburbs, the whites are leaving to the Negro the total burden of improving schools. Whites must learn to share this burden. We will force them to learn—and I say *force*." The ploy sparked a movement. Cincinnati schools emptied in a boycott, too. And Nixon, as it happened, had a speech scheduled for Cincinnati the next day.

He used the occasion to condemn the "irresponsible tactics of some of the extreme civil rights leaders" who have "created an atmosphere of hate and distrust which, if it continues to grow, will make the new law a law in name only." (He neglected to take note of the threat to the law posed by the jury that four days earlier had acquitted Byron de la Beckwith of shooting Medgar Evers, although the defendant's fingerprints were on the murder weapon; and the Alabama mayor who had just turned away six Negro students at an elementary school, because he said they would constitute a fire hazard; and the state troopers who, accompanied by a notorious local sheriff named Jim Clark, tortured a photographer with cattle prods for daring to cover the event.) For Nixon, the new civil rights militancy was a political opportunity.

He was not the only politician taking to the pulpit around Lincoln's birthday to preach moderation. In Springfield, Illinois, Adlai Stevenson declared: "Lawlessness, even verbal violence, that seeks to wound but fears to strike, destroys more than the image of America. They undermine its political foundations as well." Texas representative Henry Gonzales dug up an old issue of the Minutemen newsletter *On Target* that listed the twenty congressmen who had voted against extending HUAC's appropriation and that warned, "Traitors beware! Even now the cross hairs are on the back of your necks." Papers were filled with stories about the University of Illinois classics professor Revilo Oliver, who had published an article in Robert Welch's *American Opinion,* entitled "Marxmanship in Dallas," claiming that Kennedy had been slain for "becoming a political liability" to his Communist handlers. At the convention of the National Association for School Administrators, delegates commiserated over the Daughters of the American Revolution's campaign to ban a popular first-grade reader because of its "subtle way of undermining the American system of work and profit and replacing it with a collectivist welfare system." CBS's *The Defenders* presented a harrowing episode, entitled "The Blacklist" and starring Jack Klugman, on an innocent man ruined by homegrown fascists; *Point of Order* continued to pack theaters. America was still worried about right-wing extremism.

Unsettling things didn't issue only from the fringe. On February 7 the Beatles landed at John F. Kennedy Airport in New York for their first American tour, which would not have seemed to pose much danger to anyone—except that within two weeks of the event a *Time* cover article lamented "the Second Sexual Revolution"; the *Washington Post*'s entertainment columnist complained of "the virtual surrender of the motion picture industry to the adolescent"; novelist (and *Strangelove* screenwriter) Terry Southern's outrageous sexual satire *Candy* was burning up the best-seller lists; the FCC renounced the right to censor "provocative" television shows; the Supreme Court narrowly overturned Florida's ban on Henry Miller's *Tropic of Cancer*; and Attorney General Bobby Kennedy announced he was prosecuting a brazen "art" periodical called *Eros* under the Comstock Act. America was worried about something else, something new: rapidly changing cultural mores.

These developments brought further consuming thirst for normalcy to New Hampshire's upstanding burghers. But as more and more candidates bid fair to quench it, none seemed able to distinguish him- or herself from any of the others. Until, finally, one began pulling away from the pack.

In Boston, "the Lowells speak only to Cabots, and the Cabots speak only to God": of Henry Cabot Lodge's background, little more need be said. "Cabot," as he was known to intimates, became a Republican hero by winning a Senate seat in the 1936 Roosevelt landslide and became a national hero by resigning it to command a World War II tank brigade. Defeated in his 1952 reelection bid by Jack Kennedy (Lodge was preoccupied with campaigning for the man he personally recruited into the Republican Party, General Eisenhower), he found even greater celebrity as Eisenhower's United Nations ambassador—answering every outrage from the Soviet delegation with stinging rebukes that would invariably show up on the evening news as what a later generation would call a "sound bite." He won the vice-presidential berth on the 1960 Nixon ticket; and, in the summer of 1963, he was given the ambassadorship to Vietnam. A walking embodiment of the bipartisan principle in foreign policy, a man of peace, a bulwark at the farthest outpost of American freedom, he was tall, charismatic, debonair, handsome, reassuring. In one poll, half the respondents had strong opinions on him, and 96 percent of those were positive.

And in New Hampshire his managers—although they were not quite that, given that they were never certain whether Lodge welcomed their activity at all—put on a political campaign unlike any seen in American history: a public relations campaign. Their leader, Paul Grindle, was a Harvard dropout who had married a circus performer, gone into public relations, then settled into making a comfortable living as an importer of scientific instruments, exploiting the booming Cold War science market by mastering the new technology of computerized direct mail. New to politics, he saw no reason a candidate should be marketed any differently. That the product he was promoting was half the globe away was, if anything, an added convenience. Grindle and his associates contacted Lodge through his son, George, who had lost the 1962 Senate race to Teddy Kennedy. The ambassador agreed not to interfere. He was in the catbird seat—realizing he could take up the mantle if his managers were successful and refuse it if they were not, with no risk to his stature in the meantime.

The first step, Grindle decided, was market research. After the December 8 *Times* story naming Lodge General Eisenhower's choice for President caught them unprepared, Grindle adopted an invention of direct-marketing pioneer Lester Wunderman: the preaddressed postage-paid response card, usually bound alongside an ad in a magazine. Its simplicity was deceptive: for the first time Madison Avenue could calibrate the effectiveness of an advertising campaign. Just before Christmas, Grindle had volunteers pass out 33,000 cards to passengers on New Haven line commuter trains. They could mark a preference for Nixon, Goldwater, Rockefeller, or Lodge. Four thousand returned the cards. Over half checked Lodge. The campaign was on.

The next step was convincing New Hampshire that writing in Henry Cabot Lodge was not a wasted vote. Grindle and his team turned to Washington publicist Robert Mullen, who had ginned up the Draft Eisenhower fervor in 1952. He was able to plant a (false) item in Roscoe Drummond's *Herald Tribune* column on Christmas Eve: "My information is that the unresolved question is not whether Mr. Lodge is going to resign his ambassadorship and become an open,

active, and campaigning candidate for the nomination—but when." Mullen
then announced a fifty-state campaign to get a million signatures advocating
Lodge's nomination. It was a publicity stunt. There were no resources for
doing anything of the kind.

Next, Lodge's campaign crew rented a storefront in Boston's financial district for a "Lodge for President" headquarters. They unveiled their new office
with great fanfare on January 3 to steal the thunder from Goldwater's candidacy announcement in Arizona and the Rockefeller trip into New Hampshire.
It was another publicity stunt. Their action was illegal: Massachusetts law
required permission from the candidate to open a campaign office. Reporters
did their duty, passing on word throughout the country of an exciting new
entrant into the presidential field; the organizers did theirs and shut the place
down the next day. The president of New Hampshire's largest printing firm,
Richard Jackman (his company printed *Reader's Digest*), read the item about
the unveiling of Lodge's campaign headquarters in the *Concord Monitor* and
marched up to the state capitol with ten signatures and $100 to sign up as a
Lodge delegate candidate. Grindle read about Jackman in the *Monitor* and
recruited him as state campaign chair, giving him responsibility for coming up
with the remaining delegates—who, since every Republican luminary in the state
was already claimed by Goldwater and Rockefeller, were all friends of his.

Only then did Grindle and his cronies secure an office in Concord and set
up in earnest. They set a goal: if they won 12,000 votes and three or four delegates, they would enter the next big primary, in Oregon. Mullen sent a background memo to the D.C. press corps: Don't expect to see Lodge showing up at
any GOP fund-raisers any time soon—he had a nation to save from Communism, after all. "On the other hand," the memo continued, "I personally have no
question but that, given any sort of respite in South Vietnam and given a clear
signal that he has a fighting chance for the nomination, Cabot will make the race."

There was no respite; that very day five American helicopter crewmen died
in hard fighting over the Mekong River Delta. And Mullen, whatever his assurances, had plenty of questions about whether Lodge would come back from
Vietnam whatever the situation there. But Nelson Rockefeller didn't know
that. Around his office, his people had begun referring to the ambassador as
"Henry Sabotage." Rockefeller dispatched his Northeast regional coordinator,
Sandy Lankler, to Lodge headquarters. "I wouldn't say this if you had a chance
to win," the dapper, high-placed Washington attorney said conspiratorially.
"But as long as all you're doing is hurting us and helping Goldwater, why not
pull out?" Grindle laughed Lankler off. "How many people do you have?" he
asked. Rockefeller had sixty on staff in New Hampshire alone. Lodge had four.
Since the third and fourth were beautiful twenty-three-year-old women

(immortalized by Teddy White as "fresh with first bloom"), the office became a favorite, festive redoubt for reporters. Everyone was having a good time. The Lodge outfit thought he would make a good President. They thought Rockefeller would not. Why quit?

By the end of January they had made some progress: a former state rep told a newspaper he had endorsed Rockefeller in the interests of stopping Goldwater, but, he said, "my first personal choice is Ambassador Lodge." Reports were that the State Department had begun contingency planning in case Lodge left Saigon; the *Herald Tribune* noticed Lodge as a "conspicuous absentee" at GO-Day. Each poll revealed more undecideds than the last—potential Lodge voters, Grindle dared dream. Mullen sent out a second backgrounder: "We know that if the clear call is sounded, he will report for duty, and that he will report with the full élan of a good soldier, full of fight and spirit, and with the smell of victory in the air. His own commitment to an all-out campaign is the least of the worries."

At this point their worry was sending brochures to each of New Hampshire's 97,000 Republican voters—Lodge pictured on the front flap, standing ramrod straight behind a podium, looking presidential, and on the inside everything patriotic but the slice of apple pie: young Lodge beside an antiaircraft gun ("This military service now stands him well in Saigon, where on some days he can hear Communist gunfire through his embassy office windows"); Lodge at the UN (under his watch "Communist expansion was brought to a halt"); Lodge with Eisenhower's arm draped around his shoulder ("It was natural that this relationship should culminate in President Eisenhower's recent request that Ambassador Lodge return to the United States and seek the Republican nomination for president"). The brochure cited a Gallup poll showing Lodge running better against Johnson than Goldwater or Rockefeller (neglecting to note that Nixon ran best of all); it concluded by flattering Granite Staters' abundant political vanity by inviting them to "lead the nation in drafting Lodge." An enclosed card bore a write-in pledge to sign, preaddressed to "United States Embassy, Saigon." They were to send the card in a postage-paid envelope to Draft Lodge headquarters in Concord—where hundreds piled up each morning. The names were entered into a database, and only then were the cards forwarded to Saigon, where they served as a campaign within the campaign to convince their man he had a chance.

It worked. On February 18, Bill Loeb took a break from running photos of Rockefeller embracing Khrushchev, and proclamations of Goldwater's "holy crusade against those who have stolen the birthright of America," in order to abuse Henry Cabot Lodge on his front page. He ran a picture of a group of weeping mothers of Korean War MIAs who claimed that in 1954 they had tried to petition their UN ambassador—"an appeaser . . . partially responsible for the cynical betrayal of our missing fighting men"—only to be turned away. At Lodge headquarters there was rejoicing: now they were a threat.

Within a few days, a curious episode sent Draft Lodge past the tipping point. The mysterious goings-on in Vietnam had hardly been mentioned on the presidential stump that winter. Then Goldwater, returning to the state after ten days' break surlier than ever ("I'm not one of those baby-kissing, handshaking, blintz-eating candidates," he blurted out at a Hanover coffee hour), opined that Lodge had "kind of balled up" Vietnam. Candidates who criticized ongoing American military operations were vulnerable to backlash, by the principle that politics stopped at the water's edge. Even so oblique a criticism as Goldwater's was enough for the Lodge camp to become terrified that Rockefeller would surge into the lead any minute by impugning Goldwater's unpatriotic lapse. For two days his people waited with bated breath. They were almost ready to close up shop and go back to Boston.

Instead, Rockefeller called the Saigon embassy from the home of one of his supporters. In the age before communications satellites, such connections were hit-or-miss. He was waiting impatiently for the operator to get the call through when his hostess chirped, "If your Saigon call comes through, you can take it in my husband's office." Reporters overheard. The papers filled with speculation that Rockefeller had issued Lodge an ultimatum: Lodge should make an announcement one way or another as to whether he would campaign for the race, or Rockefeller would denounce him. When Rockefeller actually got through to him, Lodge, as he had been doing for weeks, refused to address the distracting subject. Rocky retaliated with a blistering statement on the "mess" in Vietnam. Then he called back to apologize, and made sure reporters knew it. That put Lodge's name in the papers again—as an embattled, self-sacrificing patriot, while Rockefeller came off simultaneously as bully and wimp. By taking Lodge seriously, Rockefeller spat in the wind: newsmen weary of the stalemated Goldwater-Rockefeller race now filed story after story with news of the ambassador—just as New Hampshire Republicans received their second Lodge mailing, a sample ballot showing how to write in his name and a card listing the times the one Manchester TV station, WMUR, was showing Lodge's five-minute TV commercial.

That commercial was their niftiest caper of all. Grindle had arranged to procure a copy of one of the most effective commercials from the 1960 Republican presidential campaign, "Meet Mr. Lodge." It was a quiet breakthrough in televisual technique: Lodge had sounded so snooty in scripted shoots that Nixon's television guru Gene Wyckoff had decided to use photographs of him instead, with a biographical voice-over from General Eisenhower. Wyckoff's innovation was to shoot the photos with an animation camera, panning and zooming dramatically, producing a surprising heroic effect (the technique would be copied in dozens of historical documentaries in decades to come). Grindle had the spot edited to remove the references to the Nixon presidential campaign—and fiddled with the sound over the final shot, a picture of Eisenhower literally embracing Lodge, so it sounded like Eisenhower was recommending him for the presidency, not the *vice* presidency. Livid, Goldwater implored Eisenhower to put a stop to the deception. Ike did no such thing. He wanted Goldwater to lose.

The fact that the Lodge campaign could only afford to buy time on Manchester's one TV station turned out to be an advantage. Both Rockefeller and Goldwater evaded the official spending limit of $20,000 by buying time from broadcasters in neighboring New England states. WMUR gave Lodge just enough exposure to let the people know about him without making them as sick of his face as they were of Goldwater's and Rockefeller's. Meanwhile, New Hampshire's secretary of state issued a ruling that last names only would be accepted for write-in votes—and that misspellings would be valid. It was another coup for Lodge's backers.

More ravens of disorder took wing. On February 25 in Miami, two weeks before the March 10 New Hampshire balloting, Cassius Clay, a 10-to-1 underdog, beat Sonny Liston in seven rounds. His behavior beforehand had been so flamboyant that the boxing commission's physician questioned whether he was sane enough to enter the ring. That same day it was reported that Air Force One had been accompanied on the way to Miami by fighter planes to protect the President against a suspected Cuban kamikaze-style attack—and the next day the rail line between Miami and Jacksonville was obliterated by a bomb planted by labor militants locked in a strike with the Florida East Coast Railway. Morning brought news of a school boycott in Louise Day Hicks's Boston, an hour's drive away from half of New Hampshire's population; three days later came news that black author Louis Lomax had won a standing ovation from two thousand students at California's Pomona College with the declaration "Non-violence is downright un-American." Cassius Clay suspected the same thing—which was one of the reasons he now announced membership in the Nation of Islam and chose a new name, Muhammad Ali. Against this background, the voters of New Hampshire seemed eager to fix upon old familiar Henry Cabot Lodge as the answer to every fear. "I hear him praised for views he just does not hold," a Lodge man admitted, "and I have to keep my mouth shut. But it's all to the good, as long as they like him."

One week after he had not even been included among the possibilities, the Harris poll predicted Lodge would earn 16 percent of the vote as a write-in candidate—31 percent, enough to win, if only he had let his name be printed on the ballot. It was another milestone: now Lodge was judged an option. Out went the campaign's third mailing, this one to people who had returned pledge cards. They were given names of Republicans in their district to convert to Lodge. The mailing also recruited an amazing 1,700 doorbell ringers—one for about every fifty-five Republican voters—for Election Day.

It was the beginning of March. Robert Mullen and George Lodge began traveling the byways to convince local leaders that the ambassador really truly was a candidate, and Norris Cotton was out reassuring the same people that Goldwater was an upstanding and responsible man (Cotton recalled it as "one of the most discouraging experiences of my life"). Lyndon Johnson concluded a morning of agonizing conclaves on Vietnam with a single decision—treat Henry Cabot Lodge like "Mister God." "As long as we got him there and he makes recommendations, we act on them," he told Bob McNamara. The last thing he wanted was a Republican nominee who knew how disastrous this adventure was becoming.

By that time it was hard to find a TV picture in New England absent the square jaws of Henry Cabot Lodge, Barry Goldwater, and Nelson Rockefeller. You could watch the eighteen-minute "Nelson Rockefeller Story" on WFEA at 9:30 a.m., 10:30 a.m., 11:45 a.m., and 5:00 and 6:00 p.m.; his eleven-minute show on WKBK at 8:00, 9:00, 10:30, 12:30, 3:00, and 4:00; the five-minute one on another channel at 5:00 p.m. and 5:30; the nine-minute one at 7:00 and 11:00 p.m.; the one-minute spot on WBBX at 8:15 a.m. and 12:15, 1:05, and 5:55 p.m.—sixteen ads from three different agencies in constant circulation. There were a like number of Goldwater spots—dreary where Rockefeller's were flashy, consisting of footage of their candidate standing at lecterns explaining at length why he wouldn't blow up the world, per the insistence of Kitchel and Baroody that once the electorate just got to *know* Goldwater they would love him.

His partisans agreed bad commercials didn't matter. Goldwater had finally found his voice in public appearances—Jeremiah's. "There isn't a person here who doesn't realize that something is wrong with our world today," he would cry. "This is the most powerful and prosperous nation in the world. And yet— our citizens are harassed and abused even in countries which have depended on us for aid." (A few weeks earlier in the African nation of Zanzibar rebels had kidnapped the U.S. counsel; "Death to the U.S.A." was chanted the night before by street mobs in Greece.)

"At home our crime rates soar, rising four times as fast as our population," Goldwater declared. "The quick buck, the dime-novel romances, pride and arrogance, morality that works on a sliding scale depending on your position—

and these have replaced what Teddy Roosevelt once called Americanism: 'the virtues of courage, honor, justice, truth, sincerity, and hardihood'—the virtues that made America."

This talk of crime and "morality on a sliding scale" was novel in a presidential campaign. America had begun suffering a crime wave. Violent crimes had increased from 120 per 100,000 in 1960 to 180 per 100,000 by 1964. Headline followed headline: the "Career Girl Murders" (a burglar and heroin addict on parole had beaten two young Manhattan women to death with his hands); the Boston Strangler (thirteen women had opened their doors to a man who was still at large, who sexually molested his victims, then choked them without leaving fingerprints). Chicago's Mother of the Year and her daughter were found strangled and bound facedown in their home. Goldwater's speeches now occasionally drifted into images of streets become jungles, women walking unsafe, sentimental judges giving more concern to the rehabilitation of the criminal than the vindication of his crime. The subject touched something in him. And in his crowds—who responded with electricity whenever it was raised.

The crowds were fantastic. On March 6 at the Manchester Armory, Goldwater was joined by Efrem Zimbalist Jr., Walter Brennan, and, on film—introduced as "the Gipper" in deference to his role in *Knute Rockne, All American*—Ronald Reagan. Goldwater brought the 3,500 spectators filling the seats and the aisles to a kind of communal ecstasy with a line cribbed from Richard Nixon's acceptance speech: "You are wrong, Mr. Khrushchev. Our children will not live under Communism. Your children will live under freedom!" Two nights before the March 10 election day, the Manchester speech was broadcast on TV.

Steeled by conviction against bitter cold, his volunteers performed heroic feats, contacting an astonishing 60 percent of the state's households (Lamphrey had finally prevailed upon Cotton to let the campaign workers knock on doors). Goldwater, overcome by the momentum, predicted he would get 40 percent of the vote. "I've got it made," he pronounced upon returning to D.C. At his New Hampshire headquarters on Monday there was a victory party in all but name. Outside, snow began to fall. That cheered them some more: snow would deter "moderates," not Goldwater voters.

By the time the polls opened on Tuesday morning, there was half a foot of snow on the ground. But early indications suggested a record turnout (Goldwater workers suspected a mass Rockefeller effort to wheel senior citizens into the booths to save their Social Security). By the time the polls closed, there was over a foot of snow on the ground. Voters had kept on coming. And they delivered an upset.

Goldwater was the choice of 23 percent, Rockefeller 21 (having estimated that he had shaken 50,000 hands, that worked out to 2.564 clasps per vote). Nixon got 17; Margaret Chase Smith, who had not bought any TV time or returned for a second trip, got 3. Seventy-seven souls wrote in the name of Bill Scranton, a recent *Life* and *Newsweek* cover boy.

The winner, with 35 percent, was Henry Cabot Lodge. His unknown delegates swept. A joke was coined: A backcountry farmer is asked why New Hampshire chose Lodge. "Dunno," he replied. "Mebbe 'cause he din't bother us none."

Lodge received the news while striding down the ramp of a plane upon his return from an inspection tour to Hue with Secretary McNamara. He announced, "I do not plan to go to the United States. I do not plan to leave Saigon. I do not intend to resign." (In Saigon, the day before the returns came in, Lodge made the extraordinary suggestion to Robert McNamara that South Vietnam be turned into a U.S. protectorate and that he be appointed "High Commissioner.") In D.C., Barry Goldwater's handlers were dithering with a statement backstage when Goldwater strode into the ballroom and announced: "I goofed up somewhere." It was the first loss of his political career. He toyed with quitting.

He was the only one not to declare victory. Kitchel told the press he was pleased "that a candidate from the Far West . . . could do so well in the New England state of New Hampshire." Rockefeller said he welcomed the results as a victory for moderation. Smith characterized the primary as proof that voters wanted a third choice. Nixon told reporters, "I feel that there is no man in this country who can make a case against Mr. Johnson more effectively than I can," let it be known for the benefit of conservatives looking for a new home that he had never endorsed the civil rights bill pending in the Senate—and prepared for a stature-boosting trip to the Far East. In the *New York Times*, Scotty Reston wrote that "the political pros are now betting on Gov. William W. Scranton"—he of the 77 votes—"former Vice President Richard M. Nixon or Ambassador Henry Cabot Lodge" to win the nomination. "They seem to agree": Goldwater and Rockefeller were virtually eliminated from contention.

PRESIDENT OF ALL THE PEOPLE

T he new savior of the Republican Party prepared for work every morning by strapping a sidearm to his shoulder. He stepped into the backseat
of a fortified Checker sedan, which rolled past the barbed-wire cordon
in front of his house, then started in on one of several routes, shifted at random,
to the United States Embassy at 39 Ham Nghi Boulevard. Plainclothes bodyguards at his side, he strode into the 90-degree heat and 90 percent humidity,
past the sidewalk barricades and saluting retinues of military police, then into a
lobby guarded by U.S. Marines. He took the back elevator to a sparsely furnished fifth-floor office and placed his revolver next to the .357 magnum he
kept in a desk drawer, and then he began his day as servant of a nation in Vietnam, as Lyndon Johnson put it, "at the request of a friend."

When Dwight D. Eisenhower had called Lodge to ask whether he had anything to do with the November 1, 1963, coup against the Diem government,
Lodge obligingly replied that he hadn't. He was lying. Henry Cabot Lodge had
been chosen as ambassador for his unsentimentality, for his lack of concern for
bureaucratic niceties, for his monumental ego that vouchsafed he wouldn't
leave before getting the job done—the job, in this case, being one of convincing Diem to democratize his regime. It turned out Lodge's ego was an impediment. Flying from Japan to present his credentials, Lodge had protested that the
plane the Administration sent was too small to accommodate all the reporters
he had invited. Once installed in office, Lodge refused to meet with Diem until
he detected an appropriate display of kowtowing. He much preferred, at any
rate, the course being urged by Kennedy hands Averell Harriman, Roger Hils-
man, and Mike Forrestal: a coup. Lodge was less worried about possible instability in the wake of this course of action; like his grandfather Henry Cabot
Lodge Sr. urging annexation of the Philippines in 1898, he believed "the U.S.
should be prepared to run the country" on its own. Other Vietnam policy makers despised him as a reckless fool. The in-country military chief, General Paul

Harkin, hardly spoke to him. Lodge spoke glibly of Diem's assassination, as if it pleased him.

Republican voters who responded to Lodge's victory in New Hampshire by giving him 42 percent in nationwide polls knew no more of this than they did the color of his shorts. What Americans didn't know about Vietnam was in many ways *becoming* America's Vietnam policy: an increasingly desperate military attempt to "send a message" to the North Vietnamese's supposed Soviet and Chinese masters, alongside attempts to hide any escalation from the American people.

The operative military doctrine, "graduated pressure," was a direct corollary of anxieties over nuclear escalation: Vietcong advance should be met with tit-for-tat response, carefully calibrated to simultaneously signal resolve and foreclose the possibility that China or the USSR would become directly involved. It wasn't working. By the time of Lyndon Johnson's inauguration on the tarmac of Dallas's Love Field on November 22, 1963, 16,000 American advisers, or 15,000 or 20,000—dodgy accounting methods made it hard for even the Pentagon to keep the numbers straight—were on the ground, 108 Americans were dead, and the National Liberation Front still collected taxes in all but three of South Vietnam's forty-four provinces. The Johnson Administration reacted by beginning a four-month experiment in graduated pressure set to begin on February 1, "Op Plan 34-A." The effort would include secret raids against the Ho Chi Minh Trail, the labyrinth of dirt paths the North Vietnamese had hacked out of the bush at the border with Laos and Cambodia to supply the rebels; reconnaissance flights over Laos; commando raids along the North Vietnamese coast; and naval shelling of North Vietnamese military assets from ships in the Gulf of Tonkin. These options were chosen with plausible denial in mind (on reconnaissance flights, for example, American pilots brought along Vietnamese trainees—they called them "sandbags"—so that if the plane were downed it could be claimed that a Vietnamese was the pilot).

Plausible denial to Moscow and Peking, and, as President Johnson began obsessing more and more about the upcoming election in November, to Milwaukee and Peoria. Military concerns were subordinated to public relations considerations. "We're going to rough them up a little bit in the days to come," the President explained in one of his off-the-record calls to publishers, this one to Scripps-Howard's Walker Stone. Then in his press conference the next day he said that he would welcome neutralization talks between the two countries, for, after all, we weren't at war with North Vietnam.

On February 9, as America watched those lovable moptops on the *Ed Sullivan Show* and the merry Draft Lodge band busied themselves with getting their first New Hampshire mailing out the door, graduated pressure did not deter Communist guerrillas from exploding a shrapnel bomb that killed several Americans at play on a Saigon softball diamond. Nor did it keep them from winning control of 45 percent of the land in South Vietnam by the end of the month—up a third since America's last brilliant plan, the November coup. The Joint Chiefs, whom Johnson respected no more than Kennedy had, finally succeeded in getting a memo before the President's eyes expressing their opinion that graduated pressure would mean endless American involvement with no end in sight. Only direct U.S. air attacks against the Ho Chi Minh Trail and military and industrial targets in North Vietnam, they argued, would make the Reds see reason. Retaliation from Russia or China, let alone nuclear retaliation, was unlikely; the only other alternative was "the loss of Vietnam."

This was the sort of thing that made Lyndon Johnson sit bolt upright. *The Democrats lost China*: as congressmen both he and JFK had watched as good Democrats had been carried out of Congress as if by a tidal wave when the Republicans had raised that cry in 1950. "If I tried to pull out completely now from Vietnam we would have another Joe McCarthy red scare on our hands," Kennedy had told an aide in 1963. Unfortunately, Kennedy and Johnson's other shared formative experience in foreign policy was the election of Eisenhower to the White House in 1952 on the back of the claim that the Democrats bogged us down in Korea. Holding the line against further Communist insurgency, holding it against escalating American commitment: these were the Scylla and Charybdis through which Lyndon Johnson steered his Vietnam thinking—a tortuous course that, some sleepless nights, seemed to threaten to crack open his skull. "They say, 'get in or get out,' " he moaned to Mac Bundy after coming out of a March 4 meeting with the Joint Chiefs, pictures from New Hampshire perhaps crowding the three TV screens the President kept in the Oval Office to watch all the network news shows at once. "I'm a trustee," he protested. "I've got to win an election." Until then, "let's see if we can't find enough things to do to keep them off base, and stop these shipments that are coming in from Laos, and take a few selected targets to upset them a little bit, without getting another Korea operation started."

He held off a reckoning by sending McNamara on a fact-finding mission. If McNamara could tour the countryside with the new South Vietnamese leader, General Khanh, the two men posing for pictures with their arms linked and held high to show this was Vietnam's fight but that America was behind her all the way, how much further could the Communists get? And so it went: two days before the voting in the New Hampshire primary, pudgy, goateed little General Khanh took to the jungle hustings with Bob McNamara and Cabot Lodge (who was fond of schooling the general on the fine points of American electioneering)—three LBJ proxies off on the strangest campaign trip in history.

McNamara wondered about the blank expressions on the villagers' faces. These were the reactions of a people whose national memory was wracked by hundreds of years of thwarted attempts at independence, who feared yet one more foreign power staking its claim. "The greatest gift for us was when McNamara came and toured the countryside, holding up Nguyen Khanh's arm," reflected the head of the National Liberation Front (which received only 10 percent of its weaponry from Communist allies, compared to the $1.5 million the United States pumped into Vietnam daily). "This saved our propaganda cadres a great deal of effort."

The gambit didn't work in the jungles. It did the trick at home. Even conservative *U.S. News* saw McNamara's tour as an occasion for optimism. Five hundred thousand French had been defeated in Vietnam in 1954, they allowed. "French generals, however, misunderstood the nature of the conflict"—not having McNamara to do what they presumed he had just done, earn the political loyalty of the peasantry.

Johnson breathed a sigh of relief. Now the decks were cleared for what he really cared about: continuing his remarkable string of domestic victories. His eye-popping January 8 State of the Union address was a liberal wish list: slum clearance, a mass transit program, minimum wage extensions, new public housing units—and two extraordinary initiatives inherited in various stages of vagueness from JFK: an $11 billion across-the-board tax cut and an "all-out war on human poverty and unemployment in these United States."

The latter was better remembered; the tax cut was more historic. From time immemorial politicians had been constrained by the assumption that there was only so much wealth to go around. Now economists believed the government could grow wealth as easily as turning on a spigot. It was called the "New Economics," and it heralded, said Walter Lippmann, a "post-Marxian age" where helping the poor no longer meant divisively "taxing money away from the haves and turning it over to the have-nots." With it, LBJ could fulfill his fondest dream: the corporate Pauls and the labor union Peters smiling across the bargaining table as they amicably divided a nation's bounty, with nobody taking from anyone else and no one left out. He could build, he promised to his eightieth burst of State of the Union applause, "a nation that is free from want and a world that is free from hate, a world of peace and justice, and freedom and abundance, for our time and for all time to come." Without an increase in spending—by cutting taxes.

The man responsible for this apparent miracle was John Maynard Keynes, whose *General Theory of Employment, Interest, and Money* (1935) explained that in times of economic slowdown, when people keep too much money squirreled away instead of spending it, businesses would respond to the ensuing drop in revenue by curtailing expansion. The whole economy would slow. In good times, the opposite would happen—superheating the economy, then starting the downward trend once again—dooming the economy to endless, unpredictable cyclic flutter. Unless, that is, government were to step in, as the only economic actor not obliged to respond to the laws of supply and demand, by spending more than it took in, washing consumers in cash, moving business sales into higher gear, and completing a virtuous circle of continual economic growth—so long as a wise captain was at the helm to set the process into motion when the economy looked to be braking.

Presidents were exceedingly slow to accept this wisdom. A balanced budget was judged as the symbol and substance of a sound economy; this was why Barry Goldwater stood up in the Senate in 1957 and said that Eisenhower's skyrocketing budget "not only shocks me, but weakens my faith." Even FDR was aghast, at the height of the Great Depression, at his advisers' stern counsel that he deliberately spend more than taxes took in. But slowly the economists wore the politicians down. Keynesianism answered to the spirit of an age in which liberalism, riding high, relished the opportunity to master forces formerly believed to be intractable. (Surely it was not exactly a coincidence that the same month Johnson passed his tax cut also saw teams of scientists, their bills paid by the National Science Foundation, begin a research project aimed at controlling the weather itself.) Lord Keynes's own preferred pump-prime was for the government to build massive tracts of cheap worker housing—not politic in the United States. But behind their hands, American economists suggested that massive defense expenditures served the same purpose—and that Keynesian interventions need not be disruptive at all, just a bit of innovative accounting: setting the numbers on the left side of the ledger just a little higher than those on the right. By the mid-1950s the chairman of Eisenhower's Council of Economic Advisors called it "no longer a matter of serious controversy whether the government shall play a positive role in helping to maintain a high level of economic activity"; by FY 1959 his sober boss quietly allowed a deficit of $12 billion to enter the books, the largest in peacetime history.

Tax cuts were an even more politic option.

Walter Heller urged a deficit via tax cut on President Kennedy after a dive in the stock market in the spring of 1962. JFK considered the idea and rejected it at first; even his most liberal adviser, Galbraith, said it "stretches our education in modern economics" (he preferred those tracts of worker housing) and reminded the President of the political realities: even to be labeled a tax raiser was preferable to "the worst tag of all—that of irresponsibility." Kennedy had run promising a balanced budget—a surplus, if possible. It was just after his showdown with U.S. Steel; he was eager to mend fences with businessmen, who traditionally considered deficits a bond-deflating recipe for inflation.

He overestimated the opposition. Big business, just then, was more conservative than ever, but in an entirely different sense than Barry Goldwater was: they were eager for government management as a road to the most conflictless, stable economic climate possible. If he planned a deficit, Arthur Schlesinger told Kennedy, "a large and influential part of the business community would give you enthusiastic support"—especially if it came in the palatable form of tax cuts. The Committee on Economic Development, the liberal parallel of the National Association of Manufacturers (Scranton's patron Tom McCabe was a founder), a redoubt of giant firms whereas NAM was the refuge of the medium to small (and, warned H. L. Hunt disciple Dan Smoot, was a key component of the "invisible government"), printed a Sunday supplement in the *New York Times* urging presidential authority to "make temporary countercyclical adjustments in the first-bracket rate of the personal income tax."

Soon the United States Chamber of Commerce signed on to the idea—then the National Association of Manufacturers. Only President Kennedy seemed lukewarm when he introduced his $11 billion tax-cut bill in early 1963. Conservatives bottlenecked it for over ten months—until the new President was inaugurated. Passing the tax cut, Johnson's economists informed him, would bring $30 billion in expansion to the GNP in 1964, as opposed to $12 billion if the bill wasn't passed. And by creating more wealth to be taxed, it would halve the deficit in the long run. Walter Heller only needed to explain how Eisenhower's refusal to stimulate the economy in 1959 cost Richard Nixon the election to clinch the matter. *"Business tycoons, left-wing laborites, corporation lawyers, New Dealers, anti-New Dealers, etc."*: he would be a President for all of them. He steered the tax cut through the Senate 77 to 21 in February. Federal budget deficits were now, officially, a good thing.

Then there was that other quintessential LBJ answer to the confident spirit of his age. A week earlier, Peace Corps chief Sargent Shriver had arrived back from a monthlong trip to the news that he was to direct a "war on poverty." The confidence that growth could cure all ills was secure enough for the Democrats' 1960 platform drafters to declare "the final eradication" of poverty "within reach." Wary of turning off middle-class voters in 1964, Kennedy had let Heller toil away at such a plan so long as he made sure they also did something for the suburbs, where all agreed the 1964 election would be decided.

That wasn't how Heller presented the situation when he put the memo he had prepared for Kennedy on Lyndon Johnson's desk on November 23, 1963. He implied that a poverty crusade was the martyr's last political wish. It was a rare Johnson moment, unbeclouded by political calculation. He bleated: "Push ahead full-tilt. That's my kind of program! It will help people!" The Economic Opportunity Act, coordinated by a new Office of Economic Opportunity and capitalized at $962.5 million, was presented to Congress on March 16 via a special message from the President. (The riposte from Barry Goldwater was immediate: "Under the enterprise system," America was already winning the War on Poverty, he said; federal welfare was leading to rates of fraud of 50 percent or more; the idea that people cannot find jobs because of insufficient education is "like saying that people have big feet because they wear big shoes. The fact is that most people have no skills, have no education for the same reason—low intelligence or low ambition.")

But Johnson's most precious baby was Kennedy's civil rights bill, which insiders would have no more anticipated than they would the 184,300 troops that would be stationed in Vietnam by the end of 1965. The black magazine *Jet* reported that when Johnson was sworn in, "a wave of pessimism and dejection began to build across Negro America." Would Lyndon Johnson show them!

Since Gilded Age, Supreme Court rulings had denied that the Fourteenth Amendment guaranteed equal access to public accommodations, Republicans had introduced hundreds of civil rights bills to restore its original intent—and Southern Democrats, with the tacit acquiescence of Democratic Presidents, had used every means at their disposal to annihilate them. And for most of his congressional career, Lyndon Baines Johnson had been right there with them. He dismissed President Truman's civil rights program while campaigning for Senate in 1948 as "a farce and a sham—an effort to set up a police state in the guise of liberty." But he had also seen the first civil rights bill since Reconstruction through to passage. Columnists Evans and Novak called his handiwork "The Miracle of '57"—sold to Northerners as a tiger, to Southerners and conservatives as a pussycat, and passed thanks to an amendment stipulating that all cases that fell under the bill's provisions were to be tried by local juries, cutting the bill off at the knees. He did it again in 1960—shepherding a law Pennsylvania liberal Joe Clark called "a pale ghost of our hopes."

But the price of political success in the South taxed Johnson's conscience. "The Negro fought in the war," he had been heard to admit in the 1940s. "He's not gonna keep taking the shit we're dishing out. We're in a race with time. If we don't act, we're going to have blood in the streets." Perhaps for this pragmatic reason, he was one of the few Dixie congressmen who didn't sign the 1956 "Southern Manifesto" decrying *Brown* v. *Board of Education*, and eventually calculation became conviction: weeks before Kennedy spoke out on the unfolding violence in Birmingham, Johnson delivered a brave speech echoing Martin Luther King's "Letter from a Birmingham Jail"—which rather annoyed Kennedy, who had hoped to deploy his vice president to hold the South in 1964.

Johnson had hardly returned from the Kennedy funeral when he surveyed the former Administration's legislative calendar and made civil rights his strategic priority—the South in 1964 be damned. He called Martin Luther King and told him, "I'm going to try to be all of your hopes." King's head spun; the only times that Kennedy called him were to work him over to fire his one Communist-associated deputy. "Let this session of Congress be known as the session which did more for civil rights than the last hundred sessions combined," he said at the State of the Union; congressmen exchanged knowing glances. They knew the bottom line. Of the bill's seven titles, five would likely pass as is: stiffened enforcement of voting rights and school integration, a community relations service for localities suffering racial tensions, an extension of the U.S. Commission on Civil Rights, and the withholding of federal funds from discriminatory state and local programs. Two proposals would be shaved off as they were every time to win the swing votes of conservative Republicans like Goldwater and Carl Curtis: Titles II and VII, guaranteeing equality in public accommodations and employment.

Then Johnson told his best friend, Georgia senator Richard Russell, "I'm not going to cavil and I'm not going to compromise. I'm going to pass it just as it is, Dick, and if you get in my way I'm going to run you down. I just want you to know that, because I care about you." When black leaders spoke with the President, they steeled themselves for the inevitable request for this or that compromise. It never came. He told them it would pass "without a word or a comma changed."

The proof was in the pudding. On January 30 Johnson won a petition to discharge the bill from Judge Smith's Rules Committee. His success was dismissed as a function of the eighty-year-old Smith's senility. Then, on February 10, the President won over the House, 290 to 130. That victory could be dismissed as a function of conservative House Republicans achieving morality on the cheap—the assumption being that by the time for final passage, the bill would have been watered down in the Senate under filibuster threat.

That, too, Johnson was determined would never come to pass. To pass the bill as is, he would need not just fifty-one senators, but sixty-seven—the two-thirds necessary to end Senate debate, which, under that body's infamous Rule 22, could extend indefinitely. Such "cloture" votes never succeeded. But then, the Senate had never seen a lobbyist as obstinate as Lyndon Baines Johnson.

Getting two-thirds of the senators meant getting four-fifths of the Republicans. "You're either for civil rights or you're not, you're either for the party of Lincoln or not," he would tell them; if that didn't work, there other methods. "I hope that satisfies those two goddamned bishops that called me last night," Karl Mundt exclaimed after voting the President's way on one early test vote.

Conservative Republicans like Mundt were Johnson's swing vote. Everett McKinley Dirksen, the minority leader swept to the Senate in 1950 in the front ranks of Joe McCarthy's antisubversive crusade, was the key to winning their hearts. The key to winning Dirksen's, LBJ knew, was his ego, outsized even for a senator—and since his vote for the test-ban treaty was apprized the most magnanimous act of legislating since isolationist Arthur Vandenberg voted for NATO in 1949, he had become a hungry bidder for immortality. "You drink with Dirksen," LBJ commanded his field captain, Hubert Humphrey. "You talk to Dirksen. You listen to Dirksen."

From the other side the lobbying came just as hard. The National Association of Manufacturers spooked its members with a brief on the bill's equal employment provisions: "It can be expected that the number of charges and suits under Title VII would be many times that under the National Labor Relations Act." Richard Russell proposed an amendment calling for massive resettlement of Negroes to areas where they were "underrepresented"—"inflicting on New York City, the City of Chicago, and other cities the same conditions proposed to be inflicted by this bill on the people of the community of Winder, Georgia, where I live." Citizens wrote letters to the editor—and a lawyer an article in the *American Bar Association Journal*—comparing the legislation to another noble but doomed experiment: prohibition. Southerners claimed Titles II and VII violated the Thirteenth Amendment by "enslaving" white people. A "Coordinating Committee for Fundamental American Freedoms" was financed out of the treasuries of the states of Mississippi, Alabama, and Louisiana, led by two past ABA presidents, John C. Satterfield and Loyd Wright, and two newspaper editors, James J. Kilpatrick of the *Richmond News Leader* and William Loeb of New Hampshire's *Manchester Union Leader*. One of their ads, which went out to 225 newspapers in states where senators were wavering, pictured the "socialists' omnibus bill" as a "$100 Billion Blackjack."

None of this dented the popularity of Camelot's self-anointed redeemer. Johnson enjoyed a 74 percent approval rating—among Republicans. His press rivaled Albert Schweitzer's: "Johnson Pledges Fight on Mental Retardation; Vows to Press Kennedy's Campaign to Aid Children, Battle Poverty, 'Every Other Foe.' " This would have relaxed any politician—except Lyndon Johnson. He had begun campaigning for reelection long ago. His first target was the

Republican business leaders whose checks and phone calls and subtle threats
usually vouchsafed an acceptable GOP presidential candidate every four years.
On December 7 he squeezed eighty-nine of them into the Cabinet Room,
ostensibly to win their support for his tax bill. "Call me Lyndon," he said. "I'd
like to get on a first-name basis with you." The conclaves became a regular
event. He slathered his guests in flattery, calling them the nation's life-givers,
"the symbols of the free enterprise system." Slowly he chipped away the
residue of thirty years of Democratic business bashing—Franklin Roosevelt's
resounding attacks on the nation's "economic royalists." It worked. "That was
most impressive," said one after a meeting at the White House. "Is there a citizen's group for Johnson you can join?"

November lurked behind every policy decision: whipping the tax bill into
passage in time for an autumn impact; complaining of a list of useless military
bases that might be closed, "They're all in such sensitive states." White House
staffers learned to schedule joint sessions of Congress to honor visiting Italian
leaders, to endure rants against caviling columnists, to inform the President of
poll numbers even as they rolled off the presses (right down to sub-ethnic
groups like "English Scotch"). Paranoid about imagined Kennedy restoration
plots, he ordered his people not to talk to Teddy White—one of the "agents of
the people who want to destroy me." Speeches became occasions to take on the
Republican of the moment. (In his February appearance in Miami—the target
was Goldwater—he described the presidency as "the one place where a petty
temper and narrow view cannot reside.") He defeated every setback west of the
Mekong River Delta—even the Bobby Baker affair.

Baker was a bright country boy from South Carolina who came to Washington in 1944 as a page and indefatigably worked his way up to a position as
majority secretary in the Senate by the age of twenty-six in 1955. The young
man they called "Little Lyndon" reinvented that formerly ceremonial role as
surely as his mentor did the majority leadership. Johnson was heard to say that
if he could have a son, he'd choose Bobby Baker. Baker was also the go-to guy
for senators seeking a bit of sport with the ladies, the man who knew where
every senator stood and how each could be won; he was a favorite courier for
lobbyists bearing fat envelopes. He always skimmed a bit off the top; what
were they going to do, report him? He set up a little consultantship on the side;
his customers were the kind of businesses willing to do whatever it took to win
precious government contracts. By the summer of 1963 people began wondering how a man with a salary of $20,000 had become a millionaire, and the
walls came tumbling down. Hearings began, but not before the *Des Moines
Register* spied a scoop among the thicket: a possible kickback to Lyndon Johnson laundered through the television station his wife owned, involving a com-

plex deal to secure life insurance after his 1955 heart attack. The allegations and evidence were thin enough that it would seem that the President had little to fear. But just to remind the public of the fortune the Johnson family made off KTBC, the only channel in fast-growing Austin (Goldwater's favorite opening line there was "I didn't have any trouble finding Austin, I just looked for a great big city with only one TV antenna"), threatened Johnson's appearance of propriety as much as had a Senate race won by 87 votes.

In late January, when Republicans tried to get Walter Jenkins, Johnson's most intimate aide, to testify before a Senate subcommittee investigation, Johnson put in the fix. Two psychiatrists appeared to testify that an appearance would—literally—kill him. Carl Curtis moved to call Jenkins to the stand anyway. He lost 6 to 3 in a party-line vote. That was a good thing for Johnson: "I've got considerably more detail on Reynolds's love life," Jenkins told the President about the man who linked him to Bobby Baker. "Well, get it all typed up for me," Johnson replied—not the kind of shady behavior Jenkins wanted to be asked about under oath. Curtis lost again when he moved to make the record of their session public. The investigation closed without a single Administration witness being called. A *Minneapolis Tribune* poll found that of the 80 percent of those surveyed who had heard of the Baker case, only 4 percent said it made a difference in the way they viewed the President.

He couldn't lose. A private utility executive would take to the White House lobby to announce a $1 billion expansion in Ohio, Indiana, Virginia, West Virginia, Kentucky, and Tennessee, proclaiming that the "favorable business climate" caused by the tax cut was responsible for his decision. They were supposed to be enemies: Johnson was a foremost advocate of public power plants; Goldwater was the spokesman for private ones. But this President didn't seem to have any enemies. On March 23 the *Wall Street Journal* ran an exposé estimating Johnson's fortune at $20 million. *Time* ran a piece depicting Johnson careening around his ranch at eighty miles an hour in a Cadillac full of terrified reporters, craning his neck around to bark off-color stories to the backseat, sipping Pearl beer all the while. All was forgotten after he settled a tense and violent Florida railroad strike in marathon sessions with the two parties in the White House. Shortly afterward he even won over the conservative United States Chamber of Commerce ("We haven't done anything for business this week, but please remember, this is only just Monday morning," he apologized in a speech interrupted for laughter, applause, or both sixty times). Walter Lippmann called Johnson "a healing man" whose country was "far more united and at peace with itself, except over the issue of Negro rights, than it has been for a long time." Scotty Reston praised the President's "total absence of ideology, the passionate insistence on the general welfare, the willingness to talk endlessly through the night if necessary, the vivid earthy American language and optimistic faith that problems can be solved." The public agreed: two weeks past the traditional one-hundred-day honeymoon new Presidents were supposed to enjoy, his approval rating stood at 77 percent. It was 75 percent even in the South.

It was a martyr-besotted electorate that the Republicans would have to entice in seven months. They needed a hero, the theory went, a man of the center, an antipartisan, in order to do it—a man like Henry Cabot Lodge, a selfless symbol of the principle that politics ended at the water's edge, of America's resolve to prevail over Communism at the frontier of freedom. Polls now showed Lodge to be the hands-down favorite for the Republican nomination.

The next big show was Oregon. Lodge was entered, as was almost everyone else, which was why Oregon was a big show: its election laws required Oregon secretary of state Howell Appling to place on the May 15 ballot all candidates "generally advocated and recognized" as contenders if they had not filed the functional equivalent of a Sherman statement by March 9 at 5 p.m. Dutifully he declared there were six: Goldwater, Rockefeller, Scranton, Nixon, Romney, and Lodge. He missed Mrs. Smith; it took a 1,000-name petition to get Appling to put her on the ballot. She was not being taken seriously.

Only Romney had filed a Sherman statement. When the deadline passed, the day before New Hampshire primary balloting, and Lodge had not filed one either, the sigh of relief from his backers could be heard all the way to Portland, Oregon—where, in a barnlike structure embellished with enormous photographs of their candidate ministering to wounded GIs in Vietnam, Lodge's campaign team began to set up the entire operation all over again. This time they didn't take chances. Under no circumstances, they explained, would "the commander-in-chief of American forces in the hot spot of the world, South Vietnam" come home to campaign.

Scranton was the sorcerer's apprentice: the more he tried to undo his candidacy, the more pundits suspected he was a candidate. "Intimate contact with Gov. William Scranton of Pennsylvania leads to only one conclusion," wrote Richard Wilson of the *Los Angeles Times*. "He is, in his own low-key way, an active candidate for the Republican Presidential nomination." Connecticut backers sent Scranton brochures to every fifth name in state telephone books. *Meet the Press* entertained the Pennsylvania governor on February 16; Walter Lippmann all but endorsed him on the nineteenth. Ohio governor James Rhodes was trying to whip up a Scranton delegate bloc in the Midwest. When Scranton presented an unemployment reform plan that angered union leaders, Joe Alsop called it a secret scheme to steal the hearts of conservatives—granting Scranton such extravagant conspiratorial powers that the columnist sounded like a Bircher. *Reader's Digest* reincarnated him as John F. Kennedy—telling readers that "he keeps superbly fit with vigorous tennis, skiing and other outdoor sports" and that "his manner is one of easy assurance and sophistication."

After a Scranton friend told *Time* he had just raised $25,000 for the presidential effort, the governor decided he had had enough. After he returned from a Florida vacation on April 19 (he read seventeen books), a stunning 1,200 people turned up at a press conference to hear him read a statement. This, they were sure, was the big one. It wasn't. Many "evidently believe that deep in my heart I do desire the nomination and I am only waiting until the right moment to make my move," he said. "This is not true. But it seems to be part of our American folklore to believe that every politician wants to be president." He had tears in his eyes. It is a powerful thing to have the world tell you you should be President of the United States. But he didn't *exactly* deliver a Sherman statement. His attorney general and closest political confidant warned that doing so would dishonor his pledge that he would accept an honest draft. And William Warren Scranton was an honorable man.

Nixon had come close to filing one. In early March, he convened H. R. Haldeman, John Ehrlichmann, General Mills vice president Nate Crabtree, and Crabtree's public relations chief, the wide-eyed young Len Nadasdy, to chew on the Oregon problem. Was it fertile soil for a "surprise" Nixon upset, or for a humiliating loss that would spoil his reputation for good? Nadasdy, who knew Republicans in every county from his YR work, was dispatched to the state to make discreet inquiries about Nixon's chances. He returned within the week to report that not a single candidate for delegate was likely to pledge to Nixon— and that the plurality of Oregon county chairs thought that the convention would deadlock and Nixon would end up with the nomination anyway. There was nothing to gain by orchestrating a fake grassroots groundswell as Nixon had in New Hampshire in 1956: if such a tactic were exposed, it would scotch the "elder statesman" strategy; if successful, it would likely help Goldwater by further splitting the moderate vote. And if he didn't risk such an effort but *did* win a genuinely spontaneous upsurge, so much the better. What Nadasdy proposed was that Nixon give a press conference in Portland before departing for Asia to explain that although he could not in good conscience remove his name from the ballot, Oregon voters should cast their votes for someone else. Nixon left for Asia. No such press conference was given. Nixon decided to make a stealth campaign in Oregon whatever the risks. Nadasdy reflected with wonder that so careful and shrewd a politician could also relish harebrained cloak-and-dagger schemes that could easily blow up in his face.

Rockefeller was counting on his strength in Oregon to save him. The Oregon governor, rising GOP star Mark Hatfield, had almost backed Rockefeller against Nixon in 1960; the New York governor was ahead of Goldwater in January polls; the chair of the state university's board of regents had resigned just to manage his campaign. Huge crowds fêted Nelson and Happy at every stop on a February tour of the state (it opened, per Oregon tradition, with the candidate slicing through a gargantuan log with a chain saw). College volunteers crowded his Portland campaign office. And he had a unique advantage: Oregon could be reached by commercial flight only by way of San Francisco. Rockefeller was borrowing his brother Winthrop's brand-new Sabre-Liner, which could make the direct trip from Albany in six and a half hours. Goldwater, saddled with a less impressive bird, missed one big appearance after being held up in San Francisco by mechanical difficulties.

Rockefeller pounced. His half-hour campaign film began showing two months before the May 15 balloting. A late-March tour covered 350 mountainous miles a day. He also flew in Jackie Robinson, the baseball star, now a restaurant company executive, to play bad cop: "If we have a bigot running for the presidency of the United States," Robinson said, "it will set back the course of the country."

All his ducks were in a row. Though it all seemed rather moot. National political reporters paid little attention. The polls showed Henry Cabot Lodge scoring three times higher than anyone else.

15

UNITED AND AT PEACE
WITH ITSELF . . .

Clif White had to laugh. The New Hampshire and Oregon scrambling, this obsession with Mr. Gallup—it didn't matter if *98 percent* of Republicans loved Lodge if none among their number were convention delegates. The battle for the nomination was fought in hotel ballrooms. Only greenhorns and TV anchormen thought it was fought at the ballot box.

After Goldwater's defeat in New Hampshire, White exuded the confidence of a man on top of the world: "Gentleman, off the record, don't worry—we're still going to win," he told reporters. By the day they lost New Hampshire's fourteen delegates, they had already won four times that many in North Carolina, Georgia, and the marvelous Palmetto State, from whose convention Roger Milliken had telegrammed, "SOUTH CAROLINA WILL CAST ITS 16 VOTES FOR BARRY GOLDWATER FOREVER." Let the press cite polls saying that 90 percent of the Republican rank and file wanted someone else. Besides Henry Cabot Lodge's New Hampshire delegates and Rocky's three from the Virgin Islands (where his family had extensive holdings), all the ones decided so far belonged to Goldwater. He had scores more ready to fall in during the weeks to come.

It worked like this. Prior to a state convention, White collected a goal from his chairman of how many delegates his team could harvest. He or an associate—Kleindienst, usually, although as Goldwater's designated "director of field operations," he was technically White's superior—worked the precinct committeemen and county chairs in person to line up their do-or-die support; two or three weeks before the event, White showed up again to case the ballroom for tactical purposes, parley with his local deputies, study the makeup of the committees that decided credentials and rules, and made sure arrangements had been made to bring the Goldwater delegates to San Francisco, the national convention site, in the same plane, train, or bus—as a disciplined *unit*. He would pore over the relevant rules, ponder the back-room gossip, figure out whether his people could ram through a resolution pledging the delegation to

Goldwater come hell or high water. When the day came, if the convention was contested—often it wasn't—White, Kleindienst, or both, and one of their seven regional directors, would show up to plot strategy, drum up a pep rally, seed the site with propaganda—and, if need be, engage in the black arts of convention trickery of which there was no greater master than F. Clifton White. His model was the Kennedy campaign that began in 1957; surprise was their best weapon. Springing Draft Goldwater on an unsuspecting political establishment in April of 1963 had made Goldwater look more popular than he actually was—without, *Life* was fooled into reporting, "a Kennedy-style campaign." The *Washington Post* had reported on February 8 the "flaking off" of Goldwater delegate support in Washington, Indiana, Missouri, Colorado, and Ohio. It was the kind of coverage White craved. It would only make the victory more impressive when he swept them.

But White kept on thinking of quitting. No other candidate's organization came close to the one he had built. Yet Denison Kitchel was oblivious. After the New Hampshire defeat, Joseph Alsop ("All-sop," Dean Manion said his name should be spelled) had written, "No serious Republican politician, even of the most Neanderthal type, any longer takes Goldwater seriously." Denison Kitchel chose to ignore White's briefings and believe Alsop instead. Kitchel spent the week after the New Hampshire defeat practically catatonic with grief. Perhaps he had never heard White in the first place; after all, he had that habit of switching off his hearing aid during discussions he considered tedious.

Clif White looked at the shape of Kitchel's Goldwater for President Committee offices in D.C., and he grieved, too. Goldwater had never seen White's carefully prepared advance memos for New Hampshire, he learned; the Arizona Mafia kept the candidate from "outside" advice. The campaign's fundraising had ground to a halt, stuck at a point little beyond the $500,000 White had called in from the $1 petition pledges (Marvin Liebman, charged with setting up a branch office in New York, had to do it on his American Express card). As late as February the D.C. office hadn't produced a single brochure. Disillusionment was infecting the grass roots. "For a publicity splash that should have been in preparation for three years," a friend wrote Rusher, Goldwater "has generated no excitement, no flair, no purpose, no program." The Goldwater for President finance committee demanded, and by the ukase of Barry Goldwater was refused, Kitchel's resignation.

The research, for all the team's computerized razzle-dazzle, was awful. (Couldn't someone just nail down whether the United Nations was violating either thirty-seven or forty of its covenants so Goldwater didn't have to fumble with a number every time?) The speechwriting was worse. Karl Hess had been put on the job full-time. For Goldwater, it was the beginning of a wonderful

friendship; Hess was his kind of maverick. He had left home to become a journalist at age fifteen, was a former professional gunsmith ("It would not be
America really if it did not produce men who suddenly tire of palaver and reach
for the rifle on the wall," he once wrote), had run contraband to rebels in Cuba.
On fire with ideological fervor, he had a bottomless contempt for political
operatives. And he was loyal to the point of nearly elevating his boss to the status of a god. He and Goldwater fantasized about barnstorming the nation, just
the two of them, the candidate dropping from the sky like a bronze god just as
he used to with Shadegg in 1952 and 1958. Together they wrote speeches that
were like billboards on the road to Damascus. "If we in this hour of world crisis are content to amuse ourselves with the material luxuries freedom has produced," Goldwater proclaimed in a statewide TV address in Oregon, "we stand
guilty of trading the future of all mankind for a brief moment of uncertain
safety for our generation." At which some few voters who entered the hall
seeking just enough info to pull one lever in a booth instead of another were
converted in a blinding flash. Many more just left spooked.

The trouble was rooted in a culture clash. Hess and the Arizonans' conservatism was rooted in contempt for fast-talking Easterners and their wily ways;
to their mind Goldwater's choice of a bunch of hip-shooting cowboys to run his
campaign *was* practically the message of the campaign. That couldn't have
been further from what made Clifton White and his boys tick. To them, the
thrill of politics was operating in the midst of the Establishmentarians, drinking
with them, joking with them—then stealing their party out from under their
noses. To the Arizonans, Clif White looked like just one more *operative,* feath-
ering his own nest, hogging the headlines, hedging his bets with Goldwater
until a better opportunity came his way, ready to heap scorn on a guy like
Kleindienst just because he didn't belong to the Century Club, even though he
had finished third in his class at Harvard. White did what he considered his
solemn duty ("When you get a phone call," he kept on hectoring Kitchel, "look
in the book so you know who the heck you're talking to. It's important!"); the
Arizona Mafia could only see a grasping, condescending ass; they kept talking
about "Eastern lawyers" as if they were an occupying army.

When Goldwater and his Mafia came to Chicago for a confidence-building
meeting with their state chairmen just after New Hampshire, White gathered
his original Draft Goldwater group to confront Goldwater directly about his
mistakes. But when the drafters finally got the draftee to meet with them, they
lost their nerve: the candidate was so overwrought he looked like he was ready
to snap. Charlie Barr pinioned Karl Hess instead, imploring him to seed Goldwater's speeches with local concerns and pocketbook issues. Hess looked him
in the eye and saw the enemy: an operative, a species whose craft he once dis-

missed as "whomping up spontaneous demonstrations, buying and distributing buttons and bunting; wagging their cigars and talking tough to one another as they parceled out committee assignments and head table seats." He said Goldwater could never pander to the electorate like that. "You goddamn Boy Scouts are going to ruin everything!" Barr bellowed back.

But they were grown men. The two sides needed each other. On March 18 White put aside his reservations, chose to stick out the campaign to the end, and sent a memo proposing a truce. A few days later Dick Kleindienst burst into White's office. "Get your hat. We're off to Barry's apartment." That was a surprise; White had never been there before.

The senator was aglow from his successful first tour of California. Icy Kitchel sat in a stiff, straight-backed chair, though he looked perfectly at home. White, sinking into a supple couch, looked like he was in the midst of strangers. He grew more comfortable as the meeting began. An agreement fell into place: White would run the convention, Kleindienst and White would divide up the remaining states between them as *co*-directors of field operations, access to the candidate's ear would be relaxed. On White's way out, Goldwater gave him a grapefruit. White was given to understand that it was an Arizona grapefruit. He wondered whether he hadn't been handed some ritual talisman of acceptance. Buoyed, he began a quiet second campaign: lobbying for his dream job. If Goldwater was nominated, White decided, he deserved to become chairman of the Republican National Committee.

The two directors of field operations settled into a working comity: White would handle most of the conventions and a few primaries; Kleindienst would cover most of the primaries and a few conventions. Both would help in pivotal California. Kleindienst, who was subject to constant entreaties from the experts to resign his post and hand it over to White (which Goldwater explicitly forbade), welcomed White's expertise; White respected Kleindienst as the most independent-minded of the Arizonans. (Kleindienst had recently been banned from strategy sessions after questioning one of Baroody's ideas in front of two outsiders. Not for nothing was this called a "Mafia.") The D.C. office was reorganized, which strengthened it: Karl Hess as full-time speechwriter, Chuck Lichenstein as advertising coordinator, and Lee Edwards as acting director of information.

The candidate, however, stayed the same. When Edwards called on the senator to propose exploiting his glamorous hobbies, Goldwater listened politely, then replied, "Lee, we're not going to have that kind of crap in this campaign. This is going to be a campaign of principles, not of personalities. I don't want that kind of Madison Avenue stuff, and if you try it, I will kick your ass out of this office."

"Well, Senator," young Edwards replied, "I guess you've made that very clear."

It had been a busy winter for George Wallace. There was Alabama to keep segregated, for one thing. There was his ego to attend to, for another. In November the governor had undertaken a weeklong tour of Ivy League colleges. Then he took the show national. First he honed the act, blue-penciling his speechwriters' racist turns of phrase, having his aide Bill Jones pepper him with every hostile question they could think of. Audiences, expecting a monster, were charmed by talk of how "property rights are human rights, too"—so sweet it almost sounded sensible, yet so incendiary that he led the evening news everywhere he spoke.

Wallace's people booked eight days in the West in January. At each stop Jones set up news conferences, speeches to civic groups, and three TV and radio interviews a day. Each time Wallace appeared on the air he outflanked smug liberals by mentioning the uprisings they were ignoring in their own backyards—the defeat of open housing in Berkeley ("they voted just like the people in Alabama"), the "sleep-in" in the office of liberal Republican Colorado governor John Love. Wallace said he disagreed with Abraham Lincoln when the great man said that Negroes should not vote, serve on juries, or hold public office—although he agreed with Lincoln that equality for Negroes could come only through education, uplift, and time. "Perplexed convulsions," was how one newspaper described it when half an audience exploded in laughter at one of his jokes, half the chucklers worrying whether this made them sympathizers with the Ku Klux Klan. At the University of Oregon field house the Alabama governor outdrew Goldwater by 1,500 (he got a bit carried away and shouted, "The Confederate flag will fly again!"). Vague hints were dropped about a presidential run—trial balloons ignored as too fanciful for print.

Shortly after the House passed the civil rights bill, Wallace did ten days in the heartland (on Alabama's dime; he claimed he was there to attract industry to the state). After his success in the West, politicians couldn't ignore him. Ohio senator Steve Young called him "a buffoon" who had "tarnished the image of our country throughout the world." Wallace took this remark as evidence that he was getting somewhere.

He was. Speaking in Cincinnati just before CORE's school boycott, he noted the protesters outside and said, "There are more good people like you in this country today than there are these little pinkos running around outside. But we must band together. When you and I start marching and demonstrating and carrying signs, we will close every highway in this country." Audience members leapt to their feet. Dozens made for the exits to advance on the pickets.

Richard Nixon, who knew a political opportunity when he saw one, happened to be speaking in the same city the very next day. He gave a kinder, gentler version of the same speech.

On Irv Kupcinet's TV show in Chicago, Wallace collected gubernatorial candidate Charlie Percy's scalp. "Martin Luther King said that Chicago was the most segregated city in the nation," Wallace pointed out. Percy, the blood draining from his face, was forced to grant the point. Wallace cracked his most winsome grin. At a news conference he said he might run in some primaries. "If I ran outside the South and got 10 percent, it would be a victory. It would shake their eyeteeth in Washington."

In Madison, Wisconsin, where professed socialists practically outnumbered conservatives, he awoke to the words "FUCK WALLACE" inscribed in blood-red Kool-Aid on frozen Lake Mendota outside his guesthouse room. It was February 20, a snowy day, but the weather had not kept an Oshkosh couple from making the hundred-mile drive over two-lane roads to hear him. Lloyd Herbstreith and his homemaker wife Delores wouldn't have missed the opportunity for a hurricane. The Herbstreiths had just chaired a massive, failed grassroots campaign to make Wisconsin the fifth state to ratify the Liberty Amendment. Since Wisconsin's primary on April 7 was "open"—Republicans and Democrats could vote for either party's candidates—the outcome was politically meaningless. Every Republican chose to pass it up. Conservative political junkies like the Herbstreiths were deathly bored.

Accounts vary over just when the Herbstreiths put aside their reservations about a man who, except for civil rights, had never met a government program he didn't like, and decided to approach his camp with the proposal to run a Wallace presidential primary campaign from their Oshkosh kitchen. All it took to enter, Delores explained to intrigued aides, was to file sixty delegate and alternate candidates by March 6, no signatures required, a task she could take care of with one hand tied behind her back. She laid out the odds like a seasoned Washington operative. Governor John Reynolds, President Johnson's favorite-son proxy, was unpopular among Milwaukee's hundreds of thousands of Catholic white ethnics because of his unsuccessful drive for an open housing law, and he was reviled in the rural Republican precincts that had once revered Joe McCarthy. By turning over their Liberty Amendment organization (and turning their three children over to a housekeeper), they could donate to Wallace a veritable statewide machine. Herbstreith confidently predicted a third of the vote.

Wallace didn't need much convincing. That a majority of Northerners had the same ideas about civil rights as Southerners but were chicken to say so had been a commonplace of Dixie political folklore at least since Strom Thurmond ventured to New York to scrounge up support for his Dixiecrat campaign in 1948. Thurmond's debating tricks anticipated Wallace's: "If you people in New York want no segregation, then abolish it and do away with your Harlem. Personally, I think it would be a mistake. . . . And by the same reasoning, no federal law should attempt to force the South to abandon segregation where we have it." Then, ten years later, there was Jim Johnson, writing Clarence Manion: "States' Rights have become household words in Ohio as much as in Arkansas or Mississippi. How well would Orval Faubus do in the North, the Midwest, and the West Coast states?"

A week before the filing deadline, Governor Reynolds made a mistake: he ventured a joke about Wallace's presidential ambitions at a press conference. The free publicity brought enough unsolicited calls to the Herbstreiths to round out their delegate slate. Wallace flew to Madison in his official jet (the Stars and Bars on the nose replaced by the Stars and Stripes; his motto, "Stand Up for Alabama," with "Stand Up for America"), met the couple for the first time, then formally applied for his spot on the ballot. He opened his campaign in Appleton, McCarthy's hometown, and stumbled nervously over lines the Herbstreiths scripted for him about the sellout at Yalta. The papers hardly noticed. Polls gave him 5 percent.

Senate debate on the civil rights bill began on March 8. It was as if the opening gun had been sounded for a fortnight of race skirmishes. The next day Seattle voters, juiced by a Wallace visit in January, repealed the city's open housing law. Two days later Malcolm X said that black "rifle clubs" were preferable to civil rights bills, and CORE's ultramilitant New York chapters, gathered in protest against some vague enemy they called "the System," massed at the ramps leading to the Triborough Bridge, armed with bag after bag of garbage, in an attempt to strangle traffic around the city. A second school boycott the next week roused police commissioner Michael Murphy to riot preparations against blacks seeking, he said, to "turn New York City into a battleground."

Cleveland already was a battleground. Militants who had been beaten by white vigilantes for the sin of marching with "SEPARATE IS NOT EQUAL" signs in front of an all-white school responded by sitting in at a school construction site. A bulldozer driver chose to stay the course rather than yield to the Presbyterian minister in his path, and crushed the man to death. In San Francisco, two thousand civil rights activists, most from Berkeley's hardy contingent, emboldened by a successful February action at the Lucky supermarket chain—filling their carts with groceries, they abandoned them at the checkout counter with the refrain "I'm *so* sorry, but I seem to have forgotten my purse until you hire some Negroes in public positions"—grubbed up the lobby of the Sheraton-Palace with the demand for a racial hiring agreement. Columnists Evans and Novak, recalling perhaps that at least the Young Republicans had worn suits when they had terrorized the same hotel the previous June, wrote, "Here as elsewhere the Negro is in danger of losing control over the civil rights movement to thugs and Communists." In Washington, Senator Lister Hill of Alabama hurled a pipe bomb into the Democratic coalition during his turn to filibuster by announcing that the civil rights bill would gut labor unions' seniority and apprentice systems. Segregationist Florida officials announced they would boycott Johnson's Democratic National Convention. Brooklyn congressman Emmanuel Cellers, the civil rights bill's floor manager, warned that his beloved movement was falling into the slough of "nihilism."

Suddenly it looked like the Negro revolt might rewrite every political rule. A new word was on all lips: "backlash." Governor Reynolds publicly goosed his estimate of how many votes Wallace would get—100,000 (his actual guess was 50,000)—to spur his volunteers, who now seemed worryingly unenergetic; Catholic, Jewish, and Protestant clergy united to condemn "a threat to the moral quality of our nation"; a letter from the AFL-CIO to four hundred Wisconsin affiliates denounced "one of the strongest anti-labor spokesmen in America"; COPE's brochures said that Wallace's real goal was stealing Wisconsin jobs. And Wallace surged ahead all the while.

He had an answer for every heckle: *"How many of you have read the civil rights bill? . . . I am an Alabama segregationist, not a Wisconsin segregationist. If Wisconsin believes in integration, that is Wisconsin's business, not mine. . . . You might spend a little less time worrying about Negroes in Alabama and a little more worrying about the Indians in Wisconsin and the conditions they live in on the reservations."* He bragged about how many more Negro college presidents there were in Alabama than in Wisconsin, told workers at the American Motors Corporation plant in Racine that under the civil rights bill a Japanese person could take their job by merely walking in and claiming that there weren't enough of his kind on the payroll. Horrors would ensue if well-meaning senators legislated with their hearts, not their heads, and passed this monster bill that would subject state governments, corporations, and labor unions to federal takeover, install police-state kangaroo courts, and make "government master and god over man" for all time.

It almost sounded reasonable, except when it didn't. Milwaukee's sizable Serbian community, which had raised the roof for Kennedy in 1960, hosted Wallace at their weathered, low-ceilinged meeting hall on 57th and Oklahoma. Wallace took to the podium and scanned the seven hundred bodies packed in front of him like sardines and despaired of finding any common ground on which to reach them. The band struck up the national anthem; two or three blacks in the audience refused to rise. The MC, Bronco Gruber, a burly ex-Marine and popular tavern owner, ordered them out. The shrieks and dagger-eyed glances convinced the blacks it was wise to comply. Gruber began introducing Wallace. A black minister in clerical garb cried, "Get your dogs out!"

The veins popped on Bronco Gruber's forehead. "I'll tell you something about your dogs, Padre! I live on Walnut Street and three weeks ago tonight a friend of mine was assaulted by three of your countrymen or whatever you want to call them—" (the rest of the sentence was obscured by applause). "They beat up old ladies eighty-three years old, rape our womenfolk. They mug people. They won't work. They are on relief. How long can we tolerate this? *Did I go to Guadalcanal to come back to something like this!?*"

It took a rousing chorus of "Dixie" to calm things down enough for Wallace to speak. It didn't take much to bring audience members to their feet again: "A vote for this little governor will let people in Washington know that we want them to leave our houses, schools, jobs, businesses, and farms alone—and let us run them without any help from Washington!" It took Wallace an hour to make his way out of the building for the mobbing admirers.

Lyndon Johnson was shaken. He ordered his postmaster general, John Gronouski, a local boy, to speak at a televised rally on election eve; their *President*, he told viewers, was counting on Wisconsin to turn back George Wallace. Governor Reynolds now leaked another inflated estimate, that Wallace would win 175,000 votes. And when the returns came in, Wallace parted the crowded ballroom with a war dance performed in full Indian regalia, a gift from the grateful Consolidated Tribes of Wisconsin. "We won without winning!" he cried of his 265,000 votes, a quarter of the total cast. Reynolds lost his home district. Wallace won 30 percent in rock-solid-Democratic Milwaukee. He received a startling 47 percent from the brand-new Ninth Congressional District, carved out of Milwaukee's wealthiest, best-educated suburbs.

It felt like an earthquake. But media outlets did their best to argue it meant nothing at all. "An anachronistic Southern demagogue," sniffed the *New York Times*—a strange choice of words to describe a man who seemed now to occupy politics' cutting edge.

Clif White faced the same dilemma debated in *National Review*'s editorial offices in 1961: the very anger that fed the right's fires threatened to engulf its fortunes. In the Illinois primary, Margaret Chase Smith supporters had their cars egged inside and out. In California, kids snuck in and spiked the punch and stomped on the sandwiches before a huge Rockefeller reception. Another gang of zealots began stamping "GOLDWATER IN '64" on every greenback that came through their hands. "Printing or impressing any notice or advertisement" on money was punishable by a fine of $500 per bill. The first place the Secret Service agents began looking for culprits was inside the official Goldwater campaign.

Other such mischief threatened to unweave the campaign organization itself. Back when reporters began surveying the ruins of the Young Republican convention in San Francisco in 1963 to discern whether the GOP was being overrun by its Birchite flank, they should have been paying attention to the sixth annual *Human Events* Political Action Conference two weekends later and three thousand miles away at D.C.'s Statler-Hilton. It was a huge event. Forty-one congressmen, including Goldwater, appeared. Each delegate received a thirty-page guide on how to be sure his or her state sent a conservative delegation to the Republican Convention. Most of the tips were practical, such as winning six delegates over a majority in district delegate elections, in case the Establishment stole the five at-large delegate slots.

But attendees were also warned gravely that their enemies would "attempt to split the vote for legitimate conservative delegate candidates by entering 'Trojan horse' conservatives." Word of such danger spread across the rightward fringe. And the result was splitting headaches for Clif White and Dick Kleindienst: now, no matter the state, they could be sure that at any Republican convention they would face wackos certain that White and Kleindienst were Trojan horses. At the Wyoming state convention Kleindienst was asked why, if he was *really* a conservative, he was fighting a resolution to replace the Supreme Court with a tribunal of the fifty individual state chief justices. Because, Kleindienst replied, Barry told him to. To which the militants, who preferred the expediency of assuming Goldwater's views accorded exactly with their own, were only more convinced: this Kleindienst must be an impostor.

White and Kleindienst fought sabotage attempts with preemptive strikes, asking volunteers outright if they were members of the John Birch Society. That strategy only redoubled the fringe's paranoia. Sometimes the co–field directors tried co-opting what they called the "nuts." When a Goldwater committee backed by Evan Mecham and rife with Birchers began chartering its own local Americans for Goldwater chapters around the country that, since the group was based in Phoenix, recruits assumed must be "official," White decided he couldn't afford to lose this organization—they had a membership in the thousands and rising, including a fantastic representation in vital California, sorted on IBM cards by all kinds of useful demographic categories—and he implored Mecham's group to dump the Birchers from the payroll and merge its effort into his own. They agreed, and White retreated. But that didn't work either: Americans for Goldwater brought back the Birchers and kept on establishing their maverick clubs, siphoning off volunteers and money wherever they alighted.

The biggest headache of all was in Westchester County. Rockefeller had scheduled the New York primary for June 2 to coincide with California's in the hope of sweeping 178 delegates, over a quarter of the total needed to nominate, in one hellzapoppin' day. For Goldwater to shave off just a few delegates in New York would be a public relations coup. And to win the Twenty-sixth Congressional District delegate race—the Westchester district containing the Rockefeller estate—was a holy grail. The district also happened to contain Clif White's own suburban home. He was expected to deliver it. Earlier, Birchers had taken over the county YAF chapter. Their newsletter claimed that the Soviets outlined a plan in 1931 promising to lull America, beginning in the 1960s, with "the most spectacular peace movement on record," then "smash them with our clenched fist!"—and speculated about which traitors in the government were responsible for abetting the Soviets' plan by pushing such "peace" initiatives as the visits of the Moscow Circus and the Bolshoi Ballet. Now members faced trial for infiltrating a Yonkers department store, opening packages of lingerie they claimed had been manufactured in some Iron Curtain country and inserting cards reading, "Don't patronize Klein's. Klein's is Communist." Then they reconstituted as Volunteers for Goldwater, filed a delegate slate for the New York primary—and were running a successful campaign to brand Clif White's delegate slate Rockefeller stalking-horses.

White's deputy Vince Leibell entered a credentials challenge in state court. The Birchers won. White sighed, swallowed his pride, and did the only thing he could to shut these people up. "I VERY MUCH APPRECIATE YOUR INTEREST AND SUPPORT OF MY CANDIDACY," began the telegram headed "Barry M. Goldwater, U.S. Senate, Washington." "I KNOW THAT YOU WANT THIS TO BE THE MOST EFFECTIVE CAMPAIGN POSSIBLE, THEREFORE, IT MUST BE A WELL COORDINATED PART OF OUR NATIONAL STRATEGY. TO INSURE THAT THIS WILL HAPPEN, I ASK THAT YOU COORDINATE ALL YOUR ACTIVITIES, INCLUDING DELEGATE SELECTION, UNDER THE DIRECTION OF MR. VINCENT L. LEIBELL, JR., WHO IS HANDLING MY CAMPAIGN IN THE DOWNSTATE NEW YORK AREA."

It was humiliating. Bringing in the Big Gun was the last thing White wanted to do. More setbacks like this and Goldwater might decide White was an unworthy candidate for the RNC chairmanship. So he worked harder. It was the only thing he could do.

One April day began at 5 a.m. in a hotel room in Topeka after White had wiped the sleep from his eyes from a forty-five-minute nap. He had spent the night lining up votes for a floor fight at the Kansas convention. Rockefeller, desperate to manufacture support in the Midwest, had quietly managed to secure the four at-large delegate slots traditionally chosen before the state convention convened. By customary droit du seigneur, Governor John Anderson had the right to select the remaining six at the convention, then name himself as delegation chair. White would have preferred not to have to disturb the tradition; Anderson was chairman of the Republican Governors' Conference, someone Goldwater would have to work with if he were elected President. But Anderson was also a liberal—and if he fell in line behind Rockefeller, White feared that a stampede of some dozen once-reluctant fellow governors might follow. That, White decided, could not happen. He made discreet overtures to secure Anderson's support and was rebuffed. He threatened to put up his own candidate, outgoing committeewoman Mrs. Effie B. Semple, for delegation chair, and to demolish Anderson in the roll-call vote that was supposed to be but a rubber stamp of the governor's will. Anderson laughed the threat off. White decided he had no choice but to crush him. The governor of Kansas would play ball or he would just have to watch the Republican National Convention on TV.

White had lined up his ducks quite handily. And they followed his instructions to the letter. By the time the session opened, there was nothing left but to watch from the balcony as the confusion spread before him. What guilt conservative delegates felt at double-crossing their governor was vitiated by the sentimental appeal of crowning a frilly-hatted little old lady from Baxter Springs as their chair—another brilliant move on White's part. Once Anderson's courtiers realized what had hit them, they sprang the oldest trick in the book: they tried to railroad White's pick by nominating *another* Goldwaterite to split the anti-Anderson vote. White was awfully proud to see the alacrity with which his floor runners set upon the unlucky dupe and demanded that she withdraw her name. The roll call was nip and tuck; Sedwick County's chairman—unilaterally revoking his caucus's decision to give at least half their votes to the governor—put Effie over the top. The room exploded.

White felt someone tugging at his sleeve as he retreated for the victory party. It was *Time* correspondent Murray Garst. "Clif," he said, "you were awfully nasty."

Nasty, maybe. But what other candidate had 200 delegates in the bag?

White publicly claimed 165. His strategy was to pace Goldwater's success so that it would peak by convention time—and to have a store of secret delegates to dangle before whichever other candidate should need disciplining down the line. But his plan wasn't helped when Goldwater offered, unbidden, an estimate of 435 to the press, nor when Dick Kleindienst blurted out the number 600. White sighed to see his misgivings about his bosses confirmed once more.

Kleindienst's work in the primaries was amateurish. There was a string of them in the Midwest through the spring. Since Goldwater was the choice in polls of a mere 14 percent of rank-and-file Republicans, Rockefeller of 9 percent, in each state moderate contenders made delicate maneuvers to be the one candidate entered against Rockefeller, Goldwater, or both to try to capture that huge "anything but" vote and declare a popular mandate that might inspire a delegate stampede. It put the Goldwater campaign in a tight spot. Barry had to appear in each state a few times so as not to insult the troops—but if he appeared too often and lost, and that happened in too many states, it would make his delegate victory in San Francisco look like some kind of banana republic coup. Take Illinois. He spent a weekend in Chicago dropping in at a Republican women's conference and attending a massive Captive Nations Day rally at the International Amphitheater. Four days later he scored 62 percent— a public relations disaster, because his office had predicted 80 percent. The press called him the loser. White knew the delicate game of expectations was as much a part of politics as the grip-and-grin. Kleindienst seemed either unwilling or unable to play it.

In Indiana the "anything but" vote went to the redoubtable Harold E. Stassen: boy-wonder governor of Minnesota in 1936, a presidential prospect in 1940, the loser in an upset to Dewey in 1948, sold out by a young lawyer named Warren Burger in his favorite-son bid in 1952, architect of a failed Richard Nixon purge in 1956, the losing candidate for governor of Pennsylvania and mayor of Philadelphia in the years since—the Republican Party's embarrassing old Don Quixote. (When he announced he was running for President once more, a politically precocious youngster in Queens dubbed his soapbox derby car "Harold Stassen's Ticker Tape Parade.") Stassen had managed to find his name the only other one on the Indiana Republican ballot besides Goldwater's. He financed a raft of brochures promising "progress for all along the middleway, avoiding both extremes," and asserting that a Stassen delegation would "open the door at the convention to consideration of the other five Republican candidates: Ambassador Lodge, Richard Nixon, Governor Rockefeller, Governor Romney, and Governor Scranton." Anyone-but-Goldwater and the middle-of-the-road: that was all it took for oafish Harold Stassen to siphon off an embarrassing 27 percent of the votes from Goldwater in one of the most conservative states in the country. And thanks to Kleindienst's inability to put up a publicity firewall, commentators continued to refer to Goldwater's "wretched showing" in a primary where he won upwards of 70 percent of the vote.

At any rate, few were paying attention to the Republican race. Indiana was George Wallace's stand-or-fall battle. Open-primary Wisconsin could be written off as a fluke. But party loyalty was sacred in Indiana. If Wallace could peel off significant numbers from Johnson's stand-in, Governor Matthew Welsh, that would mean the backlash was for real. Dozens of print and television correspondents descended on the Hoosier State; Walter Cronkite moved his newscast to a storefront in downtown Indianapolis. Wallace's act had been polished until it gleamed; at Butler University, his kickoff speech began to jeers and closed with 56 percent of those present saying he had their vote.

Since taking the podium in front of Bronco Gruber and his friends in Milwaukee's Serb Hall, Wallace drew sustenance from a new theme. A crime upsurge was now the obsession of barrooms and water coolers across the land: on March 27 the *New York Times* reported that in a white middle-class neighborhood in Queens, thirty-eight neighbors were awakened by the screams of a young woman named Kitty Genovese as she was raped and murdered over the course of an hour, and no one bothered to call the police. That the perpetrator was black, although the *Times* did not print the fact, soon became well known. And Wallace began playing the attendant fears like a violin.

"If you are knocked in the head on a street in a city today, the man who knocked you in the head is out of jail before you get to the hospital," he said.

"They're building a new bridge over the Potomac for all the white liberals fleeing to Virginia."

"Anyone here from Philadelphia? You know, they can't even have night football games anymore because of the trouble between the races. And that's the city of brotherly love!"

The message was moving voters. Governor Welsh warned thousands of patronage employees that they backed Wallace on pain of their jobs. Registered Republicans requesting a Democratic ballot were forced to pledge to vote for the Democratic candidate for President in November (and were threatened with having their names published). The state's two Democratic senators sent out franked letters pronouncing that a vote for Welsh was a vote for the memory of John F. Kennedy.

In Indiana Wallace beat his Wisconsin totals by 5 percentage points. He earned almost three-quarters of the vote in one Gary steelworkers' district. "The noises you hear now," he declared, "are the teeth falling out in Indiana."

It was a good thing few people were paying attention to the Republicans in Indiana, because by now it appeared that White *was* presiding over a coup. He didn't count the number of delegates he'd secured anymore; he counted *down* from the 655 needed to nominate. His secret ledger read 400, four-fifths of those chosen to date. He claimed 250 publicly. He wanted to have at least 172 with which to surprise the public if Rockefeller won California on June 2. But once more undisciplined Arizonans spilled the secret. Not long ago *Time* had declared Goldwater "flat on his back." Now the magazine reported: "Suddenly, like a brush fire racing out of control, the word crackled among informed Republicans: Goldwater's almost got it. . . . Goldwater kept collecting delegates while the unavoweds and disavowed collected press clippings."

Though how the party would sell a candidate to the nation that polls suggested only 14 percent of *Republicans* supported, White did not appear to consider.

"Far more united and at peace with itself, except over the issue of Negro rights, than it has been for a long time": future generations might be excused for wondering how many conflagrations need burn, or how few votes Bill Scranton need win, before columnists would break down and concede the point that America was a nation deeply divided against itself. But the architecture of their thought would not permit it.

As usual there was much to see that was perfectly fantastic at Flushing Park in Queens at the World's Fair that opened on April 22: the inevitable jet packs and videophones; the tractor of the future that could hew roads from unspoiled jungle as if scooping up so much ice cream; (slumless) underwater cities. But the true wonder of the 1964 World's Fair lay in the things that *weren't* futuristic, things American citizens could see right *now*, right out their windows. The candy-colored globules, hexagons, and floating wings of the great corporate pavilions were designed by the same architects, in the same manner, as their corporate headquarters downtown. The most popular attraction was simultaneously on view at your local Ford dealership: the sporty new Mustang, the first car designed and marketed as a second car for the kids. IBM's pavilion, a tribute to its speedy new Selectric typewriter, was a giant ball with raised letters across the surface; AT&T arrayed its new "Touch-Tone" phones around the grounds; RCA hosted a "Color Television Communications Center." The "audio-animatronic" tableaux Walt Disney designed for Pepsi's "It's a Small World," G.E.'s "Progressland," and Illinois's "Great Moments with Mr. Lincoln" adopted technology from the wizards in Orange County who engineered missile guidance systems. (Mr. Lincoln uttered a quote that was popular among Orange County conservatives obsessed with the menace of creeping socialism: "If destruction is our lot we must ourselves be its author and finisher.") The whole thing, *Time* observed proudly, was not so much a vision of the future as a tribute to the present—a "glittering mirror of national opulence."

It was the apotheosis of the world according to Lyndon Johnson. "Hell, we've barely begun to solve our problems," he would say. "And we can do it all. We've got the wherewithal." The World's Fair was forged by the kind of can-do middle-of-the-road industrialists he was so successfully recruiting away from Barry Goldwater's Republican Party. Everywhere it rebuked Goldwater's untoward insistence that the world was a battleground of opposing worldviews. Wycliffe Bible Translators' "2,000 Tribes" exhibit depicted the world's dark-skinned masses falling peaceably in line behind the Christian West. The pavilion sponsored by a consortium of conservative groups, the Hall of Free Enterprise (where perhaps they spent their time bemoaning the tens of millions of dollars the federal government appropriated for the fair), didn't even show up on the official map.

The future would embarrass the 1964 World's Fair. One pavilion "demonstrated" the safe harnessing of nuclear fusion. The fair's megalomaniacal promoter, Robert Moses, gutted many a peaceful Queens neighborhood to lay down his new Van Wyck Expressway in time for the opening (though the streets had been less peaceful since Parents and Taxpayers began agitating in the vicinity against the board of education's latest busing plan). Architect Philip Johnson was given free rein to commission pieces by exciting young artists outside the New York State pavilion. A funny little man called Andy Warhol contributed *Thirteen Most Wanted Men*, a mural consisting of old FBI mug shots, mostly of men who had since been exonerated. No one expected that spitting on J. Edgar Hoover's good name (instead of producing, say, sweeping, high-gloss, colorful abstract shapes) was something exciting young artists would care to do. Moses ordered the mural whitewashed. Though the Unisphere, the enormous stainless-steel globe at the center of the grounds, was not dismantled when its patron, United States Steel, was convicted in a price-fixing scheme.

John F. Kennedy had promised to open the fair when preparations began in 1961. In 1964, with the civil rights filibuster threatening to last forever, Johnson laid plans to fulfill the obligation by unveiling to the multitudes attending the fair's opening day, in the open air, live on TV, his plans for a tour of America's impoverished areas—a carefully contrived piece of symbolism designed to convey the message that the American ingenuity on display all around them could also be put to use wiping poverty from the face of the nation forever. The symbolism the speech ended up conveying was entirely different.

The Congress of Racial Equality's maverick Brooklyn chapter was promising to turn the opening into a theater of rage. Twenty-five hundred volunteers would "run out of gas" at strategic points to turn Robert Moses's beloved expressway system into so many parking lots; hundreds more would shut down the subway system by pulling the emergency brakes; meanwhile the fair's entrances would be bollixed up by activists paying their $2 entrance fee in pennies. When Lyndon Johnson rose to speak, the protesters would release sacks and sacks of rats—visiting on these privileged whites the teeming monsters that cursed black tenement dwellers every day. The Brooklyn group pledged to hold firm even after CORE leader James Farmer expelled the entire chapter and announced before the American Society of Newspaper Editors convention on April 18 his own "positive" and "focused" counterdemonstration—although Farmer's announcement was hardly placating: his people promised to mar the opening in their own fashion, by staging sit-ins, clambering up the giant stainless-steel Unisphere bearing banners, and offering ongoing educational demonstrations of the use of the Southern sheriff's favorite modern marvel, the electric cattle prod.

National CORE, and the battalions of police and tow trucks lining the expressways, won the battle of wills. The "stall-in" was abandoned; a veritable fleet of automobiles streamed into Flushing to take in the opening-day festivities. Most protesters were hauled off in time for the parade featuring Miss America, Miss Universe, and Donna Reed and family. Other protesters managed to linger. The President elected to give his vaunted speech before a small invited indoor audience. He emerged to greet the throng and began to say a few words to the malcontents—"We do not try to mask our national problems"—and was met by heckling. He perorated about a "world in which all men are equal"; that was met by laughter.

It was around then that Walter Lippmann took note in his column of his long-held conviction that as a rule, the filibuster was generally a noble device for "delaying and preventing a passionate majority from overriding a defenseless minority." Was the present filibuster against the civil rights bill principled? he asked himself rhetorically. "No more," he answered, "than would [be] a filibuster in time of war."

Goldwater wrote off Oregon, saying he needed to be in Washington for the civil rights debate. The real reason was that Lodge was polling 50 percent. At a battery of straw voting booths at the World's Fair, Lodge beat all comers combined. ("He *looks* like a President," people said.) Newspapers referred casually to his "probable victory in Oregon May 15." *Time* put "The Lodge Phenomenon" on the cover. Rumor was that if he won he would come home to campaign (a decision perhaps influenced by the Vietcong terrorist who had recently hurled a bomb in the ambassador's direction). "Anyone but" now had a name and a face. "Why go out and break your pick," demanded Dean Burch, "against someone who isn't there?" Another reason for Goldwater to avoid Oregon was to further snub Steve Shadegg, who had been named the Goldwater for President Committee's Northwest region director. Radio testimonials from five Republican congressmen, a half-hour TV film, *Meet Barry Goldwater* (pointing up the candidate's adventurous hobbies, his wishes notwithstanding), and billboards ("YOU KNOW WHERE HE STANDS," beside an ugly photo that D.C. headquarters stubbornly refused to replace, to Shadegg's professional disgust) campaigned in his stead. But so did Kent Courtney, who visited Oregon from New Orleans to distribute two of his most scabrous pamphlets yet, *How Soft on Communism Is Henry Cabot Lodge?* and *An Exposé of the Record of Former President Dwight D. Eisenhower.* Dick Kleindienst had to rush to Oregon to release a statement to once more put out a Birchite fire without burning any bridges in so doing: "Sen. Goldwater appreciates the enthusiastic support he is receiving from all Republicans—but Mr. Courtney is not authorized to speak on behalf of the Senator or on behalf of the Senator's Oregon Committee."

Nelson Rockefeller had never let another politician's hammerlock on victory deter him before. Nor the hostility of his party: in an endorsement vote at the Wisconsin Young Republican convention he trailed "Nobody" 3 votes to zero. In New York his own hand-picked delegate slate decided to officially run "uncommitted." Nor even the hostility of his old friend the Holy Father: On March 15 the two stars of *Cleopatra*, Richard Burton and Elizabeth Taylor, dumped their spouses and married each other; Pope Paul VI responded with an open letter in the Vatican newspaper condemning remarriage. Not long afterward senators began referring to "Mrs. Murphy's boarding house" as shorthand for discussing how small a business would have to be to be exempted from the civil rights law. Rockefeller begged friendly senators to *stop reminding people of his wife's maiden name.* He got nowhere. Like his campaign. World Press Syndicate had been retained to try to sell serialization of his latest campaign biography, *The Real Rockefeller*, to newspapers. Nearly every newspaper in the nation with a circulation above 25,000—1,089 in all—received the initial pitch, and 500 upper-tier papers got the hard sell. Not a single paper ordered the book. "We had assumed there would be a minimum 1 percent return just on the general law of averages," WPS's executive editor lamented. Conservative editors called him back only to shout into the phone that it was "another damned Rockefeller trick." The *Herald Tribune* didn't return his calls at all.

Rockefeller pressed harder in Oregon. After Goldwater canceled his campaign stops there, Rocky doubled his—sending out extra mailings addressed to each of Oregon's 350,000 Republicans to make sure they knew it. New York congressman John Lindsay toured the state for him. Gene Wyckoff, via the now-tried-and-true dramatic pan-over-photos method, produced a warm television biography (Rocky plays with children; patriotic medley segues into a nursery rhyme). In Grants Pass they made him an honorary Caveman; in the appropriately named town of Albany, Oregon, he became a Woodpecker. Scattered newspapers made endorsements. A Chicago newsman interviewed the candidate on the jet out to Portland and marveled at his "desperate optimism": I'll win, Rockefeller claimed, "when the convention settles down to analyzing the assets and liabilities of all the candidates."

That was Nixon's plan, too. His trip to Asia had included a dinner with his 1960 running mate. He was startled at how half-baked he found American strategy in Vietnam. He was also startled to see how close Lodge was to throwing his hat in the ring. It would appear that rivalry clouded Nixon's judgment. Immediately upon his April 15 return Nixon sent old hands Bob Finch and Cliff Folger out to Portland to raise $50,000 for a phone bank operation. An aide insisted Nixon was crazy, that Goldwater was sailing toward a certain first-ballot victory. Nixon said that was impossible. "Believe me, Dick," the exasperated deputy assured him. "*You've* been overseas, and *I've* been here." Raising the money proved difficult; once reliable donors now questioned the former vice president's integrity after his false threat to retire from politics in 1962. He finally scraped up enough to pay for fifty telephone lines, which were installed deep within an obscure Portland office building. A few days after the May 4 opening an NBC camera crew tracked down the boiler room. Nixon's managers claimed the office was taking a poll for a new magazine. When his deception was revealed on national TV, it did not make Nixon look like an elder statesman.

Confusion reigned as to where this newest New Nixon stood ideologically. Shadegg thought he would take conservative votes away from Goldwater, and negotiated for Nixon to withdraw; White thought Nixon would take liberal votes away from Rockefeller and Lodge—and worked a hustle to get Nixon to stay in. White won. He delegated one of his oldest and most loyal Draft Goldwater deputies to run Nixon's secret campaign—and keep it running to the hilt. What this all meant to Goldwater's ultimate vote totals in Oregon is not known. What it meant to the long-term health of his candidacy for the presidency that his two cleverest operatives were working at cross-purposes behind each other's backs was more clear.

Rockefeller, with 15 points to make up against Lodge, campaigned in the homestretch as if the state were a New England town: a 7:30 breakfast each morning, three or four daytime stops, and an evening rally. The speeches were dignified—he was selling moderation, after all—until the shouted conclusion: "I'm the only man who cares enough about your votes to come to Oregon!" (He hadn't cared enough to come to states like Indiana where he had feared a Goldwater rout.) Representative Lindsay's top political man put together a last-minute TV tsunami ("He Cared Enough to Come"). Still, with ten days to go, the *Oregonian* gave him only 22 percent to Lodge's 36. (Nixon was at 15, and

Goldwater at 12.) On the eve of the primary ABC had Rockefeller behind Lodge 21 to 35.

May 15 broke warm and clear. Voters poured into polling stations. They brought state-published guides to navigate through the 122 names vying for 36 delegate and alternate spots. Candidates could take out ads in these guides. Craig Truax had bought a two-pager to trumpet William Warren Scranton. The Pennsylvania governor was fresh in voters' minds at any rate: a few weeks earlier NBC afforded him a TV special and *Time* had devoted an entire page to a speech he gave at Yale.

The balloting ended at eight that evening. By nine, it is safe to say that Mr. Gallup, Mr. Truax, and Mr. Harris were taking stiff belts of something strong. Scranton won 4,000 votes—1.4 percent. Margaret Chase Smith got 7,000, Richard Nixon 48,000. Goldwater won 50,000, Lodge 78,000. Nelson Rockefeller received 94,000.

The Lodge boom had been foiled at the last minute after Shadegg discovered that the Lodge team was about to flood the airwaves with its misleading "Meet Mr. Lodge" commercial. Shadegg, a very clever man, was able to send a telegram to Eisenhower in Palm Springs that inspired the former President to wire back, "If it suggests that I have given any public indication of a preference for any person over any other in the current contest, then it is a definite misrepresentation." Shadegg released the missive to the press; Lodge managers were forced to cancel their TV time.

Lodge's campaign manager Paul Grindle's first thoughts upon hearing the Oregon returns were of a moderates' united front. If Lodge's organization merged with Rockefeller's, perhaps to be inherited by some more acceptable moderate dark horse somewhere down the line, perhaps a Scranton . . .

That was Lyndon Johnson's thought, too. Goldwater, "just as nutty as a fruitcake," *couldn't* win, Johnson told his friend Texas governor John Connally. "Rockefeller's wife ain't gonna let him get off the ground. So I guess *Time* magazine and the big ones who are really doing this job, I guess they're gonna have to go with Scranton." Robert Taft had gone into the convention in 1952 with more delegates than Dwight D. Eisenhower, after all. And look what happened to him.

16

GOLDEN STATE

C alifornia had just surpassed New York as the most populous state in the union. Its primary was like all the other ones, only more so. Goldwater didn't have to win there to clinch enough delegates to put him over the top. He did have to win there if he wanted credibility as a man who could win elections, not just snatch conventions. Rockefeller had to win California or he would die. It was holy war—to decide, as one hot-headed Goldwater pamphleteer put it, "whether Constitutional government is to be restored or if our country is going to continue to go further to the Left towards a Communist-tainted Nazi-Fascist collectivism and chaos." Rockefeller's staff would have had to edit only a few words to make that their own credo. "Even I have been shocked by the spending in this campaign. I've never seen anything like it in American politics," Clif White told a reporter. "Why, Rockefeller"—and, he should have added, Goldwater too—"is making Kennedy look like a piker."

Before turning to California in earnest, Goldwater had an errand to take care of. A crack threatened his solid South—Georgia, where his share of the at-large delegates was endangered by the only black-and-tan establishment that was strong enough not to fold under the Clif White onslaught.

The candidate landed, exhausted, to a Goldwater circus. Only after Kitchel screamed in his face, "Dammit, Barry, you're a national figure!" did Goldwater stride out to receive his adoration. A reporter poked a microphone in his snoot; Goldwater scowled. A pretty young thing tried to plop a big white cowboy hat on his head; he shoved her away. A guy was peddling a canned soft drink with the unfortunate name of "Gold Water" ("The Right Drink for the Conservative Taste") from the tailgate of his truck. Goldwater was offered a sip. He spit it out. "This tastes like piss! I wouldn't drink it with gin!"

The Georgia convention was disappointing. The opposition—weakened, reporters hastened to point out, by a Negro boycott; they refused to be in the same room as Goldwater—was tenacious. John Grenier, White's Southern field man, was weakened by the fact that the local Birch leader said his people wouldn't cooperate with Grenier no matter *what* Goldwater said. What Goldwater said from the podium disappointed most of all: he gave a dry, legalistic encomium to the coming of the two-party system to the South. When Goldwater talked about the dictator in Cuba he described as a "pygmy," he shouted. When he talked about anything touching on civil rights, he droned. When he did so in the South, he droned even more quietly. He fretted over contributing to the nation's racial divide. He didn't think his states' rights message would contribute to those divisions; to him, by honoring the concerns of the South— the new South, the progressive South, the industrial South, states that just wanted the federal government to leave them alone to prosper—he was helping make the Republicans, as he put it in Atlanta, "a truly *national* party."

By then he had honed his argument against the pending civil rights bill. He would vote for it, gladly, if Titles II and VII were struck; the Constitution just didn't allow the federal government to make private business decisions about whom to serve and whom to hire. If Washington "can tell you what to do with your property, they can take it away from you," he would say; and, "I don't think it's my right as an Arizonan to come in and tell a Southerner what to do about this thing." He would speak of good intentions gone awry: "I can see a police state coming out of that without any problem at all." In Jeremiah mode, he might say how much it sickened him to see questions of law being settled in the streets and wonder why the Democrats would sink so low as to tacitly support such tactics: "It is not understanding America or Americans that goads a man to abandon civility in this matter," he said the night after the World's Fair debacle (to an audience in Connecticut, only a commuter train ride away from the mob). He said again and again, "with the deepest possible sense of tragedy and regret," that at bottom, this was a problem of moral suasion, not of laws. Federal force only compounded the problem. "Until we have an administration that will cool the fires and the tempers of violence we simply cannot solve the rest of the problem in any lasting sense." Until then, he promised, "we are going to see more violence in our streets before we see less." All spring, Northern college students had been training with military rigor for a nonviolent assault for voting rights in Mississippi—while that state was planning to counter them with all the terror at its disposal. Goldwater bespoke his frustration with Mississippi as the state "where there is the most talk about brotherhood and the very least opportunity for achieving it." But the civil rights bill as written, he was convinced, would only make things worse. It was unconstitutional—and if Negroes didn't have a stake in the Constitution, then who did?

·   ·   ·

He plunged into the Golden State the day after leaving Georgia with a keynote address at the first annual convention of a new group, United Republicans of California, in Bakersfield.

Goldwater's official campaign headquarters was on Wilshire Boulevard in Los Angeles. To run it, the Arizona Mafia decided they needed a big name. The particular name they chose, alas, belonged to the stony, charmless man many California Republicans believed had crushed their party in 1958 when he self-ishly abandoned his Senate seat for his unsuccessful run for governor. William Knowland, now retired to the the family business, the conservative *Oakland Tribune*, was so uncomfortable around people that he worked up a routine to deal with employees with whom he was forced to share an elevator: "Taken your vacation yet?" he would ask when they entered; the answer took just long enough to deliver him to his fourth-floor office. (Once he experimented. "Don't I know you from somewhere?" he asked a photographer. "Yes, Senator," came the answer. "I've worked for you for thirty years." Knowland then went back to the routine.) Now it was Knowland's job to coordinate multitudes—and he couldn't even get the staffers who had supported Nixon in 1962 in the same room together with the ones who had been for Shell. On Wilshire Boulevard Knowland held court as a figurehead. The flesh of the Goldwater campaign in California was hung on the skeleton of the conservative volunteer groups like the one the candidate was addressing now.

The audience in Bakersfield was battle-tested. Conservatives had suffered razor-thin defeat for control of the party's premier volunteer group, the California Republican Assembly, at the convention in March of 1963—a convention, conservatives were convinced, that San Francisco union leader and Rockefeller stalwart William Nelligan had stolen from them. Redeeming that loss became the focus of conservative energies for the rest of the year. The efforts developed along three fronts. One, led by Newport Beach optometrist Nolan Frizzelle and S&L magnate Joe Crail, worked to take back the CRA. "It was like facing a howling mob," a liberal said of the one hundred conservatives who set upon the Oakland chapter's convention in December—and, after Nelligan declared the the conservatives' victory in Oakland null and void, did it again in January. The scene was repeated across the liberal northern tier of the state. And at the 1964 convention, Frizzelle won the presidency of the CRA near dawn with 363 out of 600 votes. (There were only 569 registered delegates.) The next day, portly right-wingers held sit-ins in front of the mikes. Liberals stalked out in a rage. That left the conservatives all alone to endorse Goldwater without a fight. "Fanatics of the Birch variety have fastened their fangs on the Republican Party's flanks," Nelligan told reporters, "and are hanging on like grim death."

Securing the second front, at the Young Republicans convention in February, was but perfunctory. Young Republicans had already turned back a proposed resolution denouncing "accusations, charges, and actions which tend to divide rather than unite the Republican Party." Nelson Rockefeller, one of their leaders noted, was an "international socialist." Why would they want to unite with *that*? A resolution the Young Republicans did end up passing declared liberals "regressive reactionaries" who "seek to drag the American republic into the Dark Ages." A speech by Ronald Reagan—"We can't justify foreign aid funds which went to the purchase of extra wives for some tribal chiefs in Kenya"—was received with delirium. It was the prelude to a vote of 256 to 33 to boycott the Republican presidential campaign if Barry Goldwater wasn't the nominee (which was tantamount to mutiny; the bylaws of the Young Republican National Federation outlawed participation in primaries in the first place). Regarding the thirty-three who were in the minority, a woman cried, "Everyone says they're for Goldwater—let's find out who the finks are!"

United Republicans of California was the third front. The group was masterminded by Rus Walton, the man behind Joe Shell's shockingly close gubernatorial challenge against Richard Nixon in 1962, as a sort of CRA insurance policy—an organization chartered of, for, and by conservatives, under the assumption that liberals kept the California Republican Party from the control of a conservative majority only through conspiracy. The group's paranoia was soon confirmed: the state's Republican Party chair, Caspar Weinberger, responded to the founding of UROC by invoking a party rule banning groups with the word "Republican" in their name from raising funds without approval from the California Republican Central Committee. So UROC organized to take over the Central Committee. This party governing body's membership was appointed, per state law, by a caucus of all Republican candidates running for state office. Veterans of Shell's campaign revived a dormant fund, United for California, first established in 1938 to combat the far-left Democratic gubernatorial candidate Upton Sinclair, and used it to quietly file Republican candidates for every office in the state. Since most of the incumbents were entrenched Democrats, many far-right Republicans ran in primaries unopposed. The far right would have taken over the party—if Republican and Democratic state legislators hadn't conspired in mid-June to amend the election code after the fact.

Goldwater zealots, said a harried staffer, now "ran through the woods like a collection of firebugs, and I just keep running after them, like Smokey Bear, putting out fires." Or, sometimes, helping them build fires. Outgoing California Young Republican chair Bob Gaston independently mustered eight thousand of these people to circulate petitions to put Goldwater on the primary ballot.

The first candidate to file 13,702 signatures would be listed at the top of the rolls—an automatic boon in votes that in some elections made for the margin of victory. By noon on March 4, the first day signature-gathering was allowed, Goldwater had 36,000. Learning that Rockefeller (who took weeks to get enough signatures) was paying fifty cents per name, Gaston immediately mobilized to get 7,000 Rockefeller signatures—turning the money over to Goldwater. Teddy White, whom Gaston had befriended after everyone else in the office, labeling White the enemy, refused to speak with him, had never seen anything like it. Gaston, for his part, was amazed at how easy it was; the work had already been done in the previous year. He just called a loyalist from his campaign for state YR chair in every precinct—and the job took care of itself.

And now, May 3, with the fight of their lives on their hands, over two thousand firebugs met in convention in Bakersfield. Their chairman kicked things off, from a podium draped with both the American flag and the Confederate flag, by calling Nelson Rockefeller's campaign chairman, Tom Kuchel, a "left-wing extremist." When Goldwater spoke, he begged to differ. As he did in his every California address, he urged party loyalty: "I am not interested in defeating *any* Republicans in 1964," he said. "Let me say it again: I am not afraid of what *any* Republican would do to this country." The firebugs thought entirely otherwise. But they screamed themselves hoarse for their hero nonetheless.

Nelson Rockefeller's big California push could be said to have kicked off two months earlier, on his *Face the Nation* appearance of March 8. Having ordered up enough polls to practically reproduce the state in a test tube, what Rockefeller learned was that California Republicans were terrified of increased federal spending, of Fidel Castro, and of the specter of Communist subversion of the United States from within—all issues on which Barry Goldwater enjoyed a monopoly. But Graham T. T. Molitor reminded Rockefeller of an elementary political fact: negative attacks were more effective than pushing issues anyway. Their advertising man, Nixon's Gene Wyckoff, chipped in that they needed to construct "a first-class villain to make a first-class hero." His PR man, Stu Spencer, thought they had to "destroy Barry Goldwater as a member of the human race." If all voters could think about how terrifying a Goldwater presidency would be, who would worry about something so trivial as a remarriage?

Molitor combed his Goldwater transcriptions until he found the perfect quote to begin the assault. Goldwater had argued for the development of "small, clean nuclear weapons" for battlefield use as far back as *Conscience of a Conservative*. Since then he had become enamored of a portable nuclear mortar called the "Davy Crockett"—whose relatively small punch (about as much as a sortie by a World War II bomber wing) he believed made it a marvelous

bulwark against Soviet aggression precisely because it was tame enough to be
used without fear of setting off a nuclear escalation nigh to apocalypse. Secretary McNamara—and the physicists at Lawrence Livermore who designed the
portable weapon—entirely disagreed; they thought it would incinerate civilians
no matter where in Europe it was fired. No one really knew; it was a question
of which experts you asked. So it was, one October day in 1963, that when he
was asked what he thought of a recent suggestion to cut NATO's ground force,
Goldwater opined that troops could be cut "at least by a third" simply by clari-
fying the power NATO commanders had to use the Crockett—which he called
"just another weapon"—in the event of a Soviet advance.

Or at least "commanders" was how it was quoted by the *Washington Post*,
which subheaded its report "Would Give NATO Commanders Power to Use
A-Weapons"—apparently placing that authority in the hands of dozens of officers, perhaps among them some real-life General Jack D. Ripper. Goldwater
would later insist that the word he had used was "commander"; he may have in
fact said "commanders" but meant the plural in the chronological sense—the
current commander, General Lyman Lemnitzer; then the one who came on
after he retired; and so forth. Be that as it may. Nelson Rockefeller launched his
California campaign strategy two days before the New Hampshire balloting
by casually dropping the matter into a conversation with the panel on *Face
the Nation*. He was all for a strong defense, he said. But calling nuclear arms
"just another weapon," as Goldwater had—that was "appalling," a tempting of
"world suicide."

The audacity of Rockefeller's remark was rather breathtaking. "The dis-
tinction between nuclear warfare and conventional warfare, which is para-
mount in the public mind, leads to unrealistic policy decisions": that was the
point argued in the very Rockefeller brothers report upon which he had based
his campaign strategy in 1960. He hadn't disclaimed it since; in New Hampshire, in fact, he had accepted a warm endorsement from the author of these
words, nuclear scientist Edward Teller. Eisenhower had said the identical thing
about battlefield nukes—that they could be used like "a bullet or any other
weapon"—in 1955, when Rockefeller was Ike's special assistant for psychological warfare.

But it was Goldwater who had blundered into the role of scapegoat for all
America's nuclear fears. It was an opportunity too ripe to be missed. "Respon-
sible Republicanism rejects this irresponsible approach to the conduct of
American foreign policy!" Rockefeller would cry in his speeches. Then he
would make a plea to honor "the brotherhood of man, the fatherhood of God."
Reporters began referring to the refrain as BOMFOG. At the White House,
Lyndon Johnson was taking notes.

But it wasn't enough to make California fall in love with Nelson Rocke-feller. Through back-breaking effort, Spencer-Roberts was able to drum up capacity crowds for Rockefeller's rallies, but mostly by relying on non-Republican audiences, especially blacks (whom Rockefeller urged to change their registration to Republican to stop Goldwater "and his John Birch support-ers"). But if publicists could lead the masses to Rockefeller, they could not make them drink. At Berkeley, Rocky was swamped by some five thousand students outside the university's symbolic portal, Sather Gate; he then addressed a crowd that spilled into an auditorium lobby and stood outside lis-tening to loudspeakers. They interrupted him with applause exactly once—when he praised "this great educational institution."

Molitor was desperate to raise the stakes. He had found another bombshell: Goldwater had suffered two psychological episodes in the 1930s. But higher-ups said that exploiting the fact was stepping over the line. Molitor kept on pushing the idea; the image of a mentally unstable man with his finger on the nuclear trigger would be absolutely devastating. He pointed to the Goldwater pamphlets collecting at headquarters in an ever-mounting pile accusing Rocke-feller of every sin short of congress with domestic animals. *Anything* was justi-fied, Molitor said, against a man who produced this swill. (Of course, Goldwater wasn't producing it at all: the firebugs were too numerous for the candidate to control even if he wanted to.) Then the May issue of *Good Housekeeping* hit supermarket shelves. It featured an interview with Peggy Goldwater. She described how, when working eighteen-hour days opening a new store in Prescott in 1937, her husband's "nerves broke completely." The problem abated, she said, then resurfaced two years later, never to come back again. It was the interviewer, a journalist named Alvin Toffler, who chose to describe these inci-dents with the fateful words "nervous breakdown." Muckraking liberal colum-nist and radio commentator Drew Pearson picked up the story and started the drumbeat: Goldwater wasn't mentally fit to be Commander in Chief.

If Nelson Rockefeller had been a candidate of more ordinary means, he might have begun to question the expense of maintaining an elaborate opposi-tion research operation to impugn a campaign so skilled at delivering knockout blows against itself.

Barry Goldwater would have had to have been revealed as Beelzebub himself for his partisans to abandon him. His appearances in California were festivals. In the parking lots, where cars were decked out in "ARRIBA CON BARRY" bumper stickers and "AuH$_2$O + GOP + 1964 = VICTORY!" license plates, a group of YAFers calling themselves The Goldwaters (whose banjo player, Dana Rohrabacher, organized a 120-member Goldwater club at his high school) sang selections from their LP, "Folk Songs to Bug the Liberals." Vendors hawked gold-plated jewelry, pins of every size and description, Goldwater trading stamps, Goldwater crayons, Goldwater cologne and aftershave. Then the throng would stream into sweltering halls, stuffing the "Barrels for Barry" at the entrances to bursting with small bills. Lissome young things in cowboy hats and sashes—"Goldwater Girls"—guided traffic, cooling themselves with ice-cold Gold Water (the guy from Atlanta followed the campaign in his truck) or cardboard paddles with "GOLDWATER FAN CLUB" printed on one side and a winking elephant crushing a donkey to death on the reverse.

The crowd might be warmed up with a choir singing patriotic songs, by organized cheering or an elaborate flag presentation of parade-ground proportions. When they were whipped to a fever pitch the candidate would enter with family in tow (emphasizing the integrity of his own family was one of Goldwater's few concessions to competitive strategy—Rockefeller's wife was, after all, entering her eighth month of pregnancy) flanked by a retinue that kept jubilant crowds from mobbing him. Reporters wedged themselves in for a few seconds of chitchat (after the disasters in New Hampshire, press conferences were no longer scheduled); a minister offered an invocation. There were interminable addresses by local pols. The inevitable cry: "We Want Barry! We Want Barry!" Goldwater approached the stump, suffered the noise for a few minutes. Then came the raised hand, the growl: "If you'll shut up, you'll get him."

Then he'd stick a hand in a pocket, slouch into the podium—and deliver overcooked broccoli to a crowd demanding raw meat.

Sometimes the rallies were broadcast on TV, now that there was more money coming in. The rich, well-connected, and clever Washington finance committee Clif White had put together—the one that was always calling for Denison Kitchel's head—was hitting its stride. The maximum any individual was allowed to donate to a single campaign committee being $5,000, they established ten separate paper committees—and brilliantly arranged for Goldwater's photograph book, *The Face of Arizona*, to be sold to businesses in bulk, 100 percent of the proceeds going to the campaign. California oilman Henry Salvatori had raised $1 million for the primary; the Goldwater committee in Montana, where victory was assured, turned over its treasury. Goldwater's finance crew was also knocked off guard by a new phenomenon. Small donations—the kind that in most campaigns proved mostly symbolic—were making up a considerable portion of the take. A thirteen-year-old sent $5 from his allowance, a twelve-year-old $15 earned cutting grass, a seven-year-old girl a card with three pennies taped on it and the message "I say a prayer for Senator Goldwater every night." Two young steadies pledged to give up their Saturday night movie and donated the money they saved. No one knew quite what to make of the development.

But Goldwater didn't play well on TV. Letters and numbers darkened his presentations: RS-70 and B-70 (bomber programs the Pentagon was scrapping); A-11 (a plane Lyndon Johnson claimed was a new fighter but Goldwater said was really just a reconnaissance plane); TFX (a fighter General Dynamics was building in Lyndon Johnson's Texas despite the brass's insistence it could be built better and more cheaply in California); 1970 (by which time a bomber gap would turn "the shield of the Republic into a Swiss cheese wall"). He attacked Johnson's poverty program, which, since Johnson had cleverly named it the War on Poverty, made it look like Goldwater was rooting for poverty to win. He did little better with another new theme: Vietnam. Johnson said American involvement was the same as it had been a decade before. Goldwater implored his listeners to acknowledge that America was in a war in Vietnam. *U.S. News* had printed letters from a flier killed in action, Captain Edward G. Shank Jr. of Winamac, Indiana: "The American people are being told that U.S. military forces are merely training South Vietnamese flyers and fighters," he wrote his wife and children. "We are doing the fighting." Goldwater angrily read from the dead flier's letters on the stump, and rained insults on his old enemy "Yo-Yo" McNamara (so nicknamed for his practice of jetting off to Southeast Asia every few months), who "has done more to tear down the morale of our military establishment than any secretary we've ever had." But viewers were not finding the rhetoric compelling. There was no political advantage to be gained from bringing up Vietnam; Rockefeller spoke out on it just as often and more critically. Johnson was lying about Vietnam—Goldwater knew it. But how could someone accusing the President of the United States of lying be taken seriously? It just wasn't done.

He was ahead in the polls, although his Wilshire Boulevard headquarters, which was knotted through with so many plots and subplots it could have been a Victorian triple-decker novel, had little to do with the fact; it was all they could do to nail down next week's itinerary. The firebugs helped, though sometimes they hurt. What really seemed to be winning voters were Goldwater's gentle sallies on civil rights.

Property values had become religion amidst the sun-dappled lawns of suburban southern California. "The essence of freedom is the right to discriminate," CRA's Nolan Frizzelle explained. "In socialist countries, they always take away this right in order to complete their takeover." After the state legislature passed a bill prohibiting racial discrimination in housing, it hardly took the blink of an eye for the California Real Estate Association's new "Committee for Home Protection" to collect 583,029 signatures—326,486 from L.A. County alone—to put on the November ballot Proposition 14, an amendment to the state constitution prohibiting for all time laws that impinged upon the right of individuals to sell or rent property to "any persons as he, in his absolute discretion, chooses"—segregationism in its politer, more patriotic form. The California Real Estate Association's billboards soon blanketed the state: "FREE-DOM: RENT OR SELL TO WHOM YOU CHOOSE: VOTE YES ON 14." ("DON'T LEGALIZE HATE," read the enfeebled opposition's.) The *Los Angeles Times*—which had endorsed Nelson Rockefeller—agreed, more or less, with Nolan Frizzelle: "Housing equality cannot safely be achieved at the expense of still another basic right," the "ancient right" of the property owner of "using and disposing of his private property in whatever manner he deems appropriate." The argument couldn't withstand scrutiny; after all, no one complained that owners were constrained from disposing of their private property in whatever manner they deemed appropriate when they inked formal and (after the Supreme Court outlawed them in 1948) informal racial covenants. And not all support for Prop 14 was couched so patriotically: blacks "haven't made themselves acceptable" for white neighborhoods, a Young Republican leader declared. Polls showed that 58 percent of voters of both parties supported Prop 14. Goldwater held fast to the position that it wasn't his right as an Arizonan to come in and tell a Californian what to do about this thing. But it wasn't hard to infer which side he preferred. Nor, for that matter, Nelson Rockefeller—who had seen to it that New York became one of the first states with an open housing law.

Round about May 12, rioting ensued when George Wallace, contesting his third and final primary, spoke in the racially troubled shoreline community of Cambridge, Maryland. In a bourbon-soaked meeting in Hubert Humphrey's Senate chambers, Senator Dirksen was finally won over once and for all to the civil rights bill, and he immediately set off on the task of convincing 80 percent of his fellow Republicans to vote for cloture. And Barry Goldwater was affording his audience the warm assurance, "You cannot pass a law that will make me like you—or you like me. That is something that can only happen in our hearts." Goldwater's audience was unlikely aware that this was a close paraphrase from the majority opinion in *Plessy* v. *Ferguson*: that "prejudice, if it exists, is not created by the law of the land and cannot be changed by the law." They just gave Goldwater his biggest applause of the speech.

And since he was in Madison Square Garden, that was a lot of applause indeed. Goldwater's Manhattan rally on May 12 was perhaps the most elaborate television commercial ever filmed. The buttoned-down New York audience who, according to one observer, "put the accent on the old arena's middle name"; the raft of Republican congressmen on the dais; the Negro choral group (one tenor had to sing the parts of a baritone who was boycotting the performance); the bunting, the banners, the red, white, and blue balloons—all were but props in a stage play designed to convince California moderates that Barry Goldwater was not the plaything of the kooks who dropped flyers in their mailboxes decrying the Council on Foreign Relations' plot to poison the water supply.

The effect may have been undermined when Representative John Ashbrook drew peals of laughter by referring to a certain prominent columnist as "Walter Looselippmann," or when the crowd booed every time the President's name was mentioned. But something seemed to be working. Rockefeller had been gaining. Now he was fading. It likely wasn't the literature the Goldwater campaign had finally put out—*Senator Goldwater Speaks Out on the Issues*, a booklet of one-page position statements in room-temperature prose on subjects like "Defense Strategy for the Space Age" and "Labor-Management Relations." And Goldwater certainly wasn't playing to his base. Sometimes he proclaimed an ideal that his more perfervid supporters would generally denounce as Lippmannite "one-worldism." "The next logical step" after NATO, he told one interviewer, would be "a political alliance" that "united much of the world." When asked accusingly on a radio call-in show whether he was a member of the Council on Foreign Relations, he answered, "I don't know, frankly, if it even exists anymore." Sometimes he spoke of his supporters as if they came from another planet. "I hope I'm as wrong as I could be," he spluttered in an ABC interview, "but these—this is how hard these people are. They want a conservative; they've been thwarted at convention after convention, and this time I think they're in earnest."

But he had no intention of *rejecting* the kooks. With 2.5 million registered Republicans to convince, he needed all the warm bodies and cold cash he could get. "The senator is too busy to run a security check," a candid staffer told a reporter. "Anybody who wants to carry a leaflet can carry a leaflet. We'll take the money of anybody who isn't on the Attorney General's list. They're not going to stop each check and ask, 'Does this guy think right?' All they're going to do is deposit the checks as fast as they can and hope to God they don't bounce."

Then May 15, and apparent disaster. Immediately after Rockefeller won Oregon, he leapfrogged Goldwater in California polls by 11 points. The swing, his campaign leaders were thrilled to note, came just in time for every registered Republican in California to receive a Rockefeller mailing designed to finish Goldwater off once and for all.

The brochure's cover asked, "Whom do you want in the room with the

H-bomb button?" Goldwater was pictured with the caption "This Man Stands Outside—By Himself." Rockefeller was pictured alongside Nixon, Romney, Lodge, and Scranton, with the caption "These Men Stand Together on the Party's Principles." The tag line was *"Which Do You Want, a Leader? Or a Loner?,"* which was ironic: the purpose of the pamphlet was to hint that Rockefeller would *not* necessarily be the leader that stopped Goldwater—that by voting for Rockefeller's delegation, you were really voting for whichever person moderates anointed at the convention to stop Goldwater from his first-ballot victory.

The brochure blew up in Rockefeller's face. With greater and lesser degrees of dispatch, Scranton, Nixon, and Romney, who had never given their permission for the use of their names in this tacit endorsement, all disowned themselves from the ad in open letters. And whatever Rockefeller support there had been in the GOP's highest reaches commenced to unravel. Lodge had already officially bowed out of the race and donated his organization to Rockefeller—but only a third of the California volunteers Lodge's campaign had recruited agreed to switch their allegiance to the governor. Then Eisenhower told reporters, "I personally believe that Goldwater is not an extremist as some people have made him, but in any event we're all Republicans." Goldwater responded in a triumphant press release: "Governor Rockefeller stands alone in his refusal to commit himself to support the party's choice."

Two weeks before its primary day, Mississippi responded to an epidemic of church bombings by acquitting Byron de la Beckwith for the second time and increasing bail thirtyfold for misdemeanors such as disturbing the peace, and 43 percent of Maryland Democrats gave George Wallace their vote in the largest primary turnout in state history. They "went to the polls with big grins on their faces," a local editor marveled. "I never saw anything like it." Wallace's opponent Governor Brewster said the voters had been duped by a "pack of mindless thugs . . . stewed in the vile corruption of the same ruthless power that one finds at either end of the political spectrum, right or left." Rockefeller switchboards began lighting up with callers spewing invective after his ugly "Leader or a Loner?" pamphlet—and to issue the occasional bomb, and even assassination, threat. Rockefeller changed the locks on all his campaign offices. He recited these outrages in every speech: "This is the kind of extremist tactics that have been evident throughout this campaign." Given that he employed thousands for his campaign, Rockefeller found it hard to believe that all the nastiness being hurled his way could be the work of *volunteers* acting unbidden. Goldwater, more courtly, neither mentioned nor blamed Rockefeller for the Goldwater billboards that were mysteriously chainsawed at the base in the middle of the night; the Rockefeller agents provocateurs in Goldwater buttons bellowing at TV cameras that Rocky was a nigger lover; or the black-suited security guards Goldwater's people hired to walk beside him, scan windows, and lie in wait sniper-style on rooftops as he rode his palomino in Phoenix's "Rodeo of Rodeos" parade in the face of a death threat. Since the Kennedy assassination, such threats had become relatively routine.

Many a political science professor was taking class time just then to sum up the semester's lesson on the unique genius of the American political system for quieting the voices of violence, discord, and extremism.

A television blitz for "the responsible Republican governor of New York" made it difficult to find anything else on TV in the Golden State, and Rockefeller's 1,200 paid phone solicitors made it hard to sit peacefully through dinner (though Clif White shut down the entire operation for some time by situating hundreds of volunteers at pay phones to jam the lines). Spencer-Roberts had subcontracted separate public relations agencies to court raisin growers and wine makers, Spanish speakers, blacks, and more; among their other coups was to compile the names and addresses of all graduates of Negro colleges now living in California, who were importuned once more to change their registration from Democrat to Republican. A Rockefeller "truth squad" of California assemblymen now followed Goldwater wherever he spoke ("If they will step up and say I am a liar to my face," Goldwater told reporters on his campaign plane, "they'll get the reaction of a Westerner to that kind of treatment"). Rockefeller's media men followed TV producers in Los Angeles with offers of an expense-account lunch. One day Rocky was scheduled to make six stops, and just before he headed out, his schedulers added twelve more. He sunk to (not entirely unfair) accusations that Goldwater was working to divert precious Colorado River water from California to Arizona.

It was a Rockefeller juggernaut that Dean Burch beheld when he traveled the state for an inspection tour in the middle of the month. That, and the fact that in many areas of the state an official Goldwater campaign did not exist at all. Radio and television time had been bought, but no spots had been produced; not a single ad, not even for newspapers, had been produced. Knowland's strategy appeared to be to travel around the country repeating, like a broken record, that Goldwater would win by half a million votes; the firebugs had given the campaign such a bad reputation that once-reliable conservative businessmen refused to let their names be used in ads for fear of economic backlash. Some wouldn't even contribute money lest their names be on record. Goldwater confronted Knowland at a hotel by the airport and unceremoniously dumped him. A team from the Washington office was on its way west to rescue the campaign, as if it were starting over from the very beginning.

They worked in a rented suite rumored to have once belonged to Greta Garbo. It *was* like something out of the movies—Mickey Rooney and Judy Garland throwing up a show in the old barn. Chuck Lichenstein journeyed to Los Angeles with only a toothbrush, a change of underwear, and a satchel filled with $15,000 in cash, expecting to fly back the next morning; he ended up returning to Washington two weeks later, exhausted, with an entire new wardrobe. One day, after plating a brochure responding to Rocky's "Leader or a Loner?" salvo, he called a printer, introduced himself, and said, "You don't know me and you've never heard of me. We need to print a million pamphlets. The problem is, I need them tomorrow." The printer demanded $35,000 up front. Lichenstein spent the day at the plant, signing over checks as they arrived to cover each new run of a few cartons more.

The pamphlet itself was weak: hemmed in by the diktat not to attack any Republican, it consisted of a dreary wall of quotes from worthies like Nixon, Scranton, Romney, and Eisenhower, counterpoised by Goldwater's almost identical ones, to demonstrate that it was Goldwater, not Rockefeller, who was in the Republican mainstream ("If he is, it must be a meandering stream," Rockefeller now joked superciliously in speeches). The Goldwater campaign's TV spots were little better. One opened with a shot of Goldwater upside down as a voice-over reeled off misconceptions about his positions, and the image slowly turned right side up as the record was set straight; another featured Goldwater ad-libbing rambling responses to the same points, answering questions asked by men on the street—terrible politics, letting the opponent seize the agenda by repeating his charges; the effect was mainly to remind viewers of them.

Back in Washington there was a mass mailing to supporters urging them to scour their address books for "relatives, school chums, business associates, old army buddies, and Christmas card lists for persons you know that are living in California." In the finance office, George Humphrey, Arthur Summerfield, and other very rich, prestigious, conservative Republicans availed themselves of their own Christmas-card lists to raise $500,000 in two days to pay for the homestretch push. The Greta Garbo crew hardly slept. Some even missed the candidate's appearance on Sunday morning, May 24, on Howard K. Smith's political chat show *Issues and Answers*.

Smith addressed a question of the moment. McNamara had returned from his latest trip to Vietnam (where he had almost been assassinated by a Vietcong demolition team) proclaiming, "We'll stay for as long as it takes." The situation was now clearly deteriorating; "ERROR UPON ERROR," read a recent *Wall*

Street Journal editorial headline. The Administration had just asked Congress for $125 million in new aid to the beleaguered Khanh government. And all the while, resupply and reinforcements continued to pour in for the Vietcong from the North over the infamous Ho Chi Minh Trail; if anything, they increased. How, Smith asked, did Goldwater think it could be stopped?

"It's not as easy as it sounds because these are not trails that are out in the open," Goldwater allowed, removing the glasses for emphasis, revealing uncharacteristic bags under his eyes. "There have been several suggestions made. I don't think we would use any of them. But defoliation of the forests by low-yield atomic weapons could well be done. When you remove the foliage, you remove the cover." It could be done, he added, "in a way that would not endanger life."

Wouldn't that risk a fight with China? Smith asked. "You might have to," Goldwater responded. "Either that, or we have a war dragged out and dragged out. A defensive war is never won."

Months earlier Goldwater had gone even further in an interview—*insisting* that atomic weapons should be used—and no one had paid any attention. But after *Dr. Strangelove*, a threshold had been crossed. Now merely mentioning the Bomb as a bad idea that had been proposed was enough to seal the conclusion for much of the voting public: Barry Goldwater was a maniac.

"GOLDWATER'S PLAN TO USE VIET A-BOMB," blared the *San Francisco Examiner* (subhead: "I'd Risk a War"). Bobby Kennedy joked that Goldwater had come up with "a solution for crime in Central Park. He would use conventional nuclear weapons and defoliate it." The *Herald Tribune* tendentiously, maliciously observed, "Goldwater wasn't asked, nor did he comment on, the point that U.S. use of weapons in Southeast Asia producing fallout would violate the U.S.-British-Russian pact of 1963 banning both nuclear testing and explosions except underground." The article went on to note that Goldwater had also prepared for the homestretch in California by changing "his view that it is improper for the federal government to intervene to integrate local school systems"—even though he had abandoned that view years, not days, earlier. And then, in the same issue, the *Tribune* dropped yet another bomb. Walter Thayer had prevailed upon his friend Dwight Eisenhower to write an essay setting down his views on the Republican nomination. The former President said he preferred a candidate representing "responsible, forward-looking Republicanism." The word "responsible" was unmistakable: Rockefeller repeated it so often to describe himself that it was almost a chant. In case anyone missed the message, the paper helpfully ran Roscoe Drummond's column right below Eisenhower's, in a box. It began: "If former President Eisenhower can have his way, the Republican Party will not choose Sen. Barry Goldwater as its 1964

Presidential nominee." The *Herald Tribune* waived its copyright—so Eisenhower's piece also ran on the front page of the *Los Angeles Times*. Reporters swarmed around the former President to ask if he meant to disavow Goldwater. He replied, in a trademark garbled Ike-ism, "Try to fit that shoe on that foot."

The *New York Times* said Eisenhower's words "may well be the decisive factor" in the primary. But there was nothing decisive about the California Republican electorate. Pollster Sam Lubell noted that seven of ten people agreed with Goldwater that government spending was out of control, but he'd never seen an electorate so confused as to whom to vote for. "He's just too, too—*too much*," said one housewife; another commented, "With all the men in the country, isn't it terrible that we must choose from just those two men?" A friend rang up one of those confused California Republicans, eighty-nine-year-old Herbert Hoover. "You can't pin it down," the friend said, "but the feeling is that he might get us into war." Hoover found it hard to disagree.

He might get us into war.

In Honolulu, the Pacific Command's map room was now being prepared for a conference of Lyndon Johnson's foreign policy team to discuss a long memo by Mac Bundy, "Basic Recommendations and Projected Course of Action on Southeast Asia," commissioned by a President who was now having trouble sleeping at night. "If you start doing it, they're gonna be hollerin', 'You're a warmonger,' " he told McNamara, tacitly imploring his defense secretary to find some honorable way out.

He tacitly implored Dick Russell to stiffen his backbone in case a way out was not to be found: "They'd impeach a President, though, that would run out, wouldn't they?"

He rehearsed rationalizations with his staff: "If you start running from the Communists, they may just chase you into your own kitchen," he told Bundy.

"Yeah, that's the trouble," said Bundy. "If this thing comes apart with us—that's the dilemma. That's exactly the dilemma."

"It's damn easy to get into a war," said the President, "but it's gonna be awfully hard to extricate yourself if you get in."

Firebugs ginned up their own precinct organizations. They quit school and job to work full-time; marriages were put in jeopardy. Some Goldwater freelancers were more sophisticated than others. "You've got to warn the senator right away!" one cried to a Goldwater staffer at a rally in Glendora. "There are men out there taking down every word he says!"—gesturing in the direction of the press corps.

One piece of homemade campaign literature that was circulating in California like chewing gum, *A Choice Not an Echo*, came from one of the sophisticated ones. Phyllis Schlafly claimed to be a housewife from Alton, Illinois, and in that she was busy raising five children, in a sense she was. But this housewife had worked her way through college as a test gunner in an ordnance plant, had a master's degree from Harvard, and devoted forty-plus hours a week to right-wing agitation—from chairing the Illinois Federation of Republican Women to running the Cardinal Mindzenty Society, a right-wing volunteer group, with her husband, a lawyer who operated the right's answer to the ACLU (a typical client was a farmer who refused to follow government quotas), and hosting her own radio show, *America, Wake Up!* The Schlaflys had been among the few nonbusinessmen on the Clarence Manion committee that published *Conscience of a Conservative* in 1960. Which in 1964 gave Phyllis Schlafly, home pregnant with her sixth child, an inspiration: to publish a slim little book on how "a few secret kingmakers based in New York" conspired to steal Republican conventions, "perpetuating the Red empire in order to perpetrate the high level of Federal spending and control."

She lined up the second biggest paperback printer in the country, in Cleveland, put up $3,000, invented the name of a publishing company to print on the spine—"Pere Marquette Press"—sent a flyer to the people on her extensive personal political mailing list, and set up a little order-taking office in town. Twenty-five thousand copies were delivered to the doorstep of her house in late April. A friend called April 30 and asked her to ship 5,000 copies to the UROC convention opening in two days. Within the week, UROCers were using the book to work the precincts.

Schlafly was easy on the eye—and savvy enough to put a picture of herself on the cover that intimated plunging décolletage just out of the frame. The prose was short and sharp: "Each fall 66 million American women don't spontaneously decide their dresses should be an inch or two shorter, or longer, than last year," she began. "Like sheep, they bow to the wishes of a select clique of couturiers whom they have never seen, and whose names they may not even know"—just like Republican presidential voters. She never placed an ad; she never contacted a single bookstore—and 600,000 copies were in circulation around the country by June. Most were purchased in lots greater than 100. One businessman bought 30,000. One man told her, "Your book is the first book I ever read. I couldn't even get through *Tom Sawyer*." Another, at a family Memorial Day picnic, refused to give anyone a beer (decidedly not Pearl, the President's favorite brand) unless they took a copy of *A Choice Not an Echo*. By the time of the Republican Convention in the middle of July, some delegates had received upwards of five dozen unsolicited copies in the mail.

.   .   .

Phyllis Schlafly was not the only political star from Illinois being minted in California that spring. Another was Ronald Reagan. A number of more famous pro-Goldwater celebrities worked the homestretch hustings for Goldwater. But it was Reagan, not John Wayne (a sometime Bircher) or Rock Hudson, who was chosen to narrate a half hour of testimonials from Goldwater's (especially black and Hispanic) friends on statewide television on May 29. As a regular MC for Goldwater's rallies, Reagan usually stole the show. "And good evening to all you irresponsible Republicans," he would begin, and the crowd would be won; then he would hand them off to Goldwater, and the crowd would be lost. Sometimes, when the evening's program was completed, Reagan would greedily mount the rostrum for *another* speech that brought them to their feet one last time. At a San Francisco fund-raiser a startled waitress asked Rus Walton, "I'm confused. Which one was the candidate?"

Goldwater was on national TV on May 29 as a guest of Steve Allen's. It was an ambush. Allen was a particularly smug liberal. He decided to get Goldwater's reaction to the weekly message from a far-right hotline, "Let Freedom Ring." He dialed the number, and, with Barry Goldwater looking on in embarrassment, the nation heard a frantic voice say:

"Despite an almost total blackout in the nation's mass communications news media on the serious possibilities of an internal takeover of the United States by the Communist conspiracy later during the year, a growing number of Americans have come to realize that something tragically wrong is going on over the nation.

"Reports from reliable sources indicate that large-scale recruiting on college campuses is going to secure student participation in racial agitation this summer [the reference was to the organizing for a massive, nonviolent "Freedom Summer" voter registration campaign in Mississippi]. . . . *The pattern in this country is very closely following the events which took place during the internal takeover of Czechoslovakia in 1946. . . . Keep yourself well informed. Do not trust the newspapers, radio, TV, and newsmagazines for your information. These are the main weapons the enemy has to use against us."*

To peals of laughter from the audience, Allen asked Goldwater what he thought. Barry Goldwater regained his composure and proved that conservatism could potentially be a convincing populist message.

"Instead of just laughing these people off," he said, "I recognize them as people who are concerned, people who recognize that some things in this government are not going the way they like." The audience, who had come to the studio to laugh with Steve Allen and his celebrity guests, interrupted Goldwater with heartfelt applause. In his opinion, he said, there were no more actual

Communists in America than could fit in a hatband. But the lunatic right wasn't a problem, either. "I don't worry so much about these people, frankly, as I do those people, again acting under their constitutional privileges, who subscribe to the idea that we can have a centrally controlled economy run by the government or that we can deprive the states of their powers and centralize the power of government in Washington. These people are actively engaged in government; these people like the gentleman on the phone are merely expressing their frustration and their concern—you might say, like a man standing outside the tent throwing rocks while the other bunch are inside breaking up the furniture."

The studio audience applauded louder. They were Goldwater's now.

Gallup's latest poll had him at 40 percent to Rockefeller's 49. Key Rockefeller staffers, confident they had it in the bag, boarded planes for New York. But Goldwater was gaining. For now Happy was abed at Manhattan's Lying-In Hospital, her husband shuttling back and forth between the coasts as if commuting from Westchester to Manhattan, wisecracking, as his aides cringed, "I have a show opening on both sides of the continent the same weekend"— which he chose to believe voters found quite witty.

On May 27 he had been scheduled to speak at L.A.'s Loyola University, and Dean Burch dispatched one of the Goldwater emergency team, a prominent lay Catholic trucking executive from Nebraska named Dick Herman, to remind Los Angeles's Francis Cardinal McIntyre, the most right-wing leader in the American Catholic hierarchy, of the Pope's recent comments on remarriage. The gamble paid off. Six hours before Rockefeller was to mount the podium, McIntyre announced that the Church could never host a candidate who took the sacrament of marriage so lightly. Loyola withdrew the invitation. Other venues began following suit. The next day sixteen Protestant ministers issued a statement suggesting Rockefeller should withdraw from the race.

It was agonizing. It had seemed like a clever idea a few weeks earlier to direct attention away from the issue of his wealth by cooling off his advertising campaign. His media people had shot a hair-raising little number called "The Extremist," in which victims of right-wing zealotry around the state were interviewed by the *Today* show's Dave Garroway. They had canceled it as too incendiary. Now Rockefeller had no platform—on the radio or on TV, or literally—from which to speak. Goldwater was spending $1 million in the last week. He was on TV so often it seemed like he was the only candidate running. And he finally, reluctantly, had taken off the gloves: "I would think a long time," he said, "as a Californian, before I would put a man, governor of one of the larger Eastern states, connected with some rather influential financial institutions, at the head of my government, who could, at the stroke of a pen, do what LBJ's done for Texas"—that is, pirate the best defense contracts. Eleven of fifteen Republican state senators signed a statement: now the primary campaign had crossed "the narrow line between healthy controversy and destructive charges."

It was Memorial Day afternoon—just the kind of patriotic boost Goldwater's volunteer army needed to fire themselves up to ring doorbells until they dropped. In New York, Nelson Rockefeller Jr., 7 pounds, 10 ounces, was entering the world. In Riverside, California, Barry Goldwater was proving once again that there was nothing like a homestretch to bring him to the rhetorical heights a more motivated politician would have occupied all along. Conservatives turned misty-eyed to the flag as "The Star-Spangled Banner" was sung (a group of young hotheads saw TV correspondent Robin MacNeil, a Canadian, sitting down, and had to be restrained from tearing him limb from limb). Goldwater's speech was transporting: "When you say to some bureaucrat in Washington, 'You take care of the kids' education'; when they say to you, 'Don't worry about Mom and Pop, don't lay aside any money, enjoy yourself, the Federal Government will take care . . .'; this is the ultimate destruction of the American family. When this happens, Communism will have won."

The campaign grand finale was that night at Knott's Berry Farm. On the dais sat conservative leading lights like General A. C. Wedemeyer; spread before them were 27,000 of the faithful. A million watched on live TV. John Wayne looked down from the platform, locked eyes with Howard K. Smith, and said in the throaty drawl he reserved for only the gnarliest desperadoes, *"Ah-aystarn lab'ral prasss!"* But that only made most home viewers flinch, for they did not view the handsome and authoritative men they saw on news programs as enemies. Then Ronald Reagan spoke. He was just as angry. But he made you want to stand right alongside him and shake your fist at the same things he was shaking *his* fist at. It was hard to remember exactly what they were. Clearly they were the enemy of all decent men. Howard Smith turned to Teddy White, sitting next to him, and said that Reagan had missed his calling. He should have gone into politics.

Goldwater—ignoring (or perhaps drawing dudgeon from) FBI warnings of an assassination threat—was in full prophetic mode. Woodrow Wilson had campaigned on keeping the country out of war. Goldwater's appeal was different: "I charge that today this nation is following in the most disastrous foreign policy in its entire history. . . . We are at war and we should admit it!"

Twenty-seven thousand roared back like it was welcome news. By the time he began describing "the greatest day of all, the greatest day in our history," when an American President would tell Nikita Khrushchev *"You are wrong!"*—they knew the punch line, and they roared right along with him:

"Our children will not live under socialism or communism! Your children will live under freedom!"

And for the folks watching at home, lazy, fat, and overcontent from too much Memorial Day bratwurst and beer, he seemed to have pricked some guilt.

Goldwater retreated to Phoenix to play with his ham radio. His volunteers prepared to swarm over southern California like ants. They had compiled lists of 300,000 likely Goldwater voters. On election Tuesday, 10,000 workers would make at least two checks of each voter to ensure that he or she went to the polls. Rockefeller had 2,000 precinct walkers—on the payroll, of course.

One of the Goldwater volunteers on that first canvass was none other than Hannah Milhous Nixon, Richard's sainted mother. When her son got word of it, he whisked her off for a lengthy New York vacation. He called Goldwater's headquarters. Told the candidate was on the road, he demanded he be reached by radiophone. The radio car got word that Nixon had an urgent message for the senator, and the entire caravan pulled over so Goldwater could call Nixon from a phone booth. Nixon's urgent message was that he was not now, nor had he ever been, nor would he ever be, involved in any "stop Goldwater" movement. (Then he RSVP'd to his invitation to Goldwater's daughter's wedding.) The day before the primary Nixon called again, just to make sure Goldwater understood he was serious the first time.

Eisenhower—rendered in an apposite *New York Times* typo as "Eisenhow-ever"—gave a press conference insisting he never meant to confer favor or opprobrium on any candidate. (Privately, his fondest wish was to throw his weight behind some "stop Goldwater" possibility or another. But as he complained to an old friend who still wrote many of his speeches, Bryce Harlow, "You can't canter without a horse.") James Reston once again assured his readers that there was no way the Republicans would nominate either Rockefeller or Goldwater. Rockefeller had the edge—55 percent, Lou Harris claimed in a last-minute poll. But Goldwater was still gaining. "Please keep in mind that the Rockefeller delegation is composed of moderate Republicans who like Mr. Lodge, Mr. Nixon, and Mr. Scranton and would be more inclined to support a moderate candidate during the convention," Rockefeller's phone girls read off their scripts in their final call to voters.

The greatest tension on primary Tuesday was probably in the makeshift studio CBS News had fashioned at the Biltmore Hotel. Eight months since Walter Cronkite had debuted his half-hour broadcast, six months since the networks had consoled a nation in its weekend of despair, TV news was becoming big business. The networks' "vote war" itself had become news. In Oregon each network stationed reporters at the polls in almost every precinct; CBS ran up $36,000 in phone bills, but NBC beat them to the call by a few minutes. Now, with nearly as many reporters covering the reporters as were covering the results, for the first time CBS News was using Lou Harris's new computer-sampling exit poll techniques to attempt to call the race *before* the polls closed at 7 p.m. local time—during, that is, prime time in the East.

With three hours to go, news chief Bill Leonard and Fred Friendly pored over printouts that showed Rockefeller with a small but significant lead. A few minutes later new numbers came in: Goldwater had pulled ahead with 51.6 percent. They started sweating: 51.6 was just barely on the safe side of their margin of error. A few more samples came in; the Goldwater trend was confirmed. It was 7:15 Pacific standard time.

Leonard turned to Lou Harris: "I want to be 100 percent sure." Harris shot back confidently, "We're within our guidelines."

Leonard called Cronkite in Washington—and, at 7:21 p.m., astonishment evident in his voice at both the news and speed with which he was able to deliver it, Cronkite told America that CBS News was projecting Barry Goldwater as the winner.

Several hours passed. No other network called the race. Friendly and Leonard's final samplings arrived: Goldwater, still—but this time *below* their margin of error. The actual precinct tabulations flooding in were distinctly favoring Rockefeller.

Fred Friendly had to get on a plane to make an important meeting in New York the next morning. He fell asleep and awoke to the pilot's voice: "Good morning, ladies and gentlemen. We're just about to make our approach into the New York City area, and it's going to be a beautiful day. . . . And by the way, if you're interested, Governor Rockefeller has won the California primary."

Walter Cronkite, it turned out, was not nearly as trusted a man as CBS had thought. The wire services, using their old-fashioned methods, had called the election for Rockefeller; so did the CBS local station in New York City, hours after Cronkite gave the race to the Arizonan senator on the national broadcast. It was only the counting of the absentee ballots that gave the race officially to Barry Goldwater, 1,120,403 votes to 1,052,053. The turnout was 72 percent. Rus Walton's polling suggested that Goldwater got 20 percent more votes in precincts where *A Choice Not an Echo* had been distributed. Scores of wobbling delegates in other states committed for Goldwater. It was now hard to imagine a scenario in which Barry Goldwater would not be nominated. He responded to the news by drinking so much he had to be helped onto the plane back to Washington. Rockefeller refused to quit the race, promising, "I'm going right down the line no matter what happens."

Goldwater people celebrated as if they were witnessing the risen Lord. But hating Barry Goldwater was taking on transcendent overtones, too: in Mississippi, Freedom Summer organizers found sharecroppers who were terrified that a Goldwater victory would give locals license to shoot them in their homes. Everywhere cartoonists pictured Goldwater's base as "little old ladies in tennis shoes"—an image California attorney general Stanley Mosk used in his report on the John Birch Society in 1961 to portray conservatives as the kind of people taken in by aluminum-siding salesmen (and for which Mosk received angry packages filled with loafers, sandals, and pumps for weeks on end). The *Glasgow Herald* called Goldwater "stupid to a degree that is incredible"; the *London Times* keened over "a major party endorsing and promoting a man so blatantly out of touch with reality, so wild in his foreign policy, so backward in his domestic ideas, and so inconsistent in his thinking"; and the *Frankfurter Rundschau* called Goldwater "a confused and weak man who hides his weakness and uncertainty with fiery speeches"—no small thing coming from Germany, then witnessing a dramatic suicide epidemic among old men threatened by new "de-Nazification" trials.

Graham Molitor, unwinding from the California bout at a religious retreat, confessed ashamedly to a divine that when he first came to Washington in the 1950s, Goldwater had been his hero. Now he had worked to destroy the man's very name. The priest replied that considering the gravity of the situation, Molitor had done no wrong.

DUTY

All spring, the thirteen of sixteen Republican governors who were moderates talked confidently about how Goldwater would be eliminated from the race just as soon as the party establishment got a mind to do it. Now, on the eve of the annual convention of the nation's fifty governors, the Republican moderates arrived at an uncomfortable thought: they *were* the party establishment.

It was said that Republican governors were moderates because governing a state was a moderating job. It was they who were responsible for mass transit and hospitals and housing and job training and all those other powers so generously reserved for the states by the Tenth Amendment; it was they who would have to clean up the mess if a conservative White House were able to turn off their federal funding spigot. And it was they who would have to call out the National Guard should the civil rights revolution come to blows. Such thoughts surely clouded their minds that week as Senator Robert Byrd began unspooling the longest speech of the civil rights filibuster; Martin Luther King's latest marches in St. Augustine, Florida, were met by violent mobs; the state of Mississippi was preparing to counter "Freedom Summer" with all the terror at her disposal; and Harlem militants began regularly raining debris on police from rooftops. New coinages were joining the old familiar "backlash": "Goldwater riots" (the surmise being that if Goldwater were nominated, racial violence might just rocket him to upset victory in November) and "long hot summer" (the phrase the more militant civil rights leaders used to scare recalcitrant politicians). Traditionally an untaxing weekend alternating panel discussions with golf rounds in some delightful locale like San Juan, as if in omen this year's governors' convention landed in a backlash epicenter, Cleveland. It was there that the moderate Republicans conspired to finally put a stop to the Goldwater threat.

· · ·

Fifteen Republican governors were breakfasting on June 7 at the Cleveland Sheraton. A sixteenth, William Warren Scranton, shambled in dejectedly. Politicians who had been jealously reading all year about his ruddy charm looked up from their pancakes to see someone whose face was as ashen as a hunger striker's. Earlier, Eisenhower had all but insisted to Scranton that he explicitly offer himself for a draft that afternoon on *Face the Nation*. Bill Keisling, who wore a gold-plated Scranton lapel pin, said, grinning, "I only wear this when I've got a candidate. Believe me. I've got a candidate now." But Eisenhower had just been persuaded by a friend to change his mind. The fact that it was the twentieth anniversary of D-Day did nothing to stiffen the former Allied commander's backbone. Scranton's plan had been to charge into the governors' meeting and draw first blood against Goldwater. But he had just got off the phone with Dwight Eisenhower, who had pulled the rug out from under him after seven months of encouragement. He felt dizzy, weightless.

Presently George Romney (breaking his rule against doing politics on a Sunday) piped up with a demand that the governors summon Senator Goldwater and force him to clarify his positions on a list of issues—a curious request to make of a man whose views had long appeared on the record twice a week in hundreds of newspapers; as curious as the conviction, echoing through the halls all weekend, that the Republican Party had ever been the downtrodden's last, best hope. The idea of Barry Goldwater holding their party's standard fogged moderates' brains.

The response to Romney's salvo was barely civil. Oregon's Mark Hatfield snapped, "George, you're six months too late. If you can't add, I'll add it for you." Scranton rose to speak for Romney's idea. Hatfield testily replied, "Rockefeller has been working his head off day and night for the past six months, while both of you have remained gloriously silent. Any 'stop Goldwater' movement now by you eleventh-hour warriors is an exercise in futility."

Scranton was driven to the local affiliate to face the nation. His candidacy announcement remaining folded in his lap, he blathered that the GOP must "keep to a sound footing that it had in the past under Lincoln, Roosevelt, and Dwight Eisenhower." *Does that mean you're against Goldwater?* he was asked. "No, I am not saying that. And I think you are putting words into my mouth, sir." His comments got more confusing after that.

At the Sheraton, very politic people began saying very impolitic things. "Where are his *principles*?" Romney shouted at the TV set within hearing of reporters. A reporter cornered Rockefeller: Would he consider giving Scranton his delegates if he asked? "Did *you* see him on television?" he shot back. A new nickname for Scranton spread: the Hamlet of Harrisburg.

The next morning Hamlet appeared on the *Today* show. He claimed there was still time to bring Goldwater around to a moderate platform. "Well, Governor," asked Sander Vanocur, "aren't you suggesting the greatest conversion since biblical times?" Every trace of poise deserting him, Scranton dumbly replied, "Well, I don't think it has much to do with religion, Sander, but the—but I—I have said over and over again, and I think you'll find this to be true, that in our political—with persons generally, it is much more difficult to characterize them than some people think."

This was the sound of a party slipping away.

Goldwater made a guest appearance at a reception in Cleveland that evening. He took Romney at his word. He wanted clarification; the candidate's advisers circled around the room handing out copies of *Senator Goldwater Speaks Out on the Issues*. Then he left to head back to Washington to vote against cloture.

Richard Nixon showed up shortly after midnight. His pledge to Goldwater notwithstanding, he came with a "stop Goldwater" plan: he sat up until 3 a.m. trying to convince *Romney* to enter the race. Rocky dragged Romney and Scranton to his suite; together they tried to puzzle out a statement for Romney to make that would simultaneously honor his pledge to his constituents not to actively run for President and signal his willingness to be drafted. Governors and their staff members rushed in and out of Ohio governor Jim Rhodes's suite, which he had established as a virtual "stop Goldwater" clearinghouse, bearing proposals, counterproposals, and counter-counterproposals; reporters crowding the hall outside Rhodes's suite retreated to file stories pregnant with the phrase "accounts diverged," then returned to the phones an hour later to cancel the last dispatch and send a new one. Come daylight, Nixon called a press conference and announced, "Looking to the future of the party, it would be a tragedy if Senator Goldwater's views as previously stated were not challenged—and repudiated."

The governors refueled at a private breakfast after their all-nighters. Nixon asked for the floor. He announced he had no prepared remarks and would entertain questions. Moments passed; it suddenly dawned on the men in the room that Nixon was waiting for them to ask him to run for President. Mark Hatfield mercifully broke the silence with an innocuous query about their chances of beating the Democrats in November.

It would have been a perfect week to unite for the effort. Half the Democrats were ready to fight to the death for civil rights; the other half were fighting against it. The *Washington Star* had run the most damning exposé of Johnson's business dealings yet. Two reconnaissance jets had been shot down over Vietnam. Walt Rostow of the State Department had handed the Republicans a perfect opportunity to neutralize the nuclear issue when he explained in the *New York Times* that American security depended on readiness for any eventuality, "up to and including all-out nuclear war." But this crowd of Republicans couldn't have united on what day it was. Nixon, meanwhile, left the breakfast and told reporters he detected a "very lively interest" in a "stop Goldwater" option. In Washington, Goldwater said that Nixon was "looking more like Harold Stassen every day."

Cloture passed without Goldwater's vote, 71 to 20 (Scranton said Goldwater's position made him "sick"). Commentators predicted the imminent demise of the congressional conservative coalition that had held up progressive legislation for decades. LBJ pondered a memo from RFK that terrorism in Mississippi was being actively abetted by local sheriffs. In St. Augustine a Southern Christian Leadership Conference staffer informed the FBI of death threats against Dr. King (they hardly needed the intelligence; J. Edgar Hoover had long been bugging any room the man he called a "burr-headed nigger" graced). The staffer was told that a request for protection should be referred to the local sheriff—the same sheriff who had been detaining marchers in the 90-degree heat in an unshaded pen outside the county jail with a shallow hole in the ground for a toilet. In Cleveland, the governors dressed for the closing "Parade of the States" ball. And now that Goldwater's nomination was all but inevitable, William Warren Scranton wondered whether it wasn't time to throw his hat into the ring.

Scranton had mulled it over on the flight back home Wednesday, and he had his aides arrange a dinner buffet meeting with his closest associates at the governor's mansion the following night. He brooded around the executive mansion all morning Thursday as if it were Elsinore. It was three hours into the buffet before Scranton interrupted an entreaty from Senator Hugh Scott—who had just released a statement predicting that if Goldwater was nominated he would bring down thirty Republicans with him in November—in mid-sentence, stood up, and announced, "All right, we've got a lot of work to do. I'm going to run." The convention in San Francisco was a month away. Malcolm Moos, Eisenhower's former top speechwriter, and Senator Scott drove to Gettysburg to tell Eisenhower the news. He greeted them with the incredible exclamation, "At last someone has done what I have urged."

The announcement would come the next day at the Maryland state convention—where the gung ho state chairman had already formed a campaign-organization-in-waiting for Scranton. Jock Whitney, owner of the *New York Herald Tribune*, loaned his plane. And in a garish ballroom in the Lord Baltimore Hotel, Scranton spoke stirringly of the Whigs: "Today the nation—and indeed the world—waits to see if another proud political banner will falter, grow limp, and collapse in the dust." He continued, "Lincoln would cry out in pain if we sold out our principles, but he would laugh out with scorn if we threw away an election." His dramatic words brought half the crowd to a delighted frenzy—and half, conservatives, to resounding boos.

It infuriated Goldwater. "I hope you decide to run," Scranton had written him in December. Now, seven months later, Scranton was accusing him of wrecking the party to which he had devoted his adult life. Goldwater threw his scruples about party unity to the wind and told the *New York Times*, "The Republican establishment is desperate to defeat me. They can't stand having someone they can't control." When the *Washington Star* asked Goldwater what he thought of Nixon's comment on the "tragedy" that would befall their party if his views were not repudiated—the first he had heard of it—he turned a shade of pink. "I guess he doesn't know my views. I got most of them from him."

And suddenly Bill Scranton was on the road running for President. "This is not the hour for us to join those extreme reactionaries, who are anything but conservatives, those radicals of the right who would launch a system of dime-store feudalism," he would cry; or he would say that Goldwater "has given every evidence of being a man who is seeking not to lead the Republican Party, but to start a new political party of his own," was "wreaking chaos and uproar," "talking off the top of his head," had "a cruel misunderstanding of how the American economy works." "Because of the havoc that has been spread across the national landscape by the present front-runner, the Republican Party wonders how it will make clear to the American people that it does not oppose Social Security, the United Nations, human rights, and a sane nuclear policy." "Send to the White House a man who thinks deeply, who is not impulsive," he would cry with what gusto he could muster, although it sounded like a death rattle.

When not speaking ill of Goldwater, which was rarely, Scranton spoke of curing the ravages of automation through the federal establishment of "a coordinated labor market to match available workers with available jobs." And hardly a speech went by in which he didn't indulge in a favorite new pastime among liberals: the veneration of the late, great senator Robert Taft, a legislative consensus builder whose conservatism occasionally embraced such exceptions as public housing, federal support of health and education, and public works projects. He was "the greatest conservative of all time," Scranton would say, "a conservative in the truest sense of the word. He sought to conserve all of the human values that have been carried down to us on the long stream of American history. He saw history as the foundation on which a better future might be built, not a Technicolor fantasy behind which the problems of the present might be concealed." Taft became more symbol than man; Walter Lippmann, *Time*, and Richard Rovere of *The New Yorker* were but a few of those who sounded a mighty *amen* to Scranton's necrophilia for the late Ohioan—although back when Taft was alive, Lippmann compared him to Neville Chamberlain, *Time* to a "tortoise" who "piled one ineptitude upon another," and Rovere to "a grapefruit with eyeglasses."

Scranton's desperate strategy turned on picking up a lion's share of the 200 delegates to be chosen in ten remaining primaries and conventions, then turning around the others at the convention. He hoped for Rockefeller's 144. But although Rocky gladly turned over his now skeletal campaign organization, he held on to his votes—still hoping lightning might strike in San Francisco. Manfully, Scranton professed optimism: Florida's primary was in flux because of a feud between two rival slates (he neglected to mention that both were for Goldwater); Virginia had a strong moderate presence (though only one moderate ended up winning a spot on the delegation); Idaho had a strong liberal as governor (but Bob Smylie so feared the fate of John Anderson of Kansas that he sold out to White). Scranton pointed out that although Goldwater was presumed to have more than 655 loyal delegates, most weren't legally pledged to him. Of these he claimed that 200 were "moveable." The unlucky 200 were deluged with calls, letters, telegrams, even a phonograph recording—sometimes several in a twenty-four-hour period. Scranton had what would appear to be a compelling argument: in a Gallup poll of the rank and file, he was preferred over Goldwater 55 to 34. These statistics hardly impressed conservatives. Phyllis Schlafly, for instance, claimed that Gallup asked "a lot of questions of a very few people" in order to "come up with answers that pleased the New York kingmakers." Bill Buckley called them "crazy figures" that Gallup manipulated "to say, 'Yes, Mr. President.' "

The men who were told they were kingmakers set out to make a king. On June 23 Henry Cabot Lodge, saying Vietnam was "on the right track," resigned his ambassadorship to campaign for Scranton. (He had made the decision, he claimed, when a GI told him it was his duty.) Milton Eisenhower, the most liberal of the Eisenhowers, president of Johns Hopkins University, took on the job of locking in his brother. Tom Gates of Morgan Guarantee Trust leaned on associates for funds; Tom Dewey, thrilled to be back in the game, carved the nation into districts and distributed phone lists to highly placed friends. Scranton toured with forty-two such heavy hitters in tow, who fanned out to importune delegates at every stop. (He also traveled with an impressive security detail; bomb threats, as they were for Goldwater, as they were for Rockefeller, as they were for Martin Luther King, were constant.)

The heavy hitters thought they knew what to expect of Republican convention delegates: hacks, in the main, often serving "uncommitted" at the sufferance of some boss whose support was up for sale. But Goldwater delegates were freedom fighters, not mercenaries. They remembered when these same heavy hitters had rigged the "Fair Play" resolution at the 1952 governors' conference that let them stack the deck for Eisenhower. Schlafly added a new chapter on the Scranton drive to her book and put another million copies on the street, declaiming, "The chief propaganda organ of the secret kingmakers, the *New York Times*" and the "popular national magazines" were all "goose-stepping" to "prevent Republicans from selecting their obvious candidate."

They were kingmakers no more. When Robert Alonzo Taft was routed in 1952, one-quarter of the nation's banking resources were controlled from Manhattan. By 1964 the proportion was one-eighth. And now bankers and Wall Street lawyers were not the only men who knew how to pull strings. At the American Medical Association conference in San Francisco that spring, dominated by panicked talk of the Johnson Administration's Medicare bill, four former AMA presidents formed Physicians for Goldwater and sent a $14,000 mailing to convention delegates, which brought back $500,000. Another half million dollars was raised by the AMA's political action committee to distribute to friendly congressmen.

The Scrantonites couldn't shoot straight. When Lodge flew to Harrisburg, they organized reception for him at the airport—which Goldwater partisans managed to pack. One of them slapped a Goldwater bumper sticker on the back of the governor's limousine. Lodge was dispatched to Kansas, then Missouri, to meet with supposedly wavering delegates and found that both delegations had already left for San Francisco. Friendly newspapers tried to help: the *Washington Post* rejoiced that Scranton was "calling the GOP from the land of make-believe"; the *Los Angeles Times* devoted two full pages to reprinting his opening speech; the *New York Times* treated his campaign like the return of General MacArthur to the Philippines (for the publications of Time Inc., presided over by Scranton's brother-in-law, it was more like the Second Coming). Optimistic reports were filed that delegates had been peeled off in Iowa, that Goldwater had only nine firm votes in Illinois. But when pressed to name the names of delegates who had switched, Scranton demurred, because they didn't exist. White, meanwhile, could name dozens of new Goldwater delegates in states Scranton had just visited.

Time obligingly reported that "the storied kingmakers who launched Ike into politics" had "attempted nothing of consequence in the 1964 campaign," but that once Goldwater's delegates realized that only Scranton could beat Johnson "and carry hundreds of other Republicans into office with him, their loyalty to Barry almost certainly would waver and wane." Goldwater delegates flooded their man with telegrams to assure him that that would never happen: "WILL VOTE FOR YOU IF MY VOTE ALONE IS THE ONLY VOTE YOU OBTAIN" . . .

"I AM PREPARED TO STAND BY YOU AS RESOLUTELY AS DID GENERAL THOMAS FOR THE UNION AT CHICAMAUGA" . . . "I HAVE BEEN, AND WILL BE, SUBJECTED TO PRESSURES OF TREMENDOUS FORCE. HOWEVER, I WILL BE ABLE TO STAND UP TO THIS AND COME OUT OF THE CONVENTION WITH A CLEAR CONSCIENCE TO FACE OUR GOD AND OUR PEOPLE." "I'd give Barry my blood and the marrow from my bones," one admirer remarked.

Finally Scranton spotted an opening. In Mississippi, vigilantes were setting upon black churches, tearing them apart for "weapons" they assumed were being stockpiled as a prelude to the Communist takeover, then burning them to the ground at a rate of one a week when no weapons could be found. Barry Goldwater seemed to be affording the vigilantes aid and comfort. Goldwater made a courtesy call to General Eisenhower in Gettysburg to confirm the rumors that he would vote the next day against final passage of the civil rights bill. Eisenhower, livid, suspected Goldwater was doing it for political advantage. That was the furthest thing from his intention. When Goldwater returned to his Senate office he was met by his Mississippi field man Wirt Yerger and Southern coordinator John Grenier. What they saw was a shaken man afraid he was signing his political death warrant, convinced that the Constitution offered him no other honorable choice.

In 1962, after Goldwater had proclaimed Kennedy's dispatch of troops to the University of Mississippi unconstitutional, Denison Kitchel had commissioned a brief on the subject from one of Phoenix's most prominent constitutional experts, an ally of theirs in the local party, William Rehnquist. The brief changed Goldwater's mind. (Kitchel also advised, "Make Barnett"—Governor Ross Barnett, who was holding firm for segregation—"their victim, not your hero": sage, enduring political advice that meant that he could uphold both the *principle* of integration and the principle of states' rights.) When it came time to decide how to vote on the Civil Rights Act of 1964, Goldwater turned to Rehnquist once again. Rehnquist had aggressively fought local antidiscrimination laws in Phoenix, where Goldwater had valiantly fought for them as appropriate and morally imperative. As a Supreme Court clerk, Rehnquist had even written a memo arguing that *Plessy* v. *Ferguson* should be upheld. And, not surprisingly, Rehnquist confirmed Goldwater's instincts that the Civil Rights Act of 1964 was unconstitutional. Goldwater approached Professor Robert Bork of Yale University for a second opinion. Bork was on the record already as arguing that the matter was "not whether racial prejudice or preference is a good thing but whether individual men ought to be free to deal and associate with whom they please for whatever reasons appeal to them." He reiterated that opinion to Goldwater in a seventy-five-page brief.

Their counsel to steel him, Yerger and Grenier dismissed, Goldwater changed into his darkest blue suit, made his way to the Senate floor, and gave the most closely watched speech of his political career—rapidly, tonelessly, head down, as if reading into the record. "There have been few, if any, occasions when the searching of my conscience and the reexamination of my views of our constitutional system have played a greater part in the determination of my vote than they have on this occasion," he said. He reviewed his own record fighting discrimination, his conviction that racism was fundamentally a problem of the heart and not the law. He described how Titles VII and II entailed "the loss of our God-given liberties" and would constitute a "special appeal for special welfare"; that to work, the bill would

> require the creation of a federal police force of mammoth proportions. It also bids fair to result in the development of an "informer" psychology in great areas of our national life—neighbors spying on neighbors, workers spying on workers, businessmen spying on businessmen, where those who would harass their fellow citizens for selfish and narrow purposes will have ample inducement to do so. These, the federal police force and an "informer" psychology, are the hallmarks of the police state and landmarks in the destruction of a free society.

Of the genuine police state in the nation's midst—Mississippi—he said nothing at all. Precinct day had come and gone in the Mississippi Democratic Party. Black activists dutifully showed up at the meetings at the appointed hour, found the doors locked, then retreated to form their own "Mississippi Freedom Democratic Party," following state election law to the letter. Another church burned, and three civil rights workers went to inspect the damage. They were arrested and locked up in the Neshoba County jail. They were released; then they disappeared. A few days later, Walter Cronkite announced that the search was "the focus of the whole country's concern." The regular Mississippi Democratic Party chose its delegates to the convention, extralegally and in secret, then emerged to hint that they would endorse Barry Goldwater. "It is impossible to doubt that Senator Goldwater intends to make his candidacy the rallying point of white resistance," Walter Lippmann wrote.

Everett Dirksen closed the civil rights debate on June 19 with a withering attack on Mississippi's new golden boy. Never mentioning him by name, Dirksen listed all the other reforms wrongheaded conservatives had once declared unconstitutional: child labor laws, the Pure Food and Drug Act, the minimum wage, Social Security. He thrust his arm in Goldwater's direction: "Utter all the extreme opinions that you will, it will carry forward. You can go ahead and talk about conscience! It is *man's* conscience that speaks in every generation!"

The *New York Times* found it impossible not to conclude that Dirksen was fighting against Goldwater's nomination. Scranton seized the moment. He traveled to Washington to tell the minority leader he would make a fine favorite-son presidential candidate. But whatever the wishful thinking, Dirksen had not gotten that far in life without knowing how to count. When it was time to orate, he orated. When it was time for politics, he did politics. Goldwater had the nomination; there was nothing more to discuss. Dirksen dismissed his guest summarily, telling an aide, "What do they think I am, a rookie or a patsy?"

Scranton pressed on. "It looks good in North Carolina!" he proclaimed after a trip to Charlotte. (The delegation voted against Scranton 36 to 0 at the convention.) He whistle-stopped across the Illinois prairie: if he couldn't have Dirksen, perhaps he could win over some of the senator's fifty-eight-man delegation. In Springfield Scranton planned to speak from the hall in the old state capitol where Lincoln had made his great "house divided" speech. The sheriff wouldn't let him in. In Kankakee he was egged as his train pulled away. Then he went to the O'Hare Inn, where the delegation was holding its last caucus before the convention—and there Dirksen chose to bludgeon him. In exchange for a promise from Goldwater to include a plank supporting the civil rights bill in the platform, Dirksen emerged from the proverbial smoke-filled room to announce that he would nominate Barry Goldwater at the convention.

Scranton arrived and was met by two separate groups of pickets: conservatives, including a clutch of Goldwater Girls wearing phony bandages and carrying signs that parodied the commercials for Tareyton cigarettes (slogan: "I'd rather fight than switch"), and civil rights activists for whom his Republican identification was enough to brand him as the enemy. Scranton spoke to polite applause. Goldwater spoke; the room lit up. Dirksen delivered a peroration redolent, to all present, of his famous speech nominating Robert Taft in 1952: "We followed you before," he had cried then, wagging his finger at Thomas E. Dewey, "and you took us down the road to defeat!" This time he pounded the podium and cried, "Too long have we ridden the gray ghost of me-tooism! When the roll is called, I shall cast my vote for Barry Goldwater!" The delegates were polled: 48 for Goldwater, 8 passes, 2 abstentions, no one for Scranton.

When the Civil Rights Act of 1964 was signed on July 2, Johnson told his staff, "I think we just gave the South to the Republicans for your lifetime and mine" (some among them wondered whether signing the bill could conceivably lose Johnson the election altogether). Blacks seeking to exercise their new rights at a Selma, Alabama, movie theater were assaulted by whites, and made a celebrity of an Atlanta restaurateur named Lester Maddox who chased them away with a pistol (the Los Angeles County Young Republicans unanimously passed a resolution commending Maddox and asserting that the federal government "has no legitimate business protecting civil-rights carpetbaggers in the South"). Scranton traveled to Utah and was received warmly by banner-wielding "Smith Girls for Scranton"—not exactly the Beehive State's most important voting bloc. In Seattle, he claimed there were still "literally hundreds of delegates who are still moveable"—and then his forces folded before a Clif White juggernaut that denied even the granddaughter of Theodore Roosevelt a seat at the national convention. In Oregon Scranton was desperate enough to write the Civil War out of American history: fights over racial matters, he said, are "not in our tradition, not in our custom, not in our manner!"

It was the end of the road. He had managed to peel off a grand total of two delegates in his last five meetings. Goldwater, busy riding his palomino in the Prescott Rodeo Days parade and buying drinks for the house at the Elks Club bar, would go to San Francisco with about three-quarters of the delegates, and the nomination, apparently, in his hip pocket.

It was more than some people could accept. "I doubt he's got it completely locked up," Hubert Humphrey told Lyndon Johnson. "The big money in the East there, you know, will move in, as they've done before."

"I seen 'em do it," LBJ agreed, mentioning a friend who had gone to the 1952 convention strong for Taft. "The next morning, when steel got through with him, he turned the flip."

The Eastern Establishment had no clothes. But to many it was still garbed in the cloak of limitless power.

On this, at least, the Goldwater for President Committee agreed with their President. "The 1952 tricks will be used again," Bill Middendorf warned Dean Burch: "planted 'bum dope' stories"; "whispering campaigns"; "threats and cajolery"; "shanghaiing and spiriting of delegates and alternates to distant points"; "political Mata Haris" ("Be on the lookout for any unexpectedly easy companionship from new-found female friends").

What Clif White knew told him Middendorf was paranoid. But White acted as if he were paranoid, too. He had been ensconced full-time at the Mark Hopkins Hotel, whose fifteenth and seventeenth floors Goldwater had reserved, since June. He joined an assistant, Jim Day, who had been there since April. White had an agenda over and above mere victory: when Scranton entered the race, White became determined to roll up the biggest delegate total of any contested nomination fight in history. It would be the capstone of his career. It would pave the way to his goal: to leave San Francisco as chairman of the Republican National Committee. Though there was also a lingering worry: What if the Establishment really *could* bully its way to victory?

So White created a command-and-control apparatus that put the legendary Kennedy organization in Los Angeles in 1960—his model—to shame. The platform had been drafted by Wisconsin Republican Melvin Laird to ventriloquize Goldwater's views. When the platform came up for debate the week before the opening gavel, Scrantonites could be expected to introduce sugary, "harmless" amendments in the hopes that the Goldwaterites would let them save a bit of face by granting them one or two concessions. The door thus opened a crack, a bigger amendment might follow, then another. Scranton operatives would try to discredit the chair during debate, whisper in conservative ears about business deals and called-in loans. Then they would take the platform fight. White briefed his platform committee members: This was war. If Scranton came out for motherhood and apple pie, apple pie and motherhood would just have to be voted down.

His delegates were ready to submit—they had chosen to submit—to military discipline. As they were named through the spring, White had his state chairs assign each delegate a buddy, whom they were to contact at least once a week to develop a bond—and the buddies were to travel together at all times in San Francisco lest either be led into temptation. The airport was a vulnerable flank. When they arrived at San Francisco International, delegates were to report immediately to the Goldwater hospitality room, where staffers would contact headquarters at the Mark, where the delegates' arrival was noted in the pages of big black cross-indexed loose-leaf binders which contained intelligence on each one of them ("Can be influenced and expect economic pressures can be important when the chips are down. He also is actively and economically involved in real estate in Arizona, has made several trips there in the last few years"). Neither were they to trust the transportation the RNC was providing. They would be spirited to their delegation's hotel—there were twenty-eight hotels, inconveniently scattered throughout the sprawling city—by radio-equipped cars. The routes had been timed, so if a delegate was tardy, an APB could be put out. "We can't predict the accidents," said White, "but we must be prepared for the incidents."

The key was communication. In the days before direct-dial hotel phones, whoever tied up a hotel switchboard had a distinct advantage over the competition. (White bore painful memories from the 1948 conclave in Philly, when, as a factotum for Dewey, he was assigned to feed a pay phone just off the floor with nickels at regular intervals to keep open a line to the governor's suite at the Bellevue-Stratford as angry reporters waiting outside the booth to call in their stories threatened him with castration and worse.) White wired enough new custom phone lines across San Francisco to service a small town. At each delegation's headquarters, an extra room was reserved to accommodate a phone—connected for just these two weeks—wired directly between the hotel and the campaign's mammoth switchboard in a room on the fifteenth floor of the Mark. Six regional command centers (the Southerners called theirs "Fort Sumter") were wired still more elaborately.

Telephones had been chosen over walkie-talkies because radio frequencies were easier to intercept than phone lines were to tap. (Scranton chose walkie-talkies; the Goldwater side had already cut into their frequencies.) But should the phone system be compromised, Goldwater's people had VHF walkie-talkies. Should the VHF ones fail, they had backup UHFs. They also devised a secret code for when they had to use the walkie-talkies on the convention floor, and installed a jam-resistant antenna in the rafters of the Cow Palace more powerful than the ones the networks had, to prevent interference from the iron beams. They did it in secret; nobody outside the Goldwater camp knew this setup existed.

Unwilling to trust the media, the Goldwater campaign workers had created their own. In one suite on the fifteenth floor of the hotel they built broadcast facilities. The campaign had purchased time on a local radio station every half hour, to which Goldwater delegates were to tune for general news. They tried whenever possible to interview Goldwater luminaries upon arrival, then offer them as exclusives to local TV stations, lest their words be twisted by biased reporters. They aired their televised roundup on purchased time thrice daily. Another room had a huge board on which all staffers marked their entrance and egress, even to duck out to get a pack of cigarettes; a closed-circuit television camera was trained on that board at all times, the image shown on monitors in Burch's, Kitchel's, Kleindienst's, and White's rooms. One of the original Draft Goldwater group had committed nearly to heart the arcane rules of procedure of the House of Representatives under which the convention would be governed and was on call at all times in his room, where he had a library of law books at the ready.

The seventeenth-floor Presidential Suite was reserved for the candidate and his brain trust, led by Bill Baroody. By coincidence, Scranton's headquarters (an operation of perhaps a third the size of Goldwater's, created originally for Nelson Rockefeller) was sandwiched in between, on the sixteenth. Goldwater's team barricaded the elevator exits on the fifteenth floor; all personnel had to enter on the fourteenth—then show their privilege to pass the armed Pinkertons guarding the staircase in between through an elaborate system of stickpins and ribbons. It was the most heavily guarded piece of San Francisco hotel real estate since Molotov's Soviet delegation took over a floor of the St. Francis for the founding conference of the UN. Reporters were virtually banned. One time the guards wouldn't let Mary Scranton through the stairwell on her way to her husband's offices. When not on duty, the Pinkertons slept off their shifts in a room full of cots.

When it came time to move the delegates out to the convention site, the Cow Palace, an overgrown Quonset hut set amidst the scrub hills of the nondescript San Mateo County working-class hamlet of Daly City, there would be a fleet of buses. But the only route from downtown San Francisco to the Cow Palace, the Bayshore Freeway (seeded with Goldwater billboards donated by National Airlines chairman L. B. "Bud" Maytag), might be congested. So in case of emergency, Jim Day had rented a railroad train to keep on reserve. White's pièce de résistance was perched on concrete blocks in a back corner of the Cow Palace parking lot: a green-and-white command trailer that reproduced the whole setup at the Mark in miniature—so precious it was secured not by Pinkertons but by lawyers armed with tape recorders and Polaroids, ready to file affidavits in case of enemy sabotage. Phalanxes of volunteers across the country were held in reserve if a telegram barrage was needed. A pool of eager Youth for Goldwater volunteers, shipped in from every corner of the country via chartered trains and planes, were on call for odd jobs. At the outskirts of town, warehouses bulged with mountains of Western hats, boxes of buttons, and like ephemera for the greatest demonstration an American convention had ever seen.

Clif White surveyed what he had created, and he saw that it was good. A Goldwater delegate who twitched his nose in Scranton's direction could be set upon by a swarm of friends in the time it took to drink a cup of coffee. A parliamentary double cross could be plowed under even more quickly. The Republican National Convention at last belonged to *them*.

Or so Clif White thought. To see how mistaken he was, all one needed to do was look up at the Cow Palace's tier of glass broadcast booths, swept up off the floor by spindly struts like the legs of some giant metallic spider, hoisting each superstar anchor above the firmament as if king of all he surveyed. These booths were new, a function of the cramped floor space at the Cow—and a testament to just how highly the three networks judged the stakes of winning news dominance for themselves. It made news at the 1960 Democratic Convention when there were nearly as many reporters of all kinds as there were delegates. In 1964, the number of radio and TV people alone was double that number. Their priorities had become the party's. The pageant would be broadcast almost continually (and, via the new Telstar satellite, internationally), but the

RNC scheduled key sessions for prime time—and considered calling delegates to their seats with pom-pom girls instead of a pounding gavel. General Eisenhower would be there—under contract as a commentator to ABC. Thirty-foot camera scaffolding blocked the gallery's view; meandering cameramen weighed down by fifty-pound loads of equipment threatened to knock over delegates like bowling pins. Beneath the bleachers, the networks built villages—control rooms, reception rooms, maintenance shops, copy rooms—lavishly furnished, catered around the clock, and built as if to last, in Sheetrock, not plywood. The great alabaster towers of the brand-new multibuilding Hilton downtown, convention press headquarters, were girded around by so many miles of television cable that a hotel executive joked that the building might collapse if it was removed. A correspondent marveled on camera that politicians could walk the streets unmolested, while "us television types" drew swarms.

It was one thing that Clif White had hardly given a thought: what a blitzkrieg looked like broadcast live on TV. And when the dust lifted with the Goldwater side celebrating an overwhelming victory, "pyrrhic" was hardly an adequate word to describe it.

18

CONVENTIONS

As convention day approached, San Francisco teemed like a college town the morning of the big game. The RNC first estimated that 20,000 Republicans would set upon the city. Now the guess was 35,000 and rising; even the fourth-rate motels were booked, and an emergency housing center was set up to arrange accommodations for the throngs still streaming in without reservations. All hoped to get inside an arena that seated 14,500.

The Friday before the Monday convention opening, church and labor groups sponsored a 40,000-strong civil rights march to City Hall Plaza. "DEFO-LIATE MISSISSIPPI"; "GOLDWATER FOR FÜHRER"; "GOLDWATER '64, BREAD AND WATER '65, HOT WATER '66," read signs. A casket labeled "FREEDOM IS DEAD" was borne through the crowd. One contingent marched behind the banner "PARENTS OF THE MISSISSIPPI SUMMER PROJECT"—where an FBI office had just been opened to search full-time for the three missing civil rights workers (who had, it would turn out, been shot like dogs by the Ku Klux Klan after the Neshoba police generously notified the Klan of the trio's release from their jail). Keating, Javits, Lodge, and Rockefeller made surprise appearances at the speaker's stand. It immediately became clear that in this court of opinion at least, the Republican Party was Goldwater's and Goldwater's alone. For when the speakers reminded the audience of the GOP's glorious history of advancing civil rights, they were answered by laughs and boos.

From billboards Nelson Rockefeller had rented eight months before, the smiling face of Bill Scranton looked out on a city that belonged to Barry Gold-water. From the Powell Street cable car turntable at the bottom to the jewel of San Francisco hostelries, the Mark Hopkins, at the top, Nob Hill was so bol-lixed up that trolleys and taxis sometimes had to wait half an hour for police to clear the path. Though a knot of burly partisans screaming "We are the Gold-water *armeeeee* of liberation!" had no trouble cleaving the crowd; nor did

Phyllis Schlafly, who was treated like a prophet everywhere she went. Youngsters followed Ronald Reagan's every step; the editor of *National Review* was met upon his arrival at the airport by hundreds of YAFers detonating confetti bombs and singing "Won't You Come Home Bill Buckley." (They also met Dwight D. Eisenhower as he arrived at the Santa Fe terminal after a ceremonial cross-country trek on the "Caucus Special"—a show of strength to hint what the former president would be up against should he endeavor to throw his weight behind Scranton.) Goldwater, lips pursed in annoyance, was constantly tailed by mobs chanting "We Want Barry!" So, in fact, was Scranton, by mobs chanting the very same thing.

Across town, at the intersection of Haight and Ashbury Streets, a new kind of bohemia was taking shape, although many of its most flamboyant representatives were occupied with a cross-country trip on a bus called "Further," whose riotous exterior decoration included a sign reading "A VOTE FOR BARRY IS A VOTE FOR FUN!" A stop along the way was the commune of former Harvard professor Timothy Leary, whose *The Psychedelic Experience* had come out that year. These were Ken Kesey's "Merry Pranksters," later to be immortalized as the first hippies in a book by *New York Herald Tribune* writer Tom Wolfe. The delegates, mostly gray old factory owners and club women—the butt of cabbies' jokes that San Francisco banks were running out of nickels and dimes—would have been altogether disgusted by the goings-on at the Haight, were they aware of them; but the folks who would fill the Cow's spectator galleries—the YAFers and Young Republicans—might have been amused. They were packing North Beach nightclubs dancing the swim (some might have taken in the country's first topless dancing act), snapping up comic books lampooning such trendy dances by inventing new ones like the "Eisenhower sway" ("sway back and forth. But end up in the dead center. Do not speak while performing this exercise"), and heckling lefty comedian Dick Gregory at the hungry i when they weren't laughing at his cracks at the expense of Scranton ("He reminds you of the guy who runs to John Wayne for help"). They *did* think a vote for Barry was a vote for fun. They exulted in each other, rejoiced, felt an electricity they would not experience again in their lives: it was their Woodstock.

They were a key component of Bill Scranton's strategy. The governor had not just come to win some delegates and save a bit of face. He was determined to save his beloved party from suicide—and was convinced that the way to do it was to provoke Barry Goldwater and his followers to such reckless outbursts as to make Goldwater's nomination unfathomable. And so Scranton launched his first salvo. The vehicle was an article in the magazine *Der Spiegel*. Goldwater had given an interview to the German newsmagazine at the end of June.

It came out, and was translated, on the second day of the platform hearings. By the next morning Scranton was arguing that Goldwater's answer as to whether he could win against Johnson in November—"I don't think any Republican can, as of now"—should disqualify him as a candidate (Goldwater, Scranton said, had "now decided to defoliate the Republican Party"). Scranton left it to his press office to point up the truly impolitic statements in the *Der Spiegel* article: Goldwater's contention that Germany would have won both world wars if she weren't subject to the command of men "who didn't understand war"; and that in Vietnam, "I would turn to my Joint Chiefs of Staff and say, 'Fellows, we made the decision to win, now it's your problem.' " Scranton hoped Goldwater's first press conference when he arrived in San Francisco the next day would be a panicked defense that he wasn't a bomb-throwing Nazi. Then the other shoe would drop, and his supporters would realize just how unworthy their man truly was.

In that intention Scranton failed miserably. For forty-five minutes aides briefed Goldwater on what phrases to avoid in the press conference. He sat impassively, oblivious to what it was he was supposed to be ashamed of. Then he went downstairs to the media room and, glasses skewed charmingly to the left, as they would be through the entire convention, said exactly what it was he wasn't supposed to say, calmly, without a hint of agitation. To his delegates, it only made him seem more heroic.

Within the day a startling development would rocket the momentum further in his favor. There were two big delegations still committed to favorite sons, Wisconsin and Ohio. Wisconsin was shortly expected to release its delegation to Goldwater ("Vote our wishes in San Francisco or continue westward," the Young Republicans had warned the Wisconsin delegates back home). It was assumed that Governor Jim Rhodes of Ohio—the coordinator of the "stop Goldwater" efforts at the Cleveland governors' conference—would hold his favorite-son delegates only through as many ballots as it took to deny Goldwater a majority. Instead he released them for Goldwater. Rumors swirled: Rhodes had been offered the second spot on the ticket, or had been blackmailed. The truth, as Rhodes revealed it to an incredulous Bill Scranton in a blunt hotel-room chat, was entirely more portentous: Rhodes was so impressed by the strength of backlash sentiment in Cleveland, Cincinnati, and Youngstown that he thought Goldwater might deliver a Truman-beats-Dewey-style upset.

The idea was catching. "The November outcome, if he becomes the candidate, may rest entirely with those millions of white Americans who are becoming increasingly apprehensive about the impact of civil-rights legislation in their lives," one of Martin Luther King's brain trusters advised. "If they vote on this basis, all bets are off." A California Goldwater leader put it to a reporter more plainly: "The nigger issue will put him in the White House." A Goldwater win, pronounced New York senator Jacob Javits, would "wrench the social order out of its sockets." Though Goldwater himself spent the week expressing his fervent hope that civil rights wouldn't become an issue in the campaign at all, and explaining that if he thought he could not enforce the Civil Rights Act—the law of the land—"I would withdraw from the race."

Scranton made the rounds with a secret list of 110 delegates pledged to Goldwater but said, according to Rockefeller's staff, to be "less than 100 percent." He discovered they were 99.9 percent. He began arguing that the traditional convention roll call would have to be replaced by a secret ballot to keep Goldwater operatives from bludgeoning delegates into obedience, that Goldwater's platform draft intentionally snubbed Ike, that Goldwater planned to start a new, conservative third party. The press ate it up. When Scranton managed to peel off a single Florida vote, they reported that he was on the verge of 11 more and treated it as the biggest story of the day—that, and Senator Ken Keating's announcement that he would run his tough reelection fight against Bobby Kennedy independently of the Republican Party if Goldwater were nominated. Reporters began calling the Goldwater camp apathetic for never rising to Scranton's bait. It wasn't apathy; it was discipline. They already held all the cards. They only needed to lie down, let the noise play itself out, and hold their lead.

Scranton's proxies—Milton Eisenhower, Romney, Lodge—went before the platform committee to make their stands. "Markets don't just *happen*," Romney declared with exasperation to the committee's laissez-faire majority. Declaimed Lodge: "No one in his right mind would today argue that there is no place for the federal government in the reawakening of America. Indeed, we need another Republican-sponsored Marshall Plan for our cities and schools." They received standing ovations from thirty members—and stony silence from the other seventy. Sixteen years earlier Henry Cabot Lodge had chaired this committee. Now he was being treated like an alien. He returned to the Mark Hopkins, made his way through the gilded, mirrored—and, this week, mobbed—lobby to the elevator, and found himself accosted by a raving Goldwaterite: "I voted for you in 1960, but never again. You're terrible!" Lodge shot back, "You're terrible, too." He repaired to his suite, leafed through the roll of delegates, and cried, "What in God's name has happened to the Republican Party! I hardly know any of these people!"

Scranton's operatives put motion after motion before the committee, sound and fury signifying nothing. As the desperation mounted, the press conferences became surreal: "Governor, Governor, could you give the name of any delegate who has moved over from Goldwater to join you?" "No, we are not prepared to say at this time." "Are there any?" (Titters.) "Certainly." In the back rooms his floor manager, Hugh Scott, made a deal with Thruston Morton, the convention chairman: Scranton forces would be allowed to put three sweet, sensible platform amendments—to strengthen the civil rights plank, to reiterate presidential control of nuclear weapons, and to denounce extremism—to a vote of the full convention on Tuesday. (George Romney, maverick as ever, struck a deal to offer two of his own.) Goldwater allowed the concession because it would only broadcast his dominance when 70 percent of the convention voted them down. Scranton's team was willing to take the risk to show the world the face of Goldwaterism in all its naked ignominy.

Scranton soon would receive an assist. Saturday evening, two days before the opening gavel, Walter Cronkite introduced a report from CBS's correspondent in Munich, Daniel Schorr: "Whether or not Senator Goldwater wins the nomination, he *is* going places," Cronkite said, "the first place being Germany." Schorr picked up the cue and started in: "It looks as though Senator Goldwater, if nominated, will be starting his campaign here in Bavaria, the center of Germany's right wing." He went on to report that Goldwater had accepted an invitation from his friend Lieutenant General William Quinn to visit him for a vacation at Berchtesgaden—"once Hitler's stamping ground, but now an American Army recreational center." He concluded, "It is now becoming clear that Senator Goldwater's interview with the newsmagazine *Der Spiegel* was an appeal to right-wing elements." Cronkite segued into the next piece, on the latest burning of a Negro church in Mississippi, and the Germany story hit San Francisco like a freight train.

It was false; the trip *was* a vacation. CBS president William Paley, enraged and afraid he would be outed as a Scranton supporter, ordered Schorr to correct himself on the air. Goldwater's grudge against the Tiffany Network went back to a 1962 documentary on conservatism that made him want to throw something at the screen. It flared up again in 1963 after CBS News edited a tape of a July 4 interview with him that he thought would be broadcast live; it was inflamed enormously when Cronkite misquoted him to make him appear callous after the Kennedy assassination. "I just don't trust CBS News," is what he said after the November 22 gaffe. Now he went berserk. "I don't think those people should be allowed to broadcast," he said, refusing them access to any part of his campaign organization. But the damage was done. Scranton—and the Democratic National Committee—had already distributed reams of Xeroxed transcripts of the Schorr stand-up. "You can say what you want about Gold-water's conservatism and right-wing views," columnist Herb Caen wrote, "but personally, I find him as American as apple strudel."

"I've avoided discussing the arithmetic, because, very frankly, I haven't liked the figures," Scranton now announced. "I'm beginning to like them." He had likely convinced himself he was telling the truth—even though Texas's national committeewoman, who had given $5,000 to Scranton's campaign, had become so disgusted with his tactics that she had just switched her vote to Goldwater.

That same Saturday afternoon Jim Martin, the Alabaman who had narrowly lost a Senate race against Lister Hill in 1962, was busy mowing his lawn in suburban Gadsen when his wife called him in for a phone call from his gover-nor. George Wallace instructed Martin to drive to the Gadsen airport, where a plane was waiting to fly him to Montgomery. And in Alabama, you followed your governor's instructions.

Goldwater had been publicly flattering Wallace all week to get him to drop his threat to run an independent race for President. Wallace had already gath-ered 78,000 signatures in a fortnight in North Carolina, eight times the number necessary to get on the ballot, and he was working on a dozen more. Wallace misheard Goldwater's flattery as an invitation. From the Montgomery airport, Martin was shuttled to the governor's suite at the Jefferson Davis Hotel, where he heard Wallace tell him, "It must be apparent to a one-eyed nigguh who can't see good outta his other eye that me and Goldwater would be a winning ticket." Martin was then ordered to head to San Francisco—immediately—to put the offer to Goldwater. Martin pointed out that he was still wearing his yard-work clothes. Wallace nodded to an aide, who counted a thousand dollars cash into Martin's palm. He left that night.

Convention eve, Sunday, broke unusually hot, ladies sweltering in wool suits brought to San Francisco on the unfortunate advice of the National Feder-ation of Republican Women's newsletter *The Clubwoman*. As delegates con-templated pictures in the Sunday papers of an American truck blown off the road by a Vietcong mine, a profile of the purported love child of Warren G. Harding, and a full-page ad from the Jackson Citizens Council arguing that Abraham Lincoln was a segregationist, Jim Martin was contemplating the heat waves rising off the gleaming pyramid atop the Mark Hopkins roof. "Mr. Wal-lace has suggested that he would like to be a candidate with you as your vice-presidential nominee on the Republican ticket," Martin timidly informed his hero. Goldwater winced; he thought Wallace was a racist thug, and he didn't even consider considering the offer, even though he knew this meant Wallace might run for President and draw votes from him. Martin briefed Wallace; Wallace, two days later, asked whom he preferred for President, replied, "I prefer Governor George Wallace of Alabama." He added that he would change his mind only if one of the parties adopted a segregationist platform.

Goldwater and Scranton had both been invited to appear on *Meet the Press* that Sunday morning. Goldwater exercised the front-runner's strategy of avoiding debates like the plague, and didn't show. Scranton took the opportunity to demand that Goldwater debate him on the floor of the convention instead. When he returned to the Mark, Scranton ordered his zealous young aide Bill Keisling to draft an open letter of challenge, and then he dashed off for his next exhausting round of meetings with "wavering" delegates. Keisling's letter was approved by higher-ups and was submitted to Scranton's personal secretary, who was authorized to forge her boss's signature. A courier was sent one flight up to deliver it. Scranton never saw the letter. It was 6:47. And by 7 p.m. Goldwater and his brain trust were pacing around the seventeenth floor ready to tear up the furniture.

"Will the convention choose the candidate overwhelmingly favored by the Republican voters, or will it choose you?" the letter asked. It continued, with emphasis: "With open contempt for the dignity, integrity, and common sense of the convention, your managers say in effect *the delegates are little more than a flock of chickens whose necks will be wrung at will.*" It called Clif White's roll-call estimates a fraud. "Our count differs from that of your managers because we have calculated an important element which they are incapable of comprehending. That is the element of respect for the men and women who make up the delegations to this convention"—who, the Scrantonites claimed, were deserting Goldwater in droves: because he had "too often casually prescribed nuclear war as a solution to a troubled world . . . allowed the radical extremists to use you . . . stood for irresponsibility in the serious question of racial holocaust . . . read Taft and Eisenhower and Lincoln out of the Republican Party. . . . *In short, Goldwaterism has come to stand for a whole crazy-quilt collection of absurd and dangerous positions that would be soundly repudiated by the American people in November.*" There followed the call to debate with Scranton, on Wednesday, before the balloting for the nomination began: "You must decide whether the Goldwater philosophy can stand public examination—before the convention and before the nation."

Goldwater reacted with hell's own fury. He and Scranton used to be friends; he had considered tapping Bill Scranton as his running mate. Scranton was a pilot, had served in Goldwater's National Guard unit, sat with him for long bull sessions on tours of duty abroad. Goldwater had endured his abuse all week with equanimity. But this was the last straw.

Someone pointed out that Scranton would probably release the letter to the press soon, and that their side should beat him to the punch. They cobbled together a statement, which began: "Governor Scranton's letter has been read here with amazement. It has been returned to him." Ohio State political science professor Harry Jaffa, a Lincoln expert brought to San Francisco by Baroody to spread the argument that were the Great Emancipator alive today, he would call himself a conservative, remembered a stinging rebuke Lincoln had written to Horace Greeley after a similar insult, and that was appended to the statement. Four thousand copies of Scranton's letter and Goldwater's response were run off. Clif White sparked his phone lines to life, quickly tracked down his six regional directors, and ordered them to see that the package was slipped under the door of every delegate, alternate, and Republican official within the next 120 minutes.

As minions spread out over the city like gremlins to carry out the task, Goldwater ostentatiously boycotted that night's $500-a-plate Republican Campaign Committee dinner-dance. With his absence it became, perforce, a Scranton event—which is to say, a wake. The delegates and alternates read the documents beneath their doors before turning in with nearly as much amazement as Goldwater's inner circle had. The governor had boomeranged his best issue back on himself: now he seemed the reckless one. Many of Scranton's delegates switched sides. And Goldwater's delegates, which the letter so graciously dubbed "a flock of chickens whose necks will be wrung at will," now inaugurated Scranton into the circle of contempt formerly reserved for Nelson Rockefeller, Walter Reuther, and Russia.

The Monday papers brought news of the South Vietnamese army's worst defeat yet; of two black reserve officers shot at random while driving home from Fort Benning, Georgia; and of a Lou Harris poll showing that voters disagreed with Goldwater on eight out of ten issues. At the Mark, the forty-five-minute wait for one of the three tiny elevators (the campaigns used a service elevator accessed through the hotel kitchen) was now giving zealots two chances a day at least to menace *Ah-aystarn lab'ral prasss* mainstays like Chet Huntley and David Brinkley. "You know, these nighttime news shows sound to me like they're being broadcast from Moscow," muttered one to another on the way down, loud enough so the dastardly duo could listen in. "Why can't we find Americans to do the television news?" mumbled the other. The staff at the Hilton began issuing a bottle of aspirin with every press badge. Brinkley forbade his young son to show his NBC insignia except when absolutely necessary.

In the Cow Palace parking lot, in the shadow of a giant Goldwater sign pasted on the back of a screen belonging to the Geneva Drive-In next door (the owner was a partisan), thousands of CORE activists kept vigil with apocalyptic placards: "HITLER WAS SINCERE, TOO; DEFOLIATE GOLDWATER." A security force drawn from eighteen separate police departments was there to keep them in line; 150 sergeants at arms were posted at the entrances to keep them out. A timorous black press had tried to keep the protesters from the site altogether, *Jet* accusing them of trying to "trigger a racial incident," the *Chicago Defender* complaining that only by honoring the moratorium on demonstrations recently agreed to with the White House by mainline civil rights groups could their race "escape the diabolical enslavement that the triumph of Goldwaterism would ensure for us." Down the coast in Long Beach, the NAACP's Roy Wilkins would soon address the Newspaper Guild: "We must not forget that a man from Munich rallied the rightist forces in the early 1930s." The demonstrations were still going strong as the twilight stream of automobiles trickled out of the parking lot after the closing session Thursday night.

Inside the cavernous hall the opening gavel had hardly quieted the small scattering of delegates before Scranton forces mounted their first desperate charge. For as long as anyone could remember, proud, aging Southern black men with patriotic names like George Washington Lee and Henry Lincoln Johnson had dotted the floor at these conventions—handy aids to rationalizations that the Republicans were still the party of civil rights long after blacks began deserting en masse to the Democratic Party during the New Deal. But this year, after Clif White's juggernaut had rolled over the old black-and-tans in the South, the portions of the floor reserved for Southern states were bond-paper white. G. W. Lee, a Memphis man with a trademark wide plantation hat, had been a fixture as Shelby County delegate since the 1930s and had offered a stirring second of Robert Taft's nomination in 1952. But this year, Memphis's two-hundred-member all-black Republican organization, the "Lincoln League," was deprived of its quadrennial tradition of electing Lee to represent them because John Grenier had arranged for the county convention to be held across town in a neighborhood where blacks were—to put it politely—unwelcome. A white conservative, Robert B. James, was chosen in Lee's stead. And this, Scrantonites decided, was just the outrage they needed. They would force Goldwater to explain Lee's exclusion in open session, on camera, before the eyes of the world. When the usually perfunctory opening motion was made to resolve that "this Convention be governed by the rules adopted by the National

Convention of 1960," Scranton's Maryland campaign manager, Milton Steers, popped up and moved for an amendment that no delegate be seated if "this Convention shall determine there were rules, practices, or procedures . . . which had the purpose or effect of discriminating in such selection on grounds of race, color, creed, or national origin."

The apparent nobility of the cause was misleading. The fact was, black Republican delegates often won their seats in processes less democratic than anything Clif White could dream up. Lee, for his part, was a longtime marionette of the late E. H. "Boss" Crump, who had set up the Lincoln League as a wholly owned subsidiary of his Memphis Democratic machine. The subtlety was lost on the TV cameras, which merely recorded the roar when segregation was maintained by a thunderous voice vote. It was a symbolic victory. Unfortunately, those were the only kind Scranton would win.

Mark Hatfield gave the evening's keynote speech. He attacked "bigots in this Nation who spew forth their venom of hate . . . like the Communist Party, the Ku Klux Klan, and the John Birch Society." His intended audience was not there to hear it. By order of White, Goldwater delegates skipped the speech. They were all up on top of Nob Hill at the city's WPA-style Masonic Temple screaming their heads off when Michael Goldwater explained how his father had taught his children to "be wary of any man who tries to take our land away from us or our God away from us," and that Johnson's self-professed Great Society "can only result in dictatorship."

On Tuesday—headlines: "U.S. SENDING 600 TROOPS TO SAIGON"; "2D MUTILATED BODY FOUND IN MISSISSIPPI RIVER" (tentatively identified as one of the three missing civil rights workers, but apparently the victim of another, yet unreported Klan hit)—Richard Nixon arrived by helicopter at Fisherman's Wharf, where he was met by the black D.C. lawyer William S. "Turk" Thompson. He then traveled to the Hilton for a press conference and offered the contradictory statement that he was both satisfied with the platform as drafted and that "my views are exactly today as they were in Cleveland." (CBS's Paul Niven explained to viewers that Nixon was now all but irrelevant in Republican councils, and they needn't pay much heed to him anyway.) In Scranton's next press conference—to which he shuttled after a failed attempt to win Maine from favorite daughter Margaret Chase Smith—Scranton offered, jaw-droppingly, that he agreed with Goldwater on most issues. At the St. Francis Hotel off Union Square, the Credentials Committee voted 69 to 19 against John Lindsay's motion to change the rules to prohibit racial discrimination in the choosing of delegates, and 66 to 19 that there had been no irregularities in the selection of the delegate from Shelby County, Tennessee. At the Mark Hopkins, Goldwater snuck out a secret tunnel on his way to buzz the Cow Palace in a rented airplane. The whole business bored him. Once he invited Clif White up to the Presidential Suite to "go over this delegate business." White strode in proudly with an armful of loose-leaf notebooks and began with Alabama. He was barely to the second half of the alphabet before Goldwater drifted off altogether. "From the top of the Mark Hopkins Hotel, San Francisco, California," he said into his ham microphone, "the handle is Barry—Baker Able Robert Robert Yankee. . . ."

Inside the Cow Palace his delegates were detaining warm-up speakers for minutes at a time with applause whenever his name was mentioned. The man they were warming up was Dwight D. Eisenhower, who was to deliver an appeal for party unity; it was to be the first major event of the convention schedule. It had been scheduled before the platform fight later in the afternoon for the express purpose of soothing factional passions. And, for three-fourths of his address, the former President accomplished this plodding task admirably. ("My friends, we are Republicans. If there is any finer word in the entire field of partisan politics, I have not yet heard it"; there was polite applause.) Then he went off, inadvisably, on a digression that he had worked up at the last minute. It was intended as a throwaway line: "So let us particularly scorn the divisive efforts of those outside our family, including sensation-seeking columnists and commentators—"

He could barely finish the sentence. The conservatives leapt to their feet. Many, then most, spun around and waved their fists at the broadcast booths; one group stumbled through the forest of folding chairs and made as if to storm the glass aeries themselves. Someone said Ike looked like a lion tamer who had lost his chair and whip. The outpouring only stilled when Clif White, in his magnificent green-and-white trailer, pressed his special "all-call" button that rang all his delegation chairmen's phones on the floor at once and ordered them to shut their people up.

A few paragraphs later, Ike went off on another of his digressions. It might have been annoyance at the Supreme Court's ruling three weeks ago declaring that suspects had an "absolute right to remain silent" that led him to say: "And let us not be guilty of maudlin sympathy for the criminal who, roaming the streets with switchblade knife and illegal firearm, seeking a helpless prey, suddenly becomes, upon apprehension, a poor, underprivileged person who counts upon the compassion of our society"; and to go on to deplore "the laxness or weaknesses of too many courts to forgive this offense." The floodgates opened once again. Only this time it was even louder. Eisenhower looked like he'd seen a ghost.

Now that nobody in the hall was soothed, it was time for platform debate.

Scranton managers had made the brilliant tactical move of arranging the debate for prime time to showcase the Goldwaterites' ugly displays to the greatest possible effect. Mel Laird had made the brilliant countermove of arranging to have the entire platform as it then stood read aloud. Hours passed as a team of readers traded off pages; blood did not cool in the interim. Goldwaterites had been amusing themselves all the while with a ritual that had begun in Texas Republican circles: one side of a hall would raise the ear-splitting cry *"Viva!"* The other side, challenged to scream louder, pronounced: *"Olé!"* In a rented gymnasium in Houston it sounded impressive. Over the yawning expanse of the Cow Palace, it was overwhelming—energizing to those privy to the rite, harrowing to those who were not. Norman Mailer, covering the convention for *Esquire*, heard in it "a mystical communion in the sound even as *Sieg Heil* used to offer its mystical communion."

The debate had been moved squarely out of prime time. But what followed assured it would be repeated in future prime times over and over again.

Bored delegates were milling about. The crush in the aisles became so severe that local police moved onto the floor. John Chancellor of NBC—far outpacing the other broadcasters in the ratings thanks to flashy quick-cutting while the other networks had their anchors droning on endlessly in the booth—was interviewing Alaska delegates. Strongly liberal, they had suspiciously been denied passes to the gallery for their friends. One of White's sergeants at arms told Chancellor to move along. The TV journalist pointed to his floor pass and refused. Police moved in. NBC producers ordered the scene put on the air.

"Am I going to be carried out?" Chancellor asked the cop as a sheriff's officer moved in as backup to help herd him toward the door. He was followed by one of those network cameramen in helmets sprouting a monstrous broadcast antenna, as if a visitor from outer space. "I'm in custody," Chancellor announced into the camera. "I want to assure you that NBC is fully staffed with other reporters who are not in the custody of the Daly City police and the San Mateo sheriff's office. I formally say this is a disgrace. The press, radio, and television should be allowed to do their work at a convention. I'm being taken down off the arena now. . . . I'll check in later." He signed off: "This is John Chancellor, somewhere in custody." Later an attempt was made to remove CBS's Mike Wallace from the Alaska delegates' area—although the action was thwarted when an Alaska delegate shouted into an open microphone, "This is an attempt by Goldwater or other forces to control the convention and prevent free airing of issues of the convention!"

The reading was completed, gavels were banged, order was restored. Hugh Scott was recognized to offer the first amendment, which repudiated "the efforts of irresponsible extremist groups, such as the Communists, the Ku Klux Klan, the John Birch Society, and others to discredit our Party by their efforts to infiltrate positions of responsibility in the Party or to attach themselves to its candidates." Five minutes were yielded to the first speaker for the motion, Nelson Aldrich Rockefeller. He strode to the great raised podium, beneath the enormous banner graced by the silhouette of Abraham Lincoln alongside the words "FOR THE PEOPLE," to cheers—which didn't outlast the accompanying chorus of Goldwaterite howls.

With great difficulty, Thruston Morton gaveled the crowd into silence. Rockefeller began by repeating his July 14, 1963, warning about "a radical well-financed minority . . . wholly alien to the sound and honest Republicanism that has kept this party abreast of human needs in a changing world; wholly alien to the broad middle course that accommodates the mainstream of Republican principles." His partisans applauded. He told of a year spent defending the party against extremist takeover. A lone *boo* rang out. It came from a young man from Santa Rosa who had nearly bankrupted his family that spring by working for Goldwater in the California primary when he should have been out selling real estate. Rocky had jerked them around all spring. He had lost. Now he was lording it over them like he had won. It felt damned good to boo.

Scattered voices joined him. Rockefeller smiled thinly as the ripple became a wave. A "We Want Barry!" chant proved too overpowering for him to continue. He cocked an eyebrow, smiled wider, and muttered under his breath, "That's right, that's right." They were falling into his trap; they were displaying their brutishness for all the world to see.

Clif White saw what he was up to. He pushed his all-call button. Thirty phones were picked up on the convention floor. He commanded, "If there is any booing in your delegations, stop it immediately." But he was helpless. The delegates weren't the problem. The noise came from the spectator galleries. He had drilled his regiments to the letter. There was nothing he could do about irregulars mounting a charge of their own.

Standing next to Rocky with an imploring look on his face, his oversized gavel ringing with an oddly hollow *plink*, Thruston Morton seized the microphone. "The chair must ask for order. We're going to have several speakers here on various amendments. We must proceed in an orderly manner. I think it's only fair and right to all concerned." Rockefeller continued, nodding as if to coax them on: "Their tactics have ranged from cancellation by coercion of a speaking engagement at a college, to outright threats of personal violence."

Now the noise was all-enveloping. There was a huddle at the rostrum. Rockefeller testily demanded an extension of his time; Morton granted it and turned around to return to his seat. It was as if he had given a cue: the sound now crashed the threshold of pain. "This is still a free country, ladies and gentlemen," Rockefeller simpered, relishing the moment—and they screamed some more.

Jackie Robinson was hanging back near an exit of the hall—next to the Alabama delegation, as it happened. "C'mon, Rocky!" he cheered. A burly Alabaman glared at him menacingly and rose from his seat. His wife pulled at his coat. "Turn him loose, lady!" Robinson roared. ("Luckily for him, he obeyed his wife," Robinson boasted later.)

Rocky: "You don't like to hear it, but it's true—" (a network camera cut to Happy, in pearls, a pained and embarrassed look on her face) "—they engender suspicion, they encourage disunity, and they operate from the dark shadows of secrecy—" (the camera found a row of young Goldwater partisans who rhythmically slapped their thighs with glee) "—The Republican Party must repudiate these people. . . . I move the adoption of this resolution."

The voice vote: a roar of nays. Tom Kuchel was asked how he felt. "Fine, physically," he replied sorrowfully. "God save the Union."

The next motion was called, Romney's anti-extremism amendment. The hearing was more respectful; the voice vote was the same. For the next, which would add six resounding paragraphs specifically attesting to the constitutionality and desirability of the civil rights law, Scranton had arranged for a roll-call vote, banking that some delegates would be ashamed to go on the record as being against it. The result, 897 to 409, only served to give a reliable prediction of the roll call for the Republican candidates the next day. The amendment on control of nuclear weapons was called, Romney's on civil rights (so innocuous that White even considered letting his people vote for it), speeches made for and against—two more walls of nays. The platform was ratified, as written, on the dawn side of 2 a.m.—breakfast viewing for early risers in the East. Scranton's last chance at redemption had failed. The boys who weekended in Newport Beach had ground the boys who summered in Newport to dust. The winners were not gracious. "The South took the Mason-Dixon line and shoved it right up to Canada," one Texas leader proclaimed to a *Newsweek* reporter.

The day Barry Goldwater was to be nominated Republican candidate for President of the United States he was nervous enough to cut himself shaving. He descended on the service elevator, squeezed for the umpteenth time between smelly garbage cans and the rolling carts—and was greeted in the kitchen by a brace of microphone-waving correspondents. "Do you think that the Democrats will make an issue of the GOP convention's refusal to endorse the constitutionality of the new civil rights law?" he was asked. He snapped, "After LBJ, the biggest faker in the United States, having opposed civil rights until this year—let 'em make an issue out of it. I'll just recite the thousands of words he has spoken against anti-poll-tax legislation, equal accommodations, and the FEPC [the Fair Employment Practices Commission]. Johnson is the phoniest individual that ever came around." He did not seem to be savoring his day of triumph.

In another hotel Bill Scranton was fending off his own microphone-wielding mob. "I came here to address the delegates," he said at a gathering of the Missouri caucus. "Will everyone clear the room except the live press and the Missouri press?" Each reporter considering himself either alive or from Missouri, all stayed. They saw the delegation vote 22 to 1 for Goldwater.

In the Cow Palace parking lot, all was chaos. Fifteen hundred screaming ticket holders and credential wielders were outside. The fire department had barred the doors because the hall was already thousands past capacity. Soon police had seized thousands of forged tickets, all entitling the bearer to Seat 4 in Row G of Section A. Some had been bought from scalpers; some had unwittingly been distributed by congressmen. But the lion's share were held by Scranton ringers, some recruited outside Scranton's downtown headquarters, most from a table set up on Berkeley's Bancroft Way, just off campus, the traditional spot for student politicking (advocating partisan causes on university grounds was banned).

And, unable to stomach the thought of Republicans monopolizing the news, the President of the United States chose this particular afternoon to take a very public stroll in the park across from the White House hand in hand with his wife. "I think it would look very spontaneous!" his press secretary gushed.

It was the latest move in Johnson's permanent campaign. In May he defused one potential problem—(untrue) rumors that the FBI had the goods on his once having belonged to a Texas branch of the KKK—by buying off J. Edgar Hoover by exempting him from the federal mandatory retirement law; then he defused another by goosing the economy through raising the debt ceiling and pushing through a generous federal pay increase (he also ordered his budget director to study what tricks he might use to keep unemployment down through the fall). The DNC was on its way to registering four million new voters; a "Salute to President Johnson" at the D.C. Armory raised hundreds of thousands of dollars. Then a tragedy reenergized a certain primordial advantage of the incumbent: after the civil rights vote, Senator Ted Kennedy was flying back to Massachusetts, where a roomful of Democrats were waiting to renominate him by acclamation, when his plane plowed into an apple orchard,

killing the pilot and badly injuring Kennedy's back. Everyone knew that
Joseph Kennedy Jr., the oldest Kennedy brother, had perished in a plane crash,
and sister Kathleen; the near-miss moved the cult of Kennedy martyrdom once
more to the forefront of people's minds.

Campaign planning began in earnest on July 11, when White House
deputy Bill Moyers met with representatives of Doyle Dane Bernbach, the ad
agency JFK had chosen for his campaign a year earlier. The agency's ads for
Volkswagen's goofy Beetle—headed "Think Small"—caught Kennedy's eye;
it fit his wry, ironic take on the world, his instinctive grasp of the power of
images, his compulsion to be *new*. Fifties advertising was a dogmatic art, to the
point of pretending to be a science. Industry guru Rosser Reeves—Eisenhower's adman—preached the doctrine of the "Unique Selling Proposition"
(USP): a successful ad must stake a claim as to why the company's product is
different from the competition's, then pound it in like a jackhammer. ("You
can have a lovelier complexion in fourteen days with Palmolive soap, doctors
prove!") A rival theory, David Ogilvy's, held that ads should never be entertaining. DDB set all that on its ear. It was the best agency in the business, years
ahead of its time. And Moyers—a shy, thick-spectacled ex-seminarian who at
barely thirty was the youngest of LBJ's inner circle, perhaps the most ambitious, surely the most ruthless—gave it a green light to unleash its full creative
powers on behalf of the President.

Politics would not likely emerge from DDB's clutches unchanged. In May
the networks announced that for the first time they would sell thirty-second and
one-minute spots during, instead of just at the end of, regularly scheduled programming. Under ordinary circumstances this would hardly have made a difference: the preferred lengths for political ads in the past had been five, fifteen,
and thirty minutes. Doyle Dane Bernbach, which had never handled a political
account before, never bothered to consult other agencies' precedents. In *The
Making of the President 1960*, Teddy White lamented that TV might spell the
death of serious politics: to give a thoughtful response to serious questions, a
politician needed a good thirty seconds to ponder, but television allowed only
five seconds of silence at best. DDB found nothing to lament in the fact. They
were convinced you could learn everything you needed to *know* about a product, which in this case happened to be a human being, in half a minute—the
speed not of thought but of emotion.

Bill Bernbach intuitively grasped the same insights that were making a
Canadian literature professor named Marshall McLuhan the thinker of the
moment. "The medium is the message," went his gnomic injunction. A
medium did not just neutrally deliver some preexisting bundle of information
into the viewer's brain; instead, each medium—storytelling, print, radio, tele-

vision—conditioned users' very perception in its own distinct way. A TV set was a box plunked in the middle of a living room, competing for attention with a dozen different household distractions. DDB TV commercials exploited this fact by making use of searing, disjunctive images designed to cut through the clutter. Or, because television, that most mass of media, projected built-in anxieties about conformity, other DDB spots flattered viewers by assuring them they were much too smart to be *taken in* by advertising—thus the VW ads, which mocked advertising itself by bragging about how small the car was, how ugly, what little power it had. That "cute little bug" image moved a mountain: never again would Volkswagen be primarily associated in the public mind with Nazi Germany.

From the agency's eight hundred employees, Bernbach and account executive James Graham assembled forty dedicated Democrats thrilled at the prospect of savaging Barry Goldwater. They worked twelve-hour days in their own floor of DDB's building on West 43rd Street. Through the spring of 1964 they produced a wealth of civil rights pieces; by the time of the July 11 meeting with Moyers, these had been mothballed. Civil rights, they realized, was just as likely to lose votes as to win them. Now they were kicking around the idea of associating Goldwater in voters' minds, as press secretary George Reedy put it, with the image of "kids being born with two heads."

At the Cow Palace the doors were sealed before bad tickets drove out good. The senior senator from Illinois approached the podium to place his candidate's name into nomination. But he made the mistake of uttering Goldwater's name a few minutes into the speech—and then he had to wait impatiently for the *plink* of Thruston Morton's gavel to finally shut down the delirium that followed.

At 3:10 p.m., Dirksen's voice as smooth as his face was rumpled, he intoned, "I am proud to nominate my colleague from Arizona to be the Republican nominee for President of the United States."

The heavens opened.

Thousands of tiny squares of golden foil descended in a downpour, mingled with hundreds of golden balloons on their way up, both bathed in spots that made the air shimmer. A banner fluttered down from the rafters, so big that the legend "GOLDWATER FOR PRESIDENT—655" could be read amidst its billows; from one end of the floor to the other, innumerable phosphorus yellow and orange placards ("MAN OF COURAGE") flickered like candles, and banners and flags unfurled like flowering buds (in defiance of the fire marshal's orders, which permitted neither). Californians, as the host delegation right up in front and closest to the cameras, and as the second biggest delegation, taking up a tenth of the floor space, gyrated in fluorescent vests of the sort worn by road crews at night, their faces painted gold. The air became a stew of bass drums and bugles and tubas, air horns and whistles and cowbells, the rip-roaring of a Dixieland band, the pealing of an organ, none distinguishable from the other in the thickness of the din.

Twenty minutes passed—the agreed-upon time limit for candidate demonstrations. Thruston Morton rapped his desultory *plink*s, which were ignored by throngs marching about with state standards and homemade signs reading "LA LOUISIANA DIT ALLONS AVEC L'EAU D'OR," or "INDIANA'S FAVORITE SON-IN-LAW," or "WOJEICHOWICZ AND ALL OF BROOKLYN ARE FOR BARRY," or a cutout of the state of Virginia wearing thick black Goldwater glasses. Indians paraded in full regalia, Nevadans in red silk, Texans wearing longhorns. Outside, a minister, wearing a donkey costume, pleaded with a sergeant at arms for admittance: on cue, he was supposed to be pelted with fake snowballs. But he had been locked out. So everyone just pelted one another. Morton hollered that "real friends of Barry Goldwater" would let him "get nominated this week." The crowd would not be stilled. They continued to carry on for another twenty minutes. They still had plenty of energy left to cheer seconding speeches from the likes of Bill Knowland ("He, as every delegate in this convention, knows that the road to appeasement . . . is only surrender on the installment plan") and Clare Boothe Luce ("Do you believe these pollsters?" *"No!!!"*).

The demonstration process was repeated six more times for other official candidates. Rockefeller, Margaret Chase Smith, Scranton: only Scranton was able to stretch it to a full thirty-five minutes, marred, though, by Goldwaterites who popped a ten-foot "Scranton" helium balloon just as it was released; and by incidents like the one in which two teenage girls were intercepted on their way to the floor with the admonition "Get the hell out of here, you little sons of bitches" and the one in which a CORE member was led away by the police for attempting a lie-down in front of the rostrum; and by Scranton posters featuring a faded black-and-white picture on a plain white background that could hardly be seen on TV. Then followed the favorite sons, Romney, Judd, and Lodge. (Senator Hiram Fong, the first Asian-American to be nominated for President, forwent a demonstration because the only reason for his nomination was to boost his reelection fight back home in Hawaii.) Lodge, so disgusted with events he had booked a morning flight out of town, was not present to receive the honor.

The hoopla lasted seven hours before it came time for delegates to cast their votes. The roll of states was called. Alabama: all 20 for Goldwater. Alaska: 6 votes for Scranton ("for progressive Republicanism to carry on the great tradition of our great President, Dwight D. Eisenhower"), 2 for Smith, 1 for Judd, 1 for Fong. Arizona: 16 for Goldwater. Arkansas: 9 for Goldwater, 2 for Scranton, 1 for Rockefeller. California: 86 for Goldwater. Colorado: 15 for Goldwater and 3 for Scranton. It only took to the *S*'s to put him over 655—with South Carolina, the place where a speech five years earlier had ignited the whole Draft Goldwater hoopla in the first place, casting the deciding vote.

Scranton and his wife made their way down the ramp, and the crowd *oohed* as if acknowledging the courage of a daredevil. Scranton made the traditional gesture: moving to make his opponent's nomination unanimous. Goldwater was back in his hotel room, following the tradition for putative nominees. He was shown Gallup poll results that Lyndon Johnson was favored by 80 percent of the public. "Christ," he said, "we ought to be writing a speech telling them to go to hell and turn it down." Rockefeller called to concede the nomination. Goldwater refused the phone. "Hell, I don't want to talk to that son-of-a-bitch."

The last session of the convention would include Goldwater's acceptance speech and the nominating of a VP. The choice was congressman and RNC chair William E. Miller of New York. That Miller was Catholic and an Easterner suggested he was there to balance the ticket—but for the fact that, his boom having had been organized by a coalition of Draft Goldwater vets, the New York Conservative Party, and YAF officers, he was unlikely to impress any but already conservative voters in any event. His obscurity—he was better known for snipes at President Kennedy than for anything else, especially for citing guests dancing the twist in the ballroom as an example of immorality in the White House—inspired a ditty: "Here's a riddle, it's a killer / Who the hell is William Miller?" But Goldwater liked him because he was a party man, toiling loyally as Republican Congressional Campaign Committee chair before taking over the RNC, and he was a gut fighter. He said he chose Miller "because he drives Johnson nuts." (Johnson, for his part, was barely aware of Miller's existence.)

Miller was duly anointed by 1,305 votes to 3, and a turn by Art Linkletter at the podium was enjoyed by all. *Olé*s followed *Viva*s, followed by Thruston Morton's *plink*s. Goldwater's introducer stepped up to the microphone. Dick Nixon had originally been on the schedule to speak on Tuesday. He swapped it for this chance to style himself party healer. Clearly he was positioning himself for the nomination in 1968. All agreed it was a joke. "Do you think he could make it?" a reporter asked an old Nixon hand. "Hell, no!" came the answer. "I never knew what they meant when they used to say those things about Nixon. Now, I know." Teddy White called it a moment for nostalgia.

The fallen idol gave the crowd over to the man whose candidacy he had only a month earlier labeled a "tragedy." Now he called Goldwater "Mr. Republican": "And here is the man who, after the greatest campaign in history, will be Mr. President—Barry Goldwater." Then he sat back with the rest and waited for Goldwater to usher the year's rolling waters magnanimously beneath the bridge. He would be disappointed.

Goldwater, Baroody, Hess, and the rest of the brain trust had first met to discuss the acceptance speech the previous Saturday at Goldwater's personal quarters—the seventeenth floor, which was closed to mere political operatives. Hess brought in a draft that did exactly what an acceptance speech after a divisive primary season was supposed to do: proceed as if there had never been any divisions in the first place. But it was precisely their contempt for such bromides that united these men; that was why they were the ones whom Goldwater had working on the speech. The members of the brain trust declared the draft dead on arrival. Neither Bill Scranton nor Nelson Rockefeller deserved conciliation.

Goldwater gave the task of composing a new draft to Harry Jaffa. He was impressed with Jaffa's quick thinking in invoking Lincoln during the flap over the Scranton letter and by a memorandum Jaffa had written for the platform committee on the subject of political extremism. He had argued that extremism was a nonissue—a synonym, if anything, for "principle." *"Extremism":* Goldwater was sick of the word.

The brain trust fiddled over things for the next few days in Bill Baroody's room, Goldwater testing out each new phrase on his tongue, occasionally adding lines from his own pen. (One began "Yesterday it was Korea. Tonight it is Vietnam.") Another line came from Gene Pulliam, on "the growing menace of public safety, to life, limb and property, in homes, churches, playgrounds and places of business, particularly in our great cities." Goldwater had just then read in the papers of a girl in New York who had apparently been detained for using a knife against a rapist. He was sick of this sort of thing. He thought Pulliam's contribution was splendid.

There was a major row among his deputies over one line. Jaffa had lifted it directly from his memo; Goldwater had singled it out as his favorite. But half the group thought it was way too incendiary and would be utterly misunderstood. Then Goldwater put the argument to a stop by ordering the offending passage underlined twice. And that was that.

The final text, approved before dawn on Thursday as celebrant drunks straggled up and down Nob Hill, was guarded with the sort of care usually reserved for crown jewels. Two typists simultaneously prepared clean copies of the various sections. The copies were delivered upon completion to another set of workers, locked in a room cleared of telephones and sworn to silence for good measure, who set the TelePrompTer text. Reporters begged for an advance copy. Their requests were denied. Bill Miller, Clif White, and Dean Burch didn't get to see one either. The brain trusters knew that if those three read it, they would raise hell. For this wasn't a political speech. It was a cultural call to arms.

After Nixon's introduction Goldwater strode down the ramp with his family and shook Nixon's hand. The band struck up "The Battle Hymn of the Republic." Red, white, and blue balloons fell, rat-tat-tatting jarringly as they were popped with cigarettes. Young Scrantonites bore a "STAY IN THE MAIN- STREAM" banner across the floor. The gavel banged. Goldwater gripped the podium. Deliberately, confidently, he began.

"Our people have followed false prophets," he said in a harsh, compressed tone. "We must and we shall return to proven ways—not because they are old, but because they are true." Republicans must become "freedom's missionaries in a doubting world." For there was "violence in our streets, corruption in our highest offices, aimlessness among our youth, anxiety among our elders, and there is a virtual despair among the many who look beyond material success for the inner meaning of their lives."

Words like "honesty," "destiny," and "vision" were repeated, "free," "freedom," and "liberty" some forty times. Every paragraph, sometimes every sentence, brought roars from the faithful—none more than when Goldwater declared that the nation had been founded upon the "acceptance of God as the author of freedom."

The air thickened with expectation; he was drawing to a climax. Now texts were finally distributed to reporters. "And let our Republicanism, so focused and so dedicated, not be made fuzzy and futile by unthinking and stupid labels," he said, concentrating his face. "Those who do not care for our cause we do not expect to enter our ranks in any case."

Then came the passage he had ordered double-underscored on his reading copy and the copies for the press. *"I would remind you that extremism in the defense of liberty—is—no—vice!"*

He had to wait forty-one seconds before he could continue. He pursed his lips, glanced solemnly down at the text:

"And let me remind you also—that moderation in the pursuit of justice is no virtue!"

The roar from the galleries could be heard inside the Goldwater trailer— where White was so disgusted with what he could see only as a political disas- ter that he switched off his television monitor in rage. Ken Keating bolted from the convention hall. (His later claim that he only wanted to beat the traffic was belied by the fact that he chose to exit straight up the center aisle.) Scranton glowered. A standing ovation began. Richard Nixon, making a snap political judgment, reached over to keep wife Pat in her seat. He was sick to his stomach. Frenzied delegates took hold of the struts holding up ABC's broadcast booth and shook them furiously. For five minutes Howard K. Smith endured an earthquake, floorboards creaking, objects sliding across his desk. Wirt Yerger walked up to George Romney and said, "Governor, I hope we can all unite behind Goldwater and everything." He got back nothing but a bitter stare.

What Goldwater had said hardly differed in tone from President Kennedy's vaunted inaugural address: "We shall pay any price, bear any burden, meet any hardship, support any friend, oppose any foe, to assure the survival and the success of liberty." Time and circumstance had shifted the mood. Now such words seemed a provocation to insurrection. "If a party so committed were to gain public office in this country," declared the *Washington Post*, "there would be nothing left for us to do but pray." "To extol extremism—whether 'in defense of liberty' or in 'pursuit of justice'—is dangerous, irresponsible, and frightening," read a statement released by Rockefeller. "Any sanction of lawlessness, of the vigilantes, and the unruly mob can only be deplored. The extremism of the Communists, of the Ku Klux Klan, and of the John Birch Society—like that of most terrorists—has always been claimed by such groups to be in the defense of liberty. . . . Coming as it did from the new leader of a great American political party in his first public utterance, it raises the gravest of questions in the minds and hearts and souls of Republicans in every corner of our party." Eisenhower labeled the speech an offense to "the whole American system"—although Eisenhower himself was not spared a drubbing: *Time* charged him with minting the "switchblade issue" for political expediency, because his lines on crime made sense "only if considered in conjunction with the 'white backlash.' " With all the support Goldwater "could gain from latent white resentment of militant Negro claims," worried another newspaper, who was to say that he wouldn't foment "Goldwater riots" himself?

The race to calumniate Barry Goldwater was on. To the *New York Times*'s editorialists, Goldwater had reduced "a once great party to the status of an ugly, angry, frustrated faction." Columnist C. L. Sulzberger said that if Goldwater were elected "there may not be a day after tomorrow." Governor Edmund Brown of California said, "The stench of fascism is in the air." Asked how he would run his local campaigns with Goldwater heading up the ticket, a Chicago Republican leader replied, "I'll jump off that bridge when I come to it." Senator William Fulbright stung his colleague on the Senate floor in a series of speeches calling Goldwaterism "the closest thing in American politics to an equivalent of Russian Stalinism."

NATO countries hastened to assure Americans that they regarded Goldwater's solicitude toward them with nothing but dismay. The Tory *Daily Telegraph* spied "dark eddies in American life," and Austria's *Neues Österreich* observed "shivers" sent "down the back of humanity." *Time* interviewed a Munich banker who said, "If we give you four or five years, you'll start putting on brown shirts." Goldwater's only foreign support came from South Africans, Spanish monarchists, and German neofascists—which only made sense, according to a *Washington Star* editorial perfectly encapsulating the mood: "The greatest danger may be that this reactionary takeover of the Republican machinery will induce a radical new alignment of the parties, splitting them once and for all into organizations of the right and the left." American parties traditionally united "a broad national foundation because their positions overlap widely." Were they to realign, America's "stability, which is truly one of the wonders of the political world," would crumble. For

> the nation is not likely to remain neatly divided along a conservative-liberal line—that is not man's political nature.
>
> Since the two major parties will no longer cover varying shades of opinion, various splinter parties must arise to give them expression. Our stable two-party structure thus eventually may be supplanted by the highly volatile multiple-party setup all too familiar in Europe. . . .
>
> Whether such a requirement would prove compatible with our constitutional system is a nice question.

Republicans decamped from San Francisco; the city's Democratic headquarters reported a shortage of LBJ buttons. It appeared Scrantonites were grabbing them on their way out of town.

The morning after the apotheosis of his career, Clif White tied on his bow tie at 8:15, although he had poured victory libations down his throat until dawn. He had work to do. There was a presidential campaign to organize. "White's reward if Goldwater is nominated will be the chairmanship of the GOP National Committee," *Time* had reported, only repeating what had become by then a commonplace.

Later that day, a member of the Republican finance committee buttonholed White with a tactical question: "Is this thing on Dean Burch a secret or can we let it out?"

"I don't know what you're talking about."

"Burch is the senator's choice for national chairman."

White went numb. It was inconceivable. Dean Burch—the Arizonan who wore the black ties—was only thirty-six. His expertise was in liability law. Indeed, when his name had been brought up at an earlier meeting to discuss the issue, his fellow Arizona Mafioso Dick Kleindienst said that Burch, though "one of my dearest and closest friends," just didn't have the national stature for the job. His name had not come up in press speculation. White wondered if the finance committee member had been misinformed.

White saw from the afternoon papers that the man had not. Goldwater had never even considered a non-Arizonan. Like a man on his deathbed, he wanted to be surrounded only by friends. Goldwater had never got over his lingering distrust of Clif White—he hadn't even learned to spell his name—and hadn't even made the time to kick White out of the campaign in person. For White it was 1951 again; he was watching the new Young Republican chairman harvest accolades on television, uttering not a word of recognition for the man who had manufactured his victory. He had rented the Fairmont Hotel's stunning Crystal Room for a victory celebration with the boys who had started it all—his original Draft Goldwater group. Goldwater had summarily dismissed the finance committee White had built, which raised the $3.5 million that had brought the senator to this pass. Its members were given a parting gift—wristwatches. Only one of White's seven regional directors received an invitation to stay on. The other six didn't even get watches. The party at the Fairmont went on, somberly; the victory tasted like ashes.

White had booked a Hawaiian vacation for after the convention, as a present to his long-suffering wife, Bunny, who had stood patiently behind him on the promise that great things were to come. But he was so depressed he couldn't even pack his suitcase. He could barely drag himself to the plane. Eighteen years in politics: it hardly seemed worth it anymore.

That very day the long hot summer began.

It started on East 76th Street in Manhattan, outside a high school that was holding voluntary summer remedial classes. The neighborhood was white. Most of the students were black. As they did every morning before school, they loitered on the steps of a building across the street, to the annoyance of its Irish superintendent, who sprayed them with a garden hose, saying, "I'll wash the black out of you." The kids pelted him with rocks and bottles. One of them, Jimmy Powell, followed the superintendent into the building's vestibule. A police lieutenant, off duty and in street clothes, was in a television shop next door. Accounts differed as to whether Jimmy Powell pulled a switchblade when the cop advanced to apprehend him. The cop fired three shots; Jimmy

Powell died where he stood. A crowd of angry students gathered. Police arrived. A girl cried, "Come on, shoot another nigger!" A policeman was knocked down by a flying bottle. Seventy-five steel-helmeted reinforcements arrived.

Over the next two days CORE picketed the site, then marched to a nearby station house. A story was crystallizing, and it bore little of the ambiguity that marked the eyewitness accounts. "We got a civil rights bill and along with the bill we got Barry Goldwater and a dead black boy," cried one of the soapbox-ers. "This shooting of James Powell was a murder."

By the time the story filtered fifty blocks north, no ambiguity was left. It was 92 degrees outside, closer to 100 inside Harlem's heat-soaked brick tene-ments. A crowd gathered at the Twenty-eighth Precinct, chanting about police brutality. A car bearing a white couple drove up Lenox Avenue; its headlight was smashed. Tenement roofs began raining bricks—then Molotov cocktails—at the massing police officers. White reporters arriving on the scene were socked with what one of them called "the pet Negro obscenity, an accusation of incest which turns middle-class stomachs." Fire alarms were pulled, trash cans set aflame. Store owners began pulling down the metal grates that guarded their windows at night. Looting began, and arson (one grocer put out a fire in his store with his stock of grapefruit juice). Soon a riot was raging at a scale unseen anywhere in the country since the 1940s. And in the 1940s, riots weren't tele-vised.

Police were ordered to fire into the air. The locals presumed the police were firing at them. A black witness called the *Herald Tribune*: "That Goldwa-ter stuff has started! They're shooting at people up here in Harlem!" Bayard Rustin, the civil rights leader who organized the March on Washington a year earlier, was shown on television imploring his neighbors about how little there was to gain by burning up their own neighborhood. The cameras also captured the mass surrounding him screaming that Rustin was an Uncle Tom.

The rioting continued a second night. On the third night it spread to Brook-lyn—then, through August, to three cities in New Jersey, to the Chicago suburb of Dixmoor (where armed blacks battled state troopers in the streets), to Philadelphia and Rochester (where 5 rioters died and 750 were arrested). These demonstrations were like ellipses, trailing off to mark the impending end of managerial liberalism's core vision: roll up your sleeves, dare to dream, pass a law, solve a problem. (Almost too poetically, another grand vision came a cropper in those same weeks: "Climate control is a dream that, misapplied, could lead to disaster," wrote the Reclamation Bureau project manager in clos-ing out the government's massive, confident research efforts to master the very heavens themselves.)

Goldwater's name affixed itself to events. In an op-ed piece that ran in the *Herald Tribune* while the fires were still burning, black psychologist and civil rights leader Kenneth Clark quoted Goldwater's acceptance speech—Pulliam's line about "the growing menace of public safety, to life, limb and property . . . in our great cities"—and concluded, "This type of cynical political opportunism can only add to the explosiveness of an already difficult and complex social problem. It will incite the passions and hatreds of already unstable and prejudiced citizens and police officers." Another leader, A. Philip Randolph, implored blacks to honor the White House–brokered moratorium on demonstrations, lest militancy "elect Senator Goldwater . . . the greatest disaster to befall Negroes since slavery." In the middle of it all the *New York Times Book Review* ran a piece by a member of the editorial board on Steve Shadegg's *How to Win an Election*, quoting Shadegg on Mao Tse-tung's "valuable book on the tactics of infiltration." Here was a man at the center of Goldwater's political rise, exhibiting "sublime indifference to all considerations of justice and fair play." Who knew what else Goldwater was capable of? A *Chicago Sun Times* columnist wrote: "There is considerable evidence to show that every time there is violence by Negroes, Goldwater gains supporters."

The accusation worried Barry Goldwater most of all. Rumors, from sources that Karl Hess found reliable enough to credit, said Goldwater operatives *were* musing over how they might stoke further conflagrations to swing the election. The senator himself, still enamored of the idea that he could win black voters' loyalty because of his efforts against discrimination in Arizona, was unhinged by the very thought. He met privately with reporters and said that if anyone sowed racial violence on his behalf he would withdraw from the race—even if it was the day before the election.

The President was now drowning in a flood of wires such as "I'm afraid to leave my house. I fear the Negro revolution will reach Queens." *The New Republic*'s TRB columnist had called white resentment 1964's political "X-Factor." Walter Lippmann had coined the term "Goldwater Democrats." Backlash had become Lyndon Johnson's new obsession. When Ollie Quayle prepared a fifty-five-page technical report on the blue-collar Wallace vote in Wisconsin and Indiana, Johnson devoured it in one night. When Wallace withdrew his candidacy on July 19—because, he said, the Republicans had passed a segregationist platform—Goldwater was genuinely surprised. Johnson assumed a deal had been struck: withdrawal in exchange for a weak civil rights plank. The President sought out a loyal Southern senator "to stand on his hind legs" and make the charge publicly.

In a press conference during a refueling stop on Goldwater's way back to Washington, with Harlem still smoldering, a reporter asked the candidate if he would consider a joint appeal with Johnson to ease the tensions. He said he would, and right then and there he proposed a meeting. When word of the proposed joint appeal reached the White House, Johnson's aides smelled a hustle. It was a cover, explained one strategist—Goldwater's "attempt to make a public display of his disassociation from violence for which his candidacy and supporters have, in part, been responsible."

The White House began plotting countermoves. Johnson told George Reedy to "assure everybody that we're not going to do anything to incite anybody," but "give the impression that he is, without saying so." Johnson was worried that just by meeting with Goldwater he would be dignifying him, giving him protection against charges of extremism. RFK, practically stammering, said, "Civil rights is something around our neck."

But the invitation had been public. Johnson couldn't *refuse* to see Goldwater. The White House went forward on eggshells. Fearing that Goldwater would ambush them by insisting on a conclave that very day, on a battleground of his choosing, they quickly set a date, July 24, and a place, the Oval Office. A voluminous intelligence file was prepared. The President was drilled on it over and over, schooled in the questions Goldwater would use to trap him into statements to exploit on the campaign trail. Johnson would launch a preemptive strike at the presidential press conference before the meeting by inviting the senator to join him in "rebuffing and rebuking bigots."

The day arrived. An exquisitely labored statement of the President's position sat on his desk for reference. Johnson ushered his guest into the Oval Office. There followed an awkward interval. The President was waiting for Goldwater to start, because Goldwater had called the meeting. When he didn't, Johnson uttered some banalities about how he would do nothing in the months to come that might contribute to violence in the streets. Goldwater said that was fine. Johnson lurched deskward and read his statement aloud. Goldwater thought that was fine, too, and asked for a copy. Another pause. Goldwater's face lit up like a child discussing a toy, and he said he would love to take a crack at flying the new A-11 that was in development. Johnson (hiding his incredulity) said it wouldn't be ready for a year—at which time, he joked, Goldwater might be the one issuing the orders. Chuckles were exchanged. Backs were slapped. Sixteen minutes had elapsed. The two emerged together to release a bland joint statement. Johnson's staff was stunned. "What a confrontation," someone said. "Wish we could have one like that with de Gaulle!"

Within two weeks, the Administration was wracked by another crisis. This one, though, they were better prepared for.

Op Plan 34-A had rolled on through spring to no apparent military effect.

Dean Acheson cornered a new Johnson aide to tell him, "Things are going to hell in a hack in Vietnam, and if the President does not do something that relates to getting the support of Congress in a Formosa-type resolution"—the blanket authority Eisenhower won from Congress to use military force if needed to protect Taiwan without declaring war—"it's going to be too late, and we'll go into this orgasm of a campaign period in which things will just have to stall." Johnson's men, reasoning they had to begin countering criticisms that Johnson was holding back in Vietnam because of the upcoming election, decided that proceeding with Acheson's suggestion wasn't such a bad idea. On May 22, with their boss away delivering a commencement address at the University of Michigan, they began to work on a draft.

When the first U.S. reconnaissance planes were downed during the Cleveland governors' conference in early June, William Bundy and Dean Rusk advised the President that they should begin polishing up the draft. Senate leader Mike Mansfield—coincidentally, for he knew nothing of any potential congressional resolution—gave similar advice: "If we're gonna stay in there, we're gonna have to educate the people, Mr. President." Mr. President's mind being on poll numbers showing that 63 percent of Americans were paying no attention to Vietnam, his answer to both was that he had no interest in making Vietnam an issue as the campaign approached, especially now with civil rights on the cusp of passage. But he was flexible. When GOP congressmen began chorusing against a "no-win" Vietnam policy in late June, Johnson obligingly dispatched hundreds more "military advisors." He balanced that move by coining an artful new phrase for public consumption: "We seek no wider war." The coinage left him euphoric.

When the senator from Arizona's nomination became imminent, Bill Moyers urged his boss to talk tough about Vietnam on TV to "defuse a Goldwater bomb before he ever gets the chance to throw it." Once more, Johnson demurred. As the rubble was being cleared in the streets of Harlem, he ordered secret maneuvers in the Gulf of Tonkin stepped up. The CIA assured him that would be enough to hold the line until after the election was over. The idea that North Vietnamese PT boats might challenge U.S. warships seemed too incredible to consider. Although Communist insurgents thought otherwise. They embraced the heightened American presence in the Gulf as a chance to signal their determination to fight the imperialists to the death.

On August 2, three PT boats advanced on the destroyer *Maddox*. Her captain retreated languidly out to sea. He was startled to see the scrappy little boats scooting out after him—then, twenty-five miles farther out, opening fire. Jets from a nearby aircraft carrier and the *Maddox*'s 5-inch guns made short work of these fleas, the *Maddox* emerging none the worse for the wear. It was around three in the afternoon local time, August 2—3 a.m., August 1, in Washington—when the crisis report was brought to the President's bedside. He saw not much in the incident, sending Hanoi a perfunctory diplomatic note warning that "grave consequences would inevitably result from any further unprovoked offensive military action" and ordering a second carrier and destroyer to the area to put such foolish displays of enemy bravado to a stop. The clash certainly wasn't enough to distract him from more important matters. "Raymond Guest wants to contribute to you but he still wants to be ambassador to Ireland," Florida senator George Smathers told him later in the morning. Johnson laughed and asked how much Guest was willing to pay. "Well, he'll contribute fifty. Maybe you can get more." LBJ: "He oughta give a hun'red thousand, as much as that fella's worth." Smathers: "Well, if he can get it, I can get a hundred thousand."

There followed a misunderstanding worthy of *Strangelove*. What Johnson thought was a stalling maneuver his field commanders thought was an answer to their long-stated recommendation to turn the Vietnam affair into a real fight. Admirals sent their ships—two carriers and two destroyers, sailing on instruments in the middle of a vicious storm—into the Gulf with orders to regard any vessel they encountered "as belligerents from first detection." Suspicious bleeps showed up on the *Maddox*'s sonar—what appeared to be twenty-two torpedoes heading straight at them. At 9 p.m. the sailors set their guns ablazing, then flashed news of a North Vietnamese attack to Washington.

Forty-five minutes later the President was on the phone with an old Texas pal, former Eisenhower treasury secretary Robert Anderson. Anderson was in charge of one of Johnson's pet campaign projects—swaying Republican tycoons into the Johnson column. Presuming that the President was on the phone to talk about campaign matters, Anderson rattled off the names of the esteemed executives he was lining up—including, extraordinarily, the CEO of Borg-Warner, the auto-parts empire that once belonged to Peggy Goldwater's family. Anderson brought up the name of a businessman he knew—the mobbed-up proprietor of a scandal sheet called the *National Enquirer*—who wanted to donate $250,000 to Johnson's favorite charity, the Sam Rayburn Foundation, and kick in a few thousand more to the campaign. The wealthy contributor was currently being inconvenienced by a Justice Department investigation of a merger in which he had an interest, Anderson explained. Johnson promised to make a few calls and see what he could do to help him out.

Then the President abruptly changed the subject. He told his friend about Op Plan 34-A and the retaliation it had brought on. "Make it look like a very firm stand," was Anderson's advice. "You're gonna be running against a man who's a wild man," who would surely say that if it were up to him, he "would have knocked 'em off the moon."

Johnson rang Bob McNamara. He explained that in their briefing of congressional leaders later in the day they had to "leave an impression . . . that we're gonna be firm as hell"—lest Goldwater "[raise] hell about how he's gonna blow 'em off the moon."

More storms. Three hours later the guns fell silent and the *Maddox*'s captain wired warning that what they thought were enemy attacks might well have been sonar anomalies created by freak weather effects. Johnson's meeting with congressional leaders was fast approaching. So were deadlines for the morning papers. The President was in no mood for ambiguity. "Some of our boys are floating in the water," he lied to the sixteen congressional leaders who had filed into the Cabinet Room.

The Gulf of Tonkin Resolution was approved within the week with only two dissenting votes. Hubert Humphrey helped tip the scales by conjuring up visions of General Walker and Curtis LeMay. "There are people in the Pentagon," he said, "who think we ought to send three hundred thousand troops over there." None of the congressmen were aware of Op Plan 34-A; they thought they were voting to avenge a vicious, unprovoked attack. The resolution was the sole congressional authorization for a decade of undeclared war in Vietnam.

The strikes were launched. Speechwriters prepared an address to the nation. Somewhat reluctantly, LBJ tried to reach Barry Goldwater, who was on a boat somewhere off Newport Beach, where he was vacationing instead of in Germany. Goldwater called back from the dock, his patriotic instincts kicking in, pleased that Johnson was finally doing what he had hoped for—turning the problem over to the military. He assured his President of his total support: "We're all Americans and Americans stick together." Johnson sighed with relief.

Still, Johnson found the political risk in the speech excruciating. "We don't *have* to make it, do we?" he pleaded with McNamara, who assured him that they did. The President waited until strikes were under way to speak. "We Americans know, although others appear to forget"—a reference to Goldwater—"the risk of spreading conflict. We seek no wider war."

The Gulf of Tonkin affair, he now understood, was a blessing in disguise. With the patriotic Goldwater uneager to challenge him on Vietnam, it would only become a campaign issue if Johnson made it one—on his own terms.

Racial politics was not nearly so amenable to control. Like Richard Nixon in 1960, Johnson was busy writing the script for his own coronation—the Demo-

California

LAST CHANCE POLITICAL INN

NEUTRAL NIXON'S UNDERTAKING PARLOR

"As A Lawyer, I'd Be Glad To Help You Make Out A Will"

Just in case: I hereby bequeath my convention delegates to my dear friend, Dick Nixon

GOLDWATER CANDIDACY

"Pardon Me, Did You Knock?"

VOTERS

NIXON

Richard Nixon's chances of winning the nomination were taken very seriously—though the behind-the-scenes conniving of a candidate many considered a pathetic has-been left some, including *The Washington Post*'s cartoonist Herblock, disgusted.

George Wallace's anti–civil rights run in three Democratic primaries thrilled many working-class white voters (above), while others were less than openly supportive (below). Everyone except Wallace was stunned by the Alabaman's relative success in the three races, and the word "backlash" soon dominated coverage of the presidential race.

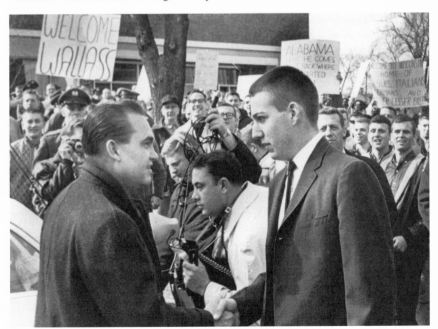

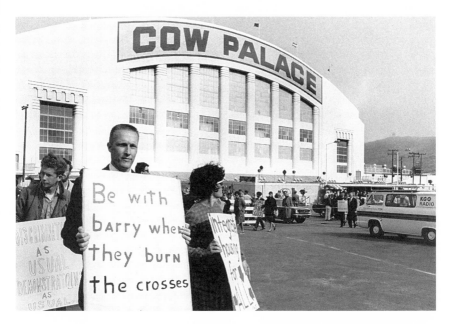

Goldwater beat William Scranton in San Francisco at a Republican National Convention that left many television viewers with enduring images of a party that seemed to have been captured by a violent fringe—an image bolstered by the civil rights protesters who flooded the city (above and bottom left). In Atlantic City, at the Democratic Convention, Lyndon Johnson was brought to the verge of withdrawing by his fears that the dispute between Fannie Lou Hamer's Mississippi Freedom Democratic Party and Mississippi's racist regular Democrats—who boycotted the convention (bottom right) and favored Barry Goldwater—portended the nation's cracking in two.

For a
Strong America
in a
World at Peace

vote for
LYNDON B. JOHNSON
and
HUBERT H. HUMPHREY

UNION WOMEN UNITED
for JOHNSON and HUMPHREY

100 MILLION LIVES
IN ONE HOUR

WHICH SHALL IT BE?

"We Americans know—although others appear to forget—the risk of spreading conflict. We still seek no wider war."
—Pres. Lyndon B. Johnson
August 4, 1964

"That word 'brinkmanship' is a great word." — Sen. Barry Goldwater
March 5, 1964

VOTE FOR JOHNSON/ HUMPHREY ON NOV. 3rd

CURES FOR
WHAT AILS
AMERICA

AU H₂O

Dr. B.M. GOLDWATER'S
ALL PURPOSE
DEFOLIATION TONIC
THE NON-TAXIC, MAGIC
COLD WAR REMEDY

A BALM FOR BOILS, BURNS, BRUISES,
BIGOTS, BIRCHERS & BUCKLEYS

Democratic campaign literature trumpeted Johnson as the candidate of peace, even though the White House had already made plans to begin a bombing campaign in North Vietnam. LBJ's supporters published literature that depicted Goldwater as, for instance, a snake oil salesman (left). Goldwater's official campaign published dry pamphlets excerpting dry Goldwater speeches, but his freelance supporters produced such pieces as a fan depicting the Republican elephant crushing the Democratic donkey to death (opposite, top).

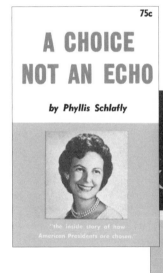

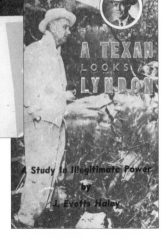

The Goldwater campaign gave birth to enormous coordinated networks of conservative activists outside official Republican Party channels. They distributed seventeen million copies of books by Phyllis Schlafly, John A. Stormer, and J. Evetts Haley, often for free.

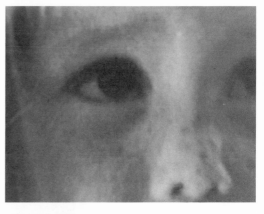

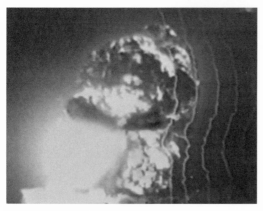

The 1964 presidential campaign came to be dominated by images of anxiety and insecurity in a fast-changing world. This page: Lyndon Johnson's advertising agency, years ahead of its competitors in media sophistication, sought to frighten viewers with the famous "Daisy" commercial, which never mentioned Barry Goldwater by name. Opposite page: Lyndon Johnson was soon being heralded, just as he desired, as a healer of all division. Goldwater's main campaign organization produced timid (and racially neutral) commercials that attempted, unsuccessfully, to do the same thing for the Republicans. More successful were the pamphlets put out by a campaign satellite run by F. Clifton White of Citizens for Goldwater-Miller, which exploited fears of racial violence in a manner similar to the way the Johnson campaign utilized fears of nuclear war, and homemade yard signs of supporters.

TO HELL WITH URBAN RENEWAL!
IT IS LEGALIZED THEFT OF PRIVATE PROPERTY
WE SHALL DEFEND OUR HOMES WITH OUR LIVES

GOLDWATER FOR PRESIDENT

It was Ronald Reagan who inherited the energies left over from the campaign with a last-minute televised campaign speech for Goldwater that commentators called "the most successful national political debut since William Jennings Bryan electrified the 1896 Democratic Convention with the 'Cross of Gold' speech." Conservatives had finally found a leader who could take them to the White House.

cratic National Convention, which was to open on August 24. And, like Nixon's, the coronation threatened to become a war. The problem wasn't Barry Goldwater. It was a Mississippi farmhand named Fannie Lou Hamer and her Mississippi Freedom Democratic Party.

Hamer had emerged as a natural leader of the courageous band of civil rights activists who planned to travel to Atlantic City to issue a credentials challenge to the regular—Goldwaterite, segregationist—Mississippi delegation. Seat the MFDP and lose the South, seat the regular Democrats and lose loyalty in the North: the dilemma cut to Lyndon Johnson's paranoid core—for surely if he showed any weakness in the face of the dilemma, that would be RFK's chance to humiliate him. On July 31 Johnson instructed an aide to relay one of an endless gauntlet of sadistic tests of loyalty to his presumptive vice-presidential choice, Hubert Humphrey: "Put a stop to this hell-raising so we don't throw out fifteen states." Two weeks later the President reached Walter Reuther. He listed the governors who were abandoning him, a Shakespearean tragic hero reciting his own dénouement: "Now today Louisiana takes her name off the ballot. Now Arkansas is on his way down to New Orleans to meet with Alabama and Mississippi and Louisiana, and they'll wind up with some serious problems. And this thing is just like a prairie fire. It spreads, and spreads fast."

"This thing's coming to pieces," Johnson moaned. "We're gonna have as much trouble as they had in San Francisco unless some of you can, can—"

He paused and sized up Reuther. It was the quintessence of his method: pinpoint his interlocutor's worst fear, then describe it coming true unless he did his President's bidding. Reuther's, Johnson realized, was the fear that his bitterest foe—they had hated each other since 1955—would ride the backlash to become a blue-collar beau ideal. "They all frighten me half to death what they say he's got in the UAW and the Steelworkers," Johnson whispered conspiratorially (his reference was to what the Steelworkers' David McDonald had told him at a recent White House dinner about a private poll of the membership showing Goldwater leading). His prey cornered, LBJ moved in for the kill. The MFDP's strategist was Joe Rauh, a bow-tied, bespectacled liberal D.C. lawyer. He was also chief counsel to Walter Reuther's United Auto Workers. "Now, Joe's been on television two or three times. . . ."

The President didn't have to say the rest. The order was plain: Deliver an ultimatum to Rauh to cease and desist or lose his practice's most lucrative client.

Like every Democratic Convention since 1940, the 1964 event was choreographed by Atlanta broadcast executive Leonard Reinsch. Reinsch knew TV. The convention would field only one session a day, at 8:30 p.m.—typically little beyond three speakers, a half-hour film, and entertainment by the likes of Peter, Paul and Mary. (The Republican Convention had featured afternoon and evening sessions, endless parliamentary tedium, and upwards of a dozen speakers a day; at one point, an interminable stretch of airtime was taken up with calling Congressman Halleck to the podium—he was bending his elbow at a bar—so he could introduce General Eisenhower.) Reinsch was desperate to keep the Democratic Convention entertaining; he was desperate to keep tension off the air. Atlantic City had been picked over Miami in the summer of 1963 out of fear of the civil rights rumblings in the South. That was well before this new terror. Blacks had rioted within the past two weeks in nearby Elizabeth and Paterson—about 90 miles away, like Cuba. Civil rights leaders had promised pickets "so long and black that they would think it was midnight in midday"—enough "to block every entrance into the convention hall."

The FBI sent a complement of twenty-seven agents, commanded by Deke DeLoach, the Bureau's second-in-command, answering to the President's top two men, Walter Jenkins and Bill Moyers (the former seminarian's code name was "Bishop"). But with six thousand media personnel on the prowl, and since the networks had invested millions to transport their elaborate temporary studios clear across the country to Atlantic City (CBS judging the stakes so high that the network replaced an incensed Walter Cronkite as commentator, since he had put people to sleep in San Francisco), it was unlikely that anything could keep tension off the air. The Beatles had just began the last leg of their American tour, at the Cow Palace. That was symbolic. Nineteen sixty-four was the year of the screaming crowd.

The Republicans erected a gargantuan eighty-foot Goldwater billboard on the boardwalk directly across from Atlantic City's Convention Hall. It featured the campaign's new slogan—"In Your Heart You Know He's Right." (Soon a placard was placed above it, reading "YES, EXTREME RIGHT." The sign painter had been hired by FCC chair Newton Minow, the scold best known for attempting to elevate the taste level of television by decrying it as "a vast wasteland.") The words sounded an abiding Goldwater theme. After Goldwater had said back in January that the reason most people were on relief was because they were stupid or lazy, he had explained on the *Today* show that when he asked those who criticized him if they thought what he said was *right*, they invariably responded, "Oh, yes, you're right, but you shouldn't say it." In the *Der Spiegel* interview, he said that if the civil rights vote had been taken in the Senate with the doors locked and the lights off, it wouldn't have gotten even twenty-five senators' support. The billboard seemed a sly reminder of the secretness of the secret ballot: behind that curtain, no one needed to know you thought the blacks were getting out of hand, too.

The Sunday before the convention, the White House released the latest in a stream of Panglossian press releases: The President's economy drive had eliminated 624 unnecessary government publications for a savings of $2.8 million annually; 11 percent of Americans had owned air conditioners in 1960 but now air conditioners were owned by 26 percent, and during the same period TV ownership had grown from 86 percent to 91 percent. It couldn't camouflage the bad news. He had invited the thirty-four Democratic governors to the White House. Louisiana, Arkansas, Mississippi, and Alabama had stood him up. As the thirty met, Fannie Lou Hamer stepped up before the platform committee—and the television cameras—and slowly, calmly, told the story of the beatings she had suffered for trying to exercise the franchise a year before. There were two Negro prisoners in the cell with her, she was explaining eight minutes into her testimony. "The policeman ordered the first Negro to take the blackjack—"

At which point the broadcast broke away. There was word of breaking news at the White House, presumably the long-awaited announcement of Johnson's vice-presidential choice. Instead of Mrs. Hamer's gut-wrenching exhortation, the nation heard Governor Connally of Texas telling reporters what a delightful meeting he and his fellow governors had just enjoyed. But Johnson's gambit backfired. Deprived of Mrs. Hamer's testimony in the afternoon, a much larger audience watched it on newscasts in the evening, full to its aching conclusion: "If the Freedom Democratic Party is not seated," she pronounced, "I question America."

There followed over the next few days a bramble of proposals and counterproposals regarding the MFDP's participation at the convention, bullying and cajoling, moral witnessing, wheeling and dealing; and since there was certainly nothing else at Lyndon Johnson's coronation worth paying attention to, the story was followed on TV. Which was enough to send the President, pacing the White House lawn, into the worst funk of his life. Perhaps he knew something about Fannie Hamer's story. The Justice Department had brought a strong case against Mrs. Hamer's tormentors in 1963. They were acquitted by a local jury in a courtroom full of Confederate flags. The reason they were being tried by a local jury was because Johnson had brokered a compromise to get the Civil Rights Acts of 1957 and 1960 past Southern obstructionists: the Justice Department could sue, but federal courts could not preside.

Long since then Johnson had converted to a civil rights crusade more fervent than any President's since Lincoln. And what had that brought? Race riots, two weeks after the Civil Rights Act was signed. What more could he do? "If you give 'em jobs and education, you stop all of it," he told Hubert Humphrey, sounding as if he were trying to convince himself. The night Hamer came on TV, Johnson drafted a statement of withdrawal: "The times require leadership about which there is no doubt and a voice that men of all parties and men of all sections and men of all color can and will follow. I have learned after trying very hard that I am not that voice, or that leader. Therefore I shall carry forward with your help until the new President is sworn in next January, and then I will go back home as I've wanted to since the day I took this job." His wife, and the thought of Barry Goldwater in the White House, convinced him to tear it up.

A compromise was finally micromanaged from the White House: the regular delegation would be seated representing Mississippi; the MFDP would be granted two "at-large" seats; future segregated delegations would be banned. "We didn't come all the way up here for no two seats!" cried Mrs. Hamer. Most of the regular Mississippi delegation boycotted rather than taking theirs. Later it would become clear that the arrangement was made at the expense of driving the flower of liberal youth from the Democratic Party; Fannie Lou Hamer was not the only civil rights activist to question America. Many were beginning to question the integrationist, nonviolent ideal altogether. "This proves the liberal Democrats are just as racist as Goldwater," cried Stokely Carmichael, leader of the Student Nonviolent Coordinating Committee.

Johnson, oblivious, blew into town in jubilant spirits to accept his crown at a united convention. But there was one more piece of business to take care of first: the evening's film, a soft-focus tribute to President Kennedy called *A Thousand Days*. Johnson had arranged to schedule it *after* the voting for the nomination. Bobby Kennedy would introduce the movie. Even more than to the MFDP activists, Johnson's FBI detail attended to his paranoid obsession that RFK was planning to stampede the convention for a Kennedy restoration. (In a clinical sense, Johnson's paranoia and bipolar tendencies bespoke far worse mental health than Goldwater's.)

RFK's introduction ended up confirming LBJ's fear. "When I think of President Kennedy, I think of what Shakespeare said . . .

> *"When he shall die*
> *Take him and cut him out in little stars*
> *And he will make the face of heaven so fine*
> *That all the world will be in love with night,*
> *And pay no worship to the garish sun."*

The garish sun. It was hard not to see the reference to a certain uncouth Texan.

The movie ended, the lights went up, Bobby took the podium—and a gut-ripping ovation pealed for almost as long as the film itself. Grown men cried—as indeed, surveys showed, half of American men had cried after John F. Kennedy was shot. It made the President's acceptance speech—spoken under banners reading "LET US CONTINUE," a cruel reminder of those old feelings of illegitimacy—to all accounts anticlimactic. And Lyndon Johnson redoubled his resolve to capture the biggest presidential landslide ever.

PART FOUR

19

DON'T MENTION
THE GREAT PUMPKIN

Goldwater opened his campaign in Prescott, Arizona, a remote mountain town of 13,000 up near the Grand Canyon, because he always opened his campaigns there. It was the original Goldwater family seat, governed for twenty-six years by Morris Goldwater, Barry's uncle and political hero. Morris had built the courthouse from whose steps Barry would speak; ahead of him, bisecting the traditional village square, would be the equestrian statue that Uncle Morris had graciously put up to honor his political enemy—Bucky O'Neill, a populist rabble-rouser who died in Teddy Roosevelt's charge up San Juan Hill.

Or so local lore had it. Actually Bucky had been the victim of a sniper's bullet whilst relieving himself in a slit-trench latrine. In Prescott, *The Atlantic Monthly* claimed, "men with revolvers on their hips or rifles in their hands are a common sight." They weren't. Prescott was like Barry Goldwater: its rough-rider image was a story the town told itself about itself. Prescott commemorated the world's first rodeo, held there in 1888, with a big-time parade each July 4, and each year its famous "Smoki Clan"—chamber of commerce types, including, most years, Barry Goldwater, who dressed up as Indians for fun and municipal profit—put on a solemn, foot-stomping display, carefully researched for "authenticity," which they proudly labeled "the premier Indian Pageant of America." On September 3 Prescott would be blending the two spectaculars, with its favorite son serving as Grand Marshal. Fifty thousand visitors were expected to show up. It would have been fantastic. If anything had gone according to plan.

Nobody bothered to check whether Prescott's airport had a runway big enough to accommodate the campaign's 727. (The passengers breathed a sigh of relief to find, upon landing, that it did.) A press room packed with typewriters and phones had been set up at the Westward Ho. But the reporters were staying at the *Valley* Ho. Then Goldwater's security detail—the events of

November 22 were still fresh in people's minds and there was a rumor that a roving gang of black militants was on its way into Prescott to join the fun—ruled it would be too dangerous for him to ride in the parade. Then the event was moved up two hours. But not in time to alert the newspapers. Only 4,000 visitors arrived in time to hear Goldwater give his speech.

It was a shame, because Goldwater was in rare form. He extended the olive branch he had withheld in San Francisco (the word "peace" was repeated twenty times). And he sharpened a theme that had run through his rhetoric like a red thread ever since he keened for the fate of the "whole man" in *Conscience of a Conservative* four years earlier. He used the story of his and his audience's pioneer forebears as the jumping-off point for his argument that the people of the nation were forgetting how to live lives of dignity, meaning, and autonomy. "There is a stir in the land," he said, "a mood of uneasiness. We feel adrift in an uncharted and stormy sea. We feel that we have lost our way." His campaign, he said, would aim America at a "greatness of soul—to restore inner meaning to every man's life in a time too often rushed, too often obsessed by petty needs and material greeds."

James Reston mocked the message as an exercise in moral philosophy, not a political speech. He was unperceptive. The average American was now seventeen years old; 2.5 million new twenty-one-year-olds were being added to the voting rolls every year. For the first time on Planet Earth, a nation was made up of more college students than farmers. The dominance of this new generation—"The Pepsi Generation," a certain beverage company called it; "the buyingest age group in history," according to the Mustang's impresario, Lee Iacocca—was registering everywhere; that very month history was made when one of those goofy dance shows, *Shindig*, ran in network prime time. Beyond the froth, however, young people were demanding new things from politics, too—a field of endeavor now conceived not merely as the place where interest groups pragmatically jostled for resources to meet their material needs, but, just as Arthur Schlesinger had predicted in 1960, as a realm devoted to the fight "for individual dignity, identity and fulfillment in an affluent society."

The spirit came from the left. In May, as Republicans dueled to the death in California, a group of folkies called Peter, Paul and Mary won a Grammy for singing "Blowin' in the Wind" and one thousand young men and women marched on the UN to assail "U.S. imperialism." Students for a Democratic Society was just breaking into public consciousness (their campaign slogan was "Part of the Way with LBJ"). A young man had recently burned his draft card in Union Square in New York City, declaring, "The basic issue is my right of free choice." And, as Young Americans for Freedom amply demonstrated—it won 5,400 new recruits in the summer of 1964, compared to SDS's total membership of 1,500—this spirit came from the right. As one young Birch leader described it, his conversion to conservative politics came in a flash, when he realized that "the man in the gray flannel suit was a devil in disguise." Which is to say that, politically, the generation seemed up for grabs.

Goldwater made a decent play for it in Prescott. "Republicans will end the draft altogether," he promised, "and as soon as possible!" He made this statement in part to drop the "warmonger" tag, in part because in his opinion the draft was an inefficient and expensive way to build an army. (The Pentagon was completing studies that strained toward the same conclusion; the thinking was that modern brushfire wars like Vietnam—"We're back to the days of Indian fighting," Goldwater once noted—wouldn't require mass deployments of soldiers.) But it was also a question of freedom: people should become soldiers because they chose to, just like the kid in Union Square said. "We will place power back to the people," as Goldwater would put it later that month.

Lyndon Johnson had made his play for the new generation back in May. It was Eric Goldman, a Princeton history professor on leave to serve as a White House special assistant, who came up with the tag "Great Society"—a vision of dignity, identity, and fulfillment in the affluent society—to bestow upon the Johnson program. The President first auditioned the phrase in April before the Democratic Club of Cook County. He had to shout to get the their attention: "We have been called upon—are you listening?—to build a great society of the highest order." To the hacks of the old school this was not politics; it was gibberish. Those who attended the commencement exercises on May 22, six months to the day after Kennedy's assassination, at the University of Michigan—where, in 1961, JFK had unveiled the Peace Corps—proved a more receptive audience. It wouldn't last long. But for a brief, shining moment, fifty-five-year-old Lyndon Johnson and these thousands of robed young grads dreaming of futures of individual dignity, identity, and fulfillment in an affluent society were thinking exactly the same thing.

"The challenge of the next half century is whether we have the wisdom to use our wealth to enrich and elevate our national life, and to advance the quality of American civilization," their President declaimed.

> For in your time we have the opportunity to move not only toward the rich society and the powerful society, but upward to the Great Society. . . .
>   The Great Society is a place where every child can find knowledge to enrich his mind and enlarge his talents. It is a place where leisure is a welcome chance to build and reflect, not a feared cause of

boredom and restlessness. It is a place where the city of man serves not only the needs of the body and the demands of commerce but the desire for beauty and the hunger for community . . . a society where the demands of morality, and the needs of the spirit, can be realized in the life of the nation.

The old ways of talking about politics were falling away. In their place, both candidates would serve up rhetoric that autumn that tingled with strains of utopianism—intercut with equal and opposite strains of apocalypticism. They told stories of hope, of a society that could not but surpass any the world had ever known. They also told stories that spoke to the dark, looming fear that the world bequeathed us by science, technology, and the Pax Americana would not make us more secure but might instead unleash the devil.

A melancholy man, Lyndon Johnson understood how souls were moved by dark thoughts that crept up on sleepless nights. "Men worry about heart attacks," he would say, clasping his chest. "Women worry about cancer of the tit" (here he jabbed the breastplate of his nearest companion). "But everybody worries about war and peace. Everything else is chickenshit."

The strategy, as it evolved through August, was for the President to take care of the chickenshit. He would campaign from the Rose Garden, pronounce upon the unprecedented good fortune being enjoyed by all, venture out once in a while before safe Union crowds, cut a ribbon or dedicate a dam, swoop down upon flood-stricken towns bearing multimillion-dollar checks.

That left the dark thoughts that crept up during sleepless nights. Which was where Doyle Dane Bernbach came in. When DDB scrapped its civil rights spots in favor of the kids-with-two-heads theme, it was Tony Schwartz whom they called upon. Schwartz was a sui generis American genius, a sculptor in sound, a manufacturer of moods. He was the inventor of the first portable tape recorder, with which he took to the streets to produce LPs that were celebrations of all things audible: cabdrivers' chatter, Times Square at rush hour, Jamaican songs sung by a shop girl at Macy's. He also produced commercials. His masterpiece was a series of radio spots for American Airlines. He sold the romance of America's great cities by crafting the aural equivalent of skylines. For one spot, Schwartz waited for an overcast day in his West Side Manhattan neighborhood and recorded Hudson River foghorns while hiring a local hobo called Moondog to walk around with the bells, drums, and pots and pans he perpetually carried on his back: instant San Francisco. The commercials brought an immediate spike in the airline's bookings.

Schwartz was also a maestro in the use of children in advertising. Enraptured by the sound of play, he had a special fascination with the intricate street games children played with numbers—cold, austere symbols, breathed life through the mouths of babes.

When DDB producer Aaron Ehrlich held up a picture and asked Schwartz, "Would you work for this product?" Schwartz, who was also a committed antinuclear activist, said he would be thrilled. They began to brainstorm. Schwartz brought an audiotape he had created for Ogilvy, Benson & Mather's IBM account that had proved too much for those two stodgy old firms. He played the segment and suggested how it might be adapted to their purposes. He described the visuals: *"You have a little girl in the middle of a field. . . ."*

VIDEO	AUDIO
Camera up on little girl in a field, picking petals off a daisy.	*Little girl: "One, two, three, four, five, seven, six, six, eight, nine, nine—"*
Girl looks up, startled; freeze-frame on girl; move into extreme close-up on her eye, until screen is black.	*Man's voice, very loud as if heard over a loudspeaker at a test site: "Ten, nine, eight, seven, six, five, four, three, two, one—"*
Cue to atom bomb exploding. Move into close-up of explosion.	*Sound of explosion. Johnson [voice-over]: "These are the stakes—to make a world in which all of God's children can live, or to go into the dark. We must either love each other, or we must die."*
Cue to white letters on black background: "Vote for President Johnson November 3."	*Announcer [voice-over]: "Vote for President Johnson on November 3. The stakes are too high for you to stay home."*

The ad ran Monday, September 7—Labor Day, for peak viewing—on NBC, a few days after Goldwater's opening speech in Prescott and a few hours after Johnson's in Detroit. Nobody had ever seen anything like it. Little girls went to bed in tears. Bill Moyers, working late in his office—as was most often the case in Lyndon Johnson's White House—was summoned by the boss. "Holy shit!" the President cried. "What in the hell do you mean putting on that ad? I've been swamped with calls!" But he was chuckling. "I guess it did what we goddamned set out to do, didn't it?" He chuckled some more.

The spot ran only once as a paid commercial. But CBS and ABC ran reports on the phenomenon on their news programs—and thus, free of charge, they aired the ad itself. Dean Burch complained to the Fair Campaign Practices Commission. "This horror-type commercial," he said, "implies that Senator Goldwater is a reckless man and Lyndon Johnson is a careful man." Moyers was thrilled. "That's exactly what we wanted to imply," he wrote the President. *"And we also hoped someone around Goldwater would say it, not us."* Local campaign leaders told Johnson's field chief, Larry O'Brien, that they hated the ad, that voters were turning off to LBJ. The White House was unfazed. They were thinking like Marshall McLuhan, like Bill Bernbach: the message people reported having gleaned from the ad bore no necessary relation to how it affected them where it counted—in the place consciousness didn't touch.

Four years earlier the Republicans might have been able to do something about it. Not now. The FCC in 1964 had begun implementing a Goldwaterite idea: turning over much of its mandate to police the broadcasting industry to the industry itself. The National Association of Broadcasters censured its members on the basis of a thirty-page "Code of Ethics" whose sole stricture against TV violence—to take one example—noted that it should be used "only as required by plot development or character delineation." (When NAB's president had proposed amending the Code to limit cigarette advertising after the Surgeon General's report, he was summarily fired.) The penalty for breaking the rules was loss of the right to display the NAB "Seal of Good Practice," which nobody noticed when it was there and nobody noticed when it was gone. "In light of this commercial," Ev Dirksen wrote their executive director, "I would hope you would read again the Code of Ethics and ask yourself whether you agree that this is unfit for children to see." He was spitting in the wind. NAB wasn't even a paper tiger. There was nothing the Goldwater campaign could do but scream.

Or so it seemed. Tony Schwartz thought that a gifted Goldwater publicist could have flipped the ad's power against itself. The spot did not make any actual reference to Goldwater. It just told people to be afraid of nuclear war and leveraged the force of a message the media was already repeating over and over like a hit Beatles song: *"Kenneth Kassel, a lean young corn and livestock farmer, paused near a hog shoot in Ayshire, Iowa, to explain why he expected to switch his vote to President Johnson this fall. 'If the Republicans had somebody a little more level-headed, I'd vote for him,' he said. 'I'm afraid of Goldwater.' "* The "warmonger" tag seemed as unchangeable as the atmosphere. But

Tony Schwartz later suggested, "Goldwater could have defused Daisy by saying, 'I think the danger of total nuclear war should be the theme of the campaign this year, and I'd like to pay half the cost of running the commercial.' If he had, the commercial would not have been perceived as being against him. He would have changed the feelings and assumptions stored within us." Perhaps it might have worked, perhaps not. But then, there were no gifted publicists in the Goldwater organization who thought to try.

Barry Goldwater was taking the unusual step of running his campaign out of Republican National Committee headquarters on Eye Street (Washingtonese for "I Street"), which already had a built-in staff, instead of from a freestanding temporary organization. But Goldwater was too busy fulfilling previous commitments—and, for the five days preceding his Prescott debut, lolling unshaven on General Wedemeyer's yacht off the Orange County coast—to supervise the changeover. Denison Kitchel, in turn, delegated the task to Dean Burch and his assistant, John Grenier. RNC mandarins feared for their positions, but Burch and Grenier insisted that their aim was "neither to reward nor to purge."

Then, they purged. The RNC's longtime executive director and half his executive committee were cut adrift; then the RNC's longtime research director, "a computer on legs," as some described him, was let go (in his stead Goldwater's research team sent form letters to the political science chairs at big state universities begging "any recent pamphlets or books . . . concerning the political situation in [your state here]"). The PR director was fired, and the finance chair left for a trip home to Ohio after the convention without a thought that he might be expendable and returned to discover someone else in his chair. The scheduling department, at least, was run by a veteran—of the first Eisenhower campaign. There were many among the new RNC staff who had not participated in as much as a campaign for class president. Kitchel, quipped a staffer afterward, "could not tell a leak from a leek"—although that staffer had little more experience himself.

Kitchel had taken the advice of Raymond Moley to gut the office's structure top to bottom. In Franklin Roosevelt's campaigns, Moley explained, the political and the policy-planning departments were strictly segregated, with a single person—that would be Kitchel—straddling the two, so the candidate's message could be disciplined against the temptations of the day-to-day electoral horse race. It was an idea Goldwater's inner circle—the Arizonans and Baroody's people—beheld with delight: that meant they could stick the grubby politicos on the second floor of the building and separate themselves on the third—ostensibly as the "Research Division," unofficially dubbed the "Think Tank," but more accurately described as the headquarters within the headquarters—and preserve the empyrean isolation they had so enjoyed while writing Goldwater's acceptance speech on the seventeenth floor of the Mark Hopkins.

What that meant practically speaking was that the month after the convention most of the work at Eye Street was being done by electricians, furniture movers, and telephone installers. Scattered around the country were the crackerjack local Goldwater outfits Clif White had put together for the primary campaigns and state conventions. Left inactive, they were now straining at the leash to get to work for the general election. Their phone calls went unanswered at headquarters; their letters piled up unopened amidst the sawdust and exposed wiring. The marketplace was being flooded with campaign kitsch— Barry Goldwater greeting cards (outside: "You made me what I am today"; inside: "A Democrat"), Barry comic books, plastic Barry dashboard dolls (splendid craftsmanship, right down to the rightward crook in his glasses), Barry soap ("4-Year Protection!"), a pamphlet in the old-timey patent medicine style: "Cures for What Ails America: Dr. B. M. Goldwater's All-Purpose Defoliation Tonic, the Non-Taxic, Magic Cold War Remedy, a Balm for Boils, Burns, Bruises, Bigots, Birchers & Buckleys." There were bumper stickers in every imaginable language and level of taste—and buttons, buttons, buttons: "METS ROOTERS! EDSEL OWNERS! BACK A REAL LOSER! GOLDWATER!"; "GOLD-WATER OR SOCIALISM"; "DOCTOR STRANGEWATER FOR PRESIDENT"; "IF I WERE 21 I'D VOTE FOR GOLDWATER." None of it came from Goldwater headquarters. Even once they had the resources to do the job, his people were paralyzed. When the Arizona Mafia took title to the Republican National Committee, they realized they had a problem on their hands. Selling such kitsch to local organizations had been their profit center during the nomination fight. But federal campaign law, it turned out, prohibited political parties from charging for the stuff. The lawyers searched for a loophole. The presses sat dormant.

Once the carpenters got finished with it, the second-floor political command center was a handsome sight. There was a map room to rival the Joint Chiefs', charts detailing sophisticated chains of command, a latticework of graphs sitting ready to mark the progress of their campaign's voter-canvass effort (they hoped to reach 75 percent of American voters in their homes). A staff of seven hundred had been assembled: tour committees, finance committees, speakers bureaus, a radio-television division, a transport department run by a former airline chief, copywriters, telephone girls. Some of Draft Goldwater's most seasoned operatives had been brought back on board (though not Clif White) to run the regional divisions. In one corner a buzzing hive was gathering and collating twenty-three different variables for each of the country's 185,000 precincts ("support of senior citizens," "vote-pulling aid from religious influences," "expected honest vote count," and so forth; the code book for Ohio alone ran to 133 pages), producing vote quotas for each, a Herculean effort; in another corner, state-of-the-art TWX and DATA teletypes were ready to clack 1,050 words per minute to offices around the country, even to the campaign plane. They had newfangled WATS long-distance lines and auto-dial phones. The communications system had awesome potential: it could relay shifting political conditions on the ground to the Washington command center and to the traveling team within minutes.

To coordinate it all there were to be meetings every Sunday with the second-floor leadership, the third-floor leadership, and Goldwater and his traveling team. This strategy board would be briefed every two weeks by the campaign's Princeton-based polling firm. And the preliminary numbers made the second floor thrum with excitement. They were counterintuitive. Only 9 percent of the sample rated Johnson "excellent"; 38 percent rated him "fair to poor." Almost three-quarters of independent voters expressed admiration for Goldwater's forthrightness; less than a quarter were worried that he "acts without thinking"—and 61 percent questioned Johnson's good judgment. Six percent thought that the President was "superficial, shallow." Forty-one percent called themselves "conservative" compared to 31 percent who called themselves "liberal"; half the sample "knew very little" about Goldwater—giving his campaign team an enormous, unexpected opportunity to shape his image in the public mind. And since the popularity trend was in Goldwater's favor—Gallup's if-the-election-were-held-today numbers gave Goldwater 19 percent in June and 34 percent in September—there came a revelation: Goldwater could ride these numbers to a historic upset and not compromise on a single conservative position—by saying the right things in the right places at the right times, lining up the right people to carry the water, and communicating in clear, attractive ways that the public could understand.

Kennedy's Irish Mafia could hardly have been better prepared.

And Goldwater's Arizona Mafia couldn't have cared less.

The people who were really running the campaign were upstairs. They were what Rowland Evans and Robert Novak called "a group of little-known academicians and publicists loosely allied with an obscure tax-exempt educational foundation in Washington, D.C., called the American Enterprise Institute for Public Policy Research." And to them, the findings of the lastest poll were beneath notice. Bill Baroody was on paid leave working eighteen-hour days running the third floor like a fiefdom. His liege men had been by his side in San Francisco: Warren Nutter, chairman of the University of Virginia's economics department; Dick Ware, who dispensed the largesse of a deceased motor oil manufacturer from Michigan as director of the Earhart-Relm Foundation; trusty Ed McCabe and his second, Chuck Lichenstein; Baroody's old AEI partner, W. Glenn Campbell, now running the Hoover Institution at Stanford University. Baroody's aristocracy were ad hoc consultants, conservative intellectuals like Milton Friedman, Robert Bork, Bill Rehnquist, and Robert Strausz-Hupé. They found the very idea of consulting polls contemptible.

Kitchel, Baroody, and Goldwater didn't bother to attend the Sunday strategy meetings. They made strategy at 33,000 feet. The campaign plane ("YIA BI KEN" [House in the Sky], read the legend above the lightning stripe running down its side) was their playhouse: Kitchel, Karl Hess, and the candidate conversed in Navajo (Hess was studying up), swapped ribald jokes, told hunting stories, yapped on the airborne ham radio. Another favorite pastime was refusing to receive top donors on board for a chance to ride along with the candidate. Occasionally, they prepared for the next stop, although that didn't take much time: Goldwater never acknowledged the locale he landed in anyway. Meanwhile the leaders on the second floor would explode once more after learning from the morning newspapers that their hard-won intelligence, relayed so assiduously by all those expensive contraptions, had been ignored while their underlings floundered, directionless, bickering, confused, because the man charged with directing them, Kitchel, was otherwise disposed.

On a wall in the Think Tank was affixed a *Peanuts* comic strip. Linus declares from a speaker's stand, "On Hallowe'en night the Great Pumpkin rises out of the pumpkin patch, and brings toys to all the good little children." His audience laughs at him. Later, Linus confides to Snoopy, "So I told them about the Great Pumpkin and they all laughed! Am I the first person ever to sacrifice political office because of belief? Of course not! I simply spoke what I felt was the truth." Snoopy walks off, muttering, "I've never pretended to understand politics, but I do know one thing. If you're going to hope to get elected, don't mention the Great Pumpkin."

LBJ's opening speech was on Labor Day in Detroit's Cadillac Square. It was Democratic tradition to ring in each presidential campaign to the roars of loyal workingmen grateful for bigger paychecks, better job security, stronger unions, and the political party that made it all possible. This year, though, the fear was that bigger paychecks and better job security would not be enough to keep the audience from Lyndon Johnson's throat.

It was a fine month for backlash. New York came close to further rioting after a grand jury refused to indict the officer whose bullet set off the July disturbance; that same week, white parents pulled their children out of New York schools to protest what the Republican platform called "federally sponsored 'inverse discrimination' . . . the abandonment of neighborhood schools, for reasons of race." Blunter, one protester carried a sign reading "YOU'LL TURN INTO A NIGGER." (The seething issue had by then earned a journalistic short-hand: "busing," sometimes spelled "bussing.") Another court ordered union locals to dismantle father-son apprenticeship programs that "automatically excluded" Negroes. One of Johnson's advance men filed a report on the comments of a New York cabbie: "He exploded—traffic terrible, Negroes pushing, city in snarl, politicians ruining country, everything a mess. Pent-up fury." He found similar sentiments among four of the seven hacks he met. The AFL-CIO budgeted $12 million for education efforts to counter the myth that the Civil Rights Act demanded hiring quotas based on race. It didn't work; polls taken at factory gates in South Chicago and Gary, Indiana, favored Goldwater 53 to 47. (It would be some time before a backlash could build up against another new civil rights program, inaugurated for the 1964–65 school year at Cornell University: intentionally increasing the representation of entering black students to 8 in a class of 2,300, from a previous high of 4.) In California, the Senate campaign between former JFK and LBJ press secretary Pierre Salinger and George Murphy was playing out as a moratorium on Proposition 14. Salinger proudly declared himself against the proposed amendment (that is, in favor of open housing). Murphy refused to take a position. Salinger, it transpired, was about as popular as the prospect of open housing—which is to say that on his whistle-stop through southern California he was pelted with eggs and tomatoes.

Johnson comforted himself with talk of the "frontlash"—the infelicitous phrase he coined to describe all the disillusioned Republicans moving over to support *him*. Members of the Establishment media comforted themselves by wishing all of it away. "In pre-campaign figuring," *Time* reported of Goldwater, "it was generally assumed that he would also gain in the North from the 'backlash' of white resentment against the excess of the Negro revolution. But if there were any such backlash, it would surely have shown itself last week in a Democratic primary in Michigan's Sixteenth Congressional District and it failed to materialize." That was a slim reed: the Sixteenth did, in fact, vote out a sluggish incumbent who voted against the Civil Rights Act. But it was also an area where racial boundaries were policed as violently as in Alabama. *Time* might just as well have chosen Massachusetts as its bellwether, where incumbent governor Endicott Peabody, an unbending civil rights supporter, was swept from office in a primary. Or Detroit itself, where a politician named Thomas Poindexter, after a decade of electoral disappointments as an economic populist, had finally won a seat on the Common Council as the "Homeowners' Champion"—first by testifying against the civil rights bill on behalf of the "99 percent of Detroit's white residents" who feared the "general lowering of moral standards" that would follow its ratification; then by becoming the all-but-official voice of a primary-ballot initiative that thumped the city's open housing laws from the books.

Fear of backlash made for no little tension in the little jet Johnson had packed with Democratic pols and AFL-CIO officials for the trip to the Motor City from the capital. They exchanged pleasantries—and thought to themselves, Would Lyndon Johnson suffer Endicott Peabody's fate?

Here was their answer. He stood side by side, hands held aloft, with Walter Reuther and—both men's fathers spinning in their graves—Henry Ford II, then wrapped up in difficult negotiations over the next UAW contract. In the crowd, 100,000 union members cheered themselves hoarse. Labor and management, allies not adversaries, reasoning together for their common good: this was Lyndon Johnson's dream.

He spoke, with a tremor in his voice, about responsibility. "I am not the first President to speak here in Cadillac Square, and I do not intend to be the last. Make no mistake, there is no such thing as a conventional nuclear weapon. . . . I believe the final responsibility for all decisions on nuclear weapons must rest with the civilian head of this government, the President of the United States, and I think and reiterate that I believe that this is the way the American people want it." These sturdy proletarians took in the words like a comforting balm. Property values, seniority systems, busing: after facing their planet's mortality, these things seemed like chickenshit indeed.

There was at least one person who blanched at this kind of talk: National Security Adviser McGeorge Bundy. He thought national security would be better served by telling the truth. Johnson's constant claim that the President was solely responsible for firing nuclear weapons was open to charges of deception, Bundy gingerly advised his boss. Bundy laid out four separate scenarios in which military commanders could authorize a nuclear strike without presidential approval, and he implored the President for the sake of the Atlantic alliance to "make a statement in which you make clear that there are indeed very specialized contingencies for which certain presidential instructions already exist." His entreaties were ignored.

Goldwater broke ground for Bill Baroody's conservative utopia on the first stop of his first tour, Los Angeles, with the help of University of Chicago economist Milton Friedman. "Every individual endeavors to employ his capital so that its produce may be of greatest value," Adam Smith famously wrote in *The Wealth of Nations* (1776), "led by an invisible hand to promote an end which has no part of his intentions. By pursuing his own interests he frequently promotes that of society more effectively than when he really intends to promote it." At Chicago, the revolutionary economics department was applying the gleaming instruments of mathematical proof to remove the qualifying "frequently" from that formulation, taking on every Keynesian orthodoxy their profession had come to hold dear. Professor Friedman, the Brooklyn-born son of an immigrant sweatshop worker, was their most fervent evangelist. By the 1950s this compact, muscular bulldog of a man was splitting his time between making pathbreaking contributions to his field (distinguished by a single-minded relentlessness in taking first principles to their logical conclusion, no matter how counterintuitive that conclusion might seem) and speaking to popular audiences around the nation (though so uncompromising was his devotion to individual liberty that when he traveled to private schools he refused to speak at compulsory chapel services).

In 1961 his schedule included a well-publicized debating victory over Pennsylvania's liberal senator Joseph Clark, who was reduced to spluttering that his opponent was a "neo-anarchist" who would make "a fine candidate for the next President of the John Birch Society." The next year Friedman published a popular treatise, *Capitalism and Freedom*. It was so iconoclastic—and so lucid in its iconoclasm—that some Keynesians successfully lobbied to have it purged from their universities' libraries. Among its off-the-deep-end arguments were that corporations should not make charitable donations (lest stockholders be defrauded by this economic irrationality); that the Post Office should be sold off; that licensing procedures for professionals like doctors should be banned (the market would take care of the problem of quackery on its own)—and that the government should disburse educational "vouchers" to force public schools to compete in the marketplace.

It seemed only a matter of time before Friedman and Goldwater should meet. Friedman first wrote Goldwater with a policy suggestion in late 1960, but he received only a perfunctory acknowledgment in return. After the professor bludgeoned Goldwater's Senate adversary Joe Clark, however, Goldwater proposed a meeting. They first got together at one of the salons Bill Baroody held at his home (Friedman served on AEI's Academic Advisory Board). Soon Goldwater took Friedman on as an informal economic adviser. Though Friedman surely never expected to see his ideas boomed over the public address system of Dodger Stadium.

Goldwater had played Dodger Stadium almost a year earlier, and then as now the event was a sellout (both times it was a rare political rally that charged admission; in southern California, people were willing to *pay* to see Barry Goldwater). Youngsters poured from buses wearing "Goldwater à Go-Go" sweatshirts. ("These niggers are trying to make me a second-class citizen," one told Stewart Alsop. "I guess a man has to be for Goldwater or be a Communist.")

Mexican-American supporters hung a huge "ARRIBA CON BARRY" banner from the upper left-field tier. Cesar Romero, Walter Brennan, Raymond Massey, and Ronald Reagan spoke, and as usual Reagan stole the show. (Another Hollywood star, Charlton Heston, would convert to Goldwaterism a few weeks later. Looking up at an "IN YOUR HEART YOU KNOW HE'S RIGHT" billboard at a Sacramento intersection, road-to-Damascus-style, on the way to a movie shoot, he thought to himself, "Son of a bitch, he *is* right.")

At Dodger Stadium, Goldwater was introduced by World War II bombing ace General James Doolittle: "I give you the leader of the modern American revolution!" The revolutionary emerged from the shadows in a blue convertible. He circled the warning track for fifteen minutes of extended cheering. It pealed on for another seven minutes as the candidate stood in front of the microphone. This was far more pleasant than his morning stop in San Diego, where hecklers pulled a fire alarm and a steel fire escape crashed right through the center of a frightened crowd.

Finally, the stadium was stilled. And Goldwater hit the ground running:

> Never in my memory have we seen an Administration running in so many ways at once. . . . This is an entire circus of politics, with the Administration ring-master trying to come up with an act to please everyone in the audience every other minute! . . . Their leader wants to forget how many friends we've lost while we have tried to cultivate our enemies. . . . We can't forget that a time when morals in general have been slipping, causing all of us concern, there has been no light in the White House. . . . While the President of the United States speaks of the Great Society, our cities and suburbs are turning into the lawless society.

The scoreboard flashed "CHARGE!" at the applause lines. The *Washington Post* described the response as a "religious revivalistic fervor."

Then Goldwater switched gears. "I will, as one of my first actions in the White House, ask the Congress to enact a regular and considered program of tax reduction," he said. "I will also ask that Congress stop the wild spending spree begun by this Administration." More applause.

"The legislation for which I will ask would provide an across-the-board reduction of 5 percent per year in all income taxes—both individual and corporate. The initial request will provide for such regular, prudent reductions in taxes in each of the next five years," he plodded. "At the end of the first year you would calculate the tax you owed under the present law. Then you would reduce it by 5 percent. At the end of the second year you would reduce the payment by 10 percent. *Each* year you would take off the 5 percent so that by the fifth year the total reduction would be 25 percent . . ."

The audience began drifting off.

"All along, of course, the amount of money that the government takes from you every payday, in withholding taxes, would be reduced at the same rate— 5 percent the first year, 10 percent the next and so on until the 25 percent mark . . ."

He went on. And on.

Economic theory predicted that Dodger Stadium should have rejoiced: the marginal utility of paying 95 percent of your tax bill instead of 100 percent was unmistakable. And one of Friedman's most treasured insights was that the unpredictability of government fiscal policy was an impediment to private investment, so knowing tax rates five years in advance would free up capital to boost economic growth.

Instead, the speech landed with a thud. Five percent, 10 percent, 25 percent, first year, fifth year, initial request, withholding taxes: it went by in a gust of confusion. Did a 5 percent tax reduction mean the 15 percent tax bracket would become 10 percent? Or that a $570 tax bill—the bite of the typical American family—would become $541.50? The answer was the latter. Those quick enough to do the back-of-the-envelope calculations couldn't have been too impressed—since that typical tax bill had just been reduced from $750 by the Johnson tax cut. Listeners were supposed to appreciate that Johnson's tax cut was designed to create a deficit, while Goldwater's would close the deficit. But *why* it would close the deficit—by forcing the government to cut spending because of reduced revenue—flew by in half a garbled sentence. Many conservatives for whom fiscal irresponsibility was the gravest sin could only agree with Treasury Secretary Dillon's assessment: "No one with the slightest understanding of fiscal affairs," he said, "could countenance the prospect of blindly binding us to annual tax cuts for many years ahead regardless of the state of the economy."

In his speech the next day Goldwater proved he could bomb just as well when he was being crystal clear. Seattle's Coliseum was full to bursting with 15,000 patrons, at $1 a pop, with a 3,000-person overflow milling outside. The speech was a screed against the doctrine of "coexistence" in the Cold War. Goldwater revived the old Republican cry that America's wars began under Democrats, scored Kennedy and Johnson for failures at the Bay of Pigs, in the Congo, Zanzibar, Panama—"Our flag, torn down, spat upon"—and warned that Vietnam was "as close as Kansas or New York or Seattle" in "the mileage of peace and freedom." The audience, packed with men who riveted Boeing warplanes together, was his. A big helium balloon trailing a "JOHNSON '64" bedsheet was stealthily released, bopped its way along the rafters, and met its end colliding with a floodlight; after it *flumph*ed to the floor the audience ripped it to shreds like mad dogs. Goldwater said that that was what he was going to do with the Johnson Administration. His audience roared.

Then he went further than they were willing to go.

Kennedy, he announced sternly, had calibrated the timing of the October 1962 Cuban missile crisis to help Democrats in the midterm elections that November. He added: "Americans must be prepared under such an Administration to be faced by a 'crisis' of some sort just before the election." He thanked Boeing for how well its planes had performed in wartime—and promised that under his Administration, the planes "will be doing so again." He meant he would distribute defense contracts to the most qualified bidder, not according to political considerations as Lyndon Johnson supposedly did. What it *sounded* like would soon be revealed when Lou Harris found that 64 percent of women and 45 percent of men believed that if elected President, Goldwater would take the United States to war; and when researchers at the University of Michigan found that there was one comment on Johnson's belligerency for every hundred about Goldwater's (people being hardly aware that in the White House, on September 8, it was decided that U.S. bombing of North Vietnam would begin just as soon as the election was out of the way).

For his next stop, Minneapolis, the second floor's Midwest experts worked up a detailed report on the mounting aggravation of wheat farmers with the federal acreage allotment system. The issue was ignored. Instead Goldwater exclaimed, "We know that it is lack of leadership that has turned our streets into jungles. . . . If it is entirely proper for government to take from some to give to others, then won't some be led to believe that they can rightfully take from anyone who has more than they?" The speech was televised across the state. The denizens of Minnesota's crime-ridden wheat farms proved nonplused. The *Washington Post*'s editorial board reacted considerably more excitedly: "Like a man looking at the world while standing on his head, he has arrived at a conclusion that the cause of crime is to be found in the excessive benevolence of the community to its unfortunate," they wrote. "This is much like asserting that the vaccination is the cause of smallpox." It was, they concluded, "hard to believe that anyone living in the 20th Century would utter it."

The next night, in Chicago, professors—those, at least, who hadn't joined a boycott called by an agitated University of Chicago don—filed into a banquet hall to hear Goldwater give the plenary address at the American Political Science Association convention. The speech was written by Harry Jaffa and Bill Rehnquist. "According to some of your learned works," Goldwater began, "a great many people make up their minds about candidates even before the convention opens." That, he continued, was why he was so glad to accept their invitation to speak at this convention. "Finding an open-minded audience to hear a discussion of fundamental issues poses a real problem."

Then he set to baiting them. He said it disgusted him that liberals admired this "power-wielding, arm-twisting President" just because he "gets his program through Congress." This, he said, was "a totalitarian philosophy that the end justifies the means." Then he turned to his main subject—what he liked to call, in less formal settings, the "jackassian" nature of recent Supreme Court decisions. "I suppose, since I am not a lawyer, that I should leave the analysis of the merits of the court's decision in these cases to the constitutional lawyers—"

Hecklers shouted their agreement. He pressed on.

"Yet, just as it has been observed that war is too important to leave to the generals . . ." (sarcastic jeers; considering what the audience members had read in their newspapers that morning of the fright Goldwater had given Seattle listeners the night before, this metaphor, which some might also have remembered as the opinion of General Jack D. Ripper in *Dr. Strangelove*, was the most injudicious imaginable). He went on to accuse the Warren Court of exercising "raw and naked power." Historically minded commentators drew attention to those words' similarity to the 1956 congressional "Southern Manifesto." Others interpreted the statement as an attack on the institution of the Supreme Court itself, perhaps even an endorsement of the Birch Society's "Impeach Warren" campaign.

By coincidence, that very same day the conservative justice John Marshall Harlan released a statement grandly explaining why he had been issuing angry dissent after angry dissent in cases that year—decrying decisions expanding the rights of criminal suspects, protecting naughty books, and broadening the public-accommodations purview of the Civil Rights Act. He railed that the federal judiciary was captive to the notion "that every major social ill in this country can find its cure in some constitutional principle." The political workers on the second floor couldn't believe their good fortune. This was cover: their man couldn't very well be accused of taking on the Supreme Court himself if he had a Supreme Court justice in his corner. They began making preparations to exploit the statement. Kitchel vetoed their efforts. He didn't think they had anything to apologize for—calling the Chicago speech "the most exciting thing we've done in the campaign so far." That Goldwater alienated audiences was taken by his inner circle as evidence he was doing something right—telling them things they needed, but didn't want, to hear. What frustrated the people on the second floor was that they believed these were things the American people *did* want to hear, if only the messages were communicated more skillfully. To them, it seemed more and more that their third-floor rivals weren't interested in winning the election at all.

It wasn't all that long ago that even liberal organs spoke of Goldwater as "an absolutely honest politician" (*Harper's*), of the "stoutness and general decency of his character" (*The Progressive*). Gone were the days. Publications were beginning to put out endorsements, and Goldwater was being pummeled. In presidential elections between 1940 and 1960, the nation's top one hundred newspapers endorsed the Republican 77 percent of the time. In 1964 only 45 percent would. *The Saturday Evening Post* was one of several organs to deliver its first Democratic endorsement in its history. Norman Rockwell it wasn't: "For the good of the Republican Party, which his candidacy disgraces, we hope that Goldwater is crushingly defeated," the editorial ran. He was "a wild man, a stray, an unprincipled and ruthless political jujitsu artist." (The language was ironic: "master of political jujitsu" had been the phrase the same magazine used back in January to praise their hero William Warren Scranton's political gifts.) Other newcomers to the Democratic column included the publications of Henry Luce ("Let me introduce myself. I am your boss," Luce once retorted to staffers who begged him to endorse Adlai Stevenson) and the Hearst Corporation (where in 1935 the boss ordered papers to substitute the phrase "Raw Deal" for the name of Franklin Delano Roosevelt's program in their news coverage). Bill Miller's little hometown paper went for Johnson; a nearby one tipped its hat to a Democrat for the first time since 1822. The unkindest cut of all came in Phoenix. You could find any number of ads for Goldwater's Department Store in Gene Pulliam's *Arizona Republic* and the *Phoenix Gazette*. You just couldn't find a kind word on behalf of Barry Goldwater. "I'll be darned," the President exhaled quietly, humbly, when he heard the news that the man who had ushered Barry Goldwater into public life was now cutting him adrift.

Clergymen and religious institutions inaugurated a new genre: the apologia for wading into presidential politics. "Readers of *The Churchman*"—a monthly of Goldwater's own Episcopal faith—"are doubtless aware that it has not been the custom of this journal to support party candidates. But they should also be certain that it could not only ever support but must strongly oppose a candidate who violates so completely the slogan which it carries on its masthead—'For the promotion of goodwill and better understanding among all peoples.' " At the Episcopalians' triennial convention, in St. Louis, delegates in the hundreds—even a bishop—signed a statement decrying Goldwater's "transparent exploitation of racism." The president of the American Jewish Congress said, "A Jewish vote for Goldwater is a vote for Jewish suicide." New York's Francis Cardinal Spellman acceded to Goldwater's request for a meeting because he didn't know how he could duck it, but he apologized to the White House for doing so, and he wouldn't let himself be photographed. A Methodist magazine devoted an entire issue to the scourge of Goldwaterism, explaining, "This journal was founded as a response to the threat of Hitlerism." Paul Tillich, with Reinhold Niebuhr one of the towering giants among U.S. theologians, pronounced: "Religion must sometimes take a side. . . . I feel as a theologian justified in calling for the defeat of the Republican candidate for the Presidency." Martin Luther King said he felt compelled to act because if Goldwater won, what would follow would be "violence and riots the like of which we have never seen before."

It didn't happen entirely spontaneously. "We have an opportunity to arouse many religious groups to oppose Goldwater," Bill Moyers advised the boss in July. The White House featured *The Churchman*'s editorial in a press release nearly before the issue was in subscribers' hands; an anti-Goldwater article in a little journal published by Niebuhr was distributed by the Johnson campaign in the thousands. ("President says he thinks they ought to put this guy on TV," White House special assistant Jack Valenti noted after the Tillich statement.) An "America's Leaders Speak" letterhead was created by the DNC to trumpet newfound fans in just about every profession. Leonard Marks, the Johnson family lawyer, worked on such matters full-time, setting up a liaison with every newspaper that made the smallest peep in opposition to the Republican candidate.

There were no Leonard Markses on Goldwater's side. They had all been thrown overboard. Thirty-one-year-old Lee Edwards had been designated director of public relations—apparently; with Kitchel ever by Goldwater's side on the campaign plane, such was the chaos that no one was certain whether the PR director's job hadn't been given to Republican ad man Lou Guylay instead. The dust settled with Guylay in charge—in charge, that is, of the staff of young, bright-eyed incompetents with which Edwards had packed the payroll, who disgorged so many press releases reporters had no idea what to write about.

The greatest flack outfit in the world would have had its hands full just dealing with the people who *did* endorse Goldwater. Robert DePugh proudly announced that his Minutemen militias would be sabotaging Democratic campaign offices on the campaign's behalf; the National Conservative Council pledged to aid Goldwater in his effort to "buy back the Federal Reserve System from the Rockefellers"; the Courtneys' anti-Johnson booklet ran a photograph of the President applauding an African drummer, captioned "Please, Massa

Lyndon, give us some of dat nice foreign aid. I need to buy two more wives."
Gerald L. K. Smith, after agonizing for months over Goldwater's Jewish
ancestry, crawled out from under his rock to declare that patriotic Americans
had "no time to lose" in joining the cause—and Georgia and Alabama KKK
leaders made their unqualified endorsements known far and wide. "We're not
in the business of discouraging votes," came Dean Burch's response; Lyndon
Johnson pounced on the opportunity. "You get on some TV up there where the
wires will quote that," he told Roy Wilkins.

And so it went. Grenier was so obsessed with control that he ordered the
entire staff not to speak to the press, on or off the record. Edwards had been
Napoleonic enough to demand that nothing be mimeographed without his
express consent. More memos, an early September memo complained, were
being circulated about how to circulate memos than about all other subjects
taken together. Only 5 percent of the Goldwater campaign's insanely ambitious
vote-quota scheme for every precinct in the nation had been fulfilled. Their
vaunted electronic communications system only speeded the pace at which
mistakes compounded: local leaders arrived at the office every morning to find
a pile of reading material on their desks, but no inkling of what they were supposed to do with it. Rome burned; and the emperors fiddled high above the
clouds, floating to the next campaign stop with blissful indifference.

CAMPAIGN TRAILS

Goldwater's next swing was through the Democrats' former Solid South. And when reporters described the crowds' receptions, words like "volcanic" and "Beatles" appeared over and over again. In Winston-Salem, the "We Want Barry" drone forced the introductions of local dignitaries to be canceled. In Charlotte, where ten thousand supporters had to be turned away, the *Observer* reported teenagers "near emotional collapse" when Goldwater walked past. "Sobbing, tears running down their faces, several girls moaned, 'Barry, Barry.' " His motorcade down Peachtree Street was showered with so much confetti that it felt like Atlanta had suffered its first blizzard. In Memphis the *Commercial Appeal* predicted a crowd between 3,000 and 7,000. "Thank God he's safe," the Memphis Chief of Police could only sigh after Goldwater escaped mauling from a throng of nearly 100,000. In Greenville, South Carolina, forty-five people required medical attention after crowds broke through the police cordon.

In contrast, Goldwater's speeches earned descriptions like "low-keyed," "listless," "monotone," and "stumbling"—as if, someone wrote, the candidate were saying, "Train 28 now leaving on Track 1." The speeches themselves were so inappropriate to their occasions that *The New Yorker*'s Richard Rovere was rubbing his eyes: "There were some times, traveling with Goldwater," he wrote, "when one wondered whether the candidate really thinks of himself as a man seeking the Presidency of the United States." Once more the second-floor units labored mightily preparing reports to help Goldwater's speechwriters: foregrounding the votes Goldwater had made to strengthen Social Security; an explanation of how TVA would be improved if it were run by the more efficient private sector; demonstration (prepared in consultation with the National Cotton Council) of how easing cotton supports would boost sales abroad. All were deposited in *Yia Bi Ken*'s circular file. The South was ground zero for

American political demagoguery—the best place, Goldwater had decided, to prove he wasn't a demagogue.

In Charlotte he gave an academic monologue on the great American system of constitutional checks and balances—before angrily denouncing the silent crowd for their indifference to their own liberty: "There have been wealthy *slaves!*" he lectured in exasperation. "You can find justice in a *prison.* We can find peace any time we say to the Communists, 'All right. We quit. We'll lie down.' " (The leader of the local Goldwater office, in the face of the alienated crowd, called Washington in sobs after seeing all their hard organizational work wasted.) In Atlanta, where business students paraded around with their arms in slings carrying signs reading "WE'D GIVE OUR RIGHT ARMS FOR BARRY," the day's lecture was on the evils of the Supreme Court's reapportionment decision. Off came the props; the speech was like a slap in the face to Atlantans who were counting on reapportionment to give the city a second, likely Republican, congressman. In St. Petersburg, a city proud of its low crime rate and where a quarter of the citizens received Social Security, Goldwater gave a speech on how American city streets were turning into jungles. (The Republican mayor immediately contacted the White House to let them know he was now for Johnson.) In Memphis and Raleigh Goldwater chastised farmers for even thinking they liked cotton subsidies, and he met the concerns of peanut farmers by noting, "I'm probably the most violent advocate of peanut butter in history. On a dare from one of my sons, I actually shaved with peanut butter and it wasn't bad, but it smells." On a rainy day in Montgomery (where, in the kind of goof that had reporters wondering whether his organizers "did graduate work at college on the arts of ineptitude," the 565 Southern belles who performed in the pageant of welcome were forced to sit on the muddy ground in their party dresses) he revealed his program for block grants to states—which might have been a good issue, if Johnson hadn't already put forward a similar proposal much earlier. In Knoxville, bumper stickers were printed up in the wake of Goldwater's visit: "SELL TVA? I'D RATHER SELL ARIZONA!" In Fort Worth, he criticized his least favorite military aircraft project, the TFX, which he believed LBJ had given to an inferior bidder, General Dynamics, a defense contractor based in—Fort Worth. In West Virginia, he called the War on Poverty "plainly and simply a war on your pocketbooks," a fraud because only "the vast resources of private business" could produce the wealth to *truly* slay penury. If he had been speaking in the boomtowns of southern California, Arizona, or Texas, he would have won the day. In the land of the tar-paper shack, the gap-toothed smile, and the open sewer—where the "vast resources of private business" were represented in the person of the coal barons who gave men black lung, then sent them off to die without pensions—the message just sounded perverse. As he left, lines of workmen jeered him.

Goldwater's hero's welcomes and the campaign's incompetence weren't the only stories from the tour. There was also the matter of Senator Strom Thurmond of South Carolina.

Strom Thurmond was perhaps the most conservative legislator in the Capitol. He was also Barry Goldwater's friend; when Thurmond broke the filibuster record during the 1957 civil rights debate, Goldwater was the only senator who spelled him for bathroom breaks. Like most of the South's politically alert demagogues, by 1964 Thurmond had stopped shy of directing scorn at blacks themselves; he proclaimed himself a constitutionalist, pure and simple. Goldwater had no compunctions about asking for Thurmond's endorsement. It was freely offered. Goldwater then dared Thurmond to go one better and become a Republican. That would make history: the only Republican senator from any state in the old Confederacy was John Tower.

Thurmond asked his cronies about the idea. They told him he was crazy. He polled South Carolina voters. They told him he wasn't crazy. A third voice tipped the decision: Roger Milliken, Thurmond's biggest benefactor. And so, in a statewide TV address on September 16, in front of a "Goldwater for President" poster bigger than he was, Senator Thurmond acted as if he had hardly given the decision a second thought. If Lyndon Johnson's Democrats prevailed, he said, "Freedom as we have known it in this country is doomed."

"My fellow extremists!" he would drawl from the podium thereafter at Goldwater's Southern stops, "I did not leave the Democratic Party. It left me!" Thurmond's example was a powerful catalyst for those lesser mortals in the crowds wondering whether to make the switch for themselves—if not at the registration table, at least in the voting booth.

George Wallace had come within days of making the same decision. He was sowing seeds for the 1968 presidential election by then, and had already received several attractive offers to turn Republican. The agent in the negotiations was none other than Roger Milliken. Then came Thurmond's announcement. Wallace felt that Milliken had betrayed him; he had no interest in sharing Strom Thurmond's thunder. He stayed a Democrat.

And what if Wallace *had* gone Republican? Could Goldwater have proudly shared his dais with a man he despised as a racist? Back when he had met with Jim Martin up on top of the Mark Hopkins Hotel, the answer would have been simple. Not now. Slowly, Goldwater seemed to be shedding his discomfort with the Southland's peculiar institutions. Another guest at his podiums at those rallies was a man named Leander Perez. Dictator of Louisiana's Plaquemines Parish since 1919, Judge Perez referred to "his" Negroes as "animals right out of the jungle," called civil rights activists "Zionist Jews," and reacted to their their arrival in his territory by outfitting a former Confederate fort into something akin to a medieval dungeon. For these sins he had been excommunicated from the Catholic church.

Perhaps Goldwater didn't know all this about Perez; perhaps he chose to ignore what he knew. Whatever he was up to, it was working. "It's been a long time since Southerners have had a presidential candidate they could support with pride and enthusiasm," the *Charleston News and Courier* gushed.

The idea on the third floor was that the President of the United States was too proud a man not to rise up in anger at Goldwater's shots. He didn't. "I'm not here to make a political speech," he would say with a smile in his occasional forays out of Washington. He was just in town "to speak to a group of workingmen who invited me."

His spots spoke for him. One showed a young girl intently licking an ice-cream cone as a maternal voice-over cooed, "Know what people used to do? They used to explode bombs in the air. You know, children should have lots of vitamin A and calcium. But they shouldn't have strontium 90 or cesium 137. . . . Now there's a man who wants to be President of the United States. . . . His name is Barry Goldwater. If he's elected, they might start testing all over again." The last words were nearly drowned out by Geiger-counter clicks.

Another, a five-minute piece that DDB had feared would not hold its audience, depicted alternating countdowns in Russian and English, each followed by a nuclear explosion, the whole cycle repeating faster and faster, converging, converging—until the unremitting tension was relieved by John Kennedy's voice announcing completion of test-ban negotiations. It held its audience.

Then there was the one that made people think the phone in their house was ringing; that got their attention. The camera panned over the phone to reveal that it had no dial; there was a flashing red light in the lower-right-hand corner, and the words WHITE HOUSE where the phone number should be. Voice-over: "This particular phone only rings in a serious crisis. Leave it in the hands of a man who has proven himself responsible."

A final spot, following a pregnant woman as she walked with her daughter through the woods as the narrator discussed nuclear fallout, was pulled. There was no evidence that fallout harmed fetuses; Moyers and the DDB people assured themselves that they didn't want to resort to scare tactics.

Johnson himself was never depicted in the ads lest he be too firmly associated with their terrible themes. Only his voice was heard—stern, comforting, fatherly. He never deigned to mention his opponent, who, when referred to at all, was never bestowed with the honorific "Senator." Nor was the Democratic Party mentioned, which was revolutionary: previous Democratic candidates' ads had tried to exploit the party's edge in registration by mentioning the party incessantly. Hubert Humphrey was ignored entirely. "We just don't feel that people vote for Vice-Presidential candidates," an account executive brazenly told the *New York Times*. "We're selling the President of the United States."

Whenever possible, the Republican Party was turned against itself. One spot panned over discarded posters on a floor littered with confetti: "Back in July in San Francisco the Republicans held a convention," the narrator said, the camera moving in on one of the posters. "Remember him? He was there. Governor Rockefeller. Before the convention, he said, 'Barry Goldwater's positions can,' and I quote, 'spell disaster for the party and the country.' Or him? Governor Scranton. The day before the convention, he called Goldwaterism a 'crazy quilt collection of absurd and dangerous propositions.' "

A five-minute spot deployed DDB's most towering contribution to the art of advertising: "Confessions of a Republican" implied that all ads were lies, except this one. A sincere, well-dressed young man spoke directly into the camera: "I don't know just why they wanted to call this a confession. I certainly don't feel guilty about being a Republican. I've always been a Republican." He twitched nervously. "But when we come to Senator Goldwater, now it seems to me we're up against a very different kind of man. . . . Those people who got a hold of that convention—who are they?" Another ad, in which the screen was filled with fiery crosses as a KKK leader was quoted—"I like Barry Goldwater; he needs our help"—was pulled at the last minute, because Goldwater had by then renounced the Klan's support—but that didn't keep the Confessing Republican from intoning worriedly, "I mean, when the head of the Ku Klux Klan with all those weird groups come out in favor of the candidate of my party, either they're not Republicans or I'm not."

One borrowed a line that Graham Molitor's indefatigable staff had unearthed that Goldwater had uttered in the 1930s upon learning he needed a New York bank account to do business in New York: that the country would be better off if the entire Eastern Seaboard were sawed off. (A graphic illustrated the very thing.)

But the ad that showed up most frequently focused on two hands taking a Social Security card from a wallet and tearing it clean in two. "On at least seven occasions," said the voice-over, "Senator Barry Goldwater said that he would change the present Social Security system. But even his running mate, William Miller, admits that Senator Goldwater's voluntary plan would destroy the Social Security system. President Johnson is working on strengthening Social Security." There was, of course, no such "voluntary plan"; the subject had barely crossed Goldwater's lips since the primary in New Hampshire.

Beyond Madison Avenue, back at the White House, the campaign operated on the same wavelength as Rockefeller's in California: the enemy was brutal, Machiavellian, justifying any savagery lest he be the first to visit the same methods on you. LBJ wanted to make JFK's victory "look like a pathetic peep." Manufacturing that landslide became a full-time cottage industry—the cottage being the West Wing of the White House.

The operation was as messy as a Texas barbecue. Any policy expert, wise man, labor leader, or cabinet secretary within shouting range of the Oval Office could expect some strange campaign assignment or another: economics hand Paul Southwick tried his hand at pamphlet design (the mushroom cloud he sketched behind the words "suburban scene" better resembled a suburban tree); Walter Heller went to work persuading Walter Lippmann and the *Washington Post* to attack the Goldwater tax plan and prepared detailed reports on each place Johnson was to speak (there would be a $1,450 loss in income to every farm in North Carolina from Goldwater's agricultural ideas, a $140 million statewide gain from Johnson's tax cut). John Bartlow Martin, an investigative journalist famed for the encyclopedic detail and geographic reach of his work, produced fifteen-page single-spaced memos on the politics of each locale so that speeches could be adjusted, presumably, according to such data as the number of "Physicians, including Osteopaths" per 10,000. Mac Bundy was assigned the task of increasing their support among Southern women. Old Johnson friends did yeoman's duty as spies: when the doyenne of New York labor activists, Anna Rosenberg, saw a TWA pilot handing out anti-Johnson literature published by *Human Events*, she immediately forwarded the relevant details—Flight 4, L.A. to New York, Captain Addick—to the White House. The boss's appetite for numbers was satisfied all the way down to a poll of the Lapeer, Michigan, Optimist Club. (They preferred him 3 to 1.) A Goldwater interview in *Time* in which the candidate admitted only intermittent church attendance was sent to lists of clergymen; a transcript of liberal Republican New Jersey senator Cliff Case's savaging of his partyman on the Sunday chat show *Opinion in the Capital* was sent to Jersey newspapers.

Lyndon Johnson was his own campaign manager. He organized his shop as he did all his endeavors: in overlapping, informal, task-oriented circles including only those advisers who knew to give him only advice he wanted to hear. Washington superlawyers Jim Rowe, Clark Clifford, and Abe Fortas combed their bulging Rolodexes for names of people to convince to become figureheads to chair twenty-six Johnson-Humphrey citizens committees (Rural Americans for Johnson-Humphrey, Women for Johnson-Humphrey, Senior Citizens, Lawyers, College Students, Union Women, Southerners, Criminologists, Republicans for Johnson and Humphrey; every imaginable ethnic group for Johnson-Humphrey . . .) set up in order to circumvent the law restricting the circulation of literature by political parties. No opportunity for advantage was missed. When Goldwater appeared in Memphis, reams of TVA brochures flooded the crowd ("If It's Socialism in the Tennessee Valley . . . How About Arizona?" they asked about the $1 billion Central Arizona Project). Outside one of Goldwater's South Carolina appearances, the pamphlets read, "He has a perfect record of having voted AGAINST every single measure that meant more bread and butter for the people of South Carolina." While Goldwater zipped through Mason City, Iowa, a press release went out over the signature of Meredith Willson, of *Music Man* fame: "The big parade comes to Mason City today, led by a political conman who makes Prof. Harold Hill look like a piker." "We ought to treat Goldwater not as an equal, who has credentials to be president," Jack Valenti wrote. "We must depict Miller as some April Fool's gag. . . . Practically all our answers ought to mantle in ridicule." He proposed hiring Hollywood joke writers to help. They contacted Bob Hope's people.

The liberal Republicans would have to be given "some useful and healing roles to play," a strategy memo suggested, "while they are driving the kooks over the skyline." Thus Johnson unveiled Bob Anderson's National Independent Committee for Johnson and Humphrey in a White House ceremony carefully scripted for the television cameras to steal Goldwater's fire in Prescott on September 3. It was a forty-five-name honor roll of Eastern Republican Establishmentarians: CEOs from companies diverse enough to fill the most conservative investment portfolio; a couple of Boston Cabots, as well as the Lodge campaign's finance chair, John Loeb; a Goldman Sachs senior partner who had raised $3 million for Eisenhower in 1952; Henry Ford II—and one future treasury secretary, one former treasury secretary, and one man who had been offered the job of treasury secretary but had turned it down. Many still bore scars from the Scranton campaign. LBJ was gracious enough to let them show their gratitude by paying the $1,000 that earned them a picture with the President and a bill-signing pen; or by signing the five-figure checks that reportedly bought a naked dip in the White House pool.

The bulwark in the maelstrom was William Moyers—as he was in most matters in Lyndon Johnson's White House. LBJ reserved his greatest affection for brilliant young climbers from the provinces who looked up to him as a father figure—as he had himself with a series of mentors culminating in House Speaker Sam Rayburn. (It betokened his insecurities; he still couldn't quite believe these geniuses were willing to yoke their fortune to *him*.) Moyers was the most brilliant and loyal climber of all. After college, divinity school, and three rural pastorates, the twenty-five-year-old former Johnson summer intern (he was hired after writing his senator in 1954 with advice on how to win the youth vote) was preparing for a job teaching Christian ethics at Baylor University when he received the call from LBJ to become his personal assistant in 1959. By 1960 Bill Moyers was running a vice-presidential campaign. Then he left for another ministry: the associate directorship of the Peace Corps. He returned, upon Johnson's accession to the presidency, as his most trusted special assistant. Convincing Bill Moyers of something, Washington soon learned, was nearly as good as convincing the President himself.

So when some aides began worrying about the "overkill effect" of all the negative sallies—"I'm wary about throwing more bombs around," wrote one—it was to Moyers that they turned. Their entreaties came to grief. The would-be professor of Christian ethics liked to play rough. "We have a few more Goldwater ads," Moyers promised the President shortly after the "Daisy" spot ran, "and then we go to the pro-Johnson, pro-Peace, Prosperity, Preparedness spots." But they never really got to them. *Anti* worked too well. "Right now, the biggest asset we have is Goldwater's alleged instability in re atom and hydrogen bombs," as Jack Valenti put it. "We *must not* let this slip away."

Moyers was instrumental in pioneering an innovation in presidential campaigning: the full-time espionage, sabotage, and mudslinging unit. The Johnson "Anti-Campaign" was an all-star Democratic team, including Daniel P. Moynihan of Labor; White House counsel Myer Feldman; the assistant postmaster; the assistant secretary of agriculture; labor lobbyist Hyman Bookbinder; a claque of top D.C. lawyers; the Pentagon's Adam Yarmolinsky (one of the Administration's strongest liberal voices); even Clifton Cooper, the CIA liaison to the White House. The group met in a conference room directly above the Oval Office, because Johnson wanted to monitor their work closely. This project was his favorite.

Some successes were catalogued in one of the few memos the Anti-Campaign left behind. "This accounting statement does not imply any obligation or commitment on your part. Copies of this are going to other major stockholders," Clifton Cooper wrote, the code humorously suggesting the CIA's internal nickname—the Company. "Our acquisition, reproduction, and dissemination of advance Goldwater texts is now flowing smoothly. In some cases we . . . have prepared a rebuttal before a speech has actually been delivered. Bob Greene is now working on an article suitable for *Life, Look,* or the *Saturday Evening Post.* It . . . will be available for someone like an Ed Murrow or other well-known, highly respected, above-the-battle figure to sign."

The operation collected off-the-record quotes from Goldwater's press corps and retained the CIA's domestic covert-actions chief, E. Howard Hunt, to place spies in the RNC (they delivered daily reports to a dummy office in the National Press Building called "Continental Press"). Democratic (or Republicans for Johnson) speakers were booked immediately before and after Goldwater appearances; letters columns of local papers were seeded to give an impression of feverish anti-Goldwater activity; sometimes the Anti-Campaign even managed to schedule "Confessions of a Republican" at the tail end of half-hour Goldwater TV spots. They considered using the Social Security list for campaign mailings (they backed off when they learned that doing so would not merely be unethical, but also illegal).

They were too good for their own good. One Friday in early October, Goldwater's inner circle kicked around the idea of promising that were Goldwater elected he would send Eisenhower to Vietnam, an echo of Eisenhower's famous 1952 campaign promise that if he were elected he would personally go to Korea. The intelligence duly found its way to the Oval Office. Johnson called up the General at Gettysburg and told him, "You don't have to wait for Senator Goldwater to get elected in order to go to Vietnam. I've got a Boeing 707 all warmed up and waiting at Andrews Air Force Base and I'll send a helicopter after you any time you care to go." The old man had no idea what Johnson was talking about. Johnson had beaten Goldwater to the call.

The Anti-Campaign's most effective agent was the Commander in Chief. Constantly, Goldwater agitated for a television showdown with Johnson. But there would be no televised debate in this election. Johnson had put in the fix—

twisting arms to kill the bill that would waive the legal requirement, under the Federal Communications Act's Section 315, of inviting every declared presidential candidate all the way down to Lar Daly, he of the Uncle Sam suit. Goldwater could still push for debate—if he was willing to share the stage with half a dozen minor-party candidates. Republicans' hopes soared on September 10 when the Senate voted 75 to 3 to reopen the investigation of the ties between Johnson and Bobby Baker, owing to the existence of new evidence. They crashed on October 12—when Johnson was able to get the investigation mysteriously postponed until after November 3. And more than one well-heeled Goldwater supporter reported answering the phone to a Texas drawl: "I have several years' worth of your tax returns in front of me, and they make most interesting reading . . ."

Meanwhile, Goldwater's critics were crossing the threshold of slander and entering the realm of the fantastic.

In 1961 a Greenwich Village huckster named Ralph Ginzburg had launched an arty semipornographic quarterly called *Eros*. His massive promotional mailing, however, backfired: it found its way into so many unsuspecting households that the postmaster general received a record number of complaints. The chair of the Post Office Operations Subcommittee denounced Ginzburg on the House floor; Attorney General Robert Kennedy revived the Comstock Act—which would mean bringing criminal, not civil charges—to try to put Ginzburg in jail. Ginzburg was convicted. There were appeals. And in 1964, in between trials, Ginzburg, casting around for something to do, decided to start a muckraking magazine. He wanted the first issue to make a big splash, and the "Eureka!" came when he read a poll showing that Goldwater was popular among medical doctors—except psychiatrists, 90 percent of whom despised him. Ginzburg rented the mailing list of the American Psychoanalytic Association and sent out a single-question poll: "Do you believe Barry Goldwater is psychologically fit to serve as President of the United States?" The returns, printed one after the other in a massive article in *Fact* magazine's first and only issue, made for one hell of a litany.

"I do not think his having two nervous breakdowns in the past should be held against him. The sickness of his character structure *now present* is his real psychological deficit," wrote one doctor. "Basically, I feel he has a narcissistic character disorder with not too latent paranoid elements." Another called the Republican candidate a "compensated schizophrenic" like Hitler, Castro, and Stalin. A colleague demurred: "Though compensated at present," he would "become more irrational and paranoid when under political attack during the campaign." A Dr. Berlin singled out Goldwater's "frustrated and malcontented" followers, who "reflect his own paranoid and omnipotent tendencies . . . as was characteristic of dictators in the '30s and '40s," because Goldwater "appeals to the unconscious sadism and hostility in the average human being." A Dr. Stillman, a bit deluded about the line between fantasy and reality himself, recognized in the candidate "a type accurately depicted by another Air Force general in the movie *Dr. Strangelove*." Another doctor, paranoid, advised, "Strategy against the paranoid fringe must be *very* carefully worked out. A frontal attack on paranoids causes them to band together and become more efficient." And one from New York decried Goldwater's "tremendous following from among . . . destructive elements of the South and West."

This went on for dozens of pages. Since only 20 percent of the doctors ever returned the survey, no statistician would ever credit its validity. It was more like a Rorschach test of what a number of educated, sophisticated professionals tended to see when the image of Barry Goldwater was put before them for comment. The fifty reporters bumping along in triple seats in the hindquarters of *Yia Bi Ken* were educated, sophisticated professionals. And they didn't think all that differently about Goldwater than the psychiatrists.

The reporters liked Barry Goldwater personally ("How could such a nice guy *think* that way?" one asked). Two traveling publicists ministered efficiently to their every need. That was far less than enough to make the experience a pleasant one. They had missed the story of how Goldwater won the nomination, which was humiliating to their professional pride; it also meant twice as much work for reporters, because none of the people in the campaign were in their little black books. Some never did learn to spell Clif White's name right. For many, memories of indignities suffered at the Cow Palace still stung; Goldwater's visits to their compartment, meanwhile, grew rarer than the Great Pumpkin's. The booing directed at them at every stop became increasingly hard to take. Once a Goldwater mob hurled stones at their bus. Their objectivity began failing them. In Montana, 10,000 stood in the freezing rain to welcome Goldwater, and the number the press somehow settled on was 2,500—an "unenthusiastic" 2,500 at that. In Atlanta—then Memphis—Jack Steel of the Scripps-Howard chain so lowballed the turnouts that Karl Hess strolled into the press quarters with a token of appreciation: a carving of a hand with the middle finger extended. Steel reported the incident in his copy—a testament to the inner circle's sublime indifference to public relations.

Lyndon Johnson's relationship with his traveling press corps was altogether different: they protected him. The President's tongue was if anything more undisciplined than his opponent's. At one point he would say that the American people wanted nuclear control "vested in a civilian. They do not expect to abandon this duty to military men in the field, and I don't think that they have ever considered that since the Founding Fathers drafted our Constitution"—though surely the control of nuclear weapons never made the Founding Fathers' agenda. "If it hadn't been for Goldwater," Johnson aide Kenny O'Donnell recalled afterward, the press would have "just murdered him." The man with his finger on the nuclear button sometimes weaved off his campaign plane stinking drunk; he made mistakes on the stump; he contradicted himself in interviews. On his way to opening day in Detroit, in order to squeeze as many VIPs into his plane as possible, he booted onto an accompanying plane the military aide who kept the briefcase handcuffed to his wrist that contained the codes to launch a nuclear strike. That plane nearly ended up crashing. Reporters looked the other way. "Thank God for Lyndon Johnson," a scribe from the *St. Louis Post-Dispatch* thought to himself, as the President lit into Goldwater once more as a "ranting, raving demagogue who wants to tear down society."

The RNC had reserved a series of half-hour blocks on CBS Friday evenings—preempting, with relish, *That Was the Week That Was,* a fiendishly witty live musical revue that sent up each week's news with a decided leftward lean. And so, in place of barbs at Barry Goldwater's expense, on Friday evening, September 18, there was Barry Goldwater, getting straight to the business at hand with hardly a "good evening"—the business being explaining why "the Republican Party is the party of peace": "*because we understand the enemy. . . .* He's the schoolyard bully. . . . Let him push you around and eventually you'll have to fight. Just stand up to him, though . . . and he'll back down and there will be no fight." The speech didn't sound very pacific. It concluded with an endless quote from Churchill—a quote that was virtually meaningless unless you knew that October 16, 1938, was when Chamberlain had promised "peace with honor" with Hitler. Even Goldwater fans judged the show a calamity.

The saving grace was a sixty-second appeal for funds tacked to the end of the half hour featuring the actor Raymond Massey, fresh from playing Abraham Lincoln in the film *How the West Was Won* and a heroic surgeon on TV's *Dr. Kildare.* The ad displayed a post-office-box address at the bottom of the screen: "TV for Goldwater-Miller, Box 80, Los Angeles 51, California."

"TV for Goldwater-Miller" was a front, incorporated in California with Walter Knott as chair to get around campaign law's spending limitations for any one "committee." No campaign had tried raising funds on television before. Baroody and Kitchel fought the idea tooth and nail as undignified. For once they were overruled, which was a good thing. So much money flowed in from that ad that the show paid for itself.

Thanks to Kitchel's incompetence, the campaign needed to save all the money it could. When Goldwater's campaign leaders purged the RNC's finance chair, the job was offered to Goldwater's friend Ralph Cordiner, the former CEO of General Electric. This was a bad enough move: Cordiner, a stony man who was widely unpopular among the very plutocrats the campaign counted on for support, was associated in the public's mind with G.E.'s recent conviction for price fixing. Even worse, Cordiner had set a condition for taking the job: that the campaign run on a balanced budget. That sounded fine to Kitchel; conservatives didn't like deficit spending when Congress did it, so why should they accept it in their campaign? It was a greenhorn mistake. Much of what a campaign needs to operate—printers, producers, pollsters, TV time—has to be hired and paid for long before the money begins rolling in. A campaign *has* to be financed on credit. But the first thing Cordiner did, congratulating himself on his rectitude, was to cancel TV time the RNC had painstakingly negotiated with the networks in advance for spots in the closing weeks of the campaign.

At least they still had their half hours. The next one was to be their Hail Mary pass—their version of John F. Kennedy's masterpiece before an audience of Protestant ministers that convinced much of the nation to vote for Kennedy to prove they weren't anti-Catholic bigots. It would feature Goldwater and General Eisenhower in informal conversation at Ike's Gettysburg farm—Americans' anxieties about Goldwater's finger on the nuclear trigger melting away while they watched Goldwater receive the blessing of the kindly man who had saved Western civilization. Even were that grand goal not achieved, at least the campaign would rake in plenty of cash from Ray Massey's appeal. Everybody, after all, liked Ike.

It was there that the problems began. Denison Kitchel put his foot down: no appeal for filthy lucre would despoil the dignity of the thirty-fourth President of the United States. The $12.166 million campaign budget was dutifully slashed by $175,000, the amount they had expected the half-hour Massey appeal would raise. Things went downhill from there.

They filmed at Eisenhower's home in Gettysburg the day before the show was to air. He would give them only a few hours, reluctantly at that. The crew moved in what seemed a ton of gear, wired the farm with yards of cable; the thirty-fourth President of the United States frowned in annoyance. Chuck Lichenstein, the producer, briefed Eisenhower on the format, a sort of directed improvisation: they would film at three different locations, and Eisenhower and Goldwater would be given rough guidelines on the topics they should cover during each scene. The climax, Lichenstein explained, would be a debunking of the charge that Goldwater was ready to release the nuclear codes to every last warrant officer in the Seventh Army.

"Oh, you know I'd say that's a lot of bullshit," Eisenhower offered. "But I can't say that on TV, can I?"

"Um . . . that wouldn't be consistent with your image, General," Lichenstein replied. He suggested "balderdash" instead. Ike said he never used the word. Then he lit up. "How about 'tommyrot'?"

And there it was. The most responsible man in the world would remove the albatross of nuclear irresponsibility from the Republican candidate's weary shoulders by vigorous application of the word "tommyrot."

They set up the shot with the two men leaning over a white picket fence, thick microphone cables protruding from their coat jackets like tails. The cameras rolled. Goldwater said something; Ike's eyes wandered. Ike began a sentence, then got lost in one of his famous syntactical thickets, never to return (we must, he said at one point, "preserve the outbreak of war"). Ike looked like he wanted to be somewhere else; Goldwater looked like a high school boy trying to engage the fickle attentions of the captain of the cheerleading squad. Goldwater started every sentence with "Well . . ." Roll, cut, roll, cut; it was a disaster.

Mercifully, the noontime break came. Goldwater awaited the invitation to join Ike back at the little white farmhouse to take lunch with Mamie. Instead Eisenhower left Goldwater standing there. The candidate swallowed his pride, sat calmly with the crew, cadged from their box lunches (they hadn't brought one along for him), and regaled them with a few dirty jokes. Behind the mask he was surely contemplating the dustbin to which General Eisenhower had just consigned him. Everyone knew Richard Nixon's famous complaint about not once having been invited inside that house in his eight years as vice president.

It took a frantic overnight editing session to pull something usable out of the morass; Kitchel was convinced Eisenhower had sabotaged the thing on purpose. But at least the ad would open nicely. An aerial camera tracked over the General's prize heard of Angus cattle. Lilting strings entered: Aaron Copland's *Appalachian Spring*. A narrator intoned in a soothing voice, "Autumn has come to the rolling hills of Gettysburg, Pennsylvania. The fragrant smell of apples ripe and ready for harvest fills the air. The leaves have just started to turn, and these are beautiful days."

If you turned the TV off then and there, you might have had a reasonably satisfying viewing experience.

It seemed like Eisenhower and Goldwater were in different rooms. More than one of Ike's remarks that aired slyly disparaged his interlocutor. ("Self-restraint is absolutely necessary to anyone who aspires to leadership of a great nation," he said. Goldwater nodded vigorously in agreement.) They repaired to the barbecue area (where, lest anyone dash the public's stereotype of the Republicans as the party of the rich, a hired hand grilled away obsequiously in the background). Goldwater lurched into the grand finale: "There's just one thing I might ask in leaving. . . . Because we constantly stress the need for a strong America, our opponents are referring to us as warmongers. And I'd like to know your opinion on that." The breeze lifted a tuft of white hair from the side of Eisenhower's head. He hit his mark and delivered his line: "Well, Barry, in this mind, this is actual tommyrot."

Then came the part where he was to sum things up with an endorsement. It turned out to be hardly an endorsement at all. It was more like an exercise in a Logic 101 class. "Now, you know about war. You've been through one," Ike said. "Any man who knows anything about war is not going to be reckless about this." *Barry Goldwater knows about war. Anyone who knows about war would not be a reckless President. Q.E.D. Barry Goldwater would not be a reckless President:* at that, viewers who were veterans could flatter themselves that Dwight D. Eisenhower thought *they* would make good Presidents, too.

The closing shot had the two men walking into the sunset. They exited the frame; the camera trained in on the five-star flag of the Supreme Commander of NATO on the General's putting green. *Appalachian Spring* sounded in the background. A sheep bleated in the foreground. This, too, was a nice shot, although by that point very few people were still watching. Of the TV sets in operation, 27.4 percent were tuned to *Petticoat Junction*; 25 percent watched *Peyton Place* ("television's first situation orgy," Jack Paar called it); and— President Johnson gleefully learned the next day—8.6 percent watched *Conversation at Gettysburg*. "I didn't have much experience with TV," Lichenstein excused himself later. He didn't mean he didn't have much experience with TV production. He meant he didn't *watch* TV.

Goldwater continued demanding debates. Johnson ignored him. And Goldwater began exhibiting the unlovely mien of a bitter man: "He will not face the issues, he will not face me—he will not face *you*," he yelped across the upper Midwest. "Can my opponent talk? What does my opponent have to say?" He besmirched the nation's highest offices: Hubert Humphrey was a "socialistic radical"; LBJ was "Light Bulb Johnson" for his scheme to save money by turning off lights in the White House ("Why doesn't he turn them *on* for once!"), "the interim president," who "knows only one thing—how to acquire fortune and power." Goldwater's supporters crowded the speaking stand and cheered him on. Much of the audience hung back in disgust.

Everyone associated with the campaign was getting bitter. Local branches began compiling affidavits on vandalism on their offices; on highways across the fruited plain, billboards admonishing "IN YOUR HEART YOU KNOW HE'S RIGHT" were subverted to read "IN YOUR GUTS YOU KNOW HE'S NUTS" (later reclaimed by conservatives with signs reading "PLEASE EXCUSE THE JOHNSON EXTREMISTS"). Stodgy *Time* printed crude jokes: "Goldwater's first major address as President: 'Ten . . . nine . . . eight . . . seven . . .' "; "What would a Goldwater presidency be like? Brief." In Tulsa, blacks crashed the hall where Goldwater was speaking and wouldn't stop singing "We Shall Overcome" for fifteen minutes straight. In Winston-Salem, civil rights activists and conservatives were booked for assaulting one another. Each had begun chanting their opposing stories about freedom, slavery, and justice at the other; things escalated from there. (Teddy White liked to ask civil rights demonstrators and Goldwater partisans what they meant by "freedom." Each camp would denounce him for even asking such a patronizing question. "It is quite possible that these two groups may kill each other in cold blood," he wrote, "both wearing banners bearing the same word.")

American campaigns had been like this before, perhaps more often than not; Lord Bryce wrote in wonderment that the presidential election of 1884 seemed to be being decided between the "copulative habits" imputed to one candidate and the "prevaricative habits" of the other. But eighty years later, the *Philadelphia Inquirer* could insist: "Presidential elections have been waged without untoward incident until this year." Historians forgot their history. "The peaceful arts of negotiation and persuasion," "our sagacity and our passion for the peaceful enjoyment of our national life": these, Columbia's Richard Hofstadter assured readers that October, were the hallmarks of political decision making in America. It was a foregone conclusion: when Goldwaterism was vanquished once and for all on November 3, civility would return, the two parties would return to their time-honored moderating role, and the nation would be restored to a healing consensus once again.

Johnson's first actual campaign trip—tarmac speeches, motorcades, rallies, the works—was a twenty-four-hour sweep through every New England state on September 28. It happened against a backdrop of extraordinary events.

On September 26, the Federal Bureau of Investigation released its report on the New York City riots. There was a kind of rhetorical protocol that usually held sway when judgment was handed down on moments when the fabric of American civility had been rent. J. Edgar Hoover's report on the students who disrupted the HUAC hearings in San Francisco in 1960, "Communist Target—Youth," was a paradigm case: it blamed the Communists, who had made students their unwitting dupes. And Nelson Rockefeller's Bastille Day proclamation: it concluded that the 1963 Young Republican convention had been upended by "vociferous and well-drilled extremist elements boring within." The story they told was: America was a good nation, a unified nation, peaceful, safe, a land of persuasion and compromise; when violence came, some exogenous toxin was always to blame.

That story was immediately and instinctually told when Harlem went up in flames in the summer of 1964. Accusations for planning and executing the disturbance were hurled at Harlem's tiny number of self-proclaimed Maoists, at its scattered bands of black nationalists, at hirelings of H. L. Hunt (LBJ's favorite theory), or (as Goldwater himself feared) at agents of the Goldwater campaign. Special attention was paid to the mysterious youths that were seen lurking at key street corners with walkie-talkies and matching berets; it was discovered that they were actually helping authorities identify the most egregious acts of looting and arson. There was no conspiracy to be found in this latest FBI report. In its place were ordinary people—" 'school dropouts,' 'young punks,' 'common hoodlums,' and 'drunken kids' " making "senseless attack on all constituted authority without purpose or objective." J. Edgar Hoover went looking for conspiracy; he always did. He just couldn't find one. It wasn't even the Communists' fault.

Then, two days later, there was the Warren Report. In later days it would be the locus for theorists propounding baroque triangulations of every imaginable group that might gain from having the President dead; its very meaning became conspiracy. But it was digested at breakfast tables on September 28, 1964—a time when three-quarters of Americans, according to surveys, trusted the government to do the right thing—differently. A conspiracy would have been far more comforting. Instead most Americans read the news at face value, and learned that all it took to rock their society to its foundations was a single man with a grievance and a gun. They had learned that all it took to fire up a riot was a bunch of rock-throwing kids—and that even a majestic Civil Rights Act would not deter them. The idea that the nation could be shielded from danger by its unique genius for conciliation and consensus was becoming a far less tenable thing.

Oswald, a magazine pointed out, "was a product of Texas (and of New York City), of the American lower-middle class, of the U.S. Marines. . . . All of those places and associations are as American as baseball. . . . There is violence in the American character, probably more than in any other national character." As if to give this new American story an exclamation point, on September 29, after four bombings in eight days in the town of McComb, Mississippi, three Klansmen were arrested off the street. They admitted that they chose bombing victims weekly out of a hat. They were released on suspended sentences. The judge ruled that they had been "unduly provoked" by "unhygienic" outsiders of "low morality." And, that same day, thirteen civil rights workers were arrested for the crime of Southern hospitality—"serving food without a license," the charge read.

And then, that same week, came Berkeley.

An unheard-of 42 percent of high school graduates sought higher education in 1964, as if reserving a spot in the knowledge-driven Great Society to come. In California 68 percent of high school graduates went to college, most of them taking advantage of the state's glittering free university system—the best of them to her crown jewel, the Berkeley campus. The system's leader, Clark Kerr, was managerial liberalism's uncrowned king. His book *The Uses of the University* was its bible.

In it he wrote that the modern "multiversity"—he also dubbed it the "knowledge factory"—was both catalyst and mirror for a society in which the objectives of myriad plural interests could be harmonized with the help of neutral, efficient, nonideological administration, delivering ever more peace and well-being to all. He also described the disasters that would befall such a system if people became *too* interested in their interests. To the best of his ability, the individual should seek "to lend his energies to many organizations and give himself completely to none." The only alternative was the conviction that some interests were irreconcilable, some principles beyond compromise. If too many people were to hold such beliefs, the outcome, in a complex, integrated social system, would be "all-out war."

Thus Clark Kerr's perennial challenge. Universities were made up of young people, and young people tended to unruly passions. Such passions led to irreconcilable interests, and they had to be reined in. Berkeley students did not always fancy these theories—a campus radical named David Horowitz had answered them in 1962 in a book called *Student* by writing "A man is not a product, nor is he an IBM record card"—and these days, the students seemed to fancy the theories less than ever. The traditional off-campus center for student politicking, a little bricked-over esplanade at the corner of Bancroft Way and Telegraph Avenue called the Bancroft Strip, had been characterized by a cacophony since July—when the Republican Convention, Mississippi Freedom Summer, Prop 14 (in the wake of Berkeley's own open-housing law campaign the year before), Johnson vs. Goldwater for President and Pierre Salinger vs. George Murphy for Senate all converged. Every side in these contests was represented in the burbling confluence of irreconcilables at Bancroft and Telegraph—sometimes two, even three factions jostling on each: lefties, liberal to Trotskyite to Maoist to Castroist; righties from Republican to anarchist. The myriad conservative groups—YAF, Young Republicans, Conservatives at Large (CAL), Cal Students for Goldwater, and the University Society of Individualists—were well stocked with hellions: a University Society of Individualists member sporting an "I AM A RIGHT-WING EXTREMIST" pin became the Rosa Parks of the San Francisco streetcars when she flamboyantly defied the unwritten rule against women standing on the running boards and caused such a disturbance that she ended up getting arrested. Berkeley political scientist Seymour Martin Lipset thought he understood what made youngsters so prone to an inappropriate overabundance of political commitment: a "relative lack of experience with the conflicting pressures derivative from varying value obligations or role demand." They would grow out of it.

But Clark Kerr didn't have time to wait. A vital construction-bond issue would be on state ballots in November. Bad publicity could kill it. Berkeley had already attracted a powerful foe who was editorializing against the "Little Red Schoolhouse" ever more frequently: William Knowland of the *Oakland Tribune*, enraged when Scrantonites used Berkeley as an organizing base, even madder now that Berkeley CORE was picketing his paper (where only 17 of 1,500 employees were black) every week. Berkeley was developing a reputation. Evans and Novak wrote after a reporting trip to San Francisco in March, "Here as elsewhere, the Negro is in danger of losing control over the civil rights movement to thugs and Communists." The thugs and Communists they referred to were Kerr's own students.

As the 1964–65 school year approached, an especially prickly administrator, suffering from the bongo drumming that drifted up from Bancroft and Telegraph to his second-floor office, began taking steps to pacify the Strip. Meanwhile one of Knowland's lackeys discovered at the county assessor's office that the Bancroft Strip was actually *inside* campus property—meaning that the presence of demonstrators was in violation of the university's mandate to keep partisan politics off campus. Subtle threats were issued through channels.

These factors converged when the university administration announced that as of the first day of school, September 21, the Bancroft Strip would be off-limits to politics "because of interference with the flow of traffic." To Clark

Kerr's shock, students, deploying organizing skills acquired in those long months of agitating for civil rights and for Barry Goldwater, struck back—forming a United Front of nineteen political organizations, from right to left, to demand negotiations with the administration. The administration, as was its wont, compromised: students could continue to distribute informational leaflets, as long as they did not encourage "action"—the university, as a state institution, was duty bound, after all, to discourage "advocacy of action without thought."

But students *had* thought, and deeply—and, in rounds of negotiations, they cut their masters to ribbons. Didn't the administration, by changing its story from "clogged traffic" to "advocacy of action without thought," demonstrate bad faith—or capitulation to outside influence, in the form of no less a partisan than William Knowland? If a campus was contaminated by the introduction of outside politics, wherefore Nelson Rockefeller's invitation to speak on campus back in March? Why had Kerr put his own administration to work politicking among voting-age students to vote for the bond-issue proposition? Why wasn't the $12 million the university received from the Atomic Energy Commission each year political? Its contributions to the American presence in Vietnam? Could it be that deciding what was neutral and what was political was *itself* political—that enforcing "neutrality" was just another way for the administration to wield its power?

So they acted. On the twenty-first, students kept an all-night vigil on the steps of the administration building, Sproul Hall. A week later, pickets flooded the school's ceremonial convocation. Tables were carted 100 yards inside campus borders, a leader announcing, "We won't stop now until we've made the entire campus a bastion of free speech." Administrators warned the eight students manning the tables that they were about to be expelled. The eight were summoned to the dean's office on September 30 for expulsion—and brought hundreds of their closest friends along with them to stage a sit-down demonstration in Sproul Hall to demand negotiations. And suddenly the administration building was playing host to a *festival* of free speech—one student following the other, Socratic-style, reasoning over the true meaning of the university, of free speech, of freedom itself.

It was near midnight when the intense, wild-maned Italian kid from New York, back from registering voters in McComb, Mississippi, stood up to speak. Mario Savio had a bad stutter that faded only when he was stirred. He wasn't stuttering now. "President Kerr has referred to the University as a factory," he said. "And just like any factory, in any industry—again, his words—you have a certain product. . . . They go in one side, as kind of rough-cut adolescents, and they come out the other side pretty smooth. . . . And never, at any point, is provision made for their taking their places as free men!" The sentiment was something with which the department store owner from Phoenix could agree (his enemy, he wrote in one of his first columns, was "a stereotyped, carbon copy society"), or William F. Buckley ("Middle-of-the-Road, *qua* Middle-of-the-Road, is politically, intellectually, and morally repugnant," the prospectus of his magazine announced in 1954). Commitments—not "interests"—were the building blocks, not the stumbling blocks, of politics. Some commitments were sacred, could not be bargained away. Sometimes the proper arena for politics was a boxing ring.

The next morning, a CORE member named Jack Weinberg set up a table (a propped-up old door, actually) at the foot of the Sproul Hall steps. Police arrested him for criminal trespass. Or at least they tried to. Weinberg went limp, civil disobedience–style (while finishing a stirring peroration about how thought, talk, and discussion were vacuous "unless we then act on the principle that we think, talk and discuss about"). Rather than break their backs carrying him to headquarters, the Berkeley campus cops rolled in a squad car and dumped him into the back—then found their way blocked by a hundred students who had gathered for a planned noon rally. The engine revved; the students raised a chorus of "We Shall Not Be Moved."

It was then that Mario Savio removed his shoes. Boston Harbor, Harpers Ferry, Omaha Beach: this time the stand for freedom would be made atop a dented squad car roof. "Be careful of the antenna! Be careful of the antenna!" the cops pleaded. Savio promised he would.

The chancellor "must agree to meet with the political organizations," Savio began. "And there must be no disciplinary action against anyone before the meeting! And, I'm publicly serving notice that we're going to continue direct action until they accede."

No one could have guessed what would happen next. Others wished to speak, so a sign-up sheet went around. One after the other, students took to the roof; more and more students straggled into the plaza—thousands, once word got around campus that something extraordinary was taking place. The speaking continued, interrupted only by singing, for another day and a half.

Jackie Goldberg, the students' lead negotiator (because she was a well-dressed sorority girl), wondered how the university could believe that the student's United Front threatened the institution's neutrality when its different groups were "at the same time supporting Goldwater and trying to defeat him." The crowd rollicked with laughter. Weinberg received the reluctant dispensation of the police to get out of, then onto, the car, where he explained that if they hung together they could never hang separately ("Fill the jails," as the SNCC motto went). A Young Republican took the floor, or roof, and joked wanly, "I am up here as an example of tokenism" (there was no question by now that events were dominated by the left wing of the United Front; conservatives drifted away as soon as laws began to be broken), and proclaimed the conservatives' solidarity "so you know that this is not protest by the same people who were washed down the steps at San Francisco." A woman, a freshman, with a squeaky voice and a nervous manner, popped onto the car; she spoke, and she seemed less a freshman and less squeaky by the minute.

By 2:30 in the afternoon hundreds of the hardest core forced their way into Sproul Hall for another sit-in. By dusk a combined 500-man police force from the cities of Oakland and Berkeley, Alameda County, and the California Highway Patrol (spluttering in on motorcycles) began mustering. Students who had worked in the South instructed those who hadn't about the Gandhian method of submitting to arrest.

There were, it turned out, no arrests—just more talk. History majors cited Founding Fathers, folkies led sing-alongs, aspiring comedians ridiculed administrative doublespeak. The occasional administrator dared take a turn. Professor Lipset lectured the crowd on how their mob tactics violated procedural democracy, rendering them cousins to the Ku Klux Klan.

It was one "second-and-a-half-year graduate dropout" who named the stakes. It was interesting, he said, that all the speakers were gravitating toward the issue of the relationship of democracy and free speech. "They're almost so much the same thing," he piped up, "that there ain't no relationship! Aristotle said if you are not a citizen you are either a beast or a god.

"Now I ask you a simple question—" (peals of laughter; his timing was impeccable).

He continued: "Johnson and Goldwater get up in front of the American people and say, 'Let's keep Vietnam out of politics,' 'Let's keep civil rights out of politics,' and 'Let's keep universal military training out of politics.' " He proclaimed, in disgust: "These are three of the most intimately *political* issues you can think of!"

Darkness fell. An administrator—the one who felt imperiled by the bongo drums—summoned a cordon of fraternity men to preserve the principle of institutional civility; they did so by pelting activists with lit cigarettes and rotten vegetables. (Savio implored them to get up on the car and present their complaints civilly, to no avail.)

Around 2:30 a.m. a near-riot was quelled by the car-top intervention of a respected campus minister. Truce negotiations stepped up inside Sproul, to the accompaniment, through the night, of speaking, chanting, and dueling renditions of "We Shall Overcome" and (from the frat boys) the Mickey Mouse Club theme, through the next morning, the next afternoon, and the dinner hour—when the members of the United Front finally declared that their terms had been met. The prisoner was released, the crowd of 7,000 broke up, the battered car rolled forth. And observers wasted no time identifying the conspiracies behind the event.

"It is regrettable that a relatively small number of students, together with certain off-campus agitators, should have precipitated so unfortunate an incident," the chair of the Regents droned. The *San Francisco Examiner* headlined its report "REDS ON CAMPUS." A columnist in the (liberal) *San Francisco Chronicle* grumbled that the instigators should be hung, then shot with arrows. A crowd photograph in Knowland's *Oakland Tribune* was artfully doctored with another picture to illustrate the caption "A textbook on Marxism was among the crowd." The article charged that the ones who started the trouble were "Cuba-trained" instigators. Clark Kerr, for his part, disagreed. He claimed that "the university was contending with a hard core of Castro–Mao Tse-tung–line Communists." The theorist of pluralism could not confront the fact that he was dealing with an ideological plurality. Or that the leaders of the United Front were just as startled as everyone else by the Squad Car Revolution.

What had happened was less conspiracy than some kind of magic: a core of a few hundred activists told a story about the hypocrisies of consensus liberalism, and it rang true for the thousands of new allies who had never given the matter any thought before. They contemplated The Story—that America was fundamentally decent, its citizens content, their differences resolved through reconciliation and persuasion and compromise—and they refused it.

And so a strange, cosmic unity bodied forth that week in American political history, as Lyndon Johnson came off his first campaign tour: the FBI and the Warren Commission asserting that all it took was one man to tear a social fabric asunder; Mississippians bombing their way past illusions about the American way of reconciling conflict; Berkeley students saying no to "neutrality"; a third of the nation still stubbornly insisting on backing Barry Goldwater—all of them, at the same time, making the idea of an American consensus seem little more than a stubborn, fanciful mythology.

There were "no basic disagreements between intellectuals, bankers, trade unionists, artists, big businessmen, beatniks, professional people, and politicians, to name a few, or between the economic classes" in America today. "There are no real critics, no new ideas, no fundamental differences of opinion."

Thus observed Richard Schlatter, provost of Rutgers University, in his contribution to "Some Comments on Senator Goldwater," a forum in the fall issue of the quarterly *Partisan Review*, for decades a leading arbiter of American intellectual taste. He concluded that the striking thing about Barry Goldwater's imminent failure "is that it has demonstrated that we are all part of the American Establishment." Richard Hofstadter wrote in the October 8 *New York Review of Books*: "It is no simple thing to account for the development and prominence of a mind so out of key with the basic tonalities of our political life. . . . When in our history has anyone with ideas so bizarre, so archaic, so self-confounding, so remote from the basic American consensus, ever got so far?" He concluded worriedly that Goldwater was "within a hair's breadth of ruining one of our great and long-standing institutions"—the Republican Party. *Partisan Review* contributors thought Goldwater was within a hair'sbreadth of something else. "The ingredients of Goldwaterism could of course be put together in such a way as to form a fascist totality," explained one (adding, with relief, that Goldwater's followers, "no better organized than is his own mind," were not up to the work involved). Wrote another, "The danger is that he might well see to it that this year's election is our last free election." His movement, with its "childish intolerance of tension," represented "a recrudescence on American soil of precisely those super-nationalistic and right-wing trends that were finally defeated in Europe at the cost of a great war, untold misery, and many millions dead."

Less empyrean publications put aside such idle speculation of what would happen in the event of a Goldwater victory to tick off the reasons that such a thing was unimaginable in the first place. "To meet the needs of the people," *Atlantic Monthly* editors explained, "the federal government must contribute to the solution of the manifold problems of modern urban life—housing, education, welfare, mass transportation, health, and civil rights." That President Johnson made these points "in language that can be easily understood" was why he was the best politician Americans were likely to see in their lifetimes. *Partisan Review*'s editor agreed, after his fashion. He warned that although one should remain "uneasy about the neanderthalism lurking in the so-called average man," we were stuck with this dreary "centrist Utopia" for the imaginable future.

To which a massed choir of the nation's editorialists could only respond: *Amen*. Then they reviewed the reports from Lyndon Johnson's New England travels and patted themselves on the back for their perspicacity.

Johnson started in Providence, Rhode Island, which suited his purposes well. It was Kennedy country, its soul divided between the martyr's two most loyal constituencies: a proud Irish-Catholic proletariat and the eggheads at Brown University. Stewart Alsop reported that Oliver Quayle, whose polls the President now carried in his pocket like a lucky rabbit's foot, found that Kennedy's "fading but much-revered memory" was LBJ's "second-greatest asset" in the campaign. (The first was "the nervous and uneasy feeling Senator Goldwater imparts to a great many voters.") Johnson was determined to show that there was so much more to his popularity than that—to show that he was loved. Although he was not exactly sure that he was.

Providence provided. The ground was marbled by frost as the President's plane made its early-morning approach. He landed; and before him at the airport was a crowd that was bigger than he had dared dream, some three thousand people. He was jumping out of his skin as he made his way down the steps. "If you want to see crowd reaction," he called giddily out to his press corps, "follow me!"

It wasn't easy. The streets of Providence were so thick with well-wishers it was like parting a sea of molasses, and just as sweet; there were more spectators on the streets, some were claiming, than the population of Providence itself. People called to him, leaned toward him, grasped at him—and, a dozen or more at a time, Johnson just pulled them onto his limousine. (He had been frightening and aggravating his Secret Service protectors with such inexcusable security risks all year.) Other times he would stretch his tall frame over the crowd and bark consensus chestnuts through a bullhorn: "We're in favor of a lot of things, and we're against mighty few!" Armor plating had been added to the sides of the presidential limousine since the assassination, and stronger shock absorbers and brakes were installed to allow for the increased stress. But no car was sturdy enough for *this*. Inching up one steep incline, flames suddenly gushed from beneath the hood of the accompanying press car. Startled Secret Service agents dove for the President's calves to pull him down below window level. Much to his annoyance: "Any dumb son of a bitch would know enough to turn off the ignition when the engine temperature gets to four hundred and fifty degrees!" he complained.

He pulled a CBS cameraman into his car during the next motorcade, through Hartford. The cameraman was motioned to lie on his back on the floorboards and shoot up through the closed bubble top—and Walter Cronkite that evening got to introduce stunning shots of the masses crawling over their President like a thousand insects. Like an addict, Johnson had had microphones attached discreetly on the exterior so that when the top was closed he could continue taking in the roar. His speech, delivered regally from the portico of the *Hartford Times* building, was a blur that bore no resemblance to the carefully calibrated remarks distributed to reporters. He spoke in a hush of the worker who "hopes someday he can have a little hospital care, he can have a little pension, he can have a little Social Security, he can have a place to take Molly and the babies when he retires. . . . His boys go to war; they fight to preserve this system. He likes his boss and respects him. He believes in free enterprise, and he does not hate the man who makes a reasonable return." He cut to the chase: "I want to talk to you today about what I know is on your minds and what I believe is in your hearts. And that is irresponsibility."

By the time he traveled the traditional Republican strongholds of Vermont and Maine (where the GOP governor rode in his car) he had shaken so many hands his cracked fingers oozed blood. By the time he arrived three hours late at the last stop, Manchester, New Hampshire, after a neurotic ramble to the crowd ("If you came out to hear me speak like I had a martyr complex and nobody loves me, you are going to be disappointed, because I think that we have the greatest system of government in the world") he confidently mentioned his opponent for the first time by name, instead of his customary reference to "these people." The context was Vietnam. "As far as I'm concerned, I want to be very cautious and careful and use it only as a last resort when I start dropping bombs around that are likely to involve American boys in a war in Asia with 700 million Chinese," he began, and since he would never dare flatter the Scylla of his Vietnam policy without paying court to Charybdis, he told a folksy story about the definition of a Texas Ranger: "A Ranger is one that when you plug him, when you hit him, he just keeps coming. . . . We must let the rest of the world know that we . . . have the will and the determination, and if they ever hit us it is not going to stop us—we just keep on comin'!"

It was a triumph. At one point he dragged the AP's Frank Cormier beside him as the people's thousand tentacles reached out for the healing touch of their chief executive: "Write *that* in your story," he said, "so the whole country can know!" Johnson was convinced, for now: when these crowds sighed, they sighed only for Lyndon Baines Johnson. Though the President's greatest rival, Bobby Kennedy, campaigning hard in a close race for Ken Keating's Senate seat, labored under a different assumption. He had stepped off a plane in Albany one night and beheld thousands before him—then thousands waiting streetside in their pajamas on the strength of only a rumor, waiting to pay their respects as he drove by on his way to somewhere else. His aides exulted. Bobby, still mourning, saw nothing to celebrate. "They're for him," he muttered softly. "They're for him."

Goldwater's next trip was a Heartland whistle-stop tour—a sentimental tradition whose origins harkened back to those pre-TV days when candidates needed to cover as many miles as humanly possible and couldn't be bothered to take the time to walk to the town's auditorium. He kicked off defiantly at Union Station, the same day Johnson left for New England. "Living in Washington, and reading newspapers that are solidly against our campaign," he said, "you might well wonder what's happening out in the real world."

Roger Mudd of CBS sent him off by calling the whistle-stop a "rendezvous with nostalgia" and a "throwback." Stewart Alsop, in that week's *Saturday Evening Post*, observed, "Goldwater's 'choice' is not really a coherent, rational alternative at all—it is hardly more than an angry cry of protest against things as they are." News cameras lingered over picket signs massed at the fringes of Goldwater's crowds: "DON'T STOP HERE, WE'RE POOR ENOUGH"; "DOWN THE DRAIN, GOLDWATER"; "FASCIST LIP IN THE WEST"; "$C_5H_4N_4O_3$ ON AuH_2O"—translated roughly from the chemical as "Piss on Goldwater" (a Texas conservative later retaliated with "LBJ DON'T PEON US"). Partisans competed in ever greater displays of devotion; in one town a kid paraded around with a sign reading "I JUST HITCHHIKED 50 MILES TO SHAKE HANDS WITH GOLDWATER." In another town blacks stood in line for the privilege of snubbing him by *not* shaking his hand. At every stop photographers and cameramen were taxed trying to keep the ubiquitous "YAF BACKS BARRY" banners out of their shots; in Lima, Ohio, they couldn't avoid shooting the three-story "LBJ-USA" banner Democrats unfurled over a building directly behind the rostrum. As Goldwater motorcaded through Sioux Falls, the Goldwater side dropped a parachuter from the sky; someone from the opposition dropped an egg from a rooftop that splattered the candidate's mohair suit. Everywhere Goldwater went, some Republican or another refused an invitation to share his platform; everywhere he left, he seemed to leave townspeople at each others' throats. "Crowds were more violent than anything a Presidential candidate has had to face in the last generation," James Reston columnized. "Supporters of Mr. Goldwater declared they could not discuss the campaign with Democrats on a rational basis," his paper's news pages reported. "Democrats said the Goldwaterites were too rabid for reason."

Each new day provided new occasions for screwups. One day a publicist convinced the candidate by painful effort to pose wearing an engineer's cap. "Senator," he said nervously, "if you'll just put this on now . . ." And so Goldwater did, glaring coldly in the cameras for a few seconds. The next day the picture didn't even show up in newspapers; the publicist had the photographers shoot directly into the sun. In Hammond, Indiana, some wag had the band play "Bye, Bye Blackbird" as parting music to humiliate the three black Republicans the organization had persuaded to sit on the platform. Goldwater's speech

at the Cincinnati Gardens on the September 29 was a scorcher that won a standing ovation ("Does he hope that he can wait until after the election to confront
the American public with the fact of total defeat or total war in Asia?"). The
speech was supposed to be nationally televised, but thanks to Ralph Cordiner
the campaign couldn't afford a network spot in time. In Frankfort, Indiana, the
public address system couldn't project Goldwater's voice thirty yards past the
platform.

Goldwater put forward new policy proposals. But his speeches mostly
demonstrated the inability or indifference of his team to communicate unfamiliar ideas. Like his previous proposals—the draft ban, the tax cut, replacing federal programmatic grants with block grants—there was no follow-through,
little repetition in future speeches, so the proposals floated around in the public's consciousness for a day or so before popping like soap bubbles. At the
University of Toledo field house he proposed federal refunds based on the
share of local property taxes allocated to schools—a complex form of uncondi-
tional grants to education—with little explanation, the essence of the proposal
buried in pages of angry, cryptic hectoring: "What would you do if I told you
you had to line up at six in the morning tomorrow and get a number?" What,
people asked, was he *talking* about?

In Moline, where the chairman of the board of John Deere had just
announced that he was a Johnson man even though he was the secretary-
treasurer for Republican gubernatorial candidate Charles Percy (a Goldwater
supporter) and local school authorities announced that they would let kids out
of school for the President's visit the following week, Goldwater finally
addressed Social Security. A reauthorization bill that would have increased
benefits had died in conference, he said, because the President held it hostage
to his insistence that it include authorization for a Medicare program. Goldwater used the opening to point out that he had voted for expanding benefits
every chance he got since 1954. "Now you know who the friends of Social
Security are," he said, "and you know why. Now you know who the enemies of
Social Security are—and you know why." To no effect. When staffers sounded
out the crowd, people could not be shaken from the conviction that they had
seen Goldwater *himself* tear up a Social Security card on TV. In Hammond,
Indiana, the candidate demonstrated his gift for terrifying people while attempting to soothe them: "We must always maintain such superiority of strength,
such devastating strike-back power, such a strong network of allies that the
Communists would be committing suicide for themselves and their society if
they push the button," he said, and then: "In all likelihood, the President . . . would
not be around at all to push the button. It would be too late for button-pushing."

The next day the *Herald Tribune* editorial page dropped a bombshell. Walter Thayer and Jock Whitney had been agonizing over the decision for months. The task of writing the endorsement fell to the *Trib*'s new editorial page chief, Ray Price. He had to down a stiff double-belt of Scotch before he could type the words:

For the Presidency: Lyndon Johnson.

Travail and torment go into those simple words, breaching as they do the political traditions of a long newspaper lifetime. But we find ourselves, as Americans, even as Republicans, with no other acceptable course.

Senator Goldwater says he is offering the nation a choice. So far as the two candidates are concerned, our inescapable choice—as a newspaper that was Republican before there was a Republican party, has been Republican ever since and will remain Republican—is Lyndon B. Johnson.

The piece went on to abuse the Republican nominee for thirty more column-inches. For decade upon decade the *Trib* could be counted on to take the business side on any issue. But the business side was changing. The day after the endorsement an economist wrote Walter Heller, "At a lunch of 11 higher echelon business executives, one hesitantly 'confessed' that he was voting for Johnson." They eventually discovered that only one of them was for Goldwater—and even he hedged his bets: following the widespread assumption that stock prices would dive in proportion to Goldwater's chances of winning, that businessman was moving funds into short-term bills. The Republicans' new fetish for balanced budgets was now judged by these sorts of men to be a formula for ruin: to cut programs that met the needs of a complex urban society would disintegrate the baseline conditions for national well-being and deteriorate that bulkhead of government fiscal intervention that was America's best defense against recession. Wall Street had joined the Democrats.

Indeed, when Milton Friedman published an article in the next Sunday's *New York Times Magazine* on "The Goldwater View of Economics," he had to protest, "No one seems to realize that Goldwater *does* have a philosophy and not merely views on particular economic problems." He proceeded to give readers of the Newspaper of Record a kindergarten primer on economic libertarianism: that providing for the common defense was a precondition for economic freedom, so that it wasn't contradictory for Goldwater to call for increased military spending; that only the free market, not the government, could produce prosperity; that governmental interventions often created baleful unintended consequences. The public clearly had a long way to go to attain even an elementary understanding of Goldwater's core ideas.

That was something the sachems atop RNC headquarters, where the chaos had stabilized at the Keystone Kops level, hardly even considered. Goldwater's old friend Dean Burch neglected functions of a party chair as basic as keeping in touch with senators up for reelection; some of them waited all the way until November without receiving so much as a single phone call. An important state leader reached John Grenier after two weeks of trying; the voice on his receiver snapped: "This is Grenier. I've got just two minutes for you over the phone." Morale was atrocious: leaks dribbled constantly, fingers pointed in every direction, and the comfort level was not helped by those mysterious clicking noises people heard on their telephones. (Regional directors began making their important calls at a pay phone outside.) Resources were squandered on expensive projects like a daily teletyped newsletter, conveying such vital information as (the best news of the day, apparently) Goldwater's endorsement by *TV Prevue*, circulating in northwest Oregon.

An advertising insert, "Senator Goldwater Speaks Out on the Issues," went out to *Reader's Digest*'s millions of subscribers with typographical errors. For the nap-inducing campaign book *Where I Stand*, instead of self-publishing à la Clarence Manion and Phyllis Schlafly, the Goldwater campaign negotiated a contract with McGraw-Hill, which printed more than 100,000 copies, didn't ship them to bookstores until late in September, and sold only 5,000. The rest of the copies were remaindered to the campaign to give away at a straight loss. (The DNC, meanwhile, sold 50,000 copies of a preexisting quickie, *Barry Goldwater: Extremist of the Right*, on commission, and made a killing.) Kitchel developed a consuming obsession with purging extremists. Beneath the obsession was dread: he himself had been a member in good standing of the John Birch Society until June 1960. The press, blessedly, never found out; campaign staffers did, and they raged at the unpardonable risk Goldwater was taking in having appointed Kitchel in the first place. But effective purges took administrative acumen. Soon the press discovered a bona fide 1930s American fascist, Allen Zoll, on the payroll—in a speaker's bureau, no less.

The next TV show, during which Goldwater answered ordinary citizens' questions, was so artless that a group of Dallas Republican leaders began an investigation "to discover who are the inside saboteurs who are mis-directing the campaign." The one after that was worse. Milwaukee Republicans moved heaven and earth to fill the city's Auditorium for a speech by Dick Nixon that they were told would be broadcast nationwide. Brooding over the fascism charges, Kitchel feared the Milwaukee rally looked a little too rousing. Instead of putting the event on TV, he put Clare Boothe Luce on the air, speaking from a studio. And Luce seemed drunk. "The calls, telegrams, letters, and stopped payments on checks have been fantastic," the RNC's Midwest regional chair raged. "Many people in Wisconsin feel it is absolutely necessary that Kitchel . . . resign." In Los Angeles the stewards of P.O. Box 80 on the TV for Goldwater-Miller committee were near to mutiny. "Republicans I talked to were not interested in listening to truck drivers, farmers, and watching cows," one wrote headquarters, referring to the man-on-the-street show and *Conversation at Gettysburg*. "Let's stop this waste of our hard-won money."

Mutinies came two a day—each expeditiously followed up by a friendly phone call from the White House (some *provoked* by a friendly phone call from the White House: "The college presidents are coming along nicely!" gushed one internal memo). Over eighty Eisenhower-era officials, seven of them cabinet secretaries, signed a stinging attack on their party's candidate; Republican senator John Sherman Cooper of Kentucky contacted Johnson with tips on how to win his key toss-up state. One fine afternoon Governor George Romney was scheduled to introduce Goldwater at the annual ox roast at the Midland County Fair. The carcasses arrived on schedule, Goldwater graciously carving off slices, dressed in an ox costume; the governor, fearing for his reelection, never arrived. (To add insult to injury, a black chef refused Goldwater's request for his recipe for barbecue sauce.) Ohio's Jim Rhodes, after melodramatically releasing his convention delegation, neglected to release an endorsement until late October. In years to come, political memorabilia collectors would notice an unusual phenomenon. Among their prized items were the "coattail" buttons that hundreds of candidates had printed up for themselves each presidential year, like "STEVENSON/PROXMIRE '52." They would search high and low for examples of the phenomenon from 1964 and find only ten. Loyal New York Republicans wearing Goldwater buttons who showed up to volunteer for Ken Keating's Senate campaign were just sent home.

The loyalists were sometimes worse than the traitors. When Scranton joined Goldwater on a swing through Pennsylvania, journalists were provided with a compendium of quotes from Scranton's nomination campaign, courtesy of the White House, called "What Scranton Really Thinks of Goldwater." But what Scranton really thought of Goldwater was plain enough to see from his half-dozen speech interjections beginning, "While I disagree with Goldwater on . . ." (Another time a reporter recorded him speculating that a Republican victory would mean recession.) Rocky and Happy joined Goldwater for a rally on the steps of the New York State Office Building, Rocky's expression thin-lipped all the while. He pocketed Goldwater buttons when they were offered.

.   .   .

One October day, the wives of Barry Goldwater and Bill Miller sat for a press conference in Chicago. They were asked how their families could possibly take all the abuse. Beneath a severe dome of hair, in a plain shift, forcing a smile, worried, as always, that her poor hearing would embarrass her, Peggy Goldwater gamely replied, "I think my skin's thicker than it used to be." Then she retreated back into a flat, distracted, is-it-over-yet look, perhaps thinking of the way she'd spent her twentieth anniversary a few weeks back, in Longview, Texas, dodging the piles released by a nearby elephant. Mrs. Miller, on the other hand, in a tailored suit and with elegantly plucked eyebrows, approached political tasks with the grace of a debutante. But even she couldn't contain the wounds. The words were polite—"It's unfortunate that people have to be the victims of unsubstantiated smears." The anger was written on her face.

Barry Goldwater, on the plane to Chicago from Missouri (where he had ripped the knee of his best mohair suit), felt hardly more at ease. He would write about the whole business later, in a 1970 memoir, his words edged with the sting of four years of enforced political idleness—because after winning the Republican nomination, he could no longer run for Senate in 1964. "Very early in the last decade," he wrote, "I found myself becoming a political fulcrum of the vast and growing tide of American disenchantment with the public policies of liberalism." There it was: controlled by events, following others' call, a horse to be ridden. Nothing had changed since those meetings with Clarence Manion and his people in 1959—back when Goldwater had all but turned them down flat. "It is true enough that I sensed it early and sympathized with it publicly, but I did not originate it. . . . I was caught up in and swept along by this tide of disenchantment." It is harder to imagine a sharper expression of political alienation.

But he was periodically swept up by enthusiasm, too. He had some things he needed to tell the country. It kept him going. Goldwater, Miller, and their wives were in Chicago for Goldwater's first major statement on civil rights, to be broadcast on TV on October 16. The project had brought the third floor to grief: no one had been able to write a civil rights speech that could satisfy Goldwater. His order to purge any taint of racism from the remarks became all the more urgent because of events in the daily news: in nearby Gary, Indiana, an alderman who had cast the tie-breaking vote for an open-housing law was now under twenty-four-hour police guard, as was a sociology professor who had filed a report on residential segregation in Chicago. (Before, such protection had been reserved for blacks who moved into the city's white neighborhoods.) There had been 71 racially motivated bombings in 1964 in the Chicago metropolitan area, Mayor Daley told the President. In deep denial, the mayor said that the city didn't have a backlash problem, although a different conclusion was suggested by the man-on-the-street quotes Johnson operatives had collected in the area: "Those kids from the slums have syphilis, gonorrhea, everything"; "Eighty-five percent of the Negroes in this town are too pushy"; "If you want a Negro in the next plot, vote Democratic"; "Every night there's a purse-snatching"; "It takes a lifetime to build a home, then the riffraff come in." The silences were even more pregnant: blue-collar bars where political arguments used to percolate were quiet, because no one knew how to discharge the bile rising up in them—where was the concern for *their* rights?—without sounding like a racist pig or starting a fight.

Harry Jaffa and Bill Rehnquist finally came up with an acceptable draft for Goldwater's speech. It was called "Civil Rights and the Common Good," and it was polished all the way up to the last minute. The venue was selected for its respectability, to prevent any throaty hollers of assent: a $100-a-plate fundraiser in the International Ballroom of the Conrad Hilton. Goldwater didn't want anything to distract him from his message: When it came to race, Americans didn't have the words to say the truth they knew in their hearts to be right, in a manner proper to the kind of men they wanted to see when they looked in the mirror each morning. Goldwater was determined to give them the words. It was a patriotic duty.

"It has been well said that the Constitution is color-blind," he began, as the glasses clinked. "And so it is just as wrong to compel children to attend certain schools for the sake of so-called integration as for the sake of segregation. . . .

"Our aim, as I understand it, is neither to establish a segregated society nor to establish an integrated society. It is to preserve a *free* society."

That line was Bill Rehnquist's mantra. Once it had been far to the right of Goldwater's customary position that his aim *was* to establish an integrated society, just not through federal coercion. That summer, Goldwater backed a local antidiscrimination ordinance in Phoenix that Rehnquist testified against. But now Goldwater debuted Rehnquist's favorite line as *his* mantra. And, evening gowns, tuxedoes, and TV cameras notwithstanding, Chicago's well-heeled conservatives responded by letting loose a hail of wolf whistles and throaty cries that raised the roof.

He continued:

> And so I endorse the position of the Republican Platform of 1964 on the busing of school children. I say with the Platform that it is wrong to take school children out of their normal neighborhood schools for the sake of achieving "racial balance," or some other hypothetical goal of perfect equality imagined by the theorists of the so-called "Great

Society." [Applause] It is wrong—*morally* wrong—because, ladies and gentlemen, *it re-introduces through the back door the very principle of allocation by race that makes compulsory segregation morally wrong and offensive to freedom.* . . .

It is often said that only the freedom of a member of a minority is violated when some barrier keeps him from associating with others in his society. But this is wrong! Freedom of association is a double freedom or it is nothing at all. It applies to both parties who want to associate with each other. . . . We must never forget that the freedom to associate means the same thing as the freedom not to associate.

He concluded to acclaim: "We have come, literally and figuratively, from the very ends of the earth to make this great nation. From many races, nations, and creeds we have made, as we shall ever more perfectly make, under God, one people."

The speech was a popular sensation. That wasn't the only reason to celebrate. Goldwater was now doing surprisingly unterribly. His numbers were trending upward. The *New York Times* reported that he led in ten states, with another eight neck and neck—and that by winning just this ten he would be more successful than most losing candidates. He was hovering near 50 percent in crucial swing states: Virginia, Kentucky, Florida, Arkansas—and vital Texas, where he had 53 percent. The Deep South was a lock. On October 12 the *Washington Post*'s headline read "PRIVATE POLL GIVES GOLDWATER 40% OF THE VOTE." The Republican Congressional Committee newsletter promptly cited a *Post* headline from October 17, 1948: "GALLUP POLL SHOWS TRUMAN WITH 40 PERCENT OF VOTE." (It was noted in hushed tones, if at all, that since Goldwater had jumped 5 points and Johnson had slipped 3 after the Harlem riots, one more conflagration could nicely slim the gap.) Once again, seasoned politicos on the second floor smelled opportunity: play the electoral college right, shift energies to just the right places, track the themes that work and dump the ones that don't—and Barry Morris Goldwater could find himself the next President of the United States.

Once again they were denied the chance. The generals were content to cruise. "Having been on the campaign trail with Barry ever since he started this activity," Kitchel wrote a friend back in Arizona, "I can assure you that the campaign is going very well and that, contrary to the indications in the polls, we have something really going which is going to produce a victory on November 3rd." On one occasion Burch decamped from riding shotgun on the campaign plane so intoxicated by the enthusiasm of Barry's supporters that he declared, "I know we're on the verge of victory." He was thinking of the crowds in the stands at the evening rallies, packed with conservatives; he ignored the fact that the general public was leaving bare patches at the sides of streets through which Goldwater motorcaded to the venues. Burch, for his part, decided that the traveling intelligence team's reports were negative and misleading and banned their circulation. He also fired the pollsters.

Lyndon Johnson, who knew how to hunt where the ducks were, was ready to write off the Deep South altogether. His wife decided that was unacceptable.

The former Claudia Alta Taylor was born a Southern belle, and she felt the Southland's glories in her bones—things like "keeping up with your kinfolk," as she put it, "long Sunday dinners after church . . . a special brand of courtesy." She was also a woman without illusions. She understood that her beloved land was not just a paradise of courtesy with a crust of sin on top, that the cult of politeness served also as a daily reminder to blacks to keep to their place—a sinister cultural matrix structured by images of the virgin on her pedestal, keeping up with kinfolk, cooking big Sunday dinners, and the savage black rapist against whom she needed constant protection. The legend *Dieu et les Dames* painted on the ceiling of the Mississippi capitol told the story at its most benign; the segregated bathroom signs—"WHITE LADIES" and "COLORED WOMEN"—at its most casually inhumane. Lady Bird understood, as other liberals—Yankees—did not, Southern fears that in sweeping away its ingrained racial hierarchies, the *South* would be swept away, too: no more family bonds thick as kudzu, no more delicacies soaked through with the fat of a freshly butchered pig, no more ladies, no more gentlemen—just assimilation into the desiccated, instrumentalist, *thin* Yankee civilization Southerners had despised since the beginning of the nineteenth century. To unvex the mind of the South, Lady Bird knew, would take the delicate, agonizing work of decades. And she felt the work as a calling.

It took physical courage for Lady Bird to do what she did—arrange a campaign tour for herself through eight Southern states. The original idea was to co-host a reception in the rotunda of each statehouse. The Secret Service nixed that proposal: closed circular spaces were a sniper's heaven. Hers would surely be the first whistle-stop in history to travel with its own minesweeper: a second train engine, traveling fifteen minutes ahead of the first, to detonate any bombs placed in its path.

The planning had been painful. Lady Bird spent eleven-hour days in September working the phones asking politicians for their participation. For the most part, only those not up for reelection offered hospitality. The Democratic nominee for North Carolina's governorship didn't return her calls. A Virginia senator scheduled a convenient hunting trip. Senator Byrd had been "jovial and courteous and darling," she reported to her husband—until she mentioned the purpose of her call, whereupon "an invisible silken curtain fell across his voice." Louisiana's governor John McKeithan embarrassedly explained that he "was working for the Democrats, you understand"—just after his own fashion. Strom Thurmond mumbled that "a really basic decision within the next two weeks" precluded his participation. As for George Wallace, she thought it would be rude even to bother.

She was unfazed. No candidate's wife had taken such a tour without her husband before. But she knew her people needed to hear some hard truths. Her husband could not do the job if he wanted to: the assassination threat was too great. But Southerners, she knew, would never shoot a lady off her pedestal.

She weighed anchor on Columbus Day, October 6. Federal employees were given time off to swell the crowd. She wouldn't stop until she'd covered 1,628 miles and made 47 stops in four days. At each depot fifteen hostesses—wives of senators and congressmen, decked out in blue shirtwaists with "LBJ" embroidered on the front—led what willing local pols they could into a Pullman car set up as a traditional Southern sitting room, where photographs would be taken and gifts exchanged. The dining car was opened for feasting upon local delicacies: shrimp Creole, biscuits and burgoo, deer-meat sausage, Mrs. Eugene Talmadge's famous Coca-Cola-marinated ham. The networks loved it. This time no one said anything about whistle-stops being nostalgic throwbacks.

The speaker's platform—the caboose—would be taken up first by Congressman Hale Boggs of Louisiana for a round of courthouse-style introductions. "How many of you-all know what red-eye gravy is?" he would say. "Well, so do I, and so does Lyndon Johnson." And then—forty times that first day—the nation's Southern Belle–in–Chief mounted her pedestal, cleared her throat, looked out at the picket signs ("FLY AWAY LADY BIRD, HERE IN RICHMOND BARRY IS THE CAT'S MEOW"; "LYNDON, WE WILL BARRY YOU"; "BRINKMANSHIP IS BETTER THAN CHICKENSHIP," a phrase Goldwater, Kitchel, and Hess happened to have pasted on a bulkhead of the Republican campaign plane), took in a few moments of "We Want Barry!" chants—and thrust her secret weapon into the air: a single, white-gloved hand. That usually was enough. If it wasn't, she would drawl, "This is a campaign trip, and I would like to ask for your vote for *both* Johnsons"—so they knew they were *insulting* both Johnsons, not just the husband. She was a lady; one continued heckling on pain of one's manhood.

She told her audience that "to this Democratic candidate and his wife, the South is a respected, valued, and beloved part of this country." She reeled off a list of what the Democrats had done for Culpeper—the roads, the factories, the navy yards, the dams—and raised the specter of Republican soup lines. And she was never too shy to remind them how proud Democrats should be of the Civil Rights Act of 1964—leavening the remark with a joke: "You might not like all I am saying, but at least you understand the way ah'm sayin' it."

It was in South Carolina where white gloves and sugared words finally failed Lady Bird Johnson. South Carolina air was now being paved over by Strom Thurmond's radio ads—"A vote for Barry Goldwater is a vote to end judicial tyranny"—and the evangelism of true believers like the minister Bob Jones Jr., whose college refused to bow to any "agnostic or materialist accrediting association," and who had adopted for his independent campaign for Barry Goldwater the apparently defeatist slogan "Turn Back America, Turn Back—Only a Divine Miracle Can Save America Now." Thanks to four years of softening by the RNC's Operation Dixie, GOP organizations were going strong in 42 of 46 South Carolina counties.

In Columbia only a maternal bark brought peace from the hecklers: "This is a country of many viewpoints. I respect your right to express your own. Now it is my turn to express mine. Thank you." The next stop, Charleston, had been chosen by Lady Bird because it had given 57 percent to the Republicans in 1960. And as her train approached, the tough old port was taking on a menacing aspect that recalled Dallas in November of 1963. Whispers shuddered through town: a band was ready to strike up a "hot beat" to incite Negroes to riot as Lady Bird arrived. The local paper pleaded with its readers for "courtesy towards the First Lady," as Nixon had pleaded with Texans for a "courteous reception" for Kennedy in Dallas papers on November 22. Twenty-four merchants failed to receive an emergency injunction to stop a rally at their shopping mall. She entered at dusk. The space in front of the platform at the mall was monopolized by the massed forces of the local John Birch Society chapters—and their children, who bore signs reading "BLACK BIRD GO HOME"; "JOHNSON IS A COMMUNIST"; "JOHNSON IS A NIGGER-LOVER."

"Jobs and a better community . . . prosperity for Charleston. . . . Polaris missile base . . . shipyard"—the words could be heard only intermittently for the wall of boos. Hale Boggs took the microphone and cried out in anguish: "This is reminiscent of Hitler! This is a Democratic gathering, not a Nazi gathering!"

Lady Bird and her entourage pressed on, shaken. In courtly Savannah, it was Johnson's seventeen-year-old daughter who was booed. That night the FBI made a yard-by-yard sweep of a seven-mile-long bridge that would convey the First Lady across a marshy expanse in north Florida.

• • •

The President would meet the train at its final stop in New Orleans. He was halfway through a trip of his own. Gone was the plan to campaign from his rocking chair on the White House porch; he hit fifteen states in the two weeks after touring New England. He needed the crowd. The crowd needed him.

A tour apparatus was hustled up from the West Wing. Advance reports ("Young—*young* men on the assembly line at Warner Gear in Muncie are pro-Goldwater. . . . White workers called the local union president 'the nigger president' ") and speech drafts blizzarded through Bill Moyers's office. "Lay low on civil rights," the strategy memos advised, suggesting instead the themes "Economic Bill of Rights for All Americans"; "Patriotism and Prosperity"; "The wrecker can wreck in a day what it takes years for the builder to build"; and "The Year 2000." The latter was the President's new favorite subject: "Think of how wonderful the year 2000 will be," he would gush. "And it is already so exciting to me that I am just hoping that my heart and stroke and cancer committee can come up with some good results that will insure that all of us can live beyond a hundred so we can participate in that glorious day when all the fruits of our labors and our imaginations today are a reality! . . . I just hope the doctors hurry up and get busy and let me live that long."

Occasionally he gave the speeches that were written for him. More often he spoke off the top of his head. Sometimes he sounded strange. In Cleveland he burbled to the $100-a-plate diners at the Convention Center: "You don't get peace by rattling your rockets. You don't get peace by threatening to drop your bombs . . . you must always have your hand out and be willing to go anywhere, talk to anybody, listen to anything they have to say, do anything that is honorable, in order to avoid pulling that trigger"—he twitched a thumb like an epileptic—"or mashing that button that will blow up the world." (This was an irony. Goldwater's obsession with manned bombers over missiles rested largely on the fact that he believed push-button warfare was hazardous and irresponsible; bombers, at least, could be called back at the last minute. And little that Goldwater said in 1964 surpassed the apocalypticism of Kennedy utterances such as "The enemy is the Communist system itself— implacable, insatiable, unceasing in its drive for world domination.") In Louisville (where, two weeks earlier, Goldwater had let loose on Vietnam: "Has there ever been a more mishandled conflict in U.S. history?"), standing at a dais bedecked with former Kentucky governors, Johnson said:

> We can't pick other people's governments. We have enough trouble picking our own. . . . Those folks who think you can have government by ultimatum are wrong. . . . There is not an ultimatum that any Presi-

dent can issue that could have produced one of these former governors on this platform, not a single ultimatum. You could take all the tanks in our combat divisions and all the planes in the sky, and all the Polaris missiles, and you couldn't have made a one of 'em come up here.

Sometimes he said that the nuclear holocaust would kill 100 million people; other times, like Joe McCarthy with his famous list of subversives in the State Department, the number was revised to 300 million. Then he would say, "I want to conclude by reminding you that you still have three more days to register."

The aide responsible for gauging crowd reaction noted "an unusual, even sometimes awe-inspiring, intensity from the audiences when he even gets close to the general theme of peace in the world." Johnson did so about as often as he drew breath. (His case was bolstered by a new picture out in theaters, *Fail-Safe*—another horrifying, helpless depiction of the nuclear Armageddon that would ensue from even the smallest error in judgment, the most minuscule breakdown in communication.) So frequently did he praise the good, decent Republicans who stood up to Goldwater—"the Republican party today," he would say, "is in temporary receivership; responsible Republicans can't do anything about it"—it was as if Dwight D. Eisenhower were the Democratic running mate. And peace. Peace was everything. "Vote for peace in the United States between labor and business and government . . . vote for peace among all people."

The President held crowds to a hush as he dramatically related the tale of sitting beside Kennedy (he hadn't) in October of 1962, as Khrushchev and Kennedy came "eyeball to eyeball, and their thumbs started getting closer to mash that nuclear button, the knife was in each other's ribs, almost literally speaking, and neither of them were flinching or quivering"—"until Mr. Khrushchev picked up his missiles and put them on his ships and took them back home." He told, in other words, bedtime stories: the child's deepest fears are aroused, to be safely assuaged when the scary monster under the bed is vanquished and everything turns out right at the end.

"Elmo Roper, polling privately for Luce," John Bartlow Martin scrawled to Moyers, "says LBJ is farther ahead than FDR in 1936. Can't believe it, is worried, but there it is." Johnson behaved as if he hadn't received the word. He constantly ordered up new billboards and ads and polls; get-out-the-vote ads ran in newspapers as early as October 1 ("No matter how good the prospect for victory on Election Day . . . a huge landslide vote will really show where our nation stands on the great issues of modern times which so deeply affect all our people and all mankind . . . a chance to eradicate the fanatical right-wing influence in our political life"). He returned to Detroit and, of course, the crowds went wild again; it wasn't enough to satisfy him. The next morning Johnson breathed fire into the phone of Chief of Staff Walter Jenkins: "Didn't I tell you I wanted every worker to have a button or an LBJ hat or sticker?" he roared. "Do you want me to lose the labor vote? I ask for things, and I expect to see them done."

Jenkins had begun working for Johnson in 1939, and had seen twenty-five years of fifteen-hour days. He was used to the abuse. He had never had another boss. If Moyers was the President's spare brain, Jenkins was his walking IBM computer. He had adopted Johnson's ambitions and made them his own—even naming his son Lyndon. Johnson reciprocated by entrusting Jenkins with about as much as a man could be entrusted with: Congressman Johnson's income taxes (Jenkins had power of signature), treasurership of Senator Johnson's holding company, presence at National Security Council meetings. "They're trying to make Walter Jenkins a criminal," Johnson complained to Bob Anderson in January as Republicans were trying to bring the aide before their tribunal on the Baker case, "and he's the best man that ever lived." Jenkins told people he was put on this earth to help make this great man's life easier. Even if that meant he was so frazzled that office wags liked to bark "Walter!" when he napped to see how high he would jump.

People's response to seeing Johnson in the flesh was primal. Sometimes security men used their fists to keep crowds from smothering the President; sometimes they had to reach for their guns when rope lines snapped. Everywhere it was the same: people packed shoulder to shoulder as far as the eye could see. The President stood on his limousine seat and seemed to float above the crowd. Photos looked like laboratory demonstrations—a million iron filings massing around an electric charge, bodies falling inward, arms outstretched, as if the President was the center of the world and his magnetism could give them life.

In the spectacle liberal intellectuals spied Newtonian perfection: the pull toward consensus, the push away from extremism, a system regressing toward a safe, steady equilibrium. The architecture of their thoughts allowing little place for such things, they missed the more mystical aspects of the transaction—the feelings sweeping these throngs that Americans, because America was not a monarchy, were not supposed to feel: their young ruler had died, and they reached out to the new one with raw, naked need, to fill an empty place, as if with his touch he could, just as he had promised, *let us continue,* as if the bad things hadn't happened at all.

And since the South was but a soon-to-be vestigial aberration from the main story of American life, the propagandists of consensus did not consider the bumpers of Southern truckers in their investigations. Their most popular new gag license plate pictured a black woman monstrous with child, admitting, "I went all de way wif LBJ."

When Lady Bird's train was about to arrive in New Orleans, the President took a dramatic half-mile walk down the track to meet it. A crowd of blacks followed alongside, doing the leaning, the reaching, the crying out. Beyond them a white crowd recoiled in disgust.

Lay low on civil rights. Especially in New Orleans. *Imperatively* in New Orleans: that had been the advice. Johnson ignored it. There was nothing about the year 2000 in the evening's speech, broadcast live throughout Louisiana and Mississippi from the Jung Hotel banquet hall. Nor was there any rambling on the rattling of rockets, or on responsible Republicans, or on Molly and the babies. An old shame rose up in the candidate, and he spoke to that instead. He glanced over at Senator Long and poured it on thick, singing songs of praise for his father, Huey, that made the old senator blush. He talked about the North—and how much Southerners *should* resent it. "All these years they have kept their foot on our necks by appealing to our animosities and dividing us." Then he twisted the knife.

"I am not going to let them build up the hate and try to buy my people by appealing to their prejudice," he said, leaning in to tell "you folks" a story. An old senator—"whose name ah won't call"—was on his deathbed, and Old Sam—House Speaker Sam Rayburn—was there beside him. His people were going hungry, the sick man said. The hospitals, the schools, the roads were deteriorating. "Sammy," he said, "I wish I felt a little better. . . . I would like to go back down there and make one more Democratic speech. I feel like I have one in me! My poor old state, they haven't heard a Democratic speech in thirty years. All they ever hear at election time is: 'Nigger! Nigger! Nigger!' "

Dryly, a Goldwater intelligence man wrote that "Johnson probably put the finishing touches on his chances of taking Louisiana with his civil rights speech in New Orleans." Johnson didn't care. The South—his South—was where his visions of the wonders that awaited a Great Society in the year 2000 ran aground. Let Goldwater talk all he wanted to about how the South's Republicans were idealistic devotees of free-market capitalism. Johnson never heard Leander Perez or George Wallace complain about what the federal government's TVA and Rural Electrification Administration had done to bring their people out of darkness and into hydro-powered electric light, or about the hospitals, schools, and roads that Washington had helped them build.

And what had Barry Goldwater done for Culpeper? He had voted against the Civil Rights Act; nothing else. For that Southerners seemed willing to turn back the clock on every social gain of the past thirty years—just for the chance to vote *nigger-nigger-nigger*. It made Lyndon Johnson heartsick. He wanted his four more years. He wanted a mandate. He wanted to do some healing.

CITIZENS

The keynote speaker for the fourth annual national convention of Young Americans for Freedom at New York's plush Commodore Hotel was the group's thirty-nine-year-old patriarch: William F. Buckley. It was YAFers' New Year's Eve and their Fourth of July. They were now a force to be reckoned with. They marched at the head of a presidential crusade.

YAFers, Young Republicans, clubs organized through the RNC's Youth for Goldwater-Miller: they worked from dawn to dusk, licking envelopes, phoning phone trees, planting yard signs, thumbing files, penciling precinct notecards, passing out literature at factory gates before the dew was off the grass. It was indescribable, the exhilaration they felt those long days, exhausting themselves for the highest cause they could imagine. It remade you; it made everything else seem small. They had no words to describe it. They could have borrowed some from the civil rights kids, who called it a "freedom high." The Commodore rang with stories of freedom highs that weekend. What there wasn't was doubt. They were young, idealistic; triumph was inevitable, for they were battling for the Lord. They couldn't but assume that their hero felt exactly the same way.

He did not. Bill Buckley had been skeptical about Goldwater presidential maneuvers since Clarence Manion invited him to join his endeavor in 1959. "I am especially anxious not to dissipate unnecessarily any conservative resources," he wrote Manion then, "and don't want to be identified with a total political failure." His position had hardly changed since, and not just because Baroody and Kitchel had humiliated him in the pages of the *New York Times* the previous September by planting a story that he was trying to take over the campaign. Buckley's approach to practical politics bore the heavy imprint of his friend the late Whittaker Chambers. In brooding, brilliant letters he used to post to Buckley from his upstate retreat in the dark days of the Eisenhower Administration, Chambers spun an argument redolent of his Marxist past:

social change was borne on tides of historical inevitability. If conservatism overreached before its time, it risked a setback of decades. Then there was the problem of Goldwater himself. Buckley had had a conversation recently with Richard Clurman, *Time*'s chief of correspondents, who had gone from an editors' lunch with Goldwater to a dinner party with Buckley—where Clurman wondered aloud just what was Barry Goldwater's appeal to this brilliant, urbane man he respected. "Barry Goldwater is a man of tremendously decent instincts, and with a basic banal but important understanding of the Constitution and what it means in American life," Buckley explained.

"But what would happen if he were elected President of the United States?" Clurman asked.

"That," Buckley quipped, "might be a serious problem."

He was making truer believers fume. "You are displaying a compulsion to proclaim, on every possible occasion, that Goldwater will be resoundingly defeated in November," Rusher implored after Buckley began seeding his columns with the Chambers argument that spring. "What you say about Goldwater's chances in November can have a measurable effect." But that was Buckley's story, and he was sticking to it. Not that his brow didn't bead with sweat, however, that September night at the YAF convention, as he took his place behind the podium at the Commodore and looked out at faces that burned with the pure blue flame of faith.

"We do not believe in the Platonic affirmation of our own little purities," he began his speech. (*Immanentizing the eschaton*: That was for the liberals.)

"To no one's surprise more than our own," he continued, "we labor under the visitation of a freedom-minded candidate for the President of the United States. . . . A great rainfall has deluged a thirsty earth, but before we had time to properly prepare for it.

"I speak, of course, about the impending defeat of Barry Goldwater."

His heresy sucked the air out of the room. The silence was broken by the sound of a single woman sobbing.

He tried to explain:

> Our morale is high, and we are marching. . . . But it is wrong to assume that we shall overcome [Martin Luther King's language, archly ironized] and therefore it is right to reason to the necessity of guarding against the utter disarray that sometimes follows a stunning defeat . . . any election of Barry Goldwater would presuppose a sea change in American public opinion; presuppose that the fiery little body of dissenters, of which you are a shining meteor, suddenly spun off no less than a majority of all the American people, who suddenly

overcome a generation's entrenched lassitude, suddenly penetrated to the true meaning of freedom in society where the truth is occluded by the verbose mystification of thousands of scholars, tens of thousands of books, a million miles of newsprint; who suddenly, prisoners of all those years, succeeded in passing blithely through the walls of Alcatraz and tripping lightly over the shark-infested waters and treacherous currents, to safety on the shore.

The point, he said in conclusion, was now to win recruits. "Not only for November the third, but for future Novembers: to infuse the conservative spirit in enough people to entitle us to look about us . . . not at the ashes of defeat, but at the well planted seeds of hope, which will flower on a great November day in the future"—ending, with a nice apocalyptic touch: "if there is a future."

There wasn't even a smattering of applause. There was trauma. This was not what this fiery little body of dissenters wanted to hear.

Even if their patriarch was correct. They were not spinning off a majority of all the American people. But the seeds were being planted.

When the *St. Louis Post-Dispatch*, one of the nation's most respected liberal dailies, sent out a team of reporters after the election for a multipart series to investigate "Who were these people who took over the Republican Party?" the reporters wrote as if describing Earth after a surprise Martian attack. The "right-wing still controls much of the party machinery and will be extremely difficult to dislodge," they reported in amazement. "Many other Americans, including some of the top figures in both parties, have yet to understand what happened." In articles with headings like "MIDWEST WAS FERTILE GROUND FOR EXTREMIST INFILTRATION; RADICAL GOLDWATERITES USED MONEY POWER TO CRUSH RIVALS," the paper uncovered a rogues' gallery of conspirators—from the fascist Allen Zoll to Buzz Lukens, to Clarence Manion, to Clif White, to Robert Welch—who had labored together "to impose its will on one of the nation's two great parties." You could have read it and presumed this gang had met somewhere in 1960 to parcel out the assignments in advance.

It could have been 27 million zombies who voted for Barry Goldwater, as far as these journalists were concerned. And as for the record 3.9 million Americans who actively *worked* for the Goldwater campaign in some capacity (Johnson had half as many, from a voter pool half again as large)—they might as well have retreated back to the planet from whence they came. In spaceships. Yet that didn't explain the fact that, by report of Johnson field men, automobile bumpers supporting Goldwater continued to outnumber those backing

LBJ on American highways by ratios of 10 to 1. Perhaps it is understandable that reporters missed the story. There had never been anything like it in their lifetimes.

Years earlier, *Fortune* had called Barry Goldwater the "favorite son of a state of mind." Gene Pulliam had recently termed the candidate's swarms a "federation of the fed-up." But a more appropriate metaphor was that of a virus. There was the original exposure. It might have come long ago: if you were a manufacturing baron, while fighting a grasping union boss or filling out your one-thousandth federal compliance form. But most people weren't factory barons. More likely it came after writing an ungodly sum on the bottom line of an income tax return. Or from watching your ancestral party, the party of Jefferson Davis and John C. Calhoun, crawl into bed with the civil rights carpetbaggers. Or after your Northern suburb became gripped by rumors of Negro families moving into your neighborhood, Negro children busing into your children's schools, Negro men taking your place at work to fulfill some egghead's idea of justice. Or from newspaper columnists asking you to "coexist" with the slavemasters of your relatives in Czechoslovakia, Poland, or Hungary. Or you caught the bug just watching the evening news, seeing citizens of countries that were perfectly happy to take our foreign aid spitting on our flag; you had not fought for that flag to put up with *that*. You felt helpless to do anything about it. You were looking for an army to march in. You saw one forming around the junior senator from Arizona. And—four years ago, three years ago, last year, last week—you took that first, fateful step.

You licked an envelope, phoned a phone tree, planted a yard sign, thumbed a file, put a bumper sticker on your car reading "GALLUP NEVER ASKED ME!" You saw others doing more. So you did more. And then some more—and the more energy you invested, the more passionate you became that your investment not go down the drain. You tried to infect friends and family (though some had been inoculated by large doses of liberal media). Others infected others. The contagion spread, and before long there were millions of you. And then there was an army—an army of true believers. And true believers work harder than any paid professional staff.

It was a culture spread via a vast literature of training manuals. (Americans for Constitutional Action's devoted fourteen pages alone on how to do a mailing, right down to the most efficient way to fold a letter.) Its rituals were passed along by word of mouth. When the campaign enlisted the theme song from *Hello, Dolly!* (the first show tune to top the pop charts in nearly a decade), the producer of the show got a court to issue a cease-and-desist order. Thereafter the tune took on an underground life:

Hello, Barry, well hello, Barry,
It's so nice to have you here with us today. . . .
The donkey brayed us into chaos
From the Bay of Pigs to Laos,
Said the Berlin Wall helped make the people free. . . .

Goldwater fans circulated elaborate accounts of a "Kennedy-Lincoln Coincidence" portending inevitable Goldwater victory: *Lincoln was assassinated and replaced by Johnson, who lost for reelection; Kennedy was assassinated and replaced by Johnson, who . . .*

Even if Goldwater supporters could not afford it, they gave money. The *Post-Dispatch* missed that story, too. Just as in the wake of the election the nation's voting booths knew only two numbers—Johnson's 61.2 percent to Goldwater's 38.8—newspapers tended to stop at two as well: the $17 million raised by Lyndon Johnson, versus the $12 million raised by Goldwater. What that ignored was that in 1960, 22,000 people donated to JFK's campaign and 44,000 to Nixon's. Over a million gave to Barry Goldwater. And that made all the difference.

For once, the Goldwater command on Eye Street had a hand in spreading the infection: ironically, thanks to Ralph Cordiner, the campaign needed a small, steady diet of new cash every day just to function. When Raymond Massey's pitch began hitting the jackpot, the finance people began looking longingly at the three-year-old RNC program selling $10 "sustaining memberships" in the party—which had reeled in $559,000 in the first quarter of 1964 alone, at the same time that traditional methods yielded but $34,000. The sustaining members were now hit up with special appeals to sustain the presidential campaign. The money proved forthcoming. Then someone had the bright idea of buying mailing lists from the brokers who sold them to catalogs and magazines. Those solicitations brought a deluge. (The campaign received thousands of gifts from customers of the Kozak Drywash Cloth Company alone, which was extraordinary, considering that the product the company made was designed for people too cheap to patronize car washes.) And the marginal utility of one hundred $10 gifts was far greater than one gift of $1,000. Political campaigning is an extraordinarily labor-intensive activity. The former signified one hundred potential laborers, whereas the latter meant only one.

Goldwater's fund-raisers were hardly averse to $1,000 checks. Or the two $1 million gifts the campaign received, one from a rogue member of the Rockefeller clan—or the $100,000 Taiwan gave to each party in those days. But the tiny gifts were talismans: small change sealed up in an envelope addressed in a childish hand; a shaky note proclaiming, "God bless you, Senator, here is my Social Security check"; a grubby paper bag filled with dollar bills, delivered to a Goldwater office on a factory hand's lunch break—these legends circulated. And like all reports of miracles, they served to further infect many more thousands of acolytes.

The spiritual army had rogue militias, hundreds of them, tiny bands for whom Goldwater was the answer to every question and every conspiracy—sometimes on topics he never addressed. These groups came in flavors like the "National Gun Alliance," whose address was a post office box in Arkansas. *"WILL YOUR GUN COLLECTION BE CONFISCATED AND DESTROYED?"* their pamphlet asked, promising a vote for Goldwater as a bulwark against the implementation of "State Department Publication 7277 detailing the *American* plan to disarm all nations." Or the "Goldwater Campaign Fund," based in Minneapolis, which published baroque handbills covering four legal-sized pages of eight-point type, underlined, boldfaced, and uppercased ("READING TIME 7 MINUTES"), wondering how Communism, considering Moscow's penury and America's plenty, could survive "WITHOUT A GREAT DEAL OF HELP!" "A Fed Up Citizen" (no address listed) announced in his flyer, *"If I were the devil and wanted to run America into a communist hell, I think I would do something like this . . ."* (the devil bore a striking resemblance to Lyndon Baines Johnson). A massive yard sign in a Boston suburb being considered for urban renewal declared "WE SHALL DEFEND OUR HOMES WITH OUR LIVES"—next to one reading "BARRY GOLDWATER FOR PRESIDENT: BECAUSE HE IS A STAUNCH DEFENDER OF PROPERTY RIGHTS."

The media ridiculed this stuff if they noticed it at all—as they did the preachments of far-right radio programs (and, sometimes, TV programs) which had once been heard mostly in rural pockets but were now more and more frequently marinating the entire country. Carl T. McIntire's *20th Century Reformation Hour*—which taught that the National Council of Churches, an umbrella organization for thirty-one separate Protestant denominations, was "the strongest ally of Russia and the radical labor movement in the U.S."—was heard on 605 stations. Clarence Manion was now heard Sunday nights on over 1,100. The "Christian Crusade" of Billy James Hargis—who preached the old Mississippi-Freedom-Summer-as-Communist-plot-to-spur-race-war gospel—reached forty-six states every evening from a superpowered radio transmitter in Mexico. Hargis, a hell-fired (and tax-exempted) fund-raiser, had just raked in $38,870 in a live evening "prayer-auction" at his Tulsa headquarters to purchase twenty-five minutes a week on the Mutual Radio Network, the nation's largest, where he would join on its airwaves R. K. Scott, who proclaimed himself the counterpoint to newsmen "knowingly or otherwise singing the praises of the welfare state, planned economy, and other forms of socialism"; and the American Security Council Report of the Air, produced by a Chicago outfit that sold corporate access to files encompassing over two million (purported) subversive Americans—more files, they claimed, than the FBI.

This kind of right-wing cultural entrepreneurship might never have been reckoned with at all had reports not begun filtering out in late September that self-published books by three conservative authors had sold enough copies to supply one out of every ten men, women, and children in the country. The head of the Fair Campaign Practices Commission called them the "dirty books": John Stormer's *None Dare Call It Treason*; J. Evetts Haley's *A Texan Looks at Lyndon*; Phyllis Schlafly's *A Choice Not an Echo*, now in a third edition, and another book she had somehow managed to squeeze out in October, *The Gravediggers*, a numbingly conspiricist indictment of the "card-carrying liberals" whose appeasement policies, not Goldwater's militarism, were "*really* risking nuclear war." Sometimes the 20 million copies of the broadside *LBJ: A Political Biography*—printed by Willis Carto, an erstwhile Birch staffer fired for his anti-Semitism—were included in the category as well. That jacked the total to one "hate book" for every four Americans. When the *New York Times* reported, "Never before have paperback books of any category been printed and distributed in such volume in such a short time," ordinary publishers began wondering what they were doing wrong. What they were doing wrong was not hiring distributors who thought of their products as billboards on the road to Damascus.

None Dare Call It Treason was written by a thirty-six-year-old former Missouri Young Republican leader who had quit his job editing an electronics trade magazine to work on the book and run its publishing company, Liberty Bell Press, which had relocated sometime in the summer of 1964 from his suburban ranch house to a building he shared with a beauty parlor down the street. The Texan behind *A Texan Looks at Lyndon* was the man who gained renown on the right in the 1950s with his lawsuit to invalidate the federal agriculture program, and in 1961 with his call to hang Earl Warren. His book was published (its pages several degrees off plumb) by Palo Dural Press, an annex to the author's 11,000-acre Panhandle ranch. *None Dare Call It Treason* was a *tour d'horizon* of Communist Trojan horses: the Revised Standard Edition of the Bible, progressive education, the Council on Foreign Relations, tax-exempt foundations; it accused the left-wing advocacy group Americans for Democratic Action, as Goldwater did, of sneaking "Fabian socialism" into the White House. Its calling card was its 818 footnotes. *A Texan Looks at Lyndon* relied on the author's unusually graceful prose style, and phases like "reported to have," "it was rumored," and "many persons believe," to argue that if law enforcement had done its job over the course of Lyndon Johnson's thirty-year political career, he would now be in the big house, not the White House.

But it was not their contents that truly made these works popular. They contained price schedules that aped the grassroots distribution methods Clarence Manion pioneered in distributing broadcasts of his radio transcripts back in the 1950s, and *Conscience of a Conservative* in 1960: "1 copy: $.75 . . . 10 copies: $5 . . . 100 copies: $30 . . . 1,000 or more copies $.10 each." The fruits of this kind of incentivizing were revealed on Stormer's copyright page: "First Printing, February, 1964—100,000"; "Second Printing, April, 1964—100,000"; "Third Printing, April, 1964—100,000"—and so on, until 6.8 million copies were accounted for by October. Haley was pumping out 50,000 copies of his book a day by November. Demand for the books, simply, was equal to the production capacity of the nation's two biggest paperback printing plants, which were manufacturing all of them. There always was another Birchite millionaire willing to spring for a lot of a few thousand more to sprinkle around like so many Gideon Bibles. At rallies they were handed out like party favors; in Arizona they were translated into Spanish; in California readings were recorded on LPs. In some areas copies disappeared from bookstore shelves as fast as murder mysteries (although to get the books stocked, the grassroots distributors sometimes resorted to unusual means, like wondering aloud whether a vacillating bookstore proprietor wasn't "Communist"). The Haley book was reportedly the number one best-seller in Virginia.

"Your letter to the President has been received," Moyers wrote in a form letter sent to those who wrote asking why, if the charges in Haley's book were not true, the White House did not sue for libel. "I have not discussed *A Texan Looks at Lyndon* with the President, and I cannot speak for him," he went on. He was almost certainly lying; books like Haley's were the West Wing's new obsession. "They are giving *A Texan Looks at Lyndon* away by the truckload all over the Southwest," reported a field man. "The hate books are all over Georgia," said another. A Kansas official declared, "We hear Haley's book quoted more than anything else in the campaign," and proudly announced that he was distributing copies of Drew Pearson's exposé of its errors to stanch the damage.

This response showed little more than the Administration's incomprehension of this strange new virus spreading in their midst: the people likely to be convinced by *A Texan* were the same people who looked upon Drew Pearson as a traitor. There was nothing more they could do to stem the tide than Goldwater's team could do about Daisy. They couldn't sue; none of the books fit within the Supreme Court's stiff new libel standard in *Sullivan* v. *New York Times*: to prove that the defendant had acted with malicious intent or reckless disregard for the truth. They were boxed in, and they knew exactly who to blame: Goldwater "has fenced with personal attacks on the President," the DNC's research chief wrote Moyers. Now, with these "slander" books, "an attempted softening up has been going on." The "all-out assault by Goldwater himself has not yet occurred," he noted. He predicted it would come in the next few weeks.

It wouldn't. Not only couldn't Eye Street intrigue its way out of a paper bag (a Xerox of what was supposed to be the single existing copy of one key strategy memo, sent from the second to the third floor and labeled with the imperative *"Destroy-After-Reading,"* was spied by its author the next day on a congressman's desk), they were too idealistic to try. They despised the books and ordered that official campaign literature should contain only Goldwater's own words—the somnolent *Where I Stand*, six brochures the RNC gave away that cut and pasted from speeches in the *Congressional Record*, booklets reprinting key campaign addresses. The rule only showed what a shambles the Goldwater campaign had become. In Dade County, Florida, the Republican Party passed out 172,000 copies of *None Dare Call It Treason* door-to-door. The only reason you couldn't get a copy of *A Texan Looks at Lyndon* at the supermarket-sized Republican headquarters in Harris County, Texas, was because the director of the state's Southern Baptist Sunday School Board had declared it a menace to the spiritual welfare of his flock. (But if you asked for a copy you would be directed to a volunteer who kept a stash hidden in her Buick.) "We have no way of controlling people out in the field," Lee Edwards protested to the *New York Times*. And the situation in the field was rather complex.

When a bug-bitten conservative endeavored to volunteer for the crusade, she might find her way to any of four centers of Goldwater activity.

There were, first, the freelancers and the outlaws: the Birch Societies and National Gun Alliances of the world, from whose precincts those who wandered in wouldn't likely leave *without* one, two, or many copies of Schlafly et al.

Second, one might stroll into an official precinct, county, or district Republican headquarters. And there things got a bit more complicated. If you were in conservative territory, you might find a Goldwater hive. In New England, except for Connecticut, no Goldwater activity existed at all; the state parties had written off the entire business in disgust to concentrate their resources on local and state campaigns. Where candidates had pledged to run without the help of their party, the office might be virtually abandoned (perhaps you might find a skeleton crew guarding the files against repossession by right-wingers). But even if you found a willing Republican office, its workers' efforts were a well-intentioned shambles, because they lacked guidance and funds from the harried home office in Washington—or, in a state like Kansas or Idaho, the offices were left in an organizational rubble after the liberal/conservative civil wars fought in the spring.

Forsaking the regular Republican office, you might locate the third center of Goldwater activity: the temporary offices parties rented for a couple of months every four years and dedicated to the presidential effort. You might look in vain. For example, when regular Republican and Goldwater leaders in New York State met at the Manhattan Harvard Club one evening in July, conservatives announced plans to set up an elaborate Goldwater network outside the party structure. Liberals—who refused to campaign for Goldwater but feared their offices would become beachheads for a wholesale conservative takeover of the Republican Party—shot back that it would happen over their dead bodies. Conservatives replied that they already controlled most of the county committees, and that any liberal who didn't cooperate with them would be crushed like a bug. They stopped just short of throwing cocktails at one another.

What that seemed to suggest was that a New Yorker wanting to volunteer for Goldwater would have a hard time of it unless the fledgling state Conservative Party (to complicate matters further) had a presence in his or her area. That didn't happen, for the fourth center of Goldwater activity arrived just in time to save the day and absorb the political orphans' energies. Its impresario was none other than the campaign's forgotten genius: long-limbed, bow-tied F. Clifton White.

When Clif White returned from his unhappy Hawaiian sojourn after finding himself shut out of the campaign's leadership at the convention, he came back to a job offer he might well have dismissed as an insult: director of Citizens for Goldwater-Miller. Citizens' groups were the traditional campaign vehicle to woo disaffected voters believed to be put off by party labels. Such groups tended to be barely tolerated by party regulars; in the GOP, conservatives considered them to be liberal Trojan horses. And Clif White knew this. But he also knew that in 1952 Citizens for Eisenhower had virtually taken over the Eisenhower campaign. Because he would only be assigned 12.1 percent of the campaign budget and given a staff of 88 compared to Eye Street's 700, such a top-down takeover would not be in the cards for him. He spied his opportunity elsewhere: at the grass roots. The precinct, county, district, and state Goldwater organizations *he* had built to win the nomination over the past three years were jamming Eye Street's bollixed switchboard and mailroom in vain to be named official auxiliaries of the Goldwater campaign. White realized that all he had to do was ring up their—his—old leaders and offer them chairmanships of Citizens for Goldwater-Miller chapters, budget them a little cash, and let them get on with doing what they had always done. Then these people could take over from below every function Burch was screwing up from above—a shadow campaign, working with the natives in the countryside like some Third World guerrilla insurgency. The Arizona Mafia, who had fought against giving White any berth whatsoever in the campaign, would be too harried to notice who was saving them from the abyss.

By the end of the first week in August, the results were arriving: Marvin Liebman's New York Goldwater for President Committee, with all his organizing expertise and a mailing list of thousands, was now New York Citizens for Goldwater-Miller; members of the Lehigh County Citizens for Goldwater-Miller were signing up members at the county fair, to the chagrin of party regulars. "300 VOLUNTEERS READY TO WORK," wired the newly christened Pomona Valley Citizens for Goldwater-Miller; "ALL WE 'ORPHANS' NOW HAVE A GOOD HOME," came word from Santa Barbara. "WE HAVE BEEN TREADING WATER WAITING FOR SOME WORD FROM OFFICIAL SOURCES"; "WE HAVE BEEN SITTING PRETTY MUCH 'ON OUR HANDS' SINCE THE NOMINATION, AWAITING INSTRUCTIONS FROM WASHINGTON"; "WE HAVE CONTACTED OUR STATE HEAD-QUARTERS NEARLY WEEKLY AND THEY SEEM TO BE IN THE DARK AS MUCH AS WE": the story was the same everywhere before White came along.

Where prenomination Goldwater organizations were strong and regular organizations were weak—as in Ohio, where the party was in a shambles over the perception that Governor Rhodes had sold the party Establishment out with his stunt of releasing the delegation for Goldwater—Citizens for Goldwater-Miller chapters practically *were* the campaign. The Ohio GOP didn't even inform the newspaper listings when Goldwater's half hours were on TV. So the Columbus Citizens chapter took out its precinct lists the night before a show and would call every undecided voter to urge him or her to watch. When the Goldwater whistle-stop chugged through the state, a Citizens volunteer flew a helicopter ahead of the train and dropped ten thousand "Follow Me to Barry Goldwater" leaflets; the state Citizens headquarters was almost evicted from its fourth-floor office until the landlord received assurances that the group would remove some of its eleven and a half tons of literature that were threatening the building's structural integrity. "TOUR PROVING TREMENDOUS SUCCESS DESPITE SHORTAGE OF ADVANCE TIMING," Vandalia, Ohio, volunteers wired after *Yia Bi Ken* swooped down for a late-October western Ohio swing without benefit of any advance work. "LOCAL COMMITTEE MEMBERS GRATEFUL FOR SHOT IN ARM . . . INJECTED BY OUR GROUP. GIVEN FULL RADIO AND TEN MINUTES TELEVISION TIME LAST NIGHT YOU COULD NOT BUY THE DEDICATED CRUSADE OF THESE

MEN AND WOMEN." In one town, two women actually lived in the Citizens office six days a week. In some places, local rivalries between Republican and Citizens organizations could end up corroding Goldwater efforts more than improving them. But even there it hardly mattered. Clif White was spreading the virus—Bill Buckley's "seeds of hope, which will flower on a great November day in the future."

Clif White would leave one more legacy to conservatism in that 1964 presidential campaign. If winning the presidential nomination and rescuing Goldwater volunteers from idleness were gifts to conservative true believers, this one would prove instrumental in the creation, one day, of a conservative governing majority. Although it would take future election years for other Republican candidates to reap the benefit, it was Clif White's shop that first refined the images and words that would tie the ravages of domestic disorder firmly to the Democratic Party's tail.

It began because of a legal loophole. When Grenier, Kitchel, and Burch discovered that it was illegal for political parties to *sell* campaign propaganda to local units, it took one of the few grizzled veterans on hand—adman Lou Guylay—to point the way out of the dilemma: a committee could be incorporated outside the party structure to front for the work—just as the Democrats had drummed up Professors for, Artists and Entertainers for, and District Attorneys for Johnson-Humphrey, and twenty-three other committees to do the same thing. They chose as their vehicle an organization they had already incorporated: Citizens for Goldwater-Miller. Then they off-loaded Rus Walton, who was on leave from running United Republicans of California, to head up the effort. And since they had enough worries just keeping their own house on Eye Street from collapsing, they hardly gave the matter another thought.

The man who ended up producing the Goldwater brochures that passed through millions of Americans' hands was an embodiment version of the third floor's nightmare. Rus Walton did not believe in the Great Pumpkin. Instead, he was possessed of an almost desperate need to burn conservative truths into an audience's heart via whatever means worked—high or low, fair or foul. In a decade spent as publicist for the National Association of Manufacturers he became ringmaster of a veritable three-ring propaganda circus: radio shows and traveling seminars, public service announcements and singing groups, full-page ads and legislative updates, itinerant debating teams and ostentatious philanthropies. When he served as Joe Shell's campaign manager, his candidate entered rallies to the angelic peal of a sixty-two-voice choir, cheered on by row after row of pom-pom-wielding "Shell's Belles." And during the Kohler strike, Walton designed a NAM booklet for women's clubs warning against the "uncontrolled power, wealth and political influence of unions and union bosses." The cover was illustrated with a picture of a woman crouching in a corner as if cowering from a rapist. Walton had a malign brilliance for that sort of thing. Singing groups and massed choirs had their uses. But voters in 1964, he instinctively understood, were afraid. To reach them you had to exploit those fears. That was the technique by which Johnson was holding crowds in the palm of his hand: convincing them that *he* was the true conservative in the race—the calmer of fears, the bringer of order, the preserver of peace; the father tucking a vulnerable electorate in after banishing the monsters from under the bed with a bedtime story.

For all the high-mindedness, that was Goldwater's goal, too. His monsters included a government "that is master not servant of the people"; a President with a "penchant for buying and bludgeoning votes"; American prestige slipping "below the peril point"; Hubert Humphrey, "the most prominent left-wing Americans for Democratic Action radical in this country . . . a heartbeat away from the Presidency," ready to "drag our nation into the swampland of collectivism"; and "a regimented society with a number for every man, woman, and child." But to conservatives' bafflement and dismay, the things that scared *them* didn't scare the average undecided voter. The candidate's exhortations just made him sound paranoid.

But Goldwater was also trying out another set of lines that were new to conservative campaigning—and these were catching fire. Lines such as "We want to make it safe to live *by* the law; enough has been done to make it safe to live life *outside* the law"; and "Our traditional values of individual responsibility . . . have been slipping away at a quickened pace"; and "Why do we see a flood of obscene literature?" These statements got applause from people who found themselves surprised to find themselves applauding Barry Goldwater. Crime, lax judges, individual responsibility, pornography: rarely did he bunch them together as a unit. He saw civilizational decline everywhere, and these things were no more evidence than were the surging power of the executive branch, rotting weapons systems, Social Security numbers, the Administration's failures in faraway countries whose names people barely recognized, and all the rest. "The theme of our campaign is clear," he would thunder in town after town: "Peace through strength. Progress through freedom. Purpose through constitutional order"—then damn the torpor, full speed ahead, he would plunge into his laundry list of things he thought Americans needed to hear whether they wanted to or not. When he did squish the "morality" themes together, his argument for why they had anything to do with why a person shouldn't vote for Lyndon Johnson was so dubious as to vitiate the power of the appeal. "Moral decay of a people begins at the top," he would say, "from the highest offices into all walks of life." But the direct line from Lyndon Johnson to Kitty Genovese was rather hard to swallow.

Only once did he devote an entire speech to how "the moral fiber of the American people is beset by rot and decay." It was broadcast on TV from the Mormon Tabernacle in Salt Lake City. It was the highest-rated nonpresidential political address in the history of television—a fact, of course, that the candidate likely ignored as a point of pride. But "morality" was political gold. It was the only Goldwater theme that the White House felt compelled to *react* to. But Johnson's people weren't exactly sure how. Memos flew back and forth: Enlist "a group of friendly criminologists"? "Judicious use of the candidate's family," "inclusion of prominent women"? Public appearances with Billy Graham and Cardinal Spellman?

They were floundering. No other presidential candidate had tried staking a political claim for these issues before Goldwater. They had never been *at issue* before.

It was a watershed year in American mores. The Supreme Court declared school prayer a menace to the Constitution; the Boston Strangler, Kitty Genovese, and other dramatic murders were forever removing America's dominant image of crime from the benign realm of the 1950s-vintage "juvenile delinquent." Adlai Stevenson told Colby College students, "In the great struggle to advance human rights even a jail sentence is no longer a dishonor but a proud achievement." It all seemed to fit together somehow. Do-gooders uprooting neighborhoods and school districts; a smut magazine like *Playboy* running interviews with politicians like some kind of cultural arbiter; marijuana smokers; what J. Edgar Hoover called "one of the most disturbing trends I have witnessed in my years in law enforcement—an overzealous pity for the criminal, and an equivalent disregard for his victim." Privileged college students in California whining like victims and holding their own university hostage; the Beatles and their long hair; topless bathing suits; climbing divorce rates; this Warhol displaying Brillo boxes as "art"; that outrageous professional atheist Madalyn Murray O'Hair—the list went on. Suddenly, it all seemed *political*—something people wanted to take a side on. Since it was a presidential year, they looked for a presidential candidate who was on their side, too.

It was hardly foreordained that it would be Goldwater. The salty high-desert rebel and nightclub habitué certainly hadn't complained when Goldwater Girls in bikinis passed the collection plate at one of his rallies in Beverly Hills back in May. One faction of conservatives, in fact, "libertarians"—exemplified by the YAFers who put their founding convention at loggerheads by decrying the Sharon Statement's reference to God and the Berkeley co-ed who was the Rosa Parks of the trolley-car running boards—*defined* their political identity by their live-and-let-live attitude on moral questions. Republicans were the party of Middle American piety. But America was a pious country. God talk on the stump wasn't so much political as pro forma; at the governors' conference in Cleveland there was hardly a peep of opposition to a resolution in favor of a school prayer amendment to the Constitution. It was a liberal Democrat who denounced Ralph Ginzburg on the House floor (the notorious sex researcher Dr. Alfred Kinsey, on the other hand, was a confirmed Republican). It was Bobby Kennedy who, besides J. Edgar Hoover, was the man most likely to be thought "tough on crime." The politician best known for crusading against smutty rock and roll was Governor Matthew Welsh of Indiana—otherwise liberal enough to earn George Wallace's full wrath in the Indiana presidential primary that spring. There was little the eminently liberal Teddy White scorned more than the Berkeley radicals at the Cow Palace: "girls with dank blond hair, parading in dirty blue jeans, college boys in sweat shirts and Beatle haircuts; shaggy and unkempt intellectuals," their rhetoric inspiring Northern Negroes to riot as "revenge for Mississippi and Alabama." And the response to Rockefeller's remarriage had been, of course, bipartisan and ecumenical.

Goldwater raised these issues as they came to concern him, on the fly, almost as a quirk. "The origin of this commendable but somewhat novel resolve is not clear," *The New Yorker*'s Richard Rovere wrote when the candidate started his morality talk at the convention. "Goldwater exegetes say that it has never been a theme in his earlier writings and speeches." (There were hints of it in the home stretch of New Hampshire, although when Walton looked for a Goldwater speech devoted to religious piety he had to go back to early 1962 to find one.) Now the candidate raised such issues constantly. All those folks who were angry at domestic disorder, at immorality, at crime—most of whom would never consider calling themselves conservatives; some of whom had long called themselves *liberals*—now had a side to join: Goldwater's. And Walton knew that for millions of undecideds and lukewarm Johnson supporters, this appeal might close the gap.

The RNC's publicity division realized it, too—and once more it badly squandered the opportunity. About half of the campaign's TV spots attacked the new morality theme, but they were sixty- and thirty-second primers on how to make even your most diehard supporters cringe with embarrassment. The most elaborate began with exclamations in jagged letters leaping out at the viewer, *Batman*-style: "GRAFT!" (Cut to a caricature of Bobby Baker, who actually looked like a rather pleasant fellow in this shot, dipping his hand into a domed building so poorly drawn it was barely recognizable as the Capitol.) "SWINDLES!" (Pictured were a barn and a silo and a photo of Billie Sol Estes, a dimly remembered grifter who had sold the Agriculture Department nonexistent fertilizer storage tanks years earlier and had once been an associate of Lyndon Johnson's.) "CRIME!" (Goofy file footage of kids "rampaging" in the streets that looked like a downmarket *Blackboard Jungle*, cops swatting nightsticks in the air as if chasing curveballs, the kids missing their dummy punches by half a foot, riotous only in the comic sense of the word.) Then the hero is shown at his desk to save the day: "The leadership of this nation has a clear and immediate challenge to go to work effectively and go to work immediately," Goldwater intones, "to restore law and order in the land." Only it looks like the hero is reading these heartfelt words off cue cards.

Walton's work was everything this was not. He gave his staff a motto: "No pale pastels." The RNC, leery of charges of racism, used white actors in those "riot" shots. Walton's rioters were not white. They were not actors. They were Harlemites caught in the act of bashing windows and attacking policemen by news photographers during the uprising in July. Bill Bernbach might have the bomb, but Rus Walton had the backlash. The brochures pressed into hands at the entrance to Goldwater rallies were propaganda masterpieces: "Lyndon Johnson's Administration Is Too Busy Protecting Itself to Protect You," one began. It showed a grocery store reduced to rubble, guarded by police in helmets. (Caption: "Johnson's Administration has whitewashed the Bobby Baker hearings. It has ordered security investigation records burned.") The photo below showed two jet-black Negroes, blurred by action, obscured by night—the eye was immediately drawn to the dead center of the image, where a set of bared teeth leaped out in a composition as exquisitely arranged as a Botticelli. (The caption, "It has asked the rioters to wait until after the election," referred misleadingly to the moratorium on demonstrations agreed to between the White House and the most timorous mainline civil rights groups.) Then the happy ending: the candidate, brow furrowed worriedly, hand on chin, glasses removed. "He will work with Federal, State, and Local authorities to restore law and order in the streets, protect your home, your family, your job—and bring moral leadership back to the White House." A Goldwater quote subtly reminded readers what to blame—the Civil Rights Act signed two weeks before the riots began. "This is the time to attend to the liberties of all," it read. "The general welfare must be considered now, not just the special appeals for special welfare."

Another pictured Goldwater in worried repose beside the words "Are you safe on the streets? What about your wife? Your kids? Your property? What about after dark? Why should we have to be afraid? This is America!" The composition suggested these were Goldwater's words. They weren't. They were things Walton and White would *want* him to say.

A poster asked: "Are you the Forgotten American?" (This evoked the brilliant appeal Goldwater had coined, then inexplicably dropped, in 1961.)

"Government officials make millions while in public service. They let crime run riot in the streets. . . .

"They sell out Cuba and let your boys die in Vietnam." (Kitchel and Baroody rejected every concept for TV commercials on Vietnam that the advertising agency offered.)

"And you—what happens to you? You pay for it: Your Sons. Your Money. Your Shame. Of course they remember you. At tax time. 30% of your income. Enough's enough!

"It's time for a new beginning."

Rus Walton explained his modus operandi at a meeting the afternoon before *Conversation at Gettysburg* provided a lesson in how not to sell a presidential candidate. "We want to just make them mad, make their stomach turn," he said, "take this latent anger and concern which now exists, build it up, and subtly turn and focus it"—focus it against the ruthless man in the White House from which all these evils had to be shown to flow.

But Johnson was more ruthless than Rus Walton knew. Unbeknownst to anyone, the meeting's shorthand reporter was an agent for the White House's Anti-Campaign. The transcript of the meeting passed to the press shortly afterward.

FOREGONE CONCLUSIONS

It was said that the presidential race only really got interesting after the World Series was out of the way. And so it was in 1964. On Thursday afternoon, October 15, the St. Louis Cardinals dispatched the New York Yankees in the seventh game. Things got plenty interesting after that.

Lyndon Johnson had just covered ten thousand miles in seven days. On October 11, a Sunday, it was Phoenix. ("I had to go to church somewhere," he said, with a straight face, in the face of criticism for making a seven-hundred-mile detour from the LBJ Ranch to campaign on the Lord's day, "and Lady Bird heard they've got a mighty fine preacher at the First Presbyterian Church here"; the congregation also happened to include the Democratic contender for Goldwater's Senate seat.) The next day it was Reno, Helena, and Denver. On October 13 it was Ohio, Kentucky, and Pennsylvania. Then, on October 14, New York. Each stop meant half a dozen speeches at least: there was the scheduled one, and then the impromptu ones when he ordered his motorcade to lurch to a halt—seven times on the way in from the Phoenix airport, ten times on the way out. "Get in your car and come on down to the speakin'," he would bark, just like he was running for Congress back in the Hill Country. "You don't have to dress. Just bring your children and dogs, anything you have with you! . . . We're gonna have a hot time in the old town tonight! . . . You take care of me in November, and I'll take care of you for the next four years! . . . Vote to save your Social Security from going down the drain. Vote to keep a prudent hand which will not mash the nuclear button. I want you all to come to my inauguration next January!" Once at the speakin', he would ramble for upwards of an hour like a country preacher. The people went wild. The press went wild. "To describe this week's work . . . as 'effective campaigning' is like calling Hurricane Hilda 'a bit of a blow,' " David Broder of the *Star* wrote. "He is no longer John Kennedy's successor. He is a towering political figure, with a constituency that is his, and his alone." "Jackson in a jetliner," concurred Scotty Reston of the *New York Times*, who had previously dismissed support for Johnson as the product of an electorate "not so much excited about Johnson as they are afraid of Goldwater." This was a triumph.

But now, Jackson-in-a-jetliner was tired. He slumped in the Presidential Suite on the thirty-fifth floor of the Waldorf-Astoria Hotel on the afternoon of October 14, wasted, summoning energy for an appearance at the Al Smith Dinner, the annual New York fund-raiser presided over by the senior prelate of the Catholic hierarchy. He told his handlers he was too hoarse to speak. They knew enough to ignore him. If you could bottle the miracles doing politics worked for Lyndon Johnson's constitution, you'd be an overnight millionaire.

The phone rang. It was Abe Fortas. What he told Johnson was about as shocking as hearing that his daughter was a KGB spy. Walter Jenkins had been arrested in a YMCA basement restroom on a "morals" charge. And the news might hit the wires at any minute.

It had happened exactly seven nights earlier. Jenkins and an old man were arrested by D.C. policemen after being spied in mid-assignation from an adjacent shower through a convenient peephole police had drilled to expedite the operation. Jenkins paid his $50 fine and went back to work. ("It was Mr. Jenkins' custom to work far into the night," the subsequent FBI report would state, "as well as on weekends.") He returned to the White House the next morning, listening dazedly as the President berated him from Detroit: "Didn't I tell you I wanted every worker to have a button or an LBJ hat or sticker?" No one noticed anything different. Walter Jenkins always looked harrowed.

A week passed quietly. Then, on the morning of the October 14, the assistant managing editor of the *Star* called Jenkins at the White House to confirm a story. Jenkins wasn't in yet. His startled secretary took the call. She called him at home, expecting soothing words: *"Of course it must be some big mistake, a confusion of identity."* And as if in a dream, she heard just the opposite. She went weak in the knees. Jenkins dragged himself to Abe Fortas's doorstep, drunk and incoherent, babbling that he didn't want to go on living. Fortas checked him into a hospital; then he summoned Clark Clifford, and the two traveled all over town to beg editors to sit on the story—Stations of the Cross to save Lyndon Johnson's presidential campaign. Many editors learned about the story from them.

Then, at four that afternoon, they gave Lyndon Johnson the news. Those who were present were quite amazed. After the initial shock, the President snapped out of his stupor, his voice now betraying not an ounce of emotion. He was doing politics. He had sprung back to life.

"You don't foresee that you can keep a lid on this, can you?" he asked Fortas. (No way.) Fortas was ordered to remove "certain confidential material" from Jenkins's office. (Perhaps it included the results of an investigation Jenkins had made on his boss's behalf of the sexual peccadilloes of their accuser in the Baker case.) And so, as two thousand well-heeled Democrats dressed for dinner (many in front of the TV, cheering the Yanks' Joe Pepitone as he blasted the grand slam that brought the Series even at three games apiece), the waiting game began. It ended at 8:02. The RNC had gotten hold of the story and released a statement: "The White House is desperately trying to suppress a major news story affecting the national security." At that, United Press ran with what it knew.

Within the hour another window of vulnerability would open up—a bay window. At 9 p.m., the diners far below eagerly awaited the evening's final speaker; that speaker, meanwhile, was in his suite, fretting that the diners would greet him as a laughingstock and the Catholic hierarchs at the head table as auxiliaries to wickedness, when another story came over the wire: Jenkins had been arrested for the same crime in 1959. At this, Johnson finally lost his cool. "Why didn't Walter tell you about it this morning?" he snapped at Fortas. This new revelation could do more damage as than the previous one.

It was a complex of the times. "The sexual pervert's . . . lack of emotional stability," as a government report put it, "and weakness of moral fiber make him susceptible to the blandishments of foreign agents." In 1953 Eisenhower signed an executive order demanding homosexuals be fired not just from all federal jobs but from all companies with federal contractors—one-fifth of the U.S. workforce. Thus the meaning of the 1959 arrest. Already official Washington was in the process of writing off the Jenkins news as a kind of temporary insanity, a product of nervous exhaustion. "I just know that he must have been a very tired—had to have been very tired—a very tired man," muttered one White House official. The beloved Kansas columnist William White called the incident "a case of combat fatigue as surely as any man ever suffered it in battle"—almost to be expected, went the implication, when the enemy is one so savage as Barry Goldwater. *Two* arrests changed the equation. Perhaps there had been three, or a dozen, and perhaps there had been dozens of other sordid assignations that had escaped the notice of the D.C. constabulary. Perhaps this wasn't a nervous breakdown but full-fledged mental illness. Had Lyndon Johnson knowingly brought a security risk into the White House, into cabinet meetings, into gatherings of the National Security Council? Had Lyndon Johnson done so *un*knowingly? So who knew how many perverts and Communists the executive mansion might be crawling with? "They're going to play this security angle big," Johnson railed at Fortas. "They're going to say, 'Here's a man that sat in the highest councils. Who else might he have something to do with? What secrets might he give away?' "

A conventional man in such matters, Lyndon Johnson must have wondered the same thing himself. He had no idea about this character-rotting failing of a man who scurried to and fro with Johnson's secrets close to his breast. He liked to repeat J. Edgar Hoover's boast: "You can spot one by the way they walk." Johnson had walked beside this one for twenty-five years. The humiliation must have been crushing.

Which made his political presence of mind within moments of learning the latest news all the more astonishing. He rang up Deke DeLoach. First—small talk—he propounded his theory that the waiters at the party Jenkins attended before the arrest must have been Republican agents who put some kind of mind-control drug in his drink. "I only wish it were true," DeLoach replied. (Perhaps he had known; he and Jenkins were close friends.) Then the President got down to business: ordering an immediate, full FBI investigation. It was a brilliant way of reminding J. Edgar Hoover that he was right there on the hook with the President. Security investigations were routine for top government officials; Jenkins had been the subject of scrutiny in 1957 upon taking an administrative job on the Preparedness Investigating Subcommittee. The FBI missed his secret then. And since they didn't even *check* White House staff, who knew how many perverts and Communists the executive mansion might have been crawling with—Johnson's White House, Kennedy's, Eisenhower's, Truman's . . . ? J. Edgar Hoover had to acquit himself. He couldn't do it without exonerating Johnson in the process. Johnson didn't even have to tell DeLoach that the report had to come forth well before November 3.

The President covered one last angle: the Pentagon was contacted, and it was learned that Jenkins's service records during his years in the Capitol Hill Air Reserve Squadron bore no blemish. Johnson gloated: wasn't his commanding officer, Lieutenant General Barry M. Goldwater, on the hook with him as well?

With matters reasonably well in hand, he went downstairs. *"And if Lincoln abolished slavery, let us abolish poverty."* (The crowd went wild.) Close to midnight, he paid a prescheduled courtesy call to Jackie Kennedy at her apartment uptown. Then he went back to work. He checked on the television reports (they had been gentle). He called Ollie Quayle down to the Waldorf from his suburban home and ordered poll numbers on the incident to be on his desk by the next afternoon. Fortas telephoned Johnson, near-whispering, "I have that material in boxes at my home." Then—for the first time—the President inquired after the well-being of his associate of a quarter century, although an instant later his thoughts were elsewhere: could the man with whom he was arrested have "gotten any secrets off him"? Fortas said the man was a bum who lived in an Army retirement home. Johnson ordered Mac Bundy to check nonetheless. Hubert Humphrey called to say he planned to tell the press about Jenkins's strong faith and big Catholic family. Johnson shot back with a start that the only thing the public needed to know about Walter Jenkins was that he was but one public servant out of three million.

A little less worried, the President got some sleep. But the next day came more bad news: a nasty Vietcong strike on an American air base outside Saigon. On the plane back to Washington, the President released to his press corps his first public statement on the Jenkins affair (based on Quayle's report that a gesture of sympathy would be advantageous to him). Then he dug into a steak sandwich. He arrived at an unmanageable clot of gristle. As his press corps looked on, he spit it into his hand and flung it clear across the cabin. It landed in a bowl of potato chips set out before Lady Bird and Mary McGrory of the *Washington Star*.

The bad news for Johnson came at just the right time for Goldwater: his people were eating their own. In California, Walter Knott's TV Committee finally became so disgusted with the drivel they were underwriting that they consulted their lawyers on how they could spend the take from P.O. Box 80 as they saw fit. The second-floor higher-ups were steadfastly plotting direct appeals to the candidate. Ralph Cordiner rode along on the plane with the plan of winning Goldwater's ear for fifteen minutes to urge him to bring back Steve Shadegg, whose black arts had brought Goldwater back from deficits almost as yawning as the one they were in now. He didn't get fifteen seconds; Kitchel and Baroody kept Cordiner out of the candidate's compartment like bodyguards. Northern California field director Bob Mardian's hijacking three days later was more successful. As Mardian slipped noiselessly into the seat next to him, Goldwater, half friendly, half accusingly, said, "You've been a very busy boy, Robert."

"I've been doing nothing more than trying to help you win this election, Senator."

"Well, whatever it is you say you're doing," Goldwater shot back with an edge, "I want you to stop it. It's too late. You go back and tell your crowd that I'm going to lose this election. I'm probably going to lose it real big. But I'm going to lose it my way."

Mardian's jaw dropped to near his belt buckle.

Then the newspapers with the blessed, sordid headlines landed on Eye

Street desks. They were an elixir. Dispirited field offices sprung back to life. Freelance printers worked overtime getting bumper stickers and buttons out the door: "LBJ—LYNDON, BAKER, JENKINS: THE FAMILY THAT PLAYS TOGETHER STAYS TOGETHER"; "LBJ—LIGHT BULB JENKINS: NO WONDER HE TURNED THE LIGHTS OUT"; "ALL THE WAY WITH LBJ, BUT DON'T GO NEAR THE YMCA"; "EITHER WAY WITH LBJ." Goldwater's snide references to the "curious crew who would run your country" were stepped up: ". . . companions like Bobby Baker, Billie Sol Estes, Matt McCloskey"—the crowd would cry in anticipation: "And? And? And?"—"and other *interesting* men." The Baroody group was even letting go of its romance with the nobility of failure—convinced that if some second Jenkins were found in the President's employ, lightning might strike. It had for Dewey in '48. It had, two times before in Arizona, for Goldwater.

The cause for optimism lasted until the newspapers landed on their desks the next day.

In the previous twenty-four hours, China had detonated its first nuclear weapon; Harold Wilson was ousted as British prime minister; and Khrushchev was removed as Soviet premier, with no heir immediately apparent. Suddenly, with the Kremlin in turmoil, warnings of imminent danger from Russia just sounded paranoid. And paradoxically, with China more dangerous than ever, the terror rubbed off on whomever should dare mention the forbidden subject of the bomb—which, of course, Goldwater continued to do. His momentum bogged down. Politics was on hold. Suddenly, the nation was interested in little more than having a steady hand on the tiller.

Johnson had canceled a campaign trip for an extended stay at the White House to parley with his foreign policy team before addressing the nation on October 18. At first the DNC bought the time. Then Johnson demanded it be given free, by all three networks—so he could speak, as Section 315 allowed, upon a nonpolitical matter of "national significance." Thus did 63 million Americans get to hear a more somber, technical version of his stump speech. ("We will demonstrate anew that the strong can be just in the use of strength," he said, smartly echoing and reversing Goldwater's convention address, "and the just can be strong in the defense of justice.") Dean Burch promptly demanded equal time to reply. All three networks refused. The FCC held that the networks were within their rights. So did the U.S. Circuit Court of Appeals in D.C. Burch asked the Supreme Court to take jurisdiction in the decision. The Court refused. Johnson's break from campaigning to take up his role as President of the United States was shaping up as his most successful campaign leg yet.

Finally NBC relented. Burch himself, not the candidate, was given fifteen minutes free for October 19. It was a rant: "This Administration repeatedly tried to manipulate the news," he said, laying out the sordid details of how Johnson had commandeered all three networks the night before. Goldwater, meanwhile, taped a talk the same day, in CBS's studios in Washington. (Johnson got his revenge by kicking Goldwater out of the studio to tape another free message, on the death of ninety-year-old former president Herbert Hoover.) Burch concluded his address by announcing that Goldwater's speech would be broadcast if $125,000 was raised in time to secure the half hour. The appeal brought in $500,000. It was amazing that the finance people were able to count it all in time—140,000 donors, an average of three and a half bucks apiece. And at this, the Goldwater campaign's flagging spirit perked up once again.

That week the Goldwater campaign owned the airwaves: Burch had spoken on Monday, October 19; the next night they planned to re-air the Mormon Tabernacle address to pound Johnson's weakened "morality" flank; on Wednesday Goldwater would deliver his response to the President, a fearsome tirade on the unity of the Communist bloc and the folly and fantasy of making friends with the Soviets in the false hope that they were moving away from the harder-line Chinese. On October 22, a half-hour film on the morality question, *Choice*, produced by Citizens for Goldwater-Miller, would be broadcast during soap-opera hours to reach housewives. The assault would conclude Friday with "Brunch with Barry," another play for the female vote bringing together Goldwater and an extremely gracious Margaret Chase Smith into an intense round-table with a Queens antibusing activist, a retiree, two housewives, and the widow of Captain Edward G. Shank Jr.—the downed flier whose letters home, published in *U.S. News*, gave lie to the fiction that America was sending only "advisers" to Vietnam.

Things looked good. So it could hardly be long before another fiasco beset them.

Clif White and Rus Walton were raring to force the lightning. In early October White had written Goldwater a memo outlining their plans. Goldwater, perhaps feeling a bit guilty at having dismissed White so rashly, wrote back: "Agree completely with you on morality issue. Believe it is the most effective we have come up with. Also agree with your program. Please get it launched immediately." He didn't realize he had just become Truman giving MacArthur what the general thought was a green light to cross the Yalu.

In Los Angeles, a film printer was fulfilling a rush order for two hundred prints of *Choice* to be sent to Citizens chapters and conservative groups around the country. A press release explained that the film had been "conceived by" a group called Mothers for a Moral America, led by thirty "prominent American mothers," with 250,000 women nationwide "taking part." That was deceit;

Mothers for a Moral America was a front. Millions of one of Walton's hairiest brochures ("YOU DO NOT HAVE TO BE AFRAID") with a neat MMA logo slapped on (a stylized flame that looked a little like a dove) were circulated from a post office in Ann Arbor. That was to soften the ground for *Choice*'s national broadcast. Then, after it had been shown on NBC, volunteers would move out with saturation showings at school auditoriums and women's clubs, and on local TV. That was what the two hundred prints were for. The idea was to crystallize another volunteer army—a real, flesh-and-blood Mothers for a Moral America, which would carry out nationwide "Mothers' Marches" shortly before the election, approaching homes with their porch lights left on for safety's sake to sell the occupants on Barry Goldwater's law-and-order message. Walton had been slaving over the editing machine with producer Robert Raisbeck for weeks, the images, sound, and music synched to the nanosecond, the emotional register as carefully orchestrated as grand opera. The film-clip research alone was monumental. (It wasn't easy to find footage of a kid giving a cop the finger in 1964.) It would be the apotheosis of Rus Walton's signature method. Which turned out to be the trouble.

Choice told its story in the opening two minutes. Under the pulse of blaring jazzy trumpets and a jungle beat, a black Cadillac careened out of control on a country road, kicking up a cloud of dust that dissolved into a scene of garishly gyrating revelers. Cut to a criminal resisting arrest. Back to the revel. Then the Cadillac; then a civil rights protest; then the revel; then the criminal; then a close-up of a shapely, twisting rump; then the Caddy spinning out of control; then a topless dancer and a chick in a poodle bikini; then the Caddy careening once more—and its owner, Lyndon Baines Johnson, was identified when an empty Pearl beer can popped out the side.

Cue "Battle Hymn of the Republic," a mass recitation of the Pledge of Allegiance, pans over the Statue of Liberty and bucolic countryside and the Declaration of Independence and the Constitution. Cue Raymond Massey: "Now there are two Americas. One is words like 'allegiance' and 'Republic.' . . . The other America—the other America is no longer a dream but a nightmare."

It was that second America that worried NBC president Robert Kintner, to whom the delicate matter of censoring a political announcement fell. He said the show could run only if the exposed breasts and close-ups of covers of books the likes of *Male for Sale, Sex and Hypnosis*, and one depicting a semi-nude woman spanking another, were excised. (He let the kid giving the cop the finger stay.) Meanwhile, Walton and White made the mistake of releasing the incendiary product to the press, which obligingly reported on every shocking image. Two hundred prints being a lot to keep track of, one found its way into the hands of the Democratic National Committee, which called the film the "sickest political program to be conceived since television became a factor in American politics." Conservatives jumped the gun with public showings (San Francisco headquarters projected theirs in its front window); Democrats directed people to these showings with sound trucks. The Wednesday re-airing of the Mormon Tabernacle morality speech hadn't happened before the Republican Party was under suspicion for trafficking in dirty movies, at the very same time that Johnson's "Confessions of a Republican" ad was drawing attention to just how perverse this new GOP was. The RNC was defenseless—for neither Goldwater nor Dean Burch had seen the thing.

Smart politics would have been to keep it that way—isolating *Choice* as the work of rogues. Instead the campaign's response was to let it be known that Goldwater had just reviewed the picture, found it "sick" and "racist," and personally ordered all showings canceled and all prints recalled. To the broad public, it seemed that the Goldwater campaign had produced a disgusting film, then disowned it when the heat was on. Half of Goldwater's diehards were flushed with shame and confusion at the idea of their hero commissioning such a thing; the other half were outraged at his weak-kneed backing away from exposing the Johnson Administration's perfidy. "AS THE RESULT OF CANCELING TV NETWORK RELEASE OF *CHOICE* THE MORALE AND ENTHUSIASM OF OUR WORKERS HAVE HIT BOTTOM," White's Northern California leadership telegrammed him. Some Citizens chapters simply held on to their prints and broadcast them locally, topless dancers, *Male for Sale*, and all, although few home viewers likely watched the whole thing; TV production was not Rus Walton's métier. Like grand opera, it was about twice too long. And the fat lady only sang—it was only identified as a *Goldwater* commercial—in the last five minutes, when John Wayne appeared, a rifle on the mantel behind him, to drawl, "You've got the strongest hand in the world . . . the hand that marks the ballot. The hand that pulls a voting lever," and clips were shown of Goldwater receiving the Republican nomination. *Choice* proved to be that unique thing: a lose-lose-lose proposition.

The withdrawal of the film was the *Post*'s banner the next day. The *New York Times* went with the headline "NO EVIDENCE IS UNCOVERED THAT EX-PRESIDENTIAL AIDE COMPROMISED NATION." Johnson was thrilled. "That was a wonderful thing you did for me and Walter," he told DeLoach, referring also to the Bureau's—illegal, fruitless—file checks on sixteen Goldwater staffers.

Lyndon Johnson still snapped between exultation and insecurity. One day he joshed with the press: "I know I'm gonna beat Goldwater. What I'm trying to do with all this travelin' is to help elect as many deserving Democrats as I can. . . . You-all know a good bit about the Republicans in Congress, and there must be at least a few of them that *you* think deserve to be defeated. Give me some names and either Hubert or I will try to get into their districts in the next few days and talk against 'em." (His press corps was stunned into silence by the cynicism—until one reporter finally piped up that he couldn't think of anyone who better deserved it than young Bob Dole of Kansas.) Another day, LBJ sent a Secret Service man to snarl at a hapless photographer for shooting the President's right side instead of his left.

He saw no reason to coast. The next race riot could break out any day. ("The crackpots must know by now Goldwater will lose," John Bartlow Martin wrote Moyers. "Some are unbalanced. One might act.") And above all Johnson lusted after that landslide that would legitimize him in the eyes of history. Press secretary George Reedy found himself increasingly disgusted with his boss's and Bill Moyers's continued boyish obsession with cloak-and-dagger schemes. "We passed out 10,000 of these outside Madison Square Garden during Goldwater's rally," an assistant wrote Moyers proudly a week before the election, referring to a flyer from an invented group they called "RAGE: Republicans Against Goldwater Extremism." A pamphlet put out by the Republican Committee in the District of Columbia (voting in its first presidential election) bemoaning the weakness of Johnson's civil rights record and the strength of Goldwater's was reproduced and graciously distributed by Johnson state committees in the most racist districts in the South.

"We are not going to send American boys nine or ten thousand miles away from home to do what Asian boys ought to be doing for themselves," Johnson repeated in Akron on October 21—but this time he didn't append his usual caveat about how America would always fight back when provoked. When John Kenneth Galbraith, three days after Gallup listed Johnson at 64 percent to Goldwater's 29 percent, conveyed the message that Governor Brown of California hoped Johnson would say "a word or two in support of open housing when you are next in California," Moyers nixed the idea: no use taking chances. (Open housing ended up losing two to one on Election Day, although Johnson won California with a cushion of well over a million votes.) Johnson even risked a dip into Florida, Georgia, and South Carolina (where feeble new local Democratic campaign offices were flailing about uselessly, because no Democratic presidential candidate ever bothered to campaign there before)—and was so enraged by anti-LBJ and pro-Goldwater pickets he ordered that they be removed by any means necessary, the means his traveling team chose being a pinch of itching powder sprinkled discreetly on the back of the offender's neck. He even shamelessly commandeered one last opportunity for a free "nonpolitical" televised address on October 24—a lecture to school-

children on American democracy. "A great strength of the two-party system,"
he explained,

> is that basically we have been in general agreement on many things and
> neither party has been the party of extremes or radicals, but temporarily
> some extreme elements have come into one of the parties and have
> driven out or locked out or booed out or heckled out the moderates.
>
> I think an overwhelming defeat for them will be the best thing that
> could happen to the Republican Party in this country in the eyes of all
> the people. Because then you would restore moderation to that once
> great party of Abraham Lincoln and the leadership then could unite
> and present a solid front to the world.

Maine had begun opening absentee ballots. It was found that a disconcert-
ing number of voters were declining to vote for either presidential candidate.

The RNC would have the chance to slap Johnson back three nights later. The
campaign had purchased a half-hour slot on NBC with the boodle left over
from Goldwater's response to LBJ's foreign policy address. The campaign had
just finished a one-day whistle-stop through Goldwater country: Los Angeles,
Orange, and San Diego Counties, where crowds were stirred to foot-stomping
frenzies. Mississippi GOP chair Wirt Yerger and Virginia finance chair Stets
Coleman were tagging along in yet one more unsuccessful attempt to hijack the
attention of the candidate from his palace guard. In San Diego's Balboa Stadium, Yerger turned to Coleman and called over the din, "Where the hell has
this been the entire campaign? They just want to show him having brunch with
a bunch of old ladies!"

This was just what was gnawing at the conservative movement potentates
watching from the VIP boxes. They had invested in this campaign in amounts
to boggle the mind. Henry Salvatori, the oilman without whose $50,000 stake
National Review might never have gotten off the ground in 1955, had raised $1
million for the June primary. Much of it had come from just a few men: Cy
Rubel of Union Oil; Holmes Tuttle, the Cheops of Southwestern car dealers;
Patrick Frawley, a frenzied acquisitions specialist with an empire worth $200
million, who had just sent out 40,000 copies of *A Choice Not an Echo* to
Catholic clergymen—and Walter Knott, whose restaurant that grew from his
wife's little berry pie stand now served ten thousand diners a day. These
friends shared several things in common. They were all either on or close to the
ostensibly "figurehead" Goldwater TV Committee. And the only thing men
like this hated more than being controlled was being controlled by anyone three

thousand miles to their east. They felt used, like bagmen. And they liked what they were hearing from their lawyers. It happened that they had convened a $1,000-a-plate fund-raiser not too long ago in L.A. that Goldwater couldn't attend. "We'll send you a surrogate speaker," a Washington factotum assured Salvatori. "Don't get a surrogate, we can get our own speaker," he responded. "No, no, you must have a surrogate." "We'll get our own speaker!" Salvatori roared back, shutting the pest up. He knew exactly who he wanted: Ronald Reagan.

Reagan was one of them. When *General Electric Theater* was suddenly canceled in September of 1962, the actor took it in stride; he was working in politics practically full-time. He had finally changed his party registration, had chaired Loyd Wright's primary campaign against Tom Kuchel (after beating back entreaties that he run himself), and had become so important to the conservative cause that the month after the cancellation of the show he was honored at a 13,000-person YAF rally in Long Island. By the time the California primary came around, he was so busy he was squeezing in noontime speeches in shopping-center parking lots. In September he was named California co-chair of Citizens for Goldwater-Miller and taped a TV commercial for the RNC (Reagan's brother was an executive in Goldwater's ad agency). It was a pip: Reagan alone on-screen, sitting casually but radiating strength, arms crossed, looking the audience in the eye, gently rebuking them that they knew better than to trust—than to trust—well, *them.* "Believe me. If it weren't for Barry keeping those boys in Washington on their toes, do you *honestly* think our national defense would be as strong as it is?" Exactly 60 seconds later, likely on the first take, he drew to a close and sucked in the audience like a tractor beam: "So join me, won't you? Let's get a real leader, and not a power politician, in the White House." Barry admired Reagan's gifts. In one of his own spots, he began his answer to an offscreen question with an attempt at a textbook-Reagan dismissive chuckle—although as usual he made it seem like he was reading it off a cue card.

By then Reagan's G.E. speech had been burnished to a blistering sheen—ineffective lines winnowed with Darwinian ruthlessness, apt examples mined from a thousand bitch sessions with fellow conservatives and hundreds of issues of his favorite magazines, *Reader's Digest* and *Human Events*, one-liners carved to a tolerance that would put Jack Benny to shame. It was a joke in SoCal circles—"The Speech," they nicknamed it, as in: " 'What are you doing tonight?' 'I'm going to the Chamber of Commerce dinner to hear Reagan give The Speech.' " They weren't mocking him; Reagan was the best they had. Few $1,000 donors felt shortchanged when they learned that he would speak in place of Goldwater at Salvatori's dinner. Many *preferred* to hear Reagan speak in place of Goldwater. And it was over cigars and brandy afterward that Salvatori et al. came up with the idea to ask Reagan if he would go into a studio to film The Speech for TV, to show as a Goldwater commercial. "Sure," he replied earnestly, "if you think it will do any good"—just the "gee-whiz, golly-shucks crap," as Frank Sinatra put it, that so endeared him to Republicans, and which annoyed the likes of Sinatra to no end. Only he had a few suggestions. He wasn't one of those cynics who believed that if you could fake sincerity you had it made, but if Ronald Reagan knew anything, it was that sincerity wouldn't come off on-screen without quite a bit of fakery.

Walter Knott, keeper of P.O. Box 80, presented the film to Eye Street with an ultimatum: it would run in the campaign's October 27 network slot. Bill Baroody hit the ceiling. These southern California loonies ruining Goldwater's dignity; this *actor* despoiling a campaign of ideas: it was an affront to everything Baroody was fighting for. Though the problem was also that The Speech contained one too many ideas: about an eighth of it was devoted to Social Security, including a passage about Goldwater's preference for "voluntary features that would permit a citizen to do better on their own." *This* was too impolitic for even Baroody to allow. The word came back to California: No way.

Walter Knott called back with a threat that Bob Mardian, Ralph Cordiner, and Wirt Yerger did not have at their disposal: the power of the purse. Baroody could run another show if he wanted to, but the RNC would have to pay for it themselves. They wouldn't get a penny from TV for Goldwater-Miller.

Baroody chose the same course Clif White had when faced with fanatics questioning his authority: he pulled out the big gun. Two days before the commercial was scheduled to show, Goldwater was persuaded to ring up Reagan. They were "uneasy" and "uncomfortable" with the bit about Social Security, he said; "some advisors" wanted to show *Conversation at Gettysburg* instead, and what did he think? Reagan could see Goldwater's heart wasn't behind his words. He pulled out a big gun of his own: his charm. "Barry," he said, "I've been making the speech all over the state for quite a while and I have to tell you, it's been very well received, including whatever remarks I've made about Social Security." Had he seen the film? Goldwater acknowledged that he hadn't. "They've got a tape here, so I'll run it and call you back," Goldwater promised. Reagan promised that his people would abide by Goldwater's decision.

Goldwater retreated to listen to Reagan's words on audiotape. "What the hell's wrong with that?" he asked Kitchel bluntly. He called Reagan back with the go-ahead. Eye Street had finally been hijacked.

A day passed. The afternoon of the broadcast, with the listings already in the papers (many of them spelling this middlingly famous figure's name "Regan"), Baroody pleaded with Knott one more time. Knott politely, firmly, said that the Californians' minds were made up. And that was that.

And so, the Tuesday before Election Day, at 8:30 p.m., this was what America saw: A nondescript title card, "TV for Goldwater-Miller." A voice-over: "Ladies and gentlemen, we take pride in presenting a thoughtful address by Ronald Reagan." There was a convention-style dais draped with red, white, and blue bunting; Goldwater posters on the walls of a hall at USC converted into a soundstage; an expectant crowd sitting in neat rows, seeded, as props, with the kind of hastily lettered signs you'd see at a "real" campaign rally; Goldwater Girls in white cowboy hats (partisans, recruited as extras). Track had been laid down for a dolly camera—one of several cameras. The extras received their instructions; action was called. Ronald Reagan hit his mark. And it was clear within five seconds that this was like no other Goldwater TV show before. Those had lost nothing in effect when they were simulcast on radio. Not so this. As Reagan began to speak, the camera dolly swooped dramatically overhead, slowly fixing on the man with the sturdy torso and the gleaming hair at the dais, eyes locked on yours like some smiling, gentler version of the prophet Jeremiah.It was hard not to pay attention.

It was harder still when Ronald Reagan started in on The Speech. He delivered lines like punches: "Thirty-seven cents out of every dollar earned in this country is the tax collector's share"; "We haven't balanced our budget in twenty-eight out of the last thirty-four years"; "Our national debt is one and a half times bigger than all the combined debts in the world"; "The dollar in 1939 will now purchase 45 cents in its total value."

Goldwater hardly ever mentioned a statistic. He hardly used an *example*. He presumed you already knew what he meant. Reagan *showed* you. How the government was cheating you: the foreign aid money that bought Haile Selassie a yacht, Greek undertakers dress suits, Kenyan government officials extra wives, and "a thousand TV sets for a place where they have no electricity"; about the Kansas county the Area Redevelopment Agency declared a depressed area even though it boasted "two hundred oil wells." ("When the government tells you you are depressed," he deadpanned, "lie down and be depressed!" That was it with Goldwater: no jokes.) How federal agents could "invade a man's property without a warrant" and "impose a fine without a formal hearing, let alone a trial"—even, he said, auctioning off the farm of a Chico County, Arkansas, man who overplanted his federal rice allotment.

The stories went by faster than thought, like a seduction: "Now we are told that 9.3 million families in this country are poverty-stricken on the basis of earning less than $3,000 a year. . . . We are spending $45 billion on welfare . . . do a little arithmetic and you will find that if we divided $45 billion equally among those 9 million poor families we would be able to give each family $4,600 a year." (In fact, of that $45 billion, only a small fraction went to the poor; the rest went to pay for programs such as Social Security and veterans' hospitals.) The camera dollied back over the crowd as they nodded, spellbound, their hand-lettered Goldwater signs resting uselessly in their laps as if they had forgotten about them altogether. Then the focus moved in on his torso, tightening so you could read the indignation on his face when he spoke of the three-year-old $1.5 million building that had been demolished in Cleveland "to make way for what government officials call a 'more compatible use of land.' " Then back to the torso as he stretched himself toward you, his passion reaching a peak: "Shouldn't we expect the government to read the score to us once in a while?!" The images danced with the words: straight-on shots intercut with profiles, then widening to take in the applauding crowd, then closing in on the radiant, intent faces as the pace of his examples quickened; then back to a close-up of Reagan so you could read the warmth in his face as he defended the honor of his friend Barry Goldwater, who—did you know?—had taken time out to sit with a dying friend in the closing weeks of the campaign.

Reagan's statements on Social Security were patient, measured, confident. Goldwater's were fragmented and defensive when he dared broach the subject again at all, let alone utter the dread word "voluntary." The liberals want you to "confess that a little intellectual elite in a far-distant capital can plan our lives for us better than we can plan them ourselves," Reagan said. But France's Medicare program was now flat bankrupt—"They've come to the end of the road." He made you understand how Social Security taxes didn't *really* go into Social Security benefits, but into the general budget instead, and that if a fellow invested his Social Security contribution in the open market he could retire ten years earlier. And suddenly Barry Goldwater didn't seem so irresponsible after all. The language had the sweep of poetry: "I would like to suggest that there is no such thing as a left or right. There is only an up or down: Up to man's age-old dream, the ultimate in individual freedom consistent with law and order; or down to the ant heap of totalitarianism." He said, "We are at war with the most dangerous enemy that has ever faced mankind in his long climb from the swamp to the stars." You might think that that sounded fine if it weren't for the fact that, as Lyndon Johnson noted, the nation was at a peace that could only be maintained by meeting the Communists halfway. Then you began reconsidering. "I wonder who among us would like to approach the wife or mother whose husband or son has died in Vietnam," Reagan said, "and ask them if they think this is a peace that should be maintained indefinitely." Goldwater never talked about wives and mothers; mostly he stuck to military hardware and deprecations of "Yo-Yo" McNamara, or Eisenhower's successful use of brinkmanship in Lebanon and the Formosa Strait— hardly victories to stir the blood.

Most of General Electric's employees were Democrats, just as most of the country was. They weren't even, necessarily, newspaper readers. Communicating with them had become Ronald Reagan's passion and his craft. He constructed a bond between "you and I" in every speech, as in: "Any time you and I question the schemes of the do-gooders, we are denounced as being against their humanitarian goals." (Everyone had questioned a scheme of the do-gooders at one point or another. And who wanted to be accused of being against humanitarianism?) And there was a "them" in every speech: condescending do-gooders; numskull bureaucrats; people like the woman whose husband made $250 a month but who asked for a divorce when she discovered she could make $330 on Aid to Dependent Children.

These were rhetorical techniques Reagan had learned from his hero, Franklin Delano Roosevelt, sitting by the radio as a young adult. In his 1936 convention acceptance speech, one of Reagan's favorites, Roosevelt attacked a "them" he labeled "economic royalists": a "small group [who] had concentrated into their own hands almost complete control over other people's property, other people's money, other people's labor—other people's lives." "Against economic tyranny such as this," he went on, "the American citizen could appeal only to the organized power of Government." . . . "Better the occasional faults of a government that lives in a spirit of charity than the consistent omissions of a government frozen in the ice of its own indifference," FDR said, before launching into his final lyrical flight: "This is a mysterious cycle in human events. To some generations much is given. Of other generations much is expected. *This generation of Americans has a rendezvous with destiny.*"

Twenty-eight years later, speaking over the nation's airwaves himself, Ronald Reagan remembered those words. "You and I have a rendezvous with destiny," he intoned in the closing peroration of the show, which was called *A Time for Choosing*:

> We will preserve for our children this, the last best hope of man on earth, or we will sentence them to take the last step into a thousand years of darkness.
>
> We will keep in mind and remember that Barry Goldwater has

faith in us. He has faith that you and I have the ability and the dignity and the right to make our own decisions and determine our own destiny.

The cheers went up and the standards were raised to the sky. But since only the backs of the audience members could be seen, an entranced mind could slip: *perhaps those signs weren't really for Barry Goldwater at all.* It was, David Broder and Steve Hess would write, "the most successful national political debut since William Jennings Bryan electrified the 1896 Democratic Convention with the 'Cross of Gold' speech."

On the coffee table of the kind of sophisticate who had no interest in tuning into the rantings of yet one more irrelevant right-wing crank that night, there might have sat the November issues of *Playboy* and *Esquire. Playboy* had an interview with George Wallace, who, asked if his campaign would soon be forgotten, replied, "That may be the case as far as I'm concerned. But the attitude of millions of people toward the trends in the country will not be forgotten." *Esquire*, meanwhile, had two articles on the Republicans: Norman Mailer on Barry Goldwater and the July convention ("The iron power of the iron people who had pushed him forth—as echoed in the iron of the Pinkertons on the 14th and 15th Floor—now pushed forth over the nation an iron regime with totalitarianism seizing the TV in every frozen dinner"), and Rowland Evans and Robert Novak on the journey that had brought Richard Nixon to the pitiable irrelevancy in which he now found himself. "Each of his carefully calculated moves in 1964," they wrote, "was followed only by his own further political destruction." The piece was illustrated by a drawing of a smiling, unsuspecting Nixon being taken down by a wrecking ball. The epigram was from the poet Dante Gabriel Rossetti: "Look in my face: my name is Might-have-been; I am also called No-More, Too-late, Farewell." Evans and Novak were the savviest judges of political horseflesh in Washington. They were also glorified gossips, perforce only as good as their sources, and they didn't burn bridges lightly. When they delivered a body blow like this, you could be sure the horse they were flogging was as good as dead.

In that case Richard Nixon was one mighty busy corpse.

The RNC put Nixon on TV live from Cincinnati the day after the Reagan speech. No jump cuts, no dolly shots, no Cross of Gold: just that familiar rumble, the plodding, algebraic exposition of points A, B, and C; lots on the glories ushered in by eight years of Republican rule from 1953 to 1960; much more on those embarrassments Lyndon Johnson and Hubert Humphrey—and, in the last paragraph, a passing mention of the man on whose behalf he spoke. Two nights earlier, before 18,000 screaming conservatives at Madison Square Garden, Nixon had taken a full six minutes and thirty-two seconds to introduce Goldwater. Two days before that he had spoken for Goldwater in Watertown, South Dakota, and Fargo, North Dakota. The day before that it had been Houston and Roswell, New Mexico. October 22, 21, 20, and 19 had brought him to Tulsa, Denver, and Casper; Lincoln, Nebraska, and Pratt, Kansas; Enid, Oklahoma, and Augusta and Presque Isle, Maine; and Manchester, Hartford, Syracuse, and Stamford. He was on his way to deliver 156 speeches for the ticket in thirty-six states. It was his new master plan.

It had begun the week after the convention, with a call to the farmhouse in Gettysburg. Nixon convinced Eisenhower to meet with Goldwater, to get to know him better, to see if he couldn't find it in his heart to see honor in the man. Nixon prepared the way by initiating a legalistic little open exchange of letters: "Since our convention, I have received several inquiries as to the intended meaning of two sentences in your acceptance speech," he began; Goldwater responded, "If I were to paraphrase the two sentences in question in the context in which I uttered them I would do it by saying that whole-hearted devotion to liberty is unassailable and that half-hearted devotion to justice is indefensible." Eisenhower was satisfied, Nixon was satisfied. So Nixon arranged a grand parley of Republicans at the Hershey Hotel in Pennsylvania for the middle of August—Goldwater and Miller, Rockefeller and Scranton, Thruston Morton and Richard Nixon, Dean Burch and Charles Percy, governor upon congressman upon senator, all histrionically declaiming on the unshakable unity of their Grand Old Party, then emerging for a press conference in which all wounds were declared healed. It was Nixon's little test. Goldwater passed. Now Nixon knew he could back him and survive.

Let Scranton and Rockefeller make their token gestures at the ticket; let Romney and Rhodes snub it altogether. Nixon had been as nauseated by the convention—literally, he would claim in his memoirs—as any of them. Only he had swallowed his bile—and swallowed the rubber chicken, the back-room whiskey, and the church-basement juice, sitting in airports, sleeping in airplanes (or not sleeping, if it was a prop plane that rattled like the end of the world), gripping and grinning just as he had for his party every two years since 1946. Once more he would pack the bags, kiss the girls goodbye, and set out to collect the chits. It was habit, strategy, a way of life.

The sophisticates would laugh and poke fun at "Tricky Dick" chasing around the country once more. They always did. But didn't Nixon always get the last laugh? While the Romneys and the Rockefellers sat on their hands, he would be the one to court the conservative foot soldiers who now owned the precincts, grateful that at least someone in the Establishment hadn't sold them out. He would get chits from moderates glad to see someone out there holding the line *against* the conservatives; and chits from county chairs in places like Enid, Oklahoma, that were saved from having to cancel half-subscribed fund-raising dinners because no other Republican of marquee stature was out there touring; chits from the local candidates who flooded his office in New York with requests for the privilege of walking the tarmac with him to the pulse of a thousand flashbulbs: conservative candidates, moderate candidates, liberal candidates. "He's one of us," they would say—again. Like that roomful of Orange County businessmen looking for a congressional candidate for 1946, when he presented himself in his Navy uniform because he didn't own a civilian suit and said that the men he talked to in the foxholes "will not be satisfied with a dole or a government handout"; like the civil rights people after "NIXON SAYS RIGHTS PLANK MUST BE MADE STRONGER" at the 1960 convention.

This year was the hardest. Day after day, candidates implored him not to associate them with their own party's presidential candidate; Nixon always managed to find some way to praise each independently of the other, an operation akin in delicacy to separating an egg yolk from the white. Liberal Republicans called him a traitor for undermining the unwritten pact to starve out the conservative wing and move in for the kill after November. Conservatives called him a traitor for evenhandedly offering his service to any candidate who asked. The scheduling office on Eye Street disdained to deal with him; but the press identified him as a loyal member of the Goldwater team nonetheless—as attested by the lowballed crowd estimates and the news cameras lingering on the empty seats or the fattest, ugliest blue-haired old lady they could find.

Nixon plowed on manfully. Goldwater would tumble into his grave on November 3. Rockefeller, Romney, Rhodes, Scranton, and the rest would stumble into theirs just as soon as the realization dawned that it wasn't Walter Lippmann and the Alsop brothers who nominated Republican presidential candidates, or television cameras, or Rowland Evans and Robert Novak. Chits did. Chits knew no ideology. And, as the campaign dragged ignobly into its final weekend and he watched his own jowly face on the TV screen boring yet one more lackadaisical audience, Richard Nixon could comfort himself that he had bagged them all. Chits lasted a long time—four years at least.

Halloween weekend, and both sides were racing for the sewer. The man whom Johnson beat in his first congressional election went on statewide TV on behalf of "Texas Doctors for Goldwater" and compared his old opponent with "Hitler and his crew of very curious people," stating that the Civil Rights Act gave the President "all the power Adolf Hitler ever had." A rumor spread that Goldwater's 9999th Air Reserve Squadron was really a cabal working for military takeover of the government, *Seven Days in May*–style. In states where black votes might provide the margin of victory, Republicans made sure that 1.4 million leaflets appeared in the ghettos urging write-in votes for Martin Luther King, the newly announced Nobel Peace Prize laureate. Bill Miller's daughter was the victim of a bomb scare. Volunteers handing out Goldwater pamphlets to passersby saw them smacked away with enough force that they feared their wrists would be broken. "Teenagers are the hard core of the trouble-makers," a shocked *Philadelphia Inquirer* political columnist wrote. "Screaming girls and yelping boys try to dominate meetings and the police seem powerless to quell the disturbances caused by these young people."

Johnson supporters wore "Goldwater for Halloween" buttons—a cryptic legend understood perfectly by the many for whom Barry Goldwater personified everything frightening and evil. For trick-or-treaters, Goldwater partisans kept by the door a store of the tiny anti-UN pamphlets the Birch Society published to be slipped into children's little UNICEF tins, or big bowls of "Barry Goldwater Taffy," and displayed huge Goldwater signs on their lawns—and teenage liberals running in packs and howling like demons made Goldwater's face an awful goulash of rotten eggs and jack-o'-lantern fragments as Goldwater teens prowled after midnight prying Johnson bumper stickers from cars with razor blades.

The candidates set the example. The President sat up all night on October 30 reading noted Republicans' FBI files, the next day burbling excitedly to Bobby Kennedy about which tidbits he planned to leak to the press. The White House was crediting a rumor that the Goldwater campaign was on the verge of springing some scandalous last-minute announcement about one of Johnson's cabinet members. The campaign team in the West Wing had a retaliatory strike planned—a statement questioning the competence of a commanding officer of an Air Reserve squadron who could give "excellent" ratings to a security risk like Walter Jenkins. Air Force One was careening around the country on whims, like a pinball. Why not Pittsburgh and Houston in one day? Salt Lake City, unscheduled and unadvanced, then Philadelphia? (Finding the 47-by-47¼-inch podiums in each city that he demanded "so it hits mah belly button" drove Johnson's road crew to distraction.) His rhetoric devolved to the level of nonsense. "I'm depending on you young folks who are going to have to fight our wars, and who are going to have to defend this country, and who are going to get blown up if we have a nuclear holocaust—I am depending on you to have enough interest in your future and what is ahead of you to get up and prod Mama and Papa and make them get up early and go vote," he pronounced at a stop in Delaware (where he was devoting enormous resources to unseating Senator John Williams, instigator of the Bobby Baker investigation). In San Diego he ranted about a sexually deviant appointment secretary in Eisenhower's Administration, bragging that back then "we Democrats didn't capitalize on a man's misfortune." (There had been no such appointment secretary, prompting an impromptu ethics seminar in the press quarters on whether it was allowable to misquote the President of the United States in order to save the real secretaries' honor.)

Goldwater's speeches were now sheer extrusions of rage. "He tells the American people in the most flagrant insult to our intelligence *I've ever heard* from a politician, that the only—*the only issue!*—is getting people up early in the morning to vote for him!" That was in Wyoming on October 30, the same day the *New York Daily News* all but withdrew its previous endorsement of Goldwater because "the Senator has made so many unfortunate remarks in public that one wonders how capable a President he would be." The next day, resting in Phoenix, Goldwater came unhinged. There was awful news from Vietnam: a mortar barrage by the Vietcong had killed four American servicemen and destroyed half a dozen B-57 bombers. Goldwater made dark hints about LBJ's complicity. "I won't make any comment about it happening just before the election," he said, "but if you will recall about three months ago I said something would happen just before the election either in Cuba or South Vietnam of this nature, and it's happened in South Vietnam." He had traveled 74,000 miles since September 3. *Yia Bi Ken* was pinballing, too: California to New York to Tennessee to Iowa to Pennsylvania, then back to California, showing up in places so irrelevant to the outcome of the election that it was as if the plane were flying itself. The strain was wearing on the candidate, and his audiences absorbed the blame. "Does this make any sense to you at all?" he would howl after outlining the perfidies of Bobby Baker and Billie Sol Estes. "Or have you already forgotten about them?"

He went on existential rambles. "I can't help but wondering, sometimes, if you've asked yourselves why my campaign is the way it is." Think of the Romans, he said. "They traded their votes for 'bread and circuses.' They traded away their Senate for an emperor." It was the only way he himself could understand this great national salivation over an opponent he now despised. He now viewed his job as just smacking people back to their senses.

> Just think about it for a moment. Do you want my opponent to "let us continue"? We *simply* can't continue!—unless we want to commit *national suicide!* . . .
> Do you want a President who will twist arms, manipulate power, and take more and more control over your lives? . . .

Do you want a President who will promise anything and every-thing, just to buy the job? Promise even to free you from all your responsibilities! . . .

You want no worries? He'll worry for you. Relax and don't worry. The *great leader* and his curious crew will do for you all those things you find unpleasant to do for yourselves. And *all* he asks is that you give him more and more power over your lives. More and more without end. . . . Put all the power in his hands, and he will give you true freedom—*which we used to call slavery!*

The old restraints fell away. Sunday evening he gave his civil rights speech, the one he once reserved for a carefully selected Chicago audience and edited and reedited for any hint of racist taint—but now gave in Columbia, South Carolina, with a covey of segregationists sitting next to him. The extrav-aganza was beamed live to eighty-seven TV stations across the South.

Few people saw it, thanks to Ronald Reagan.

In Goldwater circles a cult was quickly forming. The checks, those grubby paper bags stuffed with cash, the envelopes full of children's spare change—they came and came and came after the October 27 Reagan speech, more money, even, than could be counted. Thanks to Reagan's old boss Cordiner, who was barely speaking with Burch after the RNC pleaded with him to allow expenditures outside the organization's stingy budget, they didn't have any outstanding bills. That meant they could now buy time for a last-minute blitz of spots. But they were too late. The networks no longer had any time left to sell. And the RNC ended up with a surplus of $500,000.

But one Goldwater campaign film was on the air constantly—Reagan's *A Time for Choosing*. Dozens of local committees had spontaneously begun raising cash to run it over and over again in their towns, some half a dozen times or more. In northern California a couple took out a second mortgage on their house to help get it on the air. A kid in Kentucky watched wide-eyed with his father, a janitor. The boy pointed at the screen, and said, "That man is going to be President. And I'm gonna work for him in the White House." People called their crazy fascist Goldwaterite friends on the phone: *Now* I get it, they said. Conservatives were no less stricken; they had never heard as gripping and pithy a statement of what they believed. The Goldwater offices, down to the most ragged and irregular, were being irrigated by Reagan cash; whenever the show ran, people just sent money to whatever Goldwater outfit they could find. The Arizona Mafia fielded humiliating letters. A friend wrote Kitchel: "In my 30 years in politics I have never heard such glowing tributes as the accolades for Ronald Reagan's speech." Another dropped Kitchel a note of congratulations on how he had handled the campaign. "Incidentally," he added, "Ronald Reagan was terrific." It was one of the few times in his life that Goldwater was jealous. He never did thank Ronald Reagan, a wounded Nancy Reagan later noted.

Wirt Yerger, blunt as ever, called up one of the media chiefs in Washington and asked what it would cost to underwrite another network broadcast of the thing. It turned out that the Mississippi GOP had $120,000 left over from its own campaign fund-raising. (Mississippi's finance chair had pioneered yet another fund-raising innovation: automatically deducting a bank draft from the donor's account at set intervals.) Frantically, someone on Eye Street managed to cadge another half hour from the networks. So frantically, in fact, that no one realized that the Columbia, South Carolina, rally was running throughout the South at exactly the same time on another network.

On Monday, Goldwater traveled to San Francisco to deliver an exact reprise of his acceptance speech. ("IN YOUR HEART YOU KNOW IT'S A LOT OF TRIPE, SO GO TO THE POLLS AND DO WHAT YOU THINK IS RIGHT," read a theater marquee his motorcade passed on the way to the hall, under what was supposed to be a blizzard of ticker tape, but turned out to be gently falling flurries.) Goldwater's men made a last-ditch attempt to reclaim him as a member of the human race: a newspaper advertisement reprinted a beautiful and wise letter he wrote to his little girl, Joanne, back in 1948. It began:

> *Dearest Joanne:*
> *Those beautiful quaking aspens you have seen in the forests as we have driven along have one purpose in life. I want to tell you about them because they remind me a lot of Mommy and me and you kids. Those aspens are born and grow just to protect the spruce tree when it is born. As the spruce grows bigger and bigger, the aspens gradually grow old and tired and even die after a while, but the spruce which has had its tender self protected in its childhood grows into one of the forest's most wonderful trees. Now think about Mommy and me as aspens standing there quaking our selfs in the winds that blow, catching the cold snows of life, bearing the hot rays of the sun, all to protect you from those things until you are strong enough and wise enough to do them yourself. . . .*

Johnson ran get-out-the-vote spots: footage of an electrical storm, gale-force winds carrying umbrellas down the street, the narrator pronouncing, "If it rains on November 3, get wet. . . . The stakes are too high for you to stay home."

Another showed a voter entering the booth as the announcer told him to remember as he pulled the lever that the United States was at peace.

Behind White House doors, the commitments had been made two months earlier: American pilots would gear up for bombing raids in North Vietnam as soon as the election was won. The only question now was the dates.

On Election Day, the officials waved the Goldwater family right in at their modest local polling station in Phoenix; they insisted on waiting in line. The candidate playfully borrowed a felt-tip and penned a tic-tac-toe board on his wife's neck. The cameras wedged in for prime real estate as Goldwater entered the booth. The curtain opened; Goldwater emerged, flashbulbs popped. The pictures recorded a man who looked like he would rather be somewhere else.

Across the nation, millions of ordinary Americans did exactly the same thing at exactly the same time in exactly the same way, the glory of democracy. At a carefully marked-off legal distance from the polls, union members passed out palm cards reading "From the Hip . . . Or From the Head?" and "PRESIDENT JOHNSON . . . Soldier of Peace," and paraphrasing the President's Gulf of Tonkin speech: "We still seek no wider war." Presuming as a matter of course that Lyndon Johnson would cheat, conservatives—over one per voting booth in Chicago and Cleveland—carried out what the RNC called "Operation Eagle Eye." Poll watchers were instructed to hover over the precinct books from the opening until the closing of the polls to check that each signature corresponded to the one on record, and to tick off the names on their duplicate precinct books (the evening before, they had driven through the neighborhoods to make sure none of the addresses in the book corresponded to vacant lots or abandoned buildings). Hubert Humphrey, mindful that under the supervision of Bill Rehnquist and Dick Kleindienst in 1962, Arizona Republican Party workers attired in policelike uniforms had stalled voters in Negro and Mexican districts by forcing them to read the Constitution of the United States, called the effort "Operation Evil Eye." Employees of the three television networks swelled the crowds at some polling stations even further. It was the new ritual: viewers were glued to the big charts slowly filling up behind the anchormen all afternoon, until, four hours and twelve minutes before the close of the California polls, NBC became the first to crunch the exit-poll data and call a winner. (Afterward the networks received postcards: "*You bastards!* Election night used to be fun. You spoiled it with your goddamned gimmicks.")

It wasn't a hard election to call. No amount of cheating could run up a landslide like this. At Goldwater's D.C. election-night headquarters at the

Shoreham, reporters were swarming around Ronald Reagan, and Lee Edwards, drunker by the hour, finally wove his way to the lectern at ten or eleven after final word flashed that Goldwater had lost Illinois, that great Taftite redoubt where Edwards's father, the *Chicago Tribune*'s Washington correspondent, had been publishing articles all month with headlines like "JOHNSON'S EGO MASKS UNDERLYING CONCERN OVER ELECTION OUTCOME." He slurred something about how Goldwater would release a statement later after he'd analyzed the vote. Goldwater was back home in Arizona, where he'd been in bed for three hours, leaving Kitchel, Hess, and Paul Fannin (who won his old Senate seat) weeping in front of the TV, Goldwater never having graced either the Phoenix or Washington headquarters with his presence.

Lyndon Johnson, in Austin, was more vigilant. He was on the phone with Bill Moyers constantly, gorging himself with good news. At 5:45 p.m. he asked about Kentucky (final total: LBJ, 64 to 36), Indiana (65 to 33), New Jersey (66 to 34), and Oklahoma (56 to 44). At 5:52 he learned, unsurprisingly, that Goldwater was winning South Carolina (final total: 59 to 41), but that the Democratic ticket was on a pace toward carrying Ohio, whose governor had offloaded his convention delegates to Goldwater certain that the backlash would carry the Republican to victory, by a million and a half votes. At 6:22 the President looked into Maryland (65 to 35), Connecticut (68 to 32), Vermont (66 to 34, Democratic for the first time ever), North Carolina (a border-state landslide for LBJ, 56 to 44), Minnesota (64 to 36), and Georgia (Goldwater, 55 to 44). The news wasn't enough to cheer him. "I'm afraid of Vietnam," he told Moyers in between returns. "We're in trouble in Vietnam, serious trouble," he repeated to Hubert Humphrey. Congratulating his former attorney general on his projected New York Senate victory, Johnson, sounding perhaps a bit more pleading than he had intended, asked: "If you get any solution on Vietnam just call me direct, will you?"

Around nine, Johnson left for his Driskill Hotel headquarters to congratulate his thronging workers. From there he was driven to the Civic Center to make his victory statement. The radio was on. He heard the announcer say that President Johnson had just left the Driskill and was on his way to the Civic Center to make his victory statement. An assistant press secretary was the beneficiary of his hot Texas breath. "I didn't authorize any statement about where I'm going, when, or why!" He took the platform with the rostrum that hit his belly button and gave his victory statement. "I doubt that there has ever been so many people seeing so many things alike on decision day," he said.

So many people seeing so many things alike on Election Day. Thus the final ritual: the commentaries were published that the pundits had begun writing in their heads in July, as soon as Barry Goldwater declared that extremism in defense of liberty was no vice.

"Barry Goldwater not only lost the presidential election yesterday but the conservative cause as well," the *New York Times*'s Scotty Reston wrote. "He has wrecked his party for a long time to come and is not even likely to control the wreckage."

In embracing conservatism, proclaimed his *Times* colleague Tom Wicker, the Republicans strayed from the simple reality that "they cannot win in this era of American history" except as a "me-too" party. "With tragic inevitability," he wrote, they "cracked like a pane of glass."

"The Johnson majority," Walter Lippmann pronounced—at over 61 percent the greatest popular mandate in history—"is indisputable proof that the voters are in the center."

If the Republicans become a conservative party, "advocating reactionary changes at home and adventures abroad that might lead to war," wrote the *Los Angeles Times*'s Washington bureau chief, "they will remain a minority party indefinitely."

How could they conclude differently? The numbers were spectacular: 43,126,218 votes for Johnson to 27,174,898 for Goldwater, who won only six states—one of them, Arizona, by half a percent. William Miller lost his home district by a ratio of 2 to 1. Goldwater won only sixteen congressional districts outside the South. Republicans had devoted enormous energy to disassociating their candidacies from Dr. Strangewater's. It didn't work. People ticked the Democratic column down the line. Come January, Lyndon Johnson would enjoy a 295 to 140 majority in the House, and 68 to 32 in the Senate, with which to build his Great Society. Only one incumbent Democratic senator lost his seat. The Republicans lost 90 seats in upper chambers of state legislatures, 450 in the lower. Blacks voted upwards of 90 percent for Johnson. The truckloads of money the Democrats spent to register a million new black voters proved a windfall investment, because in many states they provided the margin of victory—and kicked out many a Republican officeholder even though he was a far greater champion of civil rights than his Democratic opponent was. According to the *Washington Post*, Goldwater had only God to thank that so many Republicans had voted for him at all. The vast majority did so "out of habit . . . despite grave fears of victory if it should come." A study of exit-poll statistics by Louis Bean and Roscoe Drummond published in *Look* was cited over and over: it concluded that the "pure" Goldwater vote was less than three million, the rest just party loyalty.

Goldwater's success in the South was historic, to be sure. In Alabama he won 70 percent, and his coattails swept in practically an entire new House delegation, five of eight representatives, wiping out some eighty years of Democratic seniority. Less dramatic shakeups transpired in South Carolina (59 percent), Louisiana (57 percent), and Georgia (55 percent). In every Southern state he lost—Texas, Tennessee, North Carolina, Arkansas, Florida (where he won 49 percent), Virginia, and Kentucky—Republicans were elected to statewide office in unprecedented numbers. In Mississippi he got 87 percent of the vote. He even won Hattiesburg, which was rather remarkable. On October 22, scientists had set off a nuclear device 2,700 feet beneath the ground a few miles southwest of Hattiesburg to study test-verification methods. The blast created a shock wave that rippled the ground ten inches high and knocked stock off warehouse shelves for miles around. ("The South shall rise again," read a placard a sardonic technician placed next to the blast site.) The blast was detected as far away as Western Europe. Hattiesburg didn't mind that Goldwater was the Senate's premier advocate of unlimited testing. They went for him 89.2 percent.

Many a Southern liberal looked upon this development with serene confidence: any step back from the big-*D* Democrats was a step forward for small-*d* democracy. A Republican institutional presence was being built that would finally force Dixiecrats to actually attend to their constituencies. Then Southern Republicans "will see that their only hope for increasing party membership and winning elections is to be 'for something' rather than to be consistently against Democratic programs which are now ingrained in the politics and life of the people of the region," asserted Sam Ragan, executive editor of the *Raleigh News and Observer.* "Emotional issues may momentarily sway, but the pinched pocketbook nerve brings even quicker reaction. . . . The disadvantaged and the dispossessed will make themselves heard, and self-preservation will dictate to the politician that he must heed the cry." Dixie's defection to conservatism, editorialized the *Washington Post,* was but a "one-shot affair." Enlightened Republicans, wrote the keeper of the *Los Angeles Times*'s Dixie beat, now recognize that the Negro vote "can be as contestable as the Chinese vote, the white Protestant vote, the Catholic vote, the Jewish vote, or the vote of the freckle-faced redheads and one-armed shortstops."

"WHITE BACKLASH DOESN'T DEVELOP": so reported the *New York Times.* The blue-collar Slavs, Italians, and others who delivered Goldwater their majorities when polled at factory gates gave him numbers in the twenties in the only poll that mattered. Democratic loyalty held in the Boston neighborhoods where Louise Day Hicks reigned supreme, and in the Queens ones in which Parents and Taxpayers led antibusing school boycotts. Scores of formerly Republican suburbs known for guarding their neighborhood boundaries like medieval castles gave Johnson a clean sweep. For over a year, backlash had loomed in the public imagination like a pit bull straining at the leash. Now it was judged the mouse that roared. "Leaders of both parties are confident," Sam Ragan wrote, "that elections will be decided on issues other than civil rights." Like most pundits, he ignored evidence around the country that didn't fit the comforting conclusion—like the fact that California decided against open housing by 2 to 1, even while going for Johnson by over a million votes. Or Goldwater's overwhelming success in hamlets with large numbers of Evangelical Christians, like Jerry Falwell's Lynchberg, Virginia.

Every Republican who wasn't a conservative—and many who were—immediately put his shoulder to the wheel to exorcise the Goldwater specter, lest Republicans be forced to run against Goldwater's rugged ghost until 1984, just as Herbert Hoover had haunted them for the twenty years until Dwight D. Eisenhower came to the rescue. "Our overriding, overwhelming distrust of big government as the Great Evil of Our Time must be abandoned," the black Republican attorney general of Massachusetts, Ed Brooke, a rising star, put it starkly. New York's Republican chair lamented the party's having paid a "shattering price for the erratic deviation from our soundly moderate, twentieth-century course." Iowa's specified the price that had been paid in his state: "Bold, drastic steps," he said, would have to be taken to keep the two-party system in Iowa. Even one of Goldwater's top captains in San Francisco, Melvin Laird, allowed that it would be "suicidal"—the word popped up again and again—"to ignore the election results and try to resist any change in the party." "The present party leadership must be replaced—all of it," Hugh Scott declared at a press conference—a process akin to tracking down a stink that lingered mysteriously weeks after the housecleaning was done. "I don't even know *where* the leadership lies in that morass down there," he said. Eisenhower placed a contrite call to Scranton: "If the Lord spares me for 1968, I am going to come out for somebody at least eighteen months ahead of time. This year I tried to do what was decent." (Nixon, virtually alone, demurred: the "strong conservative wing of the Republican Party," he said at his press conference, "deserves a major voice in party councils." Liberals like Rockefeller, he said, were not role models but spoilsports and dividers.)

The winter wasn't over before the RNC had dumped Dean Burch in favor of Ray Bliss, the phlegmatic old Ohio pro who had endeavored to shore up Republican machines in the big cities as the royal road back after the Nixon defeat in 1960. He pledged to do the same now. Lyndon Johnson always said it: A century ago 80 percent of America was rural. Now it was 70 percent urban. The new Supreme Court reapportionment decisions spelled the death knell of the decades-old "conservative coalition" of rural Republicans and Southern Democrats that had choked progress in Congress. "Legislators represent people, not trees or acres," Earl Warren said in forcing states to redraw their districts in one-man-one-vote fashion. The power was in the cities now. The Republican Party couldn't afford to court that population with nineteenth-century ideologies. As Teddy White stirringly put it in *The Making of the President 1964*: "History would have to record that the Republican Party had not submitted docilely to this new leadership, but had resisted it to the end—so that from this resistance and defeat, others, later, might take heart and resume the battle."

And so history did record. George H. Mayer concluded in a chapter added to the second edition of his *The Republican Party*, called "The Amateur Hour and After," that without besting the Democrats in meeting "the burgeoning problems of the city, the GOP seems certain to occupy its current role as a minority party for the foreseeable future." (As for Vietnam, "unless it spreads elsewhere it is no more likely to produce a lasting realignment than the Korean War.") The nation's leading students of American political behavior, Nelson Polsby and Aaron Wildavsky, speculated that if the Republicans nominated a conservative again he would lose so badly "we can expect an end to a competitive two-party system." Arthur Schlesinger put it most succinctly of all in volume 4 of his magisterial *History of American Presidential Elections, 1789–1968*: "The election results of 1964," he reflected, "seemed to demonstrate Thomas Dewey's prediction about what would happen if the parties were realigned on an ideological basis: 'The Democrats would win every election and the Republicans would lose every election.' "

At that there seemed nothing more to say. It was time to close the book.

NOTES

ABBREVIATIONS

A C : Author's Collection

A H F : Barry Goldwater Papers, Arizona Historical Foundation, Tucson

A H F A V : Barry Goldwater Audiovisual Collection, Arizona Historical Foundation

A H F C P : 1964 Campaign Photo Album and accompanying text, Arizona Historical Foundation

A R : *Arizona Republic*

B M G : Barry Morris Goldwater

C M : Clarence Manion Papers, Chicago Historical Society

C T : *Chicago Tribune*

D D E : Dwight David Eisenhower

D K : Denison Kitchel Papers, Hoover Institution, Stanford University

F C W : F. Clifton White Papers, Cornell University Special Collections

F L : Hillsdale College Freedom Library

F S A : Free Society Association Papers, in Denison Kitchel Papers, Hoover Institution

G P : George Gallup, *The Gallup Poll: Public Opinion, 1935–1971* (New York: Random House, 1972)

G R R : *Group Research Report* newsletter

H E : *Human Events*

H I : Hoover Institution, Stanford University

H R : Henry Regnery Papers, Hoover Institution

J C J : Jameson Campaigne Jr. Private Papers (unsorted)

J F K : John F. Kennedy

L B J L : Lyndon Johnson Papers, Lyndon Johnson Library, University of Texas at Austin

L B J T : Recorded LBJ phone conversations, LBJ Library

L B J W H : Johnson Papers, White House Central Files

L B J W H A : White House Central Files, Aides' Files

L B J W H A M : Aides' Files, Bill Moyers

L B J W H A M 5 3 : Aides' Files, Bill Moyers, Box 53, "Campaign, 1 of 2" and "Campaign, 2 of 2" folders

L B J W H 6 - 3 : White House Central Files, EX: PL 6-3 file

LBJWHN: White House Central Files, Name Files
LBJWHNG: Name Files: Goldwater, Barry
LN: Leonard Nadasdy Private Papers (unsorted)
MCSL: Margaret Chase Smith Library, Skowhegan, Maine
ML: Marvin Liebman Papers, Hoover Institution
MTR: Museum of Television and Radio, New York, New York
NAR: Nelson A. Rockefeller
NR: *National Review*
NYHT: *New York Herald Tribune*
NYHTEN: *New York Herald Tribune*, Rowland Evans and Robert Novak, "Inside
　　　　Report" column
NYP: *New York Post*
NYRB: *New York Review of Books*
NYT: *New York Times*
NYTM: *New York Times Magazine*
OH: Oral History
PPP: *Public Papers of the President* (Washington, D.C.: United States Government
　　　Printing Office)
RAC: Rockefeller Archive Center, New York Office, Series III 15 22, subseries 2,
　　　Sleepy Hollow, New York
SEP: *Saturday Evening Post*
SFC: *San Francisco Chronicle*
SHBGS: Barry Goldwater Scrapbook, Sharlot Hall Historical Museum, Prescott,
　　　　Arizona
SLPD: *St. Louis Post Dispatch*
TNR: *The New Republic*
USN: *U.S. News and World Report*
WAR: William A. Rusher Papers, Library of Congress
WFBJ: William F. Buckley Jr. Papers, Yale University Special Collections
WGN: WGN-TV news footage, Chicago Historical Society
WP: *Washington Post*
WS: *Washington Star*
WSJ: *Wall Street Journal*

AUTHOR INTERVIEWS

Noel Black	Jack Craddock	Milton Friedman
Alan Brinkley	Ron Crawford	Robert Gaston
William F. Buckley Jr.	Carol Dawson	Henry Geier
Jameson Campaigne Jr.	Don Devine	Patricia Geier
W. Glen Campbell	Richard Dudman	Ryan Hayes
Elsie Carper	M. Stanton Evans	Margot Henriksen
Mel Cottone	Rep. Barney Frank	Doug Henwood

John Higham	Leonard Nadasdy	Sara Jane Sayer
David Keene	Gus Owen	Phyllis Schlafly
Richard Kleindienst	Tom Pauken	William Schulz
Charles Lichenstein	Howard Phillips	Scott Stanley
Robert Love	Lou Proyect	Angie Stockwell
Wes McCune	Alfred Regnery	Richard Viguerie
John McManus	Jonathan Rosenblum	Pamela Walton
Graham T. T. Molitor	William A. Rusher	Eric Wunderman
Judge Daniel Manion	Allan Ryskind	Wirt Yerger
Steve Max	John Savage	Herbert York

ABOUT THE NOTES

Paragraphing of the source citations follows the paragraphing in the text. Page numbers indicate the page on which each paragraph begins.

Phrases in italics are passages taken from the text.

LBJ conversations reviewed and transcribed by the author are indicated by the abbreviation LBJT and a citation number; ones transcribed by Michael Beschloss are cited from his book *Taking Charge: The Johnson White House Tapes, 1963–1964* (Simon and Schuster, 1997).

PREFACE

ix   *"He has wrecked his party"*: New York Times, November 5, 1964. *"The election has finished the Goldwater school"*: Lee Edwards, *Goldwater: The Man Who Made a Revolution* (Washington, D.C.: Regnery, 1995), 344. *"By every test we have"*: NYTM, June 28, 1964.

ix   *"The Democrats would win every election"*: Arthur Schlesinger Jr., ed., *History of American Presidential Elections, 1798–1968*, vol. 4 (New York: Chelsea House, 1971), 3021. *"A recrudescence on American soil"*: Philip Rahv, "Some Comments on Senator Goldwater," *Partisan Review* (Fall 1964): 603.

ix   For 1966 off-year elections, see Andrew E. Busch, *Horses in Midstream: U.S. Midterm Elections and Their Consequences, 1894–1998* (Pittsburgh: University of Pittsburgh Press, 1999), 100–106; and M. Stanton Evans, *The Future of Conservatism* (New York: Holt, Rinehart, and Winston, 1968).

x   For DDE's preservation and extension of New Deal programs, see Samuel G. Freedman, *The Inheritance: How Three Families and the American Political Majority Moved from Left to Right* (New York: Touchstone, 1996), 162. Lippmann quote: transcript of May 1, 1963, interview on *CBS Reports*, RAC, Box 10/755. My interpretation of the sense of inevitability of progress in consensus thinking is indebted to Christopher Lasch, *The True and Only Heaven: Progress and Its Critics* (New York: Norton, 1991), especially the chapter "The Politics of the Civilized Minority," 412–75.

xi   *"To meet the needs of the people"*: "Atlantic Report on the World Today," *Atlantic Monthly*, September 1964.

xi   *"Not really a coherent, rational alternative"*: Stewart Alsop, SEP, September 29, 1964. *"A kind of vocational therapy"*: Young Americans for Freedom, *Newsletter*,

May 1962, quoting speech in Los Angeles, cited in Matthew Dallek, "Young Americans for Freedom, 1960–1964" (master's thesis, Columbia University, 1993).

xiii   *"We must assume that the conservative"*: *The Progressive,* May 1961.

xiii   *"The year 2000 has all"*: Daniel Bell and Stephen R. Graubard, eds., *Toward the Year 2000: Works in Progress* (Cambridge, Mass.: MIT Press, 1997 [original ed. 1967, reporting on conference held in 1965]), 3. *"Think of how wonderful the year 2000"*: Jack Sheppherd and Christopher S. Wren, eds., *Quotations from Chairman LBJ* (New York: Simon and Schuster, 1968), 37, 106.

xiv   *"I first learned that the government"*: Taylor Branch, *Pillar of Fire: America in the King Years, 1963–1965* (New York: Simon and Schuster, 1998), 521–22. *Three decades later, half*: David Boaz, *Libertarianism: A Primer* (New York: Free Press, 1997), 1.

I. THE MANIONITES

3   Background for Manion cadre drawn from the correspondence in CM, Boxes 69 and 70; A. G. Heinsohn, *Anthology of Conservative Writing in the United States, 1932–1960* (Chicago: Regnery, 1962), and *One Man's Fight for Freedom* (Caldwell, Idaho: Caxton Printers, 1957); Clarence Manion, *The Conservative American: His Fight for National Independence and Constitutional Government* (New York: Devon-Adair, 1964), and *The Key to Peace: A Formula for the Perpetuation of Real Americanism* (Chicago: Heritage Foundation, 1951); Frank E. Holman, *The Life and Career of a Western Lawyer, 1886–1961* (n.p., 1963), 717–31; Thomas E. Vadney, *The Wayward Liberal: A Political Biography of Donald Richberg* (Lexington: University of Kentucky Press, 1970); Fred C. Koch, "A Business Man Looks at Communism, by an American Business Man" (self-published, 1960); and David M. Oshinsky, *A Conspiracy So Immense: The World of Joe McCarthy* (New York: Free Press, 1983). For foreign policy matters, see Robert A. Taft, *A Foreign Policy for Americans* (Garden City, N.Y.: Doubleday, 1951); James T. Patterson, *Mr. Republican: A Biography of Robert Taft* (Boston: Houghton Mifflin, 1972); Justus D. Doenecke, *Not to the Swift: The Old Isolationists in the Cold War Era* (Cranbury, N.J.: Associated University Press, 1979); and Michael W. Miles, *The Odyssey of the American Right* (New York: Oxford, 1980), 57–221.

3   *"Up till then a river"*: Clarence Budington Kelland, *Mark Tidd, Manufacturer* (New York: Grosset and Dunlap, 1918). *"The man who builds a factory"*: *Publishers Weekly,* April 24, 1995, 67.

4   For the divergence in the Depression era and wartime economic interests between small and large manufacturers, see David A. Horowitz, *Beyond Left and Right: Insurgency and the Establishment* (Urbana: University of Illinois Press, 1997); Alan Brinkley, "The New Deal Experiments" and "The Late New Deal and the Idea of the State," in Brinkley, *Liberalism and Its Discontents* (Cambridge, Mass.: Harvard University Press, 1998); and Nelson Lichtenstein, *Walter Reuther: The Most Dangerous Man in Detroit* (Urbana: University of Illinois Press, 1995), 154–74.

5   On the postwar strikes, see James T. Patterson, *Grand Expectations: The United States, 1945–1974* (New York: Oxford University Press, 1996), 39–60.

5   On the GOP Eastern internationalist wing, see Wendell Willkie, *One World* (New York: Simon and Schuster, 1943); and Donald Bruce Johnson, *The Republican Party and Wendell Willkie* (Urbana: University of Illinois Press, 1960).

5   For humiliation over the Korean War truce, see General Edwin Walker's letter of resignation in "Thunder on the Far Right: Fear and Frustration," *Newsweek*, December 4, 1961.

6   *On the first day of June 1959*: Manion to various, "CONFIDENTIAL," May 27, 1959, CM, Box 69/4.

6   Manion biography: Manion, *Lessons in Liberty* (South Bend, Ind.: Notre Dame University Press, 1939), *Conservative American* (the Wilson chant is on page 25), and *Key to Peace*; William F. Buckley, "My Secret Right-Wing Conspiracy," *The New Yorker*, January 22, 1996; and author interview with Judge Daniel Manion.

7   For America First, General Robert Wood, and Colonel Robert McCormick, see Horowitz, *Beyond Left and Right*, 175–86 ("despotic" quote is on page 175).

8   For *Wickard* v. *Filburn*, see Manion, *Conservative American, 96. Manion assured high school students*: Manion, *Lessons in Liberty, 189. "Government cannot make man good"*: Manion, *Key to Peace,* 61.

8   Harry Dexter White theory in Fred J. Cook, "The Ultras: Aims, Affiliations, and Finances of the Radical Right," special issue, *The Nation*, June 30, 1962.

9   For Manion in DDE's Administration, see Robert J. Donovan, *Eisenhower: The Inside Story* (New York: Harper and Brothers, 1956), 105, 239; Manion, *Conservative American*, 93–125; and Doenecke, *Not to the Swift*, 236–38. For the Bricker Amendment, see Doenecke, 235–39; and Donovan, *Eisenhower*, 231–42.

9   The exchange with Dulles is in Manion, *Conservative American*, 118.

10   The quote from the *Fort Wayne Sentinel* is in Manion, *Conservative American*, 124.

10   TV appearance is WGN, ED 542.

10   The source throughout on Senator William Knowland is Gayle B. Montgomery and James W. Johnson, *One Step from the White House: The Rise and Fall of Senator William Knowland* (Berkeley: University of California Press, 1998). On "new nationalists" see Miles, *The Odyssey of the American Right*, 80–94. For Taftite frustration with the 1954 mutual security pact, see John Kessel, *The Goldwater Coalition: Republican Strategies in 1964* (Indianapolis: Bobbs-Merrill, 1968), 8.

11   For the founding of For America, see Cook, "The Ultras" (includes McCarran quote); and Doenecke, *Not to the Swift*, 234–35 (manifesto quoted on 234).

11   For Robotype, see Christmas letter to contributors, December 17, 1954, CM, Box 98, and Pierre Salinger, *With Kennedy* (Garden City, N.Y.: Doubleday, 1966), 52. For origins of *The Manion Forum of Opinion*, see correspondence files, Manion, HR, passim (fund-raising appeal is Patterson to Regnery September 14, 1954); and CM, Box 98.

11   For T. Coleman Andrews's presidential run, see Doenecke, *Not to the Swift*, 235; and Sara Diamond, *Roads to Dominion: Right-Wing Movements and Political Power in the United States* (New York: Guilford, 1995), 87. For massive resistance and the *Richmond News Leader*, I rely on Miles, *Odyssey of the American Right*, 275–79. For

campaign speech, listen to T. Coleman Andrews, "Income Tax—Speedway to Tyranny," FL, MF89. *Human Events* quote in Montgomery and Johnson: *One Step from the White House*, 196.

12   My main source for NR throughout is John B. Judis, *William F. Buckley, Jr.: Patron Saint of the Conservatives* (New York: Touchstone, 1990). For the 1958 electoral debacle as a crossroads for the GOP, see Andrew E. Busch, *Horses in Midstream: U.S. Midterm Elections and their Consequences, 1894–1998* (Pittsburgh: University of Pittsburgh Press, 1999), 94–100; John A. Andrew III, *The Other Side of the Sixties: Young Americans for Freedom and the Rise of Conservative Politics* (New Brunswick, N.J.: Rutgers University Press, 1997), 23–36; Richard Nixon, *RN: The Memoirs of Richard Nixon*, vol. 1 (New York: Warner Books, 1978), 228; David Glenn, article in *In These Times*, December 14, 1997; Edwards, *Goldwater*, 64; and NYT, November 5, 1958. For DDE's 1956 embrace of Modern Republicanism, see Andrew, *Other Side of the Sixties*, 32–33.

13   Manion's third-party explorations in correspondence from January 11, 1959, to March 20, 1959, in CM, Box 69/4, passim. For L. Brent Bozell, see NYT obituary, April 19, 1997; also Fellers to Manion, April 8, 1959. The DDE quote is in "The Republican Split," *Time*, May 20, 1957. Bozell's article "The 1958 Elections: Coroner's Report" ran in NR, November 22, 1958.

13   Bozell's unsuccessful fund-raising trip: Fellers to Manion, April 8, 1959, CM, Box 69/4; and Bozell to Hubbard, June 25, 1959; Bozell to Russell, June 26, 1959; and Russell to Bozell, July 2, 1959, CM, Box 69/5. The National Committee for Political Realignment: GRR, June 30, 1964. Woods's conditions are in Lee to Manion, February 4, 1959, CM, Box 69/4.

14   For Orval Faubus and Jim Johnson, see Roy Reed, *Faubus: The Life and Times of an American Prodigal* (Fayetteville: University of Arkansas Press, 1997), 169–93.

14   Johnson quote on his ballot initiative: ibid., 175.

15   The letter on Faubus is Johnson to Manion, March 24, 1959, CM, Box 69/4, which also notes the Gallup poll; see GP, 1584.

15   For W. J. B. Dorn, see Edward Cain, *They'd Rather Be Right: Youth and the Conservative Movement* (New York: Macmillan, 1963), 271; and *www.sc.edu/library/socar/mpc/dorn.html*. For South Carolina industrial history, see Eric Foner and John A. Garraty, eds., *The Reader's Companion to American History* (Boston: Houghton Mifflin, 1991), 1066–69; and "Garment Workers Union Will Attempt to Organize South," *Sumpter Daily Item*, October 26, 1959. Manion's call to Dorn is described in Manion to Buffet, March 27, 1959, CM, Box 69/4.

15   Dorn's interest in political realignment is recorded in Dorn to Purdy, January 28, 1948, General Correspondence, William Jennings Bryan Papers, University of South Carolina Special Collections. His plan is explained in Manion to Buffet, March 27, 1959; Lee to Manion, April 3, 1959; Fellers to Manion, April 8, 1959, and April 13, 1959; and Manion to Dorn, April 11, 1959—all in CM, Box 69/4; and J. Hunter Stokes, "Dorn Issues Call to Conservatives," *Greenville News*, November 20, 1959, in CM, Box 70/2.

15   *"What you tell me"*: Manion to Johnson, March 27, 1959, CM, Box 69/4. *He scrawled a note*: Manion to Wood, April 3, 1959, CM, Box 69/4.

16   *"It is all too obvious"*: Raymond Richmond to Manion, n.d., responding to Manion to various, March 10, 1959, CM, Box 69/4.

2. MERCHANT PRINCE

17   Fawning profiles of BMG include "Jet-Age Senator with a Warning," *Time*, March 7, 1955; "The Backward Look," *Time*, April 22, 1957; Paul Healy, "The Glittering Mr. Goldwater," SEP, June 7, 1958; "Personality Contest," *Time*, September 29, 1958; "This Lively Man—Goldwater," *Newsweek*, July 4, 1960; "Apostle of Conservatism," *Business Week*, March 25, 1961; "Conservatism in the U.S. . . . and Its Leading Spokesman," *Newsweek*, April 10, 1961; "Salesman for a Cause," *Time*, June 23, 1961; "The Goldwater Story—How It Is Growing," USN, August 7, 1961; "Goldwater in '64?," *Newsweek*, May 20, 1963; and "This President Thing," *Time*, June 14, 1963. Two rare demurrals include Gilbert A. Harrison, "Way Out West: An Interim Report on Barry Goldwater," TNR, November 23, 1963 (though acknowledging "Goldwater is attractive and honest"); and Gore Vidal, "A Liberal Meets Mr. Conservative," *Life*, June 9, 1961.

18   Reliable BMG sources are Robert Alan Goldberg, *Barry Goldwater* (New Haven, Conn.: Yale University Press, 1995); and Lee Edwards, *Goldwater: The Man Who Made a Revolution* (Washington, D.C.: Regnery, 1995). I am especially indebted to Goldberg's brilliant account of the entwinement of federal largesse, the rise of Arizona, and the Goldwater family's fortunes, from which all statistics are drawn. On Southwestern and Southern economic development as an explicit goal of the New Deal, see Alan Brinkley, "The New Deal and Southern Politics," in Brinkley, *Liberalism and Its Discontents* (Cambridge, Mass.: Harvard University Press, 1998), 63–78.

18   Alsop's interview is "Can Goldwater Win in '64?," SEP, August 24, 1963.

19   For descriptions of BMG's house, I rely throughout on James M. Perry, *A Report in Depth on Barry Goldwater: The Story of the 1964 Republican Presidential Nominee* (Silver Spring, Md.: National Observer, 1964); SEP, June 7, 1958; *Newsweek*, April 10, 1961; *Time*, June 14, 1963; Alsop, SEP, August 24, 1963; AHFCP vol. 3, picture 4; transcript of "ABC Reports," November 10, 1963, RAC, Box 10/773; and author visit.

19   *Barry Goldwater once wrote*: Barry Goldwater with Jack Casserly, *Goldwater* (Garden City, N.Y.: Doubleday, 1988), 28.

19   *"We didn't know the federal government"*: ibid.

19   *"Hostilities in Arizona"*: Goldberg, *Barry Goldwater*, 13.

20   BMG's open letter to Roosevelt is in Perry, *Report in Depth*, 51.

21   On his wife's trust fund, see Goldberg, *Barry Goldwater*, 55. *"There never was a lot of it"*: ibid., 89. The chamber of commerce ad and the less sanguine view on prejudice in Phoenix is in Goldberg, 37–38. Blackballing story is on 91.

21   *Like a "bronze god"*: ibid., 57. The self-portrait is reprinted in Goldberg, *Barry Goldwater*, photo plates.

22 "*It's almost*": ibid., 70.

22 *To his California vendors*: ibid., 73.

22 Battle between G. W. P. Hunt and the state economic elite, and the anemic state of the Arizona Republican Party: Richard Kleindienst, *Justice: The Memoirs of an Attorney General* (Ottawa, Ill.: Jameson Books, 1985), 5–16, which includes accounts of both Kleindienst and his grandfather being threatened with violence for supporting Republican presidential candidates; and author interview with Richard Kleindienst. See also Stephen Shadegg, *How to Win an Election: The Art of Political Victory* (New York: Taplinger, 1964), 21; and Frank H. Jonas, ed., *Political Dynamiting* (Salt Lake City: University of Utah Press, 1970), 154.

22 The Cold War expansion of Phoenix is covered in Goldberg, *Barry Goldwater*, 58, 67–68, 86. "*Altered the whole demography*": ibid., 83.

22 The story of Eugene Pulliam, his expansion to Phoenix, and his reformist crusade is told in Russell Pulliam, *Publisher: Gene Pulliam: Last of the Newspaper Titans* (Ottawa, Ill.: Jameson Books, 1984), 105–37.

23 For BMG's incredible range of acquaintances, see Goldwater with Casserly, *Goldwater*, 78. For the sweep of his board and associational memberships, see résumé in AHF, Box 33/22. For the charter reform and the city council race, see Goldberg, *Barry Goldwater*, 76–79.

23 For BMG's city council tenure and the attendant boosting of the Arizona Republican Party, consult Goldberg, 76–82. Udall quote is on 75.

23 For BMG's thwarted gubernatorial ambitions, see Goldberg, 84. For the Pyle race, see ibid., 84–85; Kleindienst, *Justice*, 18–19; Stephen Shadegg, *What Happened to Goldwater?: The Inside Story of the 1964 Republican Campaign* (New York: Holt, Rinehart, and Winston, 1965), 19; and Edwards, *Goldwater*, 36–37.

24 For BMG's decision to run for Senate, see Goldberg, *Barry Goldwater*, 88–91; Edwards, *Goldwater*, 38–41 (the quote on knowing ten thousand people is on 39); and Goldwater with Casserly, *Goldwater*, 94–95.

24 For Shadegg biography and character, I rely on Shadegg, *How to Win an Election*; *Time*, September 7, 1962; "Senator's 'Alter Ego' Seeks Hayden Seat in Arizona," NYT, July 29, 1962; review of *How to Win an Election*, NYT *Book Review*, July 26, 1964; author interviews with Ron Crawford and Richard Kleindienst; and Oscar Collier to author, March 27, 1997. "*Approached in the right fashion*": Shadegg, *How to Win an Election*, 10.

24 For Shadegg's deliberations on running BMG campaign, see Edwards, *Goldwater*, 40. For the Indifferents theory, see Shadegg, *How to Win an Election*, 13–45. His theory about why BMG could win is on 19.

25 For BMG's negotiations with Shadegg, see Edwards, *Goldwater*, 40.

25 For Shadegg's reasoning on 90 percent of Republicans and 25 percent of Democrats, see ibid., 40. Insistence that BMG fill the Republican rolls is in Shadegg, *How to Win an Election*, 90; and Kleindienst, *Justice*, 19–21. His strategy to reach Indifferents is in Shadegg, *How to Win an Election*, 19. For BMG coffees, see ibid., 21.

25   For Shadegg's " 'cheap' war" speech, see Edwards, *Goldwater*, 47–48.

25   For TV, radio, and postcard campaigns, see Shadegg, *How to Win an Election*, 21, 86–87.

26   1952 election results in Arizona are in Goldberg, *Barry Goldwater*, 98–99. *"Any son of a bitch"*: Kleindienst, *Justice, 7.*

26   For Senate Republican Campaign Committee, see Shadegg, *What Happened*, 10, 17–18; Goldberg, *Barry Goldwater*, 109–12. The *Time* profile is March 7, 1955.

27   For Paul Hoffman's *Collier's* article, see Goldberg, *Barry Goldwater*, 114.

27   The national collegiate debate topic for 1957–58 is noted in Regnery to Hall, October 18, 1957, Correspondence/Hall, Jay, HI. For BMG's consignment to the Labor and Banking Committees, see Goldberg, *Barry Goldwater*, 99–100; and Edwards, *Goldwater*, 52. BMG acknowledges a lifelong debt to Taft's decision in *With No Apologies: The Personal and Political Memoirs of United States Senator Barry M. Goldwater* (New York: William Morrow, 1979).

28   The main source for McClellan hearings is Robert F. Kennedy, *The Enemy Within* (New York: Popular Library, 1960). See also NYT obituary of William Lambert, February 16, 1998; Pierre Salinger, *With Kennedy* (Garden City, N.Y.: Doubleday, 1966), 13–29; and John McClellan, *Crime Without Punishment* (New York: Duell, Sloan, and Pierce, 1962). All hearing quotes are from the transcripts in Bureau of National Affairs, *McClellan Committee Hearings, 1957* (Washington, D.C.: Bureau of National Affairs, 1959).

28   For Kitchel biography, see NYTM, September 13, 1964; Shadegg, *What Happened*, 55; F. Clifton White with William Gill, *Suite 3505: The Story of the Draft Goldwater Movement* (New Rochelle, N.Y.: Arlington House, 1967), 199; Kitchel to BMG, November 6, 1961, DK, Box 1/BMG 1947–61; and warm personal letters to Archibald Cox and Arthur Goldberg in DK, Box 1/General 1960–65. For move to Arizona, see SEP, October 24, 1964; and *Time*, July 17, 1964. For his profound influence on BMG, see John Kessel, *The Goldwater Coalition: Republican Strategies in 1964* (Indianapolis: Bobbs-Merrill, 1968), 179; and SEP, October 24, 1964. New York's control of a quarter of the nation's bank reserves is noted in Theodore White, *Making of the President 1964* (New York: Atheneum, 1965), 85; for federal land ownership in Arizona, see Brinkley, *Liberalism and Its Discontents*, 285; information on St. Louis Cardinals is from author interview with Richard Viguerie.

29   For Phelps Dodge 1915–16, see Jonathan D. Rosenblum, *Copper Crucible: How the Arizona Miners' Strike of 1983 Recast Labor-Management Relations in America*, 2nd ed. (Ithaca, N.Y.: ILR Press, 1998), 20–30.

29   For Kitchel's immersion in labor battles, see Kitchel to Richardson ("Sometimes in the hectic turmoil . . ."), DK, Box 4, Convention Congratulations; for Kitchel's fraught relationship with Frankfurter, see Kitchel to Eastman, August 22, 1964, DK, Box 4. For *Phelps Dodge* v. *NLRB* 313 U.S. 177 (1941), I rely on Rosenblum, *Copper Crucible*, 30–33, and author interview with Jonathan Rosenblum.

29   *Dallas Morning News*'s 1941 coinage in the 1980 Annual Report, National Right to Work Committee Papers, Box 5, HI.

30   For origins and run of the "Voice of Free Enterprise" column, see DK, Box 5. The quotes are from AR, February 26, 1956.

30   My biographical source for Walter Reuther is Nelson Lichtenstein, *Walter Reuther: The Most Dangerous Man in Detroit* (Urbana: University of Illinois Press, 1995). For the sit-down revolution, see 75–103, 133. For Reuther's crusade to control the rank and file to produce bargaining leverage, see 132–53.

31   For cost of living adjustment, see ibid., 277–80; guaranteed annual wage, 284–86.

31   For the trickling down of Reuther's "Treaty of Detroit," see 286. For the reaction of smaller manufacturers, see the transcript of the "Manion Forum" for June 26, 1955, CM, Box 98; and Herb Kohler, "Are Unions Above the Law?," pamphlet of address at Executives' Club of Chicago, December 9, 1955 (n.p.; New York Public Library pamphlet collections). Kohler's speech, from which the "strict seniority" quote is drawn, is the clearest single expression of the moral vision of the Manion cadre. See also Elizabeth A. Fones-Wolf, *Selling Free Enterprise: The Business Assault on Labor and Liberalism, 1945–1960* (Urbana: University of Illinois Press, 1994), 259–69.

32   For BMG's questioning, see transcripts in Bureau of National Affairs, *McClellan Committee Hearings*, January 26, 1957; March 13, 1957; and March 21, 1957 (from which the quote is drawn); and July 18, 1957.

33   White House invitation: *Time*, April 22, 1960. Office description: *Newsweek*, April 11, 1961; Edwards, *Goldwater*, xvii; unidentified clipping, August 18, 1975, SHBGS.

33   For traditional reticence over Keynesian solutions, see David M. Kennedy, *Freedom from Fear: The American People in Depression and War* (New York: Oxford University Press, 1999), 79–82 and 357–60; for Eisenhower's openness, see Robert M. Collins, *The Business Response to Keynes, 1929–1964* (New York: Columbia University Press, 1981), 152–70. The FY 1958 budget fracas is covered in *Time*, April 22, 1957; May 13, 1957; May 20, 1957; and April 22, 1964; and USNWR, April 19, 1957.

33   BMG's speech on the FY 1958 budget is in *Congressional Record*, April 8, 1957, 5258–65.

33   *Time ran another profile*: April 5, 1957. The Knight headline is in *Time*, May 20, 1957.

34   *Throughout the spring, stories had appeared*: Kennedy, *Enemy Within*, 254. The Chamber of Commerce speech is in *Time*, May 13, 1957.

34   *Even as he did, Newsweek*: Kennedy, *Enemy Within*, 256. *"Here is a man, a socialist"*: unidentified clip, August 18, 1957, SHBGS. See also "Goldwater's Racket," TNR, September 23, 1957.

34   The story of Kohler Company and the Kohler strikes is in Walter Uphoff, *Kohler on Strike: Thirty Years of Conflict* (Boston: Beacon Press, 1966); Sylvester Petro, *The Kohler Strike: Union Violence and Administrative Law* (Chicago: Regnery, 1961); Kennedy, *Enemy Within*, 254–84; Lichtenstein, *Walter Reuther*, 347–48, 526 n. 3; and Kohler, "Are Unions Above the Law?"

35 For Lyman Conger, see Kennedy, *Enemy Within*, 262–63.

36 *"This union dictate has been and is being defied"*: Kohler, "Are Unions Above the Law?"

36 For the Hoffa testimony, consult "Goldwater's Racket," TNR, September 23, 1957; Kennedy, *Enemy Within*, 81–83; and Bureau of National Affairs, *McClellan Committee Hearings*, 268.

36 BMG's *Meet the Press* appearance is described in "Goldwater's Racket," TNR.

37 For McClellan Committee investigation and Republican counterinvestigation into Kohler, see Kennedy, *Enemy Within*, 261–368; and Salinger, *With Kennedy*, 28–29. The dry-cleaning story is in David Halberstam, *The Reckoning* (New York: Morrow, 1986), 335.

37 *"I would rather have Hoffa"*: "Goldwater's Racket," TNR. The committee's tensions and the January 8, 1958, session are on 268–70.

38 BMG's Detroit Masonic Temple speech is covered in *Time*, February 3, 1958; Edwards, *Goldwater*, 76; and Lichtenstein, *Walter Reuther*, 237.

38 The UAW's convention agenda is described in "The 1958 Bargaining Programs for the Automobile Workers," *Monthly Labor Review*, February 1958, 270–74. Reuther's speech is quoted in Jerry Chiappetta, INS news wire no. TSA3, AHF, Box 4.

38 On the preponderance of Sheboyganites in Washington, see Uphoff, *Kohler on Strike*, 171. For a general description of the Kohler hearings, see News briefs, *Monthly Labor Review*, March 1958. The Arabs and Jews comparison is in Kennedy, *Enemy Within*, 262. Reuther's quote on BMG is noted in SEP, June 7, 1958. BMG's riposte is in Edwards, *Goldwater*, 77.

38 BMG's questioning of Reuther is transcribed in Frank Cormier, *Reuther* (Englewood Cliffs, N.J.: Prentice-Hall, 1970), 349–52.

39 My account of BMG's 1958 campaign relies on the detailed chapter "The Newspaper as a Giant Public Relations Firm," by Frank Jonas and R. John Eyre, in Jonas, ed., *Political Dynamiting* (Salt Lake City: University of Utah Press, 1970), 143–81; and Stephen Shadegg, *How to Win an Election* (New York: Taplinger, 1963). Both record considerably more chicanery than there is space to recount here. See also "There Weren't Two Sides to the Story in Phoenix," TNR, December 1, 1958, by an anonymous AR staffer; and Raymond Moley, "The Test in Arizona," *Newsweek*, March 24, 1958. The exchange between BMG and Shadegg is in Edwards, *Goldwater*, 87. Arizona's population boom is characterized in "The New Millionaires of Phoenix," SEP, September 30, 1961. Shadegg's billboard purchases: Edwards, *Goldwater*, 92. One is pictured in the plates of Goldberg, *Barry Goldwater*.

39 Cell group theory and practice is described in Shadegg, *How to Win an Election*, 106–21. (Mao quote is on 106.)

39 Surveying techniques are described in Shadegg, 51.

40 Shadegg explains his brainstorm for the 1958 campaign strategy in Shadegg, *What Happened*, 19.

40 Shadegg details how the AFL-CIO organizer was exploited beginning on page 71 in *How to Win an Election*.

40 All the quotes from the AR and *Phoenix Gazette*, and the photographs, are reproduced in Jonas and Eyre, "Newspaper as a Giant Public Relations Firm."

41 The commercial with BMG breaking through the paper is in Jonas and Eyre,
160–61.

41 For Hoffa and Reuther's feud, see Shadegg, *What Happened*, 16. The story of
COPE's supposed $450,000 budget is in Jonas and Eyre, "Newspaper as a Giant
Public Relations Firm," 162–64. For Hunt and Welch's contributions, see Goldberg,
Barry Goldwater, 126. The case for the borderline illegality of obtaining Green's mug
shot is in Jonas and Eyre, "Newspaper as a Giant Public Relations Firm," 156–58.

41 For the 1958 elections nationally, refer to Andrew Busch, *Horse in Midstream:
U.S. Midterm Elections and Their Consequences, 1894–1998* (Pittsburgh: Pittsburgh
University Press, 1999).

42 *A September Time article*: "Personality Contest," *Time*, September 29, 1958. *The
Saturday Evening Post, which was outgrowing*: Paul Healy, "The Glittering Mr.
Goldwater," SEP, June 7, 1958.

3. WORKING TOGETHER FOR THE WORLD

43 For Wedemeyer, see finding aid, Albert C. Wedemeyer Papers, HI; Michele
Flynn Stenehjem, *An American First* (New Rochelle, N.Y.: Arlington House, 1976),
104–5; Clarence Manion, *The Conservative American: His Fight for National Independence and Constitutional Government* (New York: Devon-Adair, 1964); the
newspaper *The Tidings,* February 5, 1960, in HR, Box 78/1; Justus D. Doenecke, *Not
to the Swift: The Old Isolationists in the Cold War Era* (Cranbury, N.J.: Associated
University Press, 1979), 172; and I. C. B. Dear, ed., *The Oxford Companion to World
War II* (New York: Oxford University Press, 1995), 1267–68.

44 *When a columnist for the Hearst*: "Faubus—Third Party Head?," *San Francisco
Examiner*, April 22, 1959. *He arranged to meet Dorn*: Manion to Dorn, April 11,
1959, CM, Box 69/4. *He circulated a thirteen-page report*: Honorable James Johnson, "Orval Faubus Can Be Elected President," CM, Box 69/4.

44 *"This is the first step"*: Manion to various, April 28, 1959, CM, Box 69/4.

44 *Tentatively—three weeks after*: Manion to Wood, April 20, 1959; Wood to Manion, both CM, Box 4, 1959. *And when one of Manion's friends*: Pritchard to Manion,
undated, CM, Box 69/5.

44 To follow the 1959 congressional debate over labor law reform, see WSJ, January 14, 21, 27, 28, 29; March 9, 10, 11, 12, and 26; April 22, 23, 24, 27, 29, and 30;
May 14, 18, 20, and 21; June 2 and 4; July 4, 17, 22, 24, 27, and 30; August 6, 7, 13,
14, 18, 20, 24, 25, 26, 27, and 31; and September 1, 2, 3, and 11. See also legislative
history in AHF, Box W2/6. *He called the bill "a flea bite"*: Lee Edwards, *Goldwater:
The Man Who Made a Revolution* (Washington, D.C.: Regnery, 1995), 99.

45 *Manion brought in Frank Cullen Brophy*: Brophy to BMG, May 11, 1959, CM,
Box 69/4. For the Campaign for the 48 States, see GRR, July 30, 1964. For Brophy's
relationship to BMG, see Peter Iverson, *Barry Goldwater: Native Arizonan* (Norman: University of Oklahoma Press, 1997), 203: For BMG playing Indian, see ibid.,
162–67; for Brophy, see Marks to Burch, May 21, 1964, FCW, Box 8/Eric Marks.

45   *One Monday in May*: Brophy to BMG, May 11, 1959, CM, Box 69/4.

45   *The audience was May 15*: Meeting notes, "Strictly Confidential," May 15, 1959, CM, Box 69/4; and Manion to Bruce, July 1, 1959, CM, Box 69/5.

46   For BMG's mileage the first half of the year, see Robert Alan Goldberg, *Barry Goldwater* (New Haven, Conn.: Yale University Press, 1995), 136. For speeches from this period, see address to Utah State Jaycees convention, May 14, 1960, in George B. Russell, *J. Bracken Lee: The Taxpayer's Champion* (New York: Robert Spellers and Sons, 1961), 195–98; and to the Western States Republican Conference, "Wanted: A More Conservative GOP," HE, February 18, 1960.

46   For background on the rise of the Southern Republican Party see Edward G. Carmines and James A. Stimson, *Issue Evolution: Race and the Transformation of American Politics* (Princeton, N.J.: Princeton University Press, 1989), which demonstrates that 1958 was the tipping point at which more people began associating civil rights with the Democrats than with the Republicans; John Kessel, *The Goldwater Coalition: Republican Strategies in 1964* (Indianapolis: Bobbs-Merrill, 1968), 234; Alexander Lamis, *The Two-Party South* (New York: Oxford University Press, 1984), 20–43; and Bernard Cosman, *Five States for Goldwater: Continuity and Change in Southern Presidential Voting Patterns* (Tuscaloosa: University of Alabama Press, 1966). See also "Nixon's Strategy," WSJ, April 27, 1959, in which Nixon denies the accusation that he is a civil rights radical.

46   On the one-party legacy of Reconstruction, see Michael W. Miles, *The Odyssey of the American Right* (New York: Oxford University Press, 1980), 268–69.

46   On "post office parties": Kessell, *Goldwater Coalition*, 39; and author interviews with Richard Viguerie and Jack Craddock. For Mississippi GOP chair, see *Cleveland Call and Post*, July 18, 1964. For the "all rank" joke, see James T. Patterson, *Grand Expectations: The United States, 1945–1974* (New York: Oxford University Press, 1996), 538.

46   For an illustration of the party's new upwardly mobile constituency, see ads taken by the Southern Company, for example in WSJ, July 22, 1959, "In Dynamic Dixie . . . Pleasant Living Is in the Pattern of Progress!" For "Cotton Ed" Smith, see David M. Kennedy, *Freedom from Fear: The American People in Depression and War, 1929–1945* (New York: Oxford University Press, 1999), 341. For Hubert Humphrey, see Michael W. Miles, *Odyssey of the American Right* (New York: Oxford University Press, 1980), 272.

47   For Republicans moralizing on civil rights, see Carmines and Stimpson, *Issue Evolution*, 62. *Some of those gains were lost*: "Despite Its Setback by Little Rock Troops, A Dixie Two-Party System Seems Likely," WSJ, September 1959. For Operation Dixie, see Goldberg, *Barry Goldwater*, 115.

47   For Spartanburg and Kohler, see "Spartanburg, S. C., to Vote on Blue Law Repeal; Effect on Business Growth Debated," WSJ, September 1959.

48   For Shorey, see University of South Carolina Library, Modern Political Collections, Gregory D. Shorey Papers, Finding Aid. For Milliken, see *www.milliken.com*; correspondence in HR, Box 51/13; and WFBJ, Box 8. For shutting down unionizing plant, see *Textile Workers Union of America* v. *Darlington Manufacturing Co.*, 380 U.S. 263.

48   Greenville speech: J. Hunter Stokes, "Goldwater Calls GOP to Battle," *Greenville News*, May 17, 1959; Dorn to Manion, May 20, 1959, CM, Box 69/4; and F. Clifton White with William Gill, *Suite 3505: The Story of the Draft Goldwater Movement* (New Rochelle, N.Y.: Arlington House, 1967), 20.

48   Coded letter: Stratton to Manion, May 17, 1959, or May 18, 1959 (date typed over), CM, Box 69/4.

49   *"The subject of this personal"*: Clarence Manion to various, "<u>CONFIDEN-TIAL</u>," May 29, 1959, CM, Box 69/4.

50   *"A listless interlude, quickly forgotten"*: Arthur Schlesinger Jr., "The New Mood in Politics," *Esquire*, January 1960.

50   *Like sentiments*: John K. Jessup et al., *The National Purpose* (New York: Holt, Rinehart, and Winston, 1960), essays originally appearing in *Life*; William Atwood, "How America Feels as We Enter the Soaring Sixties," *Look*, January 5, 1960; "America—1960: A Symposium," TNR, February 15, 1960; and Adlai Stevenson, "Putting First Things First—A Democratic View," *Foreign Affairs*, January 1960. See also David Farber, ed., *The Sixties: From Memory to History* (Chapel Hill: University of North Carolina Press, 1994), 16–17. JFK kickoff: John A. Andrew III, *The Other Side of the Sixties: Young Americans for Freedom and the Rise of Conservative Politics* (New Brunswick: N.J.: Rutgers University Press, 1997), 3.

50   *"Do you remember that in classical times"*: Kathleen Hall Jamieson, *Packaging the Presidency: A History and Criticism of Presidential Campaign Advertising,* 3rd ed. (New York: Oxford University Press, 1996), 68. Nixon's response: Thomas C. Reeves, *A Question of Character: A Life of John F. Kennedy* (New York: Free Press, 1991), 198.

50   The YMCA-YWCA conference is noted in Doug Rossinow, *The Politics of Authenticity: Liberalism, Christianity, and the New Left in America* (New York: Columbia University Press, 1998), 6.

51   Manion's recruitment frustrations: letters from Easley and Pulliam, June 1, 1959; Sharp, Snowden, Broder, and Owsley, June 3, 1959; and Comer, June 5, 1959, CM, Box 69/4. Typical comments include "It seems to me too much of a longshot"; "I believe the Democratic Party will remain the conservative party in the state of North Carolina for years to come"; and "It would seem that Nixon ought to be the man with his background and experience." BMG associate Clarence Buddington Kelland called the effort "silly," promising he would tell Barry to steer clear of it. Their acceptances came with caveats such as "I have no illusions that outside of a miracle we could ever get him nominated."

51   *"We hope to publish"*: Manion to Bruce, July 1, 1959, CM, Box 69/7.

51   The origins of the booklet idea are documented in Brophy to Bozell, Brophy to BMG, and Manion to Roger Milliken, all persuant to a phone call between Brophy and Manion that morning, June 18, 1959, all in CM, Box 69/7. Manion's agreement with BMG is in Manion to Brophy, July 28, 1959, CM, Box 70/1, on July 24, 1959, conference with BMG in Washington, and, especially, "Proposed Program for Conservative Action," CM, Box 69/5. *"I doubt there's much money"*: Buckley to Manion, October 2, 1959, CM, Box 70/1.

51   On J. Bracken Lee, see George B. Russell, *J. Bracken Lee: The Taxpayer's Champion* (New York: Robert Spellers and Sons, 1961). For Kohler's acceptance, see Manion to various, June 29, 1959, CM, Box 69/5. For other acceptances see "PERSONAL AND CONFIDENTIAL," July 31, 1959, CM, Box 70/1. *"Dear Clarence"*: Weaver to Manion, July 6, 1959.

52   On Bozell's absence, see Manion to Brophy, July 6, 1959; Manion to Russell with enclosure, July 13, 1959, CM, Box 70/1. Announcement that book would appear in sixty days: Manion to Schwepp, July 16, 1959, CM, Box 70/1.

52   On consternation over Khrushchev visit, see Manion to Fasken, August 14, 1959, CM, Box 70/1; and Hub Russell resignation letter to Commonwealth Club of California, October 14, 1959, CM, Box 69/5. National Committee of Mourning: August 30, 1959, "Manion Forum" broadcast, FL, MF258. Committee against Summit Entanglements: Manion secretary to Buckley, August 12, 1959, WFBJ, Box 9; and Brophy to Manion, September 4, 1959. Buckley rally: Buckley to Burnham, September 22, 1959, WFBJ, Box 8/Interoffice Memos; and John B. Judis, *William F. Buckley, Jr.: Patron Saint of the Conservatives* (New York: Touchstone, 1990), 175. For Allen-Bradley ad, see WSJ, September 1959.

52   For Publishers Printing Company deal, see Manion to Brophy, September 1, 1959, Manion to Buckley, October 23, 1959, and Publishers Printing to Manion, November 3, 1959, all in CM, Box 70/1; Manion to Milliken, January 20, 1960, and Manion to Kimmel, March 22, 1960, CM, Box 70/2. Independent American Forum and New Party Rally: Manion to Phelps, September 21, 1959, and Manion to Dorn, October 22, 1959, CM, Box 69/5, and packet in CM, Box 70/2. Negotiations with Courtney: Heinsohn to Manion, November 6, 1959, CM, Box 70/2. For Hollings, see Manion to Griffith and Manion to Hanson, September 21, 1959, CM, Box 70/1; and Dorn to Manion plus attachment, October 15, 1959, CM, Box 70/2. For Wedemeyer, Manion to Bozell, July 2, 1959, Box 69/7. *"Keep after Bozell!"*: Manion to Russell, November 16, 1959, CM, Box 70/2.

53   *By then Brent Bozell*: Edwards, *Goldwater*, 114. The advantage NAR's entrance offered is noted in Manion to Haley, January 6, 1960, CM, Box 70/2. For NAR's approach to party activists, see Manion to Brophy, October 23, 1959, CM, Box 70/2; Theodore H. White, *The Making of the President 1960* (New York: Atheneum, 1961), 79–80; and Nicol C. Rae, *The Decline and Fall of the Liberal Republicans: From 1952 to the Present* (New York: Oxford University Press, 1989), 41.

53   Main biographical source for NAR is Cary Reich, *The Life of Nelson A. Rockefeller: Worlds to Conquer, 1908–1958* (New York: Doubleday, 1996). Quote is from page 16.

53   Steffens on Nelson Aldrich is quoted in Reich, 3. The "suicidal" quote is on 538.

53   The Rockefeller family good works are noted, respectively, in Reich, 11, 81, 90–91; and Theodore H. White, *The Making of the President 1964* (New York: Atheneum, 1965), 95.

54   *"Diligently attend to the Rockefeller rituals"*: Reich, *Life of Nelson A. Rockefeller*, 17. The quote on his presidential ambitions is in Reich, xvii.

55   *"The only justification for ownership"*: ibid., 169.

55   Coordinator of Inter-American Affairs: ibid., 174–244.

55   NAR's frustrated bid to become deputy secretary of state is recorded in Stewart Alsop, *Nixon and Rockefeller: A Double Portrait* (Garden City, N.Y.: Doubleday, 1960), 79. Insistence on the gubernatorial nomination: Theodore H. White, *Making of the President 1960*, 73.

56   Rockefeller Brothers Foundation's Special Studies: Reich, *Life of Nelson A. Rockefeller,* 637–67; Farber, ed., *The Sixties,* 16–17; and *Prospects for America: The Rockefeller Panel Reports* (Garden City, N.Y.: Doubleday, 1961). *It became a literary touchstone*: James E. Underwood and William J. Daniels, *Governor Rockefeller in New York: The Apex of Pragmatic Liberalism in the United States* (Westport, Conn.: Greenwood Press, 1982).

56   NAR campaigning skills: Reich, *Life of Nelson A. Rockefeller*, 742–48 (blintz quote on 745); and SEP, March 13, 1964.

56   NAR Los Angeles appearance: Kyle Palmer, LAT, November 14, 1959. NAR Manhattan campaign apparatus: White, *Making of the President 1960*, 75–79 (quote on 75).

57   BMG's wild ride to Los Angeles is recounted in Stephen Shadegg, *Barry Goldwater: Freedom Is His Flight Plan* (New York: McFadden Books, 1963), 149–51.

58   BMG speech: HE, February 18, 1960. For tumultuous reception, see Shadegg, *Barry Goldwater*, 152; Barry Goldwater, *With No Apologies: The Personal and Political Memoirs of United States Senator Barry M. Goldwater* (New York: William Morrow, 1979), 98 (for the Mazo quote); Kyle Palmer, LAT, November 14, 1959; and LAT, November 16, 1959. On the *Los Angeles Times* lunch invitation, see Stephen Shadegg, *What Happened to Goldwater?: The Inside Story of the 1964 Republican Campaign* (New York: Holt, Rinehart, and Winston, 1965), 25.

59   For early history of the *Los Angeles Times*, see David Halberstam, *The Powers That Be* (New York: Knopf, 1979), 94–122 (quote on the Rockefellers and the Sulzbergers on 94). For its late-1950s professionalization, see Halberstam, 283–86, and Rick Lyman, "Otis Regrets," NYTM, January 23, 2000. BMG column acceptance: Shadegg, *What Happened*, 26; and Goldberg, *Barry Goldwater*, 142.

59   For NAR's unsuccessful tour, see White, *Making of the President 1960*, 79–83 (quote on 83); Michael Kramer and Sam Roberts, *"I Never Wanted to Be Vice-President of Anything!": An Investigative Biography of Nelson Rockefeller* (New York: Basic, 1976), 223–25; and James Desmond, *Nelson Rockefeller: A Political Biography* (New York: Macmillan, 1964), 219–38.

60   *"Many gigantic fortunes"*: Manion Forum fund-raising appeal, Patterson to Regnery, September 14, 1954, HR, Correspondence/Manion.

60   NAR's statement of withdrawal is in White, *Making of the President 1960*, 82.

4. CONSCIENCE

61   For Manion's Goldwater committee meeting, see Lee Edwards, *Goldwater: The Man Who Made a Revolution* (Washington, D.C.: Regnery, 1995), 115–19; and Manion to committee members, March 11, 1960, CM, Box 70/2.

61   Business arrangements in handwritten note, January 27, 1960, CM, Box 68/4;

Manion to Milliken, January 29, 1960; Manion to Brewer, February 2, 1960; handwritten notes dated January 1960; typed "NOTES ON THE GOLDWATER BOOK," January 1960; and Manion to Kimmel, March 22, 1960, all in CM, Box 70/2. For Manion's bulk-selling techniques, see Patterson to various, January 10, 1955, on Social Security, and February 22, 1955, on TVA, CM, Box 98.

61   *Throughout February, pages were sent*: Stephen Shadegg, *What Happened to Goldwater?: The Inside Story of the 1964 Republican Campaign* (New York: Holt, Rinehart, and Winston, 1965), 28; Manion to Haley, January 1, 1960, CM, Box 70/2. Promotional announcement noted in Manion to Brophy, February 15, 1960, CM, Box 70/2. Bozell's visit to John Birch Society board meeting: Manion to Love, March 16, 1960, and Love to Manion, March 21, 1960, CM, Box 70/2; and author interviews with Scott Stanley and Robert Love. Publication date: Letter to 350 reviewers from L. D. Lashbrook, Victor Publishing, March 24, 1960, CM, Box 70/2. For South Carolina convention promise, see Manion to Milliken, March 12, 1960, CM, Box 70/2, and F. Clifton White with William Gill, *Suite 3505: The Story of the Draft Goldwater Movement* (New Rochelle, N.Y.: Arlington House, 1967), 20. The 10,000 figure comes from the orders in CM, Box 70/2.

62   For the 50,000-copy requirement, see Manion to Milliken, February 18, 1960; Manion to Kimmel, March 22, 1960; and pitch sent over Herb Kohler's signature to seventy-five top Manion Forum donors, February 18, 1960, CM, Box 70/2. For ads, see unidentified newspaper clip, "A New National Leader Emerges," and *New Bedford Standard-Times*, March 18, 1960, CM, Box 70/2.

62   For bookstore problems and author copies, see April 12, 1960, and April 13, 1960, typed diary, CM, Box 70/2. For BMG's lack of interest, see Edwards, *Goldwater*, 115; Russell to Manion, November 9, 1959, CM, Box 70/2; Shadegg to BMG, February 22, 1960, CM, Box 70/2; BMG to Bozell, February 24, 1960, and, most interestingly, Regnery to Hall, February 26, 1960; March 24, 1960; and April 19, 1960, HR, Correspondence/Jay Hall. There, BMG's indifference to the project is demonstrated by the fact that he had also casually agreed to sign his name to another ghostwritten book (never published), this one a collaboration between his adviser Jay Hall and Henry Regnery.

63   *The book debuted at number ten*: *Time*, June 6, 1960. *By the time voters*: WSJ, November 3, 1960. For popularity in colleges, see "Campus Conservatives," *Time*, February 10, 1961; "Conservatives on the Campus," *Newsweek*, April 10, 1961; and WSJ, November 3, 1960.

63   My discussion of the existentialist appeal of *Conscience of a Conservative* is indebted to Doug Rossinow, *The Politics of Authenticity: Liberalism, Christianity, and the New Left in America* (New York: Columbia University Press, 1998); John A. Andrew III, *The Other Side of the Sixties: Young Americans for Freedom and the Rise of Conservative Politics* (New Brunswick, N.J.: Rutgers University Press, 1997); Gerald Schomp, *Birchism Was My Business* (New York: Macmillan, 1970); and author interviews with Lou Proyect and Doug Henwood. All quotes from *Conscience of a Conservative* are from the paperback edition (New York: McFadden Books, 1961).

65   *Time* and *Barron's* review clips (n.d.) in CM, Box 70/2.

65   *"I am at a loss to understand"*: Fred C. Koch, *A Business Man Looks at Communism, by an American Business Man* (self-published, 1960).

66   For quotes from platforms, see Kirk Harold Porter, *National Party Platforms, 1840–1964* (Urbana: University of Illinois Press, 1966).

5. THE MEETING OF THE BLUE AND WHITE NILE

69   The "Flopnik" headline is in Jeremy Isaacs and Taylor Downing, *Cold War: An Illustrated History, 1945–1991* (Boston: Little, Brown, 1998), 156.

69   *Human Events* background: Justus D. Doenecke, *Not to the Swift: The Old Isolationists in the Cold War Era* (Cranbury, N.J.: Associated University Press, 1979), 39; Edward Cain, *They'd Rather Be Right: Youth and the Conservative Movement* (New York: Macmillan, 1963), 143; and author interviews with Allan Ryskind and Scott Stanley.

70   Student Committee for the Loyalty Oath: A. Whitney Griswold, " 'Loyalty': An Issue of Academic Freedom," NYTM, December 20, 1959; John A. Andrew III, *The Other Side of the Sixties: Young Americans for Freedom and the Rise of Conservative Politics* (New Brunswick, N.J.: Rutgers University Press, 1997), 26–27; and Gregory Schneider, *Cadres for Conservatism: Young Americans for Freedom and the Rise of the Contemporary Right* (New York: NYU Press, 1999), 20–23 (193–94 quotes oath).

70   The Harvard chapter petition is noted in Rebecca E. Klatch, *A Generation Divided: The New Left, the New Right, and the 1960s* (Berkeley: University of California Press, 1999), 18. The figure of thirty campuses is from Dallek, "Young Americans for Freedom, 1960–1964" (master's thesis, Columbia University, 1993), 4. TNR article is Gerald W. Johnson, "An Outburst of Servility," February 8, 1960.

70   *"I can't think of any of our students"*: Andrew, *Other Side of the Sixties*, 27.

70   My main biographical source for Buckley is John B. Judis, *William F. Buckley, Jr.: Patron Saint of the Conservatives* (New York: Touchstone, 1990). The profile of Buckley Sr. is drawn from 18–34.

71   Buckley and Bozell's relationship: ibid., 55–59.

71   Buckley's fight against the student council: ibid., 63. Henry Wallace prank: ibid., 64.

71   *One attacked a popular anthropology professor*: ibid., 67–68. Buckley's valedictory lecture is on 11–12.

72   Yale's attempts to suppress, then discredit *God and Man at Yale*: ibid., 90–94. I owe my interpretation of *McCarthy and Its Enemies* to Judis, *William F. Buckley*, 105–6.

72   My sources for ISI are Cain, *They'd Rather Be Right*, 147–69; Richard Whalen, *Taking Sides: A Personal View of America from Kennedy to Nixon to Kennedy* (Boston: Houghton Mifflin, 1974), 113–16; E. Victor Milione, "Ideas in Action: Forty Years of 'Educating for Liberty,' " *Intercollegiate Review* (Fall 1993); ISI announcement in WFBJ, Box 8/Ibele–Into; the pamphlets in JCJ, including n.a., *The ISI Story in Brief*, Admiral Ben Moreell, *The Several Faces of Communism*, and Frederich A. Hayek, *Economic Myths of Early Capitalism*; and author interviews

with M. Stanton Evans and Carol Dawson, two leaders who attribute their original involvement in conservatism to ISI. The Lippmann quote is in Whalen, *Taking Sides*, 115. Milione, an ISI founder, traced his inspiration from Friedrich Hayek's "The Intellectuals and Socialism," *University of Chicago Law Review* (Spring 1949): "The main lesson which the true liberal must learn from the success of the socialists is that it was their courage to be Utopian which gained them the support of the intellectuals and therefore an influence on public opinion which is daily making possible what only recently seemed utterly remote."

73   The story of Buckley and Schlamm and the founding of NR is in Judis, *William F. Buckley*, 114–27. *The Freeman* and its crackup: William Rusher, *The Rise of the Right* (New York: Morrow, 1984), 33–35. NR business plan is in Rusher, *Rise of the Right*, 43–44.

73   Buckley's fund-raising tour: Judis, *William F. Buckley*, 118–21; and author interview with William F. Buckley.

73   The *Harper's* review, from the March 1956 issue, is quoted in Rusher, *Rise of the Right*, 47. For similar reviews, see ibid., 47–51. For "practical liberal" and "fighting conservative," see Christopher Matthews, *Kennedy and Nixon: The Rivalry That Shaped Postwar America* (New York: Touchstone, 1996), 17. For Viereck, see E. J. Dionne Jr., *Why Americans Hate Politics* (New York: Simon and Schuster, 1991), 168–69; for Worsthorne, ibid., 173.

74   Mike Wallace interview: Judis, *William F. Buckley*, 163.

74   *"We are an opposition"*: Rusher, *Rise of the Right*, 50.

75   *"Would tax the dialectical agility"*: Whalen, *Taking Sides*, 95. My interpretation of postwar conservative intellectualism is indebted to James Allen Smith, *The Idea Brokers: Think Tanks and the Rise of the New Policy Elite* (New York: Free Press, 1991), 170–74.

75   For the Midwest Federation of College Republicans, see Schneider, *Cadres for Conservatism*, 27; and Andrew, *Other Side of the Sixties*, 27. For Youth for Goldwater for Vice President, see Marvin Liebman, *Coming Out Conservative: An Autobiography* (San Francisco: Chronicle Books, 1992), 146; Andrew, *Other Side of the Sixties*, 27–31; Schneider, *Cadres for Conservatism*, 27–30; Lee Edwards, *Goldwater: The Man Who Made a Revolution* (Washington, D.C.: Regnery, 1995), 135; and Dallek, "Young Americans for Freedom, 1960–1964," 4–5.

75   Rusher on Blue and White Nile quoted in Lisa McGirr, "Suburban Warriors: Grass-Roots Conservatism in the 1960s" (Ph.D. diss., Columbia University, 1995), 151. "Catacombs" quote in Andrew, *Other Side of the Sixties*, 27.

76   On the South Carolina convention, see F. Clifton White with William Gill, *Suite 3505: The Story of the Draft Goldwater Movement* (New Rochelle, N.Y.: Arlington House, 1967), 20; Stephen Shadegg, *What Happened to Goldwater?: The Inside Story of the 1964 Republican Campaign* (New York: Holt, Rinehart, and Winston, 1965), 30; and Brophy to Manion, March 26, 1959, CM, Box 70/2.

76   Progress of BMG column: Shadegg to Manion, March 24, 1960, CM, Box 70/2. BMG meeting with Nixon: Shadegg, *What Happened*, 30. *"In the last six weeks Dick"*: Andrew, *Other Side of the Sixties,* 46.

76   For spring 1960 Cold War scares, see Theodore H. White, *The Making of the President 1960* (New York: Atheneum, 1961), 128–29, 168.

77   NAR's bomb shelter obsession is detailed in Frank Gervasi, *The Real Rockefeller: The Story of the Rise, Decline, and Resurgence of the Presidential Aspirations of Nelson Rockefeller* (New York: Atheneum, 1964), 43; and Michael Kramer and Sam Roberts, *"I Never Wanted to Be Vice-President of Anything!": An Investigative Biography of Nelson Rockefeller* (New York: Basic Books, 1976), 219 (for quote). For the Special Studies Fund reports on defense, see Cary Reich, *The Life of Nelson A. Rockefeller: Worlds to Conquer, 1908–1958* (New York: Doubleday, 1996), 663–66; "Arms Rise Urged Lest Reds Seize Lead in 2 Years," WP, January 6, 1957; and Chesly Manly, "Anti-Red Federation Urged by Rockefeller," CT, October 4, 1961.

77   For the U2 intelligence and secrecy, see David Halberstam, *The Fifties* (New York: Fawcett, 1993), 621–25; and Isaacs and Downing, *Cold War*, 157. Republicans' attempts to still NAR's insurgency are in White, *Making of the President 1960*, 198. *"I hate the thought of Dick Nixon"*: Kramer and Roberts, *"I Never Wanted to Be Vice-President of Anything!,"* 222. NAR had worked to keep Nixon from campaigning for him in New York in 1958; see Reich, *Life of Nelson A. Rockefeller*, 758.

78   The failure of the summit and NAR's ensuing maneuverings are in Kramer and Roberts, *"I Never Wanted to Be Vice-President of Anything!,"* 227; White, *Making of the President 1960*, 200–201 (for NAR's statement); Nicol C. Rae, *The Decline and Fall of the Liberal Republicans: From 1952 to the Present* (New York: Oxford University Press, 1989), 42; and James Desmond, *Nelson Rockefeller: A Political Biography* (New York: Macmillan, 1964), 256–61.

79   Percy's trip to New York, the floor-fight threat, and Nixon's assurances are in White, *Making of the President 1960*, 210–11.

79   For the Republican National Convention generally, see Paul Tillett, ed., *Inside Politics: The National Conventions, 1960* (Dobbs Ferry, N.Y.: Oceana Publications, 1962), 53–83. Goldwater's appearance before the platform committee is described in White with Gill, *Suite 3505*, 21. Text in Stephen Shadegg, *Barry Goldwater: Freedom Is His Flight Plan* (New York: MacFadden, 1963), 183–89. The Ford Foundation testimony is in White, *Making of the President 1960*, 212.

79   The Chicago scene is set from White, *Making of the President 1960*, 206–7. For Rustin's presence, see Tillett, *Inside Politics*.

80   My interpretation on the golden age of political conventions is drawn from Alan Brinkley, "The Taming of the Political Convention," in Brinkley, *Liberalism and Its Discontents* (Cambridge, Mass.: Harvard University Press, 1998), 249–65. For Stevenson demonstration, see White, *Making of the President 1960*, 180–83.

80   NAR's secret monitoring and press statement is in White, *Making of the President 1960*, 212–15. For his headquarters, see Desmond, *Nelson Rockefeller*, 271.

81   NAR's demand for a New York meeting and Nixon's decision to kowtow is in White, *Making of the President 1960*, 215.

81   Nixon's journey to Fifth Avenue is narrated in White, 215–16; and Kramer and Roberts, *"I Never Wanted to Be Vice-President of Anything!,"* 230–35.

81 For NAR's townhouse, see Tracie Rozhon, "A Rockefeller Fixer-Upper," NYT, October 14, 1999; and Reich, *Life of Nelson A. Rockefeller*, 122–23 and 151–52.

82 For the meeting, see White, *Making of the President 1960*, 216–17. Herb Klein's denial is on page 216. The "Compact of Fifth Avenue" is reproduced in White, 424–26.

82 Nixon's ignoring hints to pay attention to conservatives: Shadegg, *What Happened*, 30; Andrew, *Other Side of the Sixties*, 44–48; Schneider, *Cadres for Conservatism*, 27–29; Robert Alan Goldberg, *Barry Goldwater* (New Haven, Conn.: Yale University Press, 1995), 143–45; NYT, July 24, 1960 (noting that Goldwater's views were "privately expressed by many influential Republican conservatives supporting the Nixon candidacy"); and *Newsweek* profile of Goldwater, July 4, 1960. Welch postcard is in Goldberg, *Barry Goldwater*, 144. National Youth for Goldwater flyer is in ML, Box 29/Barry Goldwater. *"We have worked"*: Andrew, *Other Side of the Sixties*, 298. *"Thousands and thousands of people"*: ibid., 45.

83 *Nixon took it all in*: Goldberg, *Barry Goldwater*, 144. *"They are against any change"*: Andrew, *Other Side of the Sixties*, 45. The 1 percent statistic is from Goldberg, *Barry Goldwater*, 143.

83 *The hottest ticket that weekend*: author interview with Phyllis Schlafly; and Peter Carol, *Famous in America: The Passion to Succeed: Jane Fonda, George Wallace, Phyllis Schlafly, John Glenn* (New York: Dutton, 1995). Youth for Goldwater for Vice President's activities is from Dallek, "Young Americans for Freedom, 1960–1964," 5. *Doug Caddy talked like a power broker*: Russell Baker, NYT, July 23, 1960. *On newsstands*: Barry Goldwater, "How to Win in '60: No Mollycoddling," *Newsweek*, August 1, 1960.

84 Breaking of Compact of Fifth Avenue news: Shadegg, *What Happened*, 31; NYT, July 24, 1960; White, *Making of the President 1960*, 217–18. Len Hall's reaction is in Barry Goldwater, *With No Apologies: The Personal and Political Memoirs of United States Senator Barry M. Goldwater* (New York: William Morrow, 1979), 112.

84 BMG's sense of betrayal is in Goldwater, *With No Apologies*, 110–12. BMG's sometimes naïve, blinding trust in those close to him is discussed in Goldberg, *Barry Goldwater*, 30. Nixon had also broken a promise to endorse a right-to-work plank in the platform. See Barry Goldwater with Jack Casserly, *Goldwater* (Garden City, N.Y.: Doubleday, 1988), 256.

85 *"This might cost Nixon the election!"*: Goldwater, *With No Apologies*, 112.

85 BMG's press conference: ibid., 112; NYT, July 24, 1960; White, *Making of the President 1960*, 112; and Shadegg, *What Happened*, 31.

85 Press release of the "Munich" speech is in ML, Box 27.

85 *"This man is a two-fisted, four-square liar"*: Goldwater with Casserly, *Goldwater*, 256.

85 For NAR's snub of his fans, see White, *Making of the President 1960*, 203–5.

85 The pickets against the Compact of Fifth Avenue on Michigan Avenue are pictured in NYT, July 25, 1960, A1.

86 The story of John Tower and the battle in the civil rights platform subcommittee

is told in detail in Karl A. Lamb, "Civil Rights and the Republican Platform: Nixon Achieves Control," in Tillett, *Inside Politics*, 53–83. See also White, *Making of the President 1960*, 218–24.

87   *Point nine would also, added Louisiana's flamboyant Tom Stagg*: Tillet, *Inside Politics*, 66; White, *Making of the President 1960*, 203.

87   On DDE's consternation, see White, *Making of the President 1960*, 218–19. *He called Nixon in Washington*: White, *Making of the President 1960*, 224.

88   *One of the aides Nixon brought*: author interview with Charles Lichenstein.

88   For NAR's Liberty Baptist Church appearance, see NYT, July 25, 1960, A16.

88   For platform committee chaos, see Tillett, *Inside Politics*, 76–79; White, *Making of the President 1960*, 219–20 (placard quote on 220); and White with Gill, *Suite 3505*, 21 (for Barnes story).

89   *"I've heard enough rumors"*: *Time*, August 8, 1960. *"We can't expect to come here"*: *Life*, November 1, 1963.

89   *"Get me three hundred names"*: White, *Making of the President 1964*, 112. See also White with Gill, *Suite 3505*, 22; and Shadegg, *What Happened*, 32 (for "political neck" quote).

90   For Nixon's Monday arrival, see "Nixon Says Rights Plank Must Be Made Stronger," NYT, July 26, 1960.

90   *"I believe it is essential"*: ibid.

90   For Nixon lobbying, see NYT, "Nixon Says Rights Plank"; White, *Making of the President 1960*, 223; and Edwards, *Goldwater*, 137.

91   For BMG speech Monday night, see Andrew, *Other Side of the Sixties*, 51.

91   For negotiations with DDE, see White, *Making of the President 1960*, 224.

91   *"Was it the Republicans who"*: ibid., 225.

91   *"NIXON SAYS RIGHTS PLANK"*: NYT, July 26, 1960. Platform Committee's final session: Tillett, *Inside Politics*, 80–82; Edward G. Carmines and James A. Stimson, *Issue Evolution: Race and the Transformation of American Politics* (New Brunswick, N.J.: Princeton University Press, 1989), 39 (for final platform language); and Lichenstein interview.

91   For the honoring of the Eisenhowers, DDE speech, and E. Frederic Morrow, see Taylor Branch, *Parting the Waters: America in the King Years, 1954–1963* (New York: Touchstone, 1988), 321–23.

92   *"All right. You go out"*: Edwards, *Goldwater*, 136.

92   *"We were instructed"*: Shadegg, *What Happened*, 32.

92   *"You aren't going to let"*: author interview with Richard Kleindienst.

92   For the preparation of BMG's withdrawal speech, see Shadegg, *What Happened*, 33; Edwards, *Goldwater*, 137; and Richard Kleindienst, *Justice: The Memoirs of an Attorney General* (Ottawa, Ill.: Jameson Books, 1985), 26. For BMG meeting with young backers, see SLPD, January 4, 1964; and (for quote) *Time*, June 23, 1961.

92   Nixon's acceptance speech: White, *Making of the President 1960*, 227.

93   BMG demonstration: Edwards, *Goldwater*, 138; *Life*, November 11, 1963; Schlafly interview.

93   BMG's withdrawal is printed in full in James M. Perry, *A Report in Depth on Barry Goldwater: The Story of the 1964 Republican Presidential Nominee* (Silver Spring, Md.: National Observer, 1964), 84–85. It can be seen in part on A&E Television Network, *Barry Goldwater: The Conscience of Conservatives* (1996, cat. no. AAE-14345).

95   *"That son of a bitch"*: Liebman, *Coming Out Conservative*, 159.

6. QUICKENING

99   JFK inaugural address: PPP: JFK, 1.

100   DDE farewell address: PPP: DDE, 1035–40.

100   On CIA complicity in the Lumumba assassination, see U.S. Congress, *Senate Select Committee to Study Governmental Operations with Respect to Intelligence Activities*, Frank Church, chair, final report, *Congressional Record*, 1976. Khrushchev speech, quoted in Francis X. Winters, *The Year of the Hare: America in Vietnam, January 25, 1963–February 15, 1964* (Athens: University of Georgia Press, 1997), 8. On broken arrows, see John May, *The Greenpeace Book of the Nuclear Age: The Hidden History, the Human Cost* (New York: Pantheon, 1990), 140; and Robert C. Williams and Philip L. Cantelon, eds., *The American Atom: A Documentary History of Nuclear Policies from the Discovery of Fission to the Present, 1939–1984* (Philadelphia: University of Pennsylvania Press, 1991), 239–43.

101   The Rutgers showing of *Operation Abolition* is described in Dan Wakefield, "Un-Americanism Plays the Colleges," *The Nation*, January 28, 1961. *"The Communist Party itself"*: House Committee on Un-American Activities, "The Truth about the Film 'Operation Abolition,'" supplemental report to House report no. 2228, Eighty-sixth Congress, Second Session, in JCJ.

101   The Bay Area and Berkeley roots of *Operation Abolition* are covered in David Lance Goines, *The Free Speech Movement: Coming of Age in the 1960s* (Berkeley, Calif.: Ten Speed Press, 1993), 68; Milton Viorst, *Fire in the Streets: America in the 1960s* (New York: Simon and Schuster, 1979), 168; Max Heirich, *The Spiral of Conflict: Berkeley, 1964* (New York: Columbia University Press, 1968), 78–94; and *The Nation*, January 28, 1961. The Air Force training manual incident is described in Walter Goodman, *The Committee: The Extraordinary Career of the House Committee on Un-American Activities* (New York: Farrar, Straus and Giroux, 1968), 405; quote can be found at *http://mag-net.com/~maranath/rsv.htm*.

102   The showdown at City Hall is described in Heirich, *Spiral of Conflict*, 81.

102   Production described in HUAC, "The Truth about 'Operation Abolition,'" content and distortions are described in Bay Area Student Committee for the Abolition of the House Committee on Un-American Activities, "In Search of Truth: An Analysis of the HCUA Propaganda Film 'Operation Abolition,'" both in JCJ.

102   *Communist Target—Youth* is available from International Historic Films, Chicago. *Operation Abolition*'s distribution: NR, July 28, 1961.

103   *A history professor*: John Higham, "The Cult of American Consensus: Homogenizing Our History," *Commentary* 27 (1959); and author interview with John Higham.

104   For Liebman biography, see Marvin Liebman, *Coming Out Conservative: An Autobiography* (San Francisco: Chronicle Books, 1992).

104   For the Committee of One Million, see Harry W. Ernst, "Behind the Handout Curtain," *The Nation*, March 17, 1962, which strenuously debunks Liebman's claim. For another typical Liebman product, see the full-page ad for "Fighting Aces for Goldwater," NYT, October 28, 1964.

105   The call to Sharon is in John A. Andrew III, *The Other Side of the Sixties: Young Americans for Freedom and the Rise of Conservative Politics* (New Brunswick, N.J.: Rutgers University Press, 1997), 55.

105   Hungary as a spur to conservative activism: author interviews with Tom Pauken and M. Stanton Evans; Nick Salvatore, "You Say You Want a Revolution?," *The Bookpress*, September 1997; and Liebman, *Coming Out Conservative*, 113–16.

105   *They read schoolboy equivalents*: James Michener, *The Bridge at Andau* (New York: Bantam Books, 1957), Catholic Digest Book Club edition; Thomas Dooley, *Deliver Us from Evil: The True Story of Vietnam's Flight to Freedom* (New York: Farrar, Straus and Cudahy, 1956); and Whittaker Chambers, *Witness* (New York: Random House, 1952). Lionization of JFK at parochial schools: author interview with John Savage. For young people who became conservatives in reaction against urban Democratic machine corruption, I rely on Samuel G. Freedman, *The Inheritance: How Three Families and the American Political Majority Moved from Left to Right* (New York: Touchstone, 1996), 188–89; and author interviews with Henry Geier and Patricia Geier.

106   Sharon Conference: Gregory Schneider, *Cadres for Conservatism: Young Americans for Freedom and the Rise of the Contemporary Right* (New York: NYU Press, 1999), 31–37; Andrew, *Other Side of the Sixties*, 55–60; Liebman, *Coming Out Conservative*, 151; Lee Edwards, "Rebels with a Cause," in Lee and Anne Edwards, *You Can Make the Difference* (Westport, Conn.: Arlington House, 1980), 240–52; and author interviews with M. Stanton Evans, Lee Edwards, Howard Phillips, Scott Stanley, and Carol Dawson.

106   Sharon statement reprinted in Andrew, *Other Side of the Sixties*, 221–22. Debate over including God is in Schneider, *Cadres for Conservatism*, 34; for the discussion on the name: ibid., 36; Marvin Kitman, "New Wave from the Right," *The New Leader*, September 18, 1961; and Phillips and Edwards interviews. American Youth for Democracy: David A. Horowitz, *Beyond Left and Right: Insurgency and the Establishment* (Urbana: University of Illinois Press, 1997), 192. A similar debate ensued at the founding of Americans for Democratic Action—after John Kenneth Galbraith's idea to call the new group the Liberal Union. Galbraith "Dear Friend" fund-raising letter to author, July 20, 1998.

106   For Schuchman and board of directors: Schneider, *Cadres for Conservatism*, 36–37. For Bronx Science students at von Mises's lectures: Richard Whalen, *Taking Sides: A Personal View of America from Kennedy to Nixon to Kennedy* (Boston: Houghton Mifflin, 1974), 113; and author interviews with M. Stanton Evans and William Schulz. *"Ten years ago"*: William F. Buckley, "Young Americans for Freedom," NR, September 24, 1960.

107   YAF office, and original membership claim, is described in *The New Leader*, September 18, 1961. For the first YAF wedding, see Robert E. Bauman, *The Gentleman from Maryland: The Conscience of a Gay Conservative* (New York: Arbor House, 1986), 95.

107   *The February 10 Time*: "Campus Conservatives," *Time*, February 10, 1961. *Time didn't notice*: Howard Phillips interview. For the Yale chapter's Cuba petition, see ML, Box 37/98; for Polaris march, Tom Hayden, "Who Are the Student Boatrockers?," *Mademoiselle*, August 1961.

108   *YAF soon reported 24,000 members*: The Nation, May 27, 1961. *"You walk around with"*: Time, February 10, 1961. McCarthy-Evjue lectures: David Keene to author, April 29, 1997. For the University of Wisconsin's left-wing culture, see Paul Buhle, *History and the New Left: Madison, Wisconsin, 1950–1970* (Philadelphia: Temple University Press, 1990), 111, 138, and passim.

108   *The pages of the Conservative Club's handsomely produced*: Insight and Outlook, October 1961, AC.

108   *In February YAF published*: Raymond Moley, "Youth Turns to Right," *Newsweek*, March 13, 1961. *"A flock of little Buckleys"*: E. J. Dionne Jr., *Why Americans Hate Politics* (New York: Simon and Schuster, 1991), 176. *They read twice as much*: Edwards interview. *The Michigan Daily*: January 1962 YAF newsletter cited in Matthew Dallek, "Young Americans for Freedom, 1960–1964" (master's thesis, Columbia University, 1991). Various numbers are given for SDS's membership in 1961. Nick Salvatore, "You Say You Want a Revolution?," has it at 75; James Miller, *Democracy Is in the Streets: From Port Huron to the Siege of Chicago* (Cambridge, Mass.: Harvard University Press, 1994), 65, gives the number in the fall of 1961 as 575.

108   *YAF's Greater New York Council*: Edward Cain, *They'd Rather Be Right: Youth and the Conservative Movement* (New York: Macmillan, 1963), 17, 171, 256 (which gives a membership figure of 2,200); Schneider, *Cadres for Conservatism*, 38, which claims YAF had sixty chapters in New York and New Jersey; "Breaking the Liberal Barrier," *New Guard*, March 1961; Noel Parmentel, "The Acne and the Ecstasy," *Esquire*, August 1962; Dan Wakefield, *New York in the Fifties* (Boston: Houghton Mifflin, 1992), 269–73 (for White Horse anecdote); *New Leader*, September 18, 1961 (for quote about picketing); and author interview with Don Devine.

109   Manhattan Center rally: Robert Conley, "3,200 at Rally Here Acclaim Goldwater," NYT, March 3, 1961; Cain, *They'd Rather Be Right*, 172; William Dunphy, "The YAF's Are Coming," *Commonweal*, April 14, 1961; *New Leader*, September 18, 1961; and Murray Kempton, "Growing Up Absurd," *The Progressive*, May 1961. Counterprotest: *The Nation*, May 27, 1961, and NYT, March 3, 1961.

109   For NSA, see Cain, *They'd Rather Be Right*, 261–62; Taylor Branch, *Parting the Waters: America in the King Years, 1963–1965* (New York: Simon and Schuster, 1998), 273; Alan Brinkley, "Allard Lowenstein and the Ordeal of Liberalism," in Brinkley, *Liberalism and Its Discontents* (Cambridge, Mass.: Harvard University Press, 1998), 237–48; and Nan Robertson, "A Press Release Tells Story Different from Accounts Given by Students," NYT, May 15, 1962.

109   Incursion at "Youth Service Abroad": Cain, *They'd Rather Be Right*, 171; and Hayden, "Who Are the Student Boatrockers?" *"We must assume that the conservative"*: *The Progressive*, May 1961.

110   *The day Young Americans for Freedom rallied*: "The Americanists," *Time*, March 10, 1961.

110   For the scoreboard issue, see Cain, *They'd Rather Be Right*, 80; TNR, May 28, 1962; and Welch to Regnery, December 20, 1960, HR, Box 78/1.

110   For four goals, see John D. Morris, "Birch Unit Pushes Drive on Warren," NYT, April, 1961, A1. For meetings disturbed by shouts of "republic!," see Stanley Mosk and Howard H. Jewel, "The Birch Phenomenon Analyzed," NYTM, August 20, 1961. For PTA: *The Nation*, March 11, 1961.

110   *The daily barrage of reports*: A few articles had appeared in 1960 in the *Chicago Daily News*, *Racine Journal Times*, *Amarillo News-Globe* (a positive report), and *San Marino Tribune*. The publisher of the *Santa Barbara News-Press* won a Pulitzer Prize on April 4, 1961, for his coverage in January and February. But the explosion followed the *Time* report. See above, and, for a sample, LAT, March 5, 6, 7, 8, 12 (a front-page editorial), and 18, 1961; SFC, March 9, 19, 21, 23, 28, and 30, 1961; NYT, March 19, 1961; *Boston Globe*, March 30 and 31, 1961; *Des Moines Register*, March 31, 1961; and NYHT, April 1, 1961 (editorial). See also Martin J. Fuerst, *Bibliography on the Origins and History of the John Birch Society,* 3rd ed. (Sacramento, Calif.: n.p., 1963).

110   Welch biography: *Who's Who*; author interviews with Scott Stanley, John McManus, and registrars at Naval Academy and University of North Carolina; *Time*, December 8, 1961; and Michael W. Miles, *The Odyssey of the American Right* (New York: Oxford University Press, 1980), 246.

111   *The frustrated writer's first book*: Robert H. W. Welch, *The Road to Salesmanship* (New York: Ronald Press Co., 1941); and Cain, *They'd Rather Be Right*, 70. See also Welch to Regnery, March 17, 1953, HR, Box 78/1. For work with OPA, see Cain, *They'd Rather Be Right*, 88. For his postwar investigations and travel: McManus interview; Gerald Schomp, *Birchism Was My Business* (New York: Macmillan, 1970), 54; and Robert Welch, *The Blue Book of the John Birch Society* (Appleton, Wis.: Western Islands, 1997), 131. For lieutenant governor run, see Schomp, *Birchism Was My Business*, 34; and Guild to Staley, n.d., HR, Box 78/1.

111   *"A great hunk of God in the flesh"*: David Halberstam, *The Fifties* (New York: Fawcett, 1993), 115. For Welch's 1951 travels, see Welch, *May God Forgive Us, A Famous Letter Giving the Historical Background of the Dismissal of General MacArthur* (Chicago: Regnery, 1952), 3–4; and A. E. Staley to various, May 1, 1952, HR, Box 78/1.

112   For Welch Mailing Committee: Welch to Regnery, April 9, 1952, and April 29, 1952; and Staley to various, May 1, 1952, HR, Box 78/1 (for quote).

112   For Regnery Company history, see Whalen, *Taking Sides*, 197; John B. Judis, *William F. Buckley, Jr.: Patron Saint of the Conservatives* (New York: Touchstone, 1990), 88–89; Henry Regnery, *Memoirs of a Dissident Publisher* (Washington, D.C.: Regnery, 1979); and Scott Stanley interview. For Regnery's pacifism, see A. J. Muste

Folder, HR, Correspondence. For financial troubles, see Judis, *William F. Buckley, Jr.,* 89; and HR correspondence with Jay Hall and the Erhart Foundation. Regnery went in the black in 1960, after buying out the holder of the American rights to L. Frank Baum's *Oz* series. *Welch bet Henry Regnery:* Welch to Regnery, July 7, 1952, HR, Box 78/1.

112 *At the opening meeting:* Lee Edwards, *Goldwater: The Man Who Made a Revolution* (Washington, D.C.: Regnery, 1995), 118. For the argument over *May God Forgive Us* sales figures see Regnery to Milbank, HR, Box 51/10; Welch to Regnery, April 9, 1952, April 29, 1952, and June 14, 1952; and Staley to various, May 1, 1952, all in HR, Box 78/1. *"Highlighted a definite turn back":* Welch to Regnery, December 1, 1952, HR, Box 78/1. For his allegorical novel, see correspondence with Regnery, HR, Box 78/1 for 1953, passim.

113 *Regnery accepted one more book:* Robert Welch, *The Life of John Birch: In the Story of One American Boy, the Ordeal of His Age* (Chicago: Regnery, 1954). For the composition of *The Politician:* Cain, *They'd Rather Be Right,* 77; Robert Alan Goldberg, *Barry Goldwater* (New Haven, Conn.: Yale University Press, 1995), 137; NR, April 22, 1961; and William Rusher, *The Rise of the Right* (New York: Morrow, 1984), 60. For resignations from Manion's BMG committee after receiving *The Politician,* see Thompson to Manion, September 14, 1959, CM, Box 70/1.

113 *"We have allowed our detractors":* Elizabeth A. Fones-Wolf, *Selling Free Enterprise: The Business Assault on Labor and Liberalism, 1945–1960* (Urbana: University of Illinois Press, 1994), 70. For NAM's publicity activities, see Fones-Wolf, 25, 32–57, 259–269.

113 For FEE, see Sara Diamond, *Roads to Dominion: Right-Wing Movements and Political Power in the United States* (New York: Guilford, 1995), 27–28; Milton and Rose Friedman, *Two Lucky People: Memoirs* (Chicago: University of Chicago Press, 1998), 150–52; and "An Accounting of FEE's Activities," in Milton Friedman Papers, Box 82/FEE, HI, in which the cited pamphlets can also be found. See also Barry Goldwater column, LAT, January 14, 1960, for an example of how FEE spread its message.

114 For *One Man's Opinion,* see Welch to Regnery, November 27, 1957, November 9, 1957, November 21, 1957, May 23, 1957, and June 4, 1957, HR, Box 78/1; for *American Opinion,* see Welch to Regnery, October 31, 1957, November 6, 1957, December 12, 1957, HR, Box 78/1; and McManus interview. For possible Senate run, see Cain, *They'd Rather Be Right,* 79.

114 Founding meetings of the John Birch Society are described in Heinsohn to Montgomery, March 7, 1959, CM, Box 69/4 (for quote); Welch to Manion, July 13, 1959, Box 69/7; Buffett to Manion, August 6, 1959, and Manion to Thompson, September 17, 1959, both in CM, Box 70/1; Welch to Buckley, January 2, 1959, and July 2, 1959, WFBJ, Box 9; NYT, April 1, 1961; Welch, *Blue Book,* xv–xx; Frank E. Holman, *The Life and Career of a Western Lawyer 1886–1961* (n.p., 1963); and Rusher, *The Rise of the Right,* 61. Tapes of Welch's presentations filmed in 1959, "An Invitation to Membership" and "Look at the Score," are available from the John Birch Society, Appleton, Wisconsin.

114   *"We are living in America today"*: Welch, *Blue Book*, 1. All other quotes from
Welch, *Blue Book.*

115   For Welch's salesmen, see Schomp, *Birchism Was My Business,* passim; and
Cain, *They'd Rather Be Right,* 89. *Estimates varied*: 20,000 is in "Far Right and Far
Left," NYP, April 2, 1964; 60,000 is in Alan F. Westin, "The John Birch Society:
Fundamentalism on the Right," *Commentary,* August 1961; 100,000 is in Eric Foner
and John A. Garraty, eds, *The Reader's Companion to American History* (Boston:
Houghton Mifflin, 1991), 597. Office descriptions in Donald Janson and Bernard
Eismann, *The Far Right* (New York: McGraw-Hill, 1963), 29; and Welch, *Blue
Book,* 162.

116   For the paranoia-inducing quality of everyday Cold War rhetoric and the quote
from Kennan, see Allan C. Carlson's brilliant article "Foreign Policy and 'The
American Way': The Rise and Fall of the Post-World War II Consensus," *This World*
(Spring/Summer 1983). *"Repeal of industrialism"*: Westin, "John Birch Society."
"They controlled the trade union movement": Freedman, *The Inheritance,* 159.
"Communist espionage here": attachment from *Congressional Record,* Rusher to
White, February 28, 1962, WR, Box 18/"Congressional Contact." *Army recruits saw
films*: *Red Nightmare,* available from International Historic Films, Chicago, cat. no.
273. For AEC's denials of fallout danger, see Allan M. Winkler, *Life Under a Cloud:
American Anxiety about the Atom* (New York: Oxford University Press, 1993), 103.
For Angleton, see Thomas Powers, "Spook of Spooks," NYRB, August 17, 1989.

117   *"Less government and more responsibility"*: *An Invitation to Membership* film.
Betty Friedan's book, of course, is *The Feminine Mystique* (New York: Dell, 1984
[original edition 1962]). *"I just don't have time"*: Fred J. Cook, "The Ultras: Aims,
Affiliations, and Finances of the Radical Right," special issue, *The Nation,* June 30,
1962; and *Time,* December 8, 1961. *Bulletin* dictates are in Westin, "The John Birch
Society."

118   The beginning of Welch's Impeach Warren campaign is noted in Welch to Regnery, February 22, 1961, HR, Box 78/1.

118   Stephen Young's Senate speech: *Congressional Record,* April 12, 1961, 5268f.
For Senator Eastland, see "Eastland Says John Birch Society Patriotic," SFC, March
19, 1961; and "Birch Society Leader Asks Probe by Eastland's Subcommittee," SFC,
April, 1961. For Cardinal Cushing, see "The John Birch Society: Patriotic or Irre-
sponsible," *Life,* May 12, 1961. For Hiestand and Rousselot, see "Storm Over
Birchers," *Time,* April 7, 1961. For Ezra Taft Benson, see Fred J. Cook, "The
Ultras." BMG quote is in *Time,* April 7, 1961.

118   *"On February 25, 1961"*: *Bulletin of the John Birch Society,* April 1961.

7. STORIES OF ORANGE COUNTY

120   The story of Joel Dvorman as a spark for right-wing grassroots organizing in
Orange County is told in Lisa McGirr, "Suburban Warriors: Grass-Roots Conservatism in the 1960s" (Ph.D. diss., Columbia University, 1995), 82–91.

121   For Schwarz "animal husbandry" quote, see "Will You Be Free to Celebrate

Christmas in the Future," poster of Schwarz congressional testimony, May 29, 1957, JCJ.

121   Everyday right-wing neighborhood culture is described in McGirr, "Suburban Warriors," 86–101, 114–19. For *Communism on the Map*, see Fred J. Cook, "The Ultras, Aims, Affiliations, and Finances of the Radical Right," special issue, *The Nation*, June 30, 1962; and Edward Cain, *They'd Rather Be Right: Youth and the Conservative Movement* (New York: Macmillan, 1963), 162.

121   For favorite speakers on the right-wing circuit, see "Combatting Right-Wing Activity in Your Community," ML, Box 29/Group Research. For W. Cleon Skousen's firing, see *Time*, December 8, 1961; and George B. Russell, *J. Bracken Lee: The Taxpayer's Champion* (New York: Robert Spellers and Sons, 1961).

122   For Reagan's peak, see Gary Wills, *Reagan's America: Innocents at Home* (New York: Penguin, 1988), 177. *"Going over Niagara Falls"*: Douglas Brinkley, "The President's Pen Pal," *The New Yorker*, July 26, 1999.

122   Sources for General Electric's unusual corporate culture and "Boulwarism" are Herbert R. Northrup, "The Case for Boulwarism," *Harvard Business Review* (September–October 1963); Mike Davis, *Prisoners of the American Dream* (New York: Verso, 1986), 117–21; Stanford M. Jacoby, *Modern Manors: Welfare Capitalism Since the New Deal* (Princeton, N.J.: Princeton University Press, 1997), 232, 242–47; and Lemuel R. Boulware, "The New Requirement for Business Success," speech, in HR, Boulware Folder.

123   *"Today," he would say*: Ronald Reagan and Richard Hubler, *Where's the Rest of Me?* (New York: Duell, Sloane and Pearce, 1965), 303. *"Let's give it a try"*: Anne Edwards, *Early Reagan: The Rise to Power* (New York: Morrow, 1987), 455.

123   *"Shouldn't someone tag"*: Edmund Morris, *Dutch: A Memoir of Ronald Reagan* (New York: Random House, 1999), 315–16. *"The inescapable truth"*: Edwards, *Early Reagan*, 543–46.

124   For southern California's competitive edge over the East and statistics, see James L. Clayton, "Defense Spending: Key to California's Growth," *Western Political Quarterly* 15 (June 1962). For Santa Ana lease, see McGirr, "Suburban Warriors," 34. Population boom is in McGirr, 32, 39.

124   Irvine's origins: ibid., 56–57. For James Utt and the "Liberty Amendment," see Kurt Schuparra, *Triumph of the Right: The Rise of the California Conservative Movement, 1945–1966* (Armonk, N.Y.: M. E. Sharpe, 1998), 47.

125   R. C. Hoiles: Schuppara, *Triumph of the Right*, 43–44. For residential segregation: McGirr, "Suburban Warriors," 60–61.

125   For Orange County religion, see McGirr, 120–30. *"Preachers are not called"*: Michael B. Friedland, "Giving a Shout for Freedom, Part II: The Reverend Maclolm Boyd, the Right Reverend Paul Moore, Jr., and the Civil Rights and Antiwar Movements of the 1960s and 1970s," *Viet Nam Generation* 5, nos. 1–4 (March 1994). For Billy Graham quote, see William Martin, *With God on Our Side: The Rise of the Religious Right in America* (New York: Broadway Books, 1996), 44. For Oxnam, see ibid., 38. For FCC ruling, see Sara Diamond, *Roads to Dominion: Right-Wing*

Movements and Political Power in the United States (New York: Guilford, 1995), 162. The pamphlets are ones that found their way into the vestibule of "Fighting Bob" Wells. McGirr, "Suburban Warriors," 124–25.

126   *A 1961 issue*: ibid., 77. *"Show me one, just one"*: ibid., 35. North American Aviation's lobbyist is noted in G. R. Schreiber, *The Bobby Baker Affair: How to Make Millions in Washington* (Chicago: Regnery, 1964), 10.

126   *They had two million index cards*: McGirr, "Suburban Warriors," 49.

126   For the Walter Knott legend: author interview with Gus Owen; "One Man's Crusade for Everybody's Freedom," *Reader's Digest*, June 1964; and Roger Holmes, *Fabulous Farmer* (Los Angeles: Westernlore Publishers, 1956). For an IRS judgment against him for $60,000 for falsely claiming the Freedom Center as a business expense, see GRR, June 29, 1964.

127   For the boysenberry as welfare case, see Holmes, *Fabulous Farmer*.

128   For Reagan and TVA, see Reagan and Hubler, *Where's the Rest of Me?*, 268–69.

128   For Newburgh background: Joseph P. Ritz, *The Despised Poor: Newburgh's War on Welfare* (Boston: Beacon Press, 1966); Edgar May, *The Wasted Americans: Cost of Our Welfare Dilemma* (New York: Harper and Row, 1964); Edward Berkowitz, *America's Welfare State: From Roosevelt to Reagan* (Baltimore: Johns Hopkins, 1991), 103; James T. Patterson, *America's Struggle Against Poverty, 1900–1980* (Cambridge, Mass.: Harvard University Press, 1981), 107–111; A. H. Raskin, "Newburgh's Lessons for the Nation," NYHT, December 17, 1961; *Business Week*, July 22, 1961; *The Reporter*, August 17, 1961; NYT, July 22, 1961; USNWR, July 24, 1961; *Newsweek*, July 17, 1961; *The Nation*, September 19, 1961; and *Commonweal*, February 2, 1962.

129   *"The colored people of this city"*: May, *Wasted Americans*, 34. *The city manager, convinced*: ibid., 34.

129   *"The dregs of humanity"*: ibid., 19.

129   *"Your welfare check"*: ibid., 21. The Cadillac story and the exchange between Mitchell and Ryan is in *The Nation*, September 19, 1961.

130   The commission report is quoted in NYT, July 22, 1961; NR, July 29, 1961; *Business Week*, July 22, 1961; and May, *Wasted Americans*, 22.

130   The thirteen points are quoted in May, 25–26.

131   NYT Mitchell profile ("Famous Overnight") is June 24, 1961; the "Dark Ages" editorial is June 29, 1964.

131   *"A substitute of police methods"*: Richard S. Wheeler, "The Battle of Newburgh," *Insight and Outlook: A Conservative Student Journal* (October 1961).

131   The letters to NYT are dated July 7, 1961.

131   For *Cleveland Plain Dealer* and *Detroit Free Press*, see NYT, "News of the Week in Review," July 16, 1961.

131   Liberal debunking is noted in *The Reporter*, August 17, 1961.

132   *"It's a fine commentary"*: WSJ, July 10, 1961.

132   *"I find myself in the unenviable"*: *Newsweek*, July 17, 1961.

132   I am greatly indebted to Jennifer Mittelstadt to author, March 31, 1998, for an

account of the social welfare context. *"Atomic engineers"*: Berkowitz, *America's Welfare State*, 105.

133   YAF's march through the streets of Newburgh is described, and pictured, in Ritz, *The Despised Poor*, 143–47. Liebman's scavenger work is in May, *The Wasted Americans*, 30.

133   BMG's telegram is quoted in May, 28.

133   Mitchell's trip to Washington and his meeting with BMG is in NYHT, July 19, 1961.

134   For BMG tours for Nixon, see F. Clifton White with William Gill, *Suite 3505: The Story of the Draft Goldwater Movement* (New Rockelle, N.Y.: Arlington House, 1967), 24. *"GOLDWATER SAYS DON'T DODGE": The Keynoter: The Magazine of the American Political Items Collectors* (Summer 1982): 4.

134   BMG interview in NYT: Robert Alan Goldberg, *Barry Goldwater* (New Haven, Conn.: Yale University Press, 1995), 146. For his confrontation with Nixon in Phoenix, see Theodore H. White, *The Making of the President 1960* (New York: Atheneum, 1961), 357–58.

134   BMG's letters to Nixon and Hall are in Lee Edwards, *Goldwater: The Man Who Made a Revolution* (Washington, D.C.: Regnery, 1995), 141.

135   For the New York GOP presidential strategy meeting and JFK's joke, see White, *Making of the President 1960*, 356; and Bill Adler, *More Kennedy Wit* (New York: Bantam, 1965), 19.

135   For votes for 1957 and 1960 Civil Rights Acts, see RNC Research Division, "Facts on the Civil Rights Record of Political Parties," August 1963, JCJ. For 1960 Democratic Convention walkouts, see Tom Wicker, *JFK and LBJ: The Influence of Personality upon Politics* (Baltimore: Penguin, 1968), 60; and Jack Bass and Marilyn W. Thompson, *Ol' Strom: An Unauthorized Biography of Strom Thurmond* (Atlanta: Longstreet, 1998), 190.

135   *The biggest party in Atlanta*: White, *Making of the President 1960*, 297. *In the capital of South Carolina*: Thompson to Rymer, "The Goldwater Tour of the South," n.d. (September 1964), AHF, Box W3/4.

135   On the "Big Six" and the black swing vote, see White, *Making of the President 1960*, 255, 291; and Robert Novak, *The Agony of the GOP 1964* (New York: Macmillan, 1965), 77, 106. For Graham's blandishments, see Martin, *With God on Our Side*, 52.

136   *The Democrats whistle-stopped*: Robert J. Donovan, op-ed, LAT, February 5, 1964. For "counterfeit confederate" see Goldberg, *Barry Goldwater*, 146. *But when Henry Cabot Lodge*: *Time*, May 15, 1964.

136   King's arrest, Wofford and Shriver's efforts, and RFK's horror is in Thomas C. Reeves, *A Question of Character: A Life of John F. Kennedy* (New York: Free Press, 1991), 208–211; White, *Making of the President 1960*, 251–53; and Christopher Matthews, *Kennedy and Nixon: The Rivalry That Shaped Postwar America* (New York: Touchstone, 1996), 171–73.

136   Robinson's entreaties to Nixon: Jackson Lears, TNR, February 2, 1998.

BMG's: Edwards, *Goldwater*, 141; Robert Novak, "Barry and Me," *The Weekly Standard*, June 15, 1998; *Time*, November 21, 1960.

137   *"No Comment" Nixon*: Matthews, *Kennedy and Nixon*, 173. *With a President Nixon, "there will be"*: "Georgians for Nixon-Lodge" flyer, FCW, Box 19.

137   *If Eisenhower had pump-primed*: Robert Dallek, *Flawed Giant: Lyndon Johnson and His Times, 1961–1973* (New York: Oxford University Press, 1998), 72. *If not for Henry Cabot Lodge's*: author interview with Phyllis Schlafly. *If Henry Luce hadn't*: Martin, *With God on Our Side*, 54. *They also pointed out that in Illinois*: Stephen Shadegg, *How to Win an Election* (New York: Taplinger, 1964), 18.

137   *"It's just what I've been saying"*: *Time*, November 21, 1960.

137   For Tony Smith, see NYT obituary, September 12, 1991. For Air War College speech, see Shadegg, *What Happened to Goldwater?: The Inside Story of the 1964 Republican Campaign* (New York: Holt, Rinehart, and Winston, 1965), 30; Buckley quote is Buckley to Manion, September 24, 1959, CM, Box 69/5. For speech to Congress of American Industry, see Cain, *They'd Rather Be Right*, 105. Cartoon in NYHT, December 9, 1960.

138   For the effort to dump BMG from RSCC, see William Knowland editorial, *Oakland Tribune*, January 10, 1961; and Stephen Shadegg, *What Happened*, 22. For the "Forgotten American" speech, see HE, January 27, 1961; Edwards, *Goldwater*, 145; and Robert Novak, "Barry and Me."

138   For BMG's votes in the Eighty-seventh Congress, see "Voting Record of Senator Goldwater," AHF, Box W2/4. For education, see *Congressional Record*, May 23, 1961, 8664–76, and May 24, 1961, 8720–33.

139   *"Salesman for a Cause"*: *Time*, June 23, 1961. *Conscience* sales: Andrew, *Other Side of the Sixties*, 46. *Newsweek put Goldwater on the cover*: "Conservatism in the U.S. . . . And Its Leading Spokesman," *Newsweek*, April 10, 1961. *Even the country's most liberal major daily*: NYP, May 5, 1961. For column growth: *Newsweek*, April 10, 1961; and *Time*, June 23, 1961. *His suite in the Old Senate Office Building*: "Goldwater vs. Rockefeller?," CT, September 4, 1961. *A negative profile in Life:* Gore Vidal, "A Liberal Meets Mr. Conservative," *Life*, June 1961.

139   For JFK's legislative failures, see Wicker, *JFK and LBJ*, 25–150.

139   For JFK approval ratings, see Matthews, *Kennedy and Nixon*, 194; and Reeves, *A Question of Character*, 2.

140   *Barry Goldwater gave 225 speeches*: Robert Novak, WSJ, September 14, 1962. *"The favorite son of a state of mind"*: Richard Whalen, *Taking Sides: A Personal View of America from Kennedy to Nixon to Kennedy* (Boston: Houghton Mifflin, 1974), 92.

8. APOCALYPTICS

141   *"Sometimes, I'm afraid that the Good Lord"*: interview with W. W. Rostow in CNN documentary *Cold War*, Episode IX, prod. Jeremy Isaacs.

141   *It was, said Khrushchev*: Jeremy Isaacs and Taylor Downing, *Cold War: An Illustrated History, 1945–1991* (Boston: Little, Brown, 1998), 170.

141   My main sources for the Berlin crisis are Ernest R. May and Philip D. Zelikow, eds., *The Kennedy Tapes: Inside the White House During the Cuban Missile Crisis*

(Cambridge, Mass.: Harvard University Press, 1997), 1–43; and Thomas C. Reeves, *A Question of Character: A Life of John F. Kennedy* (New York: Free Press, 1991), 292–309.

142   *In Rockford, Illinois, Barry Goldwater*: "Salesman for a Cause," *Time*, June 23, 1961.

142   *"And if that means war"*: Reeves, *A Question of Character*, 299.

142   July 25, 1961, speech is in PPP: JFK, 533–40.

143   For the bomb shelter panic in the summer of 1961 I draw on Margot A. Henriksen, *Dr. Strangelove's America: Society and Culture in the Atomic Age* (Berkeley: University of California Press, 1997), 200–217; and Allan M. Winkler, *Life Under a Cloud: American Anxiety About the Atom* (New York: Oxford University Press, 1993), 126–31.

144   *Was like talking to a statue*: *Cold War*, Episode IX.

144   *"They'd kick me in the nuts"*: Reeves, *A Question of Character*, 307.

144   *Time Inc. even helped*: Allan C. Carlson, "Foreign Policy and 'The American Way': The Rise and Fall of the Post–World War II Consensus," *This World* (Spring/Summer 1983).

145   *"Now we have a problem"*: Stanley Karnow, *Vietnam: A History* (New York: Viking Press, 1983), 248. E. M. Dealey's crack is quoted in Pierre Salinger, *With Kennedy* (Garden City, N.Y.: Doubleday, 1966), 143. My interpretation of the origins of the Vietnam escalation in nuclear fears stemming from the Berlin crisis is indebted to Francis X. Winters, *The Year of the Hare: America in Vietnam, January 25, 1963–February 15, 1964* (Athens: University of Georgia Press, 1997).

145   *"Would stimulate bitter"*: Lloyd C. Gardner and Ted Gittinger, *Vietnam: The Early Decisions* (Austin: University of Texas Press, 1997), 20. For JFK's meeting with the Joint Chiefs of Staff on Vietnam, see ibid., 101.

145   For the development of distrust between JFK and his Joint Chiefs of Staff, see George C. Herring, "Conspiracy of Silence: LBJ, the Joint Chiefs, and Escalation of the War in Vietnam," in Gardner and Ted Gittinger, *Vietnam: The Early Decisions*; H. R. McMaster, *Dereliction of Duty: Lyndon Johnson, Robert McNamara, the Joint Chiefs of Staff, and the Lies that Led to Vietnam* (New York: HarperCollins, 1997); May and Zelikow, eds., *The Kennedy Tapes*, 1–43; Curtis LeMay, *Mission with LeMay: My Story* (Garden City, N.Y.: Doubleday, 1965); and the novel by Fletcher Knebel and Charles W. Bailey II, *Seven Days in May* (New York: Harper and Row, 1962), and the film based on it (1964).

146   For the Mosk report, see Stanley Mosk and Howard H. Jewel, "The Birch Phenomenon Analyzed," NYTM, August 20, 1961.

146   For the 1956 "brain-washing" report, see Catherine Lutz, "The Psychological Ethic and the Spirit of Containment," *Public Culture* (Winter 1997): 135–59. My sources for the 1958 NSC directive, the Fulbright memo, and the right-wing response to the 1958 NSC directive are NYT, June 18, 1961; "The Radical Right," Proceedings of the Sixth Annual Intergroup Relations Conference, 1965; and Dr. Frederick Schwarz, *Beating the Unbeatable Foe: The Story of the Christian Anti-Communist Crusade* (Washington, D.C.: Regnery, 1996), 253.

146   For the Foreign Policy Research Institute, see Sara Diamond, *Roads to Dominion: Right-Wing Movements and Political Power in the United States* (New York: Guilford, 1995), 47; Louis Morton and Gene Lyons, "Schools for Strategy," *Bulletin of the Atomic Scientists*, March 1961; Fred J. Cook, "The Ultras: Aims, Affiliations, and Finances of the Radical Right," special issue, *The Nation*, June 30, 1962; and WS, November 10, 1963.

146   On Pensacola, see Intergroup Relations Conference, "The Radical Right," conference proceedings, 1965. For "preventive war," see Cook, "The Ultras" (for Wright quote); and Richard Rhodes, "The General and World War III," *The New Yorker*, June 19, 1995.

147   For General Walker, I rely on Shawn Francis Peters, " 'Did You Say That Mr. Dean Acheson Is a Pink?': The Walker Case and the Cold War," *Viet Nam Generation* 6, nos. 3–4; and "Thunder on the Far Right: Fear and Frustration," *Newsweek*, December 4, 1961.

147   For the Army's report on Walker, see NYT, June 18, 1961. For ACA: Diamond, *Roads to Dominion*, 61; and Peters, " 'Did You Say.' "

148   For Thurmond hearings: Jack Bass and Marilyn W. Thompson, *Ol' Strom: An Unauthorized Biography of Strom Thurmond* (Atlanta: Longstreet, 1998), 191–92; and Peters, " 'Did You Say' " (for "Pro-Blue" quote).

148   For James Quinlan, *New York Mirror*, the Texas state senate, Paul Harvey, and BMG reactions, see Peters, " 'Did You Say.' "

148   For Schwarz at the Hollywood Bowl, October 16, 1961, and Richfield Oil and Coast Federal funding, see Cook, "The Ultras"; and Schwarz, *Beating the Unbeatable Foe*, 226.

149   For JFK campaign against the far right, I rely on the remarkable original research in John A. Andrew III, *The Other Side of the Sixties: Young Americans for Freedom and the Rise of Conservative Politics* (New Brunswick, N.J.: Rutgers University Press, 1997). For the RFK meeting with Walter Reuther, ibid., 153; and Victor Reuther, *The Brothers Reuther and the Story of the UAW* (Boston: Houghton Mifflin, 1976), 440.

149   For original Minutemen dispatch, see "Police Seize Arms of '61 'Minutemen,' " NYT, October 22, 1961, A32; see also "Guerilla Chief Held on Coast for Violating Police Regulation," NYT, November 11, 1961, A9; and "Minutemen Guerilla Unit Found to Be Small and Loosely Knit," NYT, November 12, 1961, A6.

150   *Thirty-four had come from Texas*: Andrew, *Other Side of the Sixties*, 153.

150   For Dallas generally my source is Warren Leslie, *Dallas Public and Private* (New York: Grossman Publishers, 1964).

150   For LBJ's visit, see ibid., 179–87.

150   My sources for Yugoslavia and the founding of the National Indignation Convention are Donald Janson and Bernard Eismann, *The Far Right* (New York: McGraw-Hill, 1963), 108; *Newsweek*, December 4, 1961; and GRR, June 29, 1964.

151   For J. Evetts Haley and Texans For America's textbook crusade, and his fistfight with the history professor, see Cook, "The Ultras." For *United States* v. *J. Evetts*

Haley Jr., see "Texans for America News," June 1959, in CM, Box 69/6. His appearance in Dallas is described in *Newsweek*, December 4, 1961. For JFK's order for monthly reports on the right, IRS investigation, and speechwriting for Western tour, see Andrew, *Other Side of the Sixties*, 156–61.

151   *The radical right, he explained*: PPP: JFK, 724–28. The scene in Los Angeles is set in Tom Wicker, "Kennedy Asserts Far-Right Groups Provoke Disunity," NYT, November 19, 1961, A1. For speech, see PPP: JFK, 733–36.

152   *Time put the issue*: "Thunder Against the Right," *Time*, November 24, 1961 (for NCWC and UAHC resolutions). *"Those who take the extreme"*: *Newsweek*, December 4, 1961. The NYTM article is November 26, 1961. *Henry Luce's next Life editorial*: "Crackpots: How They Help Communism," *Life*, December 1, 1961.

152   For Harding College, see Cook, "The Ultras." For fluoride, see Robert L. Crain, Elihu Katz, and Donald B. Rosenthal, *The Politics of Community Conflict: The Fluoridation Decision* (Indianapolis: Bobbs-Merrill, 1969). For Hunt, see Jerome Tuccille, *Kingdom: The Story of the Hunt Family of Texas* (Ottawa, Ill.: Jameson Books, 1984); and William Martin, *With God on Our Side: The Rise of the Religious Right* (New York: Broadway Books, 1996), 76. For Smoot's "Siberia" claim, see Cook, "The Ultras." For the Council on Foreign Relations, see Dan Smoot, *The Invisible Government* (Dallas: Dan Smoot Report, Inc., 1962).

153   For panic over the Housing Act of 1961, see Rousselot press release, February 1962, in FCW, Box 18/"Congressional Contacts"; GRR, March 16, 1964; and Janson and Eismann, *The Far Right*, 101. For "Committee for Public Morality" and "Stay America," see pamphlets in Radical Right Collection, Box 9, HI.

153   For the beginning of Buckley and Welch's relationship, see John B. Judis, *William F. Buckley, Jr.: Patron Saint of the Conservatives* (New York: Touchstone, 1990), 193; and, for *The Politician*, NR, April 22, 1961. *"If you were smart"*: Robert Alan Goldberg, *Barry Goldwater* (New Haven, Conn.: Yale University Press, 1995), 137.

154   For the Pasternak affair, see Buckley to Welch, March 17, 1959, Welch to Buckley, March 18, 1959; and, for the donor, Carpenter to NR, April 21, 1959, and Buckley to Carpenter, May 5, 1959, all in WFBJ, Box 9. See also Gerald Schomp, *Birchism Was My Business* (New York: Macmillan, 1970), 121.

154   *"There now exists"*: Lisa McGirr, "Suburban Warriors: Grass-Roots Conservatism in the 1960s" (Ph.D. diss., Columbia University, 1995), 158.

154   The editorial office debates, and Rusher and Buckley quotes, are in Judis, *William F. Buckley*, 195–96.

154   For YAF faction fight, see Gregory L. Schneider, *Cadres for Conservatism: Young Americans for Freedom and the Rise of the Contemporary Right* (New York: NYU Press, 1999), 41–45.

155   For the Madison NSA incursion, see Dan Wakefield, *Mademoiselle*, June 1963; Steven U. Roberts, "Image on the Right," *The Nation*, May 19, 1962; and Edward Cain, *They'd Rather Be Right: Youth and the Conservative Movement* (New York: Macmillan, 1963), 264.

156   *Howard Phillips had raised*: author interview with Howard Phillips.

156   Palm Beach meeting: Judis, *William F. Buckley*, 198; and author interview with William F. Buckley.

156   The Reuther memo is reprinted as an appendix to Reuther, *The Brothers Reuther. Another White House report*: Andrew, *Other Side of the Sixties*, 166. For Group Research Inc., see GRR, especially October 29, 1964, 77–78, for an example of guilt by association with John Birch Society; also author interview with Wes McCune.

157   For the growth of BMG's column, see Goldberg, *Barry Goldwater*, 142.

9. OFF YEAR

158   *The debt from the Nixon campaign*: "GOP Hoping Dinners Will Erase Debt," WP, January 16, 1964, A19. *Every Friday night*: Arthur Schlesinger Jr., ed., *History of American Presidential Elections, 1798–1968*, vol. 4 (New York: Chelsea House, 1971), 3008; and author interview with Ryan Hayes. *"Not this corner"*: John B. Judis, *William F. Buckley, Jr.: Patron Saint of the Conservatives* (New York: Touchstone, 1990), 170. For economic projections for 1962 and the Eisenhower years: John J. Lindsay, "The '62 Legislative Outlook," *The Nation*, January 1, 1962; and Robert M. Collins, "Growth Liberalism in the Sixties: Great Societies at Home and Grand Designs Abroad," in David Farber, ed., *The Sixties: From Memory to History* (Chapel Hill: University of North Carolina Press, 1994). *A program to sell*: John Kessel, *The Goldwater Coalition: Republican Strategies in 1964* (Indianapolis: Bobbs-Merrill, 1968), 125.

158   *"When a composite"*: John Andrew III, *The Other Side of the Sixties: Young Americans for Freedom and the Rise of Conservative Politics* (New Brunswick, N.J.: Rutgers University Press, 1997), 40. For the Chicago banquet, see George B. Russell, *J. Bracken Lee: The Taxpayer's Champion* (New York: Robert Spellers and Sons, 1961), 154. My interpretation of liberal capitalism and the founding of the Republican Party is from Malcolm Moos, *The Republicans: A History of Their Party* (New York: Random House, 1956), 30; and Milton Viorst, *Fall from Grace: The Republican Party and the Puritan Ethic* (New York: New American Library, 1968), 37.

158   My sense of the development of the sectional split is from Nicol C. Rae, *The Decline and Fall of the Liberal Republicans: From 1952 to the Present* (New York: Oxford University Press, 1989).

159   *If you want to live*: E. J. Dionne Jr., *Why Americans Hate Politics* (New York: Simon and Schuster, 1991), 79. *Registered Democrats outnumbered*: Richard Nixon, *RN: The Memoirs of Richard Nixon*, vol. 1 (New York: Warner Books, 1978), 265; David M. Kennedy, *Freedom from Fear: The American People in Depression and War* (New York: Oxford University Press, 1999), 472. For Willkie's rise, see Donald Bruce Johnson, *The Republican Party and Wendell Willkie* (Urbana: University of Illinois Press, 1960). For synthetic telegram campaign, see Rae, *Decline and Fall*, 31.

160   For the 1952 convention "steal," see James T. Patterson, *Mr. Republican: A Biography of Robert Taft* (Boston: Houghton Mifflin, 1972), 547–66.

160   *"The Republican Party is just"*: Paul Tillett, ed., *Inside Politics: The National Conventions, 1960* (Dobbs Ferry, N.Y.: Oceana Publications, 1962), 133.

160   For the January 1962 RNC meeting and the urban precinct strategy, see Robert Novak, *The Agony of the GOP 1964* (New York: Macmillan, 1965), 53–65.

160   JFK quote on "great passionate movements": Dionne, *Why Americans Hate Politics*, 177.

160   For Hinman, see Stephen Shadegg, *What Happened to Goldwater?: The Inside Story of the 1964 Republican Campaign* (New York: Holt, Rinehart, and Winston, 1965), 58. For courting of conservatives, see Novak, *Agony of the GOP*, 46.

161   For NAR's appearance in Des Moines, see Novak, 66.

161   For breakfasts, see Novak, 74–75.

161   *"I have no plans for it"*: "Salesman for a Cause," *Time*, June 23, 1961.

161   For Shadegg, Milliken, and Cotton begging him to run, see F. Clifton White with William Gill, *Suite 3505: The Story of the Draft Goldwater Movement* (New Rochelle, N.Y.: Arlington House, 1967), 26.

161   For BMG cruise, see Shadegg, *What Happened*, 47; and Novak, *Agony of the GOP*, 46, 72, 102.

162   *"He's not really such"*: ibid., 74. *Though in private he complained*: Ralph de Toledano, *The Winning Side: The Case for Goldwater Republicanism* (New York: MacFadden-Bartel, 1963), 131.

162   For Viguerie hiring I rely on F. Clifton White, *Why Reagan Won: The Conservative Movement, 1964–1981* (Washington, D.C.: Regnery, 1981), 74; Marvin Liebman, *Coming Out Conservative: An Autobiography* (San Francisco: Chronicle Books, 1992), 153; Gregory Schneider, *Cadres for Conservatism: Young Americans for Freedom and the Rise of the Contemporary Right* (New York: NYU Press, 1999), 43; and author interview with Richard Viguerie (for Liebman quote).

163   Rally planning: Liebman, *Coming Out Conservative*, 154; Edward Cain, *They'd Rather Be Right: Youth and the Conservative Movement* (New York: Macmillan, 1963), 173; Dodd to Liebman, January 25, 1962, Liebman to Dodd, February 18, 1962, and Dodd to Liebman, March 14, 1962, all in ML, Box 6/Dodd, Thomas J.; and "Talk by Walker Cancelled Here," NYT, February 13, 1962; and *Time*, March 16, 1962.

163   For Tshombe: James A. Bill, *George Ball: Behind the Scenes in U.S. Foreign Policy* (New Haven, Conn.: Yale University Press, 1997), 137–50; Andrew, *Other Side of the Sixties*, 138–39; Cain, *They'd Rather Be Right*, 173; and Viguerie interview.

163   For counter-rally description: author interview with Steve Max. For rally: *Time*, March 16, 1962; "Gnostics at the Garden," *Commonweal*, March 30, 1962; NR, March 27, 1962; Cain, *They'd Rather Be Right*, 173; Lee Edwards, *Goldwater: The Man Who Made a Revolution* (Washington, D.C.: Regnery, 1995), 159; Richard Whalen, *Taking Sides: A Personal View of America from Kennedy to Nixon to Kennedy* (Boston: Houghton Mifflin, 1974); Peter Kihss, "18,000 Rightists Rally at the Garden," NYT, March 8, 1962, A1; and author interviews with William Schulz, Richard Viguerie, and Carol Dawson. For Tower Senate election and Steve Shadegg, see *Arizona Journal*, March 29, 1962.

164   *The next morning the New York Times*: NYT, March 8, 1962.

165   Nixon's temptation to run, and Weinberger quote, are in Kurt Schuparra, *Triumph of the Right: The Rise of the California Conservative Movement, 1945–1966* (Armonk, N.Y.: M. E. Sharpe, 1998), 61. His decision, and long-term strategy, are in Nixon, *RN*, 194–95.

165   For Shell, see Schuparra, *Triumph of the Right*, 61–65. The 2 percent figure is on page 68.

165   My interpretation of the importance of California's weak party system is from Theodore H. White, *The Making of the President 1964* (New York: Atheneum, 1965), 143–44. In 1959 the the system was further loosened to allow cross-filing, which was instrumental in weakening moderate Republican control. See Lisa McGirr, "Suburban Warriors: Grass-Roots Conservatism in the 1960s" (Ph.D. diss., Columbia University, 1995), 141.

165   For the LACYR rejection of Nixon, see Leonard Nadasdy to various, November 13, 1961, LN (for "galloping socialism" quote); Schuparra, *Triumph of the Right*, 66; NYT, May 3, 1964; and McGirr, "Suburban Warriors," 146. *The movement that swept Gaston*: author interview with Robert Gaston.

166   For CRA as Warren redoubt, see White with Gill, *Suite 3505*, 335; Schuparra, *Triumph of the Right*, 5; and McGirr, "Suburban Warriors," 134, 142. For Nolan Frizzelle and the right-wing takeover of the CRA, see Nolan, 142–45; and Schuparra, *Triumph of the Right*, 65–66, 177. For "dictatorial and totalitarian" quote, see LAT, March 4, 1962. *"I don't consider the John Birch Society"*: McGirr, "Suburban Warriors," 157.

166   For CRA endorsement meeting, see Schuparra, *Triumph of the Right*, 64–65; Jim Woods, "California Republicans: Are the Birchers Taking Over?," *The Reporter*, May 1964; McGirr, "Suburban Warriors," 146. For Wright and Jarvis, see Schuparra, 65. For Reagan's involvement, see White, *Why Reagan Won*, 26; and Group Research Inc., "Barry Goldwater and the American Right Wing," AC.

166   For Nixon's 1960 supporters backing Shell, see Novak, *Agony of the GOP*, 86. *At a May 23 rally*: Schuparra, *Triumph of the Right*, 66–67.

167   For Nixon's sojourn in the desert, see Novak, *Agony of the GOP*, 84. For the Birch billboards, see production draft for campaign film "The Extremist," RAC, Box 11/944. Department of State Publication 7277: Phyllis Schlafly, *A Choice, Not an Echo* (Alton, Ill.: Pere Marquette Press, 1964), 12, and AC.

167   For the Nixon-Shell meeting, see Schuparra, *Triumph of the Right*, 68. For BMG response, see White with Gill, *Suite 3505*, 71.

167   For Miller's commitment to Operation Dixie, see Rae, *Decline and Fall*, 69. *Time enshrined the Young Republican operatives*: "The New Breed," *Time*, July 13, 1962. See also Grenier to White, May 3, 1962, WAR, Box 154/4, Alabama Republican Party precinct meetings ("Today we have seen the birth of the Republican Party of Alabama as a political organization"); White, *Making of the President 1964*, 167; John Grenier Oral History, Southern Historical Collection, University of North Carolina at Chapel Hill, 4007: A-9; and "Declaration of Principles of the Republican Party of Louisiana," FCW, Box 19. For Edens's use of COPE manual, see Jack Bass

and Marilyn W. Thompson, *Ol' Strom: An Unauthorized Biography of Strom Thurmond* (Atlanta: Longstreet, 1998), 195.

168   For a copy of "Declaration of Republican Principle and Policy" read to the House of Representatives June 7, 1962, see AHF, Box 1/1. See also White with Gill, *Suite 3505*, 65. For Eisenhower's "All-Republican Conference," see Rae, *Decline and Fall*, 67; and the letters on "National Citizens Committee" letterhead in FCW, Eisenhower File. For BMG's response, see White with Gill, *Suite 3505*, 71. *"The fact that you were politically naive"*: Yerger to Eisenhower, July 23, 1962, WAR, Box 154/4.

168   My account of Bill Workman's Senate race is from Russell Merritt, "The Senatorial Election of 1962 and the Rise of Two-Party Politics in South Carolina," *South Carolina Historical Magazine* (July 1997).

169   For the integration of the University of Mississippi: Taylor Branch, *Pillar of Fire: America in the King Years, 1963–1965* (New York: Simon and Schuster, 1998), 62. For centennial of Confederacy, see Michael Kammen, *Mystic Chords of Memory: The Transformation of Tradition in American Culture* (New York: Vintage, 1993), 590–610. For General Walker's participation, see Peter Dale Scott, *Deep Politics and the Death of JFK* (Berkeley: University of California Press, 1993), 34.

169   BMG response to Ole Miss: WGN, FB 2413-A.

169   For election results, see *America Votes*, vol. 4 (New York: Macmillan, 1964).

170   For Lister Hill and James Martin's Senate race, see Ellen Proxmire, *One Foot in Washington: The Perilous Life of a Senator's Wife* (Washington, D.C.: R. B. Luce, 1964), 80; White, *Making of the President 1964*, 167–68; and Alexander Lamis, *The Two-Party South* (New York: Oxford University Press, 1984), 77. For Memphis, see David Kraslow, "Goldwater Key to All GOP Hopes in South," LAT, January 3, 1964. For Republican totals in the South generally, see *Newsweek*, May 20, 1963.

10. SUITE 3505

171   *Or so National Review publisher Bill Rusher argued*: "Crossroads for the GOP," NR, February 12, 1963.

171   For Nixon's general election campaign and "last press conference," see Kurt Schuparra, *Triumph of the Right: The Rise of the California Conservative Movement, 1945–1966* (Armonk, N.Y.: M. E. Sharpe, 1998), 68–79. For Francis Amendment, see Lisa McGirr, "Suburban Warriors: Grass-Roots Conservatism in the 1960s" (Ph.D. diss., Columbia University, 1995), 99–101. For "The Political Obituary of Richard Nixon," see Christopher Matthews, *Kennedy and Nixon: The Rivalry That Shaped Postwar America* (New York: Touchstone, 1996), 219.

172   For the success of Birch-associated candidates, see John Andrew III, *The Other Side of the Sixties: Young Americans for Freedom and the Rise of Conservative Politics* (New Brunswick, N.J.: Rutgers University Press, 1997), 167. For gerrymandering of Rousselot's district, see "The Rampant Right Invades the GOP," *Look*, July 16, 1963. For Rafferty, see Schuparra, *Triumph of the Right*, 81–82.

172 *The New York Times's top pundit*: Arthur Schlesinger Jr., ed., *History of American Presidential Elections, 1798–1968*, vol. 4 (New York: Chelsea House, 1971), 3009. For Morgenthau showing against NAR, see Rusher, "Crossroads for the GOP"; and Robert Novak, *The Agony of the GOP 1964* (New York: Macmillan, 1965), 81, 84.

172 The source for White's biography is F. Clifton White with Jerome Tuccille, *Politics as a Noble Calling* (Ottawa, Ill.: Jameson Books, 1994). The comparison to Jimmy Stewart is from author interview with William A. Rusher. For his headlong embrace of backroom politics, see E. J. Dionne Jr., *Why Americans Hate Politics* (New York: Simon and Schuster, 1991), 177.

173 *"Learn from them"*: White with Tuccille, *Noble Calling*, 58.

174 For the creation of Clif White's Young Republican machine I rely on White with Tuccille, 65–79; William Rusher, *The Rise of the Right* (New York: Morrow, 1984), 67–70, 78–79; "Old Friends," pamphlet, LN; and author interviews with Rusher and Leonard Nadasdy. John Lindsay would soon go on to work for the Justice Department to help craft the 1957 Civil Rights Act.

175 *White sat alone in his hotel room*: White with Tuccille, *Noble Calling*, 73.

176 *The resolutions committee, traditionally*: Rusher, *Rise of the Right*, 70.

176 For the business-politics movement White pioneered, see White with Tuccille, *Noble Calling*, 109–131; David J. Galligan, *Politics and the Businessmen* (New York: Pitman, 1964); "Businessmen in Politics: A GOP Candidate Is Defeated as Effort Is Made to Organize Business Behind Him," WSJ, March 6, 1959; Max P. Skelton, "Gulf's Political Program Studied by Other Firms," *Midland* (Texas) *Reporter*, July 26, 1959, clip in CM, Box 70/1.

177 *One day in the summer of 1961*: Rusher interview; Rusher, *Rise of the Right*, 98–99.

177 *Rusher called Clif White*: ibid., 100–101; Rusher interview.

178 White's astonishingly detailed organizational files for Volunteers for Nixon-Lodge are in FCW, Box 8. For his midlife crisis see White with Tuccille, *Noble Calling*, 132–33; and F. Clifton White with William Gill, *Suite 3505: The Story of the Draft Goldwater Movement* (New Rochelle, N.Y.: Arlington House, 1967), 25.

178 For the founding and first two meetings of the Draft Goldwater organization through the opening of an office: White with Tuccille, *Noble Calling*, 137–43; White with Gill, *Suite 3505*, 30–51; Rusher, *Rise of the Right*, 98–110; Jon Margolis, *The Last Innocent Year: America in 1964: The Beginning of the "Sixties"* (New York: Morrow, 1999), 22; and Rusher interview. For BMG's appearance on *Issues and Answers*, see Lee Edwards, *Goldwater: The Man Who Made a Revolution* (Washington, D.C.: Regnery, 1995), 153.

180 I draw my sense of the Rube Goldberg system for deciding Republican nominees, and White's strategy for exploiting it, from Andrew E. Busch, *Outsiders and Openness in the Presidential Nominating System* (Pittsburgh: University of Pittsburgh Press, 1997), 66–76; Nicol C. Rae, *The Decline and Fall of the Liberal Republicans: From 1952 to the Present* (New York: Oxford University Press, 1989), 55–57; and Schlesinger, ed., *History of American Presidential Elections*, 3012.

181   For Suite 3505 in the Chanin Building I rely on White with Gill, *Suite 3505*, 52–54; Rusher interview; and author visit.

181   White's materials for slide talks, including an example of his delegate map, are in FCW, Boxes 8 and 19. For his Texas, Mississippi, Louisiana, Midwestern, and Western trips, see White with Gill, *Suite 3505*, 55–56. For the bombings of ministers' homes, see "Terror Bombs," LAT, February 2, 1962, A1. For Rousselot, see Rusher to White, February 28, 1962, WAR, Box 18/"Congressional Contact." *Rousselot—a good soldier and a good spy*: in 1965 Ronald Reagan noted that Rousselot was "willing to do anything from calling me names in public to endorsement—whatever we want." Schuparra, *Triumph of the Right*, 116.

182   For the third, Minnesota, meeting: White to Rusher, March 26, 1962, WAR, Box 154/4; White to Tope, March 27, 1962, and White to Barr, April 6, 1962, FCW, Box 19; Rusher, *Rise of the Right*, 136; White and Gill, *Suite 3505*, 56–60; and Rusher interview. "Sons of Business" affair: Thomas C. Reeves, *A Question of Character: A Life of John F. Kennedy* (New York: Free Press, 1991), 331.

183   For fund-raising difficulties, see Ralph Bachenheimer correspondence in WAR, Box 154/4. For "Tope-Fernald Agency Account," see "Letter of Understanding," Fernald and Tope to Milliken, February 1962, WAR, Box 155/3. For ACA's parallel efforts for the 1962 congressional elections, see invitation to November 14, 1961, meeting in FCW, Box 3/Miscellaneous; and "Group of Conservatives Assigns Secret Aides to 46 Candidates," NYT, October 22, 1962, A1. *That was the exact amount*: White with Gill, *Suite 3505*, 62.

183   White's trip to Seattle: ibid., 68–69. For Chapman and Guilder's "flaming moderates," see *Time*, February 10, 1961; Paul Tillett, ed., *Inside Politics: The National Conventions 1960* (Dobbs Ferry, N.Y.: Oceana Publications, 1962), 46; Hayden, "Who Are the Student Boatrockers?," *Mademoiselle*, August 1961; and Rae, *Decline and Fall*, 81. For the movement to dump Goldwater, see Edward Cain, *They'd Rather Be Right: Youth and the Conservative Movement* (New York: Macmillan, 1963), 267.

183   *Washington State Republicans*: August 14, 1962, press release in WAR, Box 154/4. AP and Texas polls: White with Gill, *Suite 3505*, 78. For Chubb Fellowship, see Kitchel to BMG, November 6, 1961, Kitchel to Williams, December 14, 1961, Williams to Kitchel, December 30, 1961, Griswold to Kitchel, April 19, 1962, Kitchel to Williams, April 27, 1962, and Brown to BMG, May 16, 1962, all in DK, Box 1/Goldwater, Barry 1947–63; and Richard Brookhiser, *Weekly Standard*, July 6, 1999.

184   *He removed himself*: Robert Novak, "Boost for Rocky Seen as Goldwater Curtails Nationwide Politicking," WSJ, September 14, 1962; and Novak, *Agony of the GOP*, 76. *White, on the verge of eviction*: White with Gill, *Suite 3505*, 75.

184   For the NFRW convention, see ibid., 73–74.

185   For White's recruiting of the AMA's president, see Annis to White, November 20, 1962, in FCW, Box 18/"American Medical Association." For the AMA and right-wing politics: Schuparra, *Triumph of the Right*, 5, 18 (for Warren); Cary Reich, *The Life of Nelson A. Rockefeller: Worlds to Conquer, 1908–1958* (New York: Doubleday, 1996), 507 (for HEW); Bill Boyarsky, *The Rise of Ronald Reagan* (New

York: Random House, 1968), 101 (for Reagan and Medicare); and Tom Wicker, *JFK and LBJ: The Influence of Personality upon Politics* (Baltimore: Penguin, 1968), 34, 67. For AMA-PAC, see "Report of James L. McDevitt, National Director, Committee on Political Education, AFL-CIO," FCW, Box 19/"Campaigning." For the involvement of AMA Suite 3505, see invitation to November 14, 1961, meeting in FCW, Box 3/Miscellaneous.

185   For the Syndicate's loss of the YRs, I rely on White with Gill, *Suite 3505*, 31; and author interviews with Leonard Nadasdy and William Rusher. For Nadasdy's reign: "Young Republican National Federation: A Record of Accomplishment," "Dear Friend," letter, April 25, 1962, and "Old Friends" pamphlet, all in LN; Nadasdy to author, August 23, 1998; Nadasdy interview; and Nadasdy to Nichols, March 21, 1963, FCW, Box 18/"Young Republicans."

185   For Hutar, see John Kessel, *The Goldwater Coalition: Republican Strategies in 1964* (Indianapolis: Bobbs-Merrill, 1968), 144. For Hutar and Harff's elections, I rely on Nadasdy and Rusher interviews; and "Old Friends." For Chicago meeting of White coalition, see White to Hutar, May 3, 1962, and June 21, 1962, and meeting minutes, July 7, 1962, all in FCW, Box 18/"Young Republicans." For Hutar's travels, see Bree to Hutar, July 18, 1962, and October 10, 1962; Hutar to Bree, July 23, 1962; Rehmann to Cushing, November 5, 1962; and Hutar to Failor, February 18, 1963, all in FCW, Box 18/"Young Republicans." *And they got to work discrediting*: Bree to Hutar, August 21, 1962; Hutar to Bree, August 23, 1962; White to Barr, September 25, 1962, ibid.

186   BMG to Yerger letter: White with Gill, *Suite 3505*, 78.

186   For White's post-election meeting with BMG and plans for December meeting, see White with Gill, *Suite 3505*, 87–91.

186   *"This meeting will determine"*: White to Rusher, October 18, 1962, WAR, Box 155/5. For meeting called by Senator Case, see NYHT, November 16, 1962.

187   For the Essex Motel meeting: White with Gill, *Suite 3505*, 92–101; Theodore H. White, *Making of the President 1964* (New York: Atheneum, 1965), 116; Novak, *Agony of the GOP*, 127; colored map in FCW, White/"Primaries, maps, etc."; and Rusher interview. *"Look, everybody's been talking"*: Edwards, *Goldwater*, 164.

187   *The next morning, back in Alabama*: Grenier to White, December 5, 1962, FCW, Box 19/"Alabama."

187   *"A secret, highly confidential"*: White with Gill, *Suite 3505*, 104. *"SECRET MEET TO PUSH GOLDWATER"*: San Francisco Examiner, December 4, 1961, A1. *"GOLDWATER '64 BOOM"*: NYHT, December 4, 1962. The editorial was December 5, 1962. Alsop's conclusion—and perhaps the earliest use of the phrase "Southern strategy"—is in undated clip, WAR, Box 154/7. The spy's report, with verbatim quotes, ran in *Advance* (Spring 1963).

188   For RNC meeting, see White with Gill, *Suite 3505*, 115; and Novak, *Agony of the GOP*, 101. For the closed-door session, see *New Haven Register*, December 8, 1962; and undated Alsop clip. An exceptional source for the battle over the Southern strategy is the long exchange of letters between RNC members Katherine Neuberger of New Jersey and Charlton Lyons of Louisiana in WAR, Box 155/7.

188   On the RNC budget crisis, see Kessel, *Goldwater Coalition*, 125, 147.

188   *"I think you have summed up"*: BMG to Kellar, December 7, 1962, DK, Box 2/Kellar.

189   For the Phoenix Country Club meeting, see "Questions," December 23, 1962, DK, Box 4/Draft Goldwater Endeavor; and Edwards, *Goldwater*, 165.

189   Goldwater meeting with White on January 14: Rusher, *Rise of the Right*, 140; White with Gill, *Suite 3505*, 115–18.

189   For Scranton inauguration and his tag as "first of the Kennedy Republicans," see Murray Kempton, "Scranton of Pennsylvania," TNR, February 16, 1963; and "New Broom," *Newsweek*, January 27, 1963.

190   *Rusher wrote Goldwater*: Rusher to Goldwater, January 18, 1963, WAR, Box 18/Goldwater Correspondence. *Goldwater wrote back*: BMG to Rusher, January 22, 1963, ibid. *Frank Meyer, one of National Review's*: Meyer to BMG, February 11, 1963, ibid.

190   *"Would bend every muscle"*: NYT, November 19, 1961.

190   For February 5, 1963, meeting see Rusher interview and White with Gill, *Suite 3505*, 120–22.

191   *Half a dozen Suite 3505 leaders*: ibid., 123–26; and Rusher interview.

191   *In March he brought Denison Kitchel*: BMG to Kitchel, February 18, 1963, February 25, 1963, and Kitchel to BMG, March 5, 1963, all in AHF, Box 13/21; press release, March 19, 1963, AHF, Box 4/General Correspondence. *Jay Hall, the GM executive, prepared a confidential*: ibid., and "Program," handwritten, February 23, 1963, DK, Box 4/Draft Goldwater Endeavor.

191   *On March 22 Goldwater appeared*: transcript in RAC, Box 10/755.

192   *If it hadn't been for Goldwater's interposition*: Novak, *Agony of the GOP*, 104; and Smith to White, cc Nichols and Rusher, March 14, 1963, WAR, Box 155/5.

192   *Robert Snowden, a Manion confederate*: Kitchel to BMG, March 5, 1963, and BMG to Kitchel, March 8, 1963, in AHF, Box 21/11. *Piles of mail were forwarded*: Paraphernalia in DK, Box 4/Draft Goldwater Endeavor.

192   Dominick's refusal to chair is in White with Gill, *Suite 3505*, 128. Preparations for the National Draft Goldwater kickoff are described in Novak, *Agony of the GOP*, 129–30.

192   The press conference transcript is in FCW, Box 18.

193   *"Another 'draft Goldwater' movement"*: Novak, *Agony of the GOP*, 130. The paraphernalia is in WAR, Box 155/2. O'Donnell's comment to reporters is recalled in Middendorf to O'Donnell, FCW, Box 8/Peter O'Donnell. For reporters' incredulity at White's group, see Gilbert A. Harrison, "Way Out West: An Interim Report on Barry Goldwater," TNR, November 23, 1963. *"Barring miracles and accidents"*: *Newsweek*, April 1, 1963.

193   For Middendorf's visit to Phoenix, see Middendorf to BMG, April 5, 1963, FCW, Box 18/Goldwater Correspondence. Their strategy memo is in WAR, Box 155/6.

193   *Shortly before O'Donnell's press conference*: Kitchell to Kellar, April 8, 1963, DK, Box 2/Kellar.

194   *A band of reporters cornered him*: Novak, *Agony of the GOP*, 131. *The National Draft Goldwater Committee chose*: White, *Suite 3505*, 135. For Independence Day plans, see Viguerie to White, April 11, 1963, and Don Shafto résumé, in FCW, Box 19/Rally.

194   For NAR turning down endorsements and phone call with BMG, see Novak, *Agony of the GOP*, 115–16.

194   For NAR's unsuccessful marriage, and his affairs, see Reich, *The Life of Nelson A. Rockefeller*, 71–85, 202, 249–50, 470–76, 542–48 (the quote is on 473). *There were rumors he was dating*: Yerger to White, August 27, 1962, FCW, Box 19/Mississippi.

194   For acceptability of divorced politicians, see Ellen Proxmire, *One Foot in Washington: The Perilous Life of a Senator's Wife* (Washington, D.C.: R. B. Luce, 1964), 2; and Kathleen Hall Jamieson, *Packaging the Presidency: A History and Criticism of Presidential Campaign Advertising*, 3rd ed. (New York: Oxford University Press, 1996), 108.

195   For his marriage to Happy Murphy, see White, *Making of the President 1964*, 96–103. The *From Here to Eternity* photo is in *Newsweek*, June 3, 1963.

195   *"It is the plain fact"*: Lionel Trilling, *The Liberal Imagination: Essays on Literature and Society* (New York: Viking, 1950), ix. *Psychology of Women* and *Modern Woman: The Lost Sex* are quoted in Betty Friedan, *The Feminine Mystique* (New York: Dell, 1984), 158, 119–21. *"I think there is much"*: Adlai Stevenson, "A Purpose for Modern Woman," *Women's Home Companion*, September 1955.

196   Prescott Bush's speech is in *Time*, June 14, 1963. The minister's censure is in Novak, *Agony of the GOP*, 144. NAR's appearance at the women's conference is in Edwards, *Goldwater*, 176.

197   For NAR's supporters and the Maryland woman's club, see Novak, *Agony of the GOP*, 143. For Dewey, see Ralph de Toledano, *The Winning Side: The Case for Goldwater Republicanism* (New York: MacFadden-Bartel, 1963), 145. The Texas GOP chair and Liz Taylor quote are in *Time*, June 14, 1963.

197   Reinhold Niebuhr and the reaction of clergy is in Novak, *Agony of the GOP*, 144; Khrushchev, ibid., 146. For "deadsville" quote, see undated Frank Conniff clip in WAR, Box 154/7. Poll results are in White with Gill, *Suite 3505*, 148. Mail to New York congressmen is in NYT, May 26, 1963. The conspiracy theories of NAR and BMG are in Novak, *Agony of the GOP*, 145.

197   For NAR's slim support on the ground, see Richard Rovere, "Letter from Washington," *The New Yorker*, November 3, 1963.

197   The Cuba speech fallout is in Novak, *Agony of the GOP*, 106. For "fee" increase, liquor scandal, and newspaper strike, see ibid. and de Toledano, *The Winning Side*, 132.

198   *On April 20, Oklahoma Republicans*: resolution in DK, Box 4/Draft Goldwater Endeavor. *From Suite 3505, one million copies*: White with Gill, *Suite 3505*, 257. *White was so successful on a California trip*: Richard Burgholz, LAT, April 30, 1963. *Thruston Morton told Fortune*: Richard Whalen, *Taking Sides: A Personal View of America from Kennedy to Nixon to Kennedy* (Boston, Houghton Mifflin,

1974), 101. On the first Evans and Novak column, see Dionne, *Why Americans Hate Politics*, 381.

198   For the H. L. Hunt rumor, see BMG to Kress, May 15, 1963, DK, Box 4/Draft Goldwater Endeavor. *"Don't say that," he implored*: Novak, *Agony of the GOP*, 155.

198   For Nixon revival and Jack Paar appearance, see Matthews, *Kennedy and Nixon*, 221–22. For packaging of the ASNE speech, see FCW, Box 19/California. For Nixon's approach to White, see White with Tuccille, *Noble Calling*, 151–52.

199   *That same May 2*: Novak, *Agony of the GOP*, 156. On Romney generally, see B. J. Widdick, "Romney: New Hope for the GOP," *The Nation*, February 3, 1962. For his 1958 testimony, see Novak, *Agony of the GOP*, 90. For his mismatches with his dinner hosts, see ibid., 88. For Knight pulling the plug, see ibid., 156.

199   For "Draft Scranton" movement, McCabe quote, and speaking invitations, see George D. Wolf, *William Warren Scranton: Pennsylvania Statesman* (State College: Penn State Press, 1981), 88–89.

199   For BMG's Massachusetts appearance, see Novak, *Agony of the GOP*, 164. For the $1,000 dinner, see White with Gill, *Suite 3505*, 149; and Novak, *Agony of the GOP*, 145 (for cable).

200   *"I ask myself"*: "GOP's Goldwater: Busting Out All Over," *Newsweek*, May 20, 1963. The finding that 59 percent of Americans claimed to have voted for JFK is in Alan Brinkley, *Liberalism and Its Discontents* (Cambridge, Mass.: Harvard University Press, 1998), 213. For Kristol quote, see M. Stanton Evans, *The Future of Conservatism* (New York: Holt, Rinehart, and Winston, 1968), 94.

200   BMG's 5 percent pledge is in *Newsweek*, May 20, 1963.

11. MOBS

201   *"It shall be unlawful"*: C. Vann Woodward, *The Strange Career of Jim Crow*, 3rd ed. (New York: Oxford University Press, 1973), 118. *In 1957 a local black minister named Fred Shuttlesworth*: Dan T. Carter, *The Politics of Rage: George Wallace, the Origins of the New Conservatism, and the Transformation of American Politics* (Baton Rouge: Louisiana State University Press, 1995), 107, 230.

201   For U.S. Steel, see Carter, *Politics of Rage*, 115. For Connor's early career, see Taylor Branch, *Parting the Waters: America in the King Years, 1954–1963* (New York: Touchstone, 1988), 691.

201   My sources for the Birmingham movement are Branch, *Parting the Waters*, 689–813; and Taylor Branch, *Pillar of Fire: America in the King Years, 1963–1965* (New York: Simon and Schuster, 1998), 76–95.

202   For "mutual respect and equality of opportunity" quote, see Branch, *Parting the Waters*, 737. *"Just as we formerly pointed out"*: ibid., 737–38.

202   The drafting of King's jail letter: ibid., 737–44.

203   *"The whole world is watching"*: ibid., 757. *The New York Times displayed*: NYT, May 4, 1963.

203   *Pravda reported MONSTROUS*: Branch, *Parting the Waters*, 786. *In Massachusetts, Goldwater said*: *Time*, June 14, 1963.

204   *At the White House, Kennedy dined*: Ben Bradlee, *Conversations with Kennedy* (New York: Norton, 1975).

204   Art Hanes's quote is in Carter, *Politics of Rage*, 127.

204   *"Wherever the problem of race festered"*: "The Jitters," *Newsweek*, May 27, 1963. The garbage trucks detail is in Branch, *Pillar of Fire*, 101.

204   *The next day the Newsweek with Goldwater*: "Goldwater in '64?," *Newsweek*, May 20, 1963. The suggestion of a limitation on the right to demonstrate is in Branch, *Parting the Waters*, 808.

205   For one-hundredth anniversary of the Emancipation Proclamation, see Branch, *Pillar of Fire*, 26. For aloofness in filibuster debate, see Thomas C. Reeves, *A Question of Character: A Life of John F. Kennedy* (New York: Free Press, 1991), 348. For judicial nominees and "remarkable job" quote, see Branch, *Parting the Waters*, 700. For introduction of civil rights legislation in February and civil rights movement reaction, see Edward G. Carmines and James A. Stimson, *Issue Evolution: Race and the Transformation of American Politics* (Princeton, N.J.: Princeton University Press, 1989), 40; and Reeves, *Question of Character*, 348–49.

205   *One told him that blacks were*: Branch, *Parting the Waters*, 693. For Jackson, Mississippi, and Burke Marshall, see ibid., 745.

205   For Wallace's KKK speechwriter, see Carter, *Politics of Rage*, 106–7. For Alabama State Troopers, see ibid., 125. RFK's visit to Alabama: ibid., 120. Lingo's deployment in Birmingham is in Branch, *Parting the Waters*, 795–96.

206   The African neutralists' message is in Branch, 807. *Senator Tower promised*: *New York Daily News*, July 6, 1963. The White House action for a strong civil rights bill is in Branch, *Parting the Waters*, 808–9.

206   *But his supporters on the Los Angeles Republican Central Committee*: Waters to White, December 5, 1962, FCW, Box 19/California, and Best to O'Donald [*sic*], April 23, 1963, WAR, Box 154/7. *"Americans for Democratic Action are"*: Edward Cain, *They'd Rather Be Right: Youth and the Conservative Movement* (New York: Macmillan, 1963), 170. *Colonel Laurence E. Bunker, General MacArthur's old aide-de-camp*: "Far Right and Far Left," NYP, April 4, 1964. *The editor of The Worker*: ibid., April 3, 1964.

207   RFK's meeting is in Branch, *Pillar of Fire*, 89. For tear gas, see Branch, *Parting the Waters*, 817; for Cleveland, see Branch, *Pillar of Fire*, 88. For JFK's birthday party, see Carter, *Politics of Rage*, 133.

207   *Sunday morning the snarlingest*: Carter, *Politics of Rage*, 135–38.

208   *Declared the Winona (Kansas) Leader*: Stephan Lesher, *George Wallace: American Populist* (Reading, Mass.: Addison-Wesley, 1994), 211.

208   The White House debate is in Branch, *Pillar of Fire*, 107. JFK's American University address and the civil rights address are in PPP: JFK.

208   For Medgar Evers's assassination, see Branch, *Parting the Waters*, 825, For disturbances in its wake, see Reeves, *Question of Character*, 357.

209   For social criticism, see Michael Harrington, *The Other America: Poverty in the United States* (New York: Penguin, 1981); Betty Friedan, *The Feminine Mystique* (New York: Dell, 1984); Rachel Carson, *Silent Spring* (Boston: Houghton Mifflin, 1962); Tom Hayden, "Port Huron Statement," in James Miller, *Democracy Is in the*

Streets: From Port Huron to the Siege of Chicago (Cambridge, Mass.: Harvard University Press, 1994), 329–74; and James Baldwin, *The Fire Next Time* (New York: Dial Press, 1963).

209   *In his annual one-hour interview*: transcript of May 1, 1963, interview with Walter Lippmann on *CBS Reports*, RAC, Box 10/755.

209   The Malcolm X profile is in M. S. Handler, "Assertive Spirit Stirs Negroes, Puts Vigor in Civil Rights Drive," NYT, April 23, 1963; the *Life* photographs are cited in Branch, *Pillar of Fire*, 97. The Missouri parochial school protests are in *Newsweek*, May 20, 1963.

210   For Diem slaughter, see Francis X. Winters, *The Year of the Hare: America in Vietnam, January 25, 1963–February 15, 1964* (Athens: University of Georgia Press, 1997), 29. Kuchel's "fright mail" speech: Senator Thomas Kuchel, "The Plot to Destroy America," NYTM, July 21, 1963.

210   For the UN takeover rumor, see Kuchel and "The Rampant Right Invades the GOP," *Look*, July 16, 1963.

211   My sources for the Boston school controversy are J. Anthony Lucas, *Common Ground: A Turbulent Decade in the Lives of Three American Families* (New York: Knopf, 1985); and Ronald Formisano, *Boston against Busing: Race, Class, and Ethnicity in the 1960s and 1970s* (Chapel Hill: University of North Carolina Press, 1991).

212   The June 11, 1963, meeting is described in Lucas, *Common Ground*, 124.

212   The ensuing negotiations are in Lucas, 125. *"Our schools and our public officials"*: ibid., 127.

212   The Carl Sanders quote is in "While Most Believe in God," *Newsweek*, July 9, 1962. The Orange County electronics executive is in *Time*, December 8, 1961. Clark Kerr is quoted in Milton Viorst, *Fire in the Streets: America in the 1960s* (New York: Simon and Schuster, 1979), 277.

213   For press coverage of the self-immolation in Vietnam, see Stanley Karnow, *Vietnam: A History* (New York: Viking, 1983), 281. The scene in Sunflower County is Charles Marsh, *God's Long Summer: Stories of Faith and Civil Rights* (Princeton, N.J.: Princeton University Press, 1997), 18–24. For the construction protests in Harlem and Philadelphia, see Reeves, *Question of Character*, 357.

213   For the Berkeley ordinance, see Max Heirich, *The Spiral of Conflict: Berkeley, 1964* (New York: Columbia University Press, 1968), 85. For Ted Humes, see F. Clifton White with William Gill, *Suite 3505: The Story of the Draft Goldwater Movement* (New Rochelle, N.Y.: Arlington House, 1967), 236; and "CONFIDENTIAL" Humes survey, August 25, 1963, FCW, Box 8/Polish-American Population poll. *U.S. News editor David Lawrence reported*: David Lawrence column, SLPD, June 12, 1963. *Stewart Alsop traveled the North*: Stewart Alsop column, SEP, July 11, 1964. White's campaign plan is in FCW, Box 8.

214   The June 25, 1963, Clayton memo is in DK, Box 4/Draft Goldwater Endeavor.

214   *Goldwater was receiving so much mail*: Kitchel to BMG, July 1, 1963, AHF, Box 21/11. Texas rallies are described in White with Gill, *Suite 3505*, 157; Ralph de Toledano, *The Winning Side: The Case for Goldwater Republicanism* (New York:

MacFadden-Bartel, 1963), 107; and William Rusher, *The Rise of the Right* (New York: Morrow, 1984), 156. The Montgomery County, Maryland, rally is noted in Shafto to White, May 27, 1963, FCW, Box 19/Rally. Move to Washington suggested in O'Donnell to White, May 24, 1963, FCW, Box 18/Congressional Contacts. South Carolina county chairmen meeting is reported in press release, May 25, 1963, DK, Box 4/Draft Goldwater Endeavor. For the change in rally venue, see Chappel to White, May 20, 1963, FCW, Box 19/California. *"A surprising number"*: White with Gill, *Suite 3505*, 162. The *Time* cover is June 14, 1963.

215   *"Fine," White responded*: White with Gill, *Suite 3505*, 163.

215   *Ringing, Joe Alsop wrote*: undated clip in WAR, Box 154/7. *Which strategy, the Herald Tribune said, amounted to*: "Keep the Party Republican," NYHT July 2, 1963. For general description of Denver meeting, see White with Gill, *Suite 3505*, 163–65 (for Evans and Novak quote); and Robert Novak, *The Agony of the GOP 1964* (New York: Macmillan, 1965), 179 (for "South Africa" quote).

215   *Len Nadasdy had spent 1962*: *Young Republican National Federation: A Record of Accomplishment*, pamphlet, LN. *Hutar and Harff, meanwhile*: See correspondence in FCW, Box 18/Young Republicans, especially Rehmann to Failor, January 29, 1963. *Yet when Bruce Chapman*: NYHTEN, July 17, 1963. For Nadasdy, see memos marked "CONFIDENTIAL," April 17, 1961, to October 19, 1963, LN.

216   My reconstruction of the 1963 Young Republicans' convention is based on Morton C. Blackwell, "The 1963 Young Republican and College Republican National Conventions in San Francisco," paper draft, AC; White with Gill, *Suite 3505*, 166–73; Novak, *Agony of the GOP*, 196–201; *Time*, July 8, 1963; *Look*, July 16, 1963; NYHTEN in WAR, Box 154/7; reports to chairman from Massachusetts, Connecticut, North Dakota, Delaware, and Maryland delegations in LN; clips in LN, including NYT, June 28, 1963, *Minneapolis Tribune*, July 7, 1963, *Political Intelligence*, July 1963, WS, June 30, 1963, SFC, June 28, 1963, Drew Pearson in WP, July 19, 1963, and "Old Friends" pamphlet; exchange of letters between BMG and Nadasdy in LN; Nadasdy to author, August 23, 1998, and October 4, 1998; and author interviews with Leonard Nadasdy, John Savage, and Robert Gaston.

219   BMG speech is in *Congressional Record*, July 29, 1963, 12732–34.

221   *"Why not do it now"*: Nadasdy to BMG, August 8, 1963, LN.

222   For O'Donnell's doubts, see handwritten notes, FCW, Box 18/July 4, 1963 Rally. For Billy Graham, Eisenhower, and JFK at D.C. Armory, see William Martin, *With God on Our Side: The Rise of the Religious Right in America* (New York: Broadway Books, 1996), 30; and Lee Edwards, *Goldwater: The Man Who Made a Revolution* (Washington, D.C.: Regnery, 1995), 180. *Shortly before curtain time*: handwritten notes, FCW, Box 18/July 4, 1963 Rally.

222   For chartered buses, see Theodore H. White, *The Making of the President 1964* (New York: Atheneum, 1965), 117. Fifty-six buses came from New York and Connecticut alone. For the event I rely on USN, July 15, 1963; Mary McGrory and David Broder in WS, July 5, 1963; *Baltimore Sun*, July 5, 1963; schedule in FCW, Box 18/July 4, 1963 Rally; and author interview with Lee Edwards. For Charles Percy, see White with Gill, *Suite 3505*, 187. For Krock, see NYT, July 6, 1963.

222   For California poll, see LAT, July 29, 1963. For Pennsylvania, see White with Gill, *Suite 3505*, 178.

222   *On Independence Day in Chicago*: WP, July 5, 1963, A1; and Mike Royko, *Boss: Richard J. Daley of Chicago* (New York: Signet, 1971), 134. For the attempt to integrate Mayor Daley's neighborhood, see Royko, 139. *"The Polish-American community"*: "CONFIDENTIAL" Humes survey, August 25, 1963, FCW, Box 8/Polish-American Population Poll.

223   For Barnett and Wallace at Commerce Committee hearings and administration response, see H. W. Brand, *The Devil We Knew: Americans and the Cold War* (New York: Oxford University Press, 1993), 111; Carter, *Politics of Rage*, 157; and Branch, *Parting the Waters*, 853.

223   The Bastille Day declaration: Novak, *Agony of the GOP*, 207.

223   The *Look* article ran in the July 16, 1963, issue.

224   For Bastille Day statement transcript, see NYT, July 15, 1963.

225   *"Our party is in no position"*: Novak, *Agony of the GOP*, 213. Keating's statement is in transcript of July 15, 1963, WCBS radio and TV interview, RAC, Box 10/757. The *Newsweek* quote is July 29, 1963.

225   *"My God, we'd be the* apartheid *party"*: Stewart Alsop, "Can Goldwater Win in '64?," SEP, August 24, 1963. For Robinson, see Jackie Robinson, "The GOP: For White Men Only?," SEP, August 10, 1963. *"Barry doesn't know any more"*: Richard Reston, "A Top Republican Attacks Goldwater," SFC, n.d. clip in WAR, Box 154/7.

225   *The Harris poll had reported*: WP, August 26, 1963.

225   *"People fail to realize"*: "Goldwater the Arizonan Rides Easy," *Life*, November 1, 1963. *Newsweek soon ran a lead story*: "The Block-Goldwater Movement in the GOP," July 22, 1963.

226   *"You know, I think we ought to sell the TVA"*: SEP, August 24, 1963. For the Fulton exchange, see White with Gill, *Suite 3505*, 225; and Stephen Shadegg, *What Happened to Goldwater?: The Inside Story of the 1964 Republican Campaign* (New York: Holt, Rinehart, and Winston, 1965), 218. O'Donnell's memo is in White with Gill, *Suite 3505*, 226. The telegrams are in Novak, *Agony of the GOP*, 240.

226   White's 200,000 one-dollar petition signatures are noted in "Many in GOP See Goldwater in '64," NYT, August 26, 1963. Other fund-raising efforts: Congressional Quarterly, *The Public Records of Barry M. Goldwater and William E. Miller: The Lives, Votes and Stands of the 1964 Republican Candidates* (Washington, D.C.: Congressional Quarterly Service, 1964). *"A few race riots in the North"*: SEP, August 24, 1963.

227   For the 20 percent figure, see GP, 1836. *"I'd kill," a white South Dakota housewife*: *Newsweek*, October 21, 1963.

227   Quotes and poll numbers from *Newsweek*, October 21, 1963. *"It is an oft-repeated statement"*: Blanche Saunders, *Training You to Train Your Dog* (Garden City, N.Y.: Doubleday, 1965). *Harper's John Fischer congratulated himself*: John Fischer, "What the Negro Needs Most," Francis M. Carney and Frank H. Way, *Politics 1964* (Belmont, Calif.: Wadsworth, 1964), 245–53.

227   For fears about the march as the event approached, see Branch, *Pillar of Fire*, 131–32; and Reeves, *Question of Character*, 358.

228   The 50 percent figure on civil rights is from GP, 1832. *"Only when Christ comes again"*: LAT, August 10, 1963.

228   For the order to overthrow the Diem government, see Winters, *Year of the Hare*, 65–73. For half-hour Cronkite debut, see Branch, *Pillar of Fire*, 133.

228   For Gallup figures, see Edwards, *Goldwater*, 191. SEE THE JAPS ALMOST GET KENNEDY!: Peter O'Donnell, "Progress Report #2," September 25, 1963, WAR, Box 155/7. *"He's stirred up all the colored people"*: Newsweek, October 21, 1963. KAYO THE KENNEDYS!: Carter, *Politics of Rage*, 210. *"KENNEDY FOR KING—GOLDWATER FOR PRESIDENT"*: Summer 1982 special issue of *The Keynoter,* "A Choice, Not an Echo: The 1964 Campaign of Barry Goldwater."

229   *Polls suggested as much as 5 percent*: Jerome Himmelstein, *To the Right: The Transformation of American Conservatism* (Berkeley: University of California Press, 1992), 67. The report to the President is noted in John A. Andrew III, *The Other Side of the Sixties: Young Americans for Freedom and the Rise of Conservative Politics* (New Brunswick, N.J.: Rutgers University Press, 1997), 168; for the IRS audits, see ibid., 162–63.

229   The September 12, 1963, press conference is described by Robert J. Donovan, "North Racial Tensions Rise," LAT, February 16, 1964.

229   For Wallace and the Sixteenth Street Baptist Church bombing, see Carter, *Politics of Rage*, 174–82. For the decision against the perpetrators, see Branch, *Pillar of Fire*, 143.

229   For Cronkite's half hour with BMG, see transcript in RAC, Box 10/763. On the Mark Hopkins Hotel, see "Goldwater Reserves 51 Rooms in Hotel for GOP Convention," NYT, September 6, 1963. For Dr. Schwarz, see Fred J. Cook, "The Ultras: Aims, Affiliations, and Finances of the Radical Right," special issue, *The Nation*, June 30, 1962. For Kleindienst's conclusions, see Gilbert A. Harrison, "Way Out West: An Interim Report on Barry Goldwater," TNR, November 23, 1963. For Saltonstall, see *Boston Traveler* clip in scrapbook in WAR, Box 154/7.

230   For BMG tour, see Jack Bell AP report, *Dallas Times Herald*, September 2, 1963, and September 16, 1963; NBC documentary "The Loyal Opposition," transcript in RAC, Box 10/765. *"You leave me alone"*: White with Gill, *Suite 3505*, 223; George H. Mayer, *The Republican Party 1854–1966* (New York: Oxford University Press, 1967), 531.

230   For the Ogle County Fair, see Novak, *Agony of the GOP*, 224; NBC, "The Loyal Opposition"; and White with Gill, *Suite 3505*, 209. For NFRW convention, see ibid., 211; and Carol Felsenthal, *Sweetheart of the Silent Majority: The Biography of Phyllis Schlafly* (New York: Doubleday, 1981), 168.

230   For fund-raising, see White with Gill, *Suite 3505*, 191–92. For Youth for Goldwater: ibid., 209; and author interview with Carol Dawson.

231   For Dodger Stadium rally: *Time*, September 27, 1963; Edwards, *Goldwater*, 151; and author interview with Robert Gaston. For sabotage attempt, see Royal to Kitchel, May 21, 1963, AHF, Box 13/29.

231   *"Almost everybody in Washington"*: James Reston, NYT, September 26, 1963. *Mary McGrory followed Goldwater back to Washington*: *Time*, September 27, 1963.

231   On the American friendship with the atom, see Allan M. Winkler, *Life Under a Cloud: American Anxiety About the Atom* (New York: Oxford University Press, 1993), 27–28. For airborne test broadcast, see ibid., 91. For Project Plowshare, see Dan O'Neill, *The Firecracker Boys* (New York: St. Martin's Press, 1994).

231   For public awareness of nuclear fallout, see Winkler, *Life Under a Cloud*, 84–108; Ralph E. Lapp, "Civil Defense Faces New Perils" (1954), and W. K. Wynant Jr., "50,000 Baby Teeth" (1959), both in Robert C. Williams and Philip L. Cantelon, eds., *The American Atom: A Documentary History of Nuclear Policies from the Discovery of Fission to the Present, 1939–1984* (Philadelphia: University of Pennsylvania Press, 1991). Conservatives tended to dismiss the fallout problem as Communist propaganda. See Barry Goldwater, *Conscience of a Conservative* (Shepherdsville, Ky.: Victor Publishing, 1960), 113.

232   For test-ban negotiations and signing, see Reeves, *Question of Character*, 396. BMG's speech is reprinted in White with Gill, *Suite 3505*, 425–28.

232   For BMG's California advisory committee, see LAT, September 20, 1963, and September 21, 1963. White's visit with Goldwater: White with Gill, *Suite 3505*, 214–15.

232   For Lippmann, see Eric Alterman, *Sound and Fury: The Washington Punditocracy and the Collapse of American Politics* (New York: HarperPerennial, 1992), 21–44; and, for Scopes "monkey trial," see Ronald Steel, *Walter Lippmann and the American Century* (Boston: Little, Brown, 1980), 216–19.

233   For Eichmann, see Anthony Grafton, "Arendt and Eichmann at the Dinner Table," *American Scholar* (Winter 1999); and Hannah Arendt, *Eichmann in Jerusalem: A Report on the Banality of Evil* (New York: Viking, 1963). *"The most essential criterion"*: Dennis H. Wrong, *The Modern Condition: Essays at Century's End* (Stanford, Calif.: Stanford University Press, 1998), 35.

233   For this interpretation of Warren's *All the King's Men*, see Alan Brinkley, "Robert Penn Warren, T. Harry Williams, and Huey Long," in Brinkley, *Liberalism and Its Discontents* (Cambridge, Mass.: Harvard University Press, 1998). The quote on the Stevenson demonstration is in Theodore H. White, *The Making of the President 1960* (New York: Atheneum, 1961), 182.

233   *"Each party is like some huge bazaar"*: Daniel Bell, "Interpretations of American Politics," in Daniel Bell, ed., *The New American Right* (New York: Criterion Books, 1955). *Goldwater's candidacy "strikes at the heart"*: *Newsweek*, August 5, 1963.

234   *"It is interesting to watch him"*: *Time*, September 27, 1963. *"A fascinating political biological process"*: "TRB from Washington: The New Goldwater," TNR, September 23, 1963. Other lemmings: "Goldwater's Trend to the Center," SFC, September 21, 1963; Robert S. Boyd, "Barry Softens His Conservatism," *Detroit Free Press*, September 17, 1963; "I, too, am a middle-of-the-roader," editorial cartoon, *Detroit Free Press*, October 6, 1963; and James MacGregor Burns on David Susskind's *Open End*, October 20, 1963, WPIX-TV, transcript in RAC, Box 10/770.

234   For correction, see *Congressional Record*, October 1, 1963. *"Profits are the surest sign of responsible behavior"*: ibid., September 20, 1963. *"Barry Goldwater could give Kennedy"*: *Time*, October 4, 1963. *Look ran the banner* JFK COULD LOSE: *Look*, December 18, 1963. For reaction to Lasky book, see "Man or Myth?," *Newsweek*, September 23, 1963. *At a party celebrating the opening*: O'Donnell to Hinman, November 11, 1963, RAC, Box 12/948.

234   For JFK's "conservation trip," see White with Gill, *Suite 3505*, 233; and "Non-Political Tour," political cartoon, WS, September 26, 1963. For speeches, see PPP: JFK, 707–49.

235   *The Democratic National Committee had filled*: WP, October 2, 1963. Frank Church speech is in *Time*, September 27, 1963. Midwestern States meeting is in *Detroit News*, October 6, 1963. For Shriver's political errands, see White with Gill, *Suite 3505*, 241. Martin Luther King's concerns are in Branch, *Parting the Waters*, 863.

236   For JFK's plunging fortunes, see "The Polls: Kennedy As President," *Public Opinion Quarterly* (Summer 1964): 334–35. For Hicks and Boston: Lucas, *Common Ground*, 128–30 (for quote); and Formisano, *Boston Against Busing*, 22–30.

236   *Evans and Novak called her victory*: NYHTEN, October 3, 1963. For DNC registration drive, see White, *Making of the President 1964*, 309. For pro- and anti-integration demonstrations in New York, see Diane Ravitch, *The Great School Wars* (New York: Basic Books, 1974), 250–73.

236   For Albany protests and NAR quote, see interview in USNWR, September 23, 1963. For the examples of de facto discrimination in building trades, see Samuel G. Freedman, *The Inheritance: How Three Families and the American Political Majority Moved from Left to Right* (New York: Touchstone, 1996), 205–8.

237   For Paul Johnson's victory, see Branch, *Pillar of Fire*, 162. George Wallace's appearance at Harvard is in Carter, *Politics of Rage*, 196–99. On the Berkeley Jaycees, see Branch, *Pillar of Fire*, 494. For Berkeley activism, see Heirich, *Spiral of Conflict*, 85. For "Willis Wagons," see Royko, *Boss*, 142–43.

237   The October 31, 1963, press conference is at MTR, T83:0538.

237   The November 12, 1963, JFK campaign meeting is noted in Arthur Schlesinger Jr., *A Thousand Days* (Boston: Houghton Mifflin, 1965), 1018. For Norris Cotton, see transcript of *Capital Cloakroom*, October 20, 1963, RAC, Box 10/769; and *Open End*, RAC, Box 10/770. For Pennsylvania rally, see White with Gill, *Suite 3505*, 220–22. *"Barry Goldwater represents a valuable"*: "Barry Goldwater's Foreign Policy: Let's Hear More," *Life*, November 1, 1963.

238   *"Except for civil-rights troubles"*: *Newsweek*, October 21, 1963. *A Look feature was headlined*: *Look*, November 18, 1963. *" 'God willin' I won't vote"*: *Time*, September 27, 1963.

238   For Heller's poverty program, see Branch, *Pillar of Fire*, 175.

238   For Diem coup, see Winters, *Year of the Hare*, 91–113. For *New York Times* exposé, see review of Max Frankel, *The Time of My Life*, in *The Nation*, April 22, 1999.

NOTES

239   For JFK's unpopularity in Texas, see White with Gill, *Suite 3505*, 244. For fund-raising trip plans, see Jane Jarboe, *Lady Bird: A Comprehensive Biography of Mrs. Johnson* (New York: Simon and Schuster, 1999), 214–17.

239   On Richardson, see Richard Whalen, *Fortune*, December 1963. For UN Day, see "A City Disgraced," *Time*, November 1, 1963; and Warren Leslie, *Dallas Public and Private* (New York: Grossman, 1964), 188–99. For H. L. Hunt broadcasts, see Jerome Tuccille, *Kingdom: The Story of the Hunt Family of Texas* (Ottawa, Ill.: Jameson Books, 1984), 282.

240   For "Case History of a Rumor," see LAT, February 25, 1963. For the American Legion magazine, see GRR, January 15, 1964.

240   For CORE protests, see "CORE Pickets Freed of Contempt Charges," LAT, January 18, 1964. For Otepka developments, see White with Gill, *Suite 3505*, 242; and October 31, 1963, JFK press conference, MTR, T83:0538. The bombing at the University of Alabama is described in Carter, *Politics of Rage*, 238. For UNICEF boxes, see Gerald Schomp, *Birchism Was My Business* (New York: Macmillan, 1970), 98.

240   For Cuban rifle, see Michael Beschloss, ed., *Taking Charge: The Johnson White House Tapes, 1963–1964* (New York: Simon and Schuster, 1997), 87. JFK's Florida trip is in Branch, *Pillar of Fire*, 166. For *JFK: The Man and the Myth*, see NYT *Book Review*, November 24, 1963; for *The Winning Side*, see *Publishers Weekly*, November 12, 1963.

241   *"Don't let the President come"*: Pierre Salinger, *With Kennedy* (Garden City, N.Y.: Doubleday, 1966), 1. For Nixon trip, see Christopher Matthews, *Kennedy and Nixon: The Rivalry That Shaped Postwar America* (New York: Touchstone, 1996), 235.

241   The WANTED FOR TREASON handbill is reprinted in GRR, October 31, 1964. *"If the speech is about boating"*: Salinger, *With Kennedy*, 143. For the full-page ad in the *Dallas Morning News*, see Warren Commission, *Report on the President's Commission on the Assassination of President John F. Kennedy* (New York: St. Martin's Press, 1964), 292–96.

242   *"In dictatorships," he said*: Tuccille, *Kingdom*, 282. *The Morning News was joined on the newsstand*: Theodore White, "Rushing to a Showdown That No Law Can Chart," *Life*, November 22, 1963; White, "The Angry U.S. Negro's Rallying Cries Are Confusing His Just and Urgent Cause," *Life*, November 29, 1963.

242   The (intended) Dallas Trade Mart speech is reproduced in PPP: JFK, 890–94. The (delivered) Fort Worth speech: ibid., 888–90.

12. NEW MOOD IN POLITICS

247   For the scene at Draft Goldwater headquarters, I rely on an author interview with Lee Edwards, and Lee Edwards, *Goldwater: The Man Who Made a Revolution* (Washington, D.C.: Regnery, 1995), 196.

247   Kitchel and Smith's cab ride is in Robert Novak, *The Agony of the GOP 1964* (New York: Macmillan, 1965), 251.

247   Nixon's cab ride is in Richard Nixon, *RN: The Memoirs of Richard Nixon*, vol. I (New York: Warner Books, 1978), 312.

247   *The Voice of America's bulletin*: Arthur Krock column, NYT, November 26, 1963. *Clips of Adlai Stevenson*: Lee Edwards, *The Conservative Revolution: The Movement That Remade America* (New York: Free Press, 1999), 114. *Under the headline "DALLAS, LONG A RADICAL'S HAVEN,"*: NYHT, November 23, 1963. For John Tower, see F. Clifton White with William Gill, *Suite 3505: The Story of the Draft Goldwater Movement* (New Rochelle, N.Y.: Arlington House, 1967), 246. *Senator Maurine Neuberger of Oregon*: Jerome Tuccille, *Kingdom: The Story of the Hunt Family of Texas* (Ottawa, Ill.: Jameson Books, 1984), 283. *Walter Cronkite, on the air nonstop*: Barry Goldwater, *The Conscience of a Majority* (Englewood Cliffs, N.J.: Prentice-Hall, 1970), 178. *A deranged gunman pumped two shots*: NYT, November 24, 1963. *In man-in-the-street interviews*: ibid.

248   *"I am now satisfied that the climate of political degeneracy"*: The Nation, May 24, 1964. For Max Lerner and Bishop Pike, see Edwin McDowell, *Barry Goldwater: Portrait of an Arizonan* (Chicago: Regnery, 1964), 190.

248   For LBJ's Moscow fears and hurried convening of the Warren panel, see Michael Beschloss, ed., *Taking Charge: The Johnson White House Tapes, 1963–1964* (New York: Simon and Schuster, 1997), 31, 46–72.

249   *"I know that very often"*: cited in letter to the editor, CT, January 1, 1964. *"The savage nuts have destroyed the great myth"*: Douglas Brinkley, ed., *The Fear and Loathing Letters*, vol. I (New York: Villard, 1997), xxi. *Chief Justice Warren—a prominent target*: Beschloss, ed., *Taking Charge*, 64.

249   The classic statement of the Southern concept of liberalism as liberality is Ryhs L. Isaac, *The Transformation of Virginia, 1740–1790* (Chapel Hill: University of North Carolina Press, 1982). My account of the development of LBJ's liberalism in the context of Southwest history is drawn from Lloyd C. Gardner, "From the Colorado to the Mekong," in Lloyd C. Gardner and Ted Gittinger, eds., *Vietnam: The Early Decisions* (Austin: University of Texas Press, 1997), 37–57.

250   For the Employment Act of 1946, see Robert M. Collins, "Growth Liberalism in the Sixties: Great Societies at Home and Grand Designs Abroad," in David Farber, ed., *The Sixties: From Memory to History* (Chapel Hill: University of North Carolina Press, 1994). *The Dallas Morning News marveled*: John Kessel, *The Goldwater Coalition: Republican Strategies in 1964* (Indianapolis: Bobbs-Merrill, 1968), 253.

250   LBJ's limiting of contested votes is in Richard Franklin Bensel, *Sectionalism and American Political Development, 1880–1980* (Madison: University of Wisconsin Press, 1984), 191. See also the incisive account of LBJ's legislative strategy in Ellen Proxmire, *One Foot in Washington: The Perilous Life of a Senator's Wife* (Washington, D.C.: R. B. Luce, 1964), 24. For an excellent description of "The Treatment," see Alan Brinkley, *Liberalism and Its Discontents* (Cambridge, Mass.: Harvard University Press, 1998), 204.

251   For the Teddy White interview with Jackie Kennedy, see Christopher Matthews, *Kennedy and Nixon: The Rivalry That Shaped Postwar America* (New York: Touchstone, 1996), 243. For best-sellers, see WP *Book Week*, January 12, 1964.

251   For LBJ's martyr epiphany and the "Let Us Continue" speech, see Robert Dallek, *Flawed Giant: Lyndon Johnson and His Times, 1961–1973* (New York: Oxford University Press, 1998), 56, 63; for text, see PPP: LBJ, 8–10.

251   *The hottest political book of 1963*: John MacGregor Burns, *The Deadlock of Democracy: Four-Party Politics in America* (Englewood Cliffs, N.J.: Prentice-Hall, 1963). For wheat sale amendment, see Thomas C. Reeves, *A Question of Character: A Life of John F. Kennedy* (New York: Free Press, 1991), 403; Beschloss, ed., *Taking Charge*, 37; and Dallek, *Flawed Giant*, 70. His budget demand is in Dallek, 72.

252   For Johnson's two abiding humiliations, see Jeff Shesol, *Mutual Contempt: Lyndon Johnson, Robert Kennedy, and the Feud that Defined a Decade* (New York: Norton, 1997), 15, 88–113. LBJ's calls for guidance are in Beschloss, ed., *Taking Charge*, 19–21.

252   For new strategic calculations and "proper Republican" quote, see Novak, *Agony of the GOP*, 252. For polls see GP, 1857.

253   For Lodge, DDE, and NYT, see William J. Miller, *Henry Cabot Lodge: A Biography* (New York: Heineman, 1967), 355; and Felix Belair Jr., "Eisenhower Urges Lodge to Pursue GOP Nomination," NYT, December 8, 1963.

253   For Nixon's trip to Gettysburg, see Miller, *Henry Cabot Lodge*, 355. For book deal and cancellation, see Rowland Evans and Robert Novak, "The Unmaking of a President," *Esquire*, November 1964. For post-assassination politicking, see Evans and Novak; December 6, 1963, speech transcript in RAC, Box 10/775; and White with Gill, *Suite 3505*, 240.

253   *"I'm still wishing something"*: Time, November 22, 1963. For injury and depression, see Novak, *Agony of the GOP*, 266. *He wrote people like the editor*: Author interview with Allan Ryskind. For JFK and BMG's displays of affection and campaign proposal, see Gilbert A. Harrison, "Way Out West: An Interim Report on Barry Goldwater," TNR, November 23, 1963; and Stephen Shadegg, *What Happened to Goldwater?: The Inside Story of the 1964 Republican Campaign* (New York: Holt, Rinehart, and Winston), 81.

254   About BMG's love of flying, see, for example, *Newsweek*, April 10, 1961; for ham radio, *Time*, June 14, 1963; jazz and trombone, *Time*, March 22, 1963, Jack Paar show appearance, AHFAV, BG-C/2; for *Indian Art of the Americas* and air-conditioning, James M. Perry, *A Report in Depth on Barry Goldwater: The Story of the 1964 Republican Presidential Nominee* (Silver Spring, Md.: National Observer, 1964); about his Thunderbird, *Newsweek*, April 10, 1961; regarding the Senate machine shop, John B. Judis, *William F. Buckley, Jr.: Patron Saint of the Conservatives* (New York: Touchstone, 1990), 172; on the Heathkit, Karl Hess, *Mostly on the Edge: An Autobiography* (Amherst, N.Y.: Prometheus, 1999), 176.

254   *He had a favorite Western maxim*: transcript of Hy Gardner radio show, WOR-New York, September 26, 1963, RAC, Box 10/766. *"Doggone it," he told The Chicago Tribune*: CT, January 3, 1964, A1. *He worried whether he had*: ibid. *What would he be then*: Shadegg, *What Happened*, 79–80.

254   For fund-raising after the assassination, see Frank Kovac, "Finance Highlights Report No. 19," WAR, Box 155/7. For youth telegram campaign I rely on an author

interview with Lee Edwards, and Novak, *Agony of the GOP*, 267. For White's continuing, see Novak, 265; and White with Gill, *Suite 3505*, 252–53.

254   For White's incredulity at Kitchel's political ignorance, see ibid., 199–213. For Kitchel's personality, see Rowland Evans and Robert Novak, "The Men Around Goldwater," SEP, October 24, 1964.

255   *Then Dick Kleindienst began working*: Harrison, "Way Out West." *Then came an administrative assistant*: White with Gill, *Suite 3505*, 202. For Burch biography, see NYHT, July 17, 1964; Novak, *Agony of the GOP*, 247 (for Mississippi rumor); and Evans and Novak, "The Men Around Goldwater" (for black ties). For pride in outsider status I rely especially on author interview with Richard Kleindienst. For clannish style, see Novak, *Agony of the GOP*, 285. For AEI additions to Kitchel office: White with Gill, *Suite 3505*, 201–3, 222–23; Kitchel to Lamp, March 30, 1965, DK, Box 3; Novak, *Agony of the GOP*, 246; and author interview with Charles Lichenstein.

255   For Baroody's approach to Kitchel, see Edwards, *Goldwater*, 182; and author interview with William Rusher. For the *National Review* double cross: Shadegg, *What Happened*, 68–70; Judis, *William F. Buckley*, 183; and author interview with William F. Buckley.

255   For Baroody's personality and character I rely on author interviews with W. Glen Campbell, Milton Friedman, William Rusher, and Charles Lichenstein.

256   For AEI history I rely on James Smith, *The Idea Brokers: Think Tanks and the Rise of the New Policy Elite* (New York: Free Press, 1991); Milton Friedman and Rose Friedman, *Two Lucky People: Memoirs* (Chicago: University of Chicago Press, 1998), 343–45; GRR, April 13, 1964; the notes and documents in Richard Dudman Papers, AEI file, Library of Congress; and Friedman and Campbell interviews.

256   *"I really can't say whether"*: Evans and Novak, "The Men Around Goldwater."

256   For Recordak, see Kessel, *Goldwater Coalition*, 153; White with Gill, *Suite 3505*, 202; and NYHT, January 29, 1964. July 4, 1964. *"Who's Arthur Summerfield?"*: Shadegg, *What Happened*, 65. For the notebook White prepared for Kitchel, see F. Clifton White with Jerome Tuccille, *Politics as a Noble Calling* (Ottawa, Ill.: Jameson Books, 1994), 155. Kitchel's hearing: Evans and Novak, "The Men Around Goldwater."

257   For the meeting in BMG's apartment, see Richard Kleindienst, *Justice: The Memoirs of an Attorney General* (Ottawa, Ill.: Jameson Books, 1985), 31; Edwards, *Goldwater*, 151; Shadegg, *What Happened*, 81; White with Gill, *Suite 3505*, 254; and Edwards interview in A&E Television Network, *Barry Goldwater: The Conscience of Conservatives* (1996, cat. no. AAE-14345).

257   *Draft Goldwater met on December 11*: White with Gill, *Suite 3505*, 256.

258   For the cancellation of White's Phoenix plans, see ibid., 161.

258   For Len Hall and Kitchell, see Novak, *Agony of the GOP*, 245.

258   Kleindienst's trip back from the Rose Bowl is narrated in Kleindienst, *Justice*, 30. DDE's participation, and Kiwanis speech, are in Jon Margolis, *The Last Innocent Year: America in 1964: The Beginning of the "Sixties"* (New York: Morrow, 1999), 64.

259 BMG's joke about his daughter is from author interview with Jameson Campaigne Jr. Other details in McDowell, *Barry Goldwater*, 247; and Male to BMG planning memo, January 3, 1964, AHF, Box 13/51.

259 For BMG's wife on day of announcement, see Harold Faber, ed., *The Road to the White House: The Story of the 1964 Election by the Staff of the New York Times* (New York: McGraw-Hill, 1965), 15. For Margaret Goldwater generally: transcript of interview on *Art Linkletter's House Party*, CBS-TV, April 22, 1964, RAC, Box 10; and Robert Alan Goldberg, *Barry Goldwater* (New Haven, Conn.: Yale University Press, 1995), 115. *"If that's what you want"*: White with Gill, *Suite 3505*, 255.

259 *Kleindienst handed over his keys*: Kleindienst, *Justice*, 31; Kleindienst interview.

259 For Shadegg's Senate run and purge from Goldwater circle, see Shadegg, *What Happened*, 54; *Arizona Journal*, March 29, 1962, and April 3, 1962; NYT, September 7, 1962; and *Time*, September 7, 1962.

260 *"He'd get more space"*: Frank Cormier, *LBJ the Way He Was: A Personal Memoir* (Garden City, N.Y.: Doubleday, 1977), 32. Advice to announce from Washington noted in Shadegg, *What Happened*, 86.

260 Goldwater's meeting with Arizona Republican leaders, and his entrance onto patio, is narrated by radio announcer Ray Curtis, transcribed in RAC, Box 10/779; see also Faber, ed., *Road to the White House*, 15; Margolis, *Last Innocent Year*, 78; Perry, *A Report in Depth on Barry Goldwater*; announcement in LAT, January 3, 1964, A1; and footage in A&E Television Network, *Barry Goldwater*.

260 For press conference, see RAC, Box 10/779.

261 *"At the LBJ Ranch, meanwhile"*: Cormier, *LBJ the Way He Was*, 32. For Gallup poll and Heller statistics, see Margolis, *Last Innocent Year*, 91.

261 *"I am neither a summer soldier"*: LAT, January 4, 1964.

261 For the NAR-Nixon meeting see Nixon, *RN*, 310.

262 For NAR's November 7, 1963, announcement see Faber, ed., *Road to the White House*, 22; Novak, *Agony of the GOP*, 254; and Kessel, *Goldwater Coalition*, 45. For Maryland Republicans and McKeldin quote, see James Reston column, November 3, 1963. For Miami and St. Louis: *Time*, November 22, 1963.

262 For APSA, West Virginia, and the Indiana Bar Association, see RAC, Box 12/946. For Illinois visit, see Novak, *Agony of the GOP*, 224; for California visit, see speeches and "Dear News Editor" in RAC, Box 11/938. For audience with the Pope, see James Desmond, *Nelson Rockefeller: A Political Biography* (New York: Macmillan, 1964), 67. For cross-country staff, see Martin to Middendorf, May 5, 1964, FCW, Box 8/Wm. Middendorf. Memo on lighting is Danzig to NAR, January 14, 1964, RAC, Box 11/939.

262 For opposition research office, sources are author interview with Graham T. T. Molitor; BMG transcripts from April 1963 through June 1964 in RAC, Box 10; Molitor speech analyses in RAC, Box 11; and Issues Binder, Box 11/929.

263 For California public relations politics and Spencer-Roberts, see Bill Boyarsky, *The Rise of Ronald Reagan* (New York: Random House, 1968), 106; Gary Wills, *Reagan's America* (New York: Penguin, 1988), 292; Theodore H. White, *The Mak-*

ing of the President 1964 (New York: Atheneum, 1965), 150; and Walton to White, FCW, Box 8/Rus Walton. For Hinman's approach, see Walton to White, November 1, 1963, FCW, Box 8/Rus Walton. For Rocky closing the deal, see Danzig expense voucher, October 29, 1963, RAC, Box 11/933; "Dear News Editor" letter in Box 11/938; and George Hinman press release, November 14, 1963, Box 11. For $2 million budget, see Goldberg, *Barry Goldwater*, 190. For billboards, see Begg to White, January 17, 1964, FCW, Box 8/Baus and Ross.

264   For NAR delegates, see White, *Making of the President 1964*, 149. For Kuchel's reluctance, see Kessel, *Goldwater Coalition*, 80. For his statement: NYHT, January 28, 1964, and statement for release January 28, 1964, RAC, Box 11/939.

264   For delegates' fear of zealots, see Kessel, *Goldwater Coalition*, 81. *"There is a new wind blowing"*: Richard Whalen, *Fortune*, December 1963.

13. GRANITE STATE

265   *"COMPANY PROFITS ASTOUND EXPERTS"*: NYT, January 6, 1964. *"UCLA PUPILS NOT RADICAL"*: LAT, January 12, 1964. *In Washington, Labor Secretary Willard Wirtz*: LAT, January 1, 1964, op-ed. *The Los Angeles Times was also obliged*: LAT, January 2, 1964. For 1964 Mummers' Parade: CT, January 1, 1964, A1; LAT, January 5, 1964, A22. The magistrate said halting the parade would "do irrevocable harm to a tradition that dates back more than 100 years." He perhaps wasn't aware that the tradition began as an annual excuse for whites to terrorize Philadelphia's free blacks. See David Roediger, *The Wages of Whiteness: Race and the Making of the American Working Class* (New York: Verso, 1991), 105–9. This year they merely chanted insults directed at the president of the NAACP into ABC's cameras.

265   *There was the usual background noise*: For Chou En-lai, see LAT, January 5, 1964, A22; for Ceylon, LAT, January 2, 1964, A27; for allies selling to Cuba, LAT, February 10, 1964; for France recognizing China, LAT, February 13, 1964. *"It's been a generation or more"*: "Newsgram," USN, December 30, 1963.

266   For *Meet the Press* journey and studio scene, see Robert Novak, *The Agony of the GOP 1964* (New York: Macmillan, 1965), 279. Transcript is in DK, Box 4/*Meet the Press*.

266   For Len Hall quote, see NYHTEN, January 22, 1964.

267   For Michigan airport demonstration, see CT, January 5, 1964. For hiring of Viguerie and move to Washington: author interview with Viguerie, William Rusher, *The Rise of the Right* (New York: Morrow, 1984), 75; and Ivan Sinclair to Dr. Keating, January 8, 1964: LBJWHNG. *One letter to donors brought in $10,000*: "Dear Friend," January 18, 1963, FCW, Box 19/YAF. For five hundred new members figure, see Matthew Dallek, "Young Americans for Freedom, 1960–1964" (master's thesis, Columbia University, 1993), 55.

267   Michigan speech transcript: RAC, Box 10/781.

267   For departure from Michigan, see Novak, *Agony of the GOP*, 310.

268   For New Hampshire itinerary, see William Gill memo, FCW, Box 8/Briefing Notebook—New Hampshire.

268   For arrival, see "Fastest Gun," *Newsweek*, January 20, 1964; and F. Clifton

White with William Gill, *Suite 3505: The Story of the Draft Goldwater Movement* (New Rochelle, N.Y.: Arlington House, 1967), 284.

268　For Kefauver and the New Hampshire primary catechism, see Novak, *Agony of the GOP*, 301.

268　My sources for William Loeb and the *Manchester Union Leader* are Eric P. Veblen, *The Manchester Union Leader in New Hampshire Elections* (Hanover, N.H.: University Press of New England, 1975); "That Stinking Hypocrite," *Time*, May 20, 1957 (for McCarthy headline); *The Nation*, April 26, 1999; and *Life*, November 1, 1963. For quotes about NAR, see *Manchester Union Leader*, July 1, 1963, 1.

269　For the advice of O'Donnell and Moley, see Lee Edwards, *Goldwater: The Man Who Made a Revolution* (Washington, D.C.: Regnery, 1995), 205. For Loeb, see Edwards, "The Unforgettable Candidate," NR, July 6, 1998. White's briefing book is noted in White with Gill, *Suite 3505*, 287; copy in FCW, Box 8/Briefing Notebook—New Hampshire.

269　Opening January 8, 1964, press conference is in RAC, Box 10/782.

269　*At the Concord Monitor*: Novak, *Agony of the GOP*, 311. *"Barry Goldwater, aspirant"*: NYT, January 9, 1964.

270　For Nashua and Amherst home visits and Rotary Club: NYT, January 9, 1964, A32; *Newsweek*, January 20, 1964. For St. Anselm's: White with Gill, *Suite 3505*, 285.

270　Post–State of the Union address press conference is in RAC, Box 10/786. McNamara's response: NYT, January 10, 1964.

271　*"I think both 'em went to extremes"*: LBJ and Russell conversation, 11:25 a.m., January 10, 1964, LBJT 6401.10/26. For Stennis, see January 10, 1964, BMG statement, FSA, Box 4.

271　The culture clash between the Pentagon and JFK/LBJ Administrations is examined in George C. Herring, "Conspiracy of Silence: LBJ, the Joint Chiefs, and Escalation of the War in Vietnam," in Gardner and Ted Gittinger, eds., *Vietnam: The Early Decisions* (Austin: University of Texas Press, 1997); H. R. McMaster, *Dereliction of Duty: Lyndon Johnson, Robert McNamara, the Joint Chiefs of Staff, and the Lies That Led to Vietnam* (New York: HarperCollins, 1997); Ernest R. May and Philip D. Zelikow, eds., *The Kennedy Tapes: Inside the White House During the Cuba Missile Crisis* (Cambridge, Mass.: Harvard University Press, 1997), 1–43; Curtis LeMay, *Mission with LeMay: My Story* (Garden City, N.Y.: Doubleday, 1965); Richard Rhodes, "The General and World War III," *The New Yorker*, June 19, 1995; and the novel by Fletcher Kebel and Charles W. Bailey II, *Seven Days in May* (New York: Harper and Row, 1962), and the film based on it (1964). Thomas Power quote is in Herring, "Conspiracy of Silence."

272　The Anderson and LeMay quotes are in Herring. For their job changes, see HE clip in FCW, Box 19/Kennedy.

272　For "triad" standard, see Taylor Branch, *Pillar of Fire: America in the King Years, 1963–1965* (New York: Simon and Schuster, 1998), 147. For new emphasis on missiles, see Michael Beschloss, ed., *Taking Charge: The Johnson White House Tapes, 1963–1964* (New York: Simon and Schuster, 1997), 119. For air power inferiority complex, see April 23, 1955, BMG speech, *Congressional Record*, 5221–24. *"This is the first time in our history"*: White with Gill, *Suite 3505*, 288. For similar sentiments, see LeMay in *Life*, September 1, 1961; Stefan Possony in *National Security: Political, Economic, and Military Strategies for the Decade Ahead*, ed. David M. Abshire (New York: Praeger, 1963).

272   For B-70 and RS-70 affair, see Marquis Childs, "Why McNamara Lost His Temper," WP, January 17, 1964; "Nuclear Stalemate v. Nuclear Superiority," in Francis M. Carney and Frank H. Way, eds., *Politics 1964* (Belmont, Calif.: Wadsworth, 1964), 29; Raymond D. Senter, TNR, September 1964; and LeMay, *Mission with LeMay*. LeMay's memoir, which he wrote immediately upon retirement from the Air Force, tracks Goldwater's strategic doctrines almost identically. *"I say fear the civilians"*: LBJ handbill, FCW, Box 1/California.

273   For poll on Berlin, see GP, 1729. *"In some circumstances"*: Thomas C. Reeves, *A Question of Character: A Life of John F. Kennedy* (New York: Free Press, 1991), citing SEP, March 31, 1962.

273   *ABC Reports ran the obligatory*: transcript, RAC, Box 10/787.

273   For bad language, see George Dixon, WP, January 16, 1964.

273   Pittsfield canvass is in White with Gill, *Suite 3505*, 290.

274   BMG's call for probe is in statement released January 10, 1964, at RNC meeting in FSA, Box 4. For White demotion, O'Donnell purge, and Arizona team, see White with Gill, *Suite 3505*, 265–67; Novak, *Agony of the GOP*, 284–85. For Republicans plotting to knock him out, see *Newsweek*, January 20, 1964. For Happy at the meeting, see "GOP Has a Busy Evening," WP, January 11, 1964. For Romney, see NYT, January 8, 1964, 27.

274   For Scranton meeting, see Theodore H. White, *The Making of the President 1964* (New York: Atheneum, 1965), 109–10; George D. Wolf, *William Warren Scranton: Pennsylvania Statesman* (State College: Penn State Press, 1981), 89–90; *Time*, November 22, 1963; and White with Gill, *Suite 3505*, 385. For ratings: Richard Wilson, LAT, February 2, 1964.

275   For Scranton family biography, see White, *Making of the President 1964*, 195, 235; and Wolf, *William Warren Scranton*, 10–13.

275   For Scranton biography, see Wolf, 13–33.

275   For automation statistic, see C. Vann Woodward, *The Strange Career of Jim Crow*, 3d ed. (New York: Oxford University Press, 1973), 192. On Pennsylvania and Scranton economics, see Arthur Herzog, "A Visit with Governor Scranton," *Think* (November/December 1963); and Theodore White, *Life*, February 28, 1964. Chafee quote is from *Proceedings of the 28th Republican National Convention* (Washington, D.C.: Republican National Committee, 1964), 66. On the automation scare generally, see "Magnetic Ribbons Grab More Jobs: They Run Tools, Monitor Rockets," WSJ, June 5, 1959, 1A. For a demurral, see Barry Goldwater, "Automation Will Bring Greater Prosperity," HE, April 18, 1964.

276   The Scranton Plan is described by Wolf, *William Warren Scranton*, 35. "Private leak" quote is in Henry Brandon, "A Talk with Governor Scranton," *Saturday*

Review, April 1964. For "the best informed man" quote, see Wolf, *William Warren Scranton*, 35.

276   For Detroit statistic, see Thomas J. Sugrue, *The Origins of the Urban Crisis: Race and Inequality in Postwar Detroit* (Princeton, N.J.: Princeton University Press, 1996), 94. For Philadelphia, see Branch, *Pillar of Fire*, 296. For Kennedy's concessions on minimum wage, see Tom Wicker, *JFK and LBJ: The Influence of Personality upon Politics* (Baltimore: Penguin, 1968), 83–120.

276   For Scranton's support in Rules Committee fight, see Wicker, 77–80. For voting with Administration and depressed areas bill, see Wolf, *William Warren Scranton*, 54–58. *"What it boils down to"*: SEP, January 18, 1964. For his success in his first year as governor, see Wolf, *William Warren Scranton*, 107. Posters noted in Herzog, "A Visit with Governor Scranton."

277   *"I probably will give even deeper thought"*: White with Gill, *Suite 3505*, 259. *"Scranton appears to have opened"*: AP report cited in White with Gill, 260. NYHT editorial was December 23, 1963. For *Today* show prediction, see transcript in RAC, Box 10/811. *Life* profile ran February 28, 1964.

277   For support going into RNC meeting, and Keisling and Traux, see Wolf, *William Warren Scranton*, 94. For Ripon Society founding, see NYT, January 6, 1964; manifesto reprinted in Thomas E. Petri and Lee W. Huebner, eds., *The Ripon Papers: The Politics of Moderation, 1963–1968* (Washington, D.C.: National Press, 1968), 3–6. Also from author interview with Congressman Barney Frank.

278   Scranton's year-end address and write-in nix is in Wolf, *William Warren Scranton*, 73.

278   For scene at RNC meeting, see Wolf, 94 (for the party); "Scranton in GOP Limelight," WP, January 11, 1964; *Newsweek*, January 20, 1964 (for McCabe quote); Novak, *Agony of the GOP*, 270 (for press conference).

278   *The New York Times Magazine ran*: "Portrait of a Not-So-Dark Horse," NYTM, January 12, 1964; "Bill Scranton, a Reluctant Candidate" and "The Logical Candidate," SEP, January 18, 1964. *And opined his columnist brother Joseph*: see NYHT letter to editor, January 29, 1964.

279   For second luncheon, see White with Gill, *Suite 3505*, 361; and "GOP Pros Make Move Toward Gov. Scranton," NYHTEN, January 22, 1964. *"Only if faced with"*: LAT, January 20, 1964, A6. *"What does it show Johnson-Scranton?"*: Beschloss, ed., *Taking Charge*, 172. For Young Republican training seminar, see *The Reporter*, February 27, 1964.

279   For Pittsburgh donnybrook, see White with Gill, *Suite 3505*, 274. For Los Angeles, see "Goldwater Fans Told to Restrain 'Picketing,' " LAT, January 1, 1964. For speech transcripts, see RAC, Box 10/799.

279   For Mary Scranton's veto, see Novak, *Agony of the GOP*, 298; and "Scranton Pulls Out of Primary Race in NH," LAT, February 4, 1964.

280   NAR's New Hampshire campaigning is depicted in Harold Faber, ed., *The Road to the White House: The Story of the 1964 Election by the Staff of the New York Times* (New York: McGraw-Hill, 1965), 26; and National Broadcasting Company,

Somehow It Works: A Candid Portrait of the 1964 Presidential Election (Garden City, N.Y.: Doubleday, 1965), 12–28, which transcribes NBC news coverage. For French-Canadian gambit, see Robert Alan Goldberg, *Barry Goldwater* (New Haven, Conn.: Yale University Press, 1995), 186.

280 *"What can we tell our young people"*: *Life*, November 1, 1963. On NAR's organizational difficulties, see Novak, *Agony of the GOP*, 313. For ballot and delegates, see Charles Brereton, "1964: A Yankee Surprise," *Historical New Hampshire* 42, no. 3 (1987).

280 For NAR frugality, see Novak, *Agony of the GOP*, 317; and NYHTEV, January 29, 1964. For NBC art program: Jon Margolis, *The Last Innocent Year: America in 1964: The Beginning of the "Sixties"* (New York: Morrow, 1999), 106. *"How can there be"*: Goldberg, *Barry Goldwater*, 186; *ABC Reports*, January 9, 1964, transcript in RAC, Box 10/787. For "Robin Hood" exchange, see LAT, January 17, 1964, A1; and *Newsweek*, January 20, 1964.

281 For "Rockefeller Campaign Express," see RAC, Box 12/946. For Manhattan office: ibid., February 15, 1964. For D.C. offices: WS, February 7, 1964. *"All a public relations man has to do"*: FCW, Box 8/New York Newsmen's Opinions on Political Situation.

281 For 1962 N.H. election and Lamphrey and Cotton: Veblen, *Manchester Union Leader*, 11, 18, 163; Stephen Shadegg, *What Happened to Goldwater?: The Inside Story of the 1964 Republican Campaign* (New York: Holt, Rinehart, and Winston, 1965), 94; Brereton, "Yankee Surprise"; and White with Gill, *Suite 3505*. For schedule: ibid., 291; and author interview with Lee Edwards. The Q&As at each New Hampshire stop are meticulously transcribed in RAC, Box 10. *"The voters of the Granite State"*: January 16, 1964, Seymour address, WAR, 155/8.

282 For Goldmark case: "Libel Suit Ending as Left vs. Right Debate," WP, January 16, 1964. Shetland pony story is in SEP, March 14, 1964; and Faber, ed., *Road to the White House*, 19.

282 *"Why the hell am I doing this?"*: ibid.

282 *"I'm glad he has one foot in a cast"*: *Newsweek*, January 20, 1964. *The AP's Walter Mears*: Goldberg, *Barry Goldwater*, 185.

282 For *Point of Order* distribution, see "Film Is Surprise Hit," NYT, February 11, 1964.

283 *"The New Yorker's movie critic"*: Dwight MacDonald, *Dwight MacDonald on Movies* (Englewood Cliffs, N.J.: De Capo, 1969), 289–92.

283 *There usually followed the spectacle*: Kennedy, for example, left his Atomic Energy Commission secret briefing muttering, "And they call us the human race!" See Francis X. Winters, *The Year of the Hare: America in Vietnam, January 25, 1963–February 15, 1964* (Athens: University of Georgia Press, 1997), 5. For LBJ's AEC briefing reaction, see Beschloss, ed., *Taking Charge*, 62–63.

283 For McNamara's advice not to follow NATO policy, see interview with him in "The Gift of Time," special issue of *The Nation*, February 2, 1998. For Oppenheimer quote, see "Scorpions in a Bottle," *Defense Journal*, July 1998.

284   Appropriation hearings testimony is in Carney and Way, eds., *Politics 1964*, 296–304.

284   Kubrick's nuclear strategy reading is noted in Paul S. Boyer, *Fallout: A Historian Reflects on America's Half-Century Encounter with Nuclear Weapon* (Columbus: Ohio State University Press, 1998), 97. For narratives of the genesis of *Dr. Strangelove*, see *http:~/www.krusch.com/kubrick/Q05.html*; and Peter Bogdanovich, "What They Say About Stanley Kubrick," NYTM, July 4, 1999.

286   *By January 20, four out of ten*: Harris poll, LAT, January 20, 1964. Cartoon clip, from *Lisbon Falls* (Maine) *Enterprise* is in MCSL, Press Reports, 3 of 3 folder.

286   For New Hampshire entrance rules, see SEP, March 14, 1964.

287   *"So, because of all these impelling reasons"*: WP, January 28, 1964. Smith brought two speeches, for and against, to the meeting; she chose to announce her candidacy, she later said, so as not to spoil such a lovely luncheon. Author interview with Elsie Carper.

287   For D.C. "calling" rituals, see Ellen Proxmire, *One Foot in Washington: The Perilous Life of a Senator's Wife* (Washington, D.C.: R. B. Luce, 1964), 57. *"There are others more deserving"*: author interview with Ryan Hayes.

287   For Women's National Press Club and women, see Branch, *Pillar of Fire*, 526. For "Inquiring Camera Girls," see *Newsweek*, July 9, 1962; and Christopher Matthews, *Kennedy and Nixon: The Rivalry That Shaped Postwar America* (New York: Touchstone, 1996), 93. For sex and Civil Rights Act of 1964, see Branch, *Pillar of Fire*, 231–33.

287   *Government Girl* is in MCSL.

288   For 45th parallel, see MCSL, picture 1916. For tour see clips and materials in MCSL, "New Hampshire Campaign" and "Presidential Nomination" folders; Smith to Mrs. Gordon A. Abbot, Correspondence A folder; and LAT, February 11, 1964. For typical appearance, see Rotary Club speech, February 10, 1964, MCSL, General Materials, 2 of 4 folder. For annual Maine tours, see MCSL, scrapbook, vol. 221, 141. *"You got a lot of zip"*: *Newsweek*, February 24, 1964. *Out of earshot other men called her*: David Broder, WS, February 12, 1964.

288   For Louis Harris poll, see LAT, January 20, 1964. For 1956 "Dump Nixon" effort, see Matthews, *Kennedy and Nixon*, 104; for "spontaneous" write-in effort, see Novak, *Agony of the GOP*, 323. For Godfrey show, see LAT, January 21, 1964.

289   For typical Nixon speech from the time, hear LBJT 6404.09/10.

289   For LBJ summit plans, see Robert Dallek, *Flawed Giant: Lyndon Johnson and His Times, 1961–1973* (New York: Oxford University Press, 1998), 128. For memo: "The Inconsistent Mr. Nixon," DNC Research Division, March 3, 1964, LBJWH, Box 116.

289   For New York school boycott, see Tamar Jacoby, *Someone Else's House: America's Unfinished Struggle for Integration* (New York: Free Press, 1998), 22–23. *"By running to the suburbs"*: *Newsweek*, February 10, 1964.

289   For Cincinnati speech, see RAC, Box 11/924. For Beckwith, see Branch, *Pillar of Fire*, 213. For Alabama, see LAT, February 15, 1964.

289   Stevenson's speech is in LAT, February 13, 1964. For Minutemen, see LAT, January 21, 1964; and GRR, January 31, 1964. For "Marxmanship in Dallas," see LAT, February 13, 1964; and GRR, February 15, 1964. For DAR, see LAT, February 18, 1964. For *The Defenders*, see Margolis, *Last Innocent Year*, 104.

290   "The Second Sexual Revolution" appeared in *Time*, January 24, 1964. *The Washington Post's entertainment columnist*: WP, January 15, 1964, B13. On Terry Southern, see Margolis, *Last Innocent Year*, 146. On the FCC, see Rita Lang Kleinfelder, *When We Were Young: A Baby-Boomer Yearbook* (New York: Prentice-Hall, 1993), 382. The *Eros* case is in John Heidenry, *What Wild Ecstasy: The Rise and Fall of the Sexual Revolution* (New York: Simon and Schuster, 1997), 79–84.

290   For Lodge's UN rhetoric, and poll, see John Kessel, *The Goldwater Coalition: Republican Strategies in 1964* (Indianapolis: Bobbs-Merrill, 1968), 51.

291   Unless otherwise specified, my telling of the Lodge story in New Hampshire is collated from Eugene Vasilew, "The New Style in Political Campaigns: Lodge in New Hampshire, 1964," *Review of Politics* 30 (1968), no. 2; Brereton, "A Yankee Surprise"; Faber, ed., *Road to the White House*, 17–28; and William J. Miller, *Henry Cabot Lodge: A Biography* (New York: Heineman, 1967), 355–61.

291   On Lester Wunderman, see Malcolm Gladwell, *The New Yorker*, July 6, 1998; and author interview with Eric Wunderman.

292   For "Henry Sabotage" nickname, see Arthur Schlesinger Jr., ed., *History of American Presidential Elections, 1798–1968*, vol. 4 (New York: Chelsea House, 1971), 3015.

293   For "conspicuous absentee" quote, see NYHT, January 26, 1964.

293   For Loeb's "holy crusade" editorial, see *Manchester Union Leader*, February 17, 1964, 1. The "appeaser" piece on Lodge was the next day.

294   *"I am not one of those baby-kissing"*: White with Gill, *Suite 3505*, 292.

294   For "Meet Mr. Lodge" camera technique, see Edwin Diamond and Stephen Bates, *The Spot: The Rise of Political Advertising on Television* (Cambridge, Mass.: MIT Press, 1984), 101–2.

295   For Cassius Clay, see LAT, February 26, 1964, A1; and Branch, *Pillar of Fire*, 230, 250. For Air Force One, see ibid., 236. For school boycott, see Ronald Formisano, *Boston Against Busing: Race, Class, and Ethnicity in the 1960s and 1970s* (Chapel Hill: University of North Carolina Press, 1991), 33. Louis Lomax: LAT, February 29, 1964.

296   For LBJ conversations on Lodge, see Beschloss, ed., *Taking Charge*, 256–62.

296   NAR commercial schedules: "Radio and TV Availabilities" chart, RAC, Box 11/931. For costs, see Box 11/928. For Goldwater New Hampshire spots, see AHFAV, BG-VT/97.

296   *"There isn't a person here"*: March 3, 1964, rally at University of New Hampshire, FSA, Box 4.

297   *Violent crimes had increased*: President's Commission on Law Enforcement and Administration of Justice, *The Challenge of Crime in a Free Society* (New York: Dutton, 1968), 22. "Career Girl Murders": Daniel Goleman, *Emotional Intelligence* (New York: Bantam Books, 1995), 13. This crime occurred on the same day as the "I

Have a Dream Speech." "Boston Strangler": LAT, January 5, 1964, A17; Rita Lang Kleinfelder, *When We Were Young*, 168. Chicago: " 'Mother of Yr' Slain in Home," CT, January 23, 1964.

297   For Manchester Armory, see Branch, *Pillar of Fire*, 241; Margolis, *Last Innocent Year*, 155; and, for speech, AHF, Box 1/13.

297   *At New Hampshire headquarters on Monday*: Lee Edwards interview.

298   For New Hampshire results, see White with Gill, *Suite 3505*, 297.

298   *"I do not plan"*: Brereton, "A Yankee Surprise."

298   For Smith comment, see Smith to Jeane Dixon, March 12, 1964, in MCSL, Dixon, Jeane L., folder. For Nixon: NYT, March 12, 1964.

298   *In the New York Times*: Faber, ed., *Road to the White House*, 29.

14. PRESIDENT OF ALL THE PEOPLE

299   For Lodge's preparations for work, see "The Lodge Phenomenon," *Time*, May 15, 1964. For "at the request of the friend," see LBJ to AP luncheon, PPP: LBJ, 493–96.

299   Lodge's conversation with Eisenhower is in Francis X. Winters, *The Year of the Hare: America in Vietnam, January 25, 1963–February 15, 1964* (Athens: University of Georgia Press, 1997), 116; and Felix Belair, "Eisenhower Urges Lodge to Pursue GOP Nomination," NYT, December 8, 1964. For Lodge's colonial approach to Vietnam and prima donna behavior, see Winters, *Year of the Hare*, 2, 87, 166–73. For "run the country" quote, see Jon Margolis, *The Last Innocent Year: America in 1964: The Beginning of the "Sixties"* (New York: Morrow, 1999), 211. For Harkin, see H. R. McMaster, *Dereliction of Duty: Lyndon Johnson, Robert McNamara, the Joint Chiefs of Staff, and the Lies That Led to Vietnam* (New York: HarperPerennial, 1997), 57.

300   For 42 percent poll figure, see Charles Brereton, "1964: A Yankee Surprise," *Historical New Hampshire* 42, no. 3 (1981).

300   My interpretation of the relationship of escalation in Vietnam to nuclear anxieties is indebted to Winters, *Year of the Hare*; of the failure of "graduated pressure" and Op Plan 34-A, to McMaster, *Dereliction of Duty*. For the 20,000 figure, see Pierre Salinger, *With Kennedy* (Garden City, N.Y.: Doubleday, 1966), 348; for 15,000, Michael Beschloss, ed., *Taking Charge: The Johnson White House Tapes, 1963–1964* (New York: Simon and Schuster, 1997), 74; for 16,000, Christopher Matthews, *Kennedy and Nixon: The Rivalry That Shaped Postwar America* (New York: Touchstone, 1996), 232. *Dodgy accounting methods*: author interview with Hank Geier. For statistic on NLF tax collection and U.S. dead, see Matthews, *Kennedy and Nixon*, 232.

300   *"We're going to rough them up"*: Beschloss, ed., *Taking Charge*, 300. For next day's press conference, see PPP: LBJ, 254.

301   For softball game explosion, hear LBJT 6402.12/6. Vietcong control of land is in McMaster, *Dereliction of Duty*, 61. Joint Chiefs' memo is in McMaster, 109.

301   *"If I tried to pull out completely"*: Beschloss, ed., *Taking Charge*, 266. For LBJ's fixation on Korea example, see George C. Herring, "Conspiracy of Silence:

LBJ, the Joint Chiefs, and Escalation of the War in Vietnam," in Lloyd C. Gardner and Ted Gittinger, *Vietnam: The Early Decisions* (Austin: University of Texas Press, 1997). Ilya V. Gaiduk, "Turnabout?: The Soviet Policy Dilemma in the Vietnamese Conflict," ibid., 207–18, observes that 1964 was "the lowest point in the history of Soviet–North Vietnamese relations."

301   For McNamara and Khanh tour, see Robert S. McNamara with Brian VanDe-Mark, *In Retrospect: The Tragedy and Lessons of Vietnam* (New York: Vintage, 1995), 112; McMaster, *Dereliction of Duty*, 71; Margolis, *Last Innocent Year*, 161; and Winters, *Year of the Hare*, 119–20.

302   *"The greatest gift for us"*: Winters, *Year of the Hare*, 119. The statistics on aid are from Winters, 44.

302   *"French generals, however"*: USN, March 23, 1964, 50–52.

302   For State of the Union address, see PPP: LBJ, 112.

302   "Post-Marxian age" quote is in Margolis, *Last Innocent Year*, 142, to which I am indebted for my interpretation of LBJ's tax plan.

303   For the history of Keynes's reception in America, see David M. Kennedy, *Freedom from Fear: The American People in Depression and War* (New York: Oxford University Press, 1999), 79–82 and 357–60; and Robert Collins, *The Business Response to Keynes, 1929–1964* (New York: Columbia University Press, 1981). For weather control, see "Giant Research Effort Seeks Weather Control," LAT, February 16, 1964; Margolis, *Last Innocent Year*, 296; and Theodore H. White, *The Making of the President 1964* (New York: Atheneum, 1965), vii.

303   For "reactionary Keynesianism," see Thomas C. Reeves, *A Question of Character: A Life of John F. Kennedy* (New York: Free Press, 1991), 334. For Eisenhower's CEA and $12 billion deficit, see Collins, *Business Response to Keynes*, 152–70; and Richard Whalen, *Taking Sides: A Personal View of America from Kennedy to Nixon to Kennedy* (Boston: Houghton Mifflin, 1974), 109.

303   For tax-cut option and JFK reluctance, see Collins, *Business Response to Keynes*, 178–79. *"Stretches our education in modern economics"*: Galbraith to JFK, March 23, 1961, in John Kenneth Galbraith, *Letters to Kennedy,* ed. James Goodman (Cambridge, Mass.: Harvard University Press, 1998), 40.

304   For big business acceptance of Keynesian tax cut and CED, see Collins, *Business Response to Keynes*, 180–91.

304   For Kennedy's introduction of bill and indifference to passage, see ibid.; and Reeves, *Question of Character*, 334. For Johnson's acceptance and lobbying, see Robert Dallek, *Flawed Giant: Lyndon Johnson and His Times, 1961–1973* (New York: Oxford University Press, 1998), 70–74.

304   1960 platform quote in Kirk Harold Porter, *National Party Platforms, 1840–1964* (Urbana: University of Illinois Press, 1966).

304   For Heller's poverty program, see Taylor Branch, *Pillar of Fire: America in the King Years, 1963–1965* (New York: Simon and Schuster, 1998), 175. For Kennedy's response to Heller, see Dallek, *Flawed Giant*, 61. For preparation of poverty legislation, see ibid., 61, 74–80. For Goldwater quotes: January 15, 1964, speech to Economic Club of New York, RAC, Box 10/789.

305   For number of civil rights bills, see Edward G. Carmines and James A. Stimson, *Issue Evolution: Race and the Transformation of American Politics* (Princeton, N.J.: Princeton University Press, 1989); 150 were introduced between 1937 and 1946 alone. *He dismissed President Truman's civil rights program*: ibid., 42. *Columnists Evans and Novak called his handiwork*: Rowland Evans and Robert Novak, *Lyndon B. Johnson: The Exercise of Power: A Political Biography* (New York: New American Library, 1966), 119–40. Joe Clark quote is in Gorton Carruth, *What Happened When: A Chronology of Life and Events in America* (New York: Signet, 1991), 891.

305   *"The Negro fought in the war"*: Dallek, *Flawed Giant*, 24. For Johnson's speech echoing King, see Branch, *Pillar of Fire*, 92.

306   Call to King: Beschloss, ed., *Taking Charge,* 37.

306   *"I'm not going to cavil"*: Margolis, *Last Innocent Year*, 44. *"Without a word or a comma"*: Branch, *Pillar of Fire*, 210. For the legislative history of the Civil Rights Act of 1964, see Charles and Barbara Whalen, *The Longest Debate: A Legislative History of the 1964 Civil Rights Act* (Cabin John, Md.: Seven Locks Press, 1985).

307   *"You're either for civil rights"*: Branch, *Pillar of Fire*, 180. *"I hope that satisfies"*: Margolis, *Last Innocent Year*, 197.

307   *"You drink with Dirksen," LBJ commanded*: ibid., 158.

307   NAM's brief can be found in HR, Box 55/19. For the Richard Russell amendment, see Branch, *Pillar of Fire*, 258. For "prohibition" letter to the editor, see Felix W. Reese, LAT, February 13, 1964; for *ABA Journal* article, see David Lawrence column, LAT, February 25, 1964. For "enslavement" argument, see Branch, *Pillar of Fire*, 298. For Coordinating Committee for Fundamental Freedoms, see GRR, February 29, 1964; March 30, 1964; September 30, 1964; and Group Research Inc. 1963 roundup, AC.

307   *"Johnson Pledges Fight on Mental Retardation"*: LAT, February 6, 1964. For Johnson's business campaign, see Jack Bell, *The Johnson Treatment: How Lyndon B. Johnson Took Over the Presidency and Made It His Own* (New York: Harper and Row, 1965), 120 (for "Call me Lyndon"); Dallek, *Flawed Giant*, 73 ("Is there a citizens group").

308   *"They're all in such sensitive states"*: Beschloss, ed., *Taking Charge*, 95. For visit of Italian leaders, see ibid., 96; for "English Scotch," ibid., 172. For Teddy White, see ibid., 16. *In his February appearance in Miami*: LAT, February 28, 1964.

308   On Baker, see G. R. Schreiber, *The Bobby Baker Affair: How to Make Millions in Washington* (Chicago: Regnery, 1964); and Dallek, *Flawed Giant*, 38–44. For summary of possible Johnson kickback, see Beschloss, ed., *Taking Charge*, 92. See also Carl Curtis OH, LBJL. For Goldwater's Austin quip, see *Newsweek*, April 10, 1961.

309   For arm-twisting to take Jenkins off witness list, hear LBJT 6401.24/13 and 6401.24/15. *"I've got considerably more detail on Reynolds's love life"*: Beschloss, ed., *Taking Charge*, 191. For *Minneapolis Tribune* poll, see Dallek, *Flawed Giant*, 126. LBJ had eighty-eight recorded conversations about the Jenkins case in the month of January.

309   On the utility executive, see Bell, *Johnson Treatment*, 126. *On March 23 the*

Wall Street Journal: "The Johnson Wealth," March 23, 1964, WSJ. For *Time* piece, "Mr. President, You're Fun," see Frank Cormier, *LBJ the Way He Was: A Personal Memoir* (Garden City, N.Y.: Doubleday, 1977), 86. The chamber of commerce speech is described in Bell, *Johnson Treatment*, 127. Lippmann "healing man" quote is in Beschloss, ed., *Taking Charge*, 313; for Reston, see Beschloss, 319. Poll numbers are in LBJT 406.03/24.

310   For Oregon primary rules, see Harold Faber, ed., *Road to the White House: The Story of the 1964 Election by the Staff of the New York Times* (New York: McGraw-Hill, 1965), 34; and James M. Perry, *A Report in Depth on Barry Goldwater* (Silver Spring, Md.: National Observer, 1964). For Smith petition, see LAT, February 15, 1964.

310   For Lodge headquarters and quote, see *Time*, May 15, 1964.

310   *"Intimate contact with Gov. William Scranton"*: Richard Wilson, LAT, February 2, 1964. Connecticut backers noted in NYHTEN, February 14, 1964. For *Meet the Press*, see LAT, February 17, 1964; for Lippmann, see LAT, February 19, 1964. Rhodes's efforts are described in LAT, February 23, 1964. Alsop's column is in LAT, February 25, 1964. *Reader's Digest* quote is from April 1964 issue.

311   For $25,000 fund-raising and press conference, see George D. Wolf, *William Warren Scranton: Pennsylvania Statesman* (State College: Penn State Press, 1981), 100.

311   For Scranton's not taking name off Oregon ballot, see ibid., 94, 99.

311   For Nixon's meeting with Haldeman et al. November 1, 1964, I rely on Rowland Evans and Robert Novak, "The Unmaking of a President," *Esquire*, November 1, 1964; author interview with Leonard Nadasdy; and, for unheeded advice, Nadasdy to Nixon, March 17, 1964, LN.

311   For NAR and Oregon mutual affection, see James Desmond, *Nelson Rockefeller: A Political Biography* (New York: Macmillan, 1964), 228. For chairman of board of regents, see Sensenbrenner to Walton, FCW, Box 8/Rus Walton. For February tour: *Rockefeller Campaign Express*, February 15, 1964, RAC, Box 12/946 (for chain saw); and (Salem, Ore.) *Capital Journal* and *Oregon Statesman*, February 7, 8, and 9, 1964. For Sabre-Liner, see Villar to Douglas, January 14, 1964, RAC, Box 11/939. For Goldwater's San Francisco stop, see Stephen Shadegg, *What Happened to Goldwater?: The Inside Story of the 1964 Republican Campaign* (New York: Holt, Rinehart, and Winston, 1965), 108.

312   For Jackie Robinson in Oregon, see Arnold Rampersad, *Jackie Robinson: A Biography* (New York: Knopf, 1997), 385.

15. UNITED AND AT PEACE WITH ITSELF . . .

313   *"Gentlemen, off the record"*: Author interview with Lee Edwards. For delegate totals by March 10, 1964, see F. Clifton White with William Gill, *Suite 3505: The Story of the Draft Goldwater Movement* (New Rochelle, N.Y.: Arlington House, 1967), 301. Milliken telegram and Virgin Islands votes are in White with Gill, 304. See also Theodore H. White, *The Making of the President 1964* (New York: Atheneum, 1965), 132.

313   White's convention technique is described in John Kessel, *The Goldwater Coalition: Republican Strategies in 1964* (Indianapolis: Bobbs-Merrill, 1968), 70. *Without, Life was fooled*: "Goldwater's Foreign Policy," *Life*, November 1, 1963. *The Washington Post had just reported*: "Goldwater Aides Admit Momentum Has Changed," WP, February 8, 1964.

314   For White's mounting frustrations with the Arizona Mafia, see White with Gill, *Suite 3505*, 275–77, 293. Joe Alsop is quoted in Norman Mailer, "In a Blue Light: A History of the 1964 Republican Convention," *Esquire*, November 1964. Kitchel's mood is in White with Gill, *Suite 3505*, 301.

314   For Goldwater being kept from White memo, see White with Gill, 287. For fund-raising, see CT, January 4, 1964, 1; Bill Middendorf, "Balance Sheet per December 31, 1963," WAR, Box 155/8; and Finance Highlights Report No. 10, April 4, 1964, FCW, Box 8/G. R. Herberger. For New York office, see Marvin Liebman, *Coming Out Conservative: An Autobiography* (San Francisco: Chronicle Books, 1992), 167. *"For a publicity splash"*: "Neal" to Rusher, n.d., "RLN—PAR," WAR, Box 155/7. For Kitchel's resignation, see White with Gill, *Suite 3505*, 278; and Stephen Shadegg, *What Happened to Goldwater?: The Inside Story of the 1964 Republican Campaign* (New York: Holt, Rinehart, and Winston, 1965), 100.

314   On whether thirty-seven or forty covenants were being broken, see *ABC Reports* transcript, January 9, 1964, RAC, Box 10/787. For Hess biography, see Karl Hess, *Mostly on the Edge: An Autobiography* (Amherst, N.Y.: Prometheus, 1999). *"It would not be America really"*: *American Mercury*, May 1954. *"If we in this hour of world crisis"*: April 6, 1964, speech from Portland Hilton, AHF, Box 1/13.

315   Expressions of culture clash came in author interviews with Lee Edwards, Ron Crawford, Charles Lichenstein, and Richard Kleindienst; and Godfrey Hodgson to author, January 3, 1997. *"When you get a phone call"*: F. Clifton White with Jerome Tuccille, *Politics as a Noble Calling* (Ottawa, Ill.: Jameson Books, 1994), 155.

315   For Chicago meeting, see White with Gill, *Suite 3505*, 276–78; Shadegg, *What Happened*, 120; and Karl Hess, *In a Cause That Will Triumph: The Goldwater Campaign and the Future of Conservatism* (New York: Doubleday, 1967), 21 (for "Boy Scouts" exchange).

316   The March 18, 1964, meeting is in White with Gill, *Suite 3505*, 302–4.

316   For entreaties to Kleindienst, see Richard Kleindienst, *Justice: The Memoirs of an Attorney General* (Ottawa, Ill.: Jameson Books, 1985), 32–33. For purging from strategy sessions, see White with Gill, *Suite 3505*, 304.

316   *"Lee, we're not going to have that kind of crap"*: author interview with Lee Edwards.

317   For Wallace's Ivy League tour, see Dan T. Carter, *The Politics of Rage: George Wallace, the Origins of the New Conservatism, and the Transformation of American Politics* (Baton Rouge: Louisiana State University Press, 1995), 195–99; and Stephan Lesher, *George Wallace: American Populist* (Reading, Mass.: Addison-Wesley, 1994), 261–65.

317   For Wallace on the West Coast, see Carter, *Politics of Rage*, 200; and Lesher, *George Wallace*, 268–71 (for quotes).

317   For Cincinnati, see Lesher, *George Wallace*, 271–73.

318   For Chicago, see Lesher, loc. cit.

318   Madison appearance and the Herbstreith proposal are in Lesher, 273–74; and Carter, *Politics of Rage*, 203–4.

319   For Thurmond quote from 1948, see Alexander Lamis, *The Two-Party South* (New York: Oxford University Press, 1984), 9. *"States' Rights have become household words"*: Jim Johnson, "Orval Faubus Can Be Elected President," CM, Box 69/4.

319   For Wallace's filing trip to Wisconsin, see Carter, *Politics of Rage*, 204.

319   Malcolm X and "rifle clubs" are noted in Jon Margolis, *The Last Innocent Year: America in 1964: The Beginning of the "Sixties"* (New York: Morrow, 1999), 157. For CORE at Triborough Bridge, see Tamar Jacoby, *Someone Else's House: America's Unfinished Struggle for Integration* (New York: Free Press, 1998), 23–24. For school boycott, see Jacoby, 26.

319   For Cleveland, see Margolis, *Last Innocent Year*, 116; and Lesher, *George Wallace*, 272. For Bay Area, see Max Heirich, *The Spiral of Conflict: Berkeley, 1964* (New York: Columbia University Press, 1968), 86; David Lance Goines, *The Free Speech Movement: Coming of Age in the 1960s* (Berkeley, Calif.: Ten Speed Press, 1993), 96–97; and Margolis, *Last Innocent Year*, 157. *"Here as elsewhere the Negro"*: NYHTEN, April 4, 1964. For Emmanuel Cellers quote, see Jacoby, *Someone Else's House*, 24.

320   For Reynolds increasing votes estimate and labor and religious efforts, see Carter, *Politics of Rage*, 204–5; and Lesher, *George Wallace*, 277.

320   For speeches, hecklers, and responses: ibid., 276–79.

320   For Milwaukee Serb Hall appearance, see ibid., 282–84; and Carter, *Politics of Rage*, 206–7.

321   For LBJ and Gronouski, see Lesher, *George Wallace*, 284; and LBJT 6404.03/7. For Wallace home stretch in Wisconsin, see Lesher, *George Wallace*, 284–85 (for 175,000 figure); and Carter, *Politics of Rage*, 208 (for victory celebration and quote).

321   *"An anachronistic Southern demagogue," sniffed*: ibid., 208.

321   For the egging of Smith supporters in Illinois, see Tristram Coffin to "George," July 24, 1964, LBJWHNG; and undated draft of MCS to Joly's July 9, 1964, letter, MCSL, "Goldwater, Barry" file. For spoiled NAR reception, see Marquis Childs, WP, July 10, 1964. For vandalized currency, see "Goldwater Bills Probed," LAT, February 2, 1964.

322   For 1963 *Human Events* conference, see *Democrat*, newspaper of the Democratic National Committee, July 22, 1963, in JCJ.

322   For Wyoming GOP convention: White, *Making of the President 1964*, 113; and Kleindienst interview.

322   For screening for Birch membership, see James M. Perry, *A Report in Depth on Barry Goldwater: The Story of the 1964 Republican Presidential Nominee* (Silver Spring, Md.: National Observer, 1964), 121–22. For the rogue Phoenix organization,

Americans for Goldwater, see White with Gill, *Suite 3505*, 158; March 9, 1963, founding minutes in DK, Box 4/Draft Goldwater Endeavor; Kleindienst to Marks, February 29, 1964, Leavitt to Kitchel, February 19, 1964, and Kleindienst to O'Malley, March 2, 1964, all in AHF, Box W2/2; and Shadegg, *What Happened*, 63. For their computer work, see Chestnut to Manolis, October 8, 1963, FCW, Box 8/Jay O'Malley.

323 White's Westchester County battle is limned by the documents, including YAF newsletter and Goldwater telegram, in FCW, Box 8/Supplement, New York Nuts. For arrest and trial of Birchers, see "Foe of Reds Guilty in Retail Boycott," NYT, January 9, 1964; and Donald Janson and Bernard Eismann, *The Far Right* (New York: McGraw-Hill, 1963), 41.

323 The Kansas Republican convention is in White with Gill, *Suite 3505*, 307–11.

324 For White's delegate figuring, see White with Gill, *Suite 3505*, 312–20. For BMG boast, see speech to American Society of Newspaper Editors, AHF, Box W1/13. For Kleindienst, see April 21, 1964, statement in FCW, Box 8/Stephen Shadegg.

325 For 14 percent popularity figure, see Harold Faber, ed., *The Road to the White House: The Story of the 1964 Election by the Staff of the New York Times* (New York: McGraw-Hill, 1965), 35. For Illinois primary, see NYHTEN, May 18, 1964; David Lawrence, WS, April 16, 1964; and White with Gill, *Suite 3505*, 306–37.

325 "Harold Stassen's Ticker Tape Parade" is from author interview with Ryan Hayes. For Stassen in Indiana, see White with Gill, *Suite 3505*, 318; and Goldwater press conference in Indianapolis, April 20, 1964, RAC, Box 11/881. Stassen brochure: AC.

326 For Cronkite moving to Indianapolis, see Carter, *Politics of Rage*, 209; for Butler University, see Lesher, *George Wallace*, 287–88.

326 My source for Kitty Genovese is A. M. Rosenthal, *Thirty-Eight Witnesses: The Kitty Genovese Case* (Berkeley: University of California Press, 1999).

326 For Wallace crime quotes, see *Time*, May 15, 1964; and Lesher, *George Wallace*, 294.

326 Welsh's threats to patronage employees and the Democratic pledge are in Lesher, 289. Senator Birch Bayh and Vance Hartke letters are in Lesher, 293.

326 *"The noises you hear"*: National Broadcasting Company, *Somehow It Works: A Candid Portrait of the 1964 Presidential Election* (Garden City, N.Y.: Doubleday, 1965), 33.

326 For White's post-Indiana figuring, see White with Gill, *Suite 3505*, 319. *Not long ago Time*: "The Man to Beat," *Time*, May 8, 1964.

327 My source for the World's Fair is "A Panoramic View: The History of the New York City Building and Its Site," exhibit at the Queens Museum of Art; "A Billion-Dollar Fair Takes Shape," USN, December 30, 1963; and Margolis, *Last Innocent Year*, 198–201. *"Glittering mirror of national opulence"*: *Time*, May 1, 1964.

327 *"Hell, we've barely begun"*: David Farber, ed., *The Sixties: From Memory to History* (Chapel Hill: University of North Carolina Press, 1994), 19, 23. For the Hall of Free Enterprise, see GRR, March 16, 1964, and April 13, 1964.

328   For the board of education's latest busing plan, see NYT, March 26, 1964. For *Thirteen Most Wanted Men* story, see Rainer Crone, *Andy Warhol* (New York: Praeger, 1970), 30.

328   For CORE and World's Fair's opening day, see Jacoby, *Someone Else's House*, 15–32. For Farmer's speech before the ASNE, see "Demonstrations North and South as the Pressure for Desegregation Grows," NYT, April 19, 1964.

328   Johnson at the World's Fair is in Jacoby, *Someone Else's House*, 31.

329   Lippmann column on filibuster is quoted in Ronald Steel, *Walter Lippmann and the American Century* (Boston: Little, Brown, 1980), 553.

329   For Goldwater not campaigning in Oregon, see Shadegg, *What Happened*, 113; and John Kessel, *The Goldwater Coalition: Republican Strategies in 1964* (Indianapolis: Bobbs-Merrill, 1968), 69. For Lodge boom generally, see William J. Miller, *Henry Cabot Lodge: A Biography* (New York: Heineman, 1967), 361. World's Fair booths: *Time* cover story, May 15, 1964. For Vietnam assassination attempt, see Miller, *Henry Cabot Lodge,* 357. *"Why go out and break your pick"*: Perry, *A Report in Depth on Barry Goldwater*, 99. For evidence of snub of Shadegg, see Marks to Kleindienst, February 24, 1964, FCW, Box 8/Eric Marks; Shadegg to Kleindienst, March 6, 1964, March 20, 1964, and letter begging for cash, March 10, 1964, all in FCW, Box 8/Stephen Shadegg. *Meet Barry Goldwater* shooting script is in AHF, Box 1/8/64. Shadegg's disgust at billboard is in Shadegg, *What Happened*, 188. For Courtney in Oregon, see *Portland Reporter*, April 22, 1964.

330   For NAR trailing "Nobody," see Peter Kohler to Goldwater, May 4, 1964, FCW, Box 8. For delegates running uncommitted, see "State Delegation Bolting Rockefeller," *New York World-Telegram*, March 23, 1964. The Taylor-Burton wedding is in Margolis, *Last Innocent Year*, 97, 165. Source for "Mrs. Murphy's boarding house" embarrassment is author interview with Congressman Barney Frank. For failed attempt to syndicate *The Real Rockefeller*, see Fletcher to Gervasi, June 15, 1964, RAC, Box 12/948.

330   NAR's seizing the moment in Oregon is described in Shadegg, *What Happened*, 113; and Kessel, *Goldwater Coalition*, 77. For mailing, see Kessel, 78. For Lindsay, see *Portland Reporter*, April 25, 1964. His TV biography is described in Edwin Diamond and Stephen Bates, *The Spot: The Rise of Political Advertising on Television* (Cambridge, Mass.: MIT Press, 1984), 123. For Caveman and Woodpecker, see *Time*, May 8, 1964. *I'll win, Rockefeller claimed*: Peter Lisagor, *Chicago Daily News*, April 24, 1964.

331   For Nixon and Lodge meeting in Saigon, see Richard Nixon, *RN: The Memoirs of Richard Nixon*, vol. 1 (New York: Warner Books, 1978), 316. On the deployment of Finch and Folger to Oregon, and "Believe me, Dick" quote, see Rowland Evans and Robert Novak, "The Unmaking of a President," *Esquire*, November 1964. The film crew bursting in is in National Broadcasting Company, *Somehow It Works*, 99.

331   Shadegg's plan to neutralize Nixon is in Shadegg, *What Happened*, 113–14. The source for White's plan to boost Nixon is an author interview with Leonard Nadasdy.

331   For NAR's Oregon home stretch schedule, see Faber, ed., *Road to the White House*, 36. *"I'm the only man who cares"*: Shadegg, *What Happened*, 113. For TV

blitz, see memos in RAC, Box 11/930. NAR's 22 percent is in Portland *Oregonian*, May 5, 1964. ABC poll is in *Time*, June 12, 1964.

332   Oregon Election Day is described in Faber, ed., *Road to the White House*, 36.

332   For the failing of polls, see Earl Mazo, "California Republican Primary Trips the Polls," NYT, June 4, 1964.

332   For foiling of Lodge commercial, see Shadegg, *What Happened*, 114–15.

332   For Grindle's first thought, see Faber, ed., *Road to the White House*, 37–38.

332   *Goldwater, "just as nutty"*: LBJT, 6402.10/5.

16. GOLDEN STATE

333   *"Whether Constitutional government is to be restored"*: Joseph P. Kamp, *Goldwater MUST Be Destroyed: Who's Promoting and What's Behind the Conspiracy to Get Goldwater and to Discredit the Conservatives*, pamphlet, AC. *"Even I have been shocked"*: "Far Right and Far Left," NYP, April 5, 1964.

333   For scene on plane and tarmac at Georgia GOP convention, see National Broadcasting Company, *Somehow It Works: A Candid Portrait of the 1964 Presidential Election* (New York: Doubleday, 1965), 32; *Time*, May 15, 1964; and Peterson to White, May 19, 1964, Box 8/Other Corres. For "Gold Water": n.d., clipping in SHBGS; Goldwater on Steve Allen show, May 29, 1964, transcript in RAC, Box 11/913; and author interviews with John Savage and Lee Edwards. *"This tastes like piss!"*: Edwards interview.

333   For black boycott in Georgia, see Jon Margolis, *The Last Innocent Year: America in 1964: The Beginning of the "Sixties"* (New York: Morrow, 1999), 204. For Birch trouble, see John Grenier OH, Southern Historical Collection, University of North Carolina at Chapel Hill, 4007: A-9. Goldwater's Atlanta speech, May 2, 1964, is in AHF, Box 1/13.

334   *If Washington "can tell you"*: Goldwater on *Today* show, January 24, 1964, RAC, Box 10/799; February 13, 1964, in Reno, LAT, February 14, 1964: February 18, 1964, in Charleston, N.H., FSA, Box 4. *"I don't think it's my right"*: *Time*, June 23, 1964. *"I can see a police state"*: February 18, 1964, in Charleston, N.H. *"It is not understanding America"*: April 23, 1964, in Hartford, RAC, Box 11/884, and AHF, Box W1/8; see also January 4, 1964, in Keene, N.H., in Barry Goldwater, *Barry Speaks* (New York: McFadden Books, 1964), 5. For versions of "more violence in our streets before we see less" passage, see March 4, 1964, in Keene, FSA, Box 4; May 2, 1964, in Bakersfield, Calif., FSA, Box 4; and May 12, 1964, in New York, RAC, Box 11/888, and AHF, Box 1/11. On Mississippi: May 2, 1964, in Bakersfield. For constitutional damage civil rights bill would do to Negroes, see February 18, 1964, in Charleston, N.H.

335   For choice of Knowland, see Theodore H. White, *Making of the President 1964* (New York: Atheneum, 1965), 146. For his personality, see Gayle B. Montgomery and James W. Johnson, *One Step from the White House: The Rise and Fall of Senator William Knowland* (Berkeley: University of California Press, 1998), passim; and for elevator story, 268. For chaos in Wilshire Boulevard office, see Stephen Shadegg, *What Happened to Goldwater?: The Inside Story of the 1964 Republican Campaign*

(New York: Holt, Rinehart, and Winston, 1965), 118–19; "Neal" to Rusher, n.d. "RLN—PAR," WAR, Box 155/7; and Walton to White, March 13, 1964, and April 16, 1964, FCW, Box 8/Rus Walton.

335   For March 1963 CRA meeting, see Kurt Schuparra, *Triumph of the Right: The Rise of the California Conservative Movement, 1945–1966* (Armonk, N.Y.: M. E. Sharpe, 1998), 86; Lisa McGirr, "Suburban Warriors: Grass-Roots Conservatism in the 1960s" (Ph.D. diss., Columbia University, 1995), 149; and "The Rampant Right Invades the GOP," *Look*, July 16, 1963. *"It was like facing a howling mob"*: production script, *The Extremist*, RAC, Box 11/944. For conservative organizing and takeover at March 1964 convention, see McGirr, "Suburban Warriors," 154–56; "California Republicans: Are the Birchers Taking Over?," *The Reporter*, May 7, 1964; and *Rockefeller Campaign Express*, April 13, 1964, RAC, Box 12/946. *"Fanatics of the Birch variety"*: Schuparra, *Triumph of the Right*, 87.

336   For turning back "accusations, charges, and action resolution," see "Warnings Are Ignored; Young Republicans Spurn Unity Plea," SFC, September 23, 1963. For "international socialist," see NYT, May 3, 1964. For "regressive reactionaries" resolution, and 256 to 33 vote, see "Young GOP Endorses Goldwater," LAT, February 17, 1964. For Reagan and "finks" quote, see "Young GOP Refuses Party Loyalty Pledge," LAT, February 16, 1964.

336   For formation of UROC, see founding statement and constitution, FCW, Box 19; Walton to Miller, March 26, 1964, FCW, Box 8/Rus Walton; McGirr, "Suburban Warriors," 149; and Schuparra, *Triumph of the Right*, 80–81. For attempt to ban UROC fund-raising, see Schuparra, 97; and SFC, September 23, 1963. For Central Committee takeover attempt, see Totton J. Anderson and Eugene C. Lee, "The 1964 Election in California," *Western Political Quarterly* (June 1965).

336   "Firebugs" quote is in Theodore White, *Making of the President 1964*, 148. Gaston's petition drive: ibid., 147–48; Schuparra, "Barry Goldwater and Southern California Conservatism: Ideology, Image, and Myth in the 1964 California Republican Presidential Primary," *Southern California Quarterly* (Fall 1992); and author interview with Robert Gaston.

337   For UROC convention, see Anderson and Lee, "1964 Election in California"; and NYT, May 3, 1964. Press release with Goldwater speech excerpts is in FSA, Box 4.

337   For Rockefeller California polling, see John Kessel, *The Goldwater Coalition: Republican Strategies in 1964* (Indianapolis: Bobbs-Merrill, 1968), 81. *But Graham T. T. Molitor reminded Rockefeller*: author interview with Graham T. T. Molitor. For Wyckoff, see Edwin Diamond and Stephen Bates, *The Spot: The Rise of Political Advertising on Television* (Cambridge, Mass.: MIT Press, 1984), 124–25. For Spencer: Robert Alan Goldberg, *Barry Goldwater* (New Haven, Conn.: Yale University Press, 1995), 189.

337   For Goldwater and "small, clean nuclear weapons," see Barry Goldwater, *Conscience of a Conservative* (Shepherdsville, Ky.: Victor Publishing, 1960), 112; for Davy Crockett, see Goldwater before VFW in Cleveland, August 25, 1964, in Kessel, *Goldwater Coalition*, 190. For McNamara and nuclear scientists' opinions:

author interview with Herbert York, and transcript of interview with William F. Atwater, #S3344, at *http://www.secretsofwar.com*. For "just another weapon" and WP story, see White, *Making of the President 1964*, 353, and WS, October 22, 1964.

338   For Rockefeller *Face the Nation* appearance, see NYT, April 9, 1964.

338   For the Rockefeller brothers report quote, see Cary Reich, *The Life of Nelson A. Rockefeller: Worlds to Conquer, 1908–1958* (New York: Doubleday, 1996), 657. For later NAR confirmation, see Chesly Manly, "Anti-Red Federation Urged by Rockefeller," CT, October 4, 1961. For Teller endorsement, see NYT, January 7, 1964.

338   *"Responsible Republicanism rejects this irresponsible approach"*: See, for example, May 20, 1964, speech in Stockton, in NYHT, May 22, 1964. For BOM-FOG, see Rowland Evans and Robert Novak, SEP, May 30, 1964.

339   For Spencer-Roberts drumming up crowds, see *Time*, June 12, 1964. For appeal to blacks, see NAR to Fresno Elks, March 13, 1964, RAC, Box 11/940. For Berkeley, see *San Francisco Examiner*, March 13, 1964.

339   For attempt to break story of Goldwater's psychological episodes, I rely on Molitor interview. Peggy Goldwater interview is in Alvin Toffler, "The Woman Behind Barry Goldwater," *Good Housekeeping*, May 1964. See *Time*, June 12, 1964, for Drew Pearson.

339   For Goldwater paraphernalia generally, see Summer 1982 special issue of *The Keynoter*, "A Choice, Not an Echo: The 1964 Campaign of Barry Goldwater." For "Arriba con Barry," see Kitchel to Woodruff, April 13, 1964, AHF, Box 13/42. For trading stamps, see March 19, 1964, Walton to Kitchel, FCW, Box 8/Rus Walton. For "Folk Songs to Bug the Liberals," see *New Guard*, March 1964. Goldwater fan is from AC.

340   For a description of the California rallies, see WSJ, May 27, 1964, 18; and Schuparra, *Triumph of the Right*, 91. Nearly every California appearance is transcribed from start to finish in RAC, Box 10. For end of scheduled press conferences, see Kessel, *Goldwater Coalition*, 68; and Lee Edwards, *Goldwater: The Man Who Made a Revolution* (Washington, D.C.: Regnery, 1995), 218.

340   For finance committee, see Carl Greenberg, LAT, February 11, 1964. For statement of fund-raising rules, and how they were finessed, including *The Face of Arizona*, see Herberger to Kovac, April 9, 1964, FCW, Box 8/G. R. Herberger. For small donations, see Saltz to White, July 6, 1965, Box 18/IX-The Draft Begins; and F. Clifton White with William Gill, *Suite 3505: The Story of the Draft Goldwater Movement* (New Rochelle, N.Y.: Arlington House, 1967), 16, 192.

341   For Goldwater speech quotes, see transcripts, RAC, Box 10. For "Swiss cheese" quote, see March 25, 1964, to Detroit Economic Club, AHF, W1/3. For BMG's use of Shank letters, see May 11, 1964, to Omaha Civic Auditorium, RAC, Box 11/887, and AHF, Box 1/10. For "Yo-Yo" McNamara, see, for example, May 16, 1964, in Catalina Island, AHF, Box 1/8.

341   For Goldwater's awareness that LBJ was lying, see Karl Hess, *Mostly on the Edge: An Autobiography* (Amherst, N.Y.: Prometheus, 1999), 184; he had Hess compare the number of combat decorations against Administration claims that Americans were only in "noncombatant" roles.

341   *"The essence of freedom"*: *Time*, September 25, 1964. For Prop 14 generally: ibid. and Pierre Salinger, *With Kennedy* (Garden City, N.Y.: Doubleday, 1966), 391–92; Eric Foner, *The Story of American Freedom* (New York: Norton, 1998), 314; Margolis, *Last Innocent Year*, 117; *Californians Should Have Freedom of Choice*, pamphlet of Committee for Yes on Proposition #14 to Abolish Rumford Forced Housing Act, Radical Right Collection, Box 4, HI; and author interview with Noel Black. For proposition language, see NR, September 22, 1964. For signature collection, see LAT, February 25, 1964.

342   For billboards, see *Time*, September 25, 1964. For LAT endorsement, see February 2, 1964. For role of racial covenants, and ethnic discrimination in FHA underwriting guidelines in postwar suburbia, see George Lipsitz, "The Possessive Investment in Whiteness," *American Quarterly* (September 1995). For 58 percent figure, see *The Reporter*, July 2, 1964. For Goldwater's public agnosticism on Prop 14, see *Time*, September 25, 1964.

342   For Cambridge, Maryland, race riot, see Dan T. Carter, *The Politics of Rage: George Wallace, the Origins of the New Conservatism, and the Transformation of American Politics* (Baton Rouge: Louisiana State University Press, 1995), 213–14. For Dirksen meeting, see Margolis, *Last Innocent Year*, 208–9. *"You cannot pass a law"*: May 12, 1964, to Madison Square Garden, RAC, Box 11/888, and AHF, Box 1/11. Applause is noted in *Newsweek*, May 25, 1964.

342   For Goldwater MSG rally, see ML, Box 91, and Box 88/National Goldwater Rally. For "put the accent" quote, see *Newsweek*, May 25, 1964.

343   For "Looselippmann" quip, see John Gregory Dunne, "Marvin in Manialand," in *Quintana and Friends* (New York: Dutton, 1979). For give-and-take in polls, see White, *Making of the President 1964*, 151. *Senator Goldwater Speaks Out on the Issues*: AC. For pamphlet release date, see transcript of *ABC Reports*, May 14, 1964, RAC, Box 11/893. *"The next logical step"*: transcript of May 15, 1964, radio call-in show, RAC, Box 11/894. Council on Foreign Relations quote: ibid. *"I hope I'm as wrong as I could be"*: *ABC Reports*, May 14, 1964.

343   *"The senator is too busy"*: "Far Right and Far Left," NYP, April 15, 1964.

343   For NAR's Oregon bounce, see White, *Making of the President 1964*, 151.

343   For "H-Bomb button" brochure, see James M. Perry, *A Report in Depth on Barry Goldwater: The Story of the 1964 Republican Presidential Nominee* (Silver Spring, Md.: National Observer, 1964), 102–3; and Kessel, *Goldwater Coalition*, 85.

344   For reaction to brochure, see May 26, 1964, Goldwater press release, RAC, Box 11/908; White with Gill, *Suite 3505*, 341; and George D. Wolf, *William Warren Scranton: Pennsylvania Statesman* (State College: Penn State Press, 1981), 104. For Lodge organization's failed efforts for Rockefeller, see Kessel, *Goldwater Coalition*, 83, 85. *"I personally believe that Goldwater"*: see Goldwater speech, May 16, 1964, in Santa Rosa, RAC, Box 11/896, and AHF, Box 1/20.

344   For Beckwith and Mississippi, see Taylor Branch, *Pillar of Fire: America in the King Years, 1963–1965* (New York: Simon and Schuster, 1998), 321–33. For Wallace results in Maryland, see Carter, *Politics of Rage*, 215.

344   For threats to Rockefeller, see Anderson and Lee, "1964 Election in California." *"This is the kind of extremist tactics"*: Perry, *Report in Depth. Billboards that
were mysteriously chainsawed*: author interview with Noel Black. For agents provocateurs, see CT, June 4, 1964. For "Rodeo of Rodeos" parade, see *Phoenix Republic*,
March 13, 1964, clip in SHBGS.

345   For Rockefeller California advertising, see Bill Roberts, "General Outline,"
RAC, Box 11/935; also RAC, Box 11/937. The 1,200 phone solicitors are mentioned
in White, *Making of the President 1964*, 153. White's sabotage: author interview
with Jameson Campaigne Jr. For subcontracting publicists and black college list, see
Perry, *Report in Depth*, 99. For "truth squad" and Goldwater quote, see Scrapbook
298, MCSL, 18. For expense-account lunches, see, for example, Danzig expense
voucher, RAC, Box 11/933. For eighteen-stop schedule, see *Time*, May 29, 1964. For
Colorado River charges, see May 20, 1964, speech in Stockton, LAT, May 21, 1964.

345   For Burch inspection tour, see Richard Kleindienst, *Justice: The Memoirs of an
Attorney General* (Ottawa, Ill.: Jameson Books, 1985), 35; Harper to Baus, April 23,
1964, FCW, Box 8/Baus and Ross; and Shadegg, *What Happened*, 117, 119, 121. For
businessmen's fears, see *Time*, June 12, 1964. For Knowland's travels and predictions, see "Victory for Goldwater in California Forecast," LAT, January 20, 1964;
and Montgomery and Johnson, *One Step from the White House*, 271.

345   For Knowland's firing, see Kleindienst, *Justice*, 35.

346   The Garbo operation is described in Edwards, *Goldwater*, 219–20; Shadegg,
What Happened, 116, 121–26; and author interviews with Lee Edwards, Ron Crawford, and Charles Lichenstein.

346   Goldwater California pamphlet is in AC. Clip of "meandering stream" joke in
A&E Television Network, *Nelson Rockefeller: Passionate Millionaire* (1997, cat. no.
AAE-17506). For transcript of "upside-down" ad, see RAC, Box 11/910. For men on
the street, see Kessel, *Goldwater Coalition*, 87; transcript in RAC, Box 11/910; and
Lichenstein interview.

346   For "school chums" letter, see Goldberg, *Barry Goldwater*, 191; and White
with Gill, *Suite 3505*, 346. For finance office calls, see Perry, *Report in Depth*, 105.

346   For McNamara visit, see William J. Miller, *Henry Cabot Lodge: A Biography*
(New York: Heineman, 1967), 357.

347   For May 24, 1964, *Issues and Answers* quote, see transcript in RAC, Box 11/904.

347   For earlier Goldwater comment that nuclear weapons should be used in Vietnam, see David Susskind's *Open End* TV show, October 20, 1963, transcript in
RAC, Box 10/770.

347   For nuclear headlines, see Goldberg, *Barry Goldwater*, 191; and Karl Hess, *In a
Cause That Will Triumph: The Goldwater Campaign and the Future of Conservatism*
(New York: Doubleday, 1967), 124. RFK's quip is in Rita Lang Kleinfelder, *When
We Were Young: A Baby-Boomer Yearbook* (New York: Prentice Hall, 1993), 363.
"Goldwater wasn't asked": "Goldwater's Plan for A-Weapons in Viet, Maybe,"
NYHT, May 25, 1964. For the Eisenhower article, see White with Gill, *Suite 3505*,
242; and "On the Republicans' Choice: A Personal Statement by Eisenhower,"
NYHT, May 25, 1964. For "shoe" quote, see *Newsweek*, June 8, 1964.

348   *The New York Times said Eisenhower's words*: NYT, May 27, 1964. Lubell quotes in *Chicago Daily News*, June 1, 1964. The Hoover phone call is in Goldberg, *Barry Goldwater*, 192.

348   For Honolulu meeting, see Robert S. McNamara with Brian VanDeMark, *In Retrospect: The Tragedy and Lessons of Vietnam* (New York: Vintage, 1995), 212; and H. R. McMaster, *Dereliction of Duty: Lyndon Johnson, Robert McNamara, the Joint Chiefs of Staff, and the Lies that Led to Vietnam* (New York: HarperCollins, 1997), 99.

348   The conversation with Russell is in Michael Beschloss, ed., *Taking Charge: The Johnson White House Tapes, 1963–1964* (New York: Simon and Schuster, 1997), 363–70; with Bundy, in Beschloss, 370–73.

348   *"You've got to warn the senator"*: Harold Faber, ed., *The Road to the White House: The Story of the 1964 Election by the Staff of the New York Times* (New York: McGraw-Hill, 1965), 39.

349   For the story of *A Choice Not an Echo*, I rely on Carol Felsenthal, *Sweetheart of the Silent Majority: The Biography of Phyllis Schlafly* (New York: Doubleday, 1981), 176–77; Peter Carol, *Famous in America: The Passion to Succeed: Jane Fonda, George Wallace, Phyllis Schlafly, John Glenn* (New York: Dutton, 1995); and author interview with Phyllis Schlafly.

350   Reagan's Goldwater broadcast transcript is in RAC, Box 11/914. *"And good evening to all you irresponsible Republicans"*: Faber, ed., *The Road to the White House*, 39. For San Francisco fund-raiser, see Walton to Knowland, April 16, 1964, FCW, Box 8/Rus Walton.

350   Steve Allen transcript is in RAC, Box 11/913. For "Let Freedom Ring," see GRR, September 1, 1964.

351   For 49 to 40 percent poll, see White, *Making of the President 1964*, 151. *"I have a show opening"*: Edwards, *Goldwater*, 225.

351   For cancellation of Loyola appearance: Shadegg, *What Happened*, 125; and Lee Edwards interview. For Protestant ministers, see Goldberg, *Barry Goldwater*, 193. Rockefeller, the ministers proclaimed, had "struck a serious blow against the Christian concept of marriage."

351   For Rockefeller cutting back advertising, see Edwards, *Goldwater*, 28. For *The Extremist*, see production script, RAC, Box 11/944. For cancellation, see GRR, June 29, 1964. For $1 million in last week, see *Time*, May 29, 1964. For Goldwater's reluctance to go negative, see CT, June 4, 1964, and May 23, 1964, Goldwater statement in FSA, Box 4. *"I would think a long time"*: May 29, 1964, in Inglewood, RAC, Box 11/908. For statement on "destructive charges," see Anderson and Lee, "1964 Election in California."

352   For Goldwater's Riverside appearance, see White, *Making of the President 1964*, 154–55; and (for MacNeil story) author interview with anonymous source.

352   For Knott's Berry Farm, see McGirr, "Suburban Warriors," 167; GRR, June 12, 1964; speech transcript in RAC, Box 11/920. For John Wayne and Ronald Reagan story, see Howard K. Smith, *Events Leading Up to My Death: The Life of a Twentieth-Century Reporter* (New York: St. Martin's Press, 1996), 309–10.

353   Goldwater retreating to play with ham radio: AR, July 16, 1964. For Goldwater
canvass, see Kessel, *Goldwater Coalition*, 87; *Time*, June 12, 1964; and White with
Gill, *Suite 3505*, 338.

353   For Hannah Nixon, see White with Gill, 326; and Rowland Evans and Robert
Novak, "The Unmaking of a President," *Esquire*, November 1964.

353   Eisenhower's about-face is in Edwards, *Goldwater*, 223. *"You can't canter
without a horse"*: Goldberg, *Barry Goldwater*, 193. Final Harris polls are in White
with Gill, *Suite 3505*, 344. *"Please keep in mind"*: Kessel, *Goldwater Coalition*, 85.

353   The story of CBS on election night is told in Bill Leonard, *In the Storm of the
Eye: A Lifetime at CBS* (New York: G. P. Putnam's Sons, 1987), 95–113.

354   For California primary returns, see Anderson and Lee, "1964 Election in California." For the failing of polls, see Earl Mazo, "California Republican Primary Trips
the Polls," NYT, June 4, 1964. For the role of *A Choice, Not an Echo*, see Shadegg,
What Happened, 124. The story of Goldwater's drinking is in Edwards, *Goldwater*,
227. *"I'm going right down the line"*: *Chicago Daily News*, June 3, 1964.

355   *In Mississippi, Freedom Summer organizers*: author interview with Congress-
man Barney Frank. For "little old ladies in tennis shoes," see Stanley Mosk and
Howard H. Jewel, "The Birch Phenomenon Analyzed," NYTM, August 20, 1961.
For packages: "Mosk 'Flooded' by Shoes, Sandles," SFC, August 10, 1961. Foreign
press roundup is in *Time*, June 12, 1964. For de-Nazification trials, see "Ugly Past
Lives Again in Germany Nazi Trials," LAT, February 23, 1964.

355   Religious retreat story is from author interview with Graham T. T. Molitor.

17. DUTY

356   The theory that governors are inherently moderates is in Theodore H. White,
The Making of the President 1964 (New York: Atheneum, 1965), 176. For the governors' dread over racial disorder, see USN, June 22, 1964.

357   Narration of Cleveland governors conference is from James M. Perry, *A Report
in Depth on Barry Goldwater: The Story of the 1964 Republican Presidential Nominee* (Silver Spring, Md.: National Observer, 1964), 109–12; *Newsweek*, June 22,
1964; F. Clifton White with William Gill, *Suite 3505: The Story of the Draft Goldwater Movement* (New Rochelle, N.Y.: Arlington House, 1967), 362–68; George D.
Wolf, *William Warren Scranton: Pennsylvania Statesman* (State College: Penn State
Press, 1981), 104–7; Stephen Shadegg, *What Happened to Goldwater?: The Inside
Story of the 1964 Republican Campaign* (New York: Holt, Rinehart, and Winston,
1965), 126–28; Rowland Evans and Robert Novak, "The Unmaking of a President,"
Esquire, November 1964, esp. for Nixon's role; Murray Kempton, TNR, June 20,
1964; and *Time*, June 19, 1964.

358   Exposé of Johnson's business dealings is in "The Johnson Money," WS, June 9,
1964. Rostow's "up to and including all-out nuclear war" is in NYT, June 9, 1964.
For King in St. Augustine, see Taylor Branch, *Pillar of Fire: America in the King
Years, 1963–1965* (New York: Simon and Schuster, 1998), 326–27, 337–40.

359   Scranton's brooding and decision are in Perry, *A Report in Depth*, 113–14;
Time, June 19, 1964; and Wolf, *William Warren Scranton*, 108–10.

359   For Maryland state chair, see Robert Novak, *The Agony of the GOP 1964* (New
        York: Macmillan, 1965), 298. Scranton's entrance speech is in Walter Judd Papers,
        Box 213/Presidential Campaigns, HI.

360   For Scranton's December letter to Goldwater, see White with Gill, *Suite 3505*,
        368. *"The Republican establishment is desperate"*: NYT, June 13, 1964. *"I guess he
        doesn't know my views"*: Murray Kempton, TNR, June 20, 1964.

360   For Scranton campaign trail quotes, see John Kessel, *The Goldwater Coalition:
        Republican Strategies in 1964* (Indianapolis: Bobbs-Merrill, 1968), 101; NYT, June
        16, 1964; *Life*, June 26, 1964; *Time*, June 26, 1964, and July 3, 1964; Mary McGrory,
        WS, June 19, 1964; and Wolf, *William Warren Scranton*, 112–13.

360   "A coordinated labor market" is in *Detroit News*, June 27, 1964. For Scranton's
        Taft quotes, see *Time*, July 3, 1964. For the liberals' Taft fetish, see "Campaigner
        Goldwater," Stewart Alsop, SEP, September 19, 1964; David Riesman quote in
        "Thunder on the Far Right: Fear and Frustration," *Newsweek*, December 4, 1961;
        White, *Making of the President 1964*, 113, 117–18, 262; Richard Hofstadter, "A
        Long View: Goldwater in History," NYRB, October 8, 1964; and Bruce Chapman,
        interviewed on *ABC Reports*, November 10, 1963, RAC, Box 10/773. Lippmann,
        Time, and Rovere quotes are in James T. Patterson, *Mr. Republican: A Biography of
        Robert Taft* (Boston: Houghton Mifflin, 1972), 314, 531.

361   For Scranton's strategy, see Kessel, *Goldwater Coalition*, 99; and Wolf,
        William Warren Scranton, 114. Telegrams and so forth to delegates: White with Gill,
        Suite 3505, 379. For 55 to 34 Gallup poll, see *Time*, July 3, 1964. Schlafly on Gallup
        is in Phyllis Schlafly, *A Choice, Not an Echo* (Alton, Ill.: Pere Marquette Press,
        1964), 45. Buckley quote is in John B. Judis, *William F. Buckley, Jr.: Patron Saint of
        the Conservatives* (New York: Touchstone, 1990), 207.

361   For "on the right track" statement, hear LBJT, 6406.16/12. For what the GI told
        him, see William J. Miller, *Henry Cabot Lodge: A Biography* (New York: Heineman,
        1967), 363. For Milton Eisenhower, see TNR, June 20, 1964. For Gates, see Mid-
        dendorf to Burch, June 26, 1964, and Middendorf to Kitchel, June 26, 1964, FCW,
        Box 8/Wm. Middendorf. For Dewey, see *Newsweek*, July 6, 1964.

362   Schlafly quotes are in *A Choice Not an Echo*, 86–87.

362   For statistic on banking resources, see White, *Making of the President 1964*, 85.
        For physicians, see Jack Anderson, LAT, July 3, 1964.

362   Lodge airport reception and failed trip is in *Newsweek*, July 20, 1964. Roundup
        of media praise for Scranton campaign is in *Time*, July 3, 1964. Iowa claim is June
        16, 1964, UPI dispatch in SHBGS. For Illinois, see *Chicago Daily News* editorial,
        June 16, 1964.

362   "Storied kingmakers" quote is in *Time*, June 26, 1964. Telegrams to Goldwater:
        White with Gill, *Suite 3505*, 378.

363   For church burnings, see Branch, *Pillar of Fire*, 367–83. For Goldwater's visit
        to Eisenhower and meeting with Yerger and Grenier, see John Grenier OH, Southern
        Historical Collection, University of North Carolina at Chapel Hill, 4007: A-9.

363   For Kitchel to Goldwater in 1962, see two letters dated November 12, 1962, in
        DK, Box2/Goldwater, Barry, 1947–63. For Rehnquist in Phoenix and on *Plessy*, see

David Saraye, *Turning Right: The Making of the Rehnquist Supreme Court* (New York: John Wiley, 1992), 31–32, 35–38. For Goldwater consulting Rehnquist and Bork, see Jon Margolis, *The Last Innocent Year: America in 1964: The Beginning of the "Sixties"* (New York: Morrow, 1999), 239. For Bork brief, see Perry, *Report in Depth*. For Bork quote, see TNR, August 31, 1963.

364 Goldwater's mien on the Senate floor is described in *Time*, June 26, 1964. The full speech is in White with Gill, *Suite 3505*, 429–31.

364 For Mississippi precinct day, MFDP, Mississippi regular Democrats, and civil rights workers' disappearance, see Margolis, *Last Innocent Year*, 238, 242–55 (Cronkite quote on 254). For Lippmann column, see NYHT, June 30, 1964.

365 *The New York Times found it impossible*: "Arizona Target of GOP Leader," NYT, June 20, 1964. For Scranton courting Dirksen in Washington, see White with Gill, *Suite 3505*, 373.

365 *"It looks good in North Carolina!"*: *Birmingham World*, July 4, 1964. For Illinois whistle-stop, see Wolf, *William Warren Scranton*, 113. For Illinois delegation meeting, see White with Gill, *Suite 3505*, 372; Margolis, *Last Innocent Year*, 259; Wolf, *William Warren Scranton*, 113; and Kessel, *Goldwater Coalition*, 103.

365 For 1952 Dirksen speech, see AHF, Box W3/6.

365 For Johnson's quote upon signing the Civil Rights Act, see Branch, *Pillar of Fire*, 404. On violence, see "The Civil Rights Law Goes into Action," USN, July 20, 1964. For the LACYR's resolution, see Stewart Alsop, SEP, September 29, 1964. Scranton's trip West is in Kessel, *Goldwater Coalition*, 104. For Theodore Roosevelt's granddaughter, see White, *Making of the President 1964*, 165.

366 *"I doubt he's got it completely locked up"*: Michael Beschloss, ed., *Taking Charge: The Johnson White House Tapes, 1963–1964* (New York: Simon and Schuster, 1997), 419–20.

366 *"The 1952 tricks will be used again"*: Middendorf to Kitchel, June 26, 1964, and Middendorf to Burch, June 27, 1964, FCW, Box 8/Middendorf.

366 For White and Day at the Mark Hopkins, see White with Gill, *Suite 3505*, 381–82.

367 For White's JFK influence, see White, *Suite 3505*, 243. For JFK apparatus, see Thomas C. Reeves, *A Question of Character: A Life of John F. Kennedy* (New York: Free Press, 1991), 174; and Pierre Salinger, *With Kennedy* (Garden City, N.Y.: Doubleday, 1966), 38. For Laird, see Kessel, *Goldwater Coalition*, 107.

367 White's confidence mixed with fear is in White with Gill, *Suite 3505*, 377–78.

367 For turn-the-other-cheek strategy in platform committee, see *The GOP Constructs a Platform*, CBS News special, MTR, T78:0143.

367 For buddy system, see Shadegg, *What Happened*, 139. Transportation is described in White with Gill, *Suite 3505*, 384; and Shadegg, *What Happened*, 138, 145. For delegate binders, see Shadegg, 137. For "Can be influenced" quote, see report on Michigan delegate Robert Flood; AHF, Box W3/4.

367 For delegation command posts, see *Chicago Daily News*, July 14, 1964.

367 For communications system, see White with Gill, *Suite 3505*, 381–82; Lee Edwards, *Goldwater: The Man Who Made a Revolution* (Washington, D.C.: Reg-

nery, 1995), 254; Shadegg, *What Happened*, 137, 159; White, *Making of the President 1964*; *Time*, July 13, 1964; and author interviews with Lee Edwards and Ron Crawford.

368   For TV and radio setup: author interview with Edwards and Carol Dawson; Shadegg, *What Happened*, 145; White with Gill, *Suite 3505*, 383.

368   For security, see Drew Pearson, "A Look at Barry's 'Armed Camp,' " WP, July 15, 1964; *Time*, July 13, 1964; and White with Gill, *Suite 3505*, 383–84. See also photographs in AHFCP, vol. 3, photos 15, 16, 18, and 22.

369   The trailer is described in Shadegg, *What Happened*, 144–45; Margolis, *Last Innocent Year*, 267; White, *Making of the President 1964*, 264; and F. Clifton White with Jerome Tuccille, *Politics as a Noble Calling* (Ottawa, Ill.: Jameson Books, 1994), 159. For trailer security, see Shadegg, *What Happened*, 159. For pools of volunteers, see "Special Trains Head for S.F.," *Youth for Goldwater Newsletter*, March 1964, JCJ. For warehouses, see *Newsweek*, July 13, 1964.

369   For media setup I rely on Shadegg, *What Happened*, 134; White, *Making of the President 1964*, 231; Herb Caen, *San Francisco Chronicle*, July 16, 1964; WP, July 13, 1964, and July 15, 1964; Alan Brinkley, "The Taming of the Political Convention," in Brinkley, *Liberalism and Its Discontents* (Cambridge, Mass.: Harvard University Press, 1998), 249–65; J. Leonard Reinsch, *Getting Elected: From Radio and Roosevelt to Television and Reagan* (New York: Hippocrene, 1988), 107, 289; *The GOP Constructs a Platform*, CBS News special (for "us television types"); Norman Mailer, "In a Blue Light: A History of the 1964 Republican Convention," *Esquire*, November 1964; and author interview with Alan Brinkley.

18. CONVENTIONS

371   *The RNC first estimated that 20,000*: WP, July 12, 1964.

371   For civil rights march, see Arnold Rampersad, *Jackie Robinson: A Biography* (New York: Knopf, 1997), 86; NYT, July 13, 1964; and CBS News special, MTR, T78:0143.

371   Scranton billboards: *Newsweek*, July 13, 1964. Nob Hill traffic: WP, July 13, 1964. *"We are the Goldwater armeeeee"*: Ralph McGill column, *Atlanta Constitution*, July 11, 1964. Phyllis Schlafly: Carol Felsenthal, *Sweetheart of the Silent Majority: The Biography of Phyllis Schlafly* (New York: Doubleday, 1981), 163–78. Ronald Reagan: Gore Vidal, *United States: Essays, 1952–1992* (New York: Random House, 1993), 980. Buckley: Gregory Schneider, *Cadres for Conservatism: Young Americans for Freedom and the Rise of the Contemporary Right* (New York: NYU Press, 1999), 81–82; and WP, July 12, 1964. Eisenhower: CBS News special, MTR, T78:0143. Scranton and BMG followed by chants: AHFCP, vol. 1, picture 14.

372   For "Merry Pranksters," see Tom Wolfe, *The Electric Kool-Aid Acid Test* (New York: Farrar, Straus and Giroux, 1968). For North Beach and "Eisenhower Sway," see William J. Miller, *Henry Cabot Lodge: A Biography* (New York: Heineman, 1967), 368; and WP, July 12, 1964. Dick Gregory: author interview with Jameson Campaigne Jr.; and *Newsweek*, July 20, 1964.

372   For *Der Spiegel*, see WSJ, July 31, 1964; F. Clifton White with William Gill,

Suite 3505: The Story of the Draft Goldwater Movement (New Rochelle, N.Y.: Arlington House, 1967), 389; and, for transcript, LBJWHAM, Box 30/Clippings and Document and Departmental Refutations Book, 1 of 3. *"Now decided to defoliate"*: White with Gill, *Suite 3505*, 390.

373   For aides' briefing of BMG before his first press conference, see "Barry and the Bomb," NYHTEN, July 17, 1964. Press conference in CBS News special, MTR, T78:0143.

373   *"Vote our wishes in San Francisco"*: Peter Kohler to Goldwater, May 4, 1964, FCW, Box 8. For Rhodes's courting of Scranton, see Jack Steele column, *Washington Daily News*, October 1, 1963; LAT, February 26, 1964; SLPD, December 11, 1964; and Robert Novak, *The Agony of the GOP 1964* (New York: Macmillan, 1965), 288. For backlash theory and release of the Ohio delegation, see "The White Man's Party," NYHTEN, July 15, 1964; AR, July 10, 1964; *Cleveland Call and Post*, July 18, 1964; George D. Wolf, *William Warren Scranton: Pennsylvania Statesman* (State College: Penn State Press, 1981), 115; and Theodore H. White, *The Making of the President 1964* (New York: Atheneum, 1965), 236.

373   *"The November outcome"*: Taylor Branch, *Pillar of Fire: America in the King Years, 1963–1965* (New York: Simon and Schuster, 1998), 340. *"The nigger issue"*: Ralph McGill column, *Atlanta Constitution*, July 11, 1964. *A Goldwater win*: NYT, July 22, 1964. *"I would withdraw from the race"*: WP, July 13, 1964; and press conference in CBS News special, MTR, T78:0143.

374   List of 110 delegates: WP, July 13, 1964. For Scranton's strategy, see "The Fight That Failed," n.d. clip in LBJWHAM, Box 30/Clippings and Document and Departmental Refutations Book, 1 of 3. For the single Florida delegate, see UPI-65, wire dispatch, AHF, Box W3/4. Keating announcement: CBS News special, MTR, T78:0143.

374   *"Markets don't just happen"*: clip, ibid. *"No one in his right mind"*: Miller, *Henry Cabot Lodge*, 365. *"I voted for you in 1960"*: WP, July 13, 1964. *"What in God's name"*: Miller, *Henry Cabot Lodge*, 365.

375   *"Governor, Governor, could you"*: Norman Mailer, "In a Blue Light: A History of the 1964 Republican Convention," *Esquire*, November 1964. Hugh Scott negotiations in White, *Making of the President 1964*, 237; and John Kessel, *The Goldwater Coalition: Republican Strategies in 1964* (Indianapolis: Bobbs-Merrill, 1968), 111.

375   For Schorr report: Daniel Schorr, *Clearing the Air* (Boston: Houghton Mifflin, 1997), 7; WSJ, July 31, 1964; clip is in A&E Television Network, *Barry Goldwater: The Conscience of Conservatives* (1996, cat. no. AAE-14345).

375   BMG feud with CBS is in Barry Goldwater, *The Conscience of a Majority* (Englewood Cliffs, N.J.: Prentice-Hall, 1970), 173–81. *"You can say what you want"*: Herb Caen, SFC, July 16, 1964.

376   *"I've avoided discussing"*: AHFCP, vol. 1, pictures 14–19. For Texas's natural committeewoman: Wolf, *William Warren Scranton*, 115.

376   Jim Martin story in Dan T. Carter, *The Politics of Rage: George Wallace, the Origins of the New Conservatism, and the Transformation of American Politics* (Baton Rouge: Louisiana State University Press, 1995), 219–21.

376   Wallace's presidential plans: Stephan Lesher, *George Wallace: American Populist* (Reading, Mass.: Addison-Wesley, 1994), 306–8.

376   For *The Clubwoman*, see Dorothy Newman, "GOP Gals Play It Cool," *San Francisco News-Call Bulletin*, July 14, 1964. Sunday headlines from July 12, 1964, WP.

377   Scranton on *Meet the Press*: WP, July 13, 1964. For Scranton letter and Goldwater response, see Wolf, *William Warren Scranton*, 115–17; White, *Making of the President 1964*, 238; White with Gill, *Suite 3505*, 390–93; Lee Edwards, *Goldwater: The Man Who Made a Revolution* (Washington, D.C.: Regnery, 1995), 258; and *Time*, July 24, 1964.

377   Full text of letter is in Stephen Shadegg, *What Happened to Goldwater?: The Inside Story of the 1964 Republican Campaign* (New York: Holt, Rinehart, and Winston, 1965), 152–54.

378   For dinner-dance, see Mailer, "In a Blue Light"; and *Baltimore Afro-American*, July 25, 1964.

378   *The Monday papers*: WP, July 13, 1964. For Mark Hopkins elevators, see Mailer, "In a Blue Light." *"You know, these nighttime news shows"*: David Brinkley, *David Brinkley: 11 Presidents, 4 Wars, 22 Political Conventions, 1 Moon Landing, 3 Assassinations, 2,000 Weeks of News and Other Stuff on Television, and 18 Years Growing Up in North Carolina* (New York: Knopf, 1995), 161. Aspirin with press badge: WP, July 13, 1964. *Brinkley forbade his young son*: author interview with Alan Brinkley.

379   Geneva Drive-In: Keyston to Walton, FCW, Box 8/Rus Walton. CORE vigil: *Jet*, July 30, 1964; William F. Buckley column, LAT, July 16, 1964; Marquis Childs column, WP, July 10, 1964; and White, *Making of the President 1964*, 240–41. For security, see WP, July 12, 1964; and obituary of Wesley A. Pomeroy, NYT, May 15, 1998. *"Escape the diabolical enslavement"*: front-page editorial, *Chicago Defender*, July 25, 1964. *"We must not forget"*: LAT, July 14, 1964.

379   For "Lincoln League" and the Memphis Republican convention: Thomas Byrne Edsall and Mary D. Edsall, *Chain Reaction: The Impact of Race, Rights, and Taxes on American Politics* (New York: Norton, 1991), 43; "GOP Negroes Washed Away by the Goldwater Ocean," *Chicago Defender*, July 9, 1964; and author interview with Jack Craddock. Steers motion is in *Proceedings of the 28th Republican National Convention* (Washington, D.C.: Republican National Committee, 1964), 30.

380   *Lee, for his part*: Craddock interview.

380   Hatfield keynote: *Proceedings*, 76–80; and William Martin, *With God on Our Side: The Rise of the Religious Right in America* (New York: Broadway Books, 1996), 83. Masonic Temple rally: WP, July 15, 1964; Carroll Kilpatrick, "Goldwater Sets Off 2 Smashing Broadsides," unidentified clip in LBJWHAM, Box 30; and "Atlantic Report on the World Today," *Atlantic Monthly*, September 1964.

380   Headlines: WP, July 14, 1964. For Nixon's arrival, see *Chicago Defender*, July 24, 1964; and CBS News special, MTR, T78:0143. Scranton: WP, July 15, 1964; and n.d. clip, Presidential Nomination File/"Press Reps, 2 of 9," MCSL. Credentials Committee Vote: NYT, July 15, 1964. For Goldwater's flight, see Edwards, *Goldwater*, 263.

381   Eisenhower address in *Proceedings*, 180–87.

381   For writing and reaction to Eisenhower address, see Harold Faber, ed., *The Road to the White House: The Story of the 1964 Election by the Staff of the New York Times* (New York: McGraw-Hill, 1965), 63; Miller, *Henry Cabot Lodge*, 368; Sidney Warren, *The Battle for the Presidency* (Philadelphia: Lippincott, 1968), 354; WP, July 17, 1964; Brinkley, *David Brinkley*, 162; and Mailer, "In a Blue Light."

382   For platform-reading tactic, see Faber, ed., *Road to the White House*, 63. *Viva! Olé!*: Mailer, "In a Blue Light"; Burton Bernstein, profile of BMG, *The New Yorker*, April 25, 1988; and author interview with John Savage.

382   *Bored delegates were milling about*: *Chicago Sun Times*, July 15, 1964. Chancellor arrest: J. Leonard Reinsch, *Getting Elected: From Radio and Roosevelt to Television and Reagan* (New York: Hippocrene, 1988), 190. For attempt to remove Mike Wallace, see *Chicago Sun Times*, July 15, 1964.

382   Hugh Scott amendment introduction: *Proceedings*, 216–19.

383   Rockefeller's speech can be seen in part in A&E Television Network, *Nelson Rockefeller: Passionate Millionaire* (1997, cat. no. AAE-17506); and the video *Great American Speeches: 80 Years of Political Oratory*, vol. 2 (Pieri and Spring, 1995). Also described in Rampersad, *Jackie Robinson*, 387; Jon Margolis, *The Last Innocent Year: America in 1964: The Beginning of the "Sixties"* (New York: Morrow, 1999), 271; and *Time*, July 24, 1964. Transcript in *Proceedings*, 217–23, including interjections from crowd and Morton.

383   For beginning of booing: author interview with Noel Black.

383   For Clif White's failed "all-call," see Edwards, *Goldwater*, 261.

383   *Jackie Robinson was hanging back*: Jackie Robinson, *I Never Had It Made* (Hopewell, N.J.: Ecco Press, 1995), 162.

384   For the rest of the amendments, see *Proceedings*, 219–62. *"The South took the Mason-Dixon line"*: *Newsweek*, July 26, 1964.

384   For beginning of BMG's day and kitchen confrontation, see Edwards, *Goldwater*, 263; WP, July 16, 1964; and Faber, ed., *Road to the White House*, 65.

385   For Scranton Missouri caucus meeting, see Buckley column, LAT, July 16, 1964.

385   For ticket problems, see *Chicago Daily News*, July 16, 1964; Shadegg, *What Happened*, 162; and CT, July 16, 1964.

385   Walk with Lady Bird: LBJT, 6407.08/22; Jack Bell, *The Johnson Treatment: How Lyndon B. Johnson Took Over the Presidency and Made It His Own* (New York: Harper and Row, 1965), 236.

385   For Texas KKK rumor problem, see Robert Dallek, *Flawed Giant: Lyndon Johnson and His Times, 1961–1973* (New York: Oxford University Press, 1998), 125. Economic fine-tuning: Bell, *Johnson Treatment*, 236. For voter registration, see NYT obituary of Matt Reese, December 3, 1998. "Salute to President Johnson": Michael Beschloss, ed., *Taking Charge: The Johnson White House Tapes, 1963–1964* (New York: Simon and Schuster, 1997), 361. Ted Kennedy crash: Branch, *Pillar of Fire*, 357.

386   For July 11, 1964, DDB meeting, see Kathleen Hall Jamieson, *Packaging the Presidency: A History and Criticism of Presidential Campaign Advertising*, 3rd ed. (New York: Oxford University Press, 1996), 188, 217. For Doyle Dane Bernbach, and comparison to Rosser Reeves and David Ogilvy, see Thomas C. Frank, *The Conquest of Cool* (Chicago: University of Chicago Press, 1997), 35–73.

386   For DDB's work with the LBJ campaign, see Pete Hamill, "When the Client Is a Candidate," NYTM, October 25, 1964; Jamieson, *Packaging the Presidency*, 169–220; and Edwin Diamond and Stephen Bates, *The Spot: The Rise of Political Advertising on Television* (Cambridge, Mass.: MIT Press, 1984), 121–47.

386   For the new policy on spots within programs, see Reinsch, *Getting Elected*, 189. Teddy White's lament about the effect of TV on democracy is in *The Making of the President 1960* (New York: Atheneum, 1961), 307.

386   *"The medium is the message"*: Marshall McCluhan, *Understanding Media* (New York: Signet, 1964).

387   Structure of DDB operation described in Hamill, "When the Client Is a Candidate." Scrapping civil rights ads: Jamieson, *Packaging the Presidency*, 217. *"Kids being born with two heads"*: LBJT, 6407.11/1.

387   For interruptions of Dirksen, see AR, July 16, 1964; and WP, July 16, 1964.

387   BMG demonstration: AR, July 16, 1964; WP, July 16, 1964; Edwards, *Goldwater*, 266; and Mailer, "In a Blue Light."

388   Minister in donkey costume is from author interview with Sara Jane Sayer.

388   For Scranton demonstration, see Wolf, *William Warren Scranton*, 120.

388   Nomination roll call in *Proceedings*, 357–73.

389   For Scranton concession, see Mailer, "In a Blue Light"; and Edwards, *Goldwater*, 266 (for Goldwater quotes).

389   For Bill Miller, see "Goldwater's Running Mate," NYT, July 17, 1964; Dom Bonafede, "A Long Way from Lockport, N.Y., to . . . ," NYHT, September 20, 1964; the speeches in Bill Miller Papers, Cornell University Special Collections, Box 68; and Congressional Quarterly, *The Public Records of Barry M. Goldwater and William E. Miller: The Lives, Votes and Stands of the 1964 Republican Candidates* (Washington, D.C.: Congressional Quarterly Service, 1964). For his conservative support, see AR, July 16, 1964. His remark about dancing the twist is discussed on the CBS show *Capitol Cloakroom*, October 20, 1963, transcript in RAC III 14 22/10/769. For "riddle" ditty, see Jamieson, *Packaging of the Presidency*, 171. Goldwater states his reasons for selecting him in Congressional Quarterly, *The Public Records of Barry M. Goldwater and William E. Miller*.

389   Miller nomination and Linkletter in *Proceedings*, 392–403. For Nixon's appearance, see Rowland Evans and Robert Novak, "The Unmaking of a President," *Esquire*, November 1964; Miller, *Henry Cabot Lodge*, 367; Richard Nixon, *RN: The Memoirs of Richard Nixon*, vol. 1 (New York: Warner Books, 1978), 320; and White, *Making of the President 1964*, 258.

390   Planning for acceptance speech: Edwards, *Goldwater*, 266–69; Barry Goldwater with Jack Casserly, *Goldwater* (Garden City, N.Y.: Doubleday, 1988), 185; Shadegg, *What Happened*, 166; *Time*, July 24, 1964; *Philadelphia Bulletin*, July 22,

1964; letter to editor of *Washington Times* from Henry Jaffa, June 13, 1986; and author interview with Charles Lichenstein.

391   For delivery, see video *Great American Speeches: 80 Years of Political Oratory*, vol. 2 (Pieri and Spring, 1995); White with Gill, *Suite 3505*, 13; White, *Making of the President 1964*, 258; and Shadegg, *What Happened*, 167. Nixon and BMG transcripts in *Proceedings*, 408–19.

391   White in trailer: White with Gill, *Suite 3505*, 14. Keating: WP, July 18, 1964. Richard Nixon restraining wife: Christopher Matthews, *Kennedy and Nixon: The Rivalry That Shaped Postwar America* (New York: Touchstone, 1996), 138, 248. Earthquake in ABC booth: Howard K. Smith, *Events Leading Up to My Death: The Life of a Twentieth-Century Reporter* (New York: St. Martin's Press, 1996), 309. *Wirt Yerger walked up to George Romney*: author interview with Wirt Yerger.

392   *"If a party so committed"*: WP, July 14, 1964. *"To extol extremism"*: "Rockefeller's Words About 'Extremism,' " NYHT, July 18, 1964. *Eisenhower labeled the speech an offense*: Warren, *Battle for the Presidency*, 357. Eisenhower and "switchblade issue": *Time*, July 24, 1964. *"Latent white resentment of militant Negro claims"*: *Philadelphia Bulletin*, July 22, 1964.

392   *To the New York Times's editorialists*: NYT, July 16, 1964, A30. *"There may not be a day after tomorrow"*: cited in NR, July 6, 1998. For Fulbright's four Senate speeches against BMG, see *Congressional Record* copies in LBJWHM6-3, October 16 to October 26 Folder.

393   Roundup of world press in WP, July 18, 1964. "Brown shirts" quote in *Time*, July 24, 1964. *According to an editorial*: "The Greatest Danger," WS, July 15, 1964.

393   Republicans grabbing Democratic buttons: Herb Caen column, SFC, July 17, 1964.

393   Waking up at 8:15: F. Clifton White with Jerome Tuccille, *Politics as a Noble Calling* (Ottawa, Ill.: Jameson Books, 1994), 161. *"White's reward if Goldwater is nominated"*: *Time*, July 17, 1964.

393   *"Is this thing on Dean Burch a secret"*: White with Tuccille, *Noble Calling*, 160. *"One of my dearest and closest friends"*: Shadegg, *What Happened*, 171.

394   For wake in the Fairmont and presentation of wristwatches, see Shadegg, 167.

394   For White's depression and difficulty packing for his trip, see White with Tuccille, *Noble Calling*, 162; and interview with William Rusher.

395   New York riots sources are Fred C. Shapiro and James W. Sullivan, *Race Riots New York 1964: What Really Happened as It Happened Before the Eyes of Two Trained Observers* (New York: Thomas Y. Crowell, 1964) (Clark and Randolph quotes); and White, *Making of the President 1964*, 266–82. Rustin scene is reproduced in *Choice*, Goldwater campaign film, AC.

396   Review of *How to Win an Election*: *New York Times Book Review*, July 26, 1964. *Chicago Sun Times* columnist: Pam Rymer, mid-August state-by-state rundown, AHF, Box W3/4.

396   Goldwater meeting with reporters: Karl Hess, "An Open Letter to Barry Goldwater," *Ramparts*, August 1969.

396   *"I'm afraid to leave my house"*: LBJ and Hoover, July 21, 1964, LBJT,

6407.05/10. "X-Factor": TRB column, TNR, July 25, 1964. *Walter Lippmann had coined the term*: Lippmann, "A Realignment of Parties?," *Newsweek*, July 20, 1964. For LBJ's backlash obsession, see James Reston, "Turbulent Democratic 'Strong-holds,'" NYT, July 29, 1964; Charles M. Benjamin to LBJ, July 16, 1964, LBJWH6-3. Quayle report: White, *Making of the President 1964*, 307. *The President sought out a loyal Southern senator*: LBJ and Reedy, July 19, 1964, LBJT, 6407.10/4.

396   Goldwater press conference: *Birmingham World*, July 25, 1964. For White House suspicions, hear LBJT, 6407.11/1. *Goldwater's "attempt to make a public display"*: July 18, 1964, memo, no identification, LBJWHAM53.

397   *Johnson told George Reedy*: July 20, 1964, 7:40 p.m., LBJT, 6407.11. *"Civil rights is something around our neck"*: LBJT, 6407.12/2.

397   For meeting preparations, see Dallek, *Flawed Giant*, 134 (for "rebuffing" quote); and Bell, *Johnson Treatment*, 172.

397   For meeting: Bell ("What a confrontation" quote); Valenti OH, LBJL; and Edwards, *Goldwater*, 242.

398   *"Things are going to hell in a hack"*: H. R. McMaster, *Dereliction of Duty: Lyndon Johnson, Robert McNamara, the Joint Chiefs of Staff, and the Lies that Led to Vietnam* (New York: HarperCollins, 1997), 97–98.

398   Reconnaissance planes, Bundy, Rusk, Mansfield: Branch, *Pillar of Fire*, 333–34. The 63 percent figure is from "Vietnam and the 1964 Election," *Public Opinion Quarterly* (Fall 1995). *When GOP congressmen began chorusing*: Dallek, *Flawed Giant*, 146; and NYT, July 15, 1964. *"We seek no wider war"*: June 23, 1964, press conference, PPP: LBJ, 804.

398   *"Defuse a Goldwater bomb"*: Moyers to LBJ, July 3, 1964, LBJWH, Box 116.

398   For Gulf of Tonkin affair I rely on McMaster, *Dereliction of Duty*, 121–36; Robert S. McNamara with Brian VanDeMark, *In Retrospect: The Tragedy and Lessons of Vietnam* (New York: Vintage, 1995), 127–43. LBJ and George Smathers: LBJT, 6408.01/4.

399   LBJ and Robert Anderson: LBJT, 6408.03/8. For the *National Enquirer* contribution and evidence of quid pro quo, see May 11, 1964, LBJWH Appointment File: Diary Backup; Watson to Dormann and attached dinner invitation with handwritten note, May 4, 1965, Jenkins to Dormann, July 6, 1964, Dormann to Richard Maguire, May 15, 1964, and Watson to Dormann, August 27, 1965, Watson to Cal, May 20, 1965, and Dormann to Watson, telegram, May 20, 1965, all in LBJWHN: Pope; Jenkins to LBJ, August 1, 1964, and Valenti, "Requests for Presidential Appointments," May 4, 1964, both in LBJWHN, Box 258/Pope, F.

400   *Johnson rang Bob McNamara*: LBJT, 6408.03/10.

400   *"Some of our boys are floating"*: Branch, *Pillar of Fire*, 435.

400   *"There are people in the Pentagon"*: Margolis, *Last Innocent Year*, 292.

400   LBJ's call to BMG: LBJT, 6408.06/16.

400   *"We don't have to make it, do we?"*: LBJT, 6408.06/7. Gulf of Tonkin speech: PPP: LBJ.

401   For origins of MFDP, see Branch, *Pillar of Fire*, 296–97, 412–15, 438–69. For

the Mississippi regular Democrats, see "Mississippi Democrats Avoid Goldwater Stand," NYT, July 29, 1964.

401 *"Put a stop to this hell-raising"*: Margolis, *Last Innocent Year*, 286. Conversation with Reuther: August 14, 1964, LBJT, 6408.02

401 For TV staging of convention and civil rights threat, see Reinsch, *Getting Elected*, 194–96. Congressman Halleck story: author interview with Ryan Hayes.

402 For FBI deployment, see Branch, *Pillar of Fire*, 461; and (for "Bishop") Margolis, *Last Innocent Year*, 329.

402 For Atlantic City BMG billboard: author interview with Lee Edwards; and Alan Brinkley, *Liberalism and Its Discontents* (Cambridge, Mass: Harvard University Press, 1998), 255. Newton Minow sabotage: Brinkley, *David Brinkley*, 163. BMG on *Today* show: RAC, Box 10/797. *Der Spiegel* interview transcript: LBJWHAM, Box 30/Clippings and Document and Departmental Refutations Book, 1 of 3.

403 Panglossian press releases: LBJWH, Press Office, Box 38. For governors at White House and Fannie Lou Hamer, see Branch, *Pillar of Fire*, 458; Brinkley, *Liberalism and Its Discontents*, 256; and Margolis, *Last Innocent Year*, 301.

403 *He paced the White House lawn*: Branch, *Pillar of Fire*, 473.

403 *"If you give 'em jobs"*: LBJT, 6408.03/1,2. *"The times require"*: Jeff Shesol, *Mutual Contempt: Lyndon Johnson, Robert Kennedy, and the Feud that Defined a Decade* (New York: Norton, 1997), 217.

404 For MFDP compromise, see Branch, *Pillar of Fire*, 458–71.

404 For *A Thousand Days*, see Shesol, *Mutual Contempt*, 218–21.

19. DON'T MENTION THE GREAT PUMPKIN

409 For Morris Goldwater and his legend, see *Prescott Courier*, January 27, 1964, SHBGS, upon the occassion of being named "Prescott Man of the Century"; and *Time*, September 11, 1964.

409 *Actually Bucky was a victim*: *Time*, September 11, 1964. *"Men with revolvers"*: "Atlantic Report on the World Today," *Atlantic Monthly*, September 1964. For Prescott self-image, see Peter Iverson, *Barry Goldwater: Native Arizonan* (Norman: University of Oklahoma Press, 1997), 162–67; Sharlot M. Hall, *Arizona's First Capital* (Prescott, Ariz.: Prescott Printing Company, 1973); *Phoenix Gazette*, August 29, 1964; and Rob Wood, "From the Desk," AP column, September 26, 1964. For world's first rodeo, see timeline in front of Yavapai County Courthouse, Prescott, Arizona.

409 For opening day plans and frustrations, see *Prescott Courier* articles in SHBGS; AHFCP, vol. 2, pictures 28–46; Victor Gold, *I Don't Need You When I'm Right: The Confessions of a Washington PR Man* (New York: Morrow, 1975), 36; and SEP, October 24, 1964.

410 BMG's speech is in *Prescott Courier*, September 3, 1964, in SHBGS.

410 *James Reston mocked the message*: Stephen Shadegg, *What Happened to Goldwater?: The Inside Story of the 1964 Republican Campaign* (New York: Holt, Rinehart, and Winston, 1965), 206. The 2.5 million figure is in BMG speech in Grand Rapids, January 6, 1964, RAC, Box 10/781. The seventeen-year-old average age is in

Jon Margolis, *The Last Innocent Year: America in 1964: The Beginning of the "Sixties"* (New York: Morrow, 1999), 157. For Pepsi Generation campaign, see Rita Lang Kleinfelder, *When We Were Young: A Baby-Boomer Yearbook* (New York: Prentice-Hall, 1993), 370. *"The buyingest age group"*: Taylor Branch, *Pillar of Fire: America in the King Years, 1963–1965* (New York: Simon and Schuster, 1998), 229. For Mustang, see Margolis, *Last Innocent Year*, 157. For *Shindig*, see Kleinfelder, *When We Were Young*, 192–93. Arthur Schlesinger's prediction is in "The New Mood in Politics," *Esquire*, January 1960.

410   For Peter, Paul and Mary, see Margolis, *Last Innocent Year*, 208. The UN march is in Margolis, 194. For SDS, see James Miller, *Democracy Is in the Streets: From Port Huron to the Siege of Chicago* (Cambridge, Mass.: Harvard University Press, 1994). The draft card burning is in Margolis, *Last Innocent Year*, 211. YAF membership figure: Matthew Dallek, "Young Americans for Freedom, 1960–1964" (master's thesis, Columbia University, 1995), 55. Birch leader's quote is in Gerald Schomp, *Birchism Was My Business* (New York: Macmillan, 1970), 20.

411   For Goldwater and the draft, see Shadegg, *What Happened*, 203. *"We're back to the days of Indian fighting"*: BMG press conference, January 18, 1964, in Fayetteville, North Carolina, RAC, Box 10/790. *"We will place power back to the people"*: Theodore H. White, *Making of the President 1964* (New York: Atheneum, 1965), 388.

411   For coining of "Great Society," see Margolis, *Last Innocent Year*, 215–18. Cook County speech is in Jack Bell, *The Johnson Treatment: How Lyndon B. Johnson Took Over the Presidency and Made It His Own* (New York: Harper and Row, 1965), 234.

411   LBJ's May 22, 1964, "Great Society" speech is in PPP: LBJ, 704.

412   *"Men worry about heart attacks"*: Frank Cormier, *LBJ the Way He Was: A Personal Memoir* (Garden City, N.Y.: Doubleday, 1977), 105.

412   For LBJ's campaign strategy, see "Campaign issue strategy" (undated [June 1964], unsigned) in LBJWHAM53; Valenti to LBJ, September 7, 1964, LBJWHAM53; advance memos and speeches in LBJWHA23 for September 8, 10, 15, 16, and 25, 1964; and, for economic pronouncements, LBJHW, Press Office, Box 38, Releases 496, 497, and 517.

412   For Tony Schwartz, see Edwin Diamond and Stephen Bates, *The Spot: The Rise of Political Advertising on Television* (Cambridge, Mass.: MIT Press, 1984), 116–20; also National Public Radio profile, February 26, 1999, *www.npr.org/ramfiles/atc/19990226.atc.05.ram.*

413   Origins of daisy spot: NPR profile; also Diamond and Bates, *The Spot*, 127–31 (for script).

413   *Bill Moyers, working late in his office*: Branch, *Pillar of Fire*, 490; Kathleen Hall Jamieson, *Packaging the Presidency: A History and Criticism of Presidential Campaign Advertising*, 3rd ed. (New York: Oxford University Press, 1996), 200; Robert Dallek, *Flawed Giant: Lyndon Johnson and His Times, 1961–1973* (New York: Oxford University Press, 1998), 175.

414   *"This horror-type commercial"*: J. Leonard Reinsch, *Getting Elected: From*

Radio and Roosevelt to Television and Reagan (New York: Hippocrene, 1988), 204. *"That's exactly what we wanted to imply"*: Moyers to LBJ, September 13, 1964, LBJWHM6-3. *Local campaign leaders*: O'Brien to LBJ, October 2, 1964, LBJWHA: Wilson, Box 3/"O'Brien trips"; Rowland Evans and Robert Novak, *Lyndon B. Johnson: The Exercise of Power: A Political Biography* (New York: New American Library, 1966), 471. For similar complaint, see Hayes to Moyers, September 18, 1964, LBJWHAM53.

414   On the FCC's regulatory retreat and NAB, see Kleinfelder, *When We Were Young*, 382; Margolis, *Last Innocent Year*, 105; "Director of Television Code Considers It Voice of Public," WP, January 11, 1964, D4; and Erik Barnouw, *Tube of Plenty: The Evolution of American Television*, 2nd ed. (New York: Oxford University Press, 1982), 250. *"In light of this commercial"*: Dirksen to Washileski, LBJWHAM53, and Washileski response.

414   *"Kenneth Kassel, a lean"*: NYT quoted in Shadegg, *What Happened*, 211. For Tony Schwartz theory, see Diamond and Bates, *The Spot*, 146–47.

415   For decision to run campaign out of RNC, see WP, July 16, 1964; Lee Edwards, *Goldwater: The Man Who Made a Revolution* (Washington, D.C.: Regnery, 1995); and John Kessel, *The Goldwater Coalition: Republican Strategies in 1964* (Indianapolis: Bobbs-Merrill, 1968), 131. *"Neither to reward nor to purge"*: Time, July 26, 1964.

415   Purge detailed in Kessel, *Goldwater Coalition*, 33 (for computer quote); SLPD, December 8, 1964; and Shadegg, *What Happened*, 167, 274. For form letters to political science chairs at universities, see Thompson to "Director, Political Science Department," August 25, 1964, AHF, Box W3/2. Leak quote from author interview with Lee Edwards.

415   For Moley advice, see Karl Hess, *In a Cause That Will Triumph: The Goldwater Campaign and the Future of Conservatism* (New York: Doubleday, 1967), 31; and Kessel, *Goldwater Coalition*, 132.

415   For physicial reconstruction, see Shadegg, *What Happened*, 175, 179; and White, *Making of the President 1964*, 378. For frustrated regional offices, and law against selling material, see Shadegg, *What Happened*, 187. For kitsch, see Roger A. Fischer, *Tippecanoe and Trinkets Too: The Material Culture of Americana Presidential Campaigns, 1828–1984* (Urbana: University of Illinois Press, 1988); Summer 1982 special issue of *The Keynoter*, "A Choice, Not an Echo: The 1964 Campaign of Barry Goldwater"; and, for multilingual bumper stickers, F. Clifton White with William Gill, *Suite 3505: The Story of the Draft Goldwater Movement* (New Rochelle, N.Y.: Arlington House, 1967), 192. Dashboard doll and comic book in AC; "Cures for What Ails America" in LBJWH6-3.

416   Completed second floor described in Kessel, *Goldwater Coalition*, 132–53 (for vote quota and communications systems); Edwards, *Goldwater*, 238; White, *Making of the President 1964*, 378–80; Shadegg, *What Happened*, 170, 190; and author interview with Carol Dawson. For campaign plane communications, see Shadegg, 194. For strategy sessions, see Kessel, *Goldwater Coalition*, 147; and Shadegg, *What Happened*, 270.

417   For preliminary poll, see Shadegg, 222.

417   For third floor, see Kessel, *Goldwater Coalition*, 134, 218; Shadegg, *What Happened*, 206–13; White with Gill, *Suite 3505*, 210; "The Men Around Goldwater," SEP, October 24, 1964; undated NYT article in Richard Dudman Papers, Library of Congress, AEI Folder; Hess, *In a Cause*, 29; Grenier to BMG, February 8, 1965, DK, Box 2/Grenier, John; and author interviews with Charles Lichenstein and Thomas Pauken.

418   For campaign plane, see *Prescott Courier*, September 3, 1964, in SHBGS; AHFCP, vol. 2, picture 26; and Kitchel to Grenier, March 11, 1965, DK, Box 2/Grenier, John. For snubbing of donors, see Shadegg, *What Happened*, 268.

418   *Peanuts* cartoon is in Kessel, *Goldwater Coalition*, 218.

418   For possible New York riots, see "The Gilligan Verdict—How Harlem Feels," NYHT, September 8, 1964. For New York busing boycott, see NYT, September 3, 8, and 15, 1964. "Bussing" spelling is in September 2, 1964, press release, New Yorkers for Goldwater-Miller, ML, Box 92/Goldwater Campaign, and undated BMG speech text, pages 17–54, AHF, Box 1/8. Platform language is in *Proceedings of the 28th Republican National Convention* (Washington, D.C.: Republican National Committee, 1964), 276. "Father-son" decision is in NYT, August 25, 1964. *"He exploded"*: Martin to Moyers, September 22, 1964, LBJWHAM53. *The AFL-CIO budgeted $12 million*: Joel Seldin, "The AFL-CIO's $12 million Backlash Cost," NYHT, September 8, 1964. For 53 to 47 poll, see Pam Rymer state-by-state summary, AHF, Box W3/4. For Cornell affirmative action experiment, see Donald Alexander Downs, *Cornell '69: Liberalism and the Crisis of the American University* (Ithaca, N.Y.: Cornell University Press, 1999), 49. For Salinger: Pierre Salinger, *With Kennedy* (Garden City, N.Y.: Doubleday, 1966), 390.

419   For "frontlash" hear, for example, LBJT, 6408.39/5. *"In pre-campaign figuring"*: *Time*, September 11, 1964. Sixteenth Congressional District: author interview with Angela Dillard. Endicott Peabody is in Branch, *Pillar of Fire*, 502. For Thomas Poindexter, see Thomas J. Sugrue, *The Origins of the Urban Crisis: Race and Inequality in Postwar Detroit* (Princeton, N.J.: Princeton University Press, 1996), 209–10, 227–28.

420   Flight to Detroit: Jack Bell, *The Johnson Treatment*, 267.

420   For Cadillac Square speech, see PPP: LBJ, 1049; and Shadegg, *What Happened*, 210.

420   *Was open to charges of deception*: Bundy to LBJ, September 23, 1964, cited in "LBJ's Nuke Strike Rules Revealed," Associated Press, May 7, 1998; see also W. W. Rostow to Bundy, September 9, 1964, LBJWHM6-3.

420   *"Every individual endeavors"*: Adam Smith, *The Wealth of Nations* (1776). For Friedman biography, see Milton Friedman and Rose Friedman, *Two Lucky People: Memoirs* (Chicago: University of Chicago Press, 1998). For refusing to speak to compulsory chapel, see ibid., 342.

421   For Friedman's popular lectures and debates, see "The Economists," *Fortune*, December 1950; Edith Kermit Roosevelt, *Newark Sunday News*, February 22, 1959; *Cleveland Plain Dealer*, March 14, 1952; WP, November 18, 1963; and *Business*

Week, November 20, 1963 (all in Milton Friedman Papers, Box 1/Articles 1950–1963, HI).

421   For Joe Clark debate, see WP, June 4, 1961; and *Philadelphia Daily News*, June 4, 1961.

421   *Friedman first wrote Goldwater*: Friedman to BMG, December 6, 1960, Friedman Papers, Box 27/Goldwater, Barry; BMG response is January 17, 1961. Letter after Clark debate is BMG to Friedman, July 16, 1961. For Baroody salon, I rely on author interview with Milton Friedman.

421   For Dodger Stadium scene, see Kurt Schuparra, *Triumph of the Right: The Rise of the California Conservative Movement, 1945–1966* (Armonk, N.Y.: M. E. Sharpe, 1998), 99; Julius Duscha, WP, September 9, 1964; Edwards, *Goldwater*, 294–95; Stewart Alsop, "Campaigner Goldwater," SEP, September 26, 1964 (for "second-class citizen" quote); and AHFCP, vol. 3, pictures 24–33. Charton Heston quote is in Edwards, *Goldwater*, 356. For San Diego, see AHFCP, vol. 3, pictures 17–18. Dodger Stadium speech is in FSA, Box 4.

423   For Friedman insight on steady fiscal policy, I rely on *Business Week*, September 26, 1964; and Friedman interview.

423   For figures on Johnson tax cut, see Margolis, *Last Innocent Year*, 186–87. *"No one with the slightest understanding"*: Harold Faber, ed., *The Road to the White House: The Story of the 1964 Election by the Staff of the New York Times* (New York: McGraw-Hill, 1965), 163.

423   For Seattle scene, see AHFCP, vol. 3, pictures 42–44 (for balloon); Edwards, *Goldwater*, 294; Shadegg, *What Happened*, 297; and SEP, October 24, 1964.

423   Seattle speech in FSA, Box 4.

424   For Harris poll, see NYT, September 14, 1964. For University of Michigan researchers, see Jamieson, *Packaging the Presidency*, 204. LBJ's bombing decision is in H. R. McMaster, *Dereliction of Duty: Lyndon Johnson, Robert McNamara, the Joint Chiefs of Staff, and the Lies that Led to Vietnam* (New York: HarperCollins, 1997), 150–51; and Robert S. McNamara with Brian VanDeMark, *In Retrospect: The Tragedy and Lessons of Vietnam* (New York: Vintage, 1995), 151.

424   For second-floor agricultural memo, see Shadegg, *What Happened*, 212, 231–35. Goldwater had a strong potential in the Plains states. In 1963 wheat farmers voted in a nonbinding nationwide referendum about maintaining the wheat acreage allotment program. The farmers voted against the program; their will was unheeded by the Agriculture Department. LBJ felt vulnerable on the issue, which was never exploited by BMG. Hear LBJ and Agriculture Secretary Orval Freeman, January 13, 1964, LBJT, 6401.13/4. For Minneapolis speech, see FSA, Box 4. *"Like a man looking at the world"*: WP editorial, September 12, 1964.

424   APSA scene is in SEP, October 24, 1964; AHFCP, vol. 3, pictures 9–15; Kessel, *Goldwater Coalition*, 194; Edwards, *Goldwater*, 312; and Shadegg, *What Happened*, 214–15.

425   For Harlan statement, see Shadegg, 214.

425   *"The most exciting thing we've done"*: Kessel, *Goldwater Coalition*, 195.

426   *Harper's* and *The Progressive* quoted in precinct organization manual, Illinois

Goldwater for President Committee, AC. For endorsement statistics, see the magazine *Extra!*, July–August 1998. *"For the good of the Republican Party"*: SEP, September 19, 1964. For Bill Miller's hometown newspaper, see Valenti to Moyers, October 18, 1964, LBJWHAM, Box 30. For 1822, Luce, and Hearst, see White, *Making of the President 1964*, 398. "Raw Deal" quote is in David M. Kennedy, *Freedom from Fear: The American People in Depression and War* (New York: Oxford University Press, 1999), 276. For Pulliam on Goldwater, see Russell Pulliam, *Publisher: Gene Pulliam: Last of the Newspaper Titans* (Ottawa, Ill.: Jameson Books, 1984), 250–58; and author interview with M. Stanton Evans. Johnson quote can be heard on LBJT, 6408.42/13.

426　*"Readers of The Churchman"*: DNC press release, September 8, 1964, LBJWH6-3. Episcopalian triennial convention in Branch, *Pillar of Fire*, 515. American Jewish Congress quoted in NR, June 22, 1998. For Cardinal Francis Spellman, hear LBJ and Robert Wagner, LBJT, 6408.19/3. *"This journal was founded"*: Hess, *In a Cause*, 131. Tillich quote is in attachment to Rowe to Juanita, October 21, 1964, and Valenti memo, October 22, 1964, LBJWHAM, Box 30. King quoted in "Dr. King Foresees 'Social Disruption' If Goldwater Wins," NYT, September 13, 1964.

427　*"We have an opportunity"*: Moyers to LBJ, July 17, 1964, LBJWHAM53. *The Churchman's* editorial was distributed in a DNC press release, September 8, 1964, LBJWH6-3 (for "America's Leaders Speak" letterhead). See also "The Goldwater Candidacy and the Christian Conscience," in LBJWHNG. For Leonard Marks, see Dallek, *Flawed Giant*, 173.

427　For the confusion over RNC public relations director, see SLPD, December 8, 1964; Kessel, *Goldwater Coalition*, 139 (for hiring of inexperienced deputies); Grenier to Goldwater, February 8, 1965, DK, Box 2/Grenier, John; Kitchel to Lamb, March 30, 1966, DK, Box 2; and author interview with Lee Edwards.

427　National Conservative Council in GRR, July 15, 1964; Courtney pamphlet is cited in SLPD, December 8, 1964; Robert DePugh, Gerald L. K. Smith, and KKK are in GRR, August 15, 1964. For LBJ quote, hear conversation with Roy Wilkins, July 28, 1964, LBJT, 6407.16/1.

428　For Grenier strictures, see NYHTEN, August 23, 1964; for Edwards, see Kessel, *Goldwater Coalition*, 139. For communications snafus and memo on memos, see ibid., 145. For the communications system's failure, see Kessel, *Goldwater Coalition*, 164. For overflow from teletypes, see White, *Making of the President 1964*, 378.

20. CAMPAIGN TRAILS

429　For crowd response, Goldwater speaking style, and press accounts of Goldwater's Southern tour, see Thompson to Rymer, n.d., "The Goldwater Tour of the South," AHF, Box W3/4; and Sam Ragan, "Dixie Looked Away," *American Scholar* 34, no. 2 (1965).

429　Richard Rovere is cited in Ragan, "Dixie Looked Away." For second-floor work, see Stephen Shadegg, *What Happened to Goldwater?: The Inside Story of the*

1964 Republican Campaign (New York: Holt, Rinehart, and Winston, 1965), 216–17; and Lee Edwards, *Goldwater: The Man Who Made a Revolution* (Washington, D.C.: Regnery, 1995), 295–96. For anti-demagoguery goal, see John Kessel, *The Goldwater Coalition: Republican Strategies in 1964* (Indianapolis: Bobbs-Merrill, 1968), 197.

430   For Charlotte, see SEP, October 24, 1964. For Atlanta, see citations in Thompson to Rymer, n.d., "The Goldwater Tour of the South." For St. Petersburg, see Theodore H. White, *The Making of the President 1964* (New York: Atheneum, 1965), 398; Kessel, *Goldwater Coalition*, 196; and citations in Thompson to Rymer. For defection of mayor, see Hayes to Carter, September 18, 1964, and LBJ to Poyntner, in LBJWHAM53. For Montgomery, see Heller to LBJ, September 18, 1964, LBJWH6-3. The "ineptitude" quote and the Southern belles episode are from the *Charlotte Observer*, cited in Thompson to Rymer. For Knoxville bumper stickers, see Sidney Warren, *The Battle for the Presidency* (Philadelphia: Lippincott, 1968), 368. For Fort Worth and West Virginia, see SEP, October 24, 1964.

431   For comprehensive account of Thurmond switch, see Arjen Westerhoff, "Politics of Protest: Strom Thurmond and the Development of the Republican Southern Strategy, 1948–1972" (master's thesis, American Studies Program, Smith College, 1997).

431   For Thurmond speech, see USN, September 28, 1964. *"My fellow extremists!"*: SEP, October 24, 1964.

431   For Milliken and Wallace negotiations, see Westerhoff, "Politics of Protest."

432   For Leander Perez, see Taylor Branch, *Pillar of Fire: America in the King Years, 1963–1965* (New York: Simon and Schuster, 1998), 49; Jon Margolis, *The Last Innocent Year: America in 1964: The Beginning of the "Sixties"* (New York: Morrow, 1999), 334; and Eric Foner article in *The Nation*, November 8, 1999.

432   *Charleston News and Courier*, quoted in Thompson to Rymer, n.d., "The Goldwater Tour of the South."

432   *"I'm not here to make a political speech"*: Gil Troy, *See How They Ran: The Changing Role of the Presidential Candidate*, 2nd ed. (Cambridge, Mass.: Harvard University Press, 1996), 216; and speeches, September 10, 15, 16, and 25, 1964, LBJWHAM53.

432   For Johnson spots, see Pete Hamill, "When the Client Is a Candidate," NYTM, October 25, 1964; Kathleen Hall Jamieson, *Packaging the Presidency: A History and Criticism of Presidential Campaign Advertising*, 3rd ed. (New York: Oxford University Press, 1996), 169–220; and Edwin Diamond and Stephen Bates, *The Spot: The Rise of Political Advertising on Television* (Cambridge, Mass.: MIT Press, 1984), 121–47.

434   For "pathetic peep" quote, see Edwards, *Goldwater*, 304.

434   For mushroom cloud, see Paul Southwick to Moyers, August 3, 1964, and Southwick to Moyers, August 4, 1964, in LBJWHAM53. For Heller, see Robert Dallek, *Flawed Giant: Lyndon Johnson and His Times, 1961–1973* (New York: Oxford University Press, 1998), 173; and, for example, Heller to LBJ, September 18, 1964, LBJWH6-3, and October 6, 1964, Raleigh speech insert, LBJWHAM, Box 25.

For Bundy, see Goldman to LBJ, September 17, 1964, LBJWH6–3. For John Bartlow Martin reports, see LBJWHAM, Box 23; and September 22, 1964, Martin to Moyers, LBJWHAM53. For Anna Rosenberg, see Popple to Jenkins, September 17, 1964, LBJWH6–3. For Lapeer, Michigan, see Rural Political News Summary, September 12, 1964, LBJWHAM53. For Goldwater interview in *Time*, see Redmon to Dutton, September 16, 1964, LBJWHAM53. For Cliff Case, see Redmon to Dutton, September 22, 1964, LBJWHAM53.

435   For Johnson-Humphrey citizens committees, see Kessel, *Goldwater Coalition*, 230. For Rowe, Clifford, and Fortas assignment and campaign organization generally, see J. Leonard Reinsch, *Getting Elected: From Radio and Roosevelt to Television and Reagan* (New York: Hippocrene, 1988), 203. *"If It's Socialism"*: Dutton to Moyers, September 14, 1964, LBJWHAM53. *"He has a perfect record"*: pamphlet draft, October 26, 1964, LBJWHAM, Box 21/Material on Barry Goldwater. See also pamphlet for BMG Madison Square Garden rally, Phillips to Moyers, LBJWHAM, Box 30, Pre-election (1 of 2). *"The big parade comes to Mason City"*: draft statement from Meredith Willson, "For Goldwater's Iowa Visit, Sept. 24," LBJWHAM53. For ridicule and gag writers, see Valenti to LBJ, September 7, 1964, and Dutton to Valenti, September 14, 1964, in LBJWHAM53.

435   For giving liberal Republicans a role, see Cater to LBJ, September 21, 1964, LBJWHAM53. For National Independent Committee ceremony, see Rowland Evans and Robert Novak, *Lyndon B. Johnson: Exercise of Power: A Political Biography* (New York: New American Library, 1966), 470; and memo and speech in LBJWH, Press Office, Box 38. For committee generally, see White, *Making of the President 1964*, 418; and hear, for example, LBJT, 6408.03/9 and 6408.31/10. For $1,000 gifts, see White, *Making of the President 1964*, 309; and Edwards, *Goldwater*, 282 (for White House pool).

436   For Moyers biography, see Jeff Shesol, *Mutual Contempt: Lyndon Johnson, Robert Kennedy, and the Feud that Defined a Decade* (New York: Norton, 1997), 295; Michael Beschloss, ed., *Taking Charge: The Johnson White House Tapes, 1963–1964* (New York: Simon and Schuster, 1997), 347; and finding aid, LBJWHAM.

436   For "overkill effect" and "throwing more bombs," see Hayes to Moyers, September 18, 1964, "Reflections of New York Trip," LBJWHAM53. See also Hayes to Moyers, September 17, 1964, and September 24, 1964, and Dutton to Moyers, September 28, 1964, LBJWHAM53. *"We have a few more Goldwater ads"*: Moyers to LBJ, September 13, 1964, LBJWHAM53. *"Right now, the biggest asset"*: Dallek, *Flawed Giant*, 174.

436   For "Anti-Campaign" generally, see Dallek, 173–74; Evans and Novak, *Exercise of Power*, 468; and Clifton Carter OH, LBJL.

437   *"This accounting statement"*: Cooper to Moyers, Bundy, Reedy, and Valenti, August 24, 1964, LBJWHNG.

437   For E. Howard Hunt operation, see E. Howard Hunt, *Undercover: Memoirs of an American Secret Agent* (New York: Berkeley, 1974), 133. For "Confessions of a Republican," see Martin to White, n.d., FCW, Box 1/California. For use of the Social Security list, see Feldman to Valenti, September 22, 1964, LBJWHNG.

437   For Ike Vietnam scoop, see WS, October 11, 1964, and Frank Cormier, *LBJ the Way He Was: A Personal Memoir* (Garden City, N.Y.: Doubleday, 1977), 126.

437   For BMG's debate agitation, see "Barry Presses His Bid to Debate LBJ on TV," NYP, July 29, 1964; Gil Troy, *See How They Ran*, 218–19; and Denison Kitchel to George Humphrey, October 7, 1964, FSA, Task Force Correspondence A folder. For LBJ's throttling of the debate challenge, see Evans and Novak, *Exercise of Power*, 473. For Bobby Baker sabotage, see Evans and Novak, 478. For tax returns threat, see Karl Hess, *Mostly on the Edge: An Autobiography* (Amherst, N.Y.: Prometheus, 1999), 169.

438   For Ralph Ginzburg, see John Heidenry, *What Wild Ecstasy: The Rise and Fall of the Sexual Revolution* (New York: Simon and Schuster, 1997), 78–83. For copy of poll, see Karl Hess, *In a Cause That Will Triumph: The Goldwater Campaign and the Future of the Conservatism Movement* (New York: Doubleday, 1967), 175.

438   For quotes of psychiatrists, see "The Unconscious of a Conservative: A Special Issue on the Mind of Barry Goldwater," *Fact* (September–October 1964).

439   For Goldwater press corps generally, see White, *Making of the President 1964*, 385, 403–4.

439   *"How could such a nice guy"*: Edwards, *Goldwater*, 286. For misspelling, see Richard Dudman, "Ultrarightist Drive to Take Over GOP Was Started Four Years Ago." SLPD, December 6, 1964. For refusal to visit press compartment, see Shadegg, *What Happened*, 270. For stoning, see White, *Making of the President 1964*, 385. For Montana and Jack Steele story: Hess, *In a Cause*, 119.

440   For "Founding Fathers" gaffe, see Jack Bell, *The Johnson Treatment: How Lyndon B. Johnson Took over the Presidency and Made It His Own* (New York: Harper and Row, 1965), 267. *"If it hadn't been for Goldwater"*: O'Donnell OH, LBJL. For inebriation, see Larry Sabato, *Feeding Frenzy: How Attack Journalism Has Transformed American Politics* (New York: Free Press, 1991), 44. For Detroit story, see Bell, *Johnson Treatment*, 267. *"Thank God for Lyndon Johnson"*: author interview with Richard Dudman. For "ranting, raving" quote, see Kessel, *Goldwater Coalition*, 240.

440   For preempting *That Was the Week That Was*, see Diamond and Bates, *The Spot*, 143. Episodes on view at MTR. For September 18, 1964, Goldwater show, see transcript in FSA, Box 4; Kessel, *Goldwater Coalition*, 200; and Shadegg, *What Happened*, 247.

440   Raymond Massey appeal is in Shadegg, 248; Kessel, *Goldwater Coalition*, 212; and Jamieson, *Packaging the Presidency*, 174.

441   Cordiner hiring and financial policy is in Shadegg, *What Happened*, 178, 182; White, *Making of the President 1964*, 379; Kessel, *Goldwater Coalition*, 146; Jamieson, *Packaging the Presidency*, 174; and Kitchel to Grenier, March 11, 1965, DK, Box 2/Grenier, John.

441   For inspiration of JFK's Houston speech on Gettysburg film, see White, *Making of the President 1964*, 392.

441   For Kitchel's veto of Massey appeal, see Shadegg, *What Happened*, 248–49, and for budget figures, 253.

441   For Gettysburg film shooting: ibid., 247–48; AHFCP, vol. 5, pictures 21–25; and author interview with Charles Lichenstein.

442   Kitchel expresses sabotage conviction in Kitchel to Weiss, DK, Box 5/"Explaining Things to Ike" correspondence. *Conversation at Gettysburg* videotape at AHFAV, BG-VT/96.

443   For TV ratings, see Jamieson, *Packaging the Presidency*, 207; and Kitner memo, n.d., probably September 23, 1964, LBJWHAM53. *"I didn't have much experience with TV"*: Jamieson, *Packaging the Presidency*, 173.

443   For Goldwater's late-September bitterness, see Kessel, *Goldwater Coalition*, 198.

444   Vandalism: October 26, 1964, New Yorkers for Goldwater and Miller newsletter, ML, Box 92/Goldwater Campaign; and author interview with Noel Black. *"Goldwater's first major address"*: *Time*, September 18, 1964. *In Tulsa, blacks*: SEP, October 24, 1964; AHFCP, vol 5, pictures 31–34. *In Winston-Salem, civil rights*: AP dispatch in Thompson to Rymer, n.d., "The Goldwater Tour of the South." *"It is quite possible"*: White, *Making of the President 1964*, 395.

444   For Lord Bryce, see Paul F. Boller Jr., *Presidential Campaigns* (New York: Oxford University Press, 1984), 149. *"Presidential elections have been waged"*: John M. Cummings, "Rough Tactics by the Voters," *Philadelphia Inquirer*, October 22, 1964. *"The peaceful arts of negotiation"*: Richard Hofstadter, "A Long View: Goldwater in History," NYRB, October 8, 1964.

445   For "Communist Target—Youth," see John A. Andrew III, *The Other Side of the Sixties: Young Americans for Freedom and the Rise of Conservative Politics* (New Brunswick, N.J.: Rutgers University Press, 1997), 29. *"Vociferous and well-drilled extremist elements"*: M. Stanton Evans, *The Future of Conservatism* (New York: Holt, Rinehart, and Winston, 1968), 190.

445   For speculation on cause of riots, hear LBJT, 6407.13/3, and 6408.6/10 and 6407.11, passim (for Hoover searching for conspiracy, hear track 7); and see Branch, *Pillar of Fire*, 318, 417, 500; and advance memo for September 10, 1964, LBJ Harrisburg speech, LBJWHAM, Box 23. For Goldwater fear, see Karl Hess, "An Open Letter to Barry Goldwater," *Ramparts*, August 1969. FBI report quoted in White, *Making of the President 1964*, 728.

445   For trust survey, see Joseph Nye, Philip Zelikow, and David King, eds., *Why People Don't Trust Government* (Cambridge, Mass.: Harvard University Press, 1997).

446   *Oswald, a magazine pointed out*: *The Nation*, December 21, 1963. For McComb, Mississippi, see Branch, *Pillar of Fire*, 497–504.

446   Higher-education statistics from "University of California, Today's Multiuniversity," CT, January 4, 1964.

446   My account of the Berkeley uprising relies on David Lance Goines, *The Free Speech Movement: Coming of Age in the 1960s* (Berkeley, Calif.: Ten Speed Press,

1993), Milton Viorst, *Fire in the Streets: America in the 1960s* (New York: Simon and Schuster, 1979), 276–86; Max Heirich, *The Spiral of Conflict: Berkeley, 1964* (New York: Columbia University Press, 1968); and A. H. Raskin, "The Berkeley Affair: Mr. Kerr vs. Mr. Savio & Co.," NYTM, February 14, 1965.

447   For Lipset quote on "relative lack of experience," see Seymour Martin Lipset, *Rebellion in the University* (New Brunswick, N.J.: Transaction Publishers, 1993), 126.

447   *"Here as elsewhere, the Negro"*: NYHTEN, April 4, 1964.

449   For car-top quotes, the extraordinary live recordings available at *www.lib.berkeley.edu/MRC/FSM.html.*

452   All PR quotes from "Some Comments on Senator Goldwater," *Partisan Review*, October 1964. Richard Hofstadter quote is in "A Long View: Goldwater in History," NYRB, October 8, 1964.

452   *"To meet the needs of the people"*: "Atlantic Report on the World Today," *Atlantic Monthly*, September 1964.

453   *Stewart Alsop reported that Oliver Quayle*: SEP, October 24, 1964. For LBJ's September 28, 1964, tour I rely on Kessel, *Goldwater Coalition*, 242–43; Margolis, *Last Innocent Year*, 338; Evans and Novak, *Exercise of Power*, 474; Cormier, *LBJ the Way He Was*, 107–17; Branch, *Pillar of Fire*, 502–3; Dallek, *Flawed Giant*, 182; and Charles Brereton, "1964: A Yankee Surprise," *Historical New Hampshire* 42, no. 3 (1987)

453   For new presidential limousine, see "New Shield Around the President," USN, December 3, 1963. For Secret Service complaints, see Bell, *Johnson Treatment*, 234; and hear LBJT, 6403.01/4.

454   For RFK Albany trip, see Margolis, *Last Innocent Year*, 330.

455   For BMG's Union Station speech, see FSA, Box 4.

455   Roger Mudd quote in Troy, *See How They Ran*, 217. Alsop in SEP, September 29, 1964. Picket signs noted in Bell, *Johnson Treatment*, 265. *"I just hitch-hiked 50 miles"*: AHFCP, vol. 8, picture 4. For blacks not shaking Goldwater's hand, see SEP, October 24, 1964. For YAF and "LBJ-USA" banners, see AHFCP, vol. 7, pictures 1–10. For parachute and egg, see AHFCP, vol. 7, pictures 21 and 28.

455   For photo session in engineer's cap, see Vic Gold, NR, July 6, 1998. For "Bye, Bye Blackbird," see White, *Making of the President 1964*, 387. For Cincinnati Gardens, see Kessel, *Goldwater Coalition*, 203.

456   For University of Toledo, see Edwards, *Goldwater*, 314; and for transcript, FSA, Box 4.

456   For LBJ and Moline, see "Rock Island/Moline" memo, LBJWHAM, Box 25/10/7/64. For BMG's Social Security speech and response, see Kessel, *Goldwater Coalition*, 202; and *Time*, October 23, 1964. For Hammond, Indiana, see White, *Making of the President 1964*, 387; and Jeffrey J. Matthews, "To Defeat a Maverick: The Goldwater Candidacy Revisited, 1963–1964," *Presidential Studies Quarterly* 27, no. 4 (1997).

456   *The next day the Herald Tribune*: Richard Kluger, *The Paper: The Life and Death of the New York Herald Tribune* (New York: Knopf, 1986), 695; see also "We Choose Johnson," NYHT, October 4, 1964.

457 *An economist wrote Walter Heller*: Okun to Heller, October 5, 1964, LBJWH6-3. For Wall Street nervousness, see Heller to LBJ, August 4, 1964, "Goldwater's Impact on the Stock Market—Chapter 2," LBJWH6-3.

457 *Indeed, when Milton Friedman published*: Friedman, "The Goldwater View of Economics," NYTM, October 11, 1964.

458 For Burch's neglecting to make phone calls to senators, see Hugh Scott quote in SLPD, December 8, 1964. *"This is Grenier"*: NYHTEN, August 23, 1964. For leaks and taps, see Edwards, *Goldwater*, 305; and Shadegg, *What Happened*, 238. For newsletter and *TV Prevue*, see Kessel, *Goldwater Coalition*, 256.

458 For *Reader's Digest* insert and *Where I Stand*, see Jamieson, *Packaging the Presidency*, 205. For *Barry Goldwater: Extremist of the Right*, see "Extremist Book Sales Soar Despite Criticism in the GOP," NYT, October 4, 1964. On Kitchel's Birch Society problem, see F. Clifton White with William Gill, *Suite 3505: The Story of the Draft Goldwater Movement* (New Rochelle, N.Y.: Arlington House, 1967), 206; Shadegg, *What Happened*, 205; and Kitchel to Welch, June 8, 1960, DK, Box 3/Welch, Robert Jr. For Zoll, see SLPD, December 8, 1964.

458 For Dallas sabotage investigation, see Mayfield to Moyers, October 8, 1964, LBJWH6-3, October 1 to October 15 folder. For Milwaukee disaster, I rely on Shadegg, *What Happened*, 243–45 (for Kitchel resignation quote); Bannon to White, October 15, 1964, FCW, Box 3/Ohio; and Lichenstein interview. *"Let's stop this waste"*: Virtue to Davis, October 7, 1964, FCW, Box 3/California.

459 *"The college presidents are coming along nicely"*: Rowe to Roberts, October 21, 1964, and attached, LBJWHAM, Box 30. For Eisenhower Administration letter, see White, *Making of the President 1964*, 398. On John Sherman Cooper, see White to Jenkins, September 30, 1964, LBJWH6-3. For Romney and ox roast, see AHFCP, vol. 6, pictures 21–24. On Rhodes, see late-October field memo, AHF, Box W3/4. "Coattail" buttons noted in Robert Rouse, "Goldwater Coattails," *The Keynoter* (Summer 1982). For Keating volunteers wearing Goldwater buttons, I rely on author interview with Ryan Hayes.

459 For "What Scranton Really Thinks of Goldwater" booklet, see LBJWHAM, Box 87/Goldwater #2. Rockefeller/Goldwater rally in Albany is in AHFCP, vol. 6, picture 15; and October 2, 1964, New Yorkers for Goldwater-Miller newsletter, ML, Box 92/Goldwater Campaign. For Rockefeller's distaste, see Edwards, *Goldwater*, 312.

460 Candidates' wives' press conference on tape at WGN, FD 2555.

460 *"Very early in the last decade"*: Barry Goldwater, *Conscience of a Majority* (Englewood Cliffs, N.J.: Prentice-Hall, 1970), 29.

460 For difficulties writing Chicago speech, see Kessel, *Goldwater Coalition*, 208; and Shadegg, *What Happened*, 250. For Chicago backlash, see October 1, 1964, Martin to Moyers, briefing for LBJ October 7, 1964, Illinois trip, LBJWHAM, Box 25; and *The Reporter*, October 8, 1964. For LBJ with Daley, hear LBJT, 6408.25/1–3.

461 Taped excerpts of speech at WGN, FD 2562. Transcript in Walter Judd Papers, Box 210/5, HI.

461   For Rehnquist's use of phrase "our aim, as I understand it," see David Saraye, *Turning Right: The Making of the Rehnquist Supreme Court* (New York: John Wiley, 1992), 39. For Phoenix antidiscrimination ordinance and Rehnquist testimony, see ibid., 31–32.

462   For NYT statistics, see October 6, 1964. Other statistics in Matthews, "To Defeat a Maverick." *"PRIVATE POLL GIVES GOLDWATER 40%"*: Republican Congressional Committee Newsletter, October 17, 1964.

462   *"Having been on the campaign trail"*: Kitchel to Lawson, October 13, 1964, DK, Box 4. For Burch quote and canceling of intelligence reports, see Edwards, *Goldwater*, 329. For cancellation of polls, see White, *Making of the President 1964*, 396.

463   For Lady Bird's Southern tour I rely on Jane Jarboe, *Lady Bird: A Comprehensive Biography of Mrs. Johnson* (New York: Simon and Schuster, 1999), 244, 247–64. For *Dieu et les Dames*, see Branch, *Pillar of Fire*, 397.

465   For Thurmond radio ads, see Westerhoff, "Politics of Protest," 36. On Bob Jones, see NYT obituary, November 13, 1997; and Edward Cain, *They'd Rather Be Right: Youth and the Conservative Movement* (New York: Macmillan, 1963), 258. For progress of GOP in South Carolina, see *Time*, April 17, 1964.

466   For Warner Gear and "lay low on civil rights" quotes, see October 1, 1964, Martin briefing for LBJ October 7, 1964, Illinois trip, LBJAM, Box 25. For "Economic Bill of Rights," and so forth, see Moyers to LBJ, September 29, 1964, LBJWHAM53. *"Think of how wonderful the year 2000"*: Jack Sheppherd and Christopher S. Wren, eds., *Quotations from Chairman LBJ* (New York: Simon and Schuster, 1968), 37, 106.

466   For Cleveland speech, see Evans and Novak, *Exercise of Power*, 477; and Cormier, *LBJ the Way He Was*, 105. For Kennedy at Mormon Tabernacle, see Allan M. Winkler, *Life Under a Cloud: American Anxiety About the Atom* (New York: Oxford University Press, 1993), 125. For Louisville, see Sheppherd and Wren, *Quotations*, 70. For disparate nuclear casualties, see *Time*, September 25, 1964. *"I want to conclude"*: Cormier, *LBJ the Way He Was*, 106.

467   *"An unusual, even sometimes awe-inspiring"*: "Follow-up, Ohio Trip Speeches," October 17, 1964, LBJWHAM, Box 30. Speech quotes from Kessel, *Goldwater Coalition*, 244; and transcript of October 7, 1964, stop in Detroit, LBJWHAM, Box 25.

467   For invocations of Cuban missile crisis, see Cormier, *LBJ the Way He Was*, 105.

467   *"Elmo Roper, polling privately"*: Martin to Moyers, September 22, 1964, LBJWHAM53. For ordering billboards, ads, and polls, see Robert Divine, ed., *The Johnson Years, Volume 3, LBJ at Home and Abroad* (Lawrence: University of Kansas Press, 1994), 25. For get-out-the-vote ads, see Jamieson, *Packaging the Presidency*, 220. *"Didn't I tell you"*: Vance Muse, "LBJ's Greatest Loss," *George*, May 1999.

468   On Jenkins, see Muse; Evans and Novak, *Exercise of Power*, 479; Clifton Carter OH, LBJL; Dallek, *Flawed Giant*, 66; and Beschloss, ed., *Taking Charge*, 92. *"They're trying to make Walter Jenkins"*: Beschloss, 191.

468   For LBJ's crowds, see Bell, *Johnson Treatment*, 234, and Vance Muse, "LBJ's Greatest Loss," *George*, May 1999.

469   *"I went all de way wif LBJ"*: *The Keynoter*, Summer 1982, 10.

469   For New Orleans speech, see Branch, *Pillar of Fire*, 514–15; Dallek, *Flawed Giant*, 183; Cormier, *LBJ the Way He Was*, 124; and Valenti OH, LBJL.

469   *"Johnson probably put the finishing touches on his chances"*: late-October field memo, AHF, Box W3/4.

21. CITIZENS

471   My sense of the exhilaration of young Goldwater volunteers owes especially to a breakfast interview with William Schultz, David Keene, Allan Ryskind, and Alfred Regnery.

471   *"I am especially anxious"*: Buckley to Manion, September 24, 1959, CM, Box 69/5. For Buckley-Chambers correspondence, see John B. Judis, *William F. Buckley, Jr.: Patron Saint of the Conservatives* (New York: Touchstone, 1990), 159–80. *"Barry Goldwater is a man of tremendously decent instincts"*: ibid., 274.

472   *"You are displaying a compulsion"*: ibid., 228. For YAF convention, see Judis, *William F. Buckley, Jr.*, 230; and Gregory Schneider, *Cadres for Conservatism: Young Americans for Freedom and the Rise of the Contemporary Right* (New York: NYU Press, 1999), 85–87.

473   SLPD series is December 5, 1964 (for quote), December 6, 8, 9, 10, and 11, 1964.

473   For BMG and LBJ volunteer figures, see Milton C. Cummings, ed., *The National Election of 1964* (Washington, D.C.: Brookings Institution, 1966), 47. For bumper sticker census, see Martin to Moyers, September 22, 1964, LBJWHAM53; see also Theodore H. White, *The Making of the President 1964* (New York: Atheneum, 1965), 397.

474   For *Fortune* quote, Richard Whalen, *Taking Sides: A Personal View of America from Kennedy to Nixon to Kennedy* (Boston: Houghton Mifflin, 1974), 92. For "federation of the fed-up," see *Time*, July 24, 1964.

474   For "Gallup Never Asked Me!," see Liebman to Leithead, September 23, 1964, ML, Box 92/Goldwater Campaign.

474   ACA training manual in FCW, Box 19. The "Hello, Dolly!" ban is from author interview with Lee Edwards. Lyrics in Donald Bishop to author, November 19, 1997. For Kennedy-Lincoln coincidence, see Smith to Kitchel, "Does History Really Repeat Itself?," August 8, 1964, DK, Box 4; and "Both Presidents, Lincoln and Kennedy," in ML, Box 92/Goldwater Campaign.

475   For BMG and LBJ fund-raising totals, see Nelson Polsby and Aaron Wildavsky, *Presidential Elections: Contemporary Strategies of American Electoral Politics*, 8th ed. (New York: Free Press, 1991), 50. For 22,000 and 44,000 figures, see BMG speech in Cedar Rapids, October 28, 1964, AHF, Box 1/8. For "over a million" figure, I average Goldwater claims in Cedar Rapids speech; Barry Goldwater, *The Conscience of a Majority* (Englewood Cliffs, N.J.: Prentice-Hall, 1970), 42; and USN, December 21, 1964.

475 For "sustaining membership" program versus traditional methods, see John Kessel, *The Goldwater Coalition: Republican Strategies in 1964* (Indianapolis: Bobbs-Merrill, 1968), 147. For mailing lists generally: author interview with Ron Crawford. On Kozak Drywash Cloth Company, see George H. Mayer, *The Republican Party 1854–1966* (New York: Oxford University Press, 1967), 525.

475 Million-dollar gifts from author interview with anonymous source; Taiwan gift from author interview with W. Glenn Campbell. For small donations: author interviews with Ron Crawford, Lee Edwards, and Gus Owens; White, *Making of the President 1964*, 165; F. Clifton White with William Gill, *Suite 3505: The Story of the Draft Goldwater Movement* (New Rochelle, N.Y.: Arlington House, 1967), 16, 192; and Saltz to White, July 6, 1965, FCW, Box 18/"IX—The Draft Begins."

476 "National Gun Alliance" and "Goldwater Campaign Fund" flyers, and photo of Boston yard signs, in JCJ. "A Fed Up Citizen" in LBJWHAM53.

476 For McIntire quote, see "Far Right and Far Left," NYP, March 31, 1964; for stations, see GRR, August 15, 1964. For Manion stations, see GRR, Spring 1996. For Hargis, see "Far Right and Far Left," NYP, March 30, 1964. For R. K. Scott, see GRR, August 15, 1964; for American Security Council Report of the Air, see GRR, September 15, 1964; and Sara Diamond, *Roads to Dominion: Right-Wing Movements and Political Power in the United States* (New York: Guilford, 1995), 46–50.

477 For the "hate books," see Donald Janson, "Extremist Book Sales Soar Despite Criticism in GOP," NYT, October 4, 1964; and GRR, October 15, 1964. The books are Phyllis Schlafly, *A Choice, Not an Echo* (Alton, Ill.: Pere Marquette Press, 1964); Phyllis Schlafly, *The Gravediggers* (Alton, Ill.: Pere Marquette Press, 1964); John A. Stormer, *None Dare Call It Treason* (Florissant, Mo.: Liberty Bell Press, 1964); and J. Evetts Haley, *A Texan Looks at Lyndon: A Study in Illegitimate Power* (Canyon, Tex.: Palo Duro Press, 1964). For *LBJ: A Political Biography*, see GRR, October 31, 1964; and Diamond, *Roads to Dominion*, 153.

478 *At rallies the books were handed out*: author interview with Ann Sullivan. For Spanish, LP versions, Virginia sales, and distribution generally, see O'Brien field reports, October 1, 1964, October 2, 1964, October 6, 1964, and October 20, 1964, LBJWHA: Wilson, Box 3/Memos to the President—O'Brien Trips. Hear also LBJ and Houston Harte, August 31, 1964, LBJT, 6408.42/12. 500,000 were sent out by the Walter Knott–led group Citizens for Constructive Action; see Lisa McGirr, "Suburban Warriors: Grass-Roots Conservatism in the 1960s" (Ph.D. diss., Columbia University, 1995), 166.

478 *"Your letter to the President"*: September 16, 1964, draft for Moyers letter, LBJWHAM53. *"They are giving A Texan Looks at Lyndon"*: Garth to Finney and Sharon, "Personal Campaign Evaluation," October 2, 1964, LBJWH6-3. *"We hear Haley's book quoted"*: O'Brien field report, October 1, 1964.

478 For *Sullivan*, see Taylor Branch, *Pillar of Fire: America in the King Years, 1963–1965* (New York: Simon and Schuster, 1998), 208–9. Goldwater *"has fenced with personal attacks"*: Dutton to Moyers, September 21, 1964, LBJWHAM53. This memo was forwarded to the President.

479 "Destroy-After-Reading": Stephen Shadegg, *What Happened to Goldwater?:*

The Inside Story of the 1964 Republican Campaign (New York: Holt, Rinehart, and Winston, 1965), 271. For authorized publications at Goldwater offices, see White to Vukasin, October 7, 1964, FCW, Box 1/California, and author interview with Lee Edwards. For Dade County distribution, see October 20, 1964, O'Brien field report; for Harris County, Texas, see Janson, "Extremist Book Sales Soar Despite Criticism in GOP." *"We have no way of controlling people"*: see Janson.

479 For no Goldwater offices in New England, see White, *Making of the President 1964*, 397. For failed request for guidance see, for example, Russel and Dannemiller to White, September 24, 1964, FCW, Box 3/Ohio. For rubble from primaries, see Shadegg, *What Happened*, 200.

480 For Harvard Club meeting, see report by public relations director for Nassau County Republican Party marked *"CONFIDENTIAL,"* July 29, 1964, RAC.

480 For job offer to White, see White with Gill, *Suite 3505*, 18; and Shadegg, *What Happened*, 185. For citizens groups traditionally and in Eisenhower campaign, see ibid., 186; NYHTEN, August 10, 1964; and June 26, 1964, Clayton memo in DK, Box 4. For budget and staff, see "Citizens for Goldwater-Miller National Headquarters Staff Directory," AHF, Box W3/4; and Kessel, *Goldwater Coalition*, 146. For guerrilla strategy built on Draft Goldwater organization and Arizona Mafia's wish to purge White: Shadegg, *What Happened*, 186; and author interview with Jameson Campaigne Jr. For Arizona Mafia being too harried, see Shadegg, *What Happened*, 188.

481 For Liebman, see Liebman to Rickenbacker, August 6, 1964, and August 18, 1964, ML, Box 92/Goldwater Campaign. For Lehigh County Citizens: NYHTEN, August 10, 1964. For others, see August 11 and 12, 1964, and September 11, 1964, telegrams, FCW, Box 1/California; and late September 1964 Lake County in FCW, Box 3/Ohio.

481 For TV listings: Yurchuck to White, September 22, 1964, FCW, Box 3/Ohio. For helicopter, see *Cincinnati Inquirer*, October 3, 1964. For 11.5 tons of Goldwater material, see clipping attached to Ohio chair to White, October 5, 1964, FCW, Box 3/Ohio. *"TOUR PROVING TREMENDOUS"*: Summers to White, October 28, 1964, FCW, Box 3/Ohio.

482 For legal loophole, see Shadegg, *What Happened*, 187.

482 For Rus Walton generally I rely on Shadegg, 187; Best to O'Donald [*sic*], April 23, 1964, WAR, Box 154/7; and author interviews with Robert Gaston, Jameson Campaigne Jr., and Pamela Walton. For Shell rallies, see Kurt Schuparra, *Triumph of the Right: The Rise of the California Conservative Movement, 1945–1966* (Armonk, N.Y.: M. E. Sharpe, 1998), 63. For NAM booklet, see National Association of Manufacturers Papers, HI.

483 Goldwater quotes from October 1964 speeches in AHF, W3/4.

484 Mormon Tabernacle transcript in JCJ. See also *Salt Lake Tribune*, October 11, 1964, A1. For ratings, see Karl Hess, *In a Cause That Will Triumph: The Goldwater Campaign and the Future of Conservatism* (New York: Doubleday, 1967), 148. For "friendly criminologists," see Hayes to Moyers, September 1, 1964; for "candidate's family" and "prominent women," Dutton to Moyers, September 28, 1964; for Graham and Spellman, Dutton to Moyers, September 21, 1964; all in LBJWHAM53.

See also Dutton to RFK, July 17, 1964, LBJWHAM53; and Manatos to Moyers, October 16, 1964, LBJWHNG.

484   *"In the great struggle"*: cited in September 8, 1964, Goldwater Dodger Stadium speech. See Julius Duscha, WP, September 9, 1964. *"One of the most disturbing trends"*: quoted in *Choice*, Goldwater campaign film, AC.

484   For Goldwater's nightclub passion, see March 22, 1963, Jack Paar show appearance, AHFAV, BG-C/2. For bikinis at Beverly Hills rally, see James M. Perry, *A Report in Depth on Barry Goldwater: The Story of the 1964 Republican Presidential Nominee* (Silver Spring, Md.: National Observer, 1964), 102. For a classic expression of libertarianism, see Ronald Hamowy, " 'National Review': Criticism and Reply," *New Individualist Review* (November 1961), cited in E. J. Dionne Jr., *Why Americans Hate Politics* (New York: Simon and Schuster, 1991), 166. For Governor Welsh's crusade against the rock song "Louie, Louie," see Branch, *Pillar of Fire*, 229. For "dank blond hair" and "revenge" quotes, see White, *Making of the President 1964*, 199, 279.

485   *"The origin of this commendable"*: Richard Rovere, "Letter from San Francisco," *The New Yorker*, July 25, 1964. For Walton's brochure on Goldwater's religious piety, see "In the Image of God," text of February 6, 1962, speech to Notre Dame student body, in JCJ.

485   BMG TV spots are in AHFAV, tape BG-F/73.

486   *"No pale pastels"*: Campaigne interview. All Citizens for Goldwater-Miller brochures are from JCJ.

487   *"We want to just make them mad"*: Laurence Stern, "Goldwater Film Contrasts 'Two Americas,' " WP, October 20, 1964, which also notes transcription by LBJ spy.

22. FOREGONE CONCLUSIONS

488   For 10,000-mile figure, see Gil Troy, *See How They Ran: The Changing Role of the Presidential Candidate*, 2nd ed. (Cambridge, Mass.: Harvard University Press, 1996), 216. For LBJ Western tour, see John Kessel, *The Goldwater Coalition: Republican Strategies in 1964* (Indianapolis: Bobbs-Merrill, 1968), 243–44; Jon Margolis, *The Last Innocent Year: America in 1964: The Beginning of the "Sixties"* (New York: Morrow, 1999), 348 (for quote); and Taylor Branch, *Pillar of Fire: America in the King Years, 1963–1965* (New York: Simon and Schuster, 1998), 514. Johnson had earlier said that out of courtesy to BMG, "I wouldn't even consider campaigning in Arizona." *"To describe this week's work"*: David Broder, "Johnson Creates a Campaign Style," WS, October 13, 1964. *"Jackson in a jetliner"*: Doris Kearns Goodwin, *Lyndon Johnson and the American Dream* (New York: Harper and Row, 1976). *"Not so much excited about Johnson"*: James Reston, NYT, August 26, 1964.

489   My account of the Jenkins affair rests on Vance Muse, "LBJ's Greatest Loss," *George*, May 1999; Jane Jarboe, *Lady Bird: A Comprehensive Biography of Mrs. Johnson* (New York: Simon and Schuster, 1999), 264–68; White, *Making of the President 1964*, 436–42; FBI press release, October 22, 1964, in LBJWHA: Jenkins, Box 11; and the conversations archived at *http://www.cspan.org/lbj/lbjtest.asp*.

492   For Vietcong air strike, see Charles Brereton, "1964: A Yankee Surprise," *Historical New Hampshire* 42, no. 3 (1987). For LBJ statement, see LBJWHA: Jenkins, Box 11. For gristle, see Frank Cormier, *LBJ the Way He Was: A Personal Memoir* (Garden City, N.Y.: Doubleday, 1977), 127.

492   For TV Committee disillusionment, see Virtue to Davis, October 7, 1964, FCW, Box 3/California. Cordiner and Mardian campaign plane attempts are in Stephen Shadegg, *What Happened to Goldwater?: The Inside Story of the 1964 Republican Campaign* (New York: Holt, Rinehart, and Winston, 1965), 240–41.

493   For Jenkins-inspired kitsch, see *The Keynoter* (Summer 1982): 10. *Goldwater's snide references*: *Time*, October 30, 1964. For Baroody dropping nobility of failure, see Shadegg, *What Happened*, 241.

493   For dispute over TV time, see J. Leonard Reinsch, *Getting Elected: From Radio and Roosevelt to Television and Reagan* (New York: Hippocrene, 1988), 215; and John Kessel, *Goldwater Coalition*, 213. For figure of 63 million, see LBJWH, Press Office, Box 38, Briefing 431, October 19, 1964. *"We will demonstrate anew"*: Kessel, *Goldwater Coalition*, 237.

493   For Burch speech and $500,000 figure, see Kessel, 212. For LBJ Hoover taping, see AHFCP, vol. 8, picture 40.

494   For BMG response to LBJ, see Aaron Singer, ed., *Campaign Speeches of American Presidential Candidates, 1928–1972* (New York: Frederick Ungar, 1976), 345–51. For "Brunch with Barry" transcript, see Ranges to MCS, October 25, 1964, Barry Goldwater folder, Arizona Congressional Delegation file, MCSL.

494   *"Agree completely with you"*: Lee Edwards, *Goldwater: The Man Who Made a Revolution* (Washington, D.C.: Regnery, 1995), 329.

494   For *Choice* planning, execution, and fallout, see Laurence Stern, "Goldwater Film Contrasts 'Two Americas,' " October 20, 1964; "GOP Faces Dilemma Over 'Choice': What to Do with Morality Film," October 22, 1964; and Elsie Carper, " 'Moral Mothers' Is Paper Unit," all in WP; Kathleen Hall Jamieson, *Packaging the Presidency: A History and Criticism of Presidential Campaign Advertising*, 3rd ed. (New York: Oxford University Press, 1996), 215–16; Edwin Diamond and Stephen Bates, *The Spot: The Rise of Political Advertising on Television* (Cambridge, Mass.: MIT Press, 1984), 144–45; Karl Hess, *Mostly on the Edge: An Autobiography* (Amherst, N.Y.: Prometheus, 1999), 173; and Shadegg, *What Happened*, 254–55. For MMA pamphlet, see JCJ.

495   *Choice* film is in AC; see also AHFAV, tape BG-F/45.

496   Telegram of complaint to White is in FCW, Box 1/California.

496   NO EVIDENCE IS UNCOVERED: NYT, October 23, 1964. *"That was a wonderful thing"*: Vance Muse, "LBJ's Greatest Loss," *George*, May 1999.

496   *"I know I'm gonna beat Goldwater"*: Cormier, *LBJ the Way He Was*, 129. For photographer taking wrong side, see AHFCP, vol. 8, picture 46.

497   *"The crackpots must know"*: Martin to Moyers, October 26, 1964, LBJWHAM, Box 30/Pre-election (1 of 2). *George Reedy found himself*: Reedy OH, LBJL. *"We passed out 10,000 of these"*: Phillips to Moyers, October 30, 1964, LBJWHAM, Box

30/Pre-election (1 of 2). For District of Columbia pamphlet: Herring to DNC, October 31, 1964, ibid.

497   *"We are not going to send American boys"*: Jack Sheppherd and Christopher S. Wren, eds., *Quotations from Chairman LBJ* (New York: Simon and Schuster, 1968), 67. For Gallup poll, see Edwards, *Goldwater*, 331. For open housing, see Galbraith to LBJ and Moyers, October 22, 1964, LBJWHAM, Box 30/Pre-election (1 of 2). For itching powder, see Barry Goldwater with Jack Casserly, *Goldwater* (Garden City, N.Y.: Doubleday, 1988), 200. TV address is in Lyndon Baines Johnson, *The Vantage Point: Perspectives of the Presidency, 1963–1969* (New York: Holt, Rinehart, and Winston, 1971), 103.

498   *Maine had begun opening absentee*: "Most Disappointing," *Time*, October 30, 1964.

498   *"Where the hell has this been"*: author interview with Wirt Yerger.

498   For Salvatori raising $1 million, see NYHTEN, n.d. clip in LBJWHAM, Box 30/Refutations Book (1 of 3); for gift to NR, see John B. Judis, *William F. Buckley, Jr.: Patron Saint of the Conservatives* (New York: Touchstone, 1990), 121. For Rubel, see *Forbes*, December 1, 1962. For Frawley, see William W. Turner, *Power on the Right* (Berkeley, Calif.: Ramparts Books, 1971), 171–95. For Knott restaurant figure, see "One Man's Crusade for Everybody's Freedom," *Reader's Digest*, June 1964.

499   For Reagan chairing Wright campaign, see Group Research Inc., "Barry Goldwater and the American Right Wing," AC; for being approached to run himself, see Lou Cannon, *President Reagan: The Role of a Lifetime* (New York: Simon and Schuster, 1991), 102–7. For YAF rally on Long Island, see *New Guard*, November 1962. Noontime speeches: author interview with Noel Black.

499   For co-chairmanship of California Citizens, see Kessel, *Goldwater Coalition*, 155.

499   Reagan's 60-second spot, and Goldwater imitating Reagan chuckle: AHFAV, BG-F/73.

499   My account of origin of *A Time for Choosing* is collated from Lisa McGirr, "Suburban Warriors: Grass-Roots Conservatism in the 1960s" (Ph.D. diss., Columbia University, 1995), 235; Gary Wills, *Reagan's America: Innocents at Home* (New York: Penguin, 1988), 290; Kessel, *Goldwater Coalition*, 212; Ronald Reagan and Richard Hubler, *Where's the Rest of Me?* (New York: Duell, Sloane and Pearce, 1965); Edwards, *Goldwater*, 334; Shadegg, *What Happened*, 254; Sidney Blumenthal, *The Rise of the Counter-Establishment: From Conservative Ideology to Political Power* (New York: Times Books, 1986); and author interviews with M. Stanton Evans and Lee Edwards. For Sinatra's annoyance with Reagan, see Jane Hindle, ed., *London Review of Books: An Anthology* (New York: Verso, 1996), 73.

501   A dub of *A Time for Choosing* is in AHFAC, tape BG-VC/4, and AC.

503   For FDR's 1936 acceptance speech, see David M. Kennedy, *Freedom from Fear: The American People in Depression and War* (New York: Oxford University Press, 1999), 280.

504 The "Cross of Gold" comparison is noted in Bill Boyarsky, *The Rise of Ronald Reagan* (New York: Random House, 1968), 105; and David Broder and Stephen Hess, *The Republican Establishment: The Present and Future of the GOP* (New York: Harper and Row, 1967).

504 For text of Nixon Cincinnati speech, LBJWHAM, Box 22/Nixon. For tour dates see "Nixon Schedule—Week of Oct. 18–25," LBJWH6-3/120. For number of speeches, see Arthur Schlesinger Jr., ed., *History of American Presidential Elections, 1798–1968*, vol. 4 (New York: Chelsea House, 1971), 3020.

505 Letter exchange between Nixon and BMG in DK, Box 3/Nixon. Nixon's plans for Hershey Hotel are in Richard Nixon, *RN: The Memoirs of Richard Nixon*, vol. 1 (New York: Warner Books, 1978), 320–22; and Kessel, *Goldwater Coalition*, 186, 189. Transcript of Hershey is in Karl Hess, *In a Cause That Will Triumph: The Goldwater Campaign and the Future of Conservatism* (New York: Doubleday, 1967), 165–231.

506 For tour difficulties, see Schlesinger, *History of American Presidential Elections*, 3020; Nixon, *RN*, 324; and Shadegg, *What Happened*, 271. For distorted media coverage: Debra Livermore Turner to author, March 31, 1997.

506 For "Texas Doctors for Goldwater," see Ronnie Dugger, *The Politician: The Life and Times of Lyndon Johnson* (New York: Norton, 1982), 452. The Air Reserve Squadron rumor is noted in MCSL, Statements and Speeches, vol. 29, 148. For King leaflets, see Branch, *Pillar of Fire*, 521; and Jamieson, *Packaging the Presidency*, 218. For Miller's daughter's bomb scare, see *Harrisburg Patriot*, October 29, 1964. For broken wrist and "teenagers are the hard core" quote, see John M. Cummings, "Rough Tactics by the Voters," *Philadelphia Inquirer*, October 22, 1964.

507 For UNICEF and JBS, see Gerald Schomp, *Birchism Was My Business* (New York: Macmillan, 1970), 98. Goldwater taffy order blank in FCW, Box 3/Ohio. Vandalized BMG signs: author interview with Margot Henriksen.

507 LBJ reading Republicans' FBI reports is in Jeff Shesol, *Mutual Contempt: Lyndon Johnson, Robert Kennedy, and the Feud that Defined a Decade* (New York: Norton, 1997), 228. For statement linking BMG to Jenkins, see Shesol, *Mutual Contempt*, 227. For pinball schedule, see Kessel, *Goldwater Coalition*, 249. Podium requirements from author interview with Mel Cottone. *"I'm depending on you young folks"*: Shepherd and Wren, *Quotations from Chairman LBJ*, 13. For San Diego, see Rowland Evans and Robert Novak, *Lyndon B. Johnson: Exercise of Power: A Political Biography* (New York: New American Library, 1966), 481; and Cormier, *LBJ the Way He Was*, 128.

508 *"He tells the American people"*: AHF, Box 1/8. *"So many unfortunate remarks"*: *New York Daily News*, October 30, 1964. For BMG Phoenix interview on Vietnam, see UPI dispatches in LBJWHNG. *"Does this make any sense"*: Baltimore speech, AHF, Box 1/9.

508 *"I can't help but wondering"*: undated speech in AHF, Box 1/13.

509 For Columbia, South Carolina, speech, see Kessel, *Goldwater Coalition*, 216.

509 For Reagan surplus, see Kessel, *Goldwater Coalition*, 147; and Shadegg, *What Happened*, 24. For inability to buy time: White, *Making of the President 1964*, 397; and author interview with Charles Lichenstein.

509   Local showings of Reagan speech: William Martin, *With God on Our Side: The Rise of the Religious Right in America* (New York: Broadway Books, 1996), 87; F. Clifton White, *Why Reagan Won: The Conservative Movement, 1964–1981* (Washington, D.C.: Regnery, 1981), 24; and author interview with Noel Black (for second mortgage story). *A kid in Kentucky*: The kid was Gary Bauer, who told the story frequently while running for President in 2000. *People called their crazy*: author interview with Allan Ryskind. *"In my 30 years in politics"*: Kellar to Kitchel, January 4, 1965, DK, Box 2. *"Incidentally," he added*: Lee to Kitchel, November 20, 1964, DK, Box 4. For Goldwater's jealousy, see Edwards, *Goldwater*, 334.

510   *Wirt Yerger, blunt as ever*: author interview with Wirt Yerger. For conflict with Columbia, South Carolina, address, see AHFCP, vol. 10, pictures 28–29.

510   For San Francisco: AHFCP, vol. 10, picture 31. For rain commercial, see Jamieson, *Packaging the Presidency*, 220; and Diamond and Bates, *The Spot*, 140.

511   For bombing decision, see H. R. McMaster, *Dereliction of Duty: Lyndon Johnson, Robert McNamara, the Joint Chiefs of Staff, and the Lies That Led to Vietnam* (New York: HarperCollins, 1997), 155–78.

511   For Goldwater family at polls, see Jimmy Breslin, "Goldwater Legacy Lives On," *Newsday*, February 20, 2000; AHFCP, vol. 10, picture 41; and Edwards, *Goldwater*, 339.

511   LBJ palm cards in AC. For poll watching, see "Chairman Bailey Warns Against Republican Plans to Intimidate Voters," October 27, 1964, DNC press release, LBJWHAM, Box 22/"Operation Eagle Eye"; Cuyahoga County memo, FCW, Box 3/Ohio; and "A Word About Operation Eagle Eye," instructions to Chicago volunteers, FCW, Box 19/Illinois. For Humphrey quote, Kessel, *Goldwater Coalition*, 172. For 1962 Arizona elections, see "Memorandum to Guy Stillman, Republican Conspiracy to Deprive Citizens of Free Exercise of Franchise in Maricopa County," AHF, Box 13/32; Robert Alan Goldberg, *Barry Goldwater* (New Haven, Conn.: Yale University Press, 1995), 88; David Saraye, *Turning Right: The Making of the Rehnquist Supreme Court* (New York: John Wiley, 1992), 307; and Rehnquist confirmation hearings, *Congressional Record*, December 3, 1971, 44640. For network exit polls and postcards, see Bill Leonard, *In the Storm of the Eye: A Lifetime at CBS* (New York: G. P. Putnam's Sons, 1987), 113.

511   *At Goldwater's D.C. election-night headquarters*: author interview with Lee Edwards. *JOHNSON'S EGO MASKS:* Willard Edwards, CT, October 11, 1964. *Goldwater was back home in Arizona*: Edwards, *Goldwater*, 339.

512   *He was on the phone constantly*: LBJT, 6411.01/18, 6411.01/19, 6411.01/28, 6411.01/29, 6411.02/2, 6411.02/7. Final totals from White, *Making of the President 1964*, 480–81. For Vietnam interjections, see Karen Gullo, "Worries About Vietnam Nagged LBJ," AP dispatch, September 24, 1999.

512   For Driskell Hotel and Civic Center, see Evans and Novak, *Exercise of Power*, 483.

513   *"Barry Goldwater not only lost"*: James Reston, NYT, November 5, 1964.

513   *"They cannot win in this era"*: Harold Faber, ed., *The Road to the White House: The Story of the 1964 Election by the Staff of the New York Times* (New York: McGraw-Hill, 1965), viii.

513   " 'The Johnson majority,' Walter Lippmann pronounced": Edwards, *Goldwater*, 344.

513   *If the Republicans become a conservative party*: ibid.

513   For electoral analysis, see Schlesinger, ed., *History of American Presidential Elections*, 3021; White, *Making of the President 1964*, 451–59; Rita Lang Kleinfelder, *When We Were Young: A Baby-Boomer Yearbook* (New York: Prentice-Hall, 1993), 368; Branch, *Pillar of Fire*, 522; Thomas Byrne Edsall and Mary D. Edsall, *Chain Reaction: The Impact of Race, Rights, and Taxes on American Politics* (New York: Norton, 1991), 36; and Margolis, *Last Innocent Year*, 359. See also *America Votes*, vol. 5 (New York: Macmillan, 1966).

514   For Hattiesburg nuclear tests, see Branch, *Pillar of Fire*, 441; NYT, October 18, 1964; and NYT, October 23, 1964.

514   For liberal confidence in Southern election results, see Sam Ragan, "Dixie Looked Away," *American Scholar* 34 (1965). *"One-shot affair"*: WP, November 5, 1964. *Enlightened Republicans*: Ragan, "Dixie Looked Away."

514   *"White Backlash Doesn't Develop"*: NYT, November 5, 1964. *"Leaders of both parties are confident"*: Ragan, "Dixie Looked Away." *Or Goldwater's overwhelming*: Wayne Barrett, "Remaining the Right," *Village Voice*, February 9–15, 2000.

515   *"Our overriding, overwhelming distrust"*: Edward Brooke, *The Challenge of Change: Crisis in Our Two-Party System* (Boston: Little, Brown, 1966). *"Shattering price"*: Kessel, *Goldwater Coalition*, 308. *"Bold, drastic steps"*: ibid. Mel Laird: ibid. *"The present party leadership"*: ibid. *"If the Lord spares me for 1968"*: ibid. On Nixon: ibid., 309; and Nixon, *RN*, 325.

515   Installation of Bliss at RNC: Kessel, *Goldwater Coalition*, 315. *Lyndon Johnson always said it*: "Atlantic Report on the World Today," *Atlantic Monthly*, September 1964. For reapportionment decisions as vanquishing of congressional conservatism: Margolis, *1964*, 146; and Tom Wicker, *JFK and LBJ: The Influence of Personality upon Politics* (Baltimore: Penguin, 1968), part 2. *"History would have to record"*: White, *Making of the President 1964*, 140.

516   *"The Amateur Hour and After"*: George H. Mayer, *The Republican Party 1854–1966* (New York: Oxford University Press, 1967), 558. *The nation's leading students*: Edwards, *Goldwater*, 344. *"The election results of 1964"*: Schlesinger, ed., *History of American Presidential Elections*, 3021.

Selected Bibliography

Alsop, Stewart. *Nixon and Rockefeller: A Double Portrait*. Garden City, N.Y.: Double-day, 1960.

Andrew, John A. III. *The Other Side of the Sixties: Young Americans for Freedom and the Rise of Conservative Politics*. New Brunswick, N.J.: Rutgers University Press, 1997.

Bass, Jack, and Marilyn W. Thompson. *Ol' Strom: An Unauthorized Biography of Strom Thurmond*. Atlanta: Longstreet, 1998.

Bell, Jack. *The Johnson Treatment: How Lyndon B. Johnson Took Over the Presidency and Made It His Own*. New York: Harper and Row, 1965.

Bensel, Richard Franklin. *Sectionalism and American Political Development*. Madison: University of Wisconsin Press, 1984.

Beschloss, Michael, ed. *Taking Charge: The Johnson White House Tapes, 1963–1964*. New York: Simon and Schuster, 1997.

Boyer, Paul S. *Fallout: A Historian Reflects on America's Half-Century Encounter with Nuclear Weapons*. Columbus: Ohio State University Press, 1998.

Branch, Taylor. *Parting the Waters: America in the King Years, 1954–1963*. New York: Touchstone, 1988.

———. *Pillar of Fire: America in the King Years, 1963–1965*. New York: Simon and Schuster, 1998.

Brennan, Mary C. *Turning Right in the Sixties: The Conservative Capture of the GOP*. Chapel Hill: University of North Carolina Press, 1995.

Brinkley, Alan. *Liberalism and Its Discontents*. Cambridge, Mass.: Harvard University Press, 1998.

Brinkley, David. *David Brinkley: 11 Presidents, 4 Wars, 22 Political Conventions, 1 Moon Landing, 3 Assassinations, 2,000 Weeks of News and Other Stuff on Television, and 18 Years Growing Up in North Carolina*. New York: Knopf, 1995.

Busch, Andrew E. *Outsiders and Openness in the Presidential Nominating System*. Pittsburgh: University of Pittsburgh Press, 1997.

———. *Horses in Midstream: U.S. Midterm Elections and Their Consequences, 1894–1998*. Pittsburgh: University of Pittsburgh Press, 1999.

Cain, Edward. *They'd Rather Be Right: Youth and the Conservative Movement*. New York: Macmillan, 1963.

Carmines, Edward G., and James A. Stimson. *Issue Evolution: Race and the Trans-*
formation of American Politics. Princeton, N.J.: Princeton University Press, 1989.

Carney, Francis M., and Frank H. Way, eds. *Politics 1964*. Belmont, Calif.: Wadsworth, 1964.

Carol, Peter. *Famous in America: The Passion to Succeed: Jane Fonda, George Wal-*
lace, Phyllis Schlafly, John Glenn. New York: Dutton, 1985.

Carter, Dan T. *The Politics of Rage: George Wallace, the Origins of the New Conser-*
vatism, and the Transformation of American Politics. Baton Rouge: Louisiana State
University Press, 1995.

Collins, Robert. *The Business Response to Keynes, 1929–1964*. New York: Columbia
University Press, 1981.

Congressional Quarterly, *The Public Records of Barry M. Goldwater and William E.*
Miller: The Lives, Votes and Stands of the 1964 Republican Candidates. Washington,
D.C.: Congressional Quarterly Service, 1964.

Cormier, Frank. *LBJ the Way He Was: A Personal Memoir*. Garden City, N.Y.: Doubleday, 1977.

Cosman, Bernard. *Five States for Goldwater: Continuity and Change in Southern Pres-*
idential Voting Patterns. Tuscaloosa: University of Alabama Press, 1966.

Dallek, Matthew. "Young Americans for Freedom, 1960–1964." Master's thesis,
Columbia University, 1993.

Dallek, Robert. *Flawed Giant: Lyndon Johnson and His Times, 1961–1973*. New York:
Oxford University Press, 1998.

Desmond, James. *Nelson Rockefeller: A Political Biography*. New York: Macmillan, 1964.

de Toledano, Ralph. *The Winning Side: The Case for Goldwater Republicanism*. New
York: MacFadden-Bartel, 1964.

Diamond, Edwin, and Stephen Bates. *The Spot: The Rise of Political Advertising on*
Television. Cambridge, Mass.: MIT Press, 1984.

Diamond, Sara. *Roads to Dominion: Right-Wing Movements and Political Power in the*
United States. New York: Guilford, 1995.

Dionne, E. J., Jr. *Why Americans Hate Politics*. New York: Simon and Schuster,
1991.

Doenecke, Justus D. *Not to the Swift: The Old Isolationists in the Cold War Era*. Cranbury, N.J.: Associated University Press, 1979.

Edwards, Anne. *Early Reagan: The Rise to Power*. New York: Morrow, 1987.

Edwards, Lee. *Goldwater: The Man Who Made a Revolution*. Washington, D.C.: Regnery, 1995.

Evans, Rowland, and Robert Novak. *Lyndon B. Johnson: The Exercise of Power: A*
Political Biography. New York: New American Library, 1966.

Faber, Harold, ed. *The Road to the White House: The Story of the 1964 Election by the*
Staff of the New York Times. New York: McGraw-Hill, 1965.

Farber, David, ed. *The Sixties: From Memory to History*. Chapel Hill: University of
North Carolina Press, 1994.

Felsenthal, Carol. *Sweetheart of the Silent Majority: The Biography of Phyllis Schlafly*.
New York: Doubleday, 1981.

Fones-Wolf, Elizabeth A. *Selling Free Enterprise: The Business Assault on Labor and Liberalism, 1945–1960.* Urbana: University of Illinois Press, 1994.

Formisano, Ronald. *Boston against Busing: Race, Class, and Ethnicity in the 1960s and 1970s.* Chapel Hill: University of North Carolina Press, 1991.

Freedman, Samuel G. *The Inheritance: How Three Families and the American Political Majority Moved from Left to Right.* New York: Touchstone, 1996.

Friedman, Milton, and Rose Friedman. *Two Lucky People: Memoirs.* Chicago: University of Chicago Press, 1998.

Galligan, David J. *Politics and the Businessmen.* New York: Pitman, 1964.

Gardner, Lloyd C., and Ted Gittinger. *Vietnam: The Early Decisions.* Austin: University of Texas Press, 1997.

Gervasi, Frank. *The Real Rockefeller: The Story of the Rise, Decline, and Resurgence of the Presidential Aspirations of Nelson Rockefeller.* New York: Atheneum, 1964.

Goines, David Lance. *The Free Speech Movement: Coming of Age in the 1960s.* Berkeley, Calif.: Ten Speed Press, 1993.

Goldberg, Robert Alan. *Barry Goldwater.* New Haven, Conn.: Yale University Press, 1995.

Goldwater, Barry. *Conscience of a Conservative.* Shepherdsville, Ky.: Victor Publishing, 1960.

———. *Conscience of a Majority.* Englewood Cliffs, N.J.: Prentice-Hall, 1970.

———. *With No Apologies: The Personal and Political Memoirs of United States Senator Barry M. Goldwater.* New York: William Morrow, 1979.

Goldwater, Barry, with Jack Casserly. *Goldwater.* Garden City, N.Y.: Doubleday, 1988.

Halberstam, David. *The Fifties.* New York: Fawcett, 1993.

Haley, J. Evetts. *A Texan Looks at Lyndon: A Study in Illegitimate Power.* Canyon, Tex.: Palo Duro Press, 1964.

Heidenry, John. *What Wild Ecstasy: The Rise and Fall of the Sexual Revolution.* New York: Simon and Schuster, 1997.

Heirich, Max. *The Spiral of Conflict: Berkeley, 1964.* New York: Columbia University Press, 1968.

Henriksen, Margot A. *Dr. Strangelove's America: Society and Culture in the Atomic Age.* Berkeley: University of California Press, 1997.

Hess, Karl. *In a Cause That Will Triumph: The Goldwater Campaign and the Future of Conservatism.* New York: Doubleday, 1967.

———. *Mostly on the Edge: An Autobiography.* Amherst, N.Y.: Prometheus, 1999.

Horowitz, David A. *Beyond Left and Right: Insurgency and the Establishment.* Urbana: University of Illinois Press, 1997.

Isaacs, Jeremy, and Taylor Downing. *Cold War: An Illustrated History, 1945–1991.* Boston: Little, Brown, 1998.

Iverson, Peter. *Barry Goldwater: Native Arizonan.* Norman: University of Oklahoma Press, 1997.

Jacoby, Tamar. *Someone Else's House: America's Unfinished Struggle for Integration.* New York: Free Press, 1998.

Jamieson, Kathleen Hall. *Packaging the Presidency: A History and Criticism of Presidential Campaign Advertising*. 3rd ed. New York: Oxford University Press, 1996.

Janson, Donald, and Bernard Eismann. *The Far Right*. New York: McGraw-Hill, 1963.

Jarboe, Jane. *Lady Bird: A Comprehensive Biography of Mrs. Johnson*. New York: Simon and Schuster, 1999.

Judis, John B. *William F. Buckley, Jr.: Patron Saint of the Conservatives*. New York: Touchstone, 1990.

Kennedy, David M. *Freedom from Fear: The American People in Depression and War*. New York: Oxford University Press, 1999.

Kennedy, Robert F. *The Enemy Within*. New York: Popular Library, 1960.

Kessel, John. *The Goldwater Coalition: Republican Strategies in 1964*. Indianapolis: Bobbs-Merrill, 1968.

Kleindienst, Richard. *Justice: The Memoirs of an Attorney General*. Ottawa, Ill.: Jameson Books, 1985.

Kramer, Michael, and Sam Roberts. *"I Never Wanted to Be Vice-President of Anything!": An Investigative Biography of Nelson Rockefeller*. New York: Basic Books, 1976.

Lasch, Christopher. *The True and Only Heaven: Progress and Its Critics*. New York: Norton, 1991.

LeMay, Curtis. *Mission with LeMay: My Story*. Garden City, N.Y.: Doubleday, 1965.

Lesher, Stephan. *George Wallace: American Populist*. Reading, Mass.: Addison-Wesley, 1994.

Leslie, Warren. *Dallas Public and Private*. New York: Grossman Publishers, 1964.

Lichtenstein, Nelson. *Walter Reuther: The Most Dangerous Man in Detroit*. Urbana: University of Illinois Press, 1995.

Liebman, Marvin. *Coming Out Conservative: An Autobiography*. San Francisco: Chronicle Books, 1992.

Lucas, J. Anthony. *Common Ground: A Turbulent Decade in the Lives of Three American Families*. New York: Knopf, 1985.

Manion, Clarence. *The Conservative American: His Fight for National Independence and Constitutional Government*. New York: Devon-Adair, 1964.

Margolis, Jon. *The Last Innocent Year: America in 1964: The Beginning of the "Sixties."* New York: Morrow, 1999.

Martin, William. *With God on Our Side: The Rise of the Religious Right in America*. New York: Broadway Books, 1996.

Matthews, Christopher. *Kennedy and Nixon: The Rivalry That Shaped Postwar America*. New York: Touchstone, 1996.

May, Edgar. *The Wasted Americans: Cost of Our Welfare Dilemma*. New York: Harper and Row, 1964.

May, Ernest R., and Philip D. Zelikow. *The Kennedy Tapes: Inside the White House During the Cuban Missile Crisis*. Cambridge, Mass.: Harvard University Press, 1997.

Mayer, George H. *The Republican Party 1854–1966*. New York: Oxford University Press, 1967.

McDowell, Edwin. *Barry Goldwater: Portrait of an Arizonan*. Chicago: Regnery, 1964.

McGirr, Lisa. "Suburban Warriors: Grass-Roots Conservatism in the 1960s." Ph.D. diss., Columbia University, 1995.

McMaster, H. R. *Dereliction of Duty: Lyndon Johnson, Robert McNamara, the Joint Chiefs of Staff, and the Lies that Led to Vietnam*. New York: HarperCollins, 1997.

Miles, Michael W. *The Odyssey of the American Right*. New York: Oxford, 1980.

Miller, James. *Democracy Is in the Streets: From Port Huron to the Siege of Chicago*. Cambridge, Mass.: Harvard University Press, 1994.

Miller, William J. *Henry Cabot Lodge: A Biography*. New York: Heinemann, 1967.

Montgomery, Gayle B., and James W. Johnson. *One Step from the White House: The Rise and Fall of Senator William Knowland*. Berkeley: University of California Press, 1998.

National Broadcasting Company. *Somehow It Works: A Candid Portrait of the 1964 Presidential Election*. Garden City, N.Y.: Doubleday, 1965.

Nixon, Richard. *RN: The Memoirs of Richard Nixon*. Vol. 1. New York: Warner Books, 1978.

Novak, Robert. *The Agony of the GOP 1964*. New York: Macmillan, 1965.

Patterson, James T. *Mr. Republican: A Biography of Robert Taft*. Boston: Houghton Mifflin, 1972.

Perry, James M. *A Report in Depth on Barry Goldwater: The Story of the 1964 Republican Presidential Nominee*. Silver Spring, Md.: National Observer, 1964.

Proxmire, Ellen. *One Foot in Washington: The Perilous Life of a Senator's Wife*. Washington, D.C.: R. B. Luce, 1964.

Pulliam, Russell. *Publisher: Gene Pulliam: Last of the Newspaper Titans*. Ottawa, Ill.: Jameson Books, 1984.

Rae, Nicol C. *The Decline and Fall of the Liberal Republicans: From 1952 to the Present*. New York: Oxford University Press, 1989.

Rampersad, Arnold. *Jackie Robinson: A Biography*. New York: Knopf, 1997.

Reed, Roy. *Faubus: The Life and Times of an American Prodigal*. Fayetteville: University of Arkansas Press, 1997.

Reeves, Thomas C. *A Question of Character: A Life of John F. Kennedy*. New York: Free Press, 1991.

Reich, Cary. *The Life of Nelson A. Rockefeller: Worlds to Conquer, 1908–1958*. New York: Doubleday, 1996.

Reinsch, J. Leonard. *Getting Elected: From Radio and Roosevelt to Television and Reagan*. New York: Hippocrene, 1988.

Rosenblum, Jonathan D. *Copper Crucible: How the Arizona Miners' Strike of 1983 Recast Labor-Management Relations in America*. 2nd ed. Ithaca, N.Y.: ILR Press, 1998.

Royko, Mike. *Boss: Richard J. Daley of Chicago*. New York: Signet, 1971.

Rusher, William. *The Rise of the Right*. New York: Morrow, 1984.

Salinger, Pierre. *With Kennedy*. Garden City, N.Y.: Doubleday, 1966.

Schlafly, Phyllis. *A Choice Not an Echo*. Alton, Ill.: Pere Marquette Press, 1964.

Schlesinger, Arthur Jr., ed. *History of American Presidential Elections, 1789–1968*. Vol. 4. New York: Chelsea House, 1971.

Schneider, Gregory L. *Cadres for Conservatism: Young Americans for Freedom and the Rise of the Contemporary Right*. New York: NYU Press, 1999.

Schomp, Gerald. *Birchism Was My Business*. New York: Macmillan, 1970.

Schuparra, Kurt. *Triumph of the Right: The Rise of the California Conservative Movement, 1945–1966*. Armonk, N.Y.: M. E. Sharpe, 1998.

Shadegg, Stephen. *How to Win an Election*. New York: Taplinger, 1963.

———. *What Happened to Goldwater?: The Inside Story of the 1964 Republican Campaign*. New York: Holt, Rinehart, and Winston, 1965.

Shapiro, Fred C., and James W. Sullivan. *Race Riots New York 1964: What Really Happened As It Happened Before the Eyes of Two Trained Observers*. New York: Thomas Y. Crowell, 1964.

Shepherd, Jack, and Christopher S. Wren, eds. *Quotations from Chairman LBJ*. New York: Simon and Schuster, 1968.

Shesol, Jeff. *Mutual Contempt: Lyndon Johnson, Robert Kennedy, and the Feud that Defined a Decade*. New York: Norton, 1997.

Smith, Howard K. *Events Leading Up to My Death: The Life of a Twentieth-Century Reporter*. New York: St. Martin's Press, 1996.

Smith, James Allen. *The Idea Brokers: Think Tanks and the Rise of the New Policy Elite*. New York: Free Press, 1991.

Stormer, John A. *None Dare Call It Treason*. Florissant, Mo.: Liberty Bell Press, 1964.

Sugrue, Thomas J. *The Origins of the Urban Crisis: Race and Inequality in Postwar Detroit*. Princeton, N.J.: Princeton University Press, 1996.

Tillett, Paul, ed. *Inside Politics: The National Conventions, 1960*. Dobbs Ferry, N.Y.: Oceana Publications, 1962.

Tuccille, Jerome. *Kingdom: The Story of the Hunt Family of Texas*. Ottawa, Ill.: Jameson Books, 1984.

Uphoff, Walter. *Kohler on Strike: Thirty Years of Conflict*. Boston: Beacon Press, 1966.

Westerhoff, Arjen. "Politics of Protest: Strom Thurmond and the Development of the Republican Southern Strategy, 1948–1972." Master's thesis, American Studies Program, Smith College, 1991.

Whalen, Richard. *Taking Sides: A Personal View of America from Kennedy to Nixon to Kennedy*. Boston: Houghton Mifflin, 1974.

White, F. Clifton, with William Gill. *Suite 3505: The Story of the Draft Goldwater Movement*. New Rochelle, N.Y.: Arlington House, 1967.

———. *Why Reagan Won: The Conservative Movement, 1964–1981*. Chicago Regnery, 1981.

White, F. Clifton, with Jerome Tuccille. *Politics as a Noble Calling*. Ottawa, Ill.: Jameson Books, 1994.

White, Theodore H., *The Making of the President 1960*. New York: Atheneum, 1961.

———. *The Making of the President 1964*. New York: Atheneum, 1965.

Wicker, Tom. *JFK and LBJ: The Influence of Personality upon Politics*. Baltimore: Penguin, 1968.

Wills, Gary. *Reagan's America: Innocents at Home.* New York: Penguin, 1988.

Winkler, Allan M. *Life Under a Cloud: American Anxiety About the Atom.* New York: Oxford University Press, 1993.

Winters, Francis X. *The Year of the Hare: America in Vietnam, January 25, 1963– February 15, 1964.* Athens: University of Georgia Press, 1997.

Wolf, George D. *William Warren Scranton: Pennsylvania Statesman.* State College: Pennsylvania State University Press, 1981.

ACKNOWLEDGMENTS

It started with a notice on my project in *The New York Times Book Review*, and a lesson in how damned *generous* people are. I got missives from Goldwater workers who were so young at the time that they could barely remember the campaign (and from a one-time eleven-year-old who bravely preached on behalf of LBJ every Saturday in an Orange County shopping-center parking lot); and letters from Goldwater press secretaries, finance chairs, ad execs, press corps members, book agents—even the old lady who kept the books at his Phoenix department store. Scholars passed on their own exertions—one an Indian professor who had been on a Fulbright Fellowship to the University of Pennsylvania in 1964, another a master's student from the Netherlands whose research on Strom Thurmond was indispensable. There was even one guy who sent me Goldwater news clippings at random intervals over the course of three years—anonymously. Thanks, whoever you are.

My heart especially goes out to two of these correspondents. Andrew Szanton sent my way the arresting photograph that graces the cover of this book. And about Ryan Hayes—the great lay intellectual of Queens, New York—hardly enough can be said. His stunning command of political detail provided the seed for many of the researches herein. And without the generous loans from his bottomless collection of political paraphernalia—what would I have done without my directory of the Eighty-eighth Congress?—my scholarly life would have been much more difficult. I don't dedicate the book to him. But I do dedicate to him the sentence on his "Harold Stassen's Ticker Tape Parade" soapbox derby car.

Much thanks, too, to those who gave generously of their recollections, time, trust—and, sometimes, hospitality—in author interviews. Those who went beyond the call of duty include Jameson Campaigne Jr. (who gets triple recognition for opening his storehouse of papers to me, and for publishing so many of the biographies and memoirs of conservative figures that I relied upon), Leonard Nadasdy (his loaned dossier on his tenure as Young Republican chair was indispensable), Pam Walton, Ron Crawford, Bill Rusher, Wes McCune, Milton Friedman, Stan Evans, and Graham T. T. Molitor. The breakfast David Keene set up for me with a cadre of conservative movement veterans at the Capitol Hill Club was very helpful, and very cool.

Several scholars were invaluable to me as friends, advisers, sources, inspirations—

and, last but not least, as penners of the letters of recommendation that helped several benefactors see the merits of my case. These include Michael Kazin, Nick Salvatore, David Kennedy, Nelson Lichtenstein, David Farber, and Tom Sugrue. And thank you, thank you, to those benefactors who *did* see the merits of my case: the Rockefeller Archive Center, the LBJ Library, the Dick Goldensohn Fund—and, especially, the National Endowment for the Humanities and the Margaret Chase Smith Library. The former's contribution kept me in food, shelter, and used books for a year; the latter gave me not just a check but a hell of a good time.

The thought of my other financial benefactors brings a tear to my eye: my sister, Linda, a lifelong pillar; Jon Cohen, who taught me a thing or two about analytical precision; Allison Miller, whose middle name is Xanthe, and what else need be said?; John Palattela and Angela Dillard, who both remind me that I love to think; Lisa Bonacci, a model of courage and devotion; Amy Kossoy, a neighbor in the best sense; Eric Wunderman, who thinks, blessedly, differently; Anil Mudholkar, a friend of a lifetime; Thad Domina, not a research assistant but a mensch; and Grandma and Grandpa Perlstein, whose generosity has allowed me to follow a risky profession, not a safe one, which means everything to me.

I thank those who opened their homes to me: the Kramer family in Phoenix; and dear friends Gita Kapadia, Ben Evans, Jen Stewart, and Jefferson Decker on trips to Chicago. Two others put up with me for even longer, and I want to recognize their patience and friendship: Jon Cohen and William Duty. They are role models, both creatively and intellectually.

I also want to thank some other scholars, writers, editors, and others who gave their encouragement, solidarity, and favors large and small: David Greenberg, Matthew Dallek, Judith Broadhurst, Chris Lehmann, Jeff Shesol, Beverley Solochek, John Andrew, Gregory Schneider, Mike Leiman, Jennifer Mittelstadt, Godfrey Hodgson, Richard Ellis, Jim Sleeper, Scott Sherman, and Jim Miller (whose greatest contribution was an offhand quote in a *Lingua Franca* article about how if he had it to do over again, he might just have written about the rise of the right). And four more magnificent, unique souls: David Glenn and Scott McLemee (living rebukes to any fool who wants to talk about there not being any New York intellectuals left, even though Scott lives in Washington), and Leon Pasker and Margie Good, who have always made me feel big.

Thanks also to my friends at the New York Working Families Party, who gave me my participant-observer training in political volunteering. Knock wood, a book like this will be written about them thirty-five years from now.

Thank you to the archivists at the facilities mentioned above, and also at the Chicago Historical Society, special collections at Cornell University, and the Hoover Institution. If you love reading history, lift a glass to archivists at least once a week; they are the unsung heroes of the enterprise. And thank you, too, William F. Buckley, not only for making it possible for there to be such an interesting movement to write about in the first place, but for opening your papers at Yale to me.

I owe much to my colleagues at *Lingua Franca*: Jeffrey Kittay (for lessons in the value of *chutzpah*), Alexander Star (for lessons in the value of carefulness), and especially (for lessons in the value of volubility) Daniel Zalewski. I also owe a debt to the American Culture program at the University of Michigan.

There are four people without whom the transition from full-time magazine editor to full-time book author could not possibly have been as smooth as it was. The first is Rebecca Lowen, who commissioned the original book proposal. That our relationship ended there is owing only to the smarts, style, savvy, and friendship of my editor, Paul Elie, who saw something in a book review I wrote and decided I had what it took (ably assisted by Brian Blanchfield and Susan Goldfarb, whose work was tireless).

That review was written for Sue and John Leonard at *The Nation*. It was their mission of encouraging young writers in developing their talents in that magazine's culture section that started—to borrow an antique metaphor that an old *National Review* hand and New Lefty like John would appreciate—the domino effect.

Now I have two families, the Perlsteins (my parents Jerry and Sandi, sister Linda, and brothers Ben and Steve); and the Geiers (Hank, Patty, Frank, Kelly, Buddy, and Sean). I love them both, and thank them for their support. I have two families now because I now have my own family: Kathy Geier, my wife, a partner in every way, to whom I dedicate this book. And last but not least, our little dogs Buster and Checkers. You know, we love those dogs, and I just want to say this right now, that regardless of what they say about it, we're going to keep them.

INDEX

PERMISSIONS ACKNOWLEDGMENTS

Grateful acknowledgment is made to the following for permission to reprint photographs and other images in this book: Hillsdale College Freedom Library for the photograph of Clarence Manion; Bettmann/Corbis for the photographs of Orval Faubus, George Romney, and William F. Buckley Jr; the Arizona Historical Foundation at Arizona State University for the photographs of Barry Goldwater in an airplane cockpit and with Richard Nixon in Phoenix, Arizona, and for the image captured from a Goldwater campaign commercial; AP/Wide World Photos for the photograph of Governor and Mrs. Rockefeller on vacation, the two photographs of Alabama governor George Wallace, and the photograph of unoccupied Mississippi delegate seats at the 1964 Democratic Convention; *The New York Times* for the photograph of Barry Goldwater on stage at the Young Americans for Freedom rally; the John M. Ashbrook Center for Public Affairs at Ashland University for the photograph of F. Clifton White; TimePix for the reproduction of the September 27, 1963, cover of *Time* featuring George Wallace; the Pennsylvania State University for the photograph of William Scranton; Black Star Images for the photograph of Henry Cabot Lodge; the Bentley Historical Library at the University of Michigan for the photograph of George Romney; the Margaret Chase Smith Library and Eugene Payne for Mr. Payne's political cartoon, originally published in *The Charlotte Observer*; Herblock Cartoons for the three cartoons by Herblock involving Richard Nixon, originally published in *The Washington Post*; Ted Streshinsky for his two photographs of San Francisco during the 1964 Republican Convention; the Lyndon Baines Johnson Library for the anti-Goldwater "Cures for What Ails America" brochure; Jameson Campaigne for the photograph of the yard sign reading "To Hell with Urban Renewal" and the racially charged Goldwater brochure; the Democratic National Committee for the three images captured from the Johnson campaign's "Daisy" commercial; Phyllis Schlafly for the reproduction of the cover of her book *A Choice Not an Echo*; and Edmonds Associates for the images captured from the film *A Time for Choosing*.

Fair and reasonable effort has been made to locate the copyright holders of all other images herein.